Rivers *and the* Power *of* Ancient Rome

Studies in the

HISTORY *of* GREECE

and ROME

ROBIN OSBORNE, JAMES RIVES,

and RICHARD J. A. TALBERT, editors

Rivers *and the* Power *of* Ancient Rome

BRIAN CAMPBELL

THE UNIVERSITY OF NORTH CAROLINA PRESS

CHAPEL HILL

Set in Minion type by Tseng Information Systems, Inc.

Manufactured in the United States of America

The paper in this book meets the guidelines for permanence
and durability of the Committee on Production Guidelines for
Book Longevity of the Council on Library Resources.

The University of North Carolina Press has been a member of
the Green Press Initiative since 2003.

Library of Congress Cataloging-in-Publication Data
Campbell, J. B.
Rivers and the power of ancient Rome / Brian Campbell.
p. cm. — (Studies in the history of Greece and Rome)
Includes bibliographical references and indexes.
ISBN 978-0-8078-3480-0 (cloth : alk. paper)
1. Rivers—Rome—History. 2. Rivers—Political aspects—Rome—History.
3. Rivers—Social aspects—Rome—History. 4. Rivers in art. 5. Rivers in literature.
6. Navigation—Rome—History. 7. River life—Rome—History. 8. Rome—
Geography. 9. Rome—Politics and government. 10. Rome—Commerce. I. Title.
DG211.C28 2012
937—dc23   2012002041

Portions of this work have appeared previously, in somewhat different form, in
"Managing Disruptive Rivers," in E. Hermon (ed.), *Riparia dans L'Empire romain:
pour la définition du concept* (Oxford, 2010), and "River Definitions in Roman
Technical Literature," in R. Gianfelice (ed.), *Atti del Convegno Internazionale,
Sistemi centuriali e opere di assetto agrario tra età romana e primo medioevo.
Aspetti metodologici ricostruttivi ed interpretativi, Borgoricco (Padova)–Lugo
(Ravenna) 10–12 settembre 2009, Agri Centuriati*, in *An International Journal of
Landscape Archaeology* 6 (2009): 95–99, and are reprinted here with permission.

16 15 14 13 12   5 4 3 2 1

For Karen

CONTENTS

MAPS, FIGURES, AND DIAGRAMS

MAPS

A locator map for maps prepared by the Ancient World Mapping Center at the University of North Carolina (maps 3–15 and 19), based on the *Barrington Atlas of the Greek and Roman World*, appears on page xvii.

preface

"Of all the rivers that flow into the seas enclosed within the Roman Empire, which the Greeks call 'the internal sea,' by common consent the Nile is the greatest. Sallust wrote that the Hister (Danube) is the next biggest. Varro, however, in his discussion of that part of the world called Europe, places the Rodanus (Rhône) among the top three rivers of this area, therefore apparently making it a rival of the Hister; for the Hister also flows in Europe" (Aulus Gellius, *Attic Nights* 10.7). Gellius has done his research and offers an interesting geography lesson, setting three major rivers against the vast expanse of Roman territory and noting other factors, particularly the comparative size and status of the rivers, which presumably would then confer dignity on the areas through which they flowed. He also delves into river nomenclature, preferring *Rodanus* for the more common *Rhodanus*, and *Hister* for *Danuvius*, applying to the whole river a word of Thracian origin used by the Greeks to describe the lower course of the Danube.

This passage touches on some intriguing topics but is also typical of many of our sources in not pursuing riverine themes consistently or with the kind of precision that modern historians need. Yet rivers appear repeatedly in the works of a broad sweep of ancient writers, and geographers and surveyors in particular used rivers more methodically to measure distance, establish location, and define space and boundaries, in respect of both entire provinces and local communities. It is hard to think of a more important aspect of the natural geographical phenomena of the ancient world than rivers; permanent yet constantly in motion, they were a perplexing paradox. "Perhaps because water is irrepressibly cyclical and endlessly able to change the form it has taken, its history is varied and complex" (Squatriti, 1998, 164).

It is also inescapable that in all eras rivers have left their mark on the physical landscape and on communities that lived in the vicinity. The ancient world could not have been what it was without rivers, and individual communities were assisted or constrained by rivers, depending on local geography and their skill in exploiting and adapting to the riverine environment. In the present day, we can see the damaging consequences of the unpredictable, torrential rivers of the Mediterranean area. For example, in Spain the river Guadalmedina presents a serious problem of urban management and development at Málaga because it completely dries up for most of the year, except in cases of heavy rain, which can produce sudden surges. The riverbed, now derelict and often a disruptive eyesore, runs through the city splitting it in half. By contrast, in Valencia the river Turia with its highly variable flow was diverted after a serious flood in 1957, the old bed built over and gardens planted. Despite the modern flood precautions in Rome, days of heavy rain during December 2008 caused the Tiber to rise so high that several boats that had broken free of their moorings were jammed underneath the arches of the Ponte Sant' Angelo, and the Tiber Island was partially inundated.

Having written about land survey and the work of the Roman land surveyors (*agrimensores*) and having studied the importance of rivers in landholdings, boundary demarcation, and land disputes, I came to think that the riverine environment might offer an avenue to study people and events in the ancient world from a different perspective, and that it would be useful to try to discover how people conceptualized and described rivers, used them, and interacted with them. In fact, rivers were often not just a land boundary but served as a cultural, emotional, and psychological dividing line. At the same time they often helped to connect distant communities. The study of rivers illustrates not only wide historical themes but also more personal, individual stories, and although I have used some modern theories of analysis of riverine activity (without importing inappropriate jargon), throughout the book I have tried to keep to the forefront those ideas that ancient writers thought interesting. The result is an analysis of the ancient sources that might seem traditional, but my intention is to assess the importance of the watery environment in the life and culture of the Roman world and to look again at obscure or neglected material that sheds fresh light on Roman history.

This book, of course, is not meant to be definitive, and in the nature of the subject it is not possible to write such a book. Although it deals essentially with the Roman world, the evidence cannot be exclusively Roman because much of what happened in Roman times was informed by earlier Greek thinking about rivers and representations of rivers, and of course the nature of water as metaphor went back at least to biblical literature. Also, it is not my intention to include all the known instances of rivers or riverine communities, much of the evidence for which is in any case repetitive. Some descriptions are impressionistic because that is the best way to convey the material we have from the ancient world. Among topics not included at length in this book, it is important to note that the use of water to power machinery, especially waterwheels, has received increasing scholarly attention in recent years. However, the technicalities of construction and design of waterwheels are of peripheral relevance for the topic of rivers, even though there were sometimes important repercussions for riverine communities, and their purpose and overall significance are outside the scope of this study. Throughout the book, for Greek and Latin place names I have generally adhered to the practice of the *Barrington Atlas of the Greek and Roman World* (edited by R. Talbert, 2000), though complete consistency has not been possible. In respect of modern measurements of distance, I give the metric version. However, in quoting Latin authors I usually refer to Roman miles (one Roman mile = 1.48 kilometers), and with Greek authors sometimes to stades (normally 600 Attic feet; one Roman mile = 8⅓ Attic stades).

In compiling this study I have been helped over many years by numerous scholars who patiently answered questions or read parts of the text, notably Colin Adams, James Adams, John Curran, Simon Keay, John Patterson, Peter Thonemann, Frederick Williams, and Tony Woodman. The University College London Ancient History Seminar under Dominic Rathbone and Michael Crawford offered a useful forum in which I was able to present material from chapter 3. I express particular gratitude to Professor Richard Talbert for the invitation to give the Broughton Memorial Lecture at the University of North Carolina at Chapel Hill in 2004, which enabled me to introduce the theme of rivers; for reading the entire text and offering detailed advice that greatly improved the final version; and for arranging the production of many of the maps. For the cartography I gratefully acknowledge the superb work of Brian Turner and his colleagues at the Ancient World Mapping Center of the University of North Carolina, and also Maura Pringle of the Queen's University of Belfast. My thanks are due to the anonymous readers of the University of North Carolina Press for their diligence and many perceptive and improving comments, and the copyeditor, Brian MacDonald, for his careful scrutiny of a difficult text. Finally I thank Professor David Buck and Dr. John Curran for sharing the burden of proofreading and Ron Maner, managing editor of the University of North Carolina Press, for his patience and guidance in bringing this book to publication. For remaining errors due to my ignorance or obstinacy, I am entirely responsible.

In visiting libraries, museums, and riverine sites during the preparation of the text, I have been assisted by several grants from the Travel and Research Fund of the Queen's University of Belfast. A large part of the collection of material was carried out while I was Leverhulme Senior Research Fellow, 2002–5.

I am very grateful to The Leverhulme Trust, since its generous provision allowed me to spend three years on research away from normal university duties. Finally and most importantly, I was elected to a Visiting Fellowship at All Souls College, Oxford in 2004–5, which permitted me to complete a first draft of the text in a superb atmosphere for academic research and debate, free from the *strepitus mundi*. I record here again my thanks to the Warden and Fellows.

Belfast, September 2010

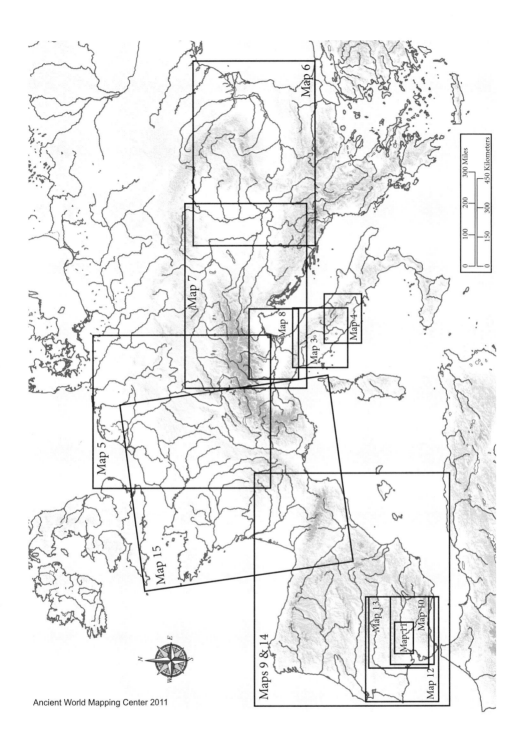

Map 6

Map 7

Map 8

Map 3

Map 4

Map 5

Map 15

Maps 9 & 14

Map 13

Map 11

Map 10

Map 12

300 Miles

450 Kilometers

200

300

100

150

0

0

N

E

S

W

Ancient World Mapping Center 2011

Rivers
and the
power *of*
Ancient
Rome

one

RIVERS PAST AND PRESENT

Nikolaos of Damascus recounts a fascinating story of how Julia, daughter of Augustus and wife of his henchman Agrippa, while on her way to Ilium was almost drowned in the waters of the Scamander, which was unusually high because of heavy rain. Agrippa was furious and imposed a crippling fine on the city. The people of Ilium did not dare to tell him that they could not foresee the storm and its effect on the river and did not know that Julia was approaching. Eventually they were rescued by a double act of patronage. Nikolaos, who was secretary of King Herod of Judaea, was impressed by the famous city and its river and persuaded the king to use his influence with Agrippa, who eventually canceled the fine.[1] This snippet illustrates important ideas. A city could benefit from the fame of its past. The Scamander, a famous river celebrated in literature, enhanced Ilium's reputation and attracted favorable attention, as well as watering its fertile plain. But the river was also an element that could never be entirely controlled or predicted and could become a bane to riverine dwellers. Furthermore, river characteristics and the rapidly changing riverine persona often intersected with historical events.

Down the ages, rivers have always excited the attention of writers and commentators, who used their continuous movement, sound, and power as illustrations and similes, as a context for philosophical speculation on the human condition, and as an explanation for the cultural complexities of local communities.[2] Rivers, being timeless, in fact seem to offer an exciting link between the ancient world and other eras. They have one obvious connection in that rivers look, sound, and behave nowadays as they did in the ancient world and in general have instantly recognizable characteristics. More particularly, for the historian features of ancient topography acquire personality and immediacy through these very characteristics. For example, to see the Tiber in full spate with floating debris moving faster than robust walking speed is to be reminded of the river's power in ancient Rome to flood and destroy. Similarly, the tawny

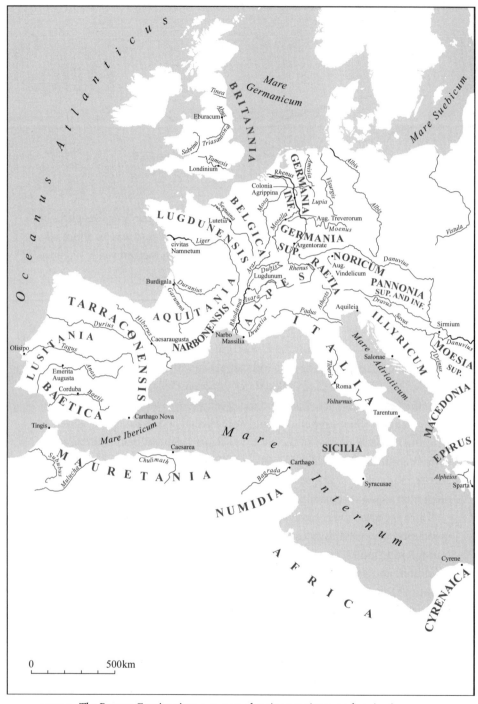

MAP 1. *The Roman Empire circa* A.D. 200, *showing provinces and main rivers.*
Prepared by Maura Pringle, cartographer, Queens University Belfast.

Mare Suebicum

Albis

Vistula

PANNONIA SUP. AND INF.

Danuvius

Dravus

Savus

ILLYRICUM

Salonae

Mare Adriaticum

ITALIA

Tarentum

DACIA

Tyras

Borythenes

Tanais

Rha

Mare Caspium

Sirmium

Danuvius

MOESIA SUP. AND INF.

Hebros

THRACIA

Strymon

MACEDONIA

Thessalonica

EPIRUS

SICILIA

Syracusae

Alpheios

ACHAEA

Athenae

Sparta

Eurotas

Mare Aegeum

ASIA

Caicus

Pergamum

Hermus

Ephesus

Maeander

GALATIA

LYCIA AND PAMPHYLIA

CILICIA

Pyramos

Tarsus

Antiochia

Orontes

Pontus Euxinus

Sinope

Nicomedia

Byzantium

BITHYNIA AND PONTUS

Sangarius

Ancyra

Halys

CAPPADOCIA

ARMENIA

Artaxata

Araxes

Euphrates

Arsanias

Tigris

MESOPOTAMIA

Tigris

S Y R I A

COELE

Palmyra

Euphrates

Ctesiphon

Babylon

PHOENICE

Tyrus

Damascus

PALAESTINA/ JUDAEA

Aelia Capitolina

Jordanes

Cyrene

Mare Internum

Alexandria

CYRENAICA

AEGYPTUS

Memphis

AFRICA

ARABIA

Nilus

Thebae

Sinus Arabicus

0   500km

yellow color that suffuses the Tiber from time to time after rainfall upstream obviously recalls the descriptions in Roman authors of the river as *flavus*. The continuity of the symbolism of rivers such as the Tiber is strikingly realized in Mussolini's erection of an inscribed column to mark the traditional location of the source of Rome's great river.[3]

At Seville (Julius Caesar's Colony of Hispalis) on the Guadalquivir (Baetis), Strabo paints a picture of a navigable river, a route of communications central to the commercial life of the town and indeed the entire province of Baetica.[4] A visitor to Seville today will be struck by the memories of the river's continuing role in the city's affairs through the ages. The Torre de Oro (Tower of Gold) built in 1220 by the Almohad rulers with its twin on the other side of the river (now destroyed) was a river fort, and a great chain stretched across the Guadalquivir between them controlled river traffic; the tower subsequently served as a port office and is now a maritime museum. Furthermore, Columbus set out from this river port on his voyage of exploration. In the twentieth century, an advertisement for a locally produced disinfectant named Zotal featured well-known characteristics of the city, such as the Torre de Oro, the Giralda, and the Alcázar, but also included prominently the Guadalquivir and its shipping.

In this chapter, I deal with the general definition and nature of rivers, including the hydrological cycle and the river environment; the relevance of changes in the long-term configuration of rivers, sea level, and climate; the tradition and significance of Rome as a great river city; the main river systems of the Roman Empire; the problems of the evidence for rivers in the ancient world; and various approaches to the study of rivers.

1   THE HYDROLOGICAL CYCLE AND RIVER DYNAMICS

Rivers and springs are ubiquitous in the Mediterranean and northern European landscape, but vary enormously in size and shape, and we must start with a basic definition. A river is a stream of water flowing along its bed toward the sea or a lake. As such, it acts as an artery in the natural drainage of the earth. A proper river must be constrained by banks, and ideally they should have a winding pattern and varied vegetation.[5] The river type is dictated by water force, which depends on a number of factors, including the size of adjacent hills, the catchment area, rock type, land use, and the nature of the water channel. A river and the alluvial corridor within which it flows can be seen as a fluvial hydrosystem, characterized by longitudinal, lateral, and vertical gradients. It has been described as a one-way flow of water generated by gravity and controlled by the gradient of its bed.[6] The longitudinal gradient develops progressively but may be interrupted or changed by geomorphologic discontinuities. The lateral gradient denotes the relationship between the permanent river channel and all adjacent areas that are inundated seasonally or spasmodically. The vertical gradient denotes the relationship of the river and the aquifers that developed in the alluvial floodplain.[7]

Rivers are part of a changing system, and over centuries they can alter position, bank, and bed, though often in a rather predictable way. The riverine area is therefore not static but dynamic, and river valley communities are consequently subject to change (in that sense, rivers are inconvenient to them), because of the connection between the river water, its banks, and the surrounding area, which included the riverine inhabitants.[8] Deposits and erosion may be on a small scale, affecting individual landholders, and arguably changes occurring within forty years are more important for farmers than large-scale changes taking place over hundreds or even thousands of years and producing great alluvial plains or steep, rocky gorges.

The river environment consists of three parts—the flowing water, the natural surroundings, and its social and cultural milieu.[9] Therefore, the entire river context is very important—water transport, river crossings, local wetlands, local river-based activities that allow people to make a living, and the whole cultural heritage of the divine and beneficent river. In more ordered times, people gradually left their hill settlements and moved to the river valleys, where agricultural land, irrigation systems, settlement sites, and routes tended to become concentrated. Consequently, river valleys have large numbers of archaeological sites, and in the landscapes of most regions, rivers and their valleys are the essential parts.[10] (For examples of river valleys, see figures 1–3.)

The origin of rivers lies in the hydrological cycle.[11] Precipitation falling on the earth is accommodated in different ways, depending on the nature of the ground. Some by evaporation returns to the air; some is absorbed into plant roots and returned to the atmosphere by the process of transpiration or evapotranspiration; and some flows downhill as runoff, which in certain cases can be stored or channeled, or enters the river system. Annual runoff equals the annual precipitation minus evaporation and evapotranspiration. The size of a river basin (drainage area) is an important control because it determines the volume of precipitation received and therefore the volume of runoff generated.[12] There is often a high runoff in the Mediterranean area, and much depends on soil texture and its ability to absorb moisture and the extent of vegetation and its capacity to store water.

If rain falls on soil that does not have or has lost the protection of trees and vegetation roots, it detaches soil particles that are then swept downhill into channels and gullies and ultimately into rivers. At the same time, soil often be-

FIGURE 1. *The Rhine near Koblenz, showing river traffic and, on the hill on the right, the Festung Ehrenbreitstein. Author's photograph.*

comes compacted by rainfall, making it harder for the water to penetrate and allowing more to run away down the hillside. The amount of runoff will be further affected by variable factors, such as the persistence and force of rainfall, the nature of underlying rock, and the composition of the soil; for example, ground that had been saturated or hard-baked in the arid months of the Mediterranean summer would encourage runoff. Climate and topography are also relevant in that the extent of precipitation and the length and severity of winters might set limits to vegetation or its regeneration. A mountainous region with steep upper slopes might have severe precipitation, encouraging runoff down the gradients. As the water gathers momentum, it removes more particles of soil. In many places, human inhabitants made their contribution to the process, though this is notoriously difficult to assess. For example, heavy use of land for agriculture will reduce vegetation cover, while uncultivated lands can allow vegetation growth, which in turn will protect against erosion. In this process there is an important distinction between normal base-flow runoff and exceptional storm-flow runoff. The remaining water enters the underground

FIGURE 2. *The Rhine valley at Braubach, with Marksburg Castle,
dating from 1117, on the hill. Author's photograph.*

water pool until the quantity of water builds up, causing movement to the surface and the appearance of springs, which duly became the source of a river.
Therefore, in the relations of ground and water in the hydrological cycle, the
river is the visible part.[13]

When the hydrological cycle becomes out of balance, excessive river action
takes place, often leading to severe contraction in volume or, by contrast, expansion and flooding. This is the result of a variety of variable factors: topographical, geological, and climatic. In the Mediterranean summer, many
smaller rivers cease to flow altogether. On the other hand, heavy rain, melting
snow on high peaks, and excessive runoff bring about flooding. Other factors
are river gradient, the nature of the river basin, rock formations, local land use,
agricultural practice, and deforestation. Flooding in the lower floodplain can
merely be a nuisance when either the river briefly overflows its banks or the
level of the groundwater rises temporarily. More destructive flooding occurs
when there is unusually high precipitation; this may be made worse by the local
geology in that impermeable rocks and soils will bring about a flooding peak

FIGURE 3. *The Thames near Binsey, north of Oxford, with Port Meadow across the river. Author's photograph.*

more quickly than areas with permeable rocks, which can allow the water to drain away and reduce the flood risk.[14] In certain cases, the river may change course, permanently or temporarily abandoning its old bed.

A particular quality of all rivers is the ability to carry substantial quantities of material in their streams, consisting of dissolved matter from the groundwater that sustains the river. Undissolved matter is either rolled along the bed of the river or carried suspended in its water. The quantity and speed of material depend on the nature of the channel, its incline, and the velocity of the water. The river first drops the heaviest material in its stream; finer material is dropped where the current is slowed by friction, for example, on the inside of river bends. The smallest material is dropped where the river meets sea or tidal currents and can form sand spits or bars at the river mouth.

During their downward course, rivers by a process of abrasion cut deeper into their bed and remove soil from their banks and advance the denudation of the land. The process is not indefinite because, as the river cuts deeper into its bed, the more it lowers that bed as it descends toward sea level, and so the lesser is its gradient; therefore, it will be able to carry less material, and its power to erode will be reduced. In its lower course, as the river's longitudinal gradient declines, the river tends to meander more, and inundation of the surrounding land happens frequently, producing a floodplain; eventually the river delta is extended by the deposition of silt, which often forms a rich farming area with a good water supply and excellent nutrients.[15] Importantly, the rate of alluviation varies notably over time, partly due to changes in climate and other variable factors.[16]

A river can increase its activity, for example, in gradient and amount of sediment carried in the stream, and when it returns to its normal balance, it may cut down into its bed, producing a smaller floodplain; the older floodplain is now abandoned and is separated from the new plain by steep escarpments. So deposits appear at various levels in the geomorphology. It should be emphasized that hydrological systems and floodplain formation proceed over a long time span. Consequently, the stratigraphy of the floodplain represents a time sequence. So if the alluvial chronology can be established, it can be linked to human activity in the floodplain or river catchment area over thousands of years.[17]

There are few substantial river systems in the Mediterranean area with stable flow and consistent volume, despite their important role in the history of the region. Local rivers tend to have narrow valleys with small catchment areas and uncertain volume; storms and winter rain and snow melt produce rapid run-off and torrential streams, which fade away in the summer drought. Perennial streams are particularly valuable. The western sides of mountain ranges often receive more rain and consequently rivers here have less variation. In general, Mediterranean rivers are dynamic, being highly active and volatile, bringing about erosion, downcutting, and deposition, and often causing floods.

2   CHANGES IN THE RIVERINE ENVIRONMENT

It is important to ask how far we can understand ancient river systems by comparing the study of modern river characteristics. Have there been significant changes in the configuration of rivers and sea-level changes? In an influential work, *The Mediterranean Valleys*, Vita-Finzi argued that over 2,000 years Mediterranean rivers modified their valleys and that the changes occurring in river valleys were of the greatest importance, because they had a large concentration of agricultural land and settlements. In general terms, from a study of valley floors in Europe, North Africa (Tripolitania, Cyrenaica, Morocco, Algeria and Tunisia), and Jordan, he contended that there were two definite periods when alluvial material was deposited synchronously, namely

Older Fill circa 8000–7000 B.C. and the Younger Fill, which began probably during the Roman period or soon afterward and continued into the twentieth century. Many streams in the Mediterranean that had previously been down-cutting began to build up their beds, producing alluvial aggradation (the filling up of an area with river-borne detritus). This aggradation produced not a continuous alluvial surface but a stairway of such surfaces, all of which gave the Mediterranean valley its characteristic form, with a well-defined channel. The long period of the Younger Fill had in his view transformed the Mediterranean environment with significant impact on life and society, though he thought that this alluviation was not directly the result of human activity. The alternation between sedimentation and erosion may be due to climate changes, because more rainfall produces more erosion and alterations in sea level. Vita-Finzi therefore contradicted the usual view that from the last age of glaciation there had been no significant change in the climatic and environmental conditions of the Mediterranean. One consequence of this argument was that the Mediterranean area before the onset of the Younger Fill had been notably different and that it was wrong to extrapolate from the subsequent conditions to explain the geomorphology of the Greco-Roman world and earlier.[18]

However, Vita-Finzi's arguments have been challenged by subsequent archaeological investigations that have suggested that the onset of the Younger Fill does not fit his precise chronology and was much more complex than he alleged, representing not continuous and synchronous periods of alluviation but a fragmented sequence of alluviation and also complete lack of alluviation. In particular, local alluvial conditions are likely to have been much more important than Vita-Finzi allowed. For example, the evidence at Narce in the Treia valley in Italy suggests the following picture: alluvial deposition before 200 B.C., a period of erosion from 200 B.C. to A.D. 200, further deposition from 200 to 800, some minor erosion from 800 to 1000, and then deposition until 1800. This sequence is now regarded as consistent with other evidence in Italy and global climate change.[19] Again, if we consider the local alluvial conditions in Britain, there may have been an increase in flooding or sustained flooding in Roman times, possibly because of the villa cultivation system and arable cultivation on clay slopes. But there was little channel change in floodplains in Britain throughout this period.[20] In general, it seems more likely that alluviation was a constant presence in Mediterranean life, but the process, though continuous, varied in effect and in different locations over a long period of time.[21] River valley characteristics changed very slowly in the ancient world, and the most significant movement will have occurred in the deltas of certain great rivers, such as the Po and the Maeander. In respect of Greece in the fifth century B.C., it has been argued that environment and landscape were similar to nowadays and that for the people working the land the ancient landscape was not rapidly changing.[22]

Overall, throughout the period of the Roman world the process of alluviation continued steadily in different ways across the Mediterranean empire, and this process alternated with erosion and downcutting in innumerable river valleys. The effects of this were, however, complicated by a wide range of local factors and conditions. Therefore, the drama of the developing relationship between communities and the environment was often played out in a relatively small local area. River action was a constant presence, removing soil and vegetation from higher ground above the valley floor, sometimes producing serious floods and over time extending fertile farmland, changing the characteristics of traditional wetlands and marshes, and altering the configuration of the coastline with consequences for maritime trade, harbors, and small river ports at the mouths of navigable rivers. Long-term changes in environmental processes will have come about through a whole nexus of variable factors. Furthermore, within these local riverine communities the inhabitants learned the river's ways, adapted to the floods, and in the main managed the consequences of the long-term changes brought about by river action. This is one reason why in this study so much attention is given to the ancient writers and what they said about rivers and their characteristics. It is important to illuminate the level of awareness and understanding of the riverine environment.

In respect of fluctuations in sea level, rivers flow into lakes or the sea, and if the sea level is raised, the gradient of the river in its lower course is reduced; consequently, its velocity declines, as does its ability to carry sediment. As a result, more is deposited near the river mouth. If the sea level falls, the river velocity should increase, and downcutting will increase. Therefore, sea-level changes will potentially have a long-term impact on the riverine environment. However, a river valley is not a uniform area and is subject to different conditions; at the head of the river, climatic conditions may have the most important impact.

Now, there have been significant fluctuations in sea level, notably during the Pleistocene era, which saw a general lowering of sea level, although there were some violent interruptions to this.[23] From the middle of the fifth millennium B.C., sea levels have in general fallen through the process of eustatic adjustment. It has been convincingly argued that the northern coastline of the Mediterranean, being deeply indented, has changed little over 5,000 years, producing many small natural harbors. In this region, only the Rhône delta has seen significant coastal advance because the river brings down about 18 million cubic meters of silt annually. The south coast has changed more, with few off-shore islands and natural harbors.[24] It is possible that the relative change in sea level in the Mediterranean region amounts to only plus or minus half a meter from the early Bronze Age, and sea-level changes throughout the world perhaps amount to between one and two meters since ancient times.[25] There were, of course, local changes, such as the volcanic activity in the Bay of Naples, where coastlines have sunk or been raised (bradyseism) by several meters in histori-cal times. But as Frederiksen has pointed out, although there was some coastal movement of this kind and some limited change in the height of the coastline, even here the relation between sea and land has not altered fundamentally since antiquity.[26] Furthermore, it is difficult to trace how specific points on the coast relate to possible different sea levels, because a number of factors influ-enced this process: inland erosion and deposition by rivers, strength of cur-rents, direction of coastwise movement of sediment, and storms, as well as the local volcanic activity.[27]

The general conclusion must be that there was not a significant change in sea level during the ancient world, and such changes as there were did not have a spectacular effect but were more a series of variations around a stable, long-term state of affairs. So river valleys and sea levels in the Mediterranean area will have been much the same in the ancient Roman world as they are today, though some rivers that were navigable then may now have silted up, and the extension of river deltas has changed the coastline in certain areas. These in the main can be identified even if the exact details of the original coast cannot be recovered. It is likely, however, that more rivers were navigable in the ancient world than now because of changes in water use and the large amount of water now abstracted from rivers for a variety of industrial and other uses. For ex-ample, in ancient times Pisa was accessible by river.[28]

In respect of climate change before A.D. 500, only the broadest generaliza-tions can be made about long-term climate trends, and historians have tended to avoid the issue.[29] In general, the type of evidence available to estimate cli-mate is not helpful.[30] For example, in North Africa archaeology can reveal Ro-man remains in areas that are now largely desert, but this by itself cannot dem-onstrate climate change. One possible avenue of research is based on the study of the pollen of plants (palynology), which can determine the geographical locations and distribution of plants known to require certain climatic condi-tions, and analysis of tree ring chronology. Most agree that it is unlikely that the ancient climate differed significantly from that of the modern.[31] I am in-clined to accept that the Mediterranean area is in the "sub-Atlantic" phase of climate, which began circa 700 B.C.[32] It is in fact very difficult to relate political and social change to climate change or other climatic events, though regional or local studies may offer some way forward.[33] In respect of North Africa, Brent Shaw has argued that agricultural developments of the Roman period, which may in any case have been exaggerated, probably took place under climatic conditions analogous to those of the present.[34]

3   THE WATERY ORIGINS OF ROME

Even at the greatest extent of its territorial control after the creation of the province of Mesopotamia by Septimius Severus in the late second century A.D., the Roman Empire remained a Mediterranean-based empire, and many of its rivers had Mediterranean characteristics, with a short course and an inconsistent, turbulent, and sometimes torrential stream. Rome itself was a river city, and its topography illustrates many riverine characteristics, the role of the river in the history and tradition of a community, the exploitation of rivers, and yet ultimate failure to master them. Rome remained throughout its history the only substantial settlement on the river Tiber, and though its site in a depression along the banks of the river was greatly subject to flooding, it retained a romantic appeal. The speech that Livy puts in the mouth of the dictator Camillus praises the splendid riverine site of Rome: "Gods and men had good reason to choose this place for founding a city, with its beneficent hills and helpful river, along which the fruits of inland places are brought, and seaborne produce from abroad. The sea is close enough to be beneficial but not close enough to expose us to the danger of foreign fleets; we are in the center of Italy in a place uniquely suited for the growth of a city."[35]

Traditional mythology about the city's foundation emphasized its watery origins. According to one account, Amulius, king of Alba Longa, having deposed his elder brother Numitor, compelled the latter's daughter, Rhea Silvia, to become a Vestal Virgin to prevent her from having children. But after she was allegedly raped by Mars and bore twins, Amulius ordered the babies to be drowned in the Tiber. But the river was in flood (perhaps reflecting a well-known occurrence in popular experience), and as the waters subsided the basket containing the twins finally drifted ashore at the Ficus Ruminalis. Here a she-wolf found and suckled them, until they were discovered by the royal shepherd Faustulus, who took them back to his wife. She named them Romulus and Remus.[36] In a sense the river rescued and protected the twins by its characteristic riverine behavior. The whole story is encapsulated in a coin issued in A.D. 71, which depicts Roma sitting on a rock, the Seven Hills of Rome, the she-wolf and twins, and the river Tiber reclining as a traditional bearded figure holding a reed.[37]

The river theme also appears in a different guise in the story of Aeneas, who was a refugee from the Greek sack of Troy and another heroic figure deeply associated with the foundation of Rome. In the third century B.C., as Rome turned its attention to Asia and increasingly encountered the Greek-speaking eastern Mediterranean, it was politically expedient to emphasize the idea of foundation by Aeneas, who had fought so nobly against the Greeks.[38] This story eventually merged with the Romulus version, and Aeneas was held to have founded Lavinium in Italy with Romulus as his distant descendant.

Virgil was the greatest exponent of the Aeneas story. In his version, as Aeneas sailed along the coast of Italy a suddenly calm sea enabled him to spot the mouth of the Tiber, whose pleasant, shady stream and birdsong proved alluring.[39] As the Trojans advanced into Latium, war broke out, and the first Italian casualties, Almo and Galaesus, bore the name of Italian rivers.[40] Symbolically, the Trojans were mastering the rivers and the countryside. However, the Tiber willingly offered a passage to the newcomers, and the personified river-god, Tiberinus, appeared to Aeneas on the bank and uttered a stirring prophecy of Aeneas's ultimate triumph and the site of the future Rome. Indeed, the river promises to lead him and allow his ships to row far upstream, a great boon since the Tiber is an outstanding landmark cutting through the fields, a source of life for great cities, and of all rivers the most favored by the gods. He commits himself to the Trojan side, and his reward will be the honors he is destined to receive. Aeneas subsequently prayed to the Horned River and asked him to be at his side.[41] Therefore, the Tiber is crucial to the founding of the city and also to the Trojan advance into Latium. For the river stilled his current, so that Trojan oars met no resistance as they powered the ships forward around long bends and through forests on the welcoming river's surface. The river becomes part of Rome's destined supremacy, flowing through an area that eventually was to be exalted to heaven by Roman might.[42] Virgil's account has successfully linked a great Roman landmark with the city's foundation and mighty imperial destiny and explains the divine honors paid to Tiberinus.[43]

The watery destiny of Rome remained a potent theme for later writers. Strabo, doubtless seeking to please his audience in Augustan Rome, spoke of Roman foresight in founding cities with adequate sewerage provision and a good water supply from aqueducts. The Tiber served as a cleansing agent by carrying away the ordure. Veritable rivers of water flowed through the aqueducts and sewers, and there were many service pipes and fountains. Although the Romans of his day admired beautiful things, the Tiber remained the city's central focus, and the grassy Campus Martius by the river remained a great attraction, while Augustus's mausoleum nestled near the riverbank. Strabo vividly describes the alluring view: "The surrounding architecture and the surface (of the Campus Martius), which is grassy throughout the year, and the summits of the hills above the river that sweep right down to its banks, offer a view just like a painting of stage scenery, from which is difficult to drag yourself away."[44] In his survey of the peoples and geography of Italy, the Elder Pliny emotionally praised the beautiful and tranquil Tiber, steadily absorbing the water of its tributaries; it was an integral part of the great city with no evil intention even in flood. For Pliny, though, the Tiber was not merely a scenic background or a source of water but provided a dynamic commercial dimension as a waterway for trade and so linked Rome with far-off peoples.[45]

The ancient hydrology of the site of Rome is recalled in the persistence of certain names and rites. Within the city, fresh springs were of great importance for drinking water in the early period, as Frontinus, in charge of the more eye-catching aqueducts, observed: "For four hundred and forty-one years from the foundation of the city, the Romans were content to use the water that they drew from the Tiber or wells or springs. Reverence for springs still endures, and they are honored and venerated. They are credited with bringing healing to the sick." Frontinus saw the aqueducts that supplied Rome in his day as the direct descendants of those early natural springs, and he mentions specifically the springs of the Camenae, Apollo, and Juturna (see map 2).[46]

Juturna is particularly interesting as a celebration of a freshwater source. In one traditional version, Juturna was associated with the river Numicus but was brought to Rome and protected "those who exercise skill with water," who kept the festival of Juturnalia. Juturna's water was salubrious, and the name allegedly came from *iuvare*, "to help."[47] In mythology, Juturna was wife of Janus, daughter of the river Volturnus and mother of Fons, although another version held that she was the sister of Turnus, Aeneas's redoubtable opponent as he struggled to found Rome. Her ancestry brought out the importance of the hydrological patterns of rivers and springs. The first temple to Juturna was built on the Campus Martius by Q. Lutatius Catulus (probably the consul of 242 B.C.). However, the *lacus Juturnae* was a spring-fed pool in the south corner of the Roman Forum. It was here that Castor and Pollux made their dramatic appearance to water their horses after the battle of Lake Regillus in 496 B.C.,[48] and a monumental basin and a shrine of the deity were constructed to the west of the spring. Castor and Pollux appeared again after the battle of Pydna in 168, and L. Aemilius Paullus adorned the basin with a marble statue of the divine brothers and their horses in celebration of his victory.[49] Further

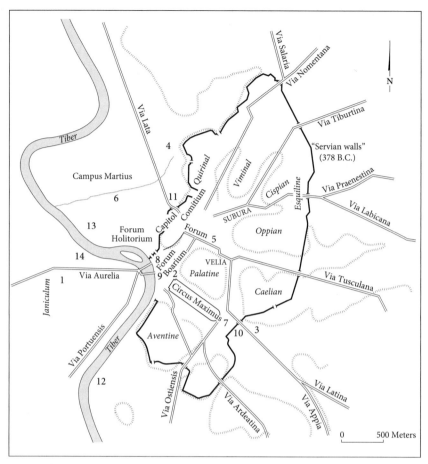

Map labels (within figure):

Via Salaria
Via Nomentana
Via Tiburtina
N
"Servian walls" (378 B.C.)
Tiber
Via Lata
4
Campus Martius
Quirinal
Viminal
Cispian
Esquiline
Via Praenestina
Via Labicana
6
11
Comitium
SUBURA
Oppian
13
Forum Holitorium
Capitol
Forum 5
14
Via Aurelia
Forum Boarium
8
9 2
VELIA
Palatine
Caelian
Via Tusculana
Janiculum
1
Circus Maximus
7
10 3
Aventine
Via Portuensis
Tiber
12
Via Ostiensis
Via Ardeatina
Via Appia
Via Latina
0   500 Meters

1. Ara of Fons	6. Petronia stream	11. *Porta Fontinalis*
2. Ficus Ruminalis	7. *Piscina publica*	12. *Porticus Aemilia*
3. *Fons Camenarum*	8. *Pons Aemilius*	13. *Prata Flaminia*
4. *Fons Cati*	9. *Pons Sublicius*	14. *Prata Quinctia*
5. *Lacus Juturnae*	10. *Porta Capena*	

MAP 2. *The center of Rome in the early third century* B.C. *Adapted from F. W. Walbank, A. E. Astin, M. W. Frederiksen, and R. M. Ogilvie (eds.),* Cambridge Ancient History, *2nd edition, vol. VII.2,* The Rise of Rome to 220 B.C. *(Cambridge, 1989), 406–7, figure 50, copyright © 1989 Cambridge University Press, with permission of Cambridge University Press.*

alterations were made by Tiberius in A.D. 6. In the third century, many dedications were made here by the curators of the water supply, who had moved their office to this area from the Campus Martius.

We have here a combination of the spiritual and mythological combined with the practical management of the city's drinking water. Associated with Rome's origins and development, its military success, and the physical well-being of the city, the spring became part of the cultural complex of an imperial people with strong respect for the importance of running water and the watery environment. The *lacus* was virtually a kind of spiritual center, which possibly contained a statue of Aesculapius and a healing shrine, while the springs continued in use into the Middle Ages.[50]

Juturna had a particularly distinguished history, but the other *fontes* and *fontani* of Rome, though more shadowy, are impressive. Some, such as the *fons Apollinis* and the *fons Camenarum*, were associated with distinguished deities. Other fountains and springs were sponsored by members of families, who bestowed their names upon them.[51] In general their names are redolent of the watery life of Rome and also its local identities, culture, and history. Above all, the *fontes* were landmarks in the topography of the city. The altar of Fons or Fontus stood out among the many springs on the Janiculum by its location close to the tomb of Numa.[52] A shrine of Fons, dedicated in 231 B.C. on the Ides of October at the feast of the Fontinalia by Cnaeus Papirius Maso from booty he had captured in Corsica, was probably situated in the southern part of the Campus Martius just outside the *porta Fontinalis*.[53] Festus thought that the gate took its name from the shrine, and whether true or not, this expresses his belief that a city landmark could be named after a spring.[54] The *fons Cati*, a spring on the western slope of the Quirinal, named after the man in whose land it emerged, was situated near the *porta Salutaris*, which apparently took its name from the Temple of Salus. This spring, which gave rise to the useful stream Petronia, benefited from its association with the healthy epithets of the vicinity.[55]

One of the most famous springs, the *fons Camenarum*, had striking topographical associations. The Camenae, originally fountain deities, were subsequently identified with the Muses. The term Camenae had wide relevance in the city of Rome, including the valley that extended northeast from the Caelian Hill, a grove, the spring itself at the southern end of the hill, and a shrine. There was also a *vicus Camenarum* in Regio I of the city, tying the spring and its celebrated health-giving water to a local area.[56] The spring was, in fact, consecrated by Vestal Virgins, and they sprinkled its water in their temple. Eventually a temple was erected, and the day of its dedication on 13 August became an annual festival.[57] At a less elevated level, we find a *vicus laci Fundani* probably between the Quirinal and Capitoline Hills. A *lacus* was a street fountain usually with a watering trough, and it is interesting that it was sometimes used to designate location and establish connections with the local area through a water source.

The springs of Rome brought great benefits to the city in fresh drinking water and pleasant watery surroundings. We have already seen the *fons Cati* near the *porta Salutaris*, to which we may add the *fons Muscosus*, whose evocative name may well convey intimations of the mossy setting of a rural spring in the heart of Rome.[58] The *piscina publica* was a more striking demonstration of the communal benefits of water. First heard of in 215 B.C., it was located on low ground between the *via Appia* and the northeast slopes of the Aventine Hill, just south of the future site of the Circus Maximus. It probably served originally as a public reservoir or pool fed by the many natural springs in the area. Later, when drinking water became generally available from aqueducts, it became a place to which people went to swim and exercise; then it fell out of use and had disappeared by the second century A.D.[59] Festus notes that the name remained in his day, and it is a reminder of the role of watery attributes in the life of the city of Rome that in Regio XII the *vicus Piscinae publicae* remained as a memory of this great public asset. In popular talk the entire Regio XII was identified with the *piscina publica*, and the local butchers were described as the *piscinenses*.[60]

The springs brought other benefits by sustaining some of the many small streams that enlivened and watered the metropolis, for example, the stream Petronia, which flowed from the southern slopes of the Quirinal Hill and contributed to the environment of the Campus Martius, before turning southward and crossing the *prata Flaminia* to enter the Tiber opposite the northern end of the Tiber Island. The stream may have formed the boundary between the Campus Martius and the *prata Flaminia*. It also marked the boundary of the city auspices, and whenever magistrates crossed it, for example in order to conduct business in the Campus Martius, they had to take the *auspicia peremnia*. These auspices were specifically linked to the crossing of a river, emphasizing the holy significance of crossing a river that might have a divine origin: "The phrase *auspicia peremnia* is applied when someone, having taken the auspices, crosses a river or water that has come from a sacred source."[61] Of course, the Tiber itself was originally the boundary marking off the Roman heartland from the Etruscan outsiders—hence, the importance of cutting down the bridge behind Horatius.[62]

Even in the time when Rome was provided with a sophisticated water supply and superbly engineered aqueducts, the *fontes* and their watery environment have an impressive presence. This is borne out by some enigmatic inscriptions from Rome celebrating the activities of people described as "masters and servants of the Spring" (*magistri* and *ministri Fontis*).[63] Several inscriptions from the vicinity of the *piscina publica* are dedicated to the *fons Scaurianus*, recording *magistri* whose names suggest that they are freedmen, and *ministri*, who are slaves. These seem to be societies given over to the worship of particular springs and their watery attributes,[64] giving us a glimpse of the respect accorded to running water by ordinary people in Rome.

Damp and grassy areas were much valued throughout the city. The term *campus* denoted land near the city just beyond the Servian wall. The various *campi* of the city were sources of moisture, either grassy spaces as Strabo observed, or water meadows, or even marshy areas. The most famous, of course, was the Campus Martius, which was the floodplain of the Tiber north of Rome, an area of low-lying ground between the river and the surrounding hills, and traversed by two streams, the Petronia, which was described earlier, and another watercourse known in modern times as the Aqua Sallustiana. The Campus Martius was a great public space for recreation, exercise, military training, and swimming in the river.[65] It contained the *palus Caprae*, a swamp perhaps located in the depression west of the spot where the *saepta Iulia* was later built; from this watery context, according to Roman tradition, Romulus was conveyed to heaven in a thundercloud.[66] The word *prata* usually designated flat land beyond the *pomerium* that was perhaps suitable for cultivation but not necessarily under cultivation. Among gardens on the west bank of the river was land once belonging to the dictator L. Quinctius Cincinnatus, which remained in the early empire with the toponym *prata Quinctia*, indicating meadows; there were also *prata Mucia*, meadows originally belonging to C. Mucius Scaevola.

Throughout the time of Rome's early development, running water continued to exert a strong pull over the minds of the Romans. This appears in the naming of newly created tribes, which celebrated the addition of new water sources; this in turn symbolized the steady increase in Rome's territory and its mastery of Italy's natural resources and attributes and ultimately over the peoples who depended on them. Livy records the addition in 387 B.C. of four new tribes after the conquest of Veii: Stellatina, Tromentina, Sabatina, and Arniensis. The names of at least three of these were clearly associated with water sources: the Arniensis can hardly refer to the river Arnus flowing in northern Etruria but perhaps may be derived from a river in southern Etruria nowadays known as the Arrone.[67] The Sabatina was named after *lacus Sabatinus*, northwest of Veii in the Tiber valley north of Rome, and the Stellatina after the *campus Stellatinus* near Capena, northeast of Veii also in the Tiber valley. The Tromentina was named after a *campus Tromentus*, which cannot be certainly identified, but which we may infer belonged to the same area, closer to the site of Veii.[68] The nomenclature reflects the geographical location of Rome's appropriation of watery resources as it advanced along the Tiber valley, including lakes, meadows, and the Tiber's tributaries.

Expansion eastward was associated with the valley of the river Anio, which rose in the Simbruini Mountains, and the creation of the Aniensis tribe in 299 B.C. marked the defeat of the Aequi and the appropriation of their water supply. In 273 Manius Curius Dentatus arranged to have the Old Anio, water from a source of the river near Tibur, brought into the city by an aqueduct built from the proceeds of booty from the war against Pyrrhus. Once again we have the connection of war, victory, and water, taken from the vanquished and given to the victors.[69]

South of Rome in Latium, Roman campaigns against the Volsci brought more territory, and in 318 the tribe Oufentina was created and named after the river Oufens in the territory of Privernum; this river flowed from Mount Lepinus to the coastal plain near Tarracina, which had been founded as a colony in 329. Once again nomenclature expresses Roman appropriation of natural assets as well as territory, including the local wetland, reclaimed from the Pomptine marshes; in 358 the tribe Pomptina had been created.[70] In 299 B.C. the tribe Teretina was named after the river Teres, which was seemingly a tributary of the Liris in Campania.[71] The Romans appreciated the importance of the river valleys in eliminating the threat from the Aurunci in the lower Liris valley, and the Hernici, who dominated the valley of its tributary. In general, it is important to note that the earlier rustic tribes, with the exception of Clustumina, tended not to have geographical names.[72] The emergence of this trend in tribal nomenclature goes with the aggressive conquest and subjugation of neighboring Italian peoples and helped the Romans to define and reinforce their claim to mastery of the land, rivers, river valleys, and the watery environment that sustained Italy. In this context the Velina tribe presents an interesting problem. Although its territory is in Picenum, it seems to take its name from the *lacus Velinus* near Reate. Manius Curius Dentatus had famously drained the waters of this lake into the river Nar, and it is possible that his original intention during his censorship of 272 B.C. was to establish a new tribe in the vicinity of Reate named after the *lacus Velinus*. The project lapsed on his death, and when the new tribe was established, it was assigned to a region where its name did not fit.[73]

The river acted as a dividing line, and on the western side of the river the Transtiberim was originally an area outside the acceptable, and rather mysterious. The earliest bridge across the Tiber was the *pons Sublicius*, traditionally built by Ancus Martius. It was constructed entirely of wood, probably for reasons of religious lore, and its maintenance and preservation were in the care of the college of *pontifices* (bridge makers).[74] It was the site of a regular ritual performed by the Vestals and *pontifices* when thirty reed dolls shaped like humans (Argei) were thrown into the river on the Ides of May.[75] It has been plausibly suggested that this was propitiation of the river-god for the building of the bridge, which probably ran south of the Tiber Island from the southern end of the Forum Boarium, possibly at the location of an old river ferry.[76] The wall built around Rome in 378, twelve years after the Gallic sack, confined the city to the east bank, and the walls abutted the riverbank only along the bend south of the Tiber Island by the slopes of the Aventine Hill.[77] It is not clear when the penetration of the west bank started; the Transtiberim region was XIV in Augustus's organization of the city, but development on this side was limited and only one surviving inscription uses the word "Transtiberim" as a noun.[78] When the district on this bank was still organized as a *pagus*, it was described as the *pagus Ianiculensis* in two inscriptions dating from about 100 B.C.[79] To the north of the Transtiberim area was the *ager Vaticanus*, and the term was also used to describe farming land on the west bank.[80] By the middle of the first century B.C., there were many *horti*, which were later absorbed into imperial estates.[81] The idea of an outside, somewhat alien area appears in the fact that the west bank of the Tiber was described as *ripa Veientana* in contrast to *ripa Romana* in the marker stones of the *curatores riparum*.[82] There were also meadows in this area.[83]

To sum up, the river Tiber was at the center of traditional stories of the foundation of Rome, in which it appeared as a benevolent collaborator. It illustrates the importance of a river in the cultural context of communities. The river or the river-god appeared intermittently in literature and art, representing Roman traditions, and effectively the essence of Rome itself, an idea that was to be remarkably long-lived.[84] Rome was a genuine river town, at an important crossing point, and on the route to the coast, which was valuable for trading in salt; therefore, it enjoyed many riverine advantages and some of the usual dangers. The potential benefits were fully exploited, especially in respect of the water meadows beyond the city along the Tiber valley, and the salt pans at the Tiber mouth.[85] Yet the city was at the mercy of the Tiber's tumultuous characteristics and was prone to severe flooding, which ultimately it failed to master despite many attempts. The hydrology of the Tiber basin and the site of Rome meant that the Romans were well acquainted with, and had great respect for, the many rivers, springs, and other manifestations of running water in the area; they expressed this in watery toponyms and got to know about the acquisition and distribution of water. They certainly understood the seminal importance, relevance, and necessity of rivers in human thinking and activity and came to appreciate what might be described as the propaganda of water, claiming and appropriating the rivers and water sources of other peoples, and adding the names to the Roman tribal nomenclature. In the context of continuing territorial expansion, it was to be an area where the Roman government became increasingly astute.

4 THE GEOGRAPHICAL SETTING

Although the empire was geographically based on the Mediterranean, some large rivers rising outside the Mediterranean area (such as the Rhine, Danube, Rhône, and Nile) influenced Mediterranean history by providing routes of communication and opening up whole areas to trade and colonization. The Nile was of course exceptional (and recognized as such in the ancient world) in the extent, regularity, and impact of the annual flood. Furthermore, the territorial extent of the empire embraced regions with river systems of distinctly different character that engendered for various reasons vastly different amounts of evidence.

For example, the geographical entity of modern Spain and Portugal, including in the imperial period the three Roman provinces of Tarraconensis, Baetica, and Lusitania, had a striking combination of Mediterranean and Atlantic characteristics; beyond the straits of Gibraltar, there is open sea, and strong winds sweep the coastline. In fact, Spain has enormous geographical diversity with great variety of landscape, from the verdant valleys of Cantabria in the north to the virtually desert terrain of Castile and Extremadura. The land is dominated by its mountains and rivers. The Meseta is an enormous inland plateau extending to more than 200,000 square kilometers, surrounded by mountains on three sides—in the north the Cordillera of Cantabria, in the east the Iberian Mountain fringe, and in the south the Sierra Morena; it is separated by the Ebro (Hiberus) basin from the Pyrenees. To the west are the mountains of eastern Portugal cut through by the valleys of the Douro/Duero (Durius), Tajo (Tagus), and Guadiana (Anas), the last two being separated by the Montes de Toledo. To the south lies Andalucía dominated by the valley of the Guadalquivir (Baetis). These four great rivers flow from east to west toward the Atlantic. Only the Ebro of the main rivers flows southward into the Mediterranean. Around the southern coastal strip, many smaller rivers flowed into the Mediterranean and down to the Cantabrian coast into the Atlantic.[86] It remains a characteristic of the main Spanish rivers that their catchment areas are in regions of low rainfall, and they flow through many arid parts. Therefore, they are subject to great variations in volume. Precipitation also varies significantly, with the north having a pluviose climate and generally cool temperatures; Andalucía and the southeast low rainfall and hot summers, with the temperature in Seville often in the mid-forties centigrade; and the Meseta a continental climate.[87] The river valleys to the south and east and also the Ebro left rich alluvial deposits.

France (comprising the Roman provinces of Gallia Narbonensis, Lugdunensis, Aquitania, and Belgica) does not have so extreme a contrast of climate and terrain as Spain. More than one-half of the surface area of France lies less than 182 meters above sea level, and only one-quarter is mountainous. The Central Massif dominates the geography of the country and generates many rivers. The river Loire rises here, also the Allier and many other tributaries that serve the river systems of the Garonne, Rhône, and Seine. France in fact resembles a series of lowland areas with interposed uplands, and river valleys provide an important linking role. In this enormously varied geography, Provence (which made up a substantial part of Gallia Narbonensis) has a Mediterranean outlook and is enclosed by a series of mountain barriers—the Alps, the Pyrenees, the Cévennes, and the Massif Central, and by the sea in the south. The dominant feature of the topography of this area is the valley of the Rhône (Rhodanus). On its journey to the Mediterranean, the river passes through a series of basins and gorges and absorbs numerous tributaries, the most important of which are the Saône (Arar), Isère (Isara), and the Durance (Druentia). The town of Arles (Arelate) stands at the Rhône delta, and the river flows into the sea through two mouths—the Great Rhône to the east and the Little Rhône to the west. Between lies the great marshy plain of the Camargue. The route to Aquitania was opened up by the important waterways of the Aude (Atax) and the Garonne (Garumna) connected by the Gate of Carcassonne. The great river systems of France are not merely self-contained regions but linked by connections between the valleys; for example, the Rhône-Saône lowland corridor is linked to the upper valley of the Loire, and the Seine, and to the east to the Rhine via the Meuse (Mosa).[88] To the east of the Rhône valley, the valley of Durance for a time provided a route through the Cottian Alps into Italy, until Augustus developed the coastal route by building the *via Julia Augusta*.

These dynamic river systems of Spain and France were central to the lives of riverine communities in the ancient world. Many ancient writers have described their characteristics or commented on them, and there is a reasonable amount of archaeological evidence, especially in respect of the production of pottery in riverine sites and the transport of goods by river and by road along river valleys; in Spain this can be linked to the production zones of olive oil and wines. The wealth and eminence of Roman settlements and river ports in Spain, such as Augusta Emerita, Hispalis, Corduba, and the seaport Gades at the mouth of the Guadalquivir, also bear witness to the importance of rivers, as do Arelate and Lugdunum in Gaul. Specialized studies on rivers as routes of communication in Spain and France have benefited from archaeological investigation over the past twenty years.[89]

But this level of evidence can be contrasted with the situation in Britain and Greece. In Britain, the analysis of physical and historical geography has traditionally employed a distinction between highland and lowland areas, the former being the west and north with higher relief, the latter being low-lying with low hills and many river valleys. The division is too rigid and does not recognize significant regional variations in relief, soil and climate.[90] However, Britain in Roman times did have an impressive river system, especially east of the Pennine watershed, where the Tyne (Tinea), Yorkshire Ouse (Abus), Trent (Trisantona), and Thames (Tamesis) were navigable, and thus important for the movement of goods and communication, and contributed to settlement patterns. Rivers to the west of the watershed were smaller and of less significance, except, for example, the Clyde (Clota), Dee (Deva), and Avon/Severn (Abona/Sabrina). Nevertheless we lack good detailed evidence for the impact of rivers on life in the river valleys, and in his history of Roman Britain, Sheppard Frere makes only a brief reference to rivers as "not negligible for transport purposes."[91] The Thames, of course, served London, where there were impressive port facilities.[92] Only in the Fens and Lincolnshire has a canal been definitely identified linking rivers — the Foss Dyke connecting Lincoln on the river Witham with the river Trent, and thence to the Humber Estuary.[93] The distribution of harbors, anchorages, and inland ports suggests the complexity of water travel in the province of Britain, which it is, however, impossible to document adequately.[94]

Greece (incorporating the Roman provinces of Achaea and Macedonia) is dominated by ranges of limestone mountains running from northwest to southeast and effectively dividing the country into series of virtually self-contained zones with differing climate and ecology.[95] The coastline is heavily indented with few good harbors, and communications are not easy. The rivers of Greece tend to be short and tumultuous and frequently dry up in the Mediterranean summer. These rivers were probably not navigable over long distances and not of significant value as routes of communication and contact on a large scale.

Although they may have served local communities well for short-term travel or transport, that is difficult to discover. Several rivers brought about important alluvial activity, for example, the Alpheios, which was eventually to bury the abandoned sanctuary of Olympia under a thick layer of alluvium. However, for riverine history in Greece, our literary evidence tends to have more of a mythological slant and to offer an illustration of the watery cultural history of the Greek communities. This reflects in part the local interest of Pausanias, one of our main sources.

The great rivers Rhine and Danube were among the most famous in the ancient world and generate much literary and archaeological evidence, though a great deal of this is of a rather general character.[96] The Danube, for example, is second only to the Volga among European rivers in volume of flow. It rises in the Black Forest and attracts many tributaries before turning east-southeast below Regensburg, where it is joined by one of its greatest tributaries, the Inn. Then it flows through a series of gorges and three large interior plains and is eventually joined by three more substantial tributaries, the Drava (Dravus) and Sava (Savus) on the right bank and the Tisza (Pathissus) on the left. At the western edge of the Carpathians, it flows through a series of mighty gorges, the greatest of which is the Iron Gates gorge, where the river narrows from one mile to 129 yards; after this it opens out into an enormous floodplain on its way to the Black Sea. Its average volume amounts to about 6,500 cubic meters per second. The river now provides an international frontier and a great waterway, as indicated by the setting up of the International Danube Navigation Commission at the Paris Conference of 1856. In 1948 the Belgrade Convention redefined free navigation on the Danube, and nowadays eleven European countries cooperate to maintain the river's navigability through their territory: Germany, Austria, Hungary, Slovakia, Croatia, Serbia, Bulgaria, Romania, Moldova, Russia, and Ukraine.[97]

Similarly, the Rhine, which stretches for 1,320 kilometers and achieves an average discharge of about 2,200 cubic meters per second, is intimately connected with the welfare of the countries through which it flows: Belgium, France, Germany, the Netherlands, and Switzerland. In the 1930s, at the height of its importance, the Rhine carried two-thirds of the waterborne traffic of Germany, as well as significant traffic from Holland and France. The main port at Duisburg-Ruhrort handled 37 million tons in 1937. Naturally, the right to use the Rhine and the means of ensuring that others used it responsibly have exercised national governments. For example, between 1648 and 1919 there were 105 separate conventions and agreements on the international use of the Rhine. As a result of decisions taken at the Congress of Vienna in 1815, a Central Commission for Navigation on the Rhine was established to ensure "the enforcement of common rules as well as to provide an authority used as a means of communication between riparian states with regard to all aspects of navigation." The provisions affecting navigation were updated at the Convention of Strasbourg in 1963.[98]

In Roman times, these great rivers were at the heart of territories crucial to the survival of the empire. Both the Rhine and the Danube ran through important military and frontier zones and for this reason were a perpetual source of interest to ancient observers. The Danube flowed past seven Roman provinces, often marking the edge of Roman control, though in Dacia providing an important transit route; the level of archaeological investigation here is as varied as the settlements along the river. But the kind of evidence is distinctive and often concerned with river fleets and the supply of armies. Similarly, the Rhine and the Danube had along their banks great legionary bases, which we know about mainly because they were hubs of military planning. We know much less about commercial activity on the rivers and how this affected riverine communities, except insofar as there were significant links between the Rhône valley and the Rhine as a route for military supplies. Symbolically, the Rhine and the Danube represent Roman acquisition of the natural environment, which then works for Rome, but the economic and social consequences for local riverine communities are more difficult to recover and remain shadowy. We would also like to know more about seemingly important tributary rivers, such as the Main, flowing into the Rhine at Mainz (Mogontiacum), the site of elaborate memorial celebrations for the dead princes Drusus and Germanicus,[99] and the Savus and Dravus flowing into the Danube at Singidunum and near Mursa.

Another great German river, the Elbe (Albis), was for a time at the center of Roman plans of conquest. Augustus claimed to have pacified the Gallic and Spanish provinces and Germany from Cadiz (Gades) to the mouth of the Elbe.[100] Tiberius's brother, the Elder Drusus, did penetrate to the banks of the Elbe only to die on the return journey at a location noted by Strabo to be between two rivers, the Rhine and the Saale (Salas). The Elbe flowed parallel to the Rhine, and between these great rivers lay other navigable rivers, notably the Ems (Amisia) and the Weser (Visurgis).[101]

The province of Noricum had a distinctive geography in which the Danube partly acted as northern boundary. It was an Alpine province where mountain ranges were traversed by river valleys that ran parallel to the high peaks of the Alps. These provided suitable areas for settlement and practical routes for communications. In the west the Rienz (Burrus) was notable, and in the east the valley of the (Austrian) Drau (Dravus). The zone between the Alps and the

Danube forms a single geographical area with many river valleys, especially the Inn (Aenus), Salzach (Ivarus), Enns (Anisus), Traisen (Tragisamus), and Erlauf (Ar(e)lape).[102]

Roman Dalmatia extended northward into the Danube basin and was bounded in the north by the valley of the Savus. The Velebit Mountains rising to more than 1,676 meters stretch southward to the hinterland of Zadar, and near the Adriatic coast generally short rivers flow to the sea. In northern Dalmatia the rivers are part of the watershed of the Savus, and the Drina (Dreinos) is the largest, flowing for 241 kilometers to join the Savus near Sirmium. The Savus served as a great route of lateral communications toward which travelers made their way up through the smaller river valleys.[103]

In the Roman province of Asia Minor the mountainous Anatolian plateau often rises to more than 3,048 meters; the coastal belt tends to be narrow but contains some of the most fertile areas. Rivers are irregular and some drain into the Black Sea, but the most important run from east to west and drain into the Aegean and Mediterranean. For example, the Scamander, Euenos, Caicus, Hermus, Meles, Cayster, and Maeander flowed down to the coast through fertile valleys, though some, such as the Maeander, produced significant alluviation, which eventually changed the relationship of river, land, and coastline. The Maeander was well known locally and associated with valley communities, as is reflected in celebration on local coinage of some cities. By combining a wide range of evidence on the Maeander, it is possible to write the history of the associated riverine communities over a long time span embracing the Byzantine period and the Middle Ages.[104]

In the Near and Middle East, the large province of Syria and, from A.D. 6, the province of Judaea were centers of Roman control. Subsequent reorganizations here saw the creation of three provinces Syria Coele, Syria Phoenice, and Syria Palaestina; in A.D. 72 Cappadocia was joined with Galatia and acquired a legionary garrison; and in the late second century the new province of Mesopotamia was created. The terrain is dominated by mountains, and there are not many rivers. The Lebanon is a limestone range on the coast extending from north of Tripoli to south of Sidon. The eastern side descends into the Bekaa valley and is in general arid, while on the western side a series of terraces and gorges stretch down to the Mediterranean and are heavily cultivated. Beyond the Bekaa valley is the Anti-Lebanon, which descends in ridges fanning out northeast to the valley of the Euphrates.

The western mountains are drained from north to south. The Litani (Litas) rises in the Bekaa valley and flows south before turning west and reaching the sea between Tyre and Sidon. The Orontes flows north, into what is now Turkey, before reaching the sea. Smaller rivers such as the Eleutheros flow from east to west to the coast. The Jordan flows for 320 kilometers in the rift valley that stretches from Antioch to the Gulf of Aqaba and is fed by springs and snow-melt on Mount Hermon; passing though the Sea of Galilee, it descends to the Dead Sea. In the ancient world, these rivers were apparently significant.

The Tigris and the Euphrates were, of course, well known, and there was much interest in how the Euphrates waterway had been manipulated by Alexander the Great. But these rivers were not as directly involved in imperial activities as the great rivers of the West, and the Euphrates valley, although from time to time a conduit for Roman invasions of Mesopotamia, did not have the same military resonance in Rome as the Rhine and the Danube, at least until the third century A.D. The Euphrates therefore did not attract the attention of our sources in the same way, although the river appears as symbolizing Parthia's military threat and its ultimate defeat by Rome, and for a time marked the boundary between Rome and the Parthian Empire; it was on an island in the river that Gaius Caesar and the Parthian king Phraataces met to ratify Augustus's foreign policy deal.[105]

North Africa offers another different picture with its many small local rivers, apart from the Bagrada valley. Here water conservation and irrigation were the principal concerns, and Roman land surveyors noticed how Africa differed from Italy in attitudes to guarding water rights: "In Italy or in certain provinces, it is a serious offense if you divert water onto someone else's land, but in the province of Africa, if you prevent water from crossing their land."[106] Africa also offers important evidence for the regulation of water supplies for irrigation and the use of small dams.[107]

Certain rivers excited special interest. In Egypt, the Nile not only dominated the entire length of the country as a waterway and route of communications but annually inundated the land with its life-giving waters, thus sustaining intensive agriculture and making the Nile valley one of the most fertile and productive areas of the ancient world.[108] The Roman province of Egypt stretched from the Mediterranean to the first cataract near Elephantine, and from here the river flowed for about 700 kilometers to Memphis at the beginning of its delta; from there it continued for another 200 kilometers to the sea by three main channels, the Canopic, Sebennytic, and Pelusiac. In the ancient world, most attention centered on the annual inundation, but navigation on the Nile dated from early times, certainly circa 3500–3200 B.C.; to go upstream, sails were used because the prevailing wind blows from the north, while to go downstream rivercraft used the current. There were different hieroglyphic symbols to depict these activities; for example, a ship with a billowing sail depicted a voyage to the south.[109] The great river was a magnet for historians and commentators and poets. It has therefore proved possible to write a kind of history of the Nile, concentrating on the inundation and the religious offerings to the beneficent river and also on the process of water management.[110]

Rivers in Italy were often not sufficiently important (apart from the Po and the Tiber) to repay study as individualities; they tended to be uncertain in volume and flow and were much affected by seasonal factors. Uneven rainfall, the limited number of natural lakes, and the size and geological composition of catchment areas meant that many rivers were torrential. The Nera (Nar), which rises in limestone springs in the Abruzzi and has substantial areas of impermeable rock in its watershed and catchment area, was one of the few rivers able to maintain a constant, vigorous flow.[111]

Of course, this is not say that the rather unstable rivers of southern Italy did not have an important impact on local communities. It is just that we cannot trace this. For example, the river Candelaro, which sweeps around the base of Mons Garganus in Apulia and helps to drain the low plain of the Tavoliere, seems to be potentially important but is difficult to put in context. According to the Antonine Itinerary and the Peutinger Map, the town of Ergitium was seemingly close to the crossing point of the river, yet has only tentatively been identified.[112] The river continued to affect the landscape and eventually, by the deposition of silt, transformed the large estuary, Lago Salso, making it into a wetland area.

Rivers in the north of Italy were influenced by an Alpine regime where ice and snow had a significant effect. Melting ice is normally important from the spring to the autumn, while melting snow is important from April to May. Therefore, Alpine rivers have maximum flow in spring and early summer and drop to a minimum in winter. There can sometimes be a second period of peak flow as a result of heavy autumn rains in the pre-Alps. The great river of northern Italy, the Po (Padus), usually reaches its highest point in late spring and early summer (May to June) and also in autumn (October to November), and reaches its lowest volume of flow in winter and summer.[113]

The Tiber shows some of the possibilities and the limitations of studying an individual river. Although its volume is very uncertain during the summer and it needs the support of its tributaries, especially the Nera (Nar), Velino (Avens), and Aniene (Anio), nevertheless it was of great significance in the Roman world in both cultural and political terms. Joël Le Gall wrote two important books about the Tiber, one a history of the river itself and its immediate environs in Rome, and the other a brief survey of the cult of the associated river-god. However, although the Tiber was the river of the principal city of a large empire, and a great route of communications and commerce with the sea and river port of Ostia, there are problems in making a convincing narrative, though in this case riverine evidence can be supplemented with useful material on the bridges in Rome, the curators of the bed and banks of the river and the sewers of the city, and the various types of riverboat in use. Even so, the detailed evidence available is limited and inconsistent, so that we have a very incomplete picture of the Tiber's role in Roman history. On the other hand, the ambitious ongoing project to survey and analyze a large section of the Tiber valley over a long time span may offer more opportunities.[114]

5   PROBLEMS AND APPROACHES

This brief survey shows the ubiquity and structure of the riverine environment in the Roman world. But why is the study of rivers important? Farming and settlement in fertile river valleys became very attractive as the rule of the state became more stable and assured, and the government eventually established secure and peaceful conditions; therefore, the need to maintain mountain towns for defense was less pressing. So many people moved to the river valleys or perhaps continued to live in hillside settlements, but they worked their land in the plains and river valleys. In the ancient world, rivers were of undeniable importance in the life of the Mediterranean area, and the history of communities' relationship with rivers can illuminate a whole range of issues and raise interesting questions even though they cannot always be answered.[115] Rivers that had once served to protect or keep communities apart could now assume a position at the heart of community life and help to connect locations, regions, and even provinces in an economic, social, and cultural nexus through routes of communication.

For many reasons, therefore, rivers were among the natural phenomena over which the Romans consciously sought mastery in one way or another. One of the most potent symbols of their control was their ability to take fresh running water from one place and deposit it by aqueduct in the center of a distant city. It is not surprising then that rivers so often caught the attention of ancient writers, though it is true that the rivers of Europe tend to receive more attention in our sources. Quite apart from the enormous practical importance of rivers in ancient life, they had great intellectual and psychological resonance. Their mysterious elements often caught the popular imagination: permanence with a changing and unpredictable nature, visible power, with life-giving yet also destructive force. Furthermore, the enigma of the hydrological cycle stimulated the imagination of writers and commentators.[116] The essential question had been posed in Ecclesiastes: "All the rivers run into the sea;

yet the sea is not full; unto the place from whence the rivers come, thither they return again."[117] This was just one part of the intellectual debate about rivers, which were not merely a source of good illustrations for writers but had a much wider significance, in stimulating analysis of nature and mankind and the relationship between water and communities. Because even the smallest streams had their resident spirits, while great rivers had correspondingly important anthropomorphic deities, who led exciting and eventful lives in mythological stories, this religious aura of rivers enhanced the status of riverine communities. What is more, running water traditionally had cleansing and healing properties, and so rivers and springs allegedly brought comfort and relief to many people, while the welcoming aspects of watery and sylvan surroundings seemingly brought spiritual uplift. Throughout the Roman Empire, rivers were an integral part of ancient culture and society, were objects of both delight and fear, and constantly stimulated interest not to say excitement.

Now, although we should not assume that modern analytical techniques will help in understanding the past,[118] nevertheless current academic study of rivers and the riverine environment can offer a guide to methods and approaches that might be of value in the examination of rivers in the ancient world. Traditionally it embraces a wide range of disciplines, including geography, natural science, history, and anthropology. The work of S. M. Haslam has exemplified a holistic approach and expounded the role of rivers in historical developments and how they can act as a kind of continuous commentary on human life. In *The Historic River: Rivers and Culture down the Ages*, she argued from the basis that "rivers show how man lived, worked and thought in the past."[119] This human connection with rivers has been excellently summed up by another modern commentator: "From the river men have drunk or lived, or they have drunk and died; from its sinuous body, ceaselessly moving yet remaining fixed, they have drawn their profoundest symbols of man's fate. Not yet fully used, never completely controlled, the river has been of all natural forces, the one most intimately involved in human development at every stage."[120] In *The River Scene: Ecology and Cultural Heritage*, Haslam dealt with the river environment by pursuing three fundamental themes: the essential element of water and water sources; the natural environment of river structure, habitat, and geomorphology; and the cultural heritage.

In Haslam's approach the analysis of the riverine environment should where possible include the structure, flow, and discharge of rivers; river sources; river types and rock formations; stream and river patterns and their changing characteristics over time; alluviation; rivers and topographical change; river vegetation and habitat; rivers as a focal point in early communities and the consequent development of river towns; the cultural heritage of people in riverine or lacustine communities; the impact of rivers on the local way of life; and river pollution geomorphology, which includes the science of river movements.

In the modern world, there are unprecedented levels of detailed scientific analysis, planning, and professional management of rivers to control pollution and safeguard and enhance the environment and riverine ecology, protect cities, and provide adequate drinking water. The control of rivers and their use often involves the law, and the creation of legal definitions of rivers sets limits to their exploitation, because private interests or government interference can remove excessive amounts of water or otherwise damage riverine benefits that could potentially be shared by all. Interestingly, the word *rivalis* in Latin, which gave rise to the English "rival" or "competitor," meant someone who shared the use of a stream or water channel (*rivus*) with another.[121] Related themes deal with the use of river water to supply city reservoirs, generate power, and provide commercial routes for the large-scale transport of goods. In these respects, rivers in heavily urbanized regions tend to be intensively used.[122] In a more unplanned way, rivers served local people and others for recreation and for health cures; in many places, they were long associated with various types of religious observance. In all ages the numerous benefits conferred by rivers have been set against their potential threat and the need for precautions against floods. Riverine communities often found themselves in a tussle with the environment as river waters advanced and retreated.

However, the study of rivers in the ancient Roman world presents an additional range of daunting problems. First, the very number and distribution of rivers of different sizes and variegated dynamics defy a complete and coherent exposition. The *Barrington Atlas of the Greek and Roman World*,[123] which is the most extensive and up-to-date review and presentation of the geographical features of the ancient world, has on a rough count between 1,300 and 1,400 rivers that can actually be named with reasonable certainty. And these are merely the rivers that ancient writers thought worth mentioning or about which we happen to know something from some other source. Naturally, therefore, rivers will have been a commonplace sight in the ancient world, as in other ages. But how can that be translated into a useful analysis or illumination of the life and culture of Rome and the peoples of the empire?

It is perhaps the type and quality of the available evidence that cause the greatest difficulty. As already noted, modern river studies embrace physical and human geography, geology, and geoarchaeology, often with detailed scientific data. Students of modern rivers have accurate records of mean annual discharge for major rivers (calculated at the basic level by multiplying the cross section of the river by its velocity), records of precipitation and other climatic activity, and the discharge ratio and the runoff deficit. For example, in the river basin of the Rhine, extending to approximately 196,840 square kilometers, it is possible to measure the variation in the volume of discharge, ranging from 1,080 cubic meters per second at Strasbourg to 2,090 at Cologne and 2,260 as the river enters the Netherlands.[124] In this way, river flow is analyzed and recorded, and chemical analysis of suspended material carried in the stream can assist in a precise calculation and measurement of alluvial activity and the extension of river estuaries. The effects of tidal rivers are now subject to close investigation, and coastal advance and changes in sea level are scientifically measured.

In the modern world there are available substantial records of economic data on the nature and quantity of goods transported by river, and analysis of this material can show how trading patterns changed over time. Historians also have records of the building of locks and other riverine engineering works and of the history and development of river ports. So, it is possible to study the impact of rivers on riverine communities and how those communities have altered the behavior of rivers over time. In addition, a detailed record of legal provisions (both national decisions and local regulations and bylaws) concerning rivers illuminates all kind of questions concerning river use and the management of riverine facilities.

Much of this kind of detailed consideration is simply not possible for the ancient world. The Romans, despite technical brilliance in many aspects of engineering and building, did not devise basic procedures for calculating rivers and water flow, though there are procedures in the texts of land surveyors for measuring the width of rivers. It is interesting that Heron of Alexandria, who probably lived in the first century A.D., by constructing a reservoir and measuring the intake of water against a time clock, worked out a way of assessing the discharge of a spring through the calculation of its velocity. He also measured the water flow by conducting it into a large pipe and recording the width of the pipe and the height of the water flowing through the mouth.[125] This method would work only for a small spring and was apparently not taken up by others interested in dealing with water management on a large scale.

Furthermore, the archaeological record of riverine communities is very uneven. Persistent alluvial activity and erosion have brought about changes in the configuration of rivers and land, and in some cases altered the shape of coastlines and deltas. River sediment has buried archaeological remains, and small river ports and wooden wharves of landing stages have completely disappeared from the record. The remains of only a few rivercraft have been recovered, and the analysis of river trade routes is developed largely by extrapolation from the location of pottery remains. Furthermore, the surviving evidence of river engineering and dam building is slight. As for settlement in river valleys, the history of riverine communities and their relation to the river and to one another can be assessed generally only in the case of some important rivers; for example, as has been noted, there has been much local interest in the navigable rivers of France and Spain, and other important projects are underway.[126] Therefore, in terms of archaeological evidence what we know tends to be related to communities living along the major European rivers, including the Rhine and Danube, which had significant connections with Roman military operations. Even here, for the historian of the Roman world, there is rarely sufficient evidence to construct a detailed history of an individual riverine environment. In fact, many of the rivers that appear in the *Barrington Atlas* remain mere names.

We do at least have abundant material from numerous Greek and Roman writers, some of whom, in writing about topics such as land survey, geography, topography, natural history, and *periegesis*, had a kind of professional interest; some writers treated rivers primarily as direction markers or convenient pointers in constructing linear itineraries. Others happened to mention rivers incidentally while pursuing other themes. Both have their value. The former at least try to describe the course and characteristics of rivers and set them in a geographical and topographical context. The latter are more impressionistic but valuable for a popular view of what interested people about rivers and how they appeared to observers. Many writers were particularly interested in the showy side of rivers, including stories of river-gods, mythology, miraculous properties, and powers of healing. But this may be what was often of interest, away from the technicalities of navigability, direction, and the measurement of distance.

One problem with our writers is vagueness in definitions of rivers. For example, in Latin and Greek several words were used virtually interchangeably to describe running water, including *amnis*: river, the current of a river; *flumen*: river, occasionally stream, current of a river; *fluvius*: stream, river, current. Other words had a more specific meaning, such as *torrens*: a torrent, tumultuous river course; *rivus*: a smaller watercourse or stream, sometimes the course of a river, artificial channel (e.g., of an aqueduct); *fons*: spring, flow of water from the ground; *alveus*: channel or bed of a river, current; *ripa*: bank of a river; *inundatio*: flooding by a river or any water source; *alluvio*: flood, addition of soil to land by river action; *abluvio*: erosion by water action. In Greek we have notably *potamos*: river, stream; *pege*: running water constituting a river or stream; *krene*: spring, well; *krounos*: spring, wellhead, watercourse; *rheuma*: the stream or current of a river, flood.

There is no obvious precision in riverine terminology among Latin writers or Greek writers of the imperial period. It seems that ancient geographical writers took over traditional riverine vocabulary and did not develop a specialist terminology to define running water and its impact. That does not necessarily indicate lack of technical interest but suggests that their approach tended to be descriptive rather than closely analytical. It was perhaps the Roman land surveyors who had most reason to define rivers, through their regular activities in dealing with measurement of land, land boundaries and disputes, and river flooding. But in their writings, too, there is little or no sign of a precise terminology in describing rivers, although that is in keeping with the general absence of precise technical definitions in the rest of their work.[127] However, surveyors, like lawyers, produce detailed descriptions where necessary of the impact of rivers on land, alluviation, and the problems of rivers' changing course. In this respect there are numerous descriptive phases for the damage or changes caused by running water.[128] Here the surveyors had to intervene and assist magistrates to restore or confirm the status of land.

In general, *amnis* and *flumen* in Latin and *potamos* in Greek seem to be used to describe more substantial rivers. Furthermore, the adjective "public" was normally attached to *amnis* or *flumen* to describe a typical river where the Roman people owned the riverbed.[129] For geographers and travel writers, one of the most important distinctions was between rivers and streams, because the former might be capable of supporting navigation whereas the latter were not and therefore were of no value of the movement of goods or people. In this case writers normally made distinctions clear by adding an appropriate definition, which might be a single adjective (*navigabilis* or, in Greek, *plotos*), or sometimes a longer exposition of how the river sustained certain types of ships.

Another major problem with our literary evidence is a lack of convincing detail. Ancient writers probably could not get hold of much good detail. What they say is often not robustly analytical but of an anecdotal nature and is thus hard to separate from reliable material. The literary evidence also tends to be repetitive and to concentrate on well-known rivers. This evidence has a cumulative value about the role of rivers in ancient communities but is still fragmentary in nature. Therefore, there are significant gaps in our knowledge of riverine communities, the precise nature of river use, and the interaction between riverine communities. Consequently, the overall impact of rivers on local life remains obscure. The evidence on navigability, provided particularly by

Strabo and the Elder Pliny, is welcome but often lacks specifics and is difficult to test, especially since many rivers have now ceased to be navigable or navigable over such long distances as in the ancient world.

Inscriptions normally offer the historian guidance in those areas which the literary sources leave obscure. But inscriptions were often the formal product of official decisions and are usually remote from the day-to-day life of riverine communities. Many of those which relate to the Tiber are a record of the posts held by senators who at some stage served as curator of the beds and banks of the Tiber and the sewers of the city, and they exhibit the usual problems associated with this kind of evidence. The inscriptions tell us what post the senators held but generally not what they did, how successful they were, or why they were appointed. In fact, a great deal of riverine activity was carried on at the local level and escaped detection by those erecting inscriptions, and we do not have a detailed or consistent picture of riverine communities. By contrast, movement along great rivers, such as the Rhône, Rhine, Danube, Po, and particularly the lower Tiber, is better known because inscriptions commemorate the role of boatmen, shippers, and traders and sometimes even depict rivercraft. Pottery remains, which reveal products carried by river, can give us an outline of how riverine trade may have been conducted, but with a very limited assessment of the scale. Apart from this, it is interesting that some private inscriptions show dedications to rivers and river-deities, providing a valuable glimpse of popular feeling. Furthermore, coins minted by Greek cities in the eastern provinces show the symbolic and emotional role of rivers in relation to the cities that they flowed past. In most areas of study, however, it is the literary evidence despite all its defects that often has most to offer.

In the context of the evidential difficulties, it is reasonable to suggest that regional studies that combine all types of evidence and set out to cover a very long expanse of time might offer a way forward. One of the most ambitious of current projects is in the Tiber valley. It covers an area of about 2,500 square kilometers from Rome on both banks of the Tiber to its confluence with the river Nera in the location of Otricoli. The methodology involves the assembling of material from field-walking expeditions, analysis of published excavations and surveys, and geophysical survey.[130] It involves much comparative work and reassessment of an earlier survey of south Etruria. On the basis of this methodology, numerous scholars have embarked on a series of studies of various aspects of the landscape in the valley. In the long term, it is hoped to piece together the history of the middle Tiber valley as part of the hinterland of Rome in a great chronological sweep from 1000 B.C. to A.D. 1300. This long time span offers one way to write the history of a river valley by observing change and comparing communities over time.

This kind of project and the relevant methodology work best in the valleys of highly significant rivers with clear patterns of settlement, good archaeological survey possibilities, and continuous occupation over millennia. The agenda is then dictated by what these rivers have to offer, which may not be typical in the light of the enormous regional variations and inconsistencies of evidence throughout the empire. My object is to approach the question in a different way by taking an empire-wide view of rivers and the interaction of local people with them. I propose to identify a number of themes that may help to explain the ancient riverine environment and try to illustrate these by citing a wide range of evidence from different rivers in various parts of the Roman world over a reasonably wide chronological range.

This study is primarily about the Roman world. That is the main area of my expertise, and clearly there must be limits to the length of the study. But in addition to these rather negative considerations, this period has the best selection of evidence, and it is from the first century A.D. onward that we have the important theme of the emergence of an imperial power and its relation to the environment and the benefits of nature. There is, it must be admitted, a further methodological or quasi-philosophical objection to my approach. Rivers are seemingly eternal, yet also are constantly in a state of change. This makes it difficult, for example, to isolate the role and significance of the river Rhône in the Roman world from what went before when the Greeks traded along it, or from what happened afterward. In practice, however, the wide range of evidence from Greco-Roman writers, who themselves had been heavily influenced by the traditions of earlier writers, the enormous geographical spread of the empire, and the longevity of Rome's domination all help to make this approach feasible. It should be possible to compare river valley communities in different parts of the Roman world, examine small communities as well as great centers, and perhaps offer a fresh approach to some much-studied topics.

It is also worth emphasizing that the work is based on what the ancients themselves wrote and thought about rivers. This book aims to place the rivers of the Roman world in their geographical, topographical, social, and cultural context, above all, by examining how the ancients described them. In this sense it is subjective, based on my interpretation of their views and prejudices. Nevertheless, I think that this approach offers an immediate flavor of riverine life and a direct and helpful route to discovering the impact that rivers had on the lives, activities, and ideas of people and communities. This study will be informed but not led by comparisons with modern river systems and modern theoretical analysis. Therefore, in general the theme of my study is the people who lived in riverine communities, who exploited rivers, and who wrote about or described rivers. In this I am working on the basis that in general river characteristics did not change much throughout the time span represented by the Greek and Roman world and retained continuity into the modern age.

There is a danger, of course, in this approach. For example, the ancient writers may have understood rivers imperfectly[131] or be subject to literary *topoi*. Therefore, we might find their comments interesting without getting an accurate account of the riverine environment. In the first place, however, this should not alter our basic question concerning what interested our writers about rivers and how they present this information. Furthermore, the cumulative effect of the evidence is important. Second, the surviving descriptions are plausible; that might mean that they are merely conventional, but in my view the conventional is valuable in reflecting what people saw and heard.

Third, some of our writers did understand, however imperfectly, the processes of alluviation, erosion, and other factors influencing river behavior. The response of Herodotus and Thucydides to alluviation involved observation, narration, and explanation.[132] Therefore, in discussing the accumulation of silt deposited by the Nile, Herodotus cites examples of other rivers with significant alluvial deposits—the Scamander at Troy, the Cayster at Ephesus, and the Caicus at Teuthrania, and the plain of the Maeander. Among other rivers he could mention, he singles out from mainland Greece the Acheloüs in Acarnania, which had already joined half of the islands of the Echinades group to the mainland. Notably, Herodotus recognizes that the process of alluviation could extend over thousands of years. Thucydides is more specific on the reasons for the silting at the mouth of the Acheloüs. The river in its course through the Acarnanian plain was powerful, mud-filled, and expansive, and the alluvial deposits were trapped by the string of islands situated close together. There is here an explicit recognition of the impact of a mighty river on the environment. Similarly, in the words of Herodotus, "The Nile is a great river and brings about great changes."

Strabo also emphasized the character of rivers and the nature of the environment they flowed through. Once again he had examples of silting at river mouths, including the famous "Breasts" at the mouth of the Danube, suggesting that the process of alluviation was well known to contemporaries. In his view, rivers tend to turn the channel in front of them into solid ground. His explanation was the volume and strength of the current (a river with many tributaries was more likely to bring down silt) and the nature of the land through which it flowed (soft soil was easily broken up and transported).[133] Arrian vaguely articulates the same idea when describing how lands were named after rivers because plains near the sea were frequently deposited by the continuous action of rivers.[134] In the same vein, the Elder Pliny, discussing the dimensions of the province of Baetica, observes topographical factors that had caused mistakes in calculating distances. "Over such a long expanse of time the seas have encroached on the land, or the shores have moved forward, or rivers have meandered or straightened a winding course."[135]

Pausanias, reflecting on the course of the Acheloüs through Aitolia and the silting up of the Echinades, added a new dimension by suggesting that man and the agricultural exploitation of the land contributed to the process of silting. He wondered if the devastation and depopulation of Aitolia (by the Romans in 167 B.C.) had reduced the scale of cultivation and hence the amount of soil that the river absorbed and then deposited. The process, therefore, had slowed, and by comparison he adduced the Maeander, which flowed though heavily cultivated agricultural land and had silted up the sea between Priene and Miletus. The anthropogenic factor emerges in Pausanias's brave attempt to explain rather than merely describe the process, though he was not in a position to assess critically other possibly relevant geomorphic and hydrological factors, changes in sea level, the gradual effects of deforestation, and the impact of irrigation and drainage works.[136] It might be the case that a stable agricultural environment rather than the abandonment of cultivation could keep alluviation at manageable levels.

In a vague way, the Roman land surveyors recognized that it was possible to define the kind of rivers where alluviation was likely to take place, and the consequences. The surveyors had also observed that the process of alluviation had enormous variations with many different forms and speeds, and that its outcome was uncertain, with immediate or long-term benefits for some people or communities but loss and distress for others.[137] In the seventh century, Isidore of Seville was content with a minimalist definition of *alluuius ager* as "that which a stream has gradually deposited on the land."[138]

Even in Strabo's measured, scholarly approach to alluviation, there is still an air of mysterious awe, which, for example, appears in an oracle about the river Pyramos in Cilicia, which stated that future generations would see the river with its silvery ripples join the mainland to Cyprus.[139] And in the work of poets and others, vague knowledge and limited observation of natural phenomena were combined with legend and mythology in a potent mix of intelligent fiction, exemplified in Ovid's colorful depiction of the endless permutations in the world, where riverine and marine power have a crucial part: "I (Pythagoras) have seen what was once solid land become sea, and I have seen land created out of what was once ocean. Seashells lie far from the ocean, and old anchors have been found on mountain peaks. What was once a plain has been turned into a valley because of water flowing down across it. Through floods, mountains have been washed away to the sea. Marshy land dries out and turns into burning sands. Thirsty deserts now drip with great pools of water. In one spot Nature sends out new springs, while in another she blocks existing ones. In one place rivers burst forth, stirred up by tremors deep in the earth, or they dry up and fade away."[140] He goes on to describe various rivers and their characteristics.[141]

Therefore, despite many interesting observations and good descriptions, our sources tend to tell us about particular situations with examples from some individual communities. It was more difficult for them to extrapolate from this to general trends and consequences spread over a long period. For example, alluviation was often the result of floods, and these could sometimes be very eye-catching, with destruction of crops and disaster for individuals. But the impact was probably temporary and over time could be accommodated. On the other hand, fertile alluvial soil eventually provided an excellent basis for agriculture, but the improved economic outlook that one might expect from this in the long run is difficult to appreciate and demonstrate. The variety of local economies across the Mediterranean basin would in any case militate against any significant overall impact of alluviation or flooding.[142] In terms of geophysics and long-term hydrology, the limitations of the ancient analysis must be recognized.

In what follows, chapter 2 examines the opinions of ancient writers who had a kind of specialist interest, such as geographers, topographers, writers of natural history and *periegesis*, land surveyors, and those who constructed itineraries of one kind or other (rivers fitted into the designation of a clear, linear route) to see how they used rivers to calculate distances, mark boundaries, define space, designate lands and peoples, and clarify maps; the ways in which they analyzed the contribution of rivers to local prosperity and development are also important. Therefore, rivers could also demarcate regions and divide and identify peoples in cultural terms, keeping some apart while putting others together. As such, they were often closely linked with the local history of riverine communities. For the adventurous, rivers also acted as a guide for travelers, merchants, and explorers.

While there was appreciation of rivers and their importance in the life of many communities and areas, ancient commentators recognized that rivers could also be extremely damaging, and it was the role of the law to manage the valuable assets of rivers and springs and contain their potentially harmful aspects, for the benefit of individuals and the common good of local communities and the Roman state. Chapter 3 examines the evidence from the work of lawyers and land surveyors, who set out to define rivers and the right to use them by different and sometimes competing interests, to ensure that the state got what it wanted in the provision of water, to put rivers to work in land settlements and the demarcation of boundaries, and to manage the consequences when they changed course or flooded the fields of neighboring landholders. Alterations in the configuration of land and water meant that there was a constant process of adjustment and rearranging of boundaries and securing access to running water. We can therefore recover the official response to a prominent feature of life in the Mediterranean area.

Chapter 4 deals with ancient writers whose comments on rivers are often incidental to their main theme and considers what they found of interest about rivers and what watery themes they pursued. In all literature, rivers were usually objects of great respect, with recognition of their awesome and potentially destructive power. From an early stage, river dwellers supplicated local rivers as deities because of their important place in the natural world. River spirits were anthropomorphic, and associated with their religious aura was a whole nexus of mythology and legend that arose from but also sustained their divine status. These ideas were translated into artistic representations that depicted rivers and springs in a variety of ways, which help to illustrate the importance of rivers in ancient life and the relation between rivers and certain cities and historical events.

The Romans' ability to control large swaths of territory and exploit natural phenomena depended on their army, and chapter 5 deals with a striking feature of ancient writing, namely the persistent interest in military affairs, tactics, and strategy, in this case with a watery dimension. Because rivers could be instruments of defense or attack, they attracted the attention of historians of warfare and play an interesting part in military textbooks and compilations of military stratagems deployed by famous commanders. Consequently we are reasonably well informed on the possible military role of rivers, and it is clear that rivers, being closely intertwined with communities, were dramatically part of the geographical rhythms of warfare and survival. In uncertain or violent times, they could sustain or help to defend a city by providing drinking water and by holding up invading forces, which had to find a way to cross. But they could also serve as a means to attack a fortified position or facilitate military transport and supply. It is no surprise, therefore, that military writers have many references to the use of waterways in the tactical maneuvering of armies, or that crossing rivers in hostile territory became a well-recognized Roman skill. In wider state policy, the riverine environment had a strategic importance in the foundation of settlements, and throughout the frontier zones, where it is a highly debated question whether the Romans viewed rivers as a form of barrier, as well as a route for supplies and communications. Linked to these tactical and strategic concepts was another view, much more difficult to define, in which rivers formed an aspect of cultural imperialism, serving the military and political interests of those powerful enough to dominate them.

Chapters 6–8 look at river navigation and the exploitation of the riverine environment that was firmly under Roman control. Rivers were seen as a great boon to communities, as the source of many economic benefits, and as routes of communication and commerce. Rivers sustained life by providing the essential fresh water for drinking, often supplying aqueducts and mills, for watering animals and irrigating pasture and crops. In fact, in the modern world the greatest use of water is for agriculture, taking up about 80 percent of consumption.[143] Rivers supported numerous watery activities that underpinned the life of riverine communities, notably fishing and the harvesting of reeds and rushes; there were opportunities for manufacture along riverbanks, particularly in pottery making, which exploited the availability of clay and water. Wetlands and water meadows offered alternative opportunities for agricultural production. Furthermore, as people mastered rivers and learned how to control their waters, they developed irrigation to put unpromising land under cultivation, to drain waterlogged areas, and to use rivers for the transport of goods.[144]

Rivers that served as waterways brought an enormous addition to the navigability of the Mediterranean Sea, as people were encouraged to devise and build suitable rivercraft. With ingenuity and hard work to propel ships upstream, the ancients used rivers extensively and fully exploited their navigability. Rivers were important contributors to the movement of goods and people, supplementing or competing with the road system, and they provided the essential connection between small and disparate communities across a large region. Waterways and the riverine environment assisted the expansion and development of settlements, and the river was the common feature in a system of connection that often included the main river's tributaries, widening access and economic opportunities.

Therefore, against this background I consider the problems, advantages, and character of river navigation. What was the perception of navigable rivers and coastal estuaries among the ancients? What was the relationship of rivers to other means of transport and how did the cost of transport by river compare with other means of transport? What attempts did the Romans make to regulate and improve river flow? Ancient writers speak enthusiastically of the benefits of navigable rivers, but how can we relate this to river ports, boats and boatmen, and methods of river navigation?

In this context, we must ask how the riverine environment presented opportunities and challenges to individual communities by examining the role of navigable rivers as thoroughfares, concentrating on their contribution to trade, commerce, and the local economy. How did rivers benefit directly or indirectly local regions and also link more distant regions? This was very important at the local level in small communities spread across a region, where the river provided continuity and essential connections. However, uncertain riverine hydrology in the Mediterranean zone meant that the benefits of a river were not constant; they might be seasonal or accompanied by periods of flooding with damage to crops and woodland, though this too might bring rich deposits of alluvium. How did people interact with the watery environment? How did rivers further local industries, and how important was the exploitation of wetlands, marshes, and alluvial deposits, and how did Rome exploit the riverine environment?

In developing this discussion, I use case studies based on a number of areas where for various reasons the use of navigable rivers, riverine commerce, and other river activities operated at a level that generated a reasonable amount of evidence. These regional surveys exploit the evidence particularly of geographical writers, archaeology, and inscriptions relating to those involved in river transport and riverine commerce.

Chapter 9 examines how respect from earliest times for running water and its divine source and cleansing power help to explain the durable interest in the Roman world in springs and rivers with curative properties. In addition, the developing empire came in contact with other peoples, especially in Gaul and Germany, who believed in the divine source and special properties of water. The Romans appropriated these ideas and quietly adapted them to suit their own presentation and exploitation. Furthermore, it seems that in everyone's view the watery environment was conducive to pleasant recreation; the seductive burbling of the river or stream, the lush vegetation and elegant trees, the striking vistas, and even the noise of birdsong had a psychological role in leisure activities quite apart from more active river pleasures. These themes involve not only literary references and *topoi* but also a wide range of evidence, including inscriptions, statues, votive offerings, and coins.

The essential connection with themes pursued in the rest of the book is, first, that all the variegated resources of the empire were potentially at the disposal of the Romans. Furthermore, rivers were often considered as divine and had strong associations with mythology, which underpinned the belief in their ability to interfere in human affairs and from time to time bring assistance, including cleansing and healing. In popular and also medical thought, spas (*aquae*) were associated with the beneficial aspects of rivers, and their origin was hot or cold springs—that is, sources of running water—which would become rivers if not channeled or caught. The whole theme of running water and cleansing and healing through the ages connects rivers and springs and connects with the intellectual and cultural traditions of the empire. The interesting difference in the case of spas is that attempts were made to organize their use.

Chapter 10 gives an overview of Roman control of waterways, which had many military, political, administrative, and economic ramifications. Mastery of rivers and streams and access to their water allowed Rome to dominate others. But the Roman government generally aimed not to destroy water resources but to develop and exploit them effectively and to assist in their distribution. This watery patronage inevitably extended their influence and was another demonstration of Roman power over nature, which was celebrated in writing and iconography. This mastery of the natural world came with military victory and the extension of conquests but went beyond that in the intellectual and cultural appropriation of the rivers of foreign peoples.

TWO

PUTTING RIVERS ON THE MAP

In Pushkin's eponymous drama, Boris Godunov, finding his son studying a map of Russia and identifying the Volga, exclaims, "How splendid! The delicious fruit of learning! Thus at a glance as from a cloud to scan our whole domain: its boundaries, towns and rivers."[1] The tsar goes on to explain that all the lands that his son had drawn on paper will someday be under his control. Pushkin establishes a link between learning, geographical knowledge, maps, and imperial power: to know exactly what you possess, where it is, how to get there, and all your potential resources, allows you confirm your control and to exploit your empire.

Geographical knowledge, therefore, was potentially valuable in the Roman world, where the establishment of colonies of settlers and the subjugation or annexation of territory became established features of the developing republic. By the mid-first century A.D. the Romans controlled or had access to territories stretching from northern Britain to Egypt and in the Near East at least up to the river Euphrates. But how could government officials, provincial governors and army commanders, not to mention ordinary people, obtain information about provinces, places, nations, routes, distances, and obstacles? And, without a map, how could travelers imagine the appearance and layout of the area described?

This chapter considers the evidence of a group of writers from widely differing backgrounds, who had a specialist or quasi-professional interest in geographical enquiry. Their work is important for showing precisely how rivers were described and how they fitted into the physical environment of provinces, regions, and communities. This includes the role of rivers in measuring distances, establishing boundaries, creating a sense of space and shape, and affirming regional identity. What are classic riverine characteristics and qualities, and how do these fit into topographical or geographical descriptions? What role did rivers and streams play in the work of the land surveyors in managing space for public and private use? If rivers were seen as more than mere lines on a map, they could add life and verve to what otherwise might seem a straightforward catalog or recital of place-names and sites. A good river description could encourage the reader to visualize the scene and the relationship of roads, mountains, and river valleys and enhance the significance of the geographer's work, as well as inspiring pride and interest in the land.

1   GEOGRAPHICAL WRITING

Doubtless many travelers or officials in the Roman world relied on word-of-mouth advice. However, it is likely that geographical writers had a role to play, because they recorded details of distances and routes and important points of topography, as well as wider subjects such as the layout of countries and the relationship of land and sea. Works on geography were not necessarily dull academic textbooks.[2] In fact, one of the most popular geography guides was a hexameter poem written by Dionysios Perigetes ("the Guide") in the time of Hadrian.[3] Although the intended audience for his description of the world remains unclear, nevertheless his work is built on many of the themes common in geographical writers. Rivers, therefore, serve as geographical locators for peoples,[4] and many riverine qualities appear, such as speed and turbulence and the potential value of a river to its surrounding territory.[5] What is more, he knows the power of rivers to act as symbols and sway the emotions. So, the Tiber is "the most kingly of all rivers"; it is wide, has a pure flow and is closely associated with the imperial city, "the mother of all cities."[6]

Early geography had in addition embraced the study of local peoples and lent itself to an ethnographic approach. However, by the fourth century B.C. geography was more scientific and based to a large extent on analysis rather than compilations of lists or simple descriptions. Eratosthenes was a leading exponent of scientific geography, and in the second century A.D. Claudius Ptolemaeus (Ptolemy) developed this approach.[7] In book 1 of the *Geography* he gave directions for drawing a world map and then, for the different regions, provided a list of towns and important topographical markers with their latitude and longitude.[8] In this he set out some basic definitions and in particular argued that "geography is the copying by drawing of the entire known world along with the features contained in it." Therefore, the role of geography was to describe the nature and position of the world, including features such as gulfs, large cities, peoples, the more important rivers, and any landmarks of particularly striking appearance. But he also thought that geography should be supplemented by chorography, which "takes certain places from the whole and examines them one by one in detail, noting even the smallest features, such as harbors, villages, hamlets, small tributaries of large rivers, and comparable features."[9] Consequently, in Ptolemy's view, both geography and the topographical studies inherent in chorography would have to deal with rivers and make use of their characteristics, and his methodology required their careful description.

Other geographers, particularly Strabo of Amaseia in Pontus (born in the late 60s B.C.), persisted with an approach that was not scientific or particularly analytical but offered straightforward descriptions of places and their importance for local peoples.[10] His *Geographia* is undoubtedly our most important source for ancient geographical information, which he collected from authors now lost. Strabo tells us how the development of the Parthian and Roman empires had greatly extended the sum of geographical knowledge and that he had to come to terms with describing a vast territorial empire on a scale not seen since the conquests of Alexander the Great.[11] He set out to describe regions, locations and natural phenomena, and the distinguishing features of countries, including everything that was elevated and noble, useful, memorable, or entertaining.[12] However, he also approved of "chorography" and included the details of limited areas and sites that went to make up the bigger picture provided by his geography.[13]

In addition, his outlook is particularly important since he was an outsider, who subsequently probably acquired Roman citizenship and certainly had the friendship of powerful individuals in the Augustan regime, notably Aelius Gallus, prefect of Egypt, with whom he visited that province. He therefore presented his material through the medium of the revolution engineered by Augustus, whom he describes as "Lord of war and peace for life."[14] Strabo viewed the developing territorial empire from close to the center of power and made a connection between geographical knowledge and government responsibilities.[15]

Furthermore, Strabo constructed a coherent intellectual justification of his work. He had a lofty view of its overall impact and identified geography as a concern of the philosopher, for which he cited three reasons. First, many early geographers were philosophers of a kind; second, the wide learning required of the geographer amounted to philosophy; third, geography was outstandingly valuable, not only assisting statesmen and commanders in their activities but also contributing to a knowledge of the heavens and of everything that could be seen on earth.[16] For Strabo, the greater part of geography served the needs of the state, "for the arena of the state's activities is land and sea, where we dwell."[17] In particular, generals needed to know about geography, because they ruled over land and sea and brought nations and cities under one rule, and of course geography provided information about seas and continents. Ignorance of the geography of a region, its characteristics, routes, and distances might be disastrous. When the Romans invaded Germany, the Germans conducted a guerrilla war in marshes and trackless forests and desolate areas; they made the unwitting Romans believe that what was close at hand was far away and concealed the roads and the means of securing supplies and other requirements.[18]

Consequently in some ways geography could intrude on the course of historical events, and in research and subject matter it could be closely associated with history, though Strabo is careful to say that writing ancient history is not the task of the geographer.[19] Furthermore, he does not seriously advocate a theory of geographical determinism or pursue a systematic analysis of how far geographical features (such as rivers) had an active role in human affairs. For example, rivers could provide protection from military action and invasion in some regions, and in others facilitate attack by offering a route for moving troops and supplies. A city in a naturally strong riverine location might have the basis for future advancement. On the other hand, land made fertile by river action might inspire war and invasion by the envious and greedy, while an unhealthy site could protect the inhabitants from outside interference. But people must work with the landscape and use their own talents to contribute to their development, and in this some displayed greater resolve and ingenuity than others.[20] For example, the Tiber and its navigable tributaries were instrumental in conveying to Rome the timber and stone of the Tiber valley for Augustus's building works. But they still needed the initiative and energy of the emperor.[21]

Sound geographical knowledge underpinned the history of regions and communities. Naturally, rivers were ubiquitous and integral to this theme, but they are presented and analyzed in a structured format, fitting into Strabo's geographical exposition in two ways. First, the spatial theme predominated— that is, distances, the location of places and their relative positions, and a sense of scale. In some ways Strabo was influenced by earlier *periplous* literature with its emphasis on linear progression along a coastline, though ultimately he developed a geographical analysis that was based on the central position of Rome and the Mediterranean.[22] Second, this spatial theme had a temporal dimension in that Strabo dealt with the peoples who dominated regions. Therefore, although his principal concern was with the present, he also studied times past in order to show how cities and peoples and regions developed or declined over a period. So, the geography of an area is linked to the history of its people.[23] Rivers not only fitted into Strabo's presentation and definition of geographical space but also contributed to considerations of time and local identity. Particularly important are riverine characteristics and their role in geographical scene painting. Other river qualities emphasized by Strabo are also relevant, particularly their navigability and alluvial deposition and, of course, their potential capacity to inundate the surrounding land. Strabo's approach and the themes he develops can be linked to other geographical writings. In fact, he provides a very useful template for descriptive geography incorporating riverine characteristics.

Among Roman writers the tradition of pure geography was rather limited as far as we can tell, but the upper classes were a receptive audience, and at all times accounts of journeys and military expeditions were potentially useful and might contain reflections on local topography and society. Julius Caesar, who was doubtless exceptional in the range of his talents and intellectual interests, nevertheless used parts of his *De Bello Gallico* to illustrate the geography of Gaul, and presumably he thought that this would be acceptable to his audience. Rivers contribute to the geographical setting of the story of Caesar's conquests, in that his description depends on rivers as markers for tribes and districts. So, the famous opening section divides Gaul into three areas, inhabited by the Belgae, the Aquitani, and the Gauls, in which the last are separated from the Aquitani by the river Garonne and from the Belgae by the Marne and the Seine. Thus, the entire territory of the Gauls was marked off by the Rhône, the Garonne, and the Atlantic Ocean.[24]

The Elder Pliny in his *Natural History* set out what he deemed the most valuable products of contemporary knowledge relating to all things animal, vegetable, and mineral. Pliny claimed, "Nature, that is Life, is my subject,"[25] and the power and generally benevolent influence of *Natura* provide a link for the disparate information he collected. His geographical synopsis in books 2–6 contains the kind of information that might appeal to Romans in the late first century A.D. Although Pliny wrote voluminously on a wide range of topics, he was not an original thinker but studied and collated the work of a large number of earlier writers. His perspective was that of an experienced military officer and administrator who understood Roman government, knew the provinces, and loved Italy.

Pliny was undoubtedly interested in rivers, and in his view the entire world was a balance of earth and water, which were locked in a perpetual embrace.[26] In his summary in book I of the topics that he intends to examine, Pliny promises that as well as towns and peoples he will deal with famous rivers,[27] mountains, islands, seas, harbors, and distances. Geography and topography were bound up with the power of Rome, since it could be argued that Rome's imperial mission extended to a responsibility for the operations of natural processes. Therefore, in welcoming the bounteous generosity of Nature, Pliny praises the endless majesty of the Roman Peace, "which displays in turn not just men with their different lands and races but also mountains and peaks towering into the clouds, their offspring and also their plants. I beg that this gift of the gods may last forever. They have apparently bestowed the Romans on human affairs as a second sun."[28] Elsewhere, he notes that Rome's imperial mission to spread civilization throughout the world is backed up by its splendid physical setting, wonderful climate, excellent produce and animals, and richly varied landscape in which rivers play a prominent part: "the numerous lakes,[29] the generous wealth of rivers and springs flowing all through it (Italy), the many seas, harbors, the heart of the country open to commercial opportunities on all sides, and the land itself stretching eagerly out into the sea as if to assist mankind."[30]

One of Pliny's sources was Pomponius Mela, who came from Tingentera in Baetica and composed the *De Chorographia* at the time of Claudius's invasion of Britain. This was a pioneering Latin geography, which set out to compile information in the tradition of Strabo.[31] Mela describes the lands and seas of the world, generally by following the line of the coasts, and names peoples and places, with a limited amount of ethnographic and mythological material; rivers appear frequently as geographical markers.

Genres of travel writing related to geography were those of *periegesis* and *periploi*. The former offered a survey of the history and traditions of various localities incorporated with a description of the topography, natural phenomena, and important buildings. The Greek writer Pausanias is the most distinguished and interesting exponent.[32] He probably came from Magnesia-ad-Sipylum in Asia Minor, and in his *Description of Greece*, written circa 155–75, limited his attention to the Roman province of Achaea, covering the areas of Attica, Megara, Argolis and its environs, Laconia, Messenia, Elis, Olympia, Achaea, Arcadia, Boeotia, Phocis, and Delphi. Pausanias wrote in a different context from that of Strabo and Ptolemy and was particularly interested in the monuments of archaic and classical Greece and in the history, culture, and religious observances of the city-states that had produced those monuments. He was much less interested in rural communities and the geography of Greece. Consequently he has less topographical material, less analysis of the environment and countryside, and much less about rivers and the integration of countryside and community. However, water, in the form of rivers or springs, does feature prominently in his work, and he understands the river's ability to benefit, change, damage, or even destroy a community. In particular, welling springs, apart from being the source of many rivers, were often associated with cults and legends that formed an important part of the cultural heritage and tradition of communities, a theme that especially interested Pausanias.[33] In fact, he gives us a closely focused account of Greek society, culture, and tradition, mediated at least partly through the geographical and topographical context. Pausanias respected rivers as part of the force of nature and in general thought that humans should not try to overturn these natural forces. Consequently, in respect of failed attempts to dig a canal across the Isthmus of Corinth and other places he says: "It is therefore difficult for men to overturn by force what has been appointed by the gods."[34]

He worked by making personal visits to sites in Greece and had himself traveled along many of the river valleys and observed the natural features he describes. For example, he contradicts an earlier writer's view that the springs on Mount Kotilion were the source of the river Lymax in Arcadia: "Whoever wrote that this spring provided the source of the river Lymax had not seen it himself or heard a report from anyone who had seen it. I myself have done both. I saw the course of the river and the water of the spring on Kotilion. It does not travel far and within a short distance disappears completely."[35]

Periploi (our surviving examples were written in Greek) were much more than a sailor's guide to coastal travel and included towns, harbors, headlands, promontories, water sources, and sometimes local winds and other climatic features.[36] Rivers feature prominently in these descriptions as part of a geographical framework marking distance and progress. *Periploi* and itineraries too followed a linear model, and their vocabulary, with phrases such as "to arrive at" or "to find," often suggests a journey in a visual sense.[37] Rivers would fit very well into this because they can be so clearly seen; therefore, named rivers that could be identified and verified on the journey might serve as highly visible landmarks. Rivers could also be measured (roughly, e.g., by volume of water and flow), and navigable rivers opened up travel and also commercial opportunities to the interior. These are important topics, involving the movement of people and goods and accessibility. What is lacking in the *periploi* is much attention to the theme of the identity and local history of communities.

The earliest known *periplous* relating to the Mediterranean is ascribed to Scylax of Caryanda (who wrote for Darius I) but probably dates from the fourth century B.C.; it offers an interesting picture of the pattern of relationships between communities, in which rivers appear frequently, for example, matched against an adjacent town,[38] or as a measure of sailing time to a destination.[39] In fact, trade along the rivers and then into the Mediterranean was an important consideration; so the river Naro in Dalmatia was wide enough to accommodate a trireme, which could sail to the *emporion*.[40] These traditional themes appear in the *Periplous Pontis Euxini*, which is substantially based around the geography of rivers, because the journey is measured from river to river, or harbor, other geographical marker, town, or trading post; rivers are used to delineate Bithynia and Cappadocia.[41] The important *Periplous* of the Red Sea, written in the first century A.D., while describing the development of routes to southern India and east Africa, also gives an important role to rivers in its geographical descriptions.[42] One of the most significant works of this kind is the *Periplous* of the Black Sea written by Arrian, who was a Greek from Bithynia and Roman senator. He served under Hadrian as governor of Cappadocia in A.D. 131–37 and his *periplous* was effectively a report to the emperor of his experiences as well as a geographical description of a journey. Therefore, as Strabo had argued, geography directly related to the work of government. The continuation of the tradition can be seen in the *Stadiasmus* or *Periplous Maris Magni*, dating from late antiquity, which uses rivers in geographical descriptions and often notes navigability.[43]

Itineraries were a specifically Roman development of the *periploi*, concerned with plotting routes by road and sometimes by river through a series of way stations and towns.[44] Largely military in origin, they retained a certain official status, and were based on the Roman road network, with distances measured in segments using milestones. Landmarks were useful for pointing the traveler in the right direction, marking the route, and assisting in the calculation of distance. Recognized stopping places (*mansiones*) and towns along the way were the most important part of itineraries, but promontories had a functional role here, and rivers in particular were useful for the traveler if they were well enough known to be easily recognized and serve as a guide. Possibly bridges and fords could also serve as landmarks. There was, however, no emotional contact or concern with the wider significance of rivers in local areas. Itineraries were above all businesslike, often with an imperial military or administrative purpose. The best preserved, the *Antonine Itinerary*, probably dating from the third century but incorporating earlier material, is a collection of itineraries along various routes, though areas of the empire are not covered and for some of those included treatment is patchy. The work is not coherently presented, and some routes are repeated, sometimes in the reverse order; there is no clear indication that the compilation was intended to facilitate travel by emperors.[45] The *Parthian Stations* of Isidore of Charax, probably written in the first century A.D., lists stopping places from the Roman province of Syria to the east, starting at Zeugma on the Euphrates.[46] In the later empire, itinerary literature came to be associated with Christian pilgrimage to the east, as in the *Itinerarium Burdigalense* (A.D. 333), which describes the routes for a journey from Bordeaux to Jerusalem.[47] The Peutinger Map, probably dating from the fourth century, depicts the inhabited Roman world, stretching from Spain to India; its carefully plotted road networks, including distances and way stations, are similar to itineraries and suggest a practical value.[48]

Although Claudius Ptolemy had intended that his geographical work should partly be a guide in the construction of regional maps, in general geography was not strictly connected to the drawing of maps. Early maps related to a world view and not local areas. However, the Roman land surveyors (*agrimensores*) employed maps (*formae*) for the depiction and recording of relatively small areas, land distributions, boundaries, and local landmarks.[49] This added a fresh dimension to the study of topography and the relationship of locations to one another. The surveyors offer a view from a different, often more intimate angle, of the role of rivers in settlements.

2   SPACE, MEASUREMENT, AND LOCATION

To find your way by sea or land, you might first look to the *periploi* and itineraries, but most people with a geographical interest would expect to be able to locate places clearly and establish their relative proximity. Consequently, distance, direction, and location were important in all geographical writers, though with considerable variation in emphasis. In terms of defining space, a river was of course highly visible in most locations and therefore of interest to surveyors and others responsible for marking out settlements, measuring distances, and arranging boundaries. It was also relatively easy to represent rivers on a map or plan for the purposes of orientation, and they could easily fit into the spatial element of the writing of itineraries. In the linear approach to geography, places and towns were enumerated in a topographical order, which was often based on the line of a road or a coast.[50] The problem was how to calibrate distances; one solution was to measure the distance between fixed points, while another was to use temporal parameters by calculating journey times in terms of days and nights. In his *Periplous*, Arrian frequently cites rivers to create a series of steps around the coast of the Black Sea, establishing a framework of distances and virtual signposts for the traveler, for example, in the area around Trapezus:

> Along the shore after Trapezus we come upon the river Hyssos, from which the harbor of Hyssos gets its name, which is one hundred eighty stades distant from Trapezus. Then there is the Ophis, which is at least ninety stades distant from the harbor of Hyssos and forms the boundary between Colchis and Thiannike. Next is the river called "Cold" (Psychros), which is thirty stades from Ophis. Then there is the river Kalos, and this is thirty stades dis-

tant from the "Cold." Next is the river Rizios, which is one hundred twenty stades distant from the Kalos. And after this about thirty stades away is another river, the Askouros. And a river called the Adienos is sixty stades from the Askouros. From there it is one hundred and eighty stades to Athenai (on the river Zagatis).[51]

In the Antonine Itinerary, although rivers and river mouths appear comparatively infrequently, they are used with other features to mark distance in Mauretania: "To Six Islands—12 miles (17.7 km); at the promontory of Cannae—30 miles (44.4 km); at the promontory of Rusaddir—15 miles (22.2 km); to Three Islands—65 miles (96.2 km); the river Malva—12 miles (17.7 km); the river Malva divides the two provinces of Mauretania; here starts Caesariensis."[52] In Spain, on the road from Olisipo to Augusta Emerita, a distance of 161 miles (238.2 km) is marked out thus: "Aquabona—12 miles (17.7 km); Caetobriga—12 miles (17.7 km); Caeciliana—8 miles (11.8 km); Malateca—26 miles (38.4 km); Salacia—12 miles (17.7 km); Ebora—44 miles (65.12 km); to the river Adrus—9 miles (13.3 km); Dione—12 miles (17.7 km); Euandria—17 miles (25.1 km); Emerita—9 miles (17.7 km)."[53] In the *Itinerarium Burdigalense* rivers also mark location: "The community of Burdigala (Bordeaux), where the river Garonna is situated, along which the Ocean advances and retreats."[54]

In Strabo's spatial measurement, distance covered or time of travel could be established between towns or landmarks along a river, between two rivers, or between a river and another natural landmark.[55] This would designate a recognizable area of land to be traversed. Rivers also featured in establishing relative locations; for example, settlements might be listed along a river or by distance from a river.[56] Furthermore, rivers, like roads and mountains, could be compared to one another in terms of size and status.[57] This helped the geographer present the concept of scale; differences in the length and width of rivers contributed to an understanding of the layout of areas and provinces and the relationship of the features that made up a landscape.[58]

Therefore, rivers contributed to making Strabo's geography more than a presentation of a mere linear connectivity of areas and regions. Roads, which were generally straight and built to last forever, could also serve as a reference point for orientation and measurement.[59] But rivers, unlike roads, were not imposed creations, but part of the natural layout and history of an area; and they had more links with the surrounding land, for example, through their tributaries, the adjacent mountains, and sea. In this way, rivers could provide a connection to the more complex creation of a map.[60] Rivers affected in various ways the space through which they flowed and established a dynamic relationship with local communities.

Naturally, the more river courses and their relationship to towns became embedded into geographical descriptions, the more valuable they were as markers for the measuring of distance. Pliny measured out the western coast of Italy from Liguria to Campania in a series of stages demarcated by rivers, from the Varus to the Macra, to the Tiber, and then on down to the coast to Surrentum, and from the river Silarus to the toe of Italy.[61] Pliny also established the breadth of Italy by calculating from the river Varus in the Maritime Alps to the Arsia in Istria as 745 miles (1,102.6 km),[62] while in Spain we find that "the Tagus is two hundred miles distant from the Durius, with the Munda coming in between."[63] Rivers were also present in defining the measurements of Europe. "Artemidorus and Isidorus give its length from the Don to Cadiz as 7,714 miles (11,416.7 km). . . . The length of Italy itself, as I pointed out, is 1,020 miles (1,509.6 km) to the Alps, and thence through Lugdunum to the harbor of the Morini (Boulogne) on the British Channel is 1,169 miles (1,730.12 km) according to the measurement used by Polybius. However, a more secure measurement and a longer one also starts from the Alps and stretches northwest through the camp of the legions in Germany to the mouth of the Rhine, a distance of 1,243 miles (1,839.6 km)."[64] More important here than the accuracy of Pliny's calculation of distance is the use of rivers as end markers for the whole process of trying to define space over a wide area.

Apart from the measurement of distance, geographers found major rivers useful in demarcating the location of the huge territory now brought within the reach of the Mediterranean world and in defining in a general kind of way continents and countries.[65] The Danube marked off northern Europe; the Elbe, which divided Germany into two parts, marked the end of western Europe; while the Dniester served to demarcate the lands beyond the Danube.[66] Appian also noted the importance of big rivers: "In Europe two rivers, the Rhine and the Danube, almost entirely bound the Roman empire."[67] The Euphrates and the Tigris embraced Mesopotamia.[68] Furthermore, rivers marked some of the limits of Roman control. "Of the continents, which number three, they hold almost all of Europe except for the part lying beyond the Danube and the parts along the ocean between the Rhine and the Don."[69] This reminds us of Tacitus's comment that "the empire was fenced in by the ocean or by distant rivers."[70]

For Pliny, with his broad Romanocentric view of the world, Rome had divided the world into provinces and districts that suited its interests, and the empire radiated out along roads and rivers, gradually crossing other rivers, for example, the Rhine, the Danube, and the Don, until it arrived at the very edge of geographical knowledge, "ten day's journey beyond the Borysthenes (Dnieper)," where dwelt cannibals who drank out of human skulls.[71] In the geography of Pomponius Mela, the whole world is divided by the Black Sea, the river Don, and the river Nile,[72] and he marked out the entire extent of the coast of northern Europe from Spain eastward by taking the mouth of the Rhine as the defining point.[73] The Rhine throughout its course marked the boundary of Germany, while in Africa the Mulucha designated peoples and kingdoms.[74]

Great rivers such as the Rhine and the Danube were particularly famous as clear-cut geographical delimiters and boundary markers. Caesar had recognized the importance of the Rhine as a physical and cultural barrier for both natives in local communities and Romans; its long course passed though the territory of many tribes and separated the Germans from the Gauls, since it often proved difficult to cross.[75] His decision to cross the river in 55 B.C. was partly influenced by the fact that he did not want it to become a kind of official or psychological barrier to Roman activities. "He wanted them to be terrified on their own account, when they realized that Roman armies had the power and the will to cross the Rhine."[76] Tacitus, who shows a good knowledge of the course of the Rhine, defines German tribes in terms of where they dwell in relation to the river.[77] He also recognized that the value of rivers in identifying locations and peoples was connected to their status, a condition that might change, as in the case of the source of the Elbe, "a river that was once famous and celebrated, but is now known only by hearsay."[78] Throughout the ancient world, the Danube with its two names (Danuvius and Hister or Ister) cast a potent spell, because of its breadth and volume, the peoples it passed on its long course, and its various religious associations. When Plautius Silvanus Aelianus, governor of Moesia circa A.D. 57, transferred a large number of people into Roman territory, they were simply described as "those living across the Danube" (Transdanuviani).[79]

At a more local level, rivers were widely employed as geographical descriptors, to orient the reader and locate districts, peoples, and communities. To someone trying to understand a region or even planning to make a journey, the location of rivers could be a very useful guide. For example, a journey might involve crossing a series of rivers running parallel or at an angle to one another, and river direction was important since traveling upstream or up a river valley would take longer. Indeed, Pliny defines the separation of Gallia Narbonensis from Italy by the parameters of the Alps and the not particularly well-known river Varus.[80] He was perhaps much influenced by what could be seen and experienced. The Alps of course are highly visible, but to the person coming along the coast on the commonly used land route, the river Varus will stand out.[81] Furthermore, rivers served to link regions within the empire, give a wider picture, and demonstrate greater geographical knowledge.[82] Of course, other factors also came into play in demarcating areas, such as the position of local tribes and landmarks.

Strabo observed: "Now a country is well demarcated when it is possible to demarcate it by rivers, or mountains, or the sea,"[83] and although he recognized that rivers could sometimes confuse boundaries by flowing through the center of a district,[84] he maintained that "rivers above all, since they are a kind of natural boundary for both the size and the shape of countries, are especially useful for our entire present enquiry."[85] Rivers appear as geographical descriptors in different ways, for example, "on this or that side of the river," or "up to the river," or "across the river," or a distance as far as a river like the Rhine or the Elbe,[86] or a marker on the river Hebrus that showed the end of the *via Egnatia*.[87]

Some areas could in fact be described as "river country" (*potamia*), as in the case of the Orontes.[88] And peoples were sometimes located through their relation to local rivers, as in the description of tribes "marked off by the river";[89] and in Gaul, "those tribes between the Loire and the Seine Rivers, which are beyond the Rhône and the Saône, are situated towards the north, close to the Allobroges and those who live near Lyon."[90] Elsewhere a community was pinpointed by its vicinity to a particular river, for example, "they dwelt around the Praktios," or "they lived beside the splendid river Kephisos," or "they had their famous estates around the Parthenios river"; the last two examples quote Homer and tie in the historical context.[91] Sometimes Strabo will precisely identify a city by its place on a river, for example, Laodicea near the river Lykos (Lycus).[92]

The value of rivers in a geographical description involving space, distance, scale, demarcation, and history is particularly well illustrated by Strabo's account of the western Iberian Peninsula:

> The coastline next to the Sacred Cape on the west is the start of the western part of Iberia, up to the mouth of the river Tagus, and on the south the start of the southern side up to another river, the Anas, and its mouth. Both rivers flow from the eastern parts, but the Tagus, which is much larger than the other river, flows straight toward the west and its mouth, whereas the Anas turns southward and demarcates the area between the rivers, which the Celtic peoples for the most part inhabit and some of the Lusitanians,

who were deported there by the Romans from the other side of the Tagus. In the inland areas dwell Carpetanians, Oretanians, and many Vettonians. This land is reasonably prosperous, but the land next to it on the east and south, when judged against the entire inhabited world, is outstanding in terms of its fertility and bounty from the land and sea. This is the land through which the river Baetis flows, which has its source in the same location as the Anas and Tagus, and is halfway between these two rivers in terms of size. Like the Anas, it first flows toward the west before turning south and reaching its mouth on the same coastline. They call the land Baetica after the river, and also Turdetania after the inhabitants.[93]

This description is based on river courses, their direction of flow, their spatial relationship to one another, and their comparative size. The rivers marked off various peoples who lived round about, but who had different backgrounds. The fertility and prosperity of the region partly depended on river action, especially in the case of the Baetis. This river, central to its region, inspired the name Baetica, though the local people were also important and hence the alternative name of Turdetania.[94]

Although Claudius Ptolemy lacks Strabo's fluent eloquence, he often has a more precise listing of locations in relative order, and in his methodology rivers provide a vital framework. Ptolemy follows a classic pattern, observing three stages: the source, the middle course, and the mouth. From this basic outline, he constructs a complex picture of a landscape including river sources, tributaries, confluences, and courses that often changed direction before a river debouched into a sea or lake.[95] This is how he sets out the course of the Rhône and its tributaries with appropriate latitude and longitude:

Below Lugdunum the river turns toward the Alps at . . . , and that section of it that is near the lake called Lemanus is at . . . , with the source of the river at. . . . Of the rivers that join the Rhône, in that part which is to the north of Lugdunum the Arar and the Dubis mingle with one another. The sources of the Arar flow from the Alps and are located at. . . . The sources of the river Dubis flowing south of this are at. . . . These rivers flow from the Alps towards the north and then turn toward the west and their juncture is at. . . . Their junction with the river Rhône is at. . . . In respect of the area south of the town of Vienna the river Isara and the river Druentia also flow from the Alps, and the source of the Isara is at . . . and the head waters of the Druentia at. . . . The junction of the Isara and the Rhône is at . . . , and the junction of the Druentia and the Rhône is at. . . .[96]

Ptolemy's coastal surveys have the recurrent theme of river mouths, which along with harbors and promontories, guide the reader forward, as in his description of the western side of Tarraconensis.[97] In fact, Ptolemy uses rivers to establish the character and layout of crucial geographical segments. Lower Pannonia is a particularly vivid example: "Lower Pannonia is bounded on the west by Upper Pannonia from that point where the river Arrabon flows (into the Danube), along those borders to which we have referred. On the south, it is bounded by Illyria, which extends from the indicated boundary as far as the bend in the Danube, near which the river Savus flows into it, the location of which is at. . . . It is bounded on the north and east by that part of the Danube that extends from the junction with the river Arrabon as far as the junction with the river Savus."[98] Here rivers mark provincial boundaries and the Danube confluence pinpoints a location; bends in the course of the river are also important. In areas such as Pannonia and European Sarmatia, where rivers are common as direction indicators in Ptolemy's account, it may be that there was a shortage of other convenient or reliable indicators.[99]

A notable feature of Ptolemy's *Geography* is the listing of principal settlements along roads.[100] However, it is worth emphasizing that in many areas the road network was closely connected to the river network, as, for example, in Gaul.[101] And in the case of river mouths and other related features, Ptolemy is careful to give coordinates. What interested him perhaps was the combination of roads and river valleys, and in some areas the latter were more important for indicating the presence of towns and communities that could give an impression of the layout of a district and show the full pattern of settlement in the context of topography, the natural environment, and man-made communications. In a way, towns fitted into Ptolemy's scheme by illustrating routes of communication through river valleys. For example, in Umbria river valleys were particularly important for communication between coast and mountain settlements, and in the northern part of Umbria few of the towns listed by Ptolemy are on a major thoroughfare. Instead towns such as Pitinum Mergens, Tifernum Mataurense, Iguvium, Aesis, Tuficum, Sentinum, and Camerinum controlled river valleys that provided access for travelers and merchants. North of Rome in Etruria, away from the coastal area, Ptolemy lists sites on major roads such as the *via Flaminia*, *via Quinctia*, and *via Cassia*, but also other communities that have no significant, or apparently limited local road access, but are positioned on a river or in a river valley—for example, Lucus Feroniae, Volaterrae, Rusellae, Perusia, Cortona, Manliana, Vetulonia, Suana, Heba, Vulci, Ferentium, and Tarquinii. Once again, he possibly envisages a pattern of local communication and connection by rivers and their valleys.[102]

We may compare Pliny's geographical descriptions in the *Natural History*, since he saw that at a local level the Mediterranean empire of Rome consisted of relatively small areas and districts with a network of towns and communities. In his businesslike account, he is more parochial than Strabo but had different objectives, which would certainly have appealed to an audience that knew its Italian regions. Roads, of course, linked settlements and helped to establish connections between small regions and prevent isolation, but rivers and river valleys also served as channels of communication, being especially valuable where roads were poor or nonexistent; there was also a network of overland routes between rivers. Pliny uses his evidence to link rivers and towns in a narrative description:

> Next there is the tenth region of Italy, on the coast of the Adriatic Sea. Here there are Venetia, the river Silis, which rises in the mountains named from Tarvisium, the town of Altinum, the river Liquentia, which rises in the mountains named from Opitergium, and the harbor of the same name, the Colony of Concordia, the river and harbor Reatinus, the Greater and Lesser Tiliaventum, the river Anaxus into which flows the Varanus, the Alsa, the Natiso with the Turrus, which flows past the colony of Aquileia located fifteen miles (22.2 km) from the sea.[103]

The pattern of communication in Venetia is based on two roads, the *via Annia*, which follows the coast, and the inland *via Postumia*, which meet at Iulia Concordia; there is also the *via Claudia Augusta* running north from Altinum. From west to east, the roads cross the rivers that run down to the coast: the Silis, Plavis, Liquentia, Reatinum, Tiliaventum Maius and Minus, Alsa, Natiso, and Timavus. The main towns tend to be along the roads—Altinum, Opitergium, and Iulia Concordia—but smaller settlements such as Tarvisium, [H]eraclia, Portus Liquentiae and Portus Reatinus are not. Pliny in fact describes a series of segments where river valleys help to provide links between centuriated lands in the inland plain and the coast.[104]

In Umbria (see map 3), Pliny's description first takes us northward along the coast before making an inland sweep, where the *via Flaminia* provides the linking element as we move along the ridge of the Apennines and into the Tiber valley. The towns mentioned are a mixture in respect of their municipal status, and many are not situated close to the Flaminia. But an additional linking factor may be their position in the river valleys on either side of the main road, which offered access to the Adriatic coast or to the Tiber valley. North of Ancona, Pliny cites the rivers Aesis, Sena, Metaurus, and Pisaurus and coastal towns Sena Gallica, Fanum Fortunae, and Pisaurum. Among inland settle-

Ancient World Mapping Center 2011

Sarsina

Crustumius

Pisaurus

Metaurus

Arnus

Pitinum Pisaurense

Sestinum

Urvinum Mataurense

Sena

Tifernum Mataurense

Pitinum Mergens

Suasa

Ostra

Misus

Aesis

Volaterrae

Sentinum

Iguvium

Attidium

Tuficum

Aesis

Caecina

Tifernum Tiberinum

Cortona

Arna

Camerinum

Manliana

Perusia

Asisium

Plestia

Umbro

Vettona

Hispellum

Clanis

Clitumnus

Vetulonia

Rusellae

Tuder

Alma

Heba

Albinia

Suana

Armenta

Spoletium

Nar

Ameria

Vulci

Marta

Ferentium

Avens

Tarquinii

Lucus Feroniae

Tiberis

Anio

Rome

Roads - - -

| 0 | 20 | 40 | 60 Miles |

| 0 | 30 | 60 | 90 Kilometers |

MAP 3. *Towns and rivers in Umbria, Etruria, and the Tiber valley*

ments that are not obviously part of the road network are Aesis (Aesis valley), Ameria (north of the junction of the Nar and Tiber), Arna (Tiber valley near Perusia), Asisium (upper Tiber valley), Attidium (upper Aesis valley), Camerinum (upper valley of Cluentus), Hispellum (Tiber valley near the headwaters of the Tinia in the Monte Subasio range), Iguvium (near the headwaters of the Clasius), Matalica (near the headwaters of the Aesis), Ostra (on the river Misus), Pitinum Pisaurense (Pisaurus valley), Plestia (on Lake Plestinus in the Apennines above the Cluentus valley), Sarsina (Sapis valley), Sentinum (upper valley of Aesis), Sestinum (upper valley of Pisaurus), Spoletium (on the *via Flaminia* at the southeast end of the valley of the Clitumnus), Suasa (between the river Sena and the modern Cesano), Tifernum Tiberinum (Tiber valley), Tifernum Mataurense (high in the valley of a tributary of the Metaurus), Tuder (on the *via Amerina* in the Tiber valley), Tuficum (upper Aesis valley), Urvinum Mataurense (in the valley of a tributary of the Metaurus), and Vettona (on the *via Amerina*, in the upper Tiber valley). Of course, many of the twelve or so communities that are on a main road have also a river connection.[105]

In his descriptions of the regions of Italy, Pliny lists towns in alphabetical order, and it could be the case that this was entirely a mechanical process. On the other hand, it can be suggested that in his choice of towns Pliny is attempting to visualize the layout of roads, rivers, valleys, and the settlements constructed around this natural setting. He wants to encourage his audience to see this wider picture in which rivers seem to be an essential part of the framework of local life. These rivers in the valleys that helped provide access to communities will have been highly visible and recognizable to the ancients, although they often seem small and insignificant to modern eyes.[106]

In the case of the provinces, to take the example of the Iberian Peninsula, Pliny's description moves along the southern coast from west to east along the putative coastal road, noting rivers and important (mainly Roman) settlements with their rivers. Roads are not important in this description; the rivers mark the districts and main towns, with the river Hiberus (Ebro) being the nodal point, and the very important settlement ("washed by the river") of Caesaraugusta.[107] It is interesting that many settlements are cited with the river on which they stand, providing its contact with the interior.[108]

3   DEMARCATING PROVINCIAL BOUNDARIES

Of the regions, districts, localities, and communities that made up the Roman world, arguably no boundaries were more important than those marking the provinces, which numbered thirty-nine by the late second century A.D. The extent to which provincial boundaries were formally marked and propagated, the movement of people between provinces, and the sense of a fresh identity inspired by a province in contrast to traditional local allegiances are challenging issues.[109] In general, rivers were convenient and highly visible landmarks, and major rivers were largely unchanging and stable, often with cultural and psychological importance in the surrounding area. Some were famous—everyone in Rome knew the river Rubico (Rubicon), after Caesar's dramatic crossing; it was also the official boundary between Cisalpine Gaul and Italy.[110] Rivers and river valleys therefore could provide a clear-cut provincial boundary marker, indicating that you were taking a significant step in crossing to the other side; it might also provide a kind of barrier, offering the government an opportunity to monitor traffic.

In the case of the Spanish territories, Strabo makes explicit an example where rivers coincided with Roman administrative structures: "The praetorian legate . . . is sent out to administer justice to the Lusitanians, who live in the land beside Baetica that stretches as far as the river Durius and its mouth." Part of the territory under the control of the consular governor of Tarraconensis lay beyond the Durius to the North.[111] The northern boundary of Baetica followed the river Anas, while at its eastern extremity an arch, the Ianus Augustus, erected beside the river Baetis, demarcated the province.[112] Furthermore, two of the three provincial capitals in the Spanish provinces were situated on major rivers: Corduba on the Baetis and Augusta Emerita on the Anas.

As Strabo points out, the mighty Danube defined boundaries on its long course from west to east,[113] and it served as the northern boundary for several provinces: Raetia, Noricum, Upper and Lower Pannonia, and Upper and Lower Moesia; it separated the last two from Dacia, which was bounded in the west by the Pathissus (Tisza) and for a distance in the north by the Muresul. For much of its course, the river Aenus (Inn) marked the boundary between Raetia and Noricum. In the Gallic provinces, the peoples of Aquitania were partly enclosed by the Garumna (Garonne) and the Liger (Loire),[114] and the boundary between Aquitania and Lugdunensis generally followed the sweep of the Loire valley. Furthermore, the boundary between Aquitania and Narbonensis ran partly along the Tarnis (Tarn). In Strabo's view, the Belgae, who inhabited the province of Belgica, were encompassed between the Liger and the Rhine, which also along its course demarcated the Roman territory of Upper and Lower Germany and free Germany.[115] In the east, the Euphrates in its middle course was recognized at least until the reign of Trajan as a quasi-formal frontier between the Parthian Empire and the Roman province of Syria and in its upper course marked the eastern extent of Cappadocia. The Jordan conveniently marked the eastern limits of Judaea from the Sea of Galilee to the Dead Sea. The northwestern border of Bithynia-Pontus and Asia briefly ran along the *lacus Artynia* and the river Rhyndakos.

Ptolemy too occasionally notes the importance of rivers in delimiting provinces. For example, in Gallia Aquitania, the river Liger (Loire) predominates in the description. "On the north it is bounded by that section of the province of Lugdunensis that runs alongside the river Liger, which we mentioned before, as far as the place where it turns south at. . . . The eastern boundary lies next to the province of Lugdunensis, running along the river Liger as far as its source, at. . . . The southern boundary lies next to part of the Pyrenees and the province of Narbonensis."[116] Similarly, rivers featured prominently in the demarcation of Noricum. "Noricum is bounded in the west by the river Aenus, and in the north by the part of the Danube that runs from the river Aenus as far as the Cetium mountains, at. . . ."[117]

But in many cases provincial boundaries cannot be clearly identified or have no obvious connection with rivers. Internal boundaries between the Greek provinces of Achaea, Epirus, and Macedonia did not follow river boundaries. Other factors will have influenced the establishment of provincial boundaries, such as ancient local traditions and rivalries, existing lines of demarcation, and administrative common sense. Geography and topography also played a part, and the absence of suitable rivers flowing along a reasonably consistent and stable course. Rivers more often served as a boundary between regions or districts within a province. In fact, some provincial boundaries cut across local rivers; the boundary between Africa Proconsularis and Numidia intersected the one substantial river in the area, the Bagrada, and it is reasonable to ask how far there was a conflict of local identity and loyalty if a provincial boundary cut across a river valley and separated riverine communities. Although our evidence does not allow us to answer this precisely, geographical writers do offer important information on riverine and local identity.

4   RIVERINE IDENTITY AND CULTURAL AFFINITY

In his discussion of the Latin language, Varro noted the origin of *flumen* and *amnis* and the derivation of some town names from their position in relation to a river. *Flumen* came from the action of flowing (*fluere*), *amnis* from the way in which a river could flow around (*am*) a place. Interamna got its name from the fact that it was established within the loop of a river, Antemnae because the river Anio where it entered the Tiber, flowed in front of it.[118] Interest in riverine names indicates how ancient writers identified rivers with the cultural and historical context of local communities. Certainly the temporal focus, so important in Strabo's geographical writing, brought together rivers, names, history, and mythology. The nomenclature of rivers might have much to tell the geographer about the history, development, and topographical aspect of a region or district. Names were very important in local and national life in the ancient world, serving to mark out ownership or control and cultural identity in the parochial world of small communities.[119]

During the early empire, the river Baetis in the Iberian Peninsula was unique in giving its name to the entire Roman province of Baetica, though according to Pliny the Greeks thought that the river Hiberus (Ebro) was so important for trade and commerce and so influential in the geography of Spain, that they called the whole of Spain by the name Iberia.[120] Mesopotamia, shaped by, and named from, its position between the Euphrates and Tigris, became a Roman province in 197.[121] In Diocletian's provincial reorganization several more provinces appeared associated directly or indirectly with rivers: Savensis in the Diocese of Pannonia was named from the river Savus, Sequania in the Diocese of Galliae from the Sequana, Augusta Euphratensis in the Diocese of Oriens from the Euphrates, and Noricum Ripensis in the Diocese of Pannoniae, and Dacia Ripensis in the Diocese of Moesiae, the last both named from their position on the bank of the Danube. After the Tiber, the Padus was the most famous river in Italy in its course through its great northern plain, and regional names reflected this, with Cispadana describing the area next to the Apennines and Liguria, Transpadana the area north of the river.[122] In fact, in official parlance we find a procurator of the taxes of the Roman people "which are on this side of the Padus."[123] The historian Cornelius Nepos was described as "Padi accola"—"dweller on the banks of the Po."[124] Elsewhere, the river Phrygios delimited Phrygia and Caria and also gave its name to the Phrygians.[125] Similarly, the people of Cappadocia, who had been called the White Syrians, subsequently took their name from the river Cappadox, which divided Cappadocia from Galatia; in Spain the Arevaci tribe took its name from the river Areva.[126] Ptolemy also can make a strong connection between rivers and peoples, noting that in Scythia a local river, the Iaxartes, shared its name with an important tribe that lived along its banks.[127]

A common feature of geographical writers is the association between rivers and towns. For example, in the district of Picenum, which itself was said to have derived its name from the woodpecker (*picus*) that had guided the settlers to their new home, a town like Castrum Truentinum was named after its river the Truentus, and Matrinum similarly named after the Matrinus.[128] In Umbria, according to Pliny, the rivers Metaurus and Tiber in adjectival form identified respectively the two settlements Tifernum Mataurense and Tifernum Tiberinum.[129] Elsewhere, entire tribes were identified by their position on the banks of the Rhine and other rivers.[130] Similarly, Ptolemy uses rivers as a way of pinpointing towns; in Gallia Belgica, we find the "Subanecti, whose town is situated to the east of the river Sequana."[131] Pomponius Mela in his descriptions often closely links rivers and towns. In Cantabria, he insists that rivers and peoples go together even when their names cannot easily be written in Latin.[132] In Picenum, "from the river Po to Ancona, the traveler passes Ravenna, Ariminum, Pisaurum, the Colony of Fanum, and the river Metaurus and Aesis."[133] Similarly, "in the Argolid there are the famous rivers Erasinos and Inachos and the famous town Lerna, and in Laconia Gythion and the river Eurotas."[134] He notes that sometimes a river and town shared the same name—Limyra, for example.[135] In emotion and sentiment, local peoples often had strong affinities built up over a long period with the rivers that flowed through their area. Rivers were part of the identity of a locality, which was important in local psychology.[136]

This sense of identity might go right back to the foundation of the city, and many stories associated city foundation with rivers.[137] River names were important to the settlers from Argos who founded Argos Amphilochikon in Acarnania and named the local river Inachos, after the famous river of the Argolid.[138] This was not just nostalgia but an affirmation of their identity as Argives. The same ideology appears in Pausanias's account of the Inachos: "As long as it runs beside the road through the mountain, the Inachos forms the frontier of Argos and Mantinea, but when its course turns away from the road, from that point on it runs through Argive territory; for this reason Aeschylus and others call the Inachos an Argive river."[139] Here the river is cited not only as a boundary marker but also as a point of identity for a local people, who established ownership of it, and as such it passed into literature. In the same way, the protracted argument over where exactly the Pylos of King Nestor was situated was partly sustained by attempts to identify local rivers.[140]

Certainly, in Pausanias's view, rivers were associated with the origins of the city-state. According to tradition, Eurotas, one of the early kings of Laconia, drained the land and named after himself the river that continued to run through the country.[141] Developing towns could take their name from rivers that traversed the countryside. Plataea in Boeotia was named after a girl named Plataea, whom the Plataeans alleged was a daughter of the mighty river Asopos.[142] So, when people had different names for the same river, it could reflect a different view of a legend, or perhaps some kind of neighborhood rivalry or claim to land.[143] Consequently, it might be argued that water was not local but as extraneous or "foreign."[144] So important was riverine identity that close to Mount Pindus two communities tussled over claims to possession of the river

Peneios.[145] For the conqueror of foreign lands, changing or adapting place-names proclaimed the reality of conquest and ownership. So rulers named water sources after themselves and members of their family; geographical imperialism involved naming and in particular renaming existing sites to proclaim cultural and military dominance. Rivers lent themselves to this kind of thinking, not least because of the strong local connections they had, and their religious and mythological overtones, which linked them closely to riverine customs. Furthermore, the river itself could be seen as a conquering force, identifying with the imperial power, though the Romans tended to use existing river names.[146]

An essential part of the association of rivers with communities was their identification with local deities and, of course, their own potential divinity. Furthermore, rivers in many areas had long been part of well-known stories of myth and legend and associated with an anthropomorphic tradition of representation. The importance of this theme in our sources, especially Strabo, Pausanias, and Pliny, owes something to the persistent interest of riverine peoples, because the link with famous places and stories was a great boost to local pride. In addition, it was convenient for writers to recount these stories since they helped to enhance the dignity of their theme and the role and importance of rivers, as well as enlivening the narrative.[147] Therefore, like other geographers, Mela distinguishes between rivers on the basis of their fame; while some were important because of sheer size, others, such as the Acheloüs, were famous by reputation in local legend and mythology. The Scamander and Simoeis were "greater" rivers by reputation as much as by nature. Here we have a useful guide to what impressed the ancients about rivers: size, reputation, historical associations, and mythology.[148]

From issues of location, history, and identity, we can see how a multifaceted geographical narrative could be constructed. Rivers were central to any geographical description not just because they were part of the landscape but because, as well as demarcating areas and defining distance, they had so many cultural and historical ramifications. In Strabo's description of Greece, he depicts a locality with an integrated narrative based on the river Peneios, but including people, history, and antiquarianism in a precise topographical context:

Now, the Peneios flows from Mount Pindus through the middle of Thessaly toward the east, and after passing the cities of the Lapithae and some of the cities of the Perrhaebians, it arrives at Tempe. It collects the water of several rivers, including the Europos, which the poet (Homer) called Titaresios, since it has its sources on Mount Titarion, which joins Mount Olympus, which from that point on begins to mark the boundary between Macedonia and Thessaly . . . (he goes on to explain that Tempe is a narrow valley between Olympus and Ossa). The Peneios flows from these narrows for forty stadia, having Olympus, the highest mountain in Macedonia, on the left, and Ossa on the right near the outlet of the river.

Another city Gyrton is then fixed by its location to the right of the mouth of the Peneios and other places in relation to the established topography.[149]

In a similar way, Pausanias makes the character of the Greek city-states emerge from a variety of factors, in which the watery environment with its associated mythology and divine attributes was often central. His account of Boeotia and the vicinity of Plataea is an example of an integrated, semigeographical description to create a strong image of the river, *polis*, countryside connection: "From Plataea on the way to Thebes is the river Oeroe. The story is that Oeroe was a daughter of Asopos. Before you cross the Asopos, follow its course downstream, and forty stades (about seven kilometers) away are the ruins of Skolos. Amid the ruins are the unfinished temple of Demeter and the Maid and the half-finished statues to the deities. Right up to the present day the Asopos divides Plataea from Thebes."[150] Here Pausanias brings together elements of history, myth, monuments, ruins, direction indicators, boundary marking, and rivers, to analyze this border district.

Interest in river names and the identification of rivers with local areas appear in Pliny's discussion of the origins of the name of the river Padus. He admits to embarrassment that he is borrowing an account of Italy from a Greek source but quotes the opinion of Metrodorus of Scepsis that the Padus got its names from the pine trees that grew around its source, which were *padi* in the Gallic dialect. The Ligurians, however, called the river Bodincus, which means "bottomless." In Pliny's view, this theory was confirmed by the fact that "the neighboring town of Industria, where the river starts to become notably deep, was called by the old name of Bodincomagum."[151]

Despite this interest in river names it seems that the Romans were not greatly concerned to exploit watery nomenclature. It is true that rulers sometimes asserted their powerful presence by naming water sources after themselves or members of their family, as Aphareos, king of Messenia, named a spring at Lepreon after his wife, Arene.[152] There was often a threatening or imperialistic aspect of this. When Philip of Macedon entered Arcadia with his army, the spring near his camp came to be known as "Philip's Spring";[153] during Alexander's advance into the Persian Empire, the Macedonians imposed the name Polytimetos on the principal river flowing through Sogdiana, "just as they imposed names on many other places, either giving them a new name or altering the spelling."[154]

Certainly from time to time the Romans used nomenclature to assert their control and demonstrate the humiliation of rebels. A striking example after the Bar Kokhba revolt was the foundation of the military colony Aelia Capitolina on the site of Jerusalem and the renaming of Judaea as Syria Palaestina; this cultural imperialism dealt a cruel blow to Jewish identity and ideology. Rivers could be part of this kind of thinking. In popular conception, they had personality and power, and at a confluence of rivers, one prevailed over the other like a victor, which was symbolized by a change of name: "The Arar (Saône) flows from the Alps . . . and later taking on the Dubis (Doubs), a navigable river that flows from the same mountains, conquers it with its name, and as the Arar, though made up of both rivers, mingles with the Rhodanus (Rhône). And in turn the Rhône is victorious and flows on to Vienna (Vienne)."[155] This could become a significant imperial metaphor. As we have seen, the Romans took water sources and transferred local watery nomenclature to their own citizen body; they appropriated local gods, who then in art and literature became allies of Rome. There is, however, little sign that the Romans normally changed the established name of rivers and natural phenomena they encountered, though Strabo casually reports that in the Troad people lost their names and dialects under Roman rule.[156]

There is, of course, a distinction between merely translating a river name to a form that is easier to pronounce (like Tiber in English for Tevere) and appropriating it in some way through the name change. The Latin Rhenus apparently comes from the Celtic Renos, and Danuvius from the Celtic or Thracian word for the river; this is also presumably the case with Ister. Rhodanus, or preferably Rodanus, may be associated with the Celtic name for the river Rhône;[157] the Romans seem to have copied the Greek effort to reproduce the native name. These cases seem to be straightforward translations or transliterations from the original. There is not the evidence to suggest that the Romans developed a consistent linguistic imperialism in Latin, at least in respect of rivers. In any case, they tended to be very receptive of loans in respect of foreign words, and not only from Greek. There are numerous Celtic, Germanic, African, Italic, and other words in Latin, though the languages to which they belonged were treated as nonexistent by the Romans.[158] It is unlikely that there was a wholesale attempt to translate river names into Latin or to find Latin terms for existing local names. Certainly, in the case of place-names in Britain, only about forty toponyms are wholly Latin; the rest are British in origin. In general, it seems that "the Roman invaders were not linguistic imperialists. When a place had a name, the Roman army, administration and settlers adopted it without question, merely Latinising its form and fitting it into a declension."[159]

5   GEOGRAPHICAL DESCRIPTIONS

Striking river images catch the reader's eye, as when Caesar observed that the Arar (Saône) flowed so gently that it was impossible to tell the direction of the current.[160] In general terms, the vivid description of river qualities and characteristics informed and enhanced geographical works and made them more palatable to the audience. More precisely, geography in a sense needed to depict the appearance of spaces and locations and help the readers to visualize a landscape that they could not see. In this, rivers had an important role to play, not just in direction and distance, but also in sight and sound and the shape of the country.[161] Furthermore, established riverine characteristics and qualities could be woven into the narrative, which contributed to the understanding of local identity, because, as we have seen before, people associated with rivers and riverine qualities were matters of local pride and proprietorship. We see the linking of river qualities, landmarks, and legend in the famous story about Mount Libethrion, situated near Koroneia in Boeotia, where there were statues of the Muses and nymphs called the Libethrian Nymphs, "and two springs called Libethrias and Petra, which are like a woman's breasts and send forth water like milk."[162]

Now, in his quasi-historical account of the topography and layout of the Greek city-states, Pausanias includes material that he thought would interest his Greco-Roman audience but also reflects the traditions of the Greek past. Although he is sparing in his use of riverine adjectives, he does convey how Greeks were interested in the appearance and feel of rivers, how much water they contained, the speed and violence of the current, and whether it moved with a smooth or swirling motion. A certain volume of water was required before a water source could be described as a river, and rivers were compared for size.[163]

Water supply was problematic in Greece especially in summer, and small rivers often dried up. River descriptions reflect this fact of life. At Corinth, a stream that continued to flow through nine years of drought when all other water sources had failed was significantly called the "golden stream";[164] similarly, the river Krathis in Achaea was called "never-failing."[165] By contrast, a river near Argos had the epithet "the winter stream," implying that it dried up in summer.[166] Therefore, Pausanias, like other writers, was interested in the sources, course, and tributaries of a river, which might contribute to good water flow.

Words such as "tumult," "torrent," "swirling," "slow-moving," "twisting," and "with deep eddies" also reflect concern for river quality and steadiness. In describing the oracle of Trophonius, Pausanias uses a striking image of a man in a deep, fast river being sucked down by the current.[167] The quality of a river is sometimes vividly demonstrated by its name, as in the river Kalliroe (Fair-flowing) in Achaea.[168] The need for reliable and suitable water for community use may underlie the fascination in Greek writers with disappearing and underground rivers.[169] The often curious mythology here had its grounding in real life. Could a stream be trusted to continue? Why did it disappear, and who was responsible? Where might it reappear? Was it the same water with the same qualities, or had it been altered?

Pausanias concentrates on strong visual imagery. Was a river good to look at and did it have a particular color? Was it pure and clean, and was it therefore good to drink? Was it cold and refreshing, or muddy with an unpleasant smell? Greeks valued a river very highly for drinking water, and a good taste was highly desirable. For example, at Aigion in Achaea, Pausanias mentions a water spring that was "delightful to see and to drink from,"[170] while in the city of Pellene the water source was called "sweet waters"; by contrast, the Anigros was notorious for its odd smell, which Pausanias thought came from the earth from which it flowed.[171] At Thermopylae, Pausanias encountered the bluest water he had ever seen flowing into the swimming bath. But elsewhere he saw water with a threatening black appearance, and at Ioppe in Judaea a spring ran red.[172]

Because good drinking water was especially highly prized in the heat of summer, it is not surprising that Pausanias has an extended discussion on the coldness of rivers. In his view, the Gortys in Arcadia was the coldest in the world. Other rivers, such as the Rhine, Danube, Hypanis (Bug), and Borysthenes (Dnieper), were true winter rivers because of the snow and frost around them for most of the time. "But those rivers that flow through a country with a pleasant climate and still cool men if they drink or wash in them in summer, without the effects of winter, these are the ones I call natural rivers of cold water. The Kydnos flowing through the territory of Tarsus and the Black River at Side in Pamphylia have cold water, and elegiac poets have celebrated the coldness of the Hales at Kolophon. But the river Gortys is far colder than any of these and especially in the summer."[173] Considerable research has gone into this celebration of the desirability of rivers with refreshingly cool qualities in their drinking water, and there is an accompanying note of river competition.

River quality certainly was a matter of rivalry, and Pausanias accepts the view that the Ladon in Arcadia had the finest water in Greece.[174] Elsewhere, he singled out this river for its beauty: "For beauty there is no foreign river and no Greek river to match it."[175] Whereas the Roman urban communities usually had aqueducts, the inhabitants of smaller Greek towns had fountains directly supplied from a local stream or went down to the riverbank to draw their drinking water, for a distance of nearly half a mile in the case of Charadra in Phocis, named after the river Charadros.[176] Even worse was the situation of Hyampolis in Phocis, where there was no source of running water nearby; the only source of water for drinking and washing, apart from winter rains, was a well.[177] By his comments and choice of material Pausanias emphasizes what was a commonly held view, that the presence of a reliable river of good water quality was enormously beneficial to the entire riverine community. Consequently in his description of Phocis he notes, "The land enclosed beside the river Kephisos is the best in Phocis for planting, for sowing, and for grazing, and this part of the land is heavily cultivated, so that the story is that there is no city called Riverside (Parapotamioi), but the poetry refers to farmers along the Kephisos: those who dwell alongside the godlike Kephisos."[178]

Strabo eloquently presents an attractive picture through the evocation of a similar range of the qualities, sights, and sounds associated with rivers. He presumably aimed to recapture the visual appearance and effect of rivers on contemporaries, for example, by using the phrases "deep-flowing" and "back-flowing," which he quotes from Homer.[179] The Tagus was wide and deep; other rivers in Spain had high banks and a good channel; the river Kephisos near Chaeronea in Boeotia was distinguished from other rivers of the same name by its twisting shape, which Hesiod compared to a dragon; the Rhine had a swift and even flow; the Padus was wide and tended to be slow flowing; the Axios was wide flowing; the Anigros was sluggish, the Inachos and Kephisos (in Attica) torrential, the Phasis violent and tumultuous; the onomatopoeic Katarraktes was a rumbustious torrent; the river Acheron apparently had sweet water, the Peneios was pure, but others were sluggish and unhealthy.[180] In this context the striking adjective "river-washed" applied to the Iberian Peninsula suggests a complex ideology, including pleasant surroundings, the boon of a river, and the idea of cleansing.[181] There was even a primitive water-quality gauge (by waiting to see if cattle would drink),[182] and the practice of immersing a javelin in a river to test the strength of the current.[183]

In Strabo's view there is therefore an element of beauty associated with rivers and the countryside that they helped to create.[184] He achieves almost a poetic tone in his presentation of rivers and the characterization of their watery qualities; a river should have a firm, clear course with no risk of flooding and be broad, deep (important for a working river), and swift flowing; its surface appearance should be clear and silvery, fresh, sweet tasting, and cool to the touch. Less pleasant qualities brought trouble: violent, turbulent torrents plunging through ravines were unstable and unusable for transport; torrents could also dry up.[185] Variation in flow was an important characteristic, and he notes one winter stream, which underwent significant variations, having at one time a dry riverbed and at other times stretching to a width of 200 feet.[186] For Strabo, the sources of rivers added to their quality and were an important topic in their own right in terms of location and establishing riverine prestige. So, he carefully describes how near the Hercynian Forest "are the sources of the Ister (Danube) and Rhine, and the lake between the sources (Lake Constance), and the marshes that spread out around the Rhine." That military tourist Tiberius went on a day's journey beyond the lake to see the sources of the Danube.[187] Given the dynamic qualities of rivers, it is no surprise that Strabo does not present them as mere passive spectators in their environment. They helped to shape their surroundings, and he has much to say about alluviation, which was generally a power for good, increasing fertility, bringing down large quantities of soil and establishing plains.[188] In this sense, the whole of Egypt could be seen in Herodotus's phrase as "the gift of the Nile."[189] The process of alluviation over time changed the land's configuration, as Strabo frequently points out, and the geographer needed to recognize those features that had become landmarks to locals, such as the famous formations at the mouth of the Danube.[190]

Rivers also had semimystical qualities, including points of technical and scientific enquiry, natural phenomena, and curiosities that helped to inform the description of the history, topography, and attributes of a region and add luster to a locality. Strabo was particularly interested in rivers that changed course and in the effect of the water table on surrounding land. Changes in the water table and river flow might lead to the creation of lakes, which could engulf entire districts and cities.[191] Part of the geographer's task was the explication of local hydrology, especially when it produced unusual events.[192] Underground rivers were a striking phenomenon, as we saw in Pausanias, and there were many theories about how they reemerged after long subterranean wanderings. Some famous rivers even flowed under the sea and allegedly emerged in a far-distant location, allowing the geographer to speculate on technical causes or supernatural possibilities.[193] This was part geology and topography, part lore and anecdote, and sometimes connected to local mythology. The question is probably more about the mystery, power, character, and distinctiveness of rivers in popular estimation. Strabo was certainly not averse to recounting unique characteristics and occasionally very unusual qualities of rivers, such as the alleged ability of the Kereus and Neleus in Euboea to change the color of sheep.[194] The serious side of this theme of river oddities was that such stories sometimes revealed the cultural and historical connections of rivers.[195]

Furthermore, rivers as a great natural force always had an air of mystery in the apparently eternal replenishment of their water sources. Strabo makes a brief reference to the hydrological cycle and the debate whether precipitation was a sufficient explanation for rivers or if there were underground sources or other factors. He quotes Homer to the effect that rivers are "heaven-fed," "not only winter torrents but all rivers equally, because they are all replenished by rainfall."[196] Strabo is also concerned with the other end of the river's life. Rivers flowed into the sea; water was subsequently absorbed from the sea and formed clouds, which fell as rain and sustained the course of rivers, which then flowed into the seas again and so renewed the process. Here Strabo takes up the view of Strato the physicist that rivers flowing into the Black Sea and the Mediterranean filled up the seabed by the quantity of their flow and eventually forced a passage, for example, at Byzantium and the Pillars of Hercules; furthermore, the process of silting had made the seabed uneven.[197] Strabo had doubts that the increase from rivers in their flood could have such a dramatic effect, especially because it did not all happen at the same time. He also believed that silting up occurred only at river mouths and that change in the seabed occurred because of seismic movements there.

In describing the Black Sea, Arrian, like Strabo, makes a fascinating observation about river quality and its effect. He believed that the river Phasis contributed to the sea's unique features. Not only was its water famed for its lightness but it had the color of lead or tin dipped in water and was partly responsible for the famed sweetness of the water of the Black Sea. Arrian saw the proof of this in the fact that animals came enthusiastically to drink from it.[198] The lighter water lay on top of the heavier salt water. He was presumably thinking of the phenomenon of the strong surface current through the Black Sea into the Mediterranean, and underneath the less strong saltwater current from the Mediterranean.

But perhaps the most important quality of rivers was their navigability and their contribution as routes of communication. Strabo is careful within the limits of his evidence to emphasize how far rivers were navigable by particular types of boats, what sort of goods could be carried, and river port facilities.[199] He is consistently interested in this topic, citing convincing detail on the distances for which rivers were navigable, seasonal variations such as winter torrents, and the importance of suitable tributary rivers for increasing water flow in the main stream. For the geographer, a network of navigable rivers inside a region was a useful guide to its wealth and economic potential, in particular for riverine communities and settlements. It is striking how often Pliny in his description of rivers in the *Natural History* discusses their navigability and their role as thoroughfares and routes of connection; for example, the Sububus is "magnificus et navigabilis."[200] In his description of Bruttium, he observes the countless rivers and then goes on to specify the navigable waterways.[201] Of course, Pliny and Strabo are also interested in other geographical markers, but the river navigability comes across as an independent subject, quite apart from the completion of geographical descriptions, the demarcation of space, and the defining of identity.

Of course, rivers were potentially very destructive, and Strabo makes two important caveats about living in river valleys. First, if rivers became torrential, they could burst their banks and cause widespread damage by flooding, creating islands, carrying away land, disrupting boundaries, and making access difficult.[202] Notably, Strabo quotes Posidonius's observation about the effect of unusually high tides on the backwater of the Baetis at Ilipa. Whereas previously the water had reached only halfway up the banks, "on this occasion the water overflowed the banks to such an extent that the soldiers (at Ilipa) got their water on the spot."[203] Further afield, changes in the course of the Indus offered a good example of riverine problems. Aristobulus in the time of Alexander noted that he had seen how a thousand cities and villages had been abandoned "because the Indus had left its normal bed and turned into the other one on the left, which was much narrower, and now plunged down like a torrent."[204] Second, some rivers did not have a good flow, were muddy and sluggish, and occasionally had a bad odor; they could generate an unhealthy atmosphere, and give rise to unproductive marshes.[205] Furthermore, rivers that were not navigable could sometimes impede access to an area. And, of course, the river Styx, traditionally associated with the realms of the dead, vividly symbolized the damaging, threatening, and sinister aspect of rivers, since it was gloomy and destructive, with life-taking rather than life-giving qualities.[206]

It is important that many of the themes discussed in this chapter appear in Roman writers of geography; there is a consistent interest in river characteristics, and the cumulative body of evidence is impressive. Given Pliny's view of the prominent role of rivers in the life of many communities and regions, it is not surprising that he was interested in river characteristics and fascinated by river phenomena, and their remarkable, not to say occasionally supernatural, qualities,[207] especially the nature of the channel, the strength of the flow, the breadth and depth of the water, a straight or sinuous course, a river's ability to change course and alter the layout of the land or bring floods, partly depending on the number and size of its tributaries.[208] The majesty of rivers counted for much with Pliny and contributed to their relative standing in the league table of rivers. He strongly emphasizes the significance of the pleasant environment that a river could create; furthermore, a river could be said to "refresh" a town.[209] Ancients liked to look at a river and appreciated the good surroundings, but these could also be combined with the idea of a working river.[210] The heavy traffic on the Tiber did not discourage the rich from building their villas along its banks.[211]

In Pliny's extended descriptions of some of what he considered the most important rivers, we can find a good indication of the ancient view of riverine qualities. The river Peneios was the most famous in all Thessaly, "rising near Gomphoi and flowing down through a wooded valley between Ossa and Olympus for 62½ miles (92.5 km), for half of which it is navigable. Part of this course is called the Vale of Tempe, 5 miles long and about an acre and a half wide, with the gently sloping hills on the left and right stretching away out of human view, while the valley between is verdant with a wooded copse. The river Peneios glides through it, glittering with its pebbles, charming with delightful greenery on the banks, and resounding with harmonious birdsong."[212] The Jordan too, in contrast to the gloomy Dead Sea, was frequently praised as "a pleasant river with a course as sinuous as the terrain allows, which offers itself for the benefit of the local inhabitants."[213]

The famous river Padus attracted Pliny as the "richest" (*ditissimus*) river,[214] by which he meant not just the fine and famous cities dotted along its course but also its majestic and imposing aspect. The source of the river on Mount Vesulus, one of the highest Alpine peaks, was well worth seeing, disappearing underground before opening out to become a river that rivaled all others in its fame and its legendary associations. Its volume was enormously increased by melting Alpine snows, and although when in full spate it caused damage to neighboring fields, the river was not greedy but left a deposit of splendidly fertile mud.[215] Its course stretched for 300 miles (444 km), with another 88 (130.2 km) in its windings, and had up to thirty navigable rivers as its tributaries. "No other river increases its volume so much over such a short distance. Indeed, the force of the water drives it on and gouges out a deep channel, causing damage to the land."[216] We may compare Polybius's striking encomium of the river, in which he set out his impressions as a Greek visiting Italy and combined topographical detail with the river's character. Noting that the river went under three names—generally the Padus, but Eridanus in the poets, and Bodincus to the local inhabitants—he deals with the source, the direction of flow through the great plain, the enormous volume of water from the many tributaries (augmented in mid-July by melting snow from the Alps), its navigability, and the safe harbor at the Olana mouth.[217]

Pliny was fascinated by what could be appreciated by the senses; he had respect for rivers, he admired their many qualities, and he knew not only the advantages they brought to riverine communities but also their potentially destructive qualities. All this contributed to his emotional tribute to the Tiber, which was a glorious symbol of imperial power. Previously it had been called the Thybris and before that the Albula. Beginning as a narrow stream, it rose near Arretium in the Apennine Mountains and was navigable only when the water was dammed and then released through sluices. Even in full spate, it was not navigable over a considerable distance because of its rugged channel. It formed boundaries along its route, notably separating Etruria from Umbria and the Sabine country, and was augmented by numerous tributaries. In its lower course, the volume of water made it navigable for even large ships from the Mediterranean. Therefore, the Tiber is "a most serene merchant of products from all over the world and has more people living close by its banks and is overlooked by more villas than any other river in the whole world. More than any other river it is entirely shut in on all sides. It does not raise any objection to this, though it is subject to frequent flash floods and the inundations particularly affect the city. However, it is regarded as a warning prophet, and the flood is in truth held to be of religious significance rather than an attack."[218] There is subtle personification here as the river begins to assume characteristics as an agent of prosperity and a wise and strong mentor and guardian of the Roman state, in which role it could be represented in human form.[219] In a way, the powerful qualities of the Tiber served to demonstrate the superiority of the dominant imperial power.

River courses, their tributaries, changes in riverine character, their visual and auditory impact, and the nature of the environment they helped to create are all part of the geography of Pomponius Mela, who reserves some of his best descriptions for rivers, for example, in his account of the area near Marathos on the coast of Syria, where the population was affluent because of the nature of the land. It was a fertile region with many navigable rivers, which promoted commercial traffic and the easy exchange of all kinds of merchandise from land and sea.[220] Mela singles out certain rivers in his geographical descriptions if he thinks that their reputation or characteristics merit. For example, the Araxes was outstanding because its fame surpassed that of other rivers in the area, and because of the striking appearance and sound of its stream. The river flowed silently and placidly across the Armenian plains, but, hemmed in by rocky gorges, it became fast flowing, with a loud roaring noise and crashing water-falls. Then it slowed down again before flowing gently to the sea.[221]

Finally, Mela's description of the qualities and character of the river Borysthenes encapsulates much of what he thought rivers could contribute to local communities, and their role in building up a geographical profile of an area: "It washes the people that shares its name and is the most pleasant of the Scythian rivers, flowing limpid clear while the others are muddy. It is more serene than the other rivers and delightful to drink. It nourishes exceptionally pleasant pastureland and large fish, which have a splendid taste and no bones. It travels over a long distance, rising from an unknown source, and the route along its banks takes forty days. It is navigable for the whole distance and it reaches the sea near the Greek city Borysthenes/Olbia."[222]

6   CREATING MAPS

The job of actually measuring rivers, assessing their impact on individual settlements and communities, and constructing a workable plan and map usually fell to the Roman land surveyors.[223] Their interest was entirely professional and limited to the local area they were surveying.[224] They recognized the many potential qualities and benefits of rivers to settlements: in the early years of establishing a new community rivers might provide protection and also offered a regular source of water for drinking and washing and watering animals. In some cases, a stretch of river might be included in the actual land allocations. Frontinus observes that in lands that had been surveyed and settled, large rivers sometimes came into the allocated area, which meant that some landholders had a river frontage to their property. He then goes on to explain how the founders of colonies fixed boundaries and decided who got what resources, particularly emphasizing that, although there was no single reason, landholders would welcome being close to what he describes as the *boon* of a water supply. This was one reason why a system of drawing lots was used, so that settlers could not complain about their allocation.[225] Consequently, there may have been some pressure from landholders for direct access to a river. Apart from anything else it offered opportunities for fishing and the easy movement of goods and people. Furthermore, through alluvial action riverine valleys often had a good supply of fertile land. The importance of rivers to individual farms comes across strongly in the *Casae Litterarum*, a late empire text in which descriptions of estates are based around letters of the alphabet.[226] Springs and streams are a regular feature of the landscape of these estates.

Surveyors therefore sought to manage and control rivers for the common benefit of settlers and communities. It was the responsibility of the founder of a settlement to arrange for the definition of the area of the river (*modus fluminis*). Surveyors when allocating the land for a new settlement measured the width of the riverbed, which was entered on the map and the map notation, on which the river would be specifically identified by name. For example at Pisaurum (Pesaro) in Umbria, the map notation read: "So much for the river Pisaurus, in which the bed (extended for so many feet)."[227] However, it became approved practice to measure an additional area around a river, which was not to be occupied by landholders, but remained as an area into which the river could flood beyond its banks after heavy rain.[228] Landholders could make what use they could of this land. In fact, rivers are relatively rarely cited by name in the surveying texts but appear routinely in the surveying operation and the distribution of land. Rivers that are mentioned, such as the Padus, the Liris in Campania, and the Anas in Spain, exemplify the problems of turbulent rivers and the details of land demarcation.

For the surveyors, one of the most useful riverine qualities was that of boundary demarcation; a river was a well-known local landmark that could not be moved or faked by landholders, and it was obviously a commonplace that rivers defined both individual properties and boundaries between communities.[229] Surveyors recorded all features relating to rivers since one of their most important duties was to draw a map (*forma*), often inscribed on bronze and set up in the settlement, while a copy on parchment or papyrus was conveyed to the record office in Rome.[230] The map, accompanied by notations giving details of landholdings and other points of interest, covered the local area of each community, its natural features, the landholdings, and other relevant details. In fact, it provided a visualization of the layout of the land after the survey and allocation, and rivers were particularly useful to catch the attention as obvious guides to finding locations. The maps served the government in providing accurate records of landholding and unused land; this information was used to resolve disputes and assess the resources of a community.[231]

Several of the surviving texts of surveying writers contain numerous drawings, diagrams, and illustrations.[232] Although these are not the work of the original surveyors, they help to show how in later ages people interested in the surveying texts interpreted the place of rivers in local communities and settlements. Everyone could appreciate how a river, drawn in blue or green, might assist in the accurate identification of a correct location or town and provide an essential framework around which the segments of the map could be connected. Rivers also added beauty and variation to a map. For example, in the case of Tarracina-Anxur on the coast of Latium, the illustration in manuscript P shows the walled town by the sea, the *via Appia*, the neighboring Pomptine marshes, and two streams, one of which flows through the town.[233]

We have a fragment of a genuine surveyor's map carved in bronze and recovered near Mérida (Augusta Emerita) in Baetica; the river Anas boldly flows though the land allocations, serving to orient the reader. At Orange (Arausio), the cadastral map carved in stone shows the land division grid and allocations clustered in the Rhône valley around the river in the territory of the Tricastini, where legionary veterans had been settled circa 35 B.C. in the Colonia Iulia Firma Secundanorum. During the Flavian dynasty, the settlement was recast as Colonia Flavia Tricastinorum, with a readjustment of the land distribution. On the map, the river and local roads provided a backdrop to the landholdings, assisted accurate identification and orientation, and contributed to a spectacular visual display in public on walls near the town forum. It is also worth mentioning the representation in a similar style of the Tiber and the Tiber Island on the marble plan of Rome, constructed between A.D. 203 and 208.[234]

We should not underestimate the value of the public display of maps in the ancient world. Their potential role in helping people to visualize and understand distant places and complex landscapes is vividly illustrated by a speech delivered by Eumenius in A.D. 297 or 298 at Augustodunum (Autun) about the rebuilding of the local school. He speaks enthusiastically of his plans for a map showing the lands, seas, cities, and peoples controlled by the emperors. "On the map, as I think that you have seen for yourself, for educating the young people so that they can learn more clearly through their own eyes material that is difficult to understand merely by hearing it, all places, areas, and distances are written in with their own names, and also the sources and mouths of all rivers, the indentations of the coastline, and places where Ocean either embraces the earth or breaks into it by force."[235]

Although surveying and related maps set rivers and other landmarks in a specifically local context, rivers easily fitted into regional maps or even world maps, which offered the ultimate depiction of space, lands, and natural phenomena. The Peutinger Map, which offers a kind of visualized guide, depicts the provinces of the Roman Empire based on roads and rivers as routes of communication, and on mountains, lakes, river tributaries, and settlements.[236] Once again, in the visualization of regions in the Roman world, the framework provided by rivers is striking. The text of Ptolemy's *Geographia* is accompanied by maps that depend on a twelfth- or thirteenth-century manuscript possibly from Constantinople, now in the Vatican Library.[237] There is no proof that it is descended from maps drawn by Ptolemy himself, and it is not even clear that Ptolemy drew maps to accompany his original work.[238] Nevertheless, the maps may well reflect later views on the various elements and topographical features that constituted the kind of map suggested by Ptolemy's analysis. Rivers, with their vivid blue color, are one of the dominating physical features of the maps along with seas, mountains, and gulfs. Major rivers are depicted with an attempt to represent their sources, tributaries, and course, which is followed through to a sea or lake. Along the river valleys are marked the principal cities, providing a framework to show the management of space, patterns of settlement, and the physical environment in the Roman Empire. Ptolemy had absorbed from earlier writers, and also from the travelers' tales that he sometimes used, the vital importance of lines of communication often via river valleys, for travel, commerce, trade, the passage of armies, and human use of space.

7   CONCLUSION: "THE BOON OF A WATER SUPPLY"

All ancient writers, including Frontinus, when writing about land allocation, thought that rivers were a benefit to local communities. Geographers and topographers repeatedly return to the theme of the location, shape, character, size, and course of rivers. Although it is true that they often tended to provide an impressionistic, anecdotal account of the riverine environment, emphasizing eye-catching detail, nevertheless rivers are discussed with a specific and coherent purpose to measure distance, to establish orientation and relative positions, and to identify towns, places, and peoples by placing them in the vicinity of a river whose name was usually permanent. Accordingly, rivers contributed to the preservation of the identity and history of communities and regions. Rivers of status and mythological pedigree brought dignity and prestige to their riverine dwellers. Geographical writers had a different range of interests from the more professional analysis of surveyors, with their special concern for the measurement of rivers, the assessment of risk, riverine boundary marking, and careful recording and mapping. They attempted to regulate land, rivers, and landholders for the benefit of the community.

The common thread among most of the writers examined is not only that a well-written river description would have a pleasing impact through the visualization of a landscape scene but that their readers would find the naming and characterization of rivers meaningful and relevant. That this idea was not entirely separate from real life we see from a moving inscription recording the fate of a retired Italian soldier murdered in Dalmatia: "Aulus Sentius, son of Aulus, of the tribe Pomptina, from Arretium, veteran of legion XI, is buried here (and) in his will ordered this to be done. He was killed here in the territory of the Varvarini in the little field beside the river Titius at Long Rock. His heir, Quintus Calventius Vitalis, son of Lucius, looked after this task."[239] Ordinary people thought it important to define a precise location in death just as in life, among rivers and mountains and familiar surroundings.

Three

RIVERS, LANDS, AND LAWS

According to a Roman land surveyor, "There is more than one type of alluvial activity through which rivers inflict loss on landholders. For example, the river Padus (Po), leaving its bed, bursts through the middle of someone's farm and makes an island between its old and new course. In this case the question concerns who should own the soil that it deposited, since the nearest landholder is suffering no small loss, as a river which is public property is flowing through his land."[1]

These comments touch on all kinds of issues: various forms of river damage, the need to protect landholders from loss, the example of the river Po with its notorious propensity to flood, and the possible legal implications that might arise when public property (i.e., the river) effectively moves to a new location. Similar issues were expressed in less scholarly tones at the beginning of the twentieth century by an American commentator: "It (the Missouri river) cuts corners, runs around at night, lunches on levees, and swallows islands and small villages for dessert. Its perpetual dissatisfaction with its bed is the greatest peculiarity of the Missouri. Time after time it has gotten out of its bed in the middle of the night with no apparent provocation, and has hunted a new bed. . . . Later it has suddenly taken a fancy to its old bed, which by this time has been filled with suburban architecture, and back it has gone with a whoop and a rush as if it had found something worthwhile. It makes farming as fascinating as gambling. You never know if you are going to harvest corn or catfish."[2]

Because of their potential destructive power, rivers, streams, springs, and their related water channels were at the heart of much Roman legal provision in respect of landholding, the management of land, relationships between neighbors, and inevitably the resolution of disputes caused by disruptive rivers. In terms valuable precisely for their melodramatic tone, the jurist Venuleius claimed that repairing aqueduct channels was more important than repairing roads, because, "if aqueducts are not repaired, the entire water provision will be stopped, and persons will be exposed to death by thirst."[3] As the state intervened more consistently in the control of water resources, there was a more formal observation of riverine activity through lawyers and other professional groups, particularly surveyors. Rivers and waterways were to be fully exploited but not allowed to disrupt rural life.

This chapter examines the legal and administrative measures taken to manage rivers, streams, water sources, and lands in the process of setting up and regulating communities and arranging relationships between landholders. There are four important themes: defining rivers and the significance of such definitions in maintaining an equitable provision of water from rivers and streams; enforcing water rights in the interests of the *res publica*; using rivers to demarcate land boundaries and the consequences of this in settlements; circumscribing and managing disruptive rivers by surveyors and lawyers for the good of the state and the local community in an attempt to achieve a balance between the benefits and potential dangers of rivers. These topics help us to appreciate some of the problems ordinary people encountered in daily life in rural communities, how they surmounted these problems, and how disputes were resolved.

Of our two main kinds of evidence, the writings of lawyers transmitted mainly in the *Digest* tend to give us a formal response on legal principle, often reflecting the view of society or the government, and the view of men of settled respectability who valued property rights but who also respected the state's authority and right to ownership. In fact, some of the headings in the *Digest* show clearly how they relate to the management of running water:

On rivers and the prevention of any action on a public river or riverbank
    that might interfere with navigation
On the prevention of any action on a public river that might make the
    water flow in a different way from the way it did in the previous
    summer
On ensuring freedom of navigation on a public river
On the requirement of strengthening riverbanks
On water for daily and summer use
On water channels
On springs
On the requirement to restrain water and rain-water[4]

There is much material to work with but it brings several problems. First, the Digest texts present the usual question of interpolations by the Justinianic compilers, who may have modified their excerpts to suit the legal opinion of their own time. In particular, some argue that lawyers under Justinian tended to give greater rights to riparian possessors in respect of claiming old riverbeds when a river had changed its course. This may distort our view of the management of disruptive rivers in the first and second centuries A.D.[5] Second, what is the status of what lawyers tell us? What they say is not necessarily a statement of the existing law but might be a legal argument or attempted definition. In many cases an advocate was probably doing his best to help his client win an uncertain case. Therefore, we have what might be seen as a statement of plausible legal argument, based on a perception of the law, to which other lawyers could sensibly respond. Not all advice or speculation of counsel makes it to court, never mind influences the development of the law. It is unlikely that by the mid-second century A.D. the law in respect of rivers had been fully codified. Litigants and their lawyers used whatever precedents they could find and persuade people to accept. At the very least the legal texts will tell us about the riverine topics that inspired most debate.

The professional work of the Roman land surveyors (*agrimensores*) gives another view. They pinpoint many of the issues associated with rivers and the practical application of the law as fairly as possible for all types of landholder. Undoubtedly rivers seem to be at the heart of many of the writings of the land surveyors. The incentive for the law to analyze and in the end prescribe solutions for the relationship of land, rivers, and landholders is found partly in the Mediterranean climate and the distinctive topography of Italy, with its narrow valleys and generally short rivers subject to enormous seasonal variation in flow and volume.[6] The writings of the land surveyors, while offering a unique record of the methodologies and practices of this increasingly professional group, are at times extremely obscure. The date of many of the authors, their relationship to one another, and their ultimate purpose in writing, are all uncertain. It is unclear to what extent the texts are didactic, historical, or an assertion of the developing role of surveyors.[7]

Our literary sources can usefully be supplemented by the evidence of inscriptions, which randomly illustrate individual cases sometimes in great detail, especially in respect of boundary determinations, descriptions of boundary marking, accounts of land disputes, and maps or plans of settlements. Inscriptions can reveal the reality of problems on the land in contrast to the generally theoretical analysis in the literary sources. For example, it is valuable to compare the recommendations of the land surveyors with what actually happened.[8] However, the evidence of inscriptions is often limited in relevance to one case, though sometimes several inscriptions, such as those relating to land disputes, can illustrate a pattern of activity.

Although most of our sources are mainly interested in the rivers of Italy and their legal problems, Roman rule extended over vast swathes of water, including the Mediterranean Sea, the Black Sea, and the entire course of major rivers such as the Rhine, Danube, Rhône, Saône, Guadiana, Guadalquivir, Ebro, Orontes, and Maeander. Other rivers such as the Nile, Euphrates, and Tigris at various times came substantially within the Roman orbit. All these rivers to some extent were the public property of the Roman people and represented the benefits of empire and Rome's dominion over the natural environment.[9]

1   DEFINITIONS

Part of the process of working with rivers and managing them was careful definition of what constituted a river, because it was not necessarily obvious if a waterway was a river or a stream, or what right people had to use it or to be protected from the actions of those who did use it. The scope, character, and area of the river (*modus fluminis*) would be part of the definition.[10] Furthermore, the language used by surveyors reflects their definition and analysis of the strength and violence of rivers and their damaging capacity to change the landscape; inundation, violent torrents, changing course, moving of earth, the creation of islands, and the unpredictable impact of storms and melting snow and ice.[11]

We start with the classic statement in the *Institutes* of Justinian of a long-established distinction between *ius civile* (civil law) and *ius gentium* (law of nations): "All peoples, who are governed by laws and customs, use law that is to some extent particular to them and to some extent held in common with the rest of mankind. For the law that every people has established for itself, that law is particular to that state and is called the *ius civile*. However, the law that natural reason has established among all mankind, that law is observed equally by all peoples and is called *ius gentium*."[12] Gaius writing in the second part of the second century cites the *ius gentium* as the basis for his confirmation of the presumably long-standing definition of a river, its use and reasonable accessibility to all: "The public use of the banks of rivers is subject to the *ius gentium* just like the river itself. Therefore, it is permissible for anyone to bring a boat to the bank, to tie ropes to trees growing there, to dry nets and to draw them up from the sea, and to place cargo on them, just as it is permissible for anyone to navigate the river."[13]

Effectively, rivers belonged to the Roman people, were part of public property, and therefore were accessible to all. However, Gaius goes on to point out that ownership of the banks belongs to those whose landholding is contiguous and that they also possess any trees on the banks. In fact, the riverbank was public property only from the point where the banks sloped down toward the water.[14] The distinction between public and private riparian ownership is vividly illustrated by boundary stones (*cippi*) erected along the Tiber at Ostia by C. Antistius Vetus and his colleagues, curators of the beds and banks of the Tiber; on the rear of the stones appears the phrase "without prejudging the rights of the state or private individuals."[15] Also five travertine *cippi* from Ostia erected along the north side of the town *decumanus* by Gaius Caninius, *praetor urbanus*, are inscribed: "He adjudicated the public area in accordance with the opinion of the senate."[16] Opposite the westernmost stone another stone apparently marks the end of the public zone: "private land to the Tiber, right up to the water."[17] It seems that Caninius was assigning to public ownership a zone between the main street and the river.[18] However, the stone designating private ownership may be later in date, and it is possible that it was set up privately to assert a local possessor's claims to land in the vicinity of the public area. That might explain the rather curious terminology "right up to the water," not "right up to the bank"; the riparian possessor wishes to emphasize possession up to the edge of the water itself, which is public. The potential conflict in such contending interests was the context in which the *ius civile* had a role in managing and arbitrating disputes. An example in a slightly different context is the response of Antoninus Pius to the fishermen of Formiae and Caieta, reminding them that whereas access to the sea for fishing was open to all, they really must keep off buildings and villas, which were not subject to the *ius gentium*.[19]

Rivers were further defined according to their recognizable characteristics. A river (*flumen*) was distinguished from a stream (*rivus*) by its size, and in an interesting concession to local knowledge, this was sometimes judged on the opinion of those who lived in the neighborhood. The other crucial characteristic, extremely significant in the context of Mediterranean lands, was the volume and nature of flow. Was the river perennial or torrential? Perennial rivers had a continuous flow, whereas torrents flowed only in winter. However, if a river dried up for a time in summer, it could still be described as perennial if it flowed normally at other times. Once again we see the value of constantly running water. The jurist Cassius gave the opinion, apparently widely approved, that a public river had to be one that flowed uninterruptedly.[20]

A river was also defined by its course and by the strength of the current. Consequently some of the praetor's regulations provided for the prevention of actions that brought about changes in the direction of a riverbed and in the strength and nature of the current from that of the previous summer. This may suggest that there was a map and also a record of the river's established characteristics, like those described by the land surveyors.[21] Another provision prevented work on the river that made it wider and so shallower, or narrower and so with a more rapid flow.[22] Ulpian also recognized the force of a river's current, even in normal circumstances, as something that could make some journeys difficult.[23] The best time to judge a river's natural course was the summer, defined as up to the autumnal equinox.[24] Presumably at this time of the year the river would have a clearly defined course and its bed could be determined; at other times it could be subject to floods that distorted its normal course.

Individuals were normally not permitted to alter the course of a river. It is interesting that the law providing for the government of the *municipium* of Irni in Spain (*lex Irnitana*) specifically gives local magistrates the right to create or alter the course of roads, ways, rivers, ditches, or drains, provided that they were within the boundaries of the community and did not infringe private interests.[25] The need to control the direction of river courses had to be set against the need to protect the interests of riparians.

Although not all rivers were public property (there were some rivers presumably entirely on private estates), lawyers generally agreed that most perennial rivers, whether navigable or not, were public. Furthermore, wherever the river went became public property. Consequently the right to enjoy the produce of a garden could be restored after the water from a river inundation had receded, but if the change in course was permanent, "I think that the usufruct is lost since that begins to be a public area of the riverbed."[26]

This insistence was in keeping with the general proviso that the running water of rivers should be available to the Roman people without fear or favor. The explanation can be seen mainly in the obvious value to communities of the natural asset of running water. But we should also recognize the determination of the senate and later of the imperial administration to set aside and manage the natural environment as it wished, as in the case of water rights; from this position of control concessions could be made as it suited them, as of course emperors were to do by controlling the distribution of water through aqueducts. With the expansion of Roman territory it was easy for the Romans to assume that any waterway coming under their control would be treated like public property. In fact, local rivers and their associated gods were subsumed as allies of the Roman state.[27]

The careful definition in the legal texts of rights of access to and use of the running water of rivers and streams confirms their value to rural communities. Of course, rivers were important as routes of communication, and all use of rivers was controlled by the provision that it must not impede riverine navigation in any way; "If a river is navigable, the praetor should not allow any water to be taken from it, according to Labeo, which might make it less navigable. That is also the case if another river is rendered navigable through this action."[28] On this condition, regular access to a *flumen publicum* was guaranteed, and the right to take water from a running source is frequently affirmed on numerous occasions;[29] water taken from a river could be used for irrigation and to provide a watering hole for cattle;[30] and several people could draw water from a river as long as they did not harm neighboring possessors, including those on the other side if the river was narrow.[31] The importance is shown by the debate over the right to take water if there was some interruption to supply. An emperor (probably Trajan) wrote as follows to Statilius Taurus: "The men who normally draw water from the Sutrine estate have approached me and explained that they have been unable to draw the water, which they have used for many years, from the spring on the Sutrine estate because it dried up, but that later it began to flow again. They have petitioned me in order that, because they had lost their right not through carelessness or any fault, but because they could not draw the water, it should be restored to them. Since their request seems to me not unreasonable, I thought that I should assist them."[32]

The right to draw water from a river often involved the issue of a servitude (*servitus*), that is, an easement (attached to land, not to a person) that permitted an individual to make use of property not belonging to him, normally in respect of a right of way. The *agrimensor* Siculus Flaccus explained as follows: "There is always right of way to all lands. Sometimes, for lack of local roads a right of way is provided through another person's land. Some landholders make a specific agreement to concede a servitude in respect of those fields, to gain access to which they are obliged to allow a right of way through their land. Moreover, water channels normally give a legal right of way across the land of others."[33] Many *Digest* texts deal with these servitudes, which were zealously protected and, in terms of water, normally related to a perennial source.[34] The needs of landholders were balanced against the need to protect the water source. For example, in drawing water from a river you could not follow if the edge of the water receded. This prevented overuse of the resource. There were also agreements to use water at certain times and careful definition of the conditions of use, with, for example, a distinction between *cottidiana* (water that was drawn constantly in summer and winter, though not always made use of) and *aestiva* (water that was used only in summer).[35]

The importance of running water for irrigation is dramatically illustrated in a reply of the emperor Claudius II to a petition: "The governor of the province will not permit you to be deprived of the of the use of the water, which, as you claim, flows from a spring belonging to you, contrary to the practice established by custom, since it would be hard and indeed virtually cruel that a body of water that rises on your estate should be unjustly taken away and distributed for the benefit of other neighboring fields when your own are thirsty."[36]

In some locations there was a system in place specifically to share a water source for irrigation. For example, near Tusculum in the Alban hills north of Rome, the famous Aqua Crabra provided water, though it is unclear if it was a natural stream or an aqueduct. It served the landholders at Tusculum, who received their water regulated according to day and quantity, and Agrippa had decided not to employ it to service the Julian Aqueduct. Later, however, abuse and corruption led to part of the Aqua Crabra being diverted for the profit of the watermen until Frontinus, with imperial permission, restored its original use.[37]

In general, access to water just like other property or holdings was guaranteed by law, but it was often up to surveyors and other adjudicators to assess and regulate the means of access by measuring and locating the exact boundary. For example, away from the countryside, in the crowded world of Rome, an inscription attached to a funeral monument gives a good vignette of the roads, paths, walls, apartments, funerary niches, and even the occasional field that contributed to city life, and the careful work of an assessor:

> To this monument a path and approach and right of way around are due in accordance with the opinion of Eros, freedman of Augustus, adjudicator, from the public road Campana on the right between the wall Calamiana and the quarter (*insula*) Eucarpiana, to a width of two and a half feet right up to this monument, and from here around the perimeter of the entire monument right up to the road which leads into the field, and similarly, the same path and approach to this monument are due from this point along the monument of Tyches Afinia, and from there along the wall Eucarpiana, in which are the funerary niches, and from there straight to the public road Campana.[38]

2   THE *RES PUBLICA* AND WATER RIGHTS

In the early period in Italy settlers often had to fight to secure running water sources, and water supply continued to be vital for Italian communities, and especially for expanding towns. But later there was more need to regulate relations between individuals over the use of, and access to, water. As we have seen, there was tension between the demands of the state and the rights of individual possessors in respect of rivers, because the state effectively owned each river (*flumen publicum*). Furthermore, wherever the river went, the state followed in claiming control, though it is true that concessions were increasingly made to possessors.

In this context, we might reasonably expect that the *res publica* could ensure, or be confident that it could ensure, the means of conducting water wheresoever it wished for the public good and making due arrangements to facilitate such distribution. The question to some extent depends on the evidence for the way in which the Romans acquired land for building and maintaining aqueducts. If the Roman state had the means to acquire land as it needed in order to exploit running-water sources, even against the wishes of neighboring landholders if necessary, though with various types of compensation, this might be relevant to our consideration of the treatment of rivers and riparian possessors.[39]

It would be extraordinary if the Romans had no means of securing vital public requirements, such as assured access to water, the building of public thoroughfares, and the construction of water channels for conducting water to urban areas over a distance. After all, the government was quite capable of treating land in an arbitrary way—hence, the confiscations of land by military dynasts and others. The Roman land surveyors, who strongly upheld the rights of individual landholders, also had to deal with the results of confiscation, arbitrary land swaps, and changes of control in the establishment of colonies expressed through the issue of jurisdiction.[40] The point is that a society in which such actions sponsored by the state are possible and not uncommon, is one in which we might surely accept that the state could take possession of land that it deemed necessary for the public good, with the appropriate legal accommodation. The interests of the people in power would predominate and favor whatever they chose to represent as the public interest. Cicero had expounded the idea (in relation to the consuls) that "the people's welfare is the highest law."[41] Emperors of course could intervene as they thought fit, and the law of A.D. 69 establishing Vespasian's powers stated "that whatever he considers to be according to the interest of the state and in accord with the majesty of things divine and human, private and public, the right and power be his to transact it." This law also exempted the emperor from laws and plebiscites, as his predecessors had been.[42] The emperors were masters of the aqueducts, through control of their finance and administration and the power to take initiatives. This included money for aqueduct repairs and appointment of "the curators of the aqueducts, whom Caesar Augustus nominated on the authority of the senate."[43] Control of resources does not imply that the government would not attempt to avoid disruption and injustice to landholders. But when it suited him, Augustus took lands from Capua in Campania and in return granted the residents a water supply (the *aqua Julia*) and land in Crete at Cnossos. Although in the end this turned out to be reasonably profitable for the Capuans, they seem not to have had a choice.[44]

A priori it is a reasonable contention that the *res publica* could acquire the land it needed by whatever method was convenient, notwithstanding the rights of landholders. This would be done by responsible officials by virtue of the power conferred on them or inherent in the office they held. Ulpian speaks of the *ius publicandi* in respect of public roads: "The land on which public roads run is public, either left (unmeasured) or with its breadth marked out between established boundaries by the man who had the right to make it public, so that people may go and travel along them."[45] It is clear enough then that an official of the state could make land public, howsoever he did it. Such a change in status is apparent in other *Digest* texts on leasing and hiring. In one case the leasing or sale of a farm was cast in doubt because the farm had been made public:

> If a farm that you have leased to me was made public, you are liable (to me) through an action of the lessee, so that I can have the benefit of it, even though you are not responsible for the fact that you cannot provide it. . . . If your tenant farmer is prevented from enjoying his property by you or by someone whom you can prevent from doing so, you must provide for him as much as he was prevented from enjoying, and this will include his profit. But if he shall be hindered by someone whom you cannot prevent because of superior force or power, you will be liable to remit or return to him nothing more than the rent.[46]

The analysis makes clear that the leaser or seller was not at fault and also that he had been subject to some outside force (*vis maior* or *potentia*). Although the exact context is unclear, nevertheless ownership of the farm was seemingly taken by the state even though the owner was not culpable.[47]

Other evidence helps to show government activity in the potentially contentious area of ensuring the smooth and effective operation of the aqueducts that served Rome. The decree of the senate in 11 B.C. provided for materials to be taken for maintenance of the aqueducts whether the owners liked it or not, although financial compensation was paid. Furthermore, a right of way through the land of adjacent landholders was insisted upon:

That when those channels, conduits, and arches, which Augustus Caesar has promised the senate to repair at his own expense, shall be repaired, from the fields of private individuals, the earth, clay, stones, potsherds, sand, wood and other materials that are necessary for this task, each of them from the nearest place from which they could be taken, removed and transported without injury to private individuals, should be taken, removed and transported, their value having been determined on the judgment of an honest man, and that for the purpose of transporting all that material for repairing those works, as often as it should be necessary, roads and thoroughfares should be open and be granted through the fields of private individuals without injury to them.[48]

The principle is clear—the government gets what it wants to secure the maintenance and operation of the aqueducts. Because Augustus paid for the repair of the channels, he presumably paid the cost of the materials, and that sum went to those from whom the raw materials were taken. The tenor of the passage suggests that the fair price will be paid to those who suffer loss, and they have no choice in the matter.[49] The *agri privatorum* must surely refer to those who own or possess land and with whom the government must deal. The government is here effectively establishing an easement by taking possession on its own terms of a marked piece of land for a certain defined purpose.

Of course, the first step was the acquisition of land for building an aqueduct. Frontinus has interesting comments on the senatorial decree of 11 B.C.:

This decree of the senate would appear to be very fair, albeit that those areas were being laid claim to only in accordance with public need. However, our ancestors, with much more admirable fairness, did not even seize from private parties those areas that pertained to the public good. Rather, when they were bringing water through, if a possessor had been reluctant in selling a necessary area, they paid money for the entire field, and after the necessary area had been measured, sold that field back again, on the condition that the state and the private parties should have their proper legal rights within their own boundaries.[50]

In my view, this clearly indicates that the state could make people sell land if it wanted. Can we really believe that acquiring land or making it public for aqueducts was a matter of persuasion? Why should they be different from roads and rivers?

The phrase "laid claim to" is a translation of the verb *vindicare*, and it has been argued that Frontinus, as "an authority on legal controversies surrounding land surveying," used *vindicare* and *vindicatio* in a precise legal sense in discussing the senatorial decree, indicating an attempt to prove existing ownership through adjudication.[51] This argument is partly based on the use of *vindicare* in his treatise on land survey in the *Corpus Agrimensorum Romanorum*. But the passages attributed to Frontinus in the *Corpus* are brief, and he was not necessarily an expert on the resolution of landholding disputes.[52] He uses the verb *vindicare* twice, in the *De Controversiis Agrorum*, a text mediated through the fifth-century Agennius Urbicus.[53] In both these instances, the word is probably employed in a nontechnical sense, as in the first example to describe a situation where individuals, who were permitted to possess certain lands in order to reap the harvest, laid claim to boundaries among themselves just as if they were dealing with private lands. In his comment in the *De Aquis* when Frontinus uses *vindicare*, he may mean merely "lay claim to," "assert a right to," with no reference to a claim to existing ownership that had been infringed.

The sense of this passage is that public utility is the dominant feature, and Frontinus congratulates Romans in the past because they did not seize (*eripere*) from private people whatever was necessary for the public good. The phrase "difficilior possessor" suggests that in the case of obstreperous private individuals the state could have taken their land but preferred another option. What follows is therefore a concession. The result is that the *res publica* measures the boundary and owns part of the land that once was all privately owned. It is also worth noting the extent of the powers of the curators of the aqueducts in protecting the area around the aqueduct in the interests of the state; they had the right to pull up trees, vines, banks, and walls and carved their name on walls that were exempt. The whole weight of action here lies with the *res publica* and its representatives.[54]

In the famous inscription from the Colony of Venafrum relating to the local aqueduct, which was established by Augustus to bring water from Monte della Rocchetta about thirty kilometers to the north, it is clear that the course of the aqueduct takes it across private land, though it is not clear how the land for its route was acquired.[55] But it clearly has been removed from private ownership — "and let there be nothing private there to prevent the water from traveling, flowing, and being brought." A width of eight feet on either side of the channel was designated, and the people of Venafrum had the right to make a road here for servicing the aqueduct. It was marked out by boundary stones, seven of which have survived inscribed "by order of Imperator Caesar Augustus."[56] It seems to assert the primacy of the community's water supply, across intervening land, even though the land comprised private farms. The edict when dealing with water distribution provides that "water not be brought through a private place against the will of the person to whom that place belongs." This raises an interesting point; does the explicit wording imply that such actions against private interests were *normally* within the power of the magistrates?[57] This must remain uncertain.

The situation in a Roman colony in the provinces can be judged from the bronze tablet containing the *lex Coloniae Genetivae*, which relates to the Roman colony at Urso in Spain, dating from 44 B.C., and sets out the rules for the management of the colony's government.[58] Chapter 99 deals with the acquisition of land for an aqueduct for conducting water into the colony: "Whatever public waters shall be brought in, in the town of Colonia Genetiva, the IIviri who shall then be (in office) are to raise with the decurions, when two-thirds shall be present, through which lands it may be lawful to bring water. Where the majority of the decurions who shall then be present shall have decreed for it to be brought, there is to be right and power to bring water through those lands, provided that water be not brought through that building, which has not yet been constructed for that purpose; and no one is to act, to the effect that water may not be brought in this way."

Therefore, when the magistrates put the question to the town councilors, they have the right to decide the route of the aqueduct, and the water will be brought along that route, provided that it is conveyed in a proper structure. The important point is that the councilors decide the best route in the interests of the community, and no one may prevent water from being brought in this way.[59] The obvious implication is that the route may lead through someone's land and that the community will take over that land. No compensation is discussed at this stage probably because that was expected to be dealt with later, when detailed provisions were made. There is a normal saving clause to ensure that the situation was not exploited to the disadvantage of landholders. The right to conduct the water is perpetual, but the actual determination of the route and the taking of the land are the decisions of *these* councilors now.

Another inscription, the Tabula Contrebiensis from the early first century B.C., shows the importance of water and the rights to channel water; the dispute concerned a watercourse and involved three communities in the valley of the Ebro.[60] The Salluienses had acted corporately to purchase land from the Sosinestani to ensure the construction of a canal in order to channel water. The degree of public intervention and the dispute itself are good evidence for the importance of the water supply for a rural community in the dry conditions of the valley, away from the Ebro itself. The transaction had in some way upset the Allavonenses. The Salluienses had marked out a course through public land of the Sosinestani and also through private land for which there was to be compensation. This therefore seems to be a case of expropriation of private land with compensation. Now, even if we agree that the sovereign law in the dispute was Iberian not Roman, and that the adjudication was based on local rights and customs, Roman legal concepts and terminology were employed. The Romans would surely not allow practices that dramatically contravened their established legal procedure, especially in a Roman *civitas*.

There is an interesting view from the private landowner's side in an inscription from Viterbo erected by a local man of senatorial family, Vegetus, celebrating the provision of water to this private estate:

> Mummius Niger Valerius Vegetus, of consular rank, brought his own water, the Vegetiana, which rises in the bigger Antonianus farm of P. Tullius Varro, from that place in which (ownership of) that spring has been transferred, over 5,950 paces to his villa Calvisiana, which is located at his Aquae Passeris, having obtained and transferred to his ownership places and routes of that water from the possessors of each individual farm through which the above-mentioned water was conducted, to a width of ten feet for structures, six feet for the width of pipes, through . . . (ten farms) and along the causeway on the left of the public highway of Ferentium, through the Scirpianum farm of Pistrania Lepida, and along the *via Cassia* to his villa Calvisiana, and also along public roads and *limites* by permission of a decree of the senate.[61]

Here we see how Vegetus had to conduct his water source over nearly six miles to his estate and secure access in the context of the competing legal rights of other landholders. The precise topographical descriptions in the inscription suggest that a survey of this area had been conducted and detailed records kept; private rights where appropriate were mapped onto public areas, and with senatorial permission Vegetus made use of public roads and *limites*, which normally were kept free of obstructions. In this case the status of the landholder was probably a help, but he has to manage relations with private and public rights.

Despite the Roman state's ability to get what it wanted for the provision of water, there will have been cases where for various reasons the government thought that compulsory appropriation of land was neither desirable nor practicable. There was the notorious case in 179 B.C. when a single landholder M. Licinius Crassus prevented the building of an aqueduct by refusing to allow it over his land.[62] But it is readily believable that at this time an influential senator from an important family could get his way against the interests of the state. In 64 B.C. Cicero, commenting on the agrarian bill of P. Servilius Rullus, said: "This good man has promised that he will not buy from the unwilling. As if indeed we did not know that a forced sale is unjust, a voluntary sale an occasion for profit."[63] But this proves nothing about the government's ability to sequester land. Not to buy from the unwilling was apparently the personal decision of Rullus, and Cicero's criticism seems to be directed more generally at the likely drain imposed on the state resources by his proposals. Similarly, in 59 B.C. Caesar ordered his officials not to purchase land from those unwilling to sell and only to pay the price recorded in official tax documents. Dio's account shows that Caesar went out of his way to win favor and act fairly (he declined to be a land commissioner himself); he clearly wanted to avoid the bad feeling created by compulsory purchase.[64]

Early in Augustus's regime there is the case of the seemingly curious route of an aqueduct constructed by Agrippa, the *aqua Virgo*. It was completed in 19 B.C. and followed a broadly circuitous path to the Campus Martius around the north of the city. It has been argued that this route was adopted because Agrippa was unable to procure land for a more direct approach and could not force possessors to sell.[65] However, it is very problematical to guess the reasons for the direction of the aqueduct. Agrippa may have made a personal decision for reasons that we cannot now recover. Perhaps he built the aqueduct privately but later made it available for public use. It is difficult to believe that Augustus and Agrippa could not get what they wanted in 21–19 B.C., and again it must be emphasized that because the right to sequester land existed does not mean that it had to be used. It may be that for reasons of goodwill and to minimize disruption Agrippa took a longer route. We may compare the interesting case of Augustus's forum. Its asymmetrical shape allegedly came about because he did not want to expropriate neighboring houses. But Suetonius presents this in a section on Augustus's general moderation, and the implication is that he could have forced possessors to sell had he wanted.[66] In any case, recent surveys suggest that the peculiar layout of the forum may have been due to the presence of drainage channels.[67] This is a warning of the uncertainties in trying to assign precise motives for the decisions of those in power.

The Roman government moved to ensure access to running water for whatever purpose it required, as well as the channeling of water to chosen sites, the building of suitable structures for the movement of water, and the maintenance of all such structures. In addition, local communities moved to assert their rights over water and water supply. All this indicates the Roman state's ultimate control of water and its use. Because the rights of private property were held in high esteem, they were protected as far as possible, and the government and its agents did their best not to disturb existing possessors. An inscription from Ammaedara in Africa is entirely in keeping with their ideology; it records how Postumius Africanus, legate of the proconsul between A.D. 160 and 180, arranged for the construction of an aqueduct, "in accordance with the legal regulations relating to the rights concerning servitudes, with a stream of water, which [flowed] by permission of the proconsul."[68] These complex relationships help to set rivers in a context where the state had a responsibility to make riverine resources reasonably available to all, to control the environment of river valleys, and to mediate fluvial relations between landholders.

3   BOUNDARIES

It needs no argument that the establishment and identification of acceptable boundaries were crucial aspects of the surveyor's services to landholders and communities. Boundaries, both private and territorial, were demarcated by a variety of methods including many natural phenomena, one of which was the course of rivers, streams, and waterways. They had an important role in the process of dividing land and establishing settlements. In this context, rivers are often mentioned by the *agrimensores*, and certain boundary markers were associated with them. For example, surveyors normally placed bigger stones called *mensales* near rivers. Again, a perforated boundary stone indicated that the boundary crossed a river or passed by a spring. Some stones were marked with letters, for example, the letter E denoted a brook or a stream in a valley in front of the stone. This could become rather complicated; a boundary stone with a horse's hoof carved on it inexplicably indicated an internal boundary marker, demarcating a boundary that ran right up to a spring. These schemes were perhaps more elaborate than could in practice be applied.[69]

But how exactly did rivers serve as boundaries? They had a great advantage in that suitable boundary-marking rivers were permanent, ubiquitous, locally well known, highly visible, and difficult to tamper with or forge, especially as they were usually marked on maps. Many rivers had been measured and recorded, the essential prerequisite for a boundary, and some had particularly good characteristics: "If the valleys include rivers, and a river is located there, which does not flow outside the land and does not change its course as it flows through the land, and if it is a river with rocky banks, which flows along a steep bed with virtually straight sides, we can establish the boundary along it."[70] When a river or stream marked a boundary it was referred to technically as *rivus rectus*, although this probably means a "proper" or "accepted" boundary rather than any indication of straightness. The surveyor had to do his homework and judge the way in which the river provided a boundary according to the lie of the land: "If boundaries are recognized by means of streams, which cannot always flow around the edges of individual fields, but can provide a boundary over a certain distance for some sides of properties, we shall have to see if there is a custom for some pieces of land to be owned on both sides of the stream, by those people who have land opposite on the other side of the stream. Some streams from their source, that is their head, provide boundaries for properties until they flow into the sea. Other streams however flow with different landholders on either side."[71] It is no surprise that rivers along with other natural landmarks like mountain peaks served as obvious territorial boundaries: "Territories are demarcated between communities . . . sometimes by rivers, or by the tops of mountain ridges or watersheds." In some areas, watersheds, because of their prominent position and natural demarcating role, served to mark land boundaries of territories.[72]

Therefore, rivers turn up frequently in boundary descriptions. For example, an inscription from Tolentinum setting out the dimensions of a tomb defines an area granted to the community of Tolentinum "between the bank of the river and the watercourse."[73] In the boundary descriptions in the *Liber Coloniarum*, rivers formed part of the boundary marking in Hadria, the land of the Sabines, Forum Novum, Falerio, and Pisaurum.[74] A river might also serve as a landmark for a series of land allocations, as the river Liris was used in descriptions of allocations at Minturnae.[75] The enigmatic but interesting estate descriptions (*Casae Litterarum*) from the late empire are partly based on the topography of local streams and springs, which help to give shape and meaning to the lie of the land and identify estates for surveyors. The text was possibly intended as a kind of guide for surveyors to help them identify the layout of estates, using the letters as mnemonic devices.[76]

Rivers, streams, and watersheds feature strongly in the surveyor Hyginus's theoretical boundary description inserted for the guidance of surveyors, which uses a combination of natural and man-made landmarks including named hills, rivers, streams, mountains, watersheds, crossroads, and monuments:

> From the small hill called such and such, to such and such a river, and along that river to such and such a stream or such and such a road, and along that road to the lower slopes of such and such a mountain, a place that has the name such and such, and from there along the ridge of the mountain to the summit, and along the summit of the mountain along the watersheds to the place that is called such and such, and from there down to such and such

a place, and from there down to such and such a place, and from there to the crossroads of such and such a place, and from there past the tomb of such and such to the place from which the description began.[77]

Surviving boundary determinations recorded and displayed on inscriptions help to show that the writings of surveyors were relevant to the real world. For example, Laberius Maximus, governor of Lower Moesia, in A.D. 100 established the territory and rights of Histria: "I have decided that the boundaries of the Histrians shall be these: [to the island] of Peuce, lake Halmyris up to the [beginning of the land] of the Argamenses, and from there along the top of the ridge [of the hills right up to] the confluence of the rivers Picusculus and Ga[branus, and from there from the] lower stretch of the Gabranus to its source, and from there [right up to the stream] Sanpaeus, and from there to the stream Turgiculus, [and from there by a straight road(?)] from the stream Calabaeus, about [. . .] miles."[78]

Similarly, in the dispute between the communities of Lamia and Hypata in Macedonia during the reign of Hadrian, the proconsul on the orders of the emperor summoned a surveyor and supervised the investigation himself before deciding "that the start of the boundary should be from that place where I understood Sides to have been, which is situated below the enclosure sacred to Neptune, from which as you go down, a straight line boundary is maintained right up to the fountain Dercynna, which is situated across the river Sperchion, so that the boundary of the people of Lamia and the people of Hypata runs through the Amphispora lands to the fountain Dercynna mentioned above, and from there on to the tomb Pelion along the downward slope called Sir [. . .] to the monument of Eurytus, which lies within the territory of the people of Lamia."[79] Here the river Sperchion acts as a crucial natural phenomenon that fixes the location of the fountain Dercynna, an important man-made landmark.

4   MANAGING DISRUPTION

Given the importance of rivers and streams in the life of ancient communities, in the demarcation of boundaries by the founders of colonies and their surveyors, in the work of lawyers, and in the considerations of agents of the government, any changes, actual or potential, to the course and characteristics of rivers had serious implications. In brief, a permanent or temporary river inundation or sometimes surplus rainwater obliterated boundaries and damaged land; a river might move to a different course and leave its old bed permanently, causing damage and loss by flowing through someone's land; a river often removed or transported land by erosion and alluviation, and in certain river deltas this brought about a large-scale deposition of silt; this alluvial activity could involve the removal of land piecemeal over time, or more substantial chunks at one instant because of a storm; a river could create new land in midstream (an *insula nata*).

These problems primarily affected landholders, but wider legal complications often ensued. The writings of lawyers and surveyors illustrate the variety of legal and practical means adopted to circumscribe and contain rivers.[80] It may seem superficially that surveyors and lawyers had contrasting views, in that the former were pragmatic compromisers, whereas the latter related what they held to be the rule of law. This in my view is simplistic and arises partly from a misunderstanding of the role of the *agrimensores*. They were not independent initiators of action or legal commentators. Although they gave advice, they were the servants of the governors and magistrates who had the appropriate legal authority.[81] Furthermore, surveyors (just like the lawyers) strongly upheld the idea of the property of the Roman people and of the local community, and the need to stop infringements by adjoining possessors: "In Italy, however, the multitude of landholders act with a great deal of dishonesty, and they appropriate sacred groves, whose land undoubtedly belongs to the Roman people, even if they are within the territories of colonies or *municipia*."[82] When Hyginus comments specifically on the work of the jurist Cassius Longinus, he is very respectful and approving.[83] The essential point is that our evidence from these two sources is often based on their answers to questions put to them. And the two groups were asked different questions; lawyers were asked to advise clients on the basis of their understanding of the law and presumably their wish to win the case, whereas surveyors were asked how the law could be effectively applied, what it meant for individuals or communities, and how they could avoid legal problems.[84]

It was part of the job of land surveyors to make an assessment of river characteristics, climatic conditions, and topographical factors, all of which contributed to the establishment of a suitable method for management of the river. Signs of this appear in the rather general assessment of the valley of the Po and the river's seasonal characteristics, which has come down to us: "Boundary disputes are very prevalent in Gallia Togata, which, crisscrossed by many rivers, carries the huge snows of the Alps to the sea, and suffers damage through the unexpected flooding that accompanies sudden thaws."[85]

The next step was to identify problems consequent upon flooding. The *Commentary* (included among the texts of the *agrimensores* and probably of the third century or later) describes what could happen when pent-up water originally from rainfall cut through its bank and created a flood: "The owner of the neighboring land wishes by false pretenses to claim for himself land right up to the stream."[86] When river water interfered with or altered boundaries, Ulpian set out the governor's duties, combining executive authority with the technical skill of the surveyor: "If a flood destroys the boundaries of a piece of land through the inundation of a river and provides the opportunity for some people to occupy places to which they have no right, the governor of the province must order them to keep their hands off the property of others, and that his own land should be restored to the owner and boundaries determined by a surveyor."[87] Even without illegality, landholders often suffered loss because they ceased to possess land occupied by a river.[88] Furthermore, the retreating river might leave land damaged and its value seriously reduced. If its character had been completely changed, it could even be argued that it had ceased to be the property of the previous possessor.[89] Stored crops were also destroyed and severe flooding could involve the loss of usufruct: "When the usufruct of a field or site has been bequeathed, if it is inundated so as to become a swamp or marsh, there is no doubt that the usufruct will be extinguished."[90]

The writings of the jurists collected in the *Digest* help to show the prevalence of river flooding and its impact on Roman life, extending beyond the loss suffered by landholders. Flooded rivers made it difficult for people to move around and interfered with main roads and rights of way. "When a public road has been lost, because of either a river flood or collapse, the nearest neighbor ought to provide a route."[91] We find Ulpian ruling on the force of a river's current, when someone alleged this as a reason for failing to make a court appearance; he noted that even without a storm the river's current could be a serious impediment if it was impossible to ford, if the bridge had been swept away, and if boats were inoperative or not available. Of course, it would be necessary to consider if the man could have found a way around the river with careful planning of his journey.[92]

There were many other problems associated with river flooding. The foundations of buildings might be undermined, though it was important to establish whether the river flood had brought about the collapse of a house or the structure had been weakened before.[93] A river in spate often swept property away, as we see in the interesting case of a ship that had been kept in lieu of debt and then lost to river action: "A man who lent money to a boatman detained the boat on the river on his own authority, when the debt was not paid on time. Later the river level rose and swept the boat away. The reply was that if the creditor had detained the boat against the wishes of the boatman, the boat was at his risk. But if the debtor had voluntarily agreed that he should keep it, he should be responsible only for negligence, not for superior force."[94] Furthermore, if a river flood had affected a tenant's activities beyond his control, he might be entitled to a reduction in rent.[95] The range of urban river problems is best seen in the Tiber floods, which were notorious for the loss of life and damage to property and continued from the republic throughout the imperial period.[96]

A linked problem that occasioned much interest in the *Digest* was the question of rainwater, which could have serious consequences when it flooded onto land. Land surveyors observed a contrast between Italy and Africa; in Italy legal measures tried to prevent the intrusion of surplus rainwater onto land, while in the dry conditions of Africa complaints came if someone tried to prevent rainwater from flowing onto a property.[97] The *Digest* heading "Concerning water and the keeping away of rainwater" establishes a definition of rainwater (*aqua pluvia*). "By rainwater we mean whatever falls from the heavens and increases after a heavy shower, whether this water from the heavens does the damage on its own, as Tubero said, or whether it is mixed with other water." On one interpretation, it could be argued that, even if water flowing from a spring became mixed with and augmented by the passage of rainwater, in terms of legal action it was subject to the action to keep away rainwater.[98] So this issue shaded into the problem of managing running water, though lawyers argued over the definition, which excluded certain features such as hot water, that is, rainwater that had been artificially heated.[99]

What steps were taken to manage disruptive rivers and control the impact of flooding on landholders? There were essentially three remedies for the river overflowing its banks: protecting the bank, careful planning at the land division stage, and modification of land use in the light of riverine disruption. In the first place, a landholder could on his own initiative strengthen the riverbank, though this should not be done to the detriment of others, as Ulpian discusses in his commentary on the praetor's edict.[100] That astute and clear-headed surveyor, Siculus Flaccus, summed up the issues: "This certainly seems a proper precaution (propping up the banks), to ensure that land remains intact for landholders, and also for the public good."[101] Emperors too supported the general principle: "Although it is not permissible to divert the natural course of a river in another direction by artificial methods, nevertheless it is not prohibited to strengthen its bank against the surge of a powerful river."[102] However, shoring up the bank might not work against a major seasonal rise in river level or after a violent storm.

Second, the surveyors recommended precautions in the management of land division. It was the responsibility of the founder of a settlement to order a calculation of the width of the riverbed enclosed by the banks. The founder also had to ensure that surveyors carried out all relevant measurements, made records, and constructed a map (*forma*) in bronze, as well as a papyrus copy, which was to be transported to the record office in Rome.[103] In the collection of writings on land survey in the *Corpus Agrimensorum Romanorum*, a work by Junius Nipsus (of uncertain date, but probably late empire) sets out a methodology for measuring the width of a river.[104]

Therefore, it was the task of surveyors when allocating the land for a new settlement to record and enter on the map the width of the riverbed, as Siculus Flaccus records at Pisaurum.[105] However, several surveyors note with approval the practice of measuring around the river an additional area, into which the river could expand when in flood: "The man responsible for the land division ensured in this precise way that whenever a storm had stirred up the river, so that it burst its banks and spread over all the region, the flood would not inflict harm on anyone. Furthermore, when the river was flowing within its banks, the adjacent landholders could use the area of land set aside for the river. This was not unjust, since unusually heavy storms sometimes force the water to flow beyond the width set aside for the river."[106] This commonsense provision offered support for the possessors in the vicinity of a river, since the land's productivity could be damaged by prolonged inundation.

This careful planning did not always work out in practice. The surveyors present the case of the river Pisaurus, which flowed into the Adriatic, as a warning against the damaging consequences when procedures were neglected. Surveyors had very sensibly established a width for the river as the widest to which it had ever been recorded as flowing beyond its banks. But later the community for profit sold off to the nearest possessors the land set aside for the river. "In this region, if there is a dispute involving harmful river action, there will be substantial arguments that, according to the bronze map, whatever was sold should be restored to the purchaser."[107] In some cases the river was included in the actual land allocations, and Frontinus pointed out the advantages to the landholder of having a river frontage.[108] There may have been some pressure from landholders for direct access to a river. The author of the late *Commentary on Types of Land* could say that in certain areas settlement by men had been completely impossible because of a shortage of water, showing the importance of access to water in the view of surveyors.[109]

The case of the river Anas at Augustus's Colony of Augusta Emerita (Mérida) in Lusitania is interesting as an example of collective action by landholders to redress the balance of some careless land distribution. Apparently, no area was assigned to the river, and lands were granted to settlers along the bank; because of the vast quantity of land available, an amount remained unallocated. These unassigned lands (*subseciua*) were occupied by neighboring landholders. Then Vespasian insisted that all *subseciua* should be claimed back by those responsible for them, including local communities where appropriate. At this point "the landholders obtained an undertaking from the governor of the province belatedly to designate a specific width for the river Anas. Because individuals were being compelled to buy back the *subseciua* that they had occupied, it was judged unfair that anyone should buy the river, which was public property or unfertile land that the river had deposited."[110] The governor responded to popular feeling, and this is a case where surveyors will have been employed to modify or rectify a previous survey.

The third possible remedy dealt with specific flooding problems by readjusting land use and possession. Two distinct but linked river activities interested the lawyers: a flood (*inundatio* or *impetus fluminis*), which could either recede pretty rapidly, restoring the status quo, or persist for a longer, undefined period. Potentially more serious was a shift in the course of a river so that it left its bed (*mutatio alvei*), possibly over a long distance. This indicated long-term or even permanent disruption, although the incident might end with the river returning to its earlier course.

In the case of an inundation, the landholder obviously lost use of the affected part of his land. However, if the water receded, in certain circumstances he could reclaim possession if his land could be recognized; the important factors were that it should have been surveyed and allocated and that there was a map against which the claim could be assessed. A surveyor would therefore be looking for landmarks and boundary markers.[111]

However, the jurists recognized that possession might be lost when a flood completely occupied an area of land. In practice it could be difficult to distinguish between a flood and a river changing its course, since a flood might involve a temporary change of direction by the river. In fact, the important point was not how the flooding had occurred but its extent; that is, if the *entire* area of the possessor's holding was overlaid by the river water, it might be judged as having lost its original character, presumably because all the boundary markers had been swept away or erased, and landmarks such as trees had been uprooted. In these circumstances, it might be impossible to identify individual holdings even with a map. Surveyors noted the problems of rivers that obliterated landmarks: "It is very difficult for unskilled people to discover whether a locality in its present appearance tallies with a map, if localities appear as scattered sheets of water and lack the visible proof of trees and other things."[112] A layer of mud and rubble left by the retreating waters would have the same

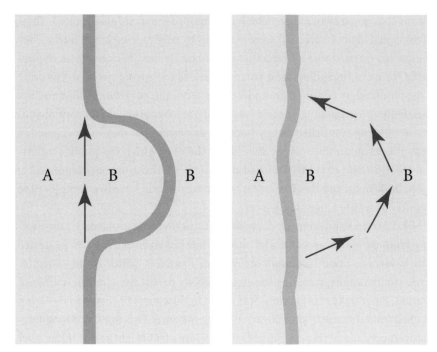

DIAGRAM 1. *Problem caused by a river changing course*

effect. The consequence was presumably that such land became *subseciuum*, and interested previous possessors could try to occupy what they thought was theirs, using markers that had no official validity but were recognized by neighboring possessors.[113] Subsequently they could hope to acquire title by keeping possession over time (*usucapio*).

It is, however, difficult to recover the precise legal position. The republican jurist Quintus Mucius, according to Pomponius, argued that the usufruct of a field was lost if it was entirely inundated by river or sea.[114] This passage goes on to say that if the flood recedes, the usufruct is restored.[115] Even if this is a hopeful interpretation by Pomponius,[116] it at least shows that by the second century A.D. the intention was to secure the minimum disruption for possessors. We see this in another passage: "While I had usufruct of a garden, a river occupied the garden and then receded from it. Labeo held that the right of usufruct was also restored, because that soil always remained in the same legal condition."[117]

These problems are obviously linked to the question of *mutatio alvei*. The point at issue was: should a landholder who had suffered loss because of the action of the river in his land (but had not had all his holding immersed) be

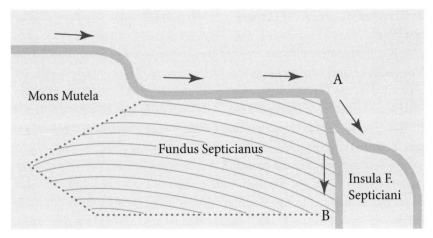

DIAGRAM 2. *A river flowing through the farm of Septicius*

permitted to claim and possess the old riverbed as a kind of compensation? If a river left its bed and flowed though someone's land, that landholder might reasonably hope to occupy the dried up area of the original bed. And if the river subsequently returned to its old course, he would also want to occupy the new bed it had been using, which after all had been part of his property.[118]

Land surveyors also wrestled with these issues. Julius Frontinus, refers to the "old bed of a river of the Roman people."[119] The river it seems was for the use of all, but the bed remained the property of the Roman people. He goes on to point out that the issue of compensation for a landholder suffering loss because of river action was not a simple one: "The question concerns who should own the soil that it deposited (that is, in the bed that it subsequently leaves), since the nearest landholder is suffering no small loss, as a river that is public property is flowing through his land. However, legal experts take a different view and argue that in no circumstances can ground that has begun to be the ground of the Roman people be acquired by *usucapio* by any mortal man."[120] Such land, if unused, was presumably classed as *subseciuum*.

However, the typical approach among surveyors was to show respect both for the property of the Roman people and for landholders, to measure carefully, to assess loss, and to arrange matters accordingly. Frontinus certainly stated the basic provision in cases of river disruption that the land boundary should remain where it had always been.[121] He intended to prevent improper land grabbing. But surveyors wished to deal fairly with the consequences of river action, and Frontinus in the passage quoted earlier shows sympathy for landholders suffering loss outside their control. This idea also emerges strongly in surveyors' discussion of changes in landholding brought about by alluvia-tion.[122]

It is unfortunately difficult to trace the development of legal thinking on how far the rights of riparian possessors extended.[123] The problem with the texts cited in the *Digest* is that, apart from the fact that it is not always clear what was the accepted legal position as distinct from a mere affirmation of a client's case, we cannot be certain about what was the view of the classical law-yers, and what changes had been made by later commentators. For example, we have a clear statement in the *Institutes* of Justinian affirming the right of land-holders to occupy an old riverbed, with no hint of the more subtle consider-ations that sometimes troubled earlier lawyers. What is more, the *Institutes* do not recognize that the complete inundation of an area of land by a river raised any doubts about ownership.[124]

However, unless there has been a complete misrepresentation in the surviv-ing texts, it seems likely that, at least by the mid-second century, lawyers were moving to an accommodation between possessors and the rights attaching to riverbeds as public property and accepted that the area of a dried up riverbed, after a change of course, appropriately belonged to those with adjoining land who had presumably suffered some disruption through river action. Pompo-nius, writing in the second century, observes: "Rivers perform the duties of officials of the census, in so far as they move land from private to public owner-ship and vice versa. Therefore, the land, which had become the bed of a river, became public, and now it should become private again (as the water receded) and revert to the original owners."[125] Ulpian in his third-century commentary on the praetor's edict said: "Similarly, if a river leaves its bed and begins to flow in another direction, whatever is constructed in the old bed does not pertain to this interdict (i.e., that nothing detrimental to navigation should be done in a public river or on its bank); for that which belongs to the neighbors on either side will not have been constructed in a public river, or, if the land has received boundaries, the bed will belong to the person who (first) appropriates it. It cer-tainly ceases to be public property. Furthermore, that (new) bed which the river made for itself, although it was previously private property, nevertheless begins to be public, because it is impossible that the bed of a public river should not be public property."[126]

Gaius, writing in the second century, had upheld the rights of landholders facing problems because of changes in the course of a river: "However, if a river entirely leaves its natural bed and begins to flow elsewhere, its old bed belongs to those who possess land along its bank, in proportion to the extent of each piece of land that is adjacent to the bank. The new bed will come under that law under which the river itself comes, that is it will become public under the law of nations. But if, after a certain lapse of time the river should return to its old bed, the new bed will again belong to those who possess land along its bank."[127] He is here thinking of a situation where several landholders had holdings along the river; although it was a point of debate whether the riparian landholders should possess the land to the midpoint of the river, the tenor of the passage is to help the riparian possessors. On the other hand, he did apparently express doubts if land was totally immersed: "However, where the new bed has occupied all of someone's land, even though the river has returned to its old bed, that man whose land that was, on a strict interpretation, is unable to possess any land in that bed, because it has ceased to be the land that it once was, having lost its original form, and because he has no adjacent land he cannot on the argument of vicinity possess any part of that bed. But it would be harsh to apply this rule." This upholds the severe view that land that had been entirely enclosed and overlaid by floodwater had completely changed its original character, with the result that the original possessor could not resume possession and had no claim to a share of the land as a riparian because he had no recognized land in the vicinity. Gaius's final comment is controversial and has been perhaps unfairly dismissed as a Justinianic interpolation. In fact, Gaius here suggests that normally (if the land had not been completely immersed) riparians could lay claim to the riverbed once the river had changed course.[128]

Although much of our evidence relates to Italy, river problems of this nature were a common feature in the empire. Strabo in an interesting passage tells us how, when the river Maeander misbehaved itself by changing its course in its great floodplain and altering land boundaries, lawsuits were brought against the river. If it were convicted, fines were paid from ferry tolls.[129] Strabo loosely ascribes this account to ancient writers, but he presents it as if the circumstances were still current in his day. So, if this relates to the Roman Empire, it is an interesting question who was responsible for the fines, the local community in the vicinity or Rome, as the owner (by conquest) of what was now effectively a *flumen publicum*. In any case, on the Maeander the rights of landholders were being vigorously pursued, just as they were in Italy.

5   ALLUVIAL ACTIVITY AND RIVER ISLANDS

The Maeander was, of course, the agent of enormous alluvial deposition, and this aspect of river action is related to the question of flooding, changes in river course, and the rights of landholders. Crucially, from the early first century A.D. lawyers sought to facilitate riparian possessors in appropriating and using alluvial land, while protecting the rights of those who suffered damage; this comes across particularly strongly in the case of river islands. The impression once again is that the rights of possessors had a high priority. Alluviation was a prominent feature in the writings of the *agrimensores* and was defined by Frontinus as one of the categories of land dispute, involving harmful river action.[130] Gradual alluviation was the slow accretion of small quantities of land brought by the river so that it was impossible to say precisely at what time it had arrived. Violent alluviation occurred when the river in a storm or in full spate broke off a large piece of land and deposited it elsewhere, visibly altering the landscape.[131] There was no legal redress for gradual loss of land by alluviation (it being open to a landholder to shore up the bank, as discussed above). In cases of significant loss through exceptional river action, in *ager occupatorius* (land occupied but not formally measured or allocated) there was no obvious redress, because there would often be no official survey or map of these lands.

In divided and allocated lands, it was at least possible to calculate the loss of land or change in shape, on the basis of the original surveyor's map. If the quantity and nature of the lost or damaged land could be assessed, the landholder could perhaps sue the local community (as happened at Pisaurum) or possibly another landholder if it was clear that an identifiable piece of land had been swept onto his property. A provision that, if alluvial land had remained in its new location long enough for trees to take root and grow up without any claim having been made, it had arguably become part of that land, suggests that substantial areas of land could be moved to a new location, even if this was unusual.[132]

The most significant legal complication was that several landholders might have lost land in the process of alluviation. How could each piece of land be identified? How were landholders to be compensated? What is more, the land added to another property might be quite different in character to that lost, having been reduced to a mess of stones and mud:

> The dispute concerns the soil that a river deposits, and complex questions are thereby produced, namely, whether it should belong to the person on the opposite bank whose land has been augmented on the retreat of the river water, or whether the man who lost some of his land should cross over and take possession of that soil that the river deposited. But against this is raised a very subtle point, namely, that the soil that one man lost does not immediately cross over to the other bank but is removed and washed away. On the other hand, the neighbor receives a very different type of soil, because, while

the former lost soil that was perhaps cultivated and fertile, the latter was left with a residue of sand, stones and mud washed up by the flood water.[133]

If lawyers insisted that land moved by river action must be reclaimed by the original owner, surveyors had the job of working out how this was to be accomplished. They presumably measured and calculated against the original map and determined some kind of compensation, either monetary or a land exchange.[134] An entry in the table of properties at Veleia apparently recognizes a change in the quantity of land on an estate as a result of alluviation; there is an account of land on the upper slopes of the valley of the Po, with a reference to the *fundus Afrianus Dextrianus* "with its outlying plots and alluvial land (*alluvionibus*)."[135]

Rights relating to fluvial action and deposition are sometimes expressed in the obscure phrase *ius alluvionis*. For example, Proculus talks of a river having *ius alluvionis* in the context of the appropriation of an island that appeared midstream.[136] Most intriguingly, Florentinus, quoting a decision of Antoninus Pius, notes that *ius alluvionis* had no place in lands that had received boundaries (*limites*). The precise meaning is doubtful, and it is possible that we do not have the full text. The intention may have been to argue that *ius alluvionis* would not apply in land that had received *limites* when an area had been set aside for the river.[137] The *limes* marked the formal boundary of landholding and any land beyond that removed by alluviation could not belong to anyone or accrue to anyone within the centuriated area. Furthermore, an opinion of Callistratus perhaps further illustrates this idea: lakes and ponds could expand or dry up, but the formal boundaries were designated and remained the same, clearly marking off the lacustine area from surrounding landholders.[138]

Other evidence shows the importance in Roman legal procedure of the concept of alluvial action, which changed the legal status quo in a number of ways. We know from Cicero that the court of *centumviri* was hearing cases relating to alluvial activity and the formation of river islands.[139] Particularly interesting examples occurred in the case of property sales: "Whatever land accrues or is diminished through alluviation in respect of an estate after purchase, pertains to the advantage or disadvantage of the purchaser. In fact, if all the land is occupied by a river after purchase, it is to the loss of the purchaser, and therefore equally he ought to be able to derive any benefit from it."[140] In this context lawyers were on their guard against fraud. "If Titius sold an estate of ninety *iugera* and in the bill of sale stated that there were one hundred *iugera* in the estate, and before the area was measured ten *iugera* were added by alluviation, I agree with the opinion of Neratius that, if someone sold the estate knowing

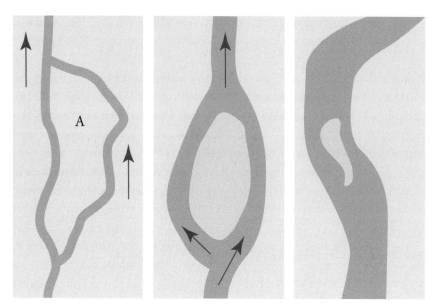

DIAGRAM 3. *The creation of river islands*

this, an action on purchase can be taken against him, even though ten *iugera* were added, because he acted fraudulently and the fraud is not expunged. But if he made the sale in ignorance an action on purchase cannot be taken against him."[141]

Alluviation and river action were particularly troublesome in the creation of islands in midstream, which attracted attention fairly early. Cassius Longinus (proconsul of Asia, A.D. 40–41, and subsequently governor of Syria) argued that the man from whose land an island had been formed should possess it. But if it had been formed from land owned in common, each person should recover his own portion.[142] We are not told how he thought that this could be implemented. Writing in the second century, Pomponius offers a more detailed explanation of river islands: "An island is formed in a river in one of three ways; first, when the river flows around land that was not part of its bed; second, when the river leaves dry the place that had been its bed and begins to flow around it; third, when by gradually removing soil, it produces a raised place above the riverbed and increases it by alluviation. In the last two cases the island becomes the property of the man whose land was closest to it when it first appeared. . . . In the first case the condition of ownership is not altered."[143]

In the first example, Pomponius means that whoever owned the land continued to own it on the basis of the original boundary because the river had formed an island in the land of one possessor. Gaius brings further analysis, arguing that an island in midstream (which in his view happened frequently) belonged to landholders on each side in proportion to their frontage; if it was closer to one bank, it was possessed entirely by the landholders on that bank in proportion (notwithstanding that soil that formed the island may have come from further upstream).[144] Surveyors were presumably expected to measure and sort out the details.

The fortuitous accretion of land through a river island and eagerness to make the most out of it appear in the splendidly detailed and lucid example expounded by Proculus in reply to the following question:

> I also enquire if, when an island has been created closer to my bank and later the entire river begins to flow between my land and the island, leaving its own bed where the larger part of it had flowed, you have any doubts that the island continues to be my property, and furthermore that part of the bed that the river left also becomes mine. I request that you write to me with your opinion on this. Proculus replied that if the island had originally been closer to your farm, and the river, leaving its main bed, which had been located between that island and the farm of a neighbor, which was located on the other side of the river, began to flow between that island and your farm, nevertheless the island remains your property. But the bed, which was between the island and the farm of a neighbor, should be divided to the middle line, so that the part that is closer to your island may be understood to be yours and the part closer to the land of your neighbor understood to be his. I realize that since the riverbed has dried up on the far side of the island, the island has ceased to exist, but so that the situation may more easily be understood, the land that had been an island is called an island.[145]

This deals with the double problem of a river island and a river leaving its original bed, showing the potential complexity of the issues involved. Landholders sought to profit from nature's generosity and to acquire even more land. The principle of proximity as an indicator of possession was preserved even when the island had technically ceased to be an island but was still regarded as an identifiable piece of land, and inherent in the response is concern that the possessor should not lose out.

Islands in the stream added an extra dimension to the problems and opportunities of dramatic river action. Even though legal opinion moved in favor of the riparian possessors, this was not a smooth process. For example, if a river island was only lightly attached to the water and not firmly rooted in earth

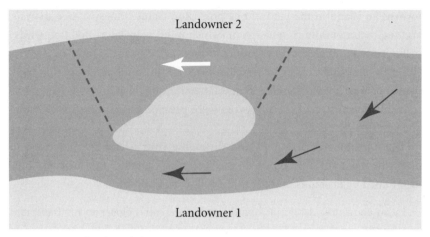

Landowner 2

Landowner 1

DIAGRAM 4. *Islands and changes in river course*

(therefore more a collection of reeds and debris), it could be argued that it was in reality part of the river, which was public property. However, the famous jurist Labeo took a more severe view that any island that appeared in a public river was bound to be public.[146] In this, however, he was not generally supported by other jurists. It is interesting that he was a dissenting voice, even though the issue had been debated since the time of Longinus, and in practice concern for possessors had long been established. Lawyers could give idiosyncratic opinions and vary arguments to suit their client's case, and we should not be surprised to find dissenting voices in other areas.

An inscription discovered at Didyma in Asia highlights the problem of river alluviation and the role of the Roman government in the later empire. It sets out a rescript of Justinian dating from A.D. 533, which deals with a dispute concerning the large quantities of new land deposited in the delta zone by the action of the Maeander. The basis of the appeal by the community of Justinianopolis (formerly the village of Didyma) was its wish to be exempt from an imposition going back to the town's original relationship with Miletus, and which was owed to the imperial authorities. They suggested a transfer of the charge to Miletus (so that the imperial treasury would suffer no loss), and that it should be levied on alluvial land that had become recently cultivable and capable of being subject to tax: "(We ask that) this sum be levied on those locations that have been turned into land, having previously been sea, and have now become subject to taxation, and be assigned to the city of Miletus and so relieve the citizens of Justinianopolis of this entire burden." When the governor of Caria pronounced the decision, he named the river Maeander specifically as the author of the new land: "those locations that have been turned into land by the Maeander river, having previously been sea."[147]

This decision on alluvial land should be set against previous legislation of the fifth century. Theodosius had apparently affirmed the rights of riparian possessors: "In respect of those lands that possessors acquire by alluviation, either in Egypt through the action of the Nile or in other provinces through different rivers, we sanction through this law that is to be eternally valid that they should not be sold by the treasury, or petitioned for by anyone, or made subject to a separate census, or have compulsory public services exacted from them, lest we should seem to ignore the damage caused by alluviation or to impose a harmful process on possessors."[148] He goes on to note that the same consideration applies to those who brought marshy land or pastureland under cultivation. Theodosius had also noted the difficulties of owning land bounded by riverbanks, since possession was at best impermanent and what had been acquired one day could be lost the next; furthermore, land moved around in this way was often damaged by the water action. This consideration had, of course, been pointed out by the surveyors. It seems that the emperor was confirming that such landholding was a risky business and that possessors must look after their own interests and be confident that the record of landholdings would not be altered to their disadvantage on each occasion. His intention was to encourage possessors to put or keep alluvial land under cultivation without fear that it would be subject to tax. Now, it is possible that Theodosius aimed merely to prevent any financial exaction on the land until it had become productive.[149] But, if so, the law as it stands does not make this clear.

Therefore, this legislation seems out of line with Justinian's decision that at Justinianopolis a tax should be imposed on the land deposited by the Maeander. The explanation may be that Justinian dealt with the Maeander delta as a unique phenomenon, because of the quantity of land being added, and also because, unlike the scenario described by Theodosius, landholders gained consistently and were unlikely to suffer any loss. The benefits from the Maeander, being permanent, should therefore be taxed.[150]

Augustus may have reached a similar decision. An inscription from Miletus confers honors on C. Julius Epikrates, friend of Augustus, who obtained from the emperor among other things some concessions relating to "an area that had become land again because of the Maeander." Either he aimed to stake a claim to it, or he was arguing that his community should not have to pay tax on it.[151] However, the exact nature of his request is uncertain. In any case, we can see over five centuries of imperial history a recognition, not only by local people but also by officials of the Roman state, of the environmental impact of the Maeander and its capacity to change the landscape, the financial and legal consequences, and the problems and the opportunities, all mediated by the imperial government.

6 CONCLUSION: MANAGING RIVERS FOR THE COMMUNITY

The writings of the land surveyors in the *Corpus Agrimensorum Romanorum*, looking back over the history of the appropriation of land, give us unique information on the early period of the Roman Republic, when virtual frontier farmers occupied land more in hope than in confidence of holding and cultivating it. They used mountain ridges and rivers as best they could for protection. Rivers also provided a vital source of water for those who managed to get access to them. These were the *agri occupatorii*, with limited survey, only informal establishment of boundaries, and little attempt to regulate or control the action of rivers.

Subsequently, when there was more settled occupancy, and lands had been subjected to formal survey and divided and allocated, rural life could not be left entirely to chance. There needed to be a fair system of allocation of set amounts of land, common pasture, woods if possible, and rivers or streams to make it all work. This eventually required an ability to understand the local region, to analyze river characteristics, assess their behavior, measure floods, draw maps, and of course keep full records. A process began where individuals and local communities and the state took responsibility for their relationship with the riverine environment and tried to regulate the use of rivers, define water rights, and institute more formal supervision. All this was more important because rivers frequently served as boundaries.

Surveyors operating in the field, as well as the state and its magistrates, who had executive authority, had important roles to play. Since the founding of settlements and land measurement and distribution were becoming more important, eventually land surveyors came to professional acceptance as demand for their services increased and they acquired an established legal status, to the extent that they could actually be sued if they made a mistake.[152] They worked out a methodology and principles of surveying practice, which they recorded, and took an increasing interest in the law, even though they were always subordinate to those with authority. The law tended to be prescriptive and could concern itself only with what had been done. Surveyors dealt with what they found on the ground and tried to devise preventative measures by working out what was likely to happen. They aimed to manage rivers so that landholders did not have to go to law.

The state played an important role in these developments in four ways.

First, in the establishment of colonies and settlements, it insisted that maps, documents, and records should be produced and formally displayed, and that a copy should be sent to Rome; this might include additional information relating to the measurement of rivers and their surrounds, and an assessment of their characteristics. Second, in the establishment of colonies, the Romans ensured that local regulations and laws dealt with the question of water use and water rights. By the mid-first century B.C. water rights were so important that we find Cicero, referring to the situation at his property in Tusculum, mentioning one Marcus Tugio, who apparently was a recognized expert in this field.[153] Third, the state accepted or sponsored the regulation of relations between individuals, and between the community and individuals, to distribute riverine benefits and protect against potential dangers and improper exploitation. It seems that a long-standing tendency to be sympathetic to riparian possessors became more pronounced, at least by the late second century A.D. In these developments, lawyers had a part to play in analyzing legal argument and precedent and advancing understanding of a complex topic. Fourth, controlled and circumscribed rivers and water sources were at the disposal of the state to exploit and conserve as it thought best.[154]

The imperial government's willingness to master the complications of a fractious riverine environment is illustrated in an inscription from Axima/ Forum Claudii Ceutronum in A.D. 163: Marcus Aurelius and Lucius Verus "restored the roads through the territory of the Ceutrones, which had been torn up by the force of the torrents, by shutting out the rivers and leading them back to their natural bed and placing embankments in numerous places, and also (restored) the temples and baths for the people of Forum Claudii at their own expense."[155] Here we see the determination of emperors to master natural forces and where necessary deploy government funds for a provincial community. Ranged against them was the river as a force of nature, moving its bed, smashing man-made facilities, causing disruption, and needing to be managed, in this case by the planned construction of levees to reinforce the banks.

Four

RIVERS IN LITERATURE, RELIGION, AND ART

In A.D. 15 the consuls Lucius Arruntius and Gaius Ateius Capito initiated a discussion in the senate about whether the problem of the Tiber flooding the center of Rome should be addressed by diverting the rivers and lakes that fed it. Deputations from the municipalities and colonies in the Tiber valley argued passionately against the proposal. The people of Florentia did not want the Clanis to be diverted from its usual course into the Arnus since this might bring destruction to their community. The inhabitants of Interamna had the same view about their own river Nar; if it were diverted into smaller channels, it would flood and destroy some of the best farming land in Italy. In Reate, they objected to the damming of the Veline Lake where it flowed out into the Nar because it would flood the surrounding land. The spokesmen of the rural communities then moved the argument onto a higher plane: "Nature had looked after mortals very well by giving every river its own source, course, outlet, and limits. They should take account of the religious views of local people, who had honored the rivers close to their homes with sacred rites, groves, and altars. Even Tiber himself would not take kindly to flowing with his majesty diminished if he were deprived of the tributary rivers." The senate finally decided to preserve the status quo.[1]

Tacitus was presumably using the record of senatorial business, and this incident shows the commitment of local riverine communities, which had undertaken the expense of sending a deputation to Rome to plead their case. We can only guess that there will have been many other instances, about which we hear nothing, where communities fought for their rivers. The spokesmen for the rural communities show an impressive grasp of river dynamics, lakes, and water systems. The psychology encouraged by the watery environment was that rivers brought many benefits but also potential dangers if their systems were disrupted. Communities were built around the ancestral rivers (*amnes patrii*), which in tradition and emotion became the center of local life, receiving regular offerings, groves, and altars. Rivers enhanced the status and dignity of a small community, and traditional, long-standing respect for rivers was based on the belief that nature was beyond human control and that the entire course of the river was best left to its own devices. There is an interesting contrast here with surveyors and engineers, who took the scientific and technical view that they should control, manage, and manipulate rivers to suit the government's requirements. Finally, the delegates cleverly invoked the river Tiber, personified in all his majesty, whose mighty flow depended on the tributary rivers, a view that frequently appears elsewhere.[2] They hint that the Tiber's status in the riverine world reflects the imperial grandeur of Rome.

In Tacitus's cool analysis, the senate's vote to do nothing could have been based on religious scruples, respect for local views, or technical difficulties. But he grants the story a reasonable amount of space and gives due weight to the feelings and beliefs of small-town riverine communities in Italy. This is invaluable for anyone trying to recover what the ancients, and particularly perhaps those outside the articulate upper classes, thought about rivers. His account also provides an introduction to important, wider themes of rivers and people, and the significance of rivers and springs in religious observances.

In this chapter, I discuss how different people observed and wrote about rivers. Such descriptions with their watery stories and themes, whether or not enhanced by poetic imagination, reflect psychological responses to the riverine environment. They therefore tell us why rivers were important in the ancient world, in a way perhaps not clearly recognized or expressed by geographers, land surveyors, and other specialists, who tended to emphasize the prosaic geographical and topographical setting. Furthermore, in common belief, rivers were divine, often possessing special powers, and had participated in the legends associated with many rural communities. From an early stage, river dwellers supplicated local rivers because of their crucial place in the natural world, and some rivers such as the Tiber and the Nile became objects of particular attention or reverence. The religious aura of the watery environment assisted the anthropomorphic characterization of rivers and the whole nexus of mythology and legend that arose from but also sustained their divine status. Finally, observation of water sources, legendary stories, imagination, and reverence were translated into a series of representations of rivers in sculpture and mosaics and on coinage. The many artistic images of rivers indicate not just their ubiquity in the landscape but also their place in the thinking of individuals and of the Roman government.

The response to the riverine environment has been of great cultural significance in many societies in different ages. Naturally, rivers meant different things to different groups in different places. In many areas they offered clean drinking water for people and their animals, irrigation for crops, an avenue of trade and the movement of goods, commercial opportunities, boundary demarcation, and often a quasi-mystical inspiration.[3] The Persians, for example, had an enormous reverence for rivers, which they refused to pollute by spitting or urinating or even washing their hands. The king drank the water of only one river, the Choaspes, which flowed past Susa.[4] On the other hand, the nomadic tribes in Mesopotamia in Roman times found their physical world entirely defined by the Tigris and Euphrates, which enclosed the land. They were so convinced that they were islanders that "when they are journeying to the rivers they talk about going down to the sea, thinking that the circle made by the rivers marks the land's boundary."[5] Here rivers were integral to the way of life that they circumscribed.

It needs no lengthy demonstration that rivers were an important theme in ancient writers of the Roman period. Suetonius wrote about weather signs, the names of seas and rivers, and the names of winds.[6] Among the collection of the minor Greek geographers, the so-called Pseudo-Plutarch wrote on the names of rivers and mountains and refers to several other writers on rivers.[7] Writers make many passing references and often use rivers in comparisons, illustrations, and analogies. Running water was a very useful metaphor for violent or serene movement, conflict or peace. Writers, by emphasizing a river's qualities and characteristics and by evoking the sight and sound of its many changing moods, could create a pleasant, stimulating picture of the natural world. It is striking that they so often express respect and even reverence for rivers as beneficiaries of mankind and local communities. Therefore, riverine themes cover a wide spectrum, ranging from the replenishment of the seas in the hydrological cycle and the mystery of rivers' ever-changing apparent immutability, to impressions of river appearance and characteristics and related curiosities and legends.

Lucretius perhaps has the most eloquent if rather vague account of how sea, rivers, and springs are eternally replenished; one way was the seeping of seawater underground, whence, with the salt filtered out, it entered underground aquifers before welling up again: "Hence it flows above ground, a steady column of sweet fluid marching down the highway already hewn with liquid foot for the guidance of waves."[8] Vitruvius, in his handbook on architecture knows about the pluvial aspects of the hydrological cycle, arguing that valleys with their dense forests collect snow, which eventually melts, percolates through the earth, and becomes the source of mountain springs. But he also indulges in quasi-romantic speculation, emphasizing the importance of rainfall brought by the moist winds from the south and deposited in the north; therefore he believed the largest rivers had their sources in the northern area, citing the map of Agrippa as evidence.[9]

Many commentators were impressed by rivers as an awe-inspiring elemental power of nature with qualities of constant movement yet enigmatic timelessness that allowed a quasi-philosophical comparison with human life. Marcus Aurelius expresses this most vividly, singling out the ceaseless flow of rivers. Time is like a river, a rushing torrent; no sooner do you see something than it is swept past; then another object is passing, but it too will be carried away.[10] So, all being is like a river in endless flow, and the body of man is as a river, and the life of man is only a point.[11] Again, the changing pattern of life resembles a river where it is difficult to get a foothold.[12]

Seneca also thought that rivers, ever-changing but retaining the same outward appearance, resembled the human body. Heraclitus had already taken up the philosophical implications of this great enigma. He noted that we may seem to descend into the same river twice, but in fact we cannot because the water has moved past.[13] Furthermore, in Seneca's view the natural force of rivers had religious significance. "We venerate the sources of great rivers; we erect altars where a mighty river bursts forth unexpectedly from its subterranean hiding place; we pay our respects at the source of hot springs."[14]

Similarly, the Greek philosopher Epictetus compared the varied life of man to rivers. A life touched by ill fortune was like a winter torrent—rough, full of debris, hard to access, tyrannical, noisy, and short-lived; a life lived with virtue resembled an ever-flowing spring—pure, clear, drinkable, palatable, enjoyed in common, rich, harmless, and bringing no ruin.[15] Of course, from the Christian standpoint rivers had a fundamental place in the world alongside seas and mountains as God's creations, and the divinity would set rivers where there was no water. God's control over the natural world was complete.[16] The great, eternal flow of a river could be seen as taking man back to the beginning not only of his own existence but of time itself.[17] Rivers might contain or represent the vitality of men and of empires. By contrast, when rivers dried up, it was a sign of the end of days or destruction of societies, in the reversal of such a vital natural process.

The quasi-mystical, philosophical view of rivers in some writers as a commentary on life certainly does not mean that they regarded rivers as remote from the real world. In fact, the comments noted above reveal an acute observation of the nature and characteristics of rivers as an integral part of society and community life. This is the key to understanding the way in which most writers described rivers. They wrote about what they saw and heard, which often involved an emotional or intellectual response, overlaid at times with elements of literary tradition. All this, so it might be argued, is the view of the articulate thinking classes. Nevertheless, ordinary people would surely have recognized the essential features of rivers. It is another difficulty that such themes may contain an element of a literary commonplace or *topos*, emphasizing riverine and sylvan pleasures such as plashing water, beautiful scenery, and birdsong. But the very fact that riverine material does appear so frequently indicates in my view that authors were writing about immediately recognizable features of the watery environment, even if they expressed this in a traditional way.

Although writers in the Roman world express appreciation, even love, and respect for the benefits the riverine environment, they do not trouble to give a detailed discussion of river action. Instead they make passing comments, using adjectives (ranging from the physical to personified human attributes) to characterize individual rivers; for example, the Eurotas is "cold," the Padus is "rich in poplars," the Tagus "gold-bearing," the Maeander "exceedingly winding," the Anio where it joined the Tiber was "good to look at and sweet to drink," the Marsyas "exceptionally clear," the Baetis "most remote," the Nar at Narnia "white with a sulfurous surge," the Tiber "tawny" or sometimes "blue."[18]

Many writers were fascinated by the changing face of the watery environment. So Horace memorably spoke of how winter's bitter frost paralyzed rivers, while in the spring they were able to flow quietly again when the melting snow had gone.[19] A river in full spate was an awesome sight, just like Pindar's style, as Horace put it.[20] Lucretius's description of a fast-flowing river may owe much to personal observation: "In the way they (particles of air) flow and the havoc they spread they are no different from a torrential flood of water when it rushes down in a sudden spate from the mountain heights, swollen by heavy rains, and heaps together wreckage from the forest and entire trees." The roaring, surging river rolls along huge rocks and flattens bridges.[21] At all times, variation in river flow was important, especially for rural communities, and Seneca and others devoted learned discussion to the reasons for seasonal changes.[22]

Those writers who had the leisure to celebrate the pleasure given by their favorite river or spring, or who treated rivers as a recreation or a plaything, sometimes offer an interesting discussion of the riverine environment and its relation to people. The Younger Pliny famously celebrated the source of the river Clitumnus, between Spoletium and Trebiae, which flowed into the Tinia, a tributary of the Tiber.[23] The source had a solemn, almost religious aura as people threw offerings of coins into the spreading pool of water. The water itself was as clear as glass and, with a strong flow, soon became a river that was as cold and sparkling as snow. It was navigable, allowing two boats to pass, although its current was so strong that boats going upstream had to use oars and poles. The riverine environment was delightful, with the green ash and poplar trees mirrored in the stream where the locals went boating for pleasure. There were strong religious associations, and a statue of Clitumnus himself had pride of place. Pliny probably did not deliberately make a detour to see the Clitumnus. His careful and vivid description, however, is no literary commonplace but shows genuine interest and originality and awareness of the varied role of rivers. Other writers, while noting the beauty of the Clitumnus, concentrate on its famous white oxen.[24]

Horace addressed one of his most famous Odes to the spring of Bandusia, which he presents as a deity receiving offerings. He highlights the appearance ("more shining than glass"), feel ("cold stream"), and sound ("chattering waters leap down") of the spring. Bandusia retained good flow even in the hottest weather and provided cool drinking water for tired flocks. In an interesting comment on the status of water sources, Horace claims that his poetry will add Bandusia to the list of famous springs.[25] Here the physical appearance of the spring and the real benefits it offered shade into a spiritual dimension. Similarly, in a splendid descriptive passage in Aelian we hear that the Peneios flows gently and leisurely like olive oil, shaded from the sun by trees, with a pleasant environment for sailing and religious observances on the banks.[26]

There was a widespread recognition among ancient writers not only of the physical assistance offered by rivers (cool water and shade) but also of the potential for restoring the spirits and intellectual peace through enjoyment of this environment. In this case the *topos* may genuinely reflect real life. Lucretius expressed the idea in a moralizing commonplace: men do not need a lavish banquet to find enjoyment; it is sufficient to lie in good company on soft grass by a running stream under the shade of a tall tree and refresh their bodies at small expense.[27] Catullus in a striking simile creates a similar picture of a mountain stream tumbling down a sloping valley beside a busy road and bringing sweet relief to the exhausted traveler in blazing hot weather.[28] Cicero, struggling to accept the realities of politics under Caesar's sole rule, wrote from

Arpinum in 45 B.C. that he was seeking rivers and solitude to make life more endurable.[29] These watery delights were available to all country dwellers and travelers. On the other hand, in Statius's description of the villa of Manilius Vopiscus at Tibur, which straddled the river Anio, the river is now a plaything of the rich.[30] At the villa, the river's turbulent flow became gentle, serving its master and the layout of the buildings amid pleasant sylvan surroundings.

An imaginative poetic context also helps us to see how contemporaries perceived riverine status, identity, and character. Silius Italicus imagines a confrontation between the river Trebia and the advancing Carthaginians led by Hannibal, in which he threatens the river with disgrace in rather interesting terms. Its stream will be dispersed through the countryside, its sources will be blocked up, and its name will be taken away; it will no longer serve as a tributary of the Padus and will lose the status inherent in that.[31] So apparently the ancients saw the importance of rivers as coming partly from their volume of water, their established bed, and their association with other famous rivers. Furthermore, riverine names were important.

Some similar ideas appear in Ovid's *Amores* in the long address of a lover to a river, which incidentally gives an excellent picture of how people viewed rivers in their local context. The lover is eager to get to his girlfriend, but the swollen river is in the way.[32] There was no bridge or chain ferry close by, and it was difficult to ford the river without a boat, since it was now in full spate because of melting snow and had turned into a muddy torrent. Ovid, doubtless echoing the sentiments of many country folk, wishes that the river would stay within its banks. Under the guise of arguing that rivers should help young lovers, Ovid gives a lengthy survey of the legendary amorous activities of famous rivers. But as the stream spreads further beyond its banks, Ovid becomes abusive—it is not a proper river at all, famous with a name renowned throughout the world; it has no proper source and no home; it depends on the accident of melting snows—a mud bath in winter and a dusty desert in summer. It is no use to travelers, cattle, or crops and is just a nondescript trickle. These insults further illustrate the roll call of river qualities and attributes in popular emotion and sentiment.

We can see this too in Statius's poem celebrating the construction of Domitian's road from Sinuessa to Naples. He strikingly personifies the river Volturnus, which the road crossed on a bridge.[33] Volturnus appears as a man with long, flowing yellow tresses, leaning against the new bridge and addressing the emperor. He had once been a threatening river, accustomed to flood and create mayhem in the fields, having no set channel and being difficult to navigate. The emperor has given him firm banks and a bridge for people to cross. "I who to my shame used to snatch up and whirl away land and trees am now starting to be a river." The emperor is the master of the riverbank and has cleaned up the river, which used to carry much detritus and stain the waters of the Gulf of Naples, like the awful Bagrada in Africa. Now the Volturnus promises to flow with a sparkling stream that will challenge the neighboring Liris. This riverine monologue gives a fascinating summary of the good and bad impact of rivers on the environment, local and international riverine competition, and also imperial control over the natural world.

In the fourth century A.D., Ausonius's poem addressed to the Mosella (Moselle) stands out among river encomia as the longest and most emotionally charged, and it is worthy of extended treatment.[34] Ausonius came from Bordeaux and was praising a famous even if rather distant Gallic river, and so we must expect some conventional enthusiasm. Yet he strikes a fresh note with his vigorous and imaginative approach. The poet greets the river (lines 23–32), which is praised by the surrounding fields and by the farmers, and treats it as a person with human characteristics; at the confluence with the Rhine there will be no jealousy since the rivers are brothers and the Rhine is a generous host (417–37). The rivers once joined together will be powerful enough to make hostile peoples quake. But in its own right the Moselle had typical watery qualities in abundance; it was deep as a lake but matched smaller rivers with its lively flow, and surpassed cool springs with its crystal-clear drinking water; its glasslike surface (55–61) showed the pebbles and gravel on its bed and various types of underwater plants and grasses. The visual impact of the river was very important to Ausonius, and he dwells on its beauty as it reflected and mirrored the surrounding greenery, which was particularly impressive in the glow of the setting sun (189–95). The Moselle managed to avoid the problems that afflicted many rivers, such as shallows, rocks and rapids, muddy banks, and islands in midstream, and was not a threatening river, but flowed gently with a subdued murmuring (33–47).

The Moselle encouraged a vibrant riverine life: the many great estates along its banks, the rich farmland, the extensive vines, and the numerous fish nurtured in its waters (75–81), which gave rise to a fishing industry (240–82). Yet the Moselle was also a working river since it was navigable for large ships for part of its course and bargemen plied their trade, either using the current or pulling their craft by a rope (36–42). In Ausonius's view the surrounding estates were an adornment to the river (318–20), which also enhanced its majestic aura and reputation through its mighty tributaries; they sacrificed their own names to enhance its volume and power, but also gained from merging with the powerful Moselle (349–58). Finally, the river was the outstanding centerpiece of a fruitful land, with many fine young men and a splendid culture (381–88). Ausonius boasts of the roll call of watery elements that will do reverence to the Moselle, whose fame will spread though many lands, even though it had to concede preeminence to the Tiber, which guarded the seat of empire and the homes of the Romans (374–81, 469–83). This is a striking reversal of the usual status of the Rhône as the preeminent Gallic river, along with the Rhine. It is important that the idea of a river where satyrs and nymphs sport on the banks (169–88) does not take center stage, since Ausonius wants us to share his appreciation of the Moselle through its genuinely admired visual delights and splendid riverine environment, rather than through conventional legends and supernatural elements.

These sentiments are echoed in the sixth century by Venantius Fortunatus, who was well aware of literary precedents when he described a voyage in an oared boat along the "fertile" Moselle from Metz (Divodurum) to Trier (Colonia Augusta Treverorum) and on to the "foaming" Rhine. Elsewhere he celebrates the river, which "softly rolls along its great waters; it laps the banks, scented with the verdant sward, and the wave gently washes the grassy blades"; at Metz, "besieged by fish," its course is swelled by the gentler waters of a tributary, the Seille.[35]

3   STATUS, CHARACTER, AND IDENTITY

Respect for the natural environment combined with love and thoughtful veneration for, and identification with, a homeland at the local or national level have been defined in theoretical terms by scholars of human geography as geopiety and topophilia.[36] Dio Chrysostomos put it in simpler terms when he came to address the people of Tarsus. He wondered what they expected to hear from him—perhaps praise of their country and the river Cydnus, how it was the most splendid and beautiful of all rivers, and that those who drank from it were "rich and blessed."[37] As we have seen in the geographical writers, rivers were of immense importance in establishing not only direction, distance, and place but also identity.[38] Precisely because rivers had their own status, which they could win, increase, or forfeit to another river, they could confer fame and a tag of identity on peoples associated with them. Lucan memorably described the course of the Isara (Isère), which traveled a long distance with its own waters but then slipped into the stream of a river of greater fame (Rhône) "and lost its name before it reached the sea."[39] The Rhône then assumed the role of dominant regional river. There was usually a competitive edge to river comparisons. When King Darius during the invasion of Europe came to the river Tearos in Thrace, which the locals claimed was the best in the world for its curative properties, he was so impressed that he erected an inscribed pillar at its source noting that the Great King had visited the Tearos, "the best and most beautiful of all rivers."[40]

In the context of ownership of rivers and territoriality, it is easy to understand how mighty rivers came to represent their lands and peoples and how a bond of affection was established. Rivers are often used to represent cultures, peoples, or regions. Virgil, describing threats to Roman peace, treats the Euphrates as a Parthian warlord—"from one side the Euphrates starts a war, from the other Germany."[41] Propertius admits that he is a poet of soft themes and not of war, and will not describe how Rome drives back the German hordes, while the barbaric river Rhine stained with German blood carries the mangled bodies in its sad waters.[42] Virgil, emphasizing the stability of customs, says that change will happen sooner than the Parthian will drink the Arar or the German the Tigris, while Horace speaks of how his poetry will eventually be known in the provinces, including by the Gauls who drink the Rhône.[43] In a different vein, the satirist Juvenal sneers that "for a long time now the Syrian Orontes has been pouring its filth into our native Tiber," symbolizing the home-grown, decent Romans submerged beneath a tide of decadent easterners represented by their famous river.[44]

Therefore, rivers can represent nations, peoples and even ideologies, and they appear with affection and pride in Virgil's famous description of the typical landscape of the Italian hill towns: "See our noble cities, labor's crown, / built breathlessly upon steep mountainsides, / deep rivers flowing under ancient walls," where the calm majesty of the rivers is contrasted with the precipitous towns.[45] Virgil has a particular affinity for the lakes and rivers near his native Mantua. He emphasizes the preeminent role of water in the local landscapes of northern Italy, especially the Po valley. This large, impressive river was subject to seasonal flooding, partly inspired by torrential Alpine rivers, but was nevertheless navigable, offering pleasant surroundings with oaks and its famous poplar trees. Virgil also speaks warmly of the river Mella and, of course, the Mincius, which flowed languidly past Mantua with its banks festooned with reeds.[46]

Lucan expresses a similar pride in the geography of Italy based on a framework of rivers. He wonders where Pompey and Caesar will fight the civil war. Perhaps it would be near the mighty Apennines, which divide sea from sea and whose watershed sends rivers flowing to the east and west: "Toward the east flow the swift Metaurus and the tumultuous Crustumius, the Sapis along with the Isaurus, the Sena and the Aufidus, which strikes the waters of the Adriatic. There is also the Eridanus (Po), as large as any river produced by earth, which whirls uprooted trees down to the sea and drains Italy." This river could match the Nile and the Danube, at least in a Roman's imagination.[47] Toward the west the Apennines ushered forth the Tiber; the deep Rutuba; the swift Volturnus; the Sarnus, which produced nocturnal breezes; the Liris, which from Mount Vestinus passed through the sylvan domain of the nymph Marica; the Siler in its rugged terrain; and the Macra, which allowed no navigation in its stream.[48] In this passage, geography, hydrology, legend, and a series of pithy adjectives come together in the affectionate characterization of these well-known rivers in the heartland of Italy.[49]

Augustus too in his own way exploited the reputation, romance, and powerful geographical associations of mighty rivers. In the *Res Gestae* he mentions four of the great rivers of Europe: the Elbe, Rhine, Danube, and Don. The remote Elbe marks the furthest extent of Augustus's pacification of northern Europe "from Cadiz to the mouth of the Elbe." The mouth of the Rhine launched the Roman fleet on its eastward exploration, and the Danube briefly marked the limit of Roman military activity before, on the emperor's orders, the army crossed the river in order to chastise the Dacians. Distant peoples dwelling on both sides of the river Don sent embassies seeking friendship with Rome.[50] The emperor displays knowledge and respect, though in the context of Roman power and mastery of all elements of the environment, no matter how remote. These ideas were also expressed in Agrippa's world map, which was on display in the *porticus Vipsaniae* in Rome and seems to have included the main rivers. This was a superb demonstration of the prestige and status of Rome, whose great men had the knowledge and power to construct such a map and launch campaigns of conquest to bring these mighty rivers and their peoples within the Roman orbit.[51]

4   DIVINE RIVERS AND SPRINGS

Servius observed that "there is no spring that is not sacred."[52] Rivers, springs, and water sources received worship in various forms. What was the basis of this, and how important were water sources in popular feeling toward sacred rites? Even if it is true that the animistic element of early Roman religion has been exaggerated, we can recognize that people had genuine respect for the power of nature and the awe-inspiring appearance and strength of rivers and welling sources of water.[53] Spatial relationships, landscapes, and places of sacred phenomena and religious practices were part of the complex pattern of the geography of religion. The connection between the clearly perceived, everyday characteristics of rivers and divine intervention in human affairs appears in the work of Artemidorus of Ephesus, who in late second century A.D. wrote a work on dreams that predicted the future. Rivers appear in these dreams and show us how people identified riverine behavior with the course of life itself; rivers are good when they are clear, transparent, and flowing gently; but they can also be muddied and troubled, violent, noisy, and swollen; they can take away pieces of land, and they can sweep people out to sea. In general they were like judges because "they do what they want with impunity and in accord with their own inclination." They are like trips abroad because the water does not stand still but flows on. He also says that all men need a river and that there is nothing so nourishing as water.[54]

Ordinary people would directly see a divine element in rivers because of their protean qualities, by which they were potentially lethal (through violent floods) or, by contrast, bringers of fertility and prosperity. They were literally the water of life, vital for human existence and for the success of the surrounding area. In this context we can understand why rivers are often portrayed with the horn of plenty.[55] They not only supported life in rural communities but also provided the pure water so prized in big cities, which depended on water distribution by aqueducts.[56] Ovid, through the medium of the goddess Leto, gives a powerful statement of the value of water. Leto upbraids local people who tried to prevent her from drinking the cool waters of a lake. "Why do you keep me away from the water? Water is for everybody to use. Nature did not make gentle streams, any more than air and sunlight, for the benefit of individuals. I come for something to which all people have a right."[57]

The religious aura of water therefore derived from a variety of factors but undoubtedly owed much to its appearance. It often seems sparkling and vibrant, especially in sunlight; it can be deep yet transparent, almost as if it has nothing to hide, yet at times dark and gloomy. By its very movement, the running water of a river suggests a cleansing quality, in both the literal and metaphorical sense; as such it had an important role in religious ritual.[58] Then, the traditional beauty of the watery environment evoked reverence and awe; rivers and pools were often surrounded by shady and cool trees and peaceful groves with grassy banks, as idyllically described by Ovid.[59] The noise of river water had its own attraction and mystery, moving from sonorous plashing to insistent roaring, announcing the river's presence even if the river itself could not be seen. The enormous influence of rivers on the lives of rural communities reminded men of the divine power to intervene in human affairs and the mutability of human fortune. What is more, some rivers shocked local people by disappearing into a chasm, drying up, or reappearing.[60] In addition, traditional stories insisted that many rivers had supernatural or magical qualities and could bring about dramatic changes in those who quaffed them.[61] Many local communities were more exposed to, or dependent on, rivers than others, and so the nature of a river and its power to influence events might determine the kind of worship it received. Where there was a close bond between the rural riverine communities and their rivers, we might expect to find a close connection between religious veneration of rivers and traditional legends. The divine element would then be fostered by the whole complex of local conditions and emotions. It is worth noting that in areas of mainland Greece and particularly among the Greek communities of Asia Minor, potamophoric names are common, and although diluted by time and convention, these are a guide to local feelings and traditions and the original connection to river spirits. This nomenclature derived from rivers indirectly associated its bearer with the divine aspect of the riverine environment.[62]

Finally, rivers were linked to cult and religious observances (not necessarily directly associated with watery things) by geographical location, because rural shrines tended to be placed close to the site of springs for refreshment or bathing or cleansing, or along river valleys in the interests of easier communications, or at river crossing points. In the history of Greek colonies in Italy, rivers served as territorial boundaries and also offered protection; sanctuaries were sometimes placed at the mouths of rivers.[63] River water may have had an indirect importance in religious observances; for example, Demeter was associated with agriculture, which used water extensively.[64]

Ancient writers routinely attribute divine powers to rivers and treat them as objects of veneration. To some extent, this is literary convention linked to mythological tales that provided such good material for writing. Therefore, for Ovid it was virtually commonplace to set a sacred spring in a cavern in a verdant wood.[65] Or when Poseidon wants to cause a flood, he summons all the rivers to a council meeting and orders them to flow with uninhibited force to the sea.[66] After noting the sacred source of the Peneios, Virgil adopts a tone closer to the beliefs of the rural communities of Italy when he has Aeneas on first arriving in Latium pray to the spirit of the place, the earth, the nymphs, and the rivers as yet unknown to him.[67] This reminds us of the importance of locality and the mysterious natural forces in the countryside. The deputation from the rural communities of Italy in A.D. 15 had voiced the simple piety of country folk; rivers were part of nature's grand plan; local people observed sacred rites, with groves and altars for their ancestral rivers, which had a more immediate relevance than the lordly Tiber.[68] Similarly, Pliny's description of the Clitumnus shows an active riverine cult in the second century A.D. The site contained an ancient, hallowed temple and a statue of Clitumnus in human form with the adornment of a real toga. The presence of his divinity produced prophecies. There were other small shrines of lesser deities dotted around, with their own name and rites, which were often associated with springs, for the river had many small tributaries. A bridge marked the dividing point between the water held to be sacred and the ordinary river, and in the sacred area, sailing only (not swimming) was permitted.[69] The many votive inscriptions that Pliny mentions celebrating the god indicate that this shrine was very much in business and that people continued to approach the god. Of course, there was an element of commercialism in that the neighboring town of Hispellum, by gift of Augustus, organized bathing in the river.[70]

Vitruvius confirms the general significance of rivers in the planning of temples. In his view the temple and statue should normally look toward the western part of the sky. But if a temple were built on the banks of a river, it ought to appear to look toward the river, as on the banks of the Nile.[71] The purpose of this may have been a mark of respect to the divine spirit of the river, or perhaps to allow river travelers to observe the temple, in the same way that if temples were near public roads they should be located so that travelers could take note of them. But river crossing was also a crucial and perhaps dangerous moment for someone moving from one place to another across the watery barrier. It was therefore entirely in keeping with contemporary respect for the special position of rivers for Arrian to relate without comment that Alexander the Great sacrificed and prayed to the Danube for permitting his crossing.[72]

Pausanias certainly conveys the idea that springs and rivers with special qualities assisted life and work in the Greek communities he describes. The greater the perceived boon from the river the greater the divine power must be. The relevance of rivers and springs to local life and culture helps to explain why they continued to receive offerings and ceremonial observances from antiquity to Pausanias's day. In Attica there was an altar to Acheloüs, who was conventionally represented with a bull's head.[73] At Olympia the Alpheios had two altars, one shared with Artemis,[74] and the river was also associated with the altar of Zeus. Every year in March the priest brought ash soaked with river water from the council house, and plastered it over the altar. No other water could be used—"that is why they believe that Alpheios is the most pleasant of all rivers to Olympian Zeus."[75] Apart from the Alpheios, the Kladeos had more honors in Elis than any other river, and an altar at Olympia.[76] At Psophis in Arcadia, the Erymanthos had a riverside temple with a statue of white marble. According to Pausanias, riverine images were always of white marble except the Nile, which had images of black stone.[77] Statues were also set up in rivers as a mark of honor.[78]

Many observances in honor of rivers were probably at a very personal level.

It was, for example, a long-standing Greek tradition for boys to cut their hair in honor of rivers, and Pausanias had observed individual commemorations of this. In Arcadia the boys cut their hair in honor of the river Neda at the point where it came closest to the town of Phigaleia, neatly tying the observance in with the local community.[79] By the river Kephisos was a statue showing a boy cutting his hair for the river.[80] Garlands too were offered in worship,[81] and at the temple of the river Pamisos in Messenia annual offerings were made.[82] Cakes were presented to the Kephisos on certain special days by local people, who believed they appeared at the Kastalian spring.[83] The importance of rivers in local life can be seen in offerings made to mark where a water source burst out of the ground or an underground river reappeared, and also to appease the river after flooding. Springs too were closely associated with the local community, and their importance can be seen from the association with major deities, such as the sanctuary of Athene of the Springhead near Elateia.[84] In Italy, the river Numicus, which flowed past Lavinium into the Tyrrhenian Sea, received offerings from the consuls.[85]

In terms of the divine element of watery sources, the evidence of inscriptions offers a fresh outlook and a different dimension. Inscriptions are particularly valuable since they have no literary affectation and are not normally conditioned by traditional literary themes. Most were set up by people who were not necessarily part of the highly literate elite, though they were probably well-off because of the expense involved. Inscriptions provide a random selection of material, which is not contaminated by a tendency to concentrate on major rivers. Precisely because the erection of an inscription was relatively expensive, dedications to rivers and springs should indicate real interest and commitment, and perhaps also an expectation that something could be gained from it. This kind of evidence might indicate that it is unwise to argue that Romans did not give great weight to the divine element of water, even though running water was important for purposes of purification and *fontes* were sacred.[86]

On the other hand, although many inscriptions refer to dedications or the honoring of vows to springs (*fontes*), waters (*aquae*), nymphs (*nymphae* or *nimphae*), or, in fewer cases, named rivers, there are problems in trying to assess their significance. We have no idea how many similar inscriptions have been lost. And, of course, not all nymphs were connected to the watery environment of pools, springs, and rivers. They inhabited many different parts of the natural world, including mountains, trees, groves, and rural places in general. Most inscriptions are very brief and provide few helpful details. Therefore, it is difficult to establish the context of the occasion and to assess the feelings of the dedicant and the degree of convention in conforming to social and cultural pressures in commemorative expenditure. Furthermore, the status of the person setting up the inscription is not always clear. Since the date is often unknown, it is impossible to trace any trends or developments in the honoring of watery sources. Whereas some inscriptions can be linked to certain thermal sites, in many other cases the original location is unclear. Nevertheless, evidence of this kind by its very repetition does have some cumulative force. It shows a prevailing concern with water sources, the regular availability of running water, the purificatory role of water in religious ritual, and also the curative properties of hot and cold waters.[87] It is clear that some springs and rivers acquired attention and reverence because of their location and their inherent value and cultural significance in a local context that was too parochial to attract the attention of our usual literary sources.

Dedications that imply some form of religious engagement with the watery environment are found in most parts of Italy from *lacus Benacus* (Lake Como) and the Padus (Po) to Naples and Campania.[88] Offerings and vows in many provinces, including the three Spanish provinces (Lusitania, Baetica, Tarraconensis), Gaul, Germany, Dalmatia, Pannonia, Moesia, Dacia, Asia, and Africa suggest that in rural communities throughout the empire water sources and springs were revered and venerated in a traditional way, at least by Romans or Romanized individuals who set up most of the inscriptions. An inscription from near Verona refers to the Augustan nymphs and the *genius* of the *pagus Arusnatium*, suggesting a close association between the watery environment and rural life.[89] From Gaul there is a rare combination of Silvanus and the "nymphs of the place."[90] Although many dedications refer vaguely to "nymphs," leaving it to the reader to associate the spirits with the locality, sometimes the nymphs are linked to a named spring.[91]

Virtually all elements of the population are found to have erected dedications to springs, nymphs, or rivers. We find slaves, slaves of the emperor, imperial freedmen, freedmen, soldiers, legions, and women and men up to senatorial rank. Many set up a dedication when they were holding office, though not usually as a function of that office. At Caere, Lucius Pontilius Duurus, a standard-bearer, set up a dedication to the "Spring of the Waters of Caere." Claudius Marcellinus, a *beneficiarius consularis*, at Rigomagus (Remagen) in A.D. 190 fulfilled his vow to "Jupiter Best and Greatest, and the Spirit of the Place and the Rhine"; a *speculator* Cassius Severus paid his respects to Aquae Aponi near Patavium; a *dispensator* in Sabine country welcomed the restoration of a spring, Granius Priscus; a *sevir Augustalis* and *praefectus iure dicundo* dedicated his building of a fountainhead to the nymphs and the *Vires Augusti* at Veleia; and at Aquae Flavianae in Numidia, Abidius Bassus, curator, paid his vow to the "spirit of the nymphs and Draco."[92] The entire legion XX Valeria Victrix made a dedication "Nymphis et fontibus" at Deva (Chester).[93]

At a higher social level, we find legionary commanders and provincial governors making offerings. At Legio (León), Terentius Homullus Junior, legate of legion VII Gemina, "willingly and properly fulfilled his vow to the nymphs of the spring Amevus." A *legatus Augusti* in Numidia commemorated the springs at Sinuessa in Campania on behalf of himself, his wife, and his two children, while in Dacia the governor of Lower Moesia paid his vow to Hercules, the spirit of the place, and the hot springs.[94] The prefect of Egypt, Sulpicius Similis, named a spring at *mons Claudianus* after Trajan—*fons Felicissimus Traianus Dacicus.*[95] Two brothers who were *curatores aquarum* made an offering to Fons and Tellus at Volsinii (Bolsena).[96]

There were also local officials such as Arruntius Faustus, *magister pagi* at Cirta, who set up with his own money a memorial to the spirit of the local river Ampsaga.[97] At Formiae, Fufius Alexander, master of a *collegium*, erected an altar at his own expense on behalf of the *collegium*, dedicated to Fontanus.[98] Rather mysteriously, a group of five delegates who came to Rome from Dacia on official business made a dedication on their safe return to "the gods and spirits of the waters."[99] Perhaps they had sailed along or crossed the Danube. At Nemausus in Gaul, we get a glimpse of enthusiastic local religious practice when the worshipers of the spring Ura (river Eure) combined to make a dedication.[100] Most of those making dedications were men, but women and freedwomen and slaves also made offerings.[101] In the main, the form and content of these vows and dedications were simple and straightforward, perhaps suggesting a degree of convention, though that does not preclude sincere belief and respect.

This is an important point, because it is often difficult to see why a spring or river is celebrated. However, many inscriptions remind us of the importance of the water supply. In the Mediterranean area, despite water's importance in divine rituals and purification, it was often a rare commodity and existing springs could dry up in the summer months. Inscriptions celebrating a perennial water source, or a more generous flow, or the reappearance of a river or spring, or a new source that had never been seen before tell us something about the importance of water in life and society and can help explain the apparent enthusiasm for venerating watery things.[102] For example, Antonius Victorinus, town councilor of Aquincum, celebrated the local "perennial spring," while Pomponius Cornelianus, a young man from a senatorial family, celebrated the return of the water at Vicetia (Vicenza) with a dedication to the Augustan nymphs and waters. On the island of Arba off the coast of Dalmatia in A.D. 173, Raecius Leo celebrated the provision for the town of a supply of water that "none of the old people remembered to have existed in the community," at the expense and wish of his senatorial patron. Sometimes the restoration of a water source might have involved digging or the building of a suitable outlet. An intriguing inscription from Rome dated to A.D. 123 mentions a group of people called masters and servants of the *fons*.[103] The significance of this is unclear, but we might have here a private society in honor of one water source, rather than some state-sponsored officials to supervise fountains.[104]

Normally the spirit (*genius* or *numen*) of a watery source is vaguely addressed, and divinity is implied rather than stated. However, several dedications are more specific (such as "Fonti Divino" or "dea" or "sacer"), and a spring or nymph is sometimes associated with other spirits and gods including Apollo and Jupiter.[105] A nymph too is sometimes called "divine," or "most holy" (*sanctissima*), and there was also a temple of the nymphs at civitas (S)edetanorum in Spain.[106] This scattered evidence confirms the importance of the sanctity of water in its various manifestations. The personal response of individuals sometimes provides sharper illumination, as in the case of one Laetus at Lambaesis, who burst into poetry in honor of the spirit of the "Aqua Alexandriana." He set up an altar when he was holding office in his community, and what pleased him most about his year of office was that during it the water flowed with a particularly generous stream.[107] The same kind of emotion for a less benevolent purpose appears in a curse tablet from Arretium, in which Letinius Lupus seeks to encompass the death of someone within the year through "you surging waters or you nymphs, or by whatever name you want to be called."[108]

Reverence and respect for water spirits and a belief in their capacity to intervene in human affairs illustrate many aspects of local life. At Ostia, a well was built at the expense of three officials in local *collegia* "on the advice of Ceres and the Nymphs."[109] At Aquae Sulis (Bath), a family swore an oath at the spring of the goddess Sulis, invoking retribution on anyone who broke the oath.[110] On a sadder note, a funeral monument from Rome speaks of a young boy who had presumably drowned. "Here lies M. Ulpius Firmus, whose good spirit has returned to heaven, snatched away by the nymphs; he lived nine years and six months, betrayer of his parents. Ulpius Nymphicus to his dearest son."[111]

Official, state-sponsored offerings to the tutelary deities of springs to a limited extent directed worship of watery sources. Each year on 13 October the Romans celebrated the *Fontinalia* in honor of Fons and natural water sources. "They throw wreaths into springs and place crowns on wells."[112] Fons had an altar on the Janiculum near the alleged burial place of Numa,[113] and outside the Porta Capena was a grove with a spring of the Camenae from which the Vestals drew water daily by hand to sprinkle in the temple.[114] There was also a god Fontanus and a goddess Fontana, associated with springs. At Villaviçosa in Lusitania we find a dedication "pro salute" to Fontanus and Fontana.[115] Formal offerings by individuals to springs and water sources will also have consisted of flowers and garlands accompanied by libations of wine. Horace, however, in addressing the Fons Bandusiae, speaks of the sacrifice of a kid whose red blood will stain the gelid water of the spring.[116]

By contrast with nymphs and springs, rivers come to our attention much less often and are comparatively rarely mentioned in inscriptions. However, they are usually explicitly named and dedications appear in Italy and in many provinces, including Spain, Gaul, Germany, Pannonia, Moesia, Greece, Asia, and Numidia.[117] Of course, many rivers will have been worshiped by the local population without leaving any trace for the historian. It is only by chance that we hear how at Nuceria the river Sarnus was specially favored and had a cult; similarly, at Naples the river Sebethus was worshiped as a god.[118] The immediate background to the popular veneration of rivers lies first in the respect in which they were held. Consequently, rivers are usually mentioned in terms of honor, such as "Father Padus,"[119] or "Father Rhine."[120] Second, there was often an emotional identification with them as markers of domicile or birthplace. An inscribed poem from Moesia shows how a river served as a means of identity: "son of Postumus, prefect of the fleet, I was a Roman child brought up by the Iberian river."[121] Similarly, the funeral monument of Julia Secunda in Rome celebrates her birthplace, "where the Tagus and the noble river Hiberus arise and flow in different directions, one toward the east and one toward the west."[122] From this it was a short step to seeing the local river as a quasi-divine presence.

Few rivers, however, had a bigger or more dramatic economic impact than the Nile. The most important aspect was the annual inundation, lasting generally from June or July to September, which sustained agriculture, fertility, and abundance, all concepts normally associated with rivers.[123] The unique position of the Nile in the pattern and rhythm of life in the Nile valley meant that it was closely bound up with the emotions and psychology of the population. The Nile's gradual inundation was in contrast to the torrential characteristics of many other Mediterranean rivers and produced an enormous amount of interested debate in ancient writers.[124] The Egyptian god Ha'py was originally associated with the river's inundation, which was also linked to the legend of Isis and Osiris, and Nile water was used to purify and invigorate.[125] It is in some respects unclear if devotions were addressed to the river itself or to the inundation. However, a long time before the conquest of Alexander there was a Greek divinization of the Nile, and in the Ptolemaic and Roman period Nilos received worship in the form of a Greek river-god and was represented in the way that rivers normally were in Greco-Roman art: a male, bearded figure generally reclining.[126] The Nile was also associated with Greek mythology, with strong emphasis on his amorous exploits and fecundity; in this way the Ptolemies imparted a Greek ambience to the cult of the Nile.

In the Roman Empire, the Nile was treated with respect, for example, appearing as Nilus Pater in the time of Augustus.[127] Within Egypt, worship concentrated on the river's fertilizing qualities, and the Nile, though lacking a distinctive personality, was associated with Euthenia, that is, the prosperity and plenty brought by its waters. An incantation to Isis in the early second century addresses her as "Ruler of the world, protector and guide, lady of the mouths of seas and rivers. . . . who also bring back the Nile over all the land."[128] Therefore, in Egypt the Nile, through its annual inundation, remained the power that sustained and enriched the country, also enhancing navigability with its generous flow and canals. Outside Egypt, in the imperial period the Nile lost this personality and became the traditional river of Egypt with its trademark crocodile or hippopotamus.[129] It is in this context that we can place the prayer that Pliny offers to the Nile in his Panegyric to Trajan: "If there is any divinity in the land or any spirit in rivers, I invoke that land and the very river."[130] There were important festivals in honor of the Nile in late June or early July when the waters rose, involving offerings of various kinds and prayers; there was also a priest of the Nile. A papyrus of the second century A.D. lists articles for a sacrifice in June to a "most sacred Nile, 1 calf, 2 jars of sweet wine, 16 wafers, 16 garlands, 16 pine cones, 16 cakes, 16 green palm branches, similarly 16 reeds, oil, honey, milk, every spice except frankincense."[131] Official recognition came in the annual sacrifice to the Nile by the Roman prefect of Egypt, continuing the tradition of the Pharaohs. It was also considered improper for the prefect to sail on the river when it was rising.[132] Veneration of the Nile's regenerative qualities was important and notably long-lived, since the Christian religion assimilated some of the features of the worship of the Nile inundation to Christian practice.[133] By the sixth century, the fertilizing river was sustained by "the power of Christ."[134]

Among European rivers, the Rhine and the Danube received many dedications, presumably partly because of their size and length, and the Rhine was particularly popular in the military environment around Argentorate (Strasbourg). As fully fledged gods, rivers were part of the anthropomorphic view of the divine and were represented as men; for example, the river-god Hiberus at

Tarraco received a statue.[135] The city of Tymhiada(?) in Pisidia described the Eurymedon River as a "manifest god."[136] At Aquincum, a legionary legate set up a dedication to Danuvius, while on the bank of the river Q. Veranius(?) had dedicated an altar to the same deity.[137] Elsewhere, the spirit residing within the river received observances as in a dedication in Spain to "genius Baetis."[138] An inscription records how P. Sempronius Tuditanus, consul in 129 B.C. who defeated the Histrians and Iapudians, made some kind of offering to the river Timavus, perhaps for his successful crossing.[139]

Rivers, like springs, were regularly associated with other, more important gods. In an inscription on an altar from Dorylaion dating to the second or third century A.D., the Sangarius River is identified with Poseidon.[140] The Danube and the Rhine are coupled with Jupiter, which will greatly have enhanced their status.[141] A legionary legate, of legion XXX Ulpia, offering a vow for his own safety and that of his family, took no chances by including "Jupiter Optimus Maximus, the ancestral gods, and the protectors of this place, and Ocean and the Rhine."[142] The great rivers of Greece, as Pausanias makes clear, had from early times been treated as divinities in local tradition and worship, as well as in famous mythological stories.

The Romans in common with other peoples apparently attached special significance to the confluence of rivers. A dedication from Croatia on the river Sava near its confluence with the Sann, "Sacred to the Savus and the Adsalluta, P. Ant(onius) Secundus willingly and properly paid his vow," suggests that the meeting of great rivers was a special place.[143] The temple of Augustus at Lugdunum was positioned opposite the confluence of the Rhône and Saône, and it is notable that priests specifically mention this fact—"priest of Rome and Augustus at the altar and temple at the confluence of the Arar and the Rhodanus."[144] Furthermore, among the honors granted outside Italy to Germanicus, who died in A.D. 19, there was to be a commemorative site on the bank of the Rhine near Mogontiacum (Mainz) at the confluence of the Rhine and the Main, close to the monument for Drusus, who had died in 9 B.C. Mogontiacum was an important road junction, the site of a Rhine bridge, and eventually the seat of the governor of Upper Germany. Rites were to be observed on the day of Germanicus's death by the Gallic and German communities living on the left bank of the Rhine, just as they had been ordered to carry out annual observances for Drusus.[145] Mogontiacum was a crucial location both emotionally and topographically at the river confluence and as a place of easy access. We must look here to the psychological importance, to Romans, Gauls, and Germans, of this location amid the rivers, where, as Cassius Dio says, the initial honoring of Drusus consisted of statues and a cenotaph "beside the Rhine itself."[146] What we have is a Roman viewpoint, but I wonder if the Romans were not also exploiting German respect for this confluence (river spirits were worshiped by the German and Gallic peoples). The local people dwelling on the riverbank are involved in the ceremony and in a complex web of cultural and religious beliefs, all brought within the Roman orbit.

It is certainly the case that many peoples with whom the Romans came in contact in the Celtic world had a long tradition of venerating rivers and springs. For example, Nemausus (Nîmes) was named after the sacred spring, which had a sanctuary predating the Roman occupation, and hosted a spirit that acted as patron of the community.[147] The Romans were not imposing an alien idea on indigenous Celtic communities but rather responding to and assimilating local religious practice.[148] In Gaul there was a cult of the river Marne and the Saône, and at Chalon to *dea Souconna*. Similarly, the Meuse and Rhine and many smaller water sources were venerated by the local riverine populations.[149] In Gaul, worship was largely aniconic, and temples to river-divinities were rare, but at the source of the river Seine (Sequana) there was a temple and at the site was discovered an *ex voto* figurine of a riverboat supporting the goddess. It may have been an offering from a river sailor to the goddess for rescue from some danger. Other offerings relate to cures from illnesses. The site was both a sanctuary and a thermal spa. Consequently, one could pray to the goddess for prosperity in trade, a cure from illness, and security from danger.[150] A traditional deity had been partly assimilated to Roman practice. North of Lugdunum too at the sacred springs near Mavilly, local sculptors had carved Roman deities including Jupiter and Neptune, but in a distinctly native style.[151] In another important example from Pouillé in Gaul, a man gratefully fulfills his vow to a river because he had been rescued from some kind of life-threatening danger; although he has a Celtic name, Virtigombo, he has adopted Roman religious practice.[152]

In Britain, Coventina was a water-goddess of Carrawburgh on Hadrian's Wall. Although originally a native goddess, she became assimilated to the Roman ideology of nymphs, and appears as Dea nimfa Coventina in a dedication erected by Mahudus, a German probably serving in the auxiliaries.[153] She had a small shrine in which a well replaced the usual central chamber. In the well were found more than 13,000 Roman coins, with many pots, carved stones, incense burners, and other objects. These votive offerings had continued for centuries, and soldiers, officers, and civilians participated in the worship of Coventina.[154] Africa was also outside the Greco-Roman tradition, and here a consistent water supply was very important, with the veneration of many local water sources.[155] These local cults were eventually largely replaced by Neptune (representing fresh water) and the nymphs, both for normal water sources and for thermal or medicinal springs, since healing waters were important in Africa. In the case of rivers, dedications tend to be addressed to their *genius*.[156] Many of those making dedications were Romanized Africans perhaps recalling earlier Libyan traditions, and it is possible that in rural shrines earlier forms of worship continued. Some local water-divinities did survive, like the mysterious Draco, and Lilleus, who received a dedication at Madaura.[157]

The many small sanctuaries associated with water sources not only confirm the religious feeling generated by the qualities of running water but also contribute to regional history; worship of rivers and springs, often facilitated by the Romans, was consequently part of the history of the Roman Empire.[158] The evidence considered in this section suggests that veneration of rivers and watery sources continued at many levels of society in the Roman world and was not undermined by the increasingly scientific analysis of rivers in terms of their types of fish and purity of water or the increasing ability of Roman engineering to control and channel rivers for the benefit of the state.

One river deserves special mention because of its unique position in the Roman world: the Tiber.

5   THE TIBER

Among the watery divinities of Italy, the Tiber was supreme and had a special place in Roman affections, combining three important elements in Roman life by serving as a divinity, a legend, and a national symbol. There was a truly Roman cult present from early times in which the river itself was the object of worship. The river was a dynamic force, with the power to sustain life in its fertile valley, provide drinking water, bring trade and prosperity on its navigable waters, remove the detritus of the city of Rome, but also bring destruction with its surging floods. Therefore, ordinary people needed the river's help and approval through its 199-mile course and across its great basin stretching for 6,847 square miles through north-central Italy. From an early period, the Tiber was seen as a healing river, because many votive dedications have been discovered in numerous places in the riverbed indicating attempts to find relief from various types of illnesses.[159]

Furthermore, numerous riverine dwellers, such as boatmen and fishermen, who made a living from the Tiber, made offerings to it. On 8 June each year the Ludi Piscatorii were held by the urban praetor across the Tiber opposite the Forum Boarium on behalf of the fishermen of the Tiber, "whose catch does not go to market but to a large extent to the area of Vulcan, for this kind of small fish is given to this god on behalf of humankind." These fishermen through their homage showed their gratitude to the river, and they formed a *collegium* in imperial times.[160] Although part of the catch was destined for Vulcan, the festival was based around the river, and Vulcan had no role as a god of the Tiber.[161] There was also a festival on 27 August in honor of Volturnus, who, according to the *Fasti Vallenses* in Rome, was a river-god. He may have been regarded as a god of all rivers.[162]

The Tiber could bring literal as well as metaphorical cleanliness, though the role of the river as a purificatory agent is controversial since the ancient sources are not clear.[163] The sacred waters of the river flowed down to the sea, conveying away from the city anything that was held to be a stain or contamination. This seems to be the point of the obscure festival of the *Argea* on 15 and 16 March when human effigies were thrown into the Tiber from the *pons Sublicius*, representing the purification of the citizens from each part of the city.[164] Similarly, at the end of the Vestalia festival in June, the accumulated refuse from the temple of Vesta was ceremonially deposited in the Tiber and so conveyed away to the sea.[165] Unwelcome prodigies and anything out of the ordinary could be speedily disposed of with the benefit of a purifying rite. State priests organized all these activities, showing official involvement in dealing with the divine element of the river. However, the practice of throwing bodies into the river, such as those of Tiberius Gracchus and his supporters, and of various emperors who had been murdered, was probably a spontaneous act by political enemies. It was an expression of contempt and an attempt to humiliate and deny burial rather than any act of purification.[166]

State involvement in riverine religious observances can be seen elsewhere in Rome, and worship may have been concentrated in certain areas of the city. There were three areas where the Tiber name was attached—the Campus Tiberinus, that is, part of the Campus Martius at the sacred precinct Tarentum; the Forum Boarium, where the *vicus Tiberini* may have been situated; and the *insula Tiberina*.[167] Traces of the river cult in the Campus Martius appear in the Ludi Saeculares, since some of the rites were conducted specifically on the riverbank. It may be that worship was originally conducted on the alluvial plain at low water because this allowed people to penetrate the sacred watery domain from which they were normally excluded. The likely site of the Ludi Piscatores was at the river bend opposite the Forum Boarium and Cloaca Maxima, where the *vicus Tiberini* was probably located.[168] The Tiber island (*insula Tiberina*), which because of alluvial action at the bend in the river seemed to emerge directly from riverine activity, was sacred because of the old cult of the Tiber and was particularly associated with healing processes, becoming the site of the temple of the god of healing Asclepius, which was erected circa 291 B.C.[169]

There are many grateful dedications to the god, and later there was a shrine to Tiberinus on the island with a festival on 8 December.[170] Numerous *ex voto* finds have been discovered opposite it.

Despite elements of state intervention, it was probably ordinary people living in close proximity to the river who carried out most acts of homage to the Tiber, not just in Rome, as the finds of coins in the river testify, but also throughout the Tiber valley.[171] Doubtless many nameless people threw cups, coins, and other small offerings into the river. They did not have the resources for expensive memorials, and there are very few examples of dedications in honor of the Tiber. When we do have one example from Horta (Orte) on the Tiber, it belonged to a man of status, a veteran soldier and imperial reservist, Sex. Atusius Priscus, who claims that he "was first of all to set up to Tiberinus the altar that he had vowed as a soldier."[172] Furthermore, there is little evidence that the Tiber was associated with other gods; no temple or *cella* was provided for Tiberinus at least until the second century A.D., and there was no formal cult statue, though of course the river appears as a sturdy, mature man in artistic representations. There may even be a hint of cynicism in the upper classes about Tiberinus in the story about how the hated emperor Elagabalus was nicknamed Tiberinus after his body had been thrown in the river.[173]

The name "Tiberis" or "Tiberinus" was certainly ancient, since it appears in the augural prayer cited by Cicero.[174] Other forms, Thybris or Tybris, also appear, and Roman writers were unsure about the history of the name, explaining that an original name, Albula, had been changed on the hypothesis that a Tiberinus, a king of Alba, had drowned while crossing the river.[175] Eventually, while *Tiberis* was normally used to describe the river, Tiberinus, or Pater Tiberinus particularly served to identify the god, as the original worship of the river itself was overlaid at least by the second century B.C. by developed Greek anthropomorphic concepts of the river-god, through which people worshiped a god dwelling in the river rather than the river.[176]

The Tiber was also linked to the numerous foundation myths of Rome and traditional fables of Romulus and Remus; the river and the characteristics of its course played its part in what Livy described as the fateful founding of a mighty city and the beginning of the greatest empire next to heaven itself, and fresh water was integral to the traditions of Rome.[177] The river Tiber in the works of Roman writers is either specifically or by implication a god. So, Martial refers to "sacred Tiber."[178] In the *Aeneid* the Tiber, as the god of the place, appears to Aeneas, wearing a gray linen cloak and with reeds in his hair.[179] He promises Aeneas ultimate victory and the founding of a mighty realm. In return, the Tiber will receive great honors from the Romans; most loved by heaven of all rivers, he flows though the rich farmland and sustains the life of powerful cities. Aeneas, taking water from the river in his hands, accepts the prophecy and greets Father Tiber as the ruler of all the western waters.[180] As we have already seen, it could be argued that the venerable Tiber was enhanced by the waters of other rivers in central Italy.[181]

The Tiber, with its status as an object of religious homage, its place in the foundation myth of Rome, and its impact on the lives of many people, was a ready-made national symbol. In human form, the Tiber appeared on imperial coins and was represented on important temples such as Mars Ultor, where he emerges as a strong mentor and guardian of the Roman state and a symbol and guarantor of Rome's prosperity and success.[182] Of course, a river with these powerful qualities, which flowed though a mighty city, could be seen as demonstrating the superiority of the dominant imperial power. Even a simple poetic phrase, as when Statius speaks of the "Thybris lord of rivers" (*ductor aquarum*), could contain the idea of Rome's imperial domination with implications of cultural and environmental imperialism.[183]

The sanctity of the Tiber usefully gives us a perspective on Roman society and beliefs. Overall, it seems that the upper classes and emperors viewed the river as a great national symbol, where it could acquire a personality in the Greek style. It was not of enormous significance in the religious practice of the Roman state, since it had no temple and no cult statue. It was ordinary people who lived in the Tiber valley or in the riverine districts in Rome who had real psychological and emotional connection with the river, a river that they both needed and feared. And they have left few memorials. It is a reasonable point that throughout the empire particular interest and religious significance lay with the local rivers and springs, which had a more direct bearing on life in rural communities and on the water supply of towns and cities.

6   RIVERINE LEGENDS

Myths help to define and interpret human experience of the environment, however exaggerated the stories may be. Rivers were ubiquitous, highly visible, and sometimes dangerous, and local communities wanted to claim ownership of them, assert territoriality, magnify their river's identity, and rationalize their relationship with running water. Therefore, they gave rivers human form and, where possible, associated them with legendary stories, which enhanced not only the river's status but also the community's individual identity. Colorful stories of riverine mythology and the exploits of rivers that had assumed anthropomorphic form, historical associations, and a complex cultural and intellectual process sustained the visual and spiritual image of rivers that was so common to many.

Writers routinely make rivers men, suggesting that they live in caverns and have families. They are often addressed directly with questions or appeals and, in turn, can speak to others. They can have debates and arguments with outsiders and one another.[184] They witness historical events, such as invasions and battles, and can at times intervene.[185] They can express and represent patriotic sentiments, as does the Trebia in argument with Hannibal in Silius Italicus's epic of the Punic Wars.[186] They can even address an emperor, as does the Volturnus with his long tawny locks while leaning on the bridge built by Domitian over his stream.[187] They can act as an ally of emperors and take part in major historical events. So, in traditional panegyric the Tiber acted as Constantine's ally at the battle of the Milvian Bridge.[188] They are therefore potentially powerful agents for good or ill and, like other deities, could benefit a local community. They might pay tribute,[189] watch the military situation, or even ferry extraneous rubbish and corruption, as Juvenal imagines the Orontes emptying its filthy contents into the pure Tiber.[190]

The idea of a river in human form was of course a literary device in order to enliven a narrative or add poetic color. But the fact that writers had their own agenda does not rob the concept of wider significance. For the idea of rivers in the shape of a man was deep-seated in popular consciousness and fitted easily into the existing ideology of deities intervening in human affairs. Personification was also part of an intellectual process in illustrating or reinforcing a historical point or judgment, which was often bound up with local life and culture. Therefore, personification blended with the divine spirit of the watery environment and linked directly to river legends, in which well-known rivers were portrayed as forceful agents in either the local or the international arena.

In the colorful riverine legends, anthropomorphic rivers generally mimic the behavior of men, appearing as lovers, rapists, and pursuers of women, as warriors, healers, prophecy makers, state builders, and protectors of local communities; in this way they could ensure the status and even survival of people who identified with the local river and who might owe their livelihood to it. In this fantasy world, there was a deep yearning in local communities for strong protectors and people who could intercede with the deities who might intervene in human life at any time. Riverine mythology has much to tell us about the sincere veneration of rivers by local people, which was then greatly elaborated by sophisticated writers. The stories confirm the special element in rivers that will also have been an object of reverence in smaller rivers and springs that we do not often hear about in ancient writers, though we have seen some sign of this in the inscriptions noted previously and the numerous dedications to nymphs and springs unacknowledged in literature.

It is in this context that we need to understand the importance in Pausanias's work of the theme of rivers and legends and divine intervention.[191] Pausanias's survey of Greek communities is woven around topography and surviving monuments, which were often associated with legendary events and could then be linked to local history and tradition, producing a coherent and self-contained topographical description and cultural analysis based on the local river and the known landscape. As Pausanias points out, all rivers are different, and the many stories about them reflect different regional traditions. However, we need to identify the common themes in these stories, and assess the importance of Greek riverine mythology that persisted to the imperial period.

Pausanias's description of the river Alpheios sums up many of the characteristics and qualities traditionally associated with rivers. "As you arrive at Olympia you are already at the water of the Alpheios, the greatest of rivers in its volume of water, and the most pleasure-giving to the sight, because there are seven important rivers among the streams that run into it." His account encompasses the river's size, appearance, sources, and tributaries, which help establish the geographical framework of the entire local area and the position of nearby cities and sanctuaries.[192] From this emerge the many associated popular legends that underpin Pausanias's narrative.

The role of the rivers in these legends takes several forms. In some cases, the river itself in the shape of a man is a leading player. The river then performed actions that affected the surrounding area or fathered children who subsequently participated in important events. Therefore, the river, directly or indirectly, actually made the legend, and more important rivers, such as the Asopos and Alpheios, were particularly active. Children of rivers were autochthonous and could claim rights over the land in question. Asopos, a legendary son of Poseidon, discovered in the Corinthia the river that was then named after him and bore several local nymphs, who were later abducted by Zeus. The spring on the Acrocorinth was allegedly a bribe to Sisyphos for information about the episode.[193] Alpheios, a huntsman, had a dalliance with Arethusa, but she did not want to marry and crossed over to the island of Ortygia opposite Syracuse, where she turned into a water spring. In pursuit, Alpheios turned into a river, and Pausanias notes with approval the story that the Alpheios flowed uncontaminated through the sea to mingle its waters with the spring of Arethusa.[194]

Many other rivers fathered children—the Asterion, the Inachos, the Kaikinos (who bore a famous boxer), the Kephisos, the Maeander (in Asia), and the

Peneios.[195] These stories included the idea of propagation and renewal, associated with the fertility of river valleys. Great rivers by their activities enhanced the fame of the areas through which they flowed and made sure that they were thoroughly integrated in Greek cultural tradition. On other occasions, the river was a witness to supernatural events or accidentally provided the location as the story was played out—for example, the hunt of the Erymanthean Boar beside the river Erymanthos.[196]

Common legendary riverine themes involve love, pursuit, and abduction, in many cases because rivers seemed to offer an escape route or a means of rapid travel, either along them or through their depths. In one story Pluto carried Persephone off beside the Kephisos to his subterranean kingdom.[197] We also find stories of overwhelming grief, where a weeping person could even be changed into a spring or river. The legend of the spring Peirene was that as she wept for her son Kenchrias, who had been accidentally killed by Artemis, she turned into a spring.[198] This may be related to the importance of a water provider in a country usually short of water. The love stories involving ill-stared or unrequited love and dramatic change convey in exciting terms the story of everyday emotional life connected with the watery environment, in which there was eternal movement over the same course. For example, in Achaea the spring of Argyra and the river Selemnos gave rise to the legend that Selemnos, a shepherd, had been in love with the nymph Argyra but died when she eventually rejected him. Aphrodite turned him into a river and granted forgetfulness.[199] A splendid story combines the important notion of the mingling of sources of running water and water as a kind of deliverance.

Some legends explained the characteristics of a river, its flow, course, and direction, or even its color. So, the river Po's trademark poplar trees were associated with the lament of the daughters of the Sun for their dead brother Phaethon. The fact that the Inachos, Kephisos, and Asterion dried up in summer was ascribed to the anger of Poseidon because they had helped to grant Hera suzerainty over the Argolid. A spring near Ioppe in Judaea flowed red allegedly because Perseus had washed off the blood of the sea monster there. The very direction of the course of the Kephisos was said to be the work of Herakles.[200] This kind of story might have some root in a rational effort to explain local riverine phenomena. Similarly, legends of river monsters might owe something to popular ideas about enormous fish that lurked in the depths.[201]

Sometimes an interesting tension appears between local willingness to accept a distinguished legend and a less dramatic explanation, which of course would not bring such honor and possibly extra visitor revenue to an area. Lucian tells us about one local phenomenon; the river Adonis, which flowed from Mount Libanus and into which Adonis had allegedly fallen and stained with his blood, was said on certain days to flow blood red into the sea in memory of him. But Lucian discovered another account from a local man from the town of Byblos, who said that the river flowed from the mountain, which had tawny red soil and that on these days the winds blew strongly and churned up the water so that the soil came to the surface making it seem like blood.[202]

We also find that a legendary character or event played a part in establishing a water source's name or nickname. For example, the story of Makaria, a daughter of Herakles, who killed herself so that Athens could win a victory, explains the name of the spring Makaria at Marathon and is also part of the early history and noble tradition of the Athenian state.[203] On a lighter note, after Herakles had destroyed Elis, the women prayed to Athene to make them conceive as soon as they slept with their men, to repopulate the country. Their prayer was granted and "as both the women and the men experienced extreme pleasure in that first intercourse, they named the place Sweet and they called the river that flows past it in their dialect Sweetwater."[204] Rivers brought authenticity and honor to local names.

Elsewhere, rivers were named directly after the action of some legendary figure, for example the Balyra (Lyrethrow) in Messenia got its name because Thamyris threw his harp into it when he was blinded.[205] In some cases, a legend was woven into local customs and names. So, at the shrine of Triklarian Artemis, a strange custom had prevailed in antiquity. Two lovers Melanippos and Komaitho, forbidden to marry by their parents, met for secret sex in the sanctuary of Artemis. The goddess responded with plagues; the oracular response demanded the execution of the two lovers and the annual sacrifice of the boy and the virgin with the most beautiful bodies. Consequently, the nearby river was named Implacable. But later the city was rescued from the cruel obligation, and the river assumed its name Placation.[206]

The cleansing power of running water is conspicuous in many riverine legends. In a literal sense, Herakles famously diverted the waters of the Menios to clear away the dung of Augeas's animals.[207] But in a supernatural sense, water brought invigorating purity and release from contamination. Two rivers in Arcadia contain the root of the verb "to wash" (*louein*): the Lymax, where Rhea washed herself after giving birth to Zeus, and the Lousios, where Zeus was washed at birth.[208] Those who wished to consult the oracle of Trophonios, apart from other ritual observances, washed in the river Herkyna. Before entering the oracle they drank first the water of Forgetfulness to purify their minds, and then the water of Memory, so as to remember the entire experience.[209] At the spring Kanathos in the Argolid, local legend had it that Hera washed every year to renew her virginity. Ritual purification in the Anigros caused the river's unpleasant smell, as it took onto itself infected material.[210] The strong belief in the purifying power of water can also be seen in the story explaining the course of the river Helikon, which flowed underground for a distance. The women who had murdered Orpheus tried to wash away his blood in the river, which dived underground "in case its water should purify murderers."[211] The mystical, elevating power of rivers or welling springs appears too in the belief that water contributed to or at least accompanied prophetic powers.[212] In day-to-day life, the special status of running water and ritual washing is illustrated by an inscription from Keos setting out rules to stop people from misusing a spring on the way to the temple of Demeter.[213]

The cleansing effect of rivers was, of course, also part of Roman ideology. Therefore, Aeneas could not touch religious objects until he had washed away the blood of battle with running water.[214] Purificatory rites normally were to be carried out with river water.[215] In this way, we can make sense of the legend in which a Sabine, receiving a prophecy that the country of whoever sacrificed a white cow would establish a great empire, went to Rome to carry out the sacrifice at the altar of Diana. However, the temple doorkeeper deceived him by pointing out that he must first wash in river water and directed him to the Tiber. The doorkeeper then sacrificed the cow, so establishing Rome's domination of the world.[216] The cleansing power of water and ritual washing may have contributed to later Christian baptismal practice.[217]

Why are so many legends associated with rivers? The answers must surely lie in the ubiquitous nature of rivers, which extended over long distances, were ever present, but also constantly changing; they were often considered divine, life enhancing with the power to effect recovery from disease; river names often had important local connections but carried within them the threat of destructive flooding and therefore needed to be supplicated; stories of immersion in rivers and metamorphosis through their agency may be related to more profound ideas of death and redemption. Many stories are clearly related to the appearance or disappearance of water sources, or the discovery of a new river, or a water source endlessly renewed. Linked to all this was the strong mythological tradition about the rivers of the underworld. In some ways, these behaved as normal rivers would, but they had special characteristics as suited their role and status in the realms of the dead. The river Styx (the only female river, though in part a spring), which was thought to flow in Arcadia, was a preeminent mythological location, with its water presumed to be fatal to both men and animals.[218] The Arcadians swore oaths by it. The Acheron in Thesprotia was also identified as one of the underground rivers, along with Lethe, the river of forgetfulness. All the rivers of the underworld constituted an impenetrable barrier, often being seen as rivers of fire stoking up the flames of hell.[219]

Despite occasional moments of skepticism, Pausanias clearly believed that riverine legends were a crucial part of the rhythms of Greek society, and continued to be relevant to any account of regional history in the imperial period, in which myth, legend, and heroic genealogies were used to provide a sense of identity and purpose.[220] It is an intriguing question how the Romans reacted to such stories, which must have been prevalent when they occupied Greece. They seem to have left them undisturbed and did not attempt to claim them or give them a Roman dimension. In fact, their interests lay elsewhere, namely in the domination and exploitation of major rivers valuable to them in commercial or strategic terms, and through which they could exercise and assert their control.[221]

Instead, Greek riverine legends passed into polite letters in Rome. Pliny shows only limited interest in the legendary associations of rivers, although he mentions a number of stories concerning important figures or incidents in mythology connected with rivers.[222] He is critical of the gullibility of the Greeks in terms of watery legends, referring to "the extravagant lies of Greece about these (legendary serpents) and the river Lixus," and claiming that Greek myths often changed their location.[223] Nevertheless, Pliny himself is quite capable of telling us that rivers flowed backward on Nero's death.[224]

Ovid in the *Metamorphoses* used the traditional exploits of Greek river-gods to illustrate his topic.[225] His main themes are familiar: love; pursuit; rivers with divine powers that can bring about transformations; according to Ovid, rivers have families and human emotions; other rivers share their feelings; they arrange weddings; rivers live under their streams in vast caverns from which many other rivers start to flow; nymphs actually live in the stream and wait upon the rivers in the same way that servants or young daughters would; the traditional sylvan setting for rivers and pools inspires veneration and awe. For Ovid, rivers usually appear in the shape of a man, although Acheloüs has the horns of a bull. Despite his generally playful approach, Ovid vividly describes the potential destructive power of rivers when he depicts the Acheloüs in flood.[226] In Ovid's version of the story of Alpheios and Arethusa, the river falls in love with Arethusa as she swims naked in a romantic pool, which is silent, smooth, and clear, shady and cool, surrounded by pleasant foliage. But Alpheios murmurs from the depth and pursues Arethusa in the form of a man. When Arethusa becomes a spring, Alpheios threatens to catch her by turning back into a river, until she plunges into a separate cavern and eventually emerges in Sicily.[227] This gave rise to a large group of stories about rivers and springs flowing under the sea or through lakes, while maintaining their individual qualities uncontaminated. This kind of story was just as relevant in Italy as in Greece, because of the fear of local people that seasonal rivers that dried up during the hot summer months would not reappear.[228]

What place do riverine stories and legends like those related by Pausanias and Ovid have in a work of history? They seem to have little to do with a particular view of history, concerned with establishing facts and narrating events. Yet history is also about people and their thought world. In a recently discovered inscription, we find Hadrian writing in A.D. 137/8 to the small Greek community of Naryka asserting that no one will dispute its status as a *polis*. Among the supporting reasons, he cites the fact that "you have been mentioned by certain of the most celebrated poets, both Roman and Greek, as Narykians, and they also name certain of the heroes as having started from your *polis*."[229] In the cultural context of the ancient world, an appearance in literary works and links with legendary events or people often served as the early history of rural communities in Greece and Italy and a kind of proof of identity. And people never lost interest in watery sources, rivers, and springs. Pausanias chose to include many of these stories, and the prevalence of riverine legends shows a continuing fascination and a need to see rivers as quasi-human and approachable because they were so important in everyday life, even in cities distant from rivers but which perhaps received river water brought by aqueducts. Pausanias portrays a layer of Greek local life below the level normally noticed by the imperial administration. The point of connection is that communities had to compete as they strove to catch the emperor's attention, receive benefactions, and move ahead of their rivals in civic status. Life-sustaining, conspicuous waterways, and the nexus of traditional stories attached to them, helped to establish identity and territory, enhance public standing, tourism, and revenue. Each local community had its own mythological tradition but would also want to claim a wider audience for its myths, which could serve to put it on the map. Riverine culture was the product of, and responded to, a variety of emotions, extending from simple respect and awe to the exploitation of business opportunities; but even those with a vested economic interest took the local traditions very seriously.

7   ART

One of the most common artistic forms in the ancient world is that of a reclining male figure representing a river or river-god.[230] Numerous examples have survived in various media, though the most striking are figures carved in the round as individual statues or as part of a larger group. Such elaborate artwork is comparatively rare, but there are also several important mosaics, some of which probably go back to original paintings. The painting of rivers in rural scenes was often part of private decoration in the villas of the rich. According to Vitruvius, among the styles of Pompeian painting in covered walkways "they use different landscapes, fitting the image to the appropriate characteristics of different places; for they paint harbors, promontories, shores, rivers, springs, straits, shrines, groves, mountains, cattle, and shepherds."[231] However, the most common source of river illustrations in both quality and chronological spread is certainly the coinage, principally coins minted by Greek cities in the empire as well as those issued directly by the Roman government.

The depiction of rivers in the Greco-Roman world, though commonplace, inspired interest in contemporary observers. Dio Chrysostomos, commenting on the skill of artists, noted that not only did they represent gods in human shape but they also sometimes depicted rivers as men and springs as women, often with certain attributes that helped to identify them. Typically, a river had a beard and was crowned with reeds or tamarisks, since these plants enjoyed the watery environment.[232] In a very interesting passage, Aelian, writing in the late second or early third century A.D., discusses the nature of rivers and their streams and how communities took differing views when they made representations of them. It is a splendid evocation of the enthusiasm among Greek communities (and this was apparently still relevant toward the end of the second century A.D.) to depict their rivers while offering acts of homage:

> For the Stemphalians depict as bulls the Erasinos and the Metopes, the Lacedaimonians the Eurotas, the Sicyonians and Phliasians the Asopos, and the Argives the Kephisos. The Psophidians (depict) the Eurymanthos in the shape of a man and the Heraeans the Alpheios. The Cheronesians from Knidos treat the same river in the same way. The Athenians depict the Kephisos with the face of a man, with horns in the background. In Sicily, the Syracusans depict the Anapos as a man but worship the spring Kuane with the image of a woman. The Aegestaioi worship the Porpax, the Kremisos, and the Telmessos in the form of men. The people of Akragas sacrifice to the river that shares the city's name in the form of a beautiful youth. The same people set up a statue in Delphi carved in ivory and inscribed on it the name of the river. The statue is of a boy.[233]

It is unclear exactly how the portrayal of rivers by the Greeks and the Romans developed from zoomorphic, using bulls with a man's head, to full anthropomorphic images.[234] Earliest representations in the seventh century B.C. are of the river Acheloüs in bull form; bulls perhaps represented strength and unpredictability.[235] In the sixth century appeared an intermediate style depicting the river with human face or mask complemented with horns. The earliest fully anthropomorphic image (a bronze figurine from Euboea from the second quarter of the fifth century) shows the Acheloüs standing as a bearded figure with no horns, holding a cornucopia.[236] His fruit and waters were particularly relevant to riverine communities and also to colonies in southern Italy and Sicily. Thereafter, not much change occurred in the iconography, and the Romans did not interfere. Probably in the late fifth and early fourth centuries, images of reclining rivers became established, and eventually these were to predominate throughout the Roman period, though they do not appear in the coinage of Hellenistic cities.[237]

In the anthropomorphic depiction of water sources in Greco-Roman art, there was a fundamental distinction between a river, which was almost always depicted as a man, and a spring, which was always feminine. Within the male river category, there was a further distinction between an older, corpulent, bearded man and a younger, slimmer man, sometimes (though rarely) without a beard. This distinction owed more to tradition and artistic variation than to any attempt to differentiate bigger and smaller rivers.[238] In the case of springs, the representative nymph was usually portrayed standing or seated, often holding an urn from which came a flow of water. A billowing robe could also suggest watery movement. Hellenistic and Roman art confirmed the connection between nymphs and water.[239] Roman artists normally portrayed rivers as men with no animal characteristics; the format was either a head or bust, or a figure standing, seated, or reclining; sometimes the figure floats, swims, or emerges from waves.[240]

Typical riverine characteristics come across most clearly in statues carved in the round.[241] The male figures are shown reclining or semireclining on one elbow, or sometimes supported on a rock, with both legs stretched out, or with one bent beneath them. They are usually naked, or seminaked, with the lower body covered by a cloak, which can help to suggest the undulating flow of water. These images convey the idea of the languid but potentially enormous power of rivers, and we are also reminded of their tremendous reputation in legend for procreation. The generally benevolent demeanor of the river as depicted may indicate an apotropaic element, as river dwellers would pray to the river to avoid flooding. Various attributes and symbols accompany the reclining figure and indicate the watery environment. Long, flowing locks of hair suggest water, while the scene sometimes contains rocks and an urn (as we saw before), which may have water flowing from it. Reeds and other aquatic plants adorn the god's head.

Artists also depict rivers with attributes showing the benefits they conferred on the riverine community or the whole country. So, we find the horn of plenty, symbolizing fertility and prosperity, and perhaps again suggesting rivers' traditional role in producing offspring. There was a link with myth since the origin of the association of rivers and the horn of plenty was the story that Hercules had torn off one of the horns of Acheloüs when the river was in the form of a bull, and this was transformed into the horn of plenty.[242] More directly, grain and other crops were used to symbolize the fertilizing power of rivers. Rivercraft or a ship's oar symbolized the river's role in providing a thoroughfare for transport and the movement of goods. That these artistic forms and symbols in depicting rivers became a stereotype in the Roman Empire does not necessarily deprive them of significance.[243]

Only the Tiber and the Nile, and also Oceanos, which had riverine characteristics and in mythology was regarded as the father of all rivers, had specific attributes associated with them.[244] The Tiber was marked out by a wolf and the twins Romulus and Remus, along with the usual reed crown, steering oar, and urn. Once established, the iconography and attributes of the river did not change much throughout the imperial period. The Tiber is represented by several full-size statues, the most famous of which is that now in the Louvre, probably of late-Hadrianic date (for a sixteenth-century representation by Baldassare Peruzzi, see figure 4).[245] The by now traditional attributes of the Tiber appear on coins issued by Antoninus Pius; the river is an old man, half-draped and crowned with reeds, reclining either on an urn, from which water flows, or on a rock; he holds a reed in his left hand while the right rests on the prow of a ship (figure 5).[246] The appearance of the Tiber in the pediment of the Augustan Temple of Mars Ultor and also in the forum of Nerva gives some idea of the importance of the Tiber's public perception in human form.[247] Furthermore, the river's watchful role in Roman life can be seen on the arch of Constantine, where, after the defeat of Maxentius at the Milvian Bridge, the Tiber observes the drowning emperor.[248]

As we have seen, the representation of the Nile was directly created by the Greeks and did not correspond in any significant way with the religion of the Pharaonic age. The Romans took over his representation, although there are numerous variations. The earliest known Roman image dates from 25–19 B.C. The river appears as a male, bearded figure generally in a reclining pose on a rock or sometimes on a crocodile or a hippopotamus. However, some representations on coins show the Nile as a seated figure, which seems to be especially connected with the inundation.[249] The famous statue of the Nile in the round at Rome probably dates from the first century A.D. The Nile occasionally

FIGURE 4. *Drawing of the Tiber river-god by Baldassare Peruzzi (1496–1536).*
The Tiber is depicted with the horn of plenty, Romulus and Remus, and a she-wolf.
The model was probably the ancient statue of the Tiber now in the Louvre Museum.
The drawing is held in the British Museum. Image copyright © Trustees of the
British Museum, used by permission of the Trustees of the British Museum.

has reeds, a garland of roses or lotus, and sometimes leans on the sphinx; his favored attribute is the horn of plenty and the inundation of the river explains the concept of fruitful fertility (for the statue of the Nile from the Palazzo Senatorio in Rome, see figure 6).[250] The annual inundation also came to have certain attributes, and from the reign of Vespasian sixteen small children are represented climbing over the river's recumbent form.[251] A famous mosaic from Praeneste shows not the Nile itself but the effects of the Nile inundation with scenes from the Nile valley; it perhaps dates from the second century B.C. and is likely to be based on an original painting.[252] Here the artist or artists set out to show the wide range of activities in the river valley and the surrounding hills and to exhibit the plants, animals, and geographical layout of Egypt. It offers a panorama with a bird's-eye view of the Nile from its source in Africa through Egypt to the Delta. In the lower part of its course, the river is in flood, indicating the annual inundation and the attendant activities and celebrations. Portions of dry land have various temples, priests, and, in one case, a nilometer. There are also dwellings for the rural population. Numerous boats appear on the water, including small papyrus craft for local trips and larger merchant

FIGURE 5. Sestertius of Antoninus Pius, A.D. 140–44, depicting the bearded figure of the Tiber reclining on an urn from which water flows; he places his right hand on a ship and holds a reed in his left. Reverse legend: TIBERIS SC (RIC III, p. 118, no. 706). Image reproduced by kind permission of Spink and Son, London.

FIGURE 6. Statue of the Nile river-god from the Palazzo Senatorio, Rome. The Nile is depicted leaning on a sphinx, with the horn of plenty. The statue, along with a matching statue of the Tiber, was originally part of the decoration of the baths of Constantine on the Quirinal Hill and was moved in 1518. By permission of iStockphoto.com.

ships. Ship-borne hunters pursue crocodiles and hippopotamus. At the bottom of the mosaic in the Delta area, a fully manned warship is depicted, and an alfresco party is in progress under a pergola, while nearby soldiers and priests assemble at a large temple. Throughout the mosaic, there are numerous local fauna. The river Nile is central in the artist's conception, since its annual inundation brought fertility and prosperity to the country and many activities took place around it—fishing, agriculture, hunting, and social and civic life, which were conditioned by the riverine characteristics and environment. Here, despite the flood the river is the friend of the people, and the temples suggest the religious context of the natural environment.[253]

Other major rivers assumed human form in the traditional Roman way. The Danube made a great impression on the ancients,[254] and although it had not been represented before the Roman era, it came to be venerated in the empire as a bearded man with naked torso, accompanied by a cornucopia and aquatic plants, occasionally with his hand on the prow of a ship. Sometimes he leans on his arm, from which water flows. It is rare for a river figure to participate in the action, but on Trajan's Column the Danube rises from his stream and seems to usher the legionaries across the bridge.[255] The Rhine in the few surviving representations of the Roman period appears with long beard and hair and horns, and sometimes also crab's claws. These depictions embrace two main themes: the Rhine as bringer of prosperity to riverine communities, and the reality of Roman control of the waterway, expressed especially in imperial coinage.[256]

The Euphrates had no specific attribute, but because of its majestic and tumultuous course had been from early antiquity an object of veneration to riverine communities. Anthropomorphic representations may be linked to the arrival of the Roman legions, and in Roman art the Euphrates was depicted as a bearded figure, seminude, often sitting on a rock, with an urn and flowing water. The Tigris is represented in much the same way.[257] For other rivers we have less evidence,[258] but the typical representation of the river-god spread quite widely in Gaul, modeled perhaps on representations of the Tiber.[259] There are few representations of the Rhône, but the river seems to have gained human form without the usual nexus of myth and legend and appears in the traditional way as a bearded man holding a reed or urn. Lugdunum is closely linked to the river.[260] Among the important rivers of Spain, the Hiberus is known as a river-divinity from only one inscription (with a fragment of a marble statue in human form) from Tarragona; the base was inscribed *flumen Hiberus* with water flowing from an urn.[261] In Italy the Eridanos (or Padus) in Roman ideology appears with Italia, and is sometimes characterized by a swan and an urn.[262]

Coins are the greatest source of evidence for the representation of rivers in human form and offered a significantly different medium.[263] The designer had a smaller area in which to represent the river and ensure that it could be recognized, but possibly the opportunity to blend the river into a wider scene. Coin types, despite the traditional format, manage to retain vitality in the depiction of rivers. In those coins minted for the Roman government, the only river to appear consistently, from the Flavians onward, is the Tiber. Vespasian celebrated the river as one of the great symbols of Rome. Coins of Antoninus Pius and Marcus Aurelius show the Tiber with his hand on a ship, which might indicate the role of the river in bringing food to Rome.[264] The general import is the fertility, prosperity, and wealth that come to Rome from the river. In one coin of Pius, the river appears in designs showing the arrival of the sacred snake of Asclepius, perhaps suggesting the river's association with healing.[265] We also have a unique type showing the Tiber and Nile shaking hands, with the legend *homonoia*. This may symbolize imperial concord in the cooperation between Egypt as a supplier of grain and the Tiber as the waterway that brought it to Rome (figure 7).[266] The Nile appears in its own right in a coin of Hadrian showing its famous attributes associated with fertility.[267] Other coins depicting rivers have a more grandiose style, and there is a strong military and imperialistic element since a river could signify a defeated country, and mastery over the river demonstrated Roman territorial control.

The coins struck by Greek cities under the empire were an expression not of autonomy from Rome but of local identity and tradition, in which a river was often a city's emblem. A large number of these coins celebrated local water sources in one way or another, either with horned animal representations or in human form, generally as bearded men. This tradition was maintained throughout the Roman period.[268] For example, we have a notable coin of Istros in the Roman period with the bearded river Istros reclining.[269] Many coins have a legend specifically linking the river to the town, for example, Prusias on Hypios (the bearded river holds a horn or plenty and leans on a rock), Imbrasos at Samos (the river-god has a reed and horn of plenty), Stratonicea/Hadrianopolis (the river-god Caicus has a reed and water container), Antioch and the river Anthios (the young river-god has a horn of plenty and a water jug, and behind is a reed).[270] At Antioch on the Orontes, a completely new dimension of river representation was introduced, in which the river was closely associated with Tyche (Fortune) of Antioch. There is a statue of Tyche as the city's protecting goddess with the Orontes swimming beneath her feet. So the city dominates the river but seems to gain strength from it.[271] The Maeander was particularly important and was associated with many cities throughout its

FIGURE 7. *Bronze coin of Antoninus Pius, A.D. 154, minted in Alexandria, depicting the Tiber standing, holding a reed and clasping the right hand of the Nile, who stands opposite holding ears of corn and the horn of plenty. Reverse legend:* TIBERIS OMONOIA *(J. M. C. Toynbee,* The Hadrianic School: A Chapter in the History of Art *(Cambridge, 1934), plate XVI.6 = Catalogue of Greek Coins in the British Museum: Alexandria, p. 138, no. 1167). Copyright © 1934 Cambridge University Press. Image reprinted with permission of Cambridge University Press.*

valley; with only minor variations, it appears bearded, recumbent, with reeds and a horn of plenty. It was most notably honored by Antioch, and the identification of the city through its river comes out clearly in an inscription offering thanks to a high priest of Asia who came from Antioch "from the Maeander."[272] In Sicily river images on coin types are particularly frequent, though this may be largely due to the eponymous character of most rivers, since many cities were named after them. Such coin types may not have a great religious significance, but they do show how rivers were thought to represent a city, to the extent that a community might resent an outsider bearing a name associated with "their" river.[273] Elsewhere in the western part of the empire, clearly identified river coins are quite rare. In the Spanish provinces, the river Hiberus appears as a young bearded figure with water flowing from his mouth.[274] The river Baetis, so important to the province of Baetica, and the Danube also appear.[275] In many examples there is no strong impression of devotion or veneration of watery sources, and some issues seem rather to celebrate the generally benevolent role of rivers in contributing to commerce and prosperity and providing water.[276]

8   CONCLUSION: "A STEADY COLUMN OF SWEET FLUID"

Rivers were a fruitful source of imagery and literary description, not least in Lucretius's splendid depiction of riverine movement. They were also a kind of metaphor for life itself, but despite elements of the conventional *topos*, writers present an array of recognizable characteristics that seem to derive from genuine interest and observation. A common theme in writing was the river as a living being with a personality, who acted as an agent and intervened in the world. Water was a dangerous factor that could affect natural processes and benefit or disrupt mankind. It could readily be accepted that a spirit was inherent in this great power of nature, and thus it received worship in various degrees of sincerity and enthusiasm. Though big rivers receive most attention, it is likely that religious observances were most sincerely carried out in local riverine communities. The divinity of the river spirit was bound up with the framework of legends about rivers or river-gods in the form of men. Such stories sustained the divine aura of rivers but also took strength from the supernatural power of rivers and, through anthropomorphic presentation, emphasized the ability of rivers to intervene directly in human affairs. The combination of literary descriptions, legendary tales, and divine attributes contributed to riverine status and the identity of local peoples in a complex cultural nexus. The depiction of rivers in art is an expression of all these aspects. It was partly an act of veneration of the mysterious qualities of rivers but also purely artistic in conveying what had come to be the accepted attributes of rivers. So, although statues could be part of the process of the worship of watery sources, it is difficult to see many of the surviving sculptures of rivers in the round as cult statues. The religious elements should not be exaggerated, and the Tiber, for example, was probably much more of a cultural and emotional symbol of the Roman state than a present divinity. Like much other artistic work, river statues also served as a decoration and adornment of public places, a channel of benefaction, and a reinforcement of the common and legendary tradition about riverine prowess. Furthermore, there was also a commercial angle in that in some cases statues were probably set up by merchants who used the waterways, which points to the theme of the exploitation of rivers as routes of communication and sources of prosperity. Finally, in literature and art representations of mighty foreign rivers also demonstrated Rome's imperial splendor through the extent of its geographical domain, and propagated the ruling power's ideology. The military exploitation of rivers was a further aspect of this.

Five

RIVERS, ARMIES, FLEETS, AND FRONTIERS

"Then Cocles shouted, 'Father Tiberinus, I solemnly pray to you; receive these weapons and this soldier in your auspicious stream.'" This is the climax to Livy's version of the story of Horatius Cocles, who saved Rome by defending the Sublician Bridge against the invading forces of the Etruscan king Lars Porsenna until it could be cut down behind him.[1] The truth of this romantic tale is immaterial; it was both nobly inspirational and symbolic of the Tiber as a last line of defense for the young city; a river bridge could provide a means of access, but at the same time deny it, if it could be defended or destroyed. In the story, the Tiber has cultural and emotional significance, in that the river-god himself is invoked to save a Roman hero in his waters. The whole episode was celebrated in a medallion with graphic images minted in the reign of Antoninus Pius.[2]

It was a feature of ancient warfare that rivers could be the instruments of defense or attack, and they naturally attracted the attention of compilers of military stratagems. There was therefore a strong practical element in the attitude of commanders to rivers and, in wider state policy, to the strategic importance of the riverine environment in the foundation of settlements and in frontier zones, where a river might conceivably serve as a form of barrier. Of course, rivers might serve as a route to imperial control.[3] In this way, a defeated people was represented by its river, which had been humiliated and bridged, and which subsequently came to identify with the Roman conquerors and symbolize the imperial power. Now transformed, it could be depicted as an ally of Rome.

This chapter considers the role played by rivers in military tactics as a means of either defending or attacking a position, the place of rivers in the strategic location of settlements and military camps, the part played in the imperial period by river fleets and the importance of rivers in the supply of armies, the significance of rivers in strategic thinking in frontier zones, and how the

Romans used water to further their military and imperialist objectives. What was implied in some writing about the watery environment received its clearest expression in military terms, namely the mastery of rivers and land and their subordination to the Romans.

1   MILITARY TACTICS

The great natural power of rivers, which could be harnessed by the military for its own objectives, was a traditional theme that went back to mythological stories. The authors of military handbooks and collections of stratagems wrote to provide instruction and guidance and were no mere purveyors of antiquarian anecdotes. Those placed in charge of troops apparently really did seek instruction from what previous commanders had done.[4] Frontinus, who had governed provinces and commanded armies in the late first century, set out his purpose in the *Strategemata*: "For in this way army commanders will be equipped with examples of good planning and foresight, and this will develop their own ability to think out and carry into effect similar operations. An added benefit will be that the commander will not be worried about the outcome of his own stratagem when he compares it with innovations already tested in practice."[5]

The value of this kind of largely anecdotal evidence about armies and rivers is that it illustrates events about which we are otherwise poorly informed—namely, the preparations by commanders to get around or exploit the constraints of rivers and waterways. A prominent theme for military writers was how generals had to deal with problems of the natural environment, and how rivers, waterways, and springs could be exploited or circumvented where necessary. In fact, rivers, like mountains and swamps, were part of the geographical limitations of warfare. For example, Roman invasions of Parthia inevitably meant a campaign from the north down a river valley, usually the Euphrates, but occasionally the Tigris. This contributed to the fairly speedy capture of Ctesiphon at the confluence of the two rivers, but that was often inconclusive. Wider strategic opportunities were curbed partly by the geography and riverine topography. A successful military campaign depended on making contact with the enemy, and moving sufficient numbers of troops into the most advantageous position to outmaneuver and defeat them in open battle or wear them down by siege. Commanders at all times will have needed to understand local topography, a wider geographical outline, and the possibilities and dangers of the riverine environment. To this end, they will have needed to obtain or construct maps.[6]

Interfering with river dynamics was a well-established part of military trickery. Aeneas Tacticus, writing in the fourth century B.C., gave the general advice that, when faced with the invasion of a numerically superior force, the defenders should impede enemy operations as far as possible and "make the rivers hard to cross and increase their flow."[7] Xenophon, an experienced officer, describes how rivers were used to attack cities, as when the Spartan Agesipolis, frustrated by the well-supplied defenders during the siege of Mantinea, damned the river Ophis that flowed through the city. The resulting flood undermined the foundations of the city wall. Xenophon observes that men learned from this that it was inadvisable to allow a river to flow though a city.[8]

Frontinus, in book 3 of the *Strategemata* has an entire section entitled "On diverting rivers and contaminating waters."[9] This covers a wide chronological span, and several stories were attached to the site of Babylon, which was divided in two by the river Euphrates. By diverting the river it was possible to attack along the dried-up bed.[10] In the same way, Polyaenus, who addressed his *Strategemata* to Marcus Aurelius and Lucius Verus, apparently as practical guidance for their campaign in Parthia, resorted to an example from mythology to demonstrate how, by diverting a river, cavalry could be made ineffective because of the boggy ground.[11] Typical of the Roman period is the ploy of Metellus, who, fighting in Spain in 143–142 B.C., diverted a river from higher ground and directed it into the enemy camp, which was on low ground. During the confusion caused by the sudden flood he was able to launch a successful attack.[12] Roman forces operating in Germany under Caecina Severus in A.D. 15 received the same treatment from the enemy, who diverted local streams onto the low-lying ground where the legions had taken up position.[13]

A famous story in Herodotus tells how during Xerxes' invasion of Greece in 480 B.C. his massive army drank rivers dry. This was perhaps not an exaggeration if we think of some of the small rivers of Greece, with their uncertain summer flow. Rivers were important sources of drinking water for armies on the move, and this is supported by anecdotes in military handbooks and by historical accounts of military campaigns.[14] Control of watery resources was therefore crucial to military operations, as was, conversely, the denial of water to others, especially those under siege, by interfering with a river or spring.[15] Not everyone was as ingenious or as ruthless as Kleisthenes of Sikyon, who first cut off the water supply of the town Krisa and then restored it after contamination, so that the inhabitants were physically ill with stomach cramps and unable to defend the walls.[16]

A more coherent account of rivers, springs, and water supply as a serious topic of military strategy and tactics appears in Julius Caesar's *Commentaries on the Gallic War and the Civil Wars*. We get a view of the battlefield through a commander's eyes, and his detailed and self-congratulatory description of the siege of Uxellodunum, a town of the Cadurci, in 51 B.C., strikingly confirms the attention to detail in denying a source of water to the town. Caesar first noted that it was impossible to divert or drain away the river that flowed around the site of the town. However, the way down to the river for the townspeople was very difficult, and Caesar therefore posted archers, slingers, and artillery to harass those who set out to get water.

> Then all the multitude of the townspeople converged on a single water source at a spot right underneath the city wall, where an abundant spring gushed out at the side of the town where for a distance of three hundred feet there was a gap in the circuit of the river. Everyone wanted to find a way to keep the townspeople away from this spring, but only Caesar saw how it could be done. Opposite the spring he began to erect mantlets up the hillside and to construct a terrace. . . . our men were not prevented from pushing on with the mantlets and overcame the difficulties of terrain by hard work and effort. Simultaneously they dug hidden mines toward the watercourses and the source of the spring. They carried on this kind of work without any danger to themselves since they could work without the enemy's suspecting it. They constructed a terrace sixty feet high and placed on it a ten-story tower. This was not intended to reach the height of the walls (no amount of work could achieve that), but to allow them to dominate the spring. When engines fired missiles from the tower at the approaches to the spring, the townspeople could not collect water without risk, and not only cattle and pack animals but also a great crowd of the enemy were tormented by thirst.

Caesar's final move was to cause the spring to fail by digging mines, producing consternation among the population, which suspected divine intervention.[17]

As well as providing vital drinking water, rivers with a little ingenuity might be siege-breakers, as at Casilinum in Campania, which was under attack by the Carthaginians. The Romans used the river Volturnus to float jars of wheat into the city, and when Hannibal prevented this by stretching a chain across the river, they scattered nuts on the water. There is a similar story about the siege of Mutina in 43 B.C. by Antony. Hirtius sent in a supply of salt in jars floated along the river Scultenna; he also floated the carcasses of animals down the river to supply the garrison.[18]

On the battlefield a skillful general might find an opportunity to use a river's characteristics to his best advantage. According to one version of the battle of Cannae, Hannibal exploited the local dynamics of the river Volturnus, which in the mornings produced a swirling wind that carried sand and dust, by maneuvering so that this was in the face of the Romans.[19] In the same way commanders exploited the course of a river to execute a particular tactical ploy; for example, Fulvius Nobilior, operating in Samnium in 217 B.C. and observing that a river was fordable, though with difficulty, posted part of his force in ambush on the near side and took the rest across; the Lucanians despising his small numbers tried to attack immediately and were caught in the ambush as they tried to cross the river.[20]

Caesar's commentaries show the salient points of mobile military campaigns, in which rivers feature prominently and were exploited by an alert tactician. Caesar made use of the river Rhône as he tried to bring the Helvetii to battle on favorable ground; he built a fortification sixteen feet high and a ditch along the bank of the river for nineteen miles from Lacus Lemannus to the Iura to prevent their crossing.[21] Subsequently he used the river to set up the Helvetii for an attack. Only a small portion of their forces made the difficult crossing, and Caesar was able to defeat them in a night attack before they could recover.[22] He used similar tactics in the war against the Belgae by positioning his camp on the Axona (Aisne) with its back to river; when the Belgae tried to force their way across a ford, Caesar crushed them by attacking in the river where they were hampered by the water.[23] His lieutenants were equally adept, and in 51 B.C. C. Fabius outmaneuvered Dumnacus, leader of the Andes, who "thought that his only hope of safety lay in getting his army across the Liger, which because of its width could be crossed only by bridge."[24] Fabius, however, correctly worked out the strategic requirements and got to the vital bridge first. Labienus, in 53 B.C., showed equal skill and awareness of the possibilities when he feigned retreat and lured the Gauls into crossing a river in pursuit; then he wheeled about and caught them as they tried to cross.[25]

In many of these maneuvers, river crossing was crucial, and it is a commonplace in the works of Frontinus and Polyaenus that river crossing points were central to strategic planning; the commander who crossed a river aggressively could gain the initiative and demoralize the enemy or sometimes achieve the same objectives by preventing hostile forces from crossing. A general could develop a tactical plan taking account of the presence of a river and the enemy's need to cross it. There was scope for ingenuity, elaborate maneuvers, and deception. For example, Q. Lutatius Catulus, confronting the Cimbri near Tridentum in 102 B.C. and finding them in possession of the riverbank, pretended to encamp on a neighboring hill and, when the enemy dispersed, got his troops across safely.[26] Sertorius, while on the retreat during the war in Spain, cleverly arranged to get his troops across a river by building a crescent-shaped palisade on the riverbank and setting fire to it to keep away enemy troops.[27] The same kind of thinking appears in a letter written by L. Munatius Plancus (consul 42 B.C.) to Cicero in 43, describing his military operations in Gaul against Antony and Lepidus; he pointed out that one factor in his choice of position for his army was the need to keep a river in front, as an effective shield to delay the enemy troops by forcing them to cross it; later he brought his army across the Isara (Isère) and then broke the bridge to provide everyone with a breathing space.[28]

Once a commander had decided to cross a river, he had to work out how. If the river was fordable, troops could try to wade across, and an expert commander could use the natural characteristics of a river to help his men; the heavy infantrymen would cross at the deepest point, where the water came up to their chest, and put their shields over their heads as protection against missiles; then the other troops could cross in the shallower parts.[29] Another device was to position the sturdiest cavalry horses upstream to break the current and allow the infantry to cross downstream.[30] During his invasion of Britain, Caesar emphasized the importance of crossing the Thames at the only available ford, strongly defended by the British; the legionaries had to cross up to their necks in water.[31]

It is worth emphasizing that the basic military training recommended for Roman soldiers by Vegetius recognized the potential importance of rivers in military operations.[32] Recruits were prepared for every eventuality by frequent exercise at swimming, because rivers had to be crossed without bridges, and sudden storms produced floods which were potentially more dangerous than force of arms. In the old republic, the Campus Martius had been chosen for military training because of its proximity to the Tiber, where the soldiers swam after their weapons training.[33] Swimming skills in the Roman imperial army are proudly celebrated in an inscription recording the achievement of a soldier of the cohort of Batavians, who claimed that "with Hadrian watching I succeeded in swimming in full armor across the vast waters of the mighty Danube."[34]

However, where possible the Romans preferred to build a bridge of boats or a permanent wooden bridge. This facilitated the transport of large numbers of troops and their equipment and also demonstrated a permanent Roman presence, wider strategic objectives, and domination of the local environment.[35] Caesar normally did not expect to be held up by rivers. As he followed up this initial success over the Helvetii, he built a bridge over the slow-flowing Arar (Saône) and led his army across in a single day, causing despair among his opponents, who had taken twenty days to cross the river on rafts and small boats joined together.[36] Even in appalling conditions, Caesar maintained communications. While fighting the Pompeians in Spain, he encountered problems

when a mighty storm and melting snow made the river Sicoris (Segre) torrential and destroyed two bridges; the state of the river and enemy action made
it very difficult for him to repair them, with damaging consequences for his
supply line. However, Caesar used improvised boats constructed of light wood
and wickerwork to transport troops across the river, built a new bridge, and
brought in supplies.[37] Where necessary he outwitted his opponents in order to
effect a safe crossing. So, in the maneuvering before Gergovia in 52 B.C., Vercingetorix tried to use the river Elaver (Allier) to block Caesar's advance by cutting down the bridges and marching a parallel course to prevent any attempt
at constructing a bridge. Caesar was hemmed in because the river could not be
forded again until the autumn. However, he got across by a ruse, leaving two
legions in hiding, which, when the rest of the army had moved on and drawn
Vercingetorix with it, emerged to rebuild a previously destroyed bridge.[38]

Obviously a permanent river crossing offered the best approach to enemy
territory, and a line of withdrawal if necessary, and wherever possible Roman
bridge-building techniques were brought into play. These were skillfully developed, and ancient writers described them with an enormous sense of pride.
Caesar himself has the archetypal description of building a wooden bridge in
difficult conditions and also affirms the symbolic importance of constructing a
proper bridge:

> For the reasons that I have mentioned, Caesar decided to cross the Rhine
> but thought that it was too risky to cross by ship and also not in keeping
> with his own dignity or that of the Roman people. Therefore, although the
> building of a bridge presented enormous difficulties because of the breadth,
> speed, and depth of the river, nevertheless he thought that he should at-
> tempt it or not take the army across. He adopted the following method of
> building the bridge. He took two wooden piles, each one and a half feet thick
> and sharpened close to its end and with a length measured to suit the river
> depth, and joined them at intervals of two feet. He used machinery to lower
> these into the river and then fixed them in position with pile drivers; these
> supports were not set upright but angled so as to provide a sloping surface
> to fit in with the direction of the current. Opposite these, forty feet lower
> down the river he then set up two piles constructed in the same way, but this
> time set against the direction of the current. The two pairs were then kept
> apart by the insertion into their tops of beams two feet thick, which were
> the same length as the gaps between the two piles, and they were secured by
> two iron braces at the outer side (of each pile). Since the pairs of piles were
> both kept apart and secured together, the construction was so sturdy and

such was its nature that the greater the force of the current the more tightly the bridge supports were held fastened together. These piles were connected with cross beams, and these were then covered over with poles and bundles of sticks. Nonetheless, more wooden supports were added obliquely on the downstream side, which jutted out like a buttress and joined with the whole structure in resisting the force of the water. Other supports were positioned a short distance above the bridge, so that if tree trunks or ships were floated down by the barbarians to break down the bridge, their force would be reduced by these defenses and the bridge protected from harm.[39]

This entire operation took only ten days. Arrian, writing in the second century A.D., describes another method; the quickest way to build a bridge was by floating ships downstream, which were then anchored side by side at the appropriate spot with prows facing the current; then linking timbers were laid down from ship to ship to form a continuous walkway.[40] The most ambitious structure was a stone bridge, and Cassius Dio proudly describes the impressive structure built by Trajan across the Danube.[41]

2   SETTLEMENTS AND MILITARY BASES

The writings of the Roman land surveyors help to explain the role of the riverine environment in the foundation and protection of settlements. "Neighboring townspeople or landholders, when nothing was yet being demarcated by *limites*, had the presupposition that in battle when they were fighting against one another in disputes over sites, the physical boundary of victory would be wherever one side retreated to when defeated, or wherever it had succeeded in making a stand; and that the protection of a hill or the barrier of a stream or the shelter of a ditch would allow the defeated side to make a stand, and that guided by this type of natural (obstacle) or a river, they would achieve the secure and permanent possession of their land."[42] This is how Hyginus, describes the origin of *agri occupatorii* (lands occupied without formal survey). The theme is taken up by another writer on surveying technique: "Men of old, because of the danger of sudden outbreaks of war, were not satisfied with building walls around their cities, but also chose sites in rocky high ground, where their best defense lay in the very topography of the site."[43] As we have seen, access to water was also important for settlers, and the founder of a new community tried to assess a fair distribution of natural assets.[44] These comments by writers experienced in the practice and history of land measurement, suggest that in their view early settlements and occupation of land were not an orderly process. Amid violence and open warfare, choice of site in part depended on the protection offered by the terrain, including mountain ridges, streams, and rivers. The position of Vesontio (Besançon) is an excellent example; it was strategically crucial because of the strength of its natural position, since the river Dubis (Doubs) wound around the town, virtually enclosing it, leaving only a gap of 500 yards. This was protected by a hill, the slopes of which came right down to the riverbank.[45]

Early foundations of colonies by Rome naturally reflected the concerns of the developing state. The Latin colonies were founded for military and strategic reasons, and aimed to control river crossings, river confluences, land transport routes, and access to sources of water, while denying possession to hostile forces or opening a way for Rome to advance further. Rivers were intimately connected with the location of early settlements. Rome's earliest colony, Fidenae, traditionally ascribed to Romulus, was strategically situated at the last Tiber crossing above Rome, controlling routes along the Tiber valley from the coast to the interior; for that reason it was believed to have been a bone of contention between Rome and Veii in the fifth century B.C.[46] North of Fidenae, the Latin colonies of Sutrium and Nepet, founded in 383 or 382, also protected the Tiber valley route. In 299 Narnia was established at a crossing point over the river Nar at a place called Nequinum (subsequently renamed after the river); the Nar was an important tributary of the Tiber, offering access to Umbria. Typical of these early settlements were their strong defensive features, particularly a hilltop position, guarded by ravines and rivers and streams.[47] To the east of Rome, Carsioli (298) occupied a lofty position near the river Tolenus and was well suited to watch over the Aequi. In 241 Spoletium was founded on an eminence at the southeast end of the valley of the river Clitumnus and guarded the valley, keeping a watchful eye on the Etruscans and Umbrians (see map 4).

The rich area of Campania became increasingly important to the Romans as they struggled to overcome the Samnites in the fourth century. In this region, the Volturnus and Liris Rivers were particularly significant, providing access from the coastal route to the interior. Cales (334 B.C.), founded on a tributary of the Volturnus, had its city plain protected by streams. Several other foundations sought to dominate the communications route along the valley of the Liris, leading northward though Aquinum toward Rome (eventually along the *via Latina*). In 328 Fregellae had been set up on the east bank in the middle Liris valley, at the junction with the Trerus (Sacco) and where the line of the *via Latina* from northwest to southeast crossed the route down to the Liris valley through the mountains to the coast. It was strategically placed to guard Campania, both controlling the access land routes and dominating the Apennine river valley routes to the southwest.[48] Its position was so powerful that the

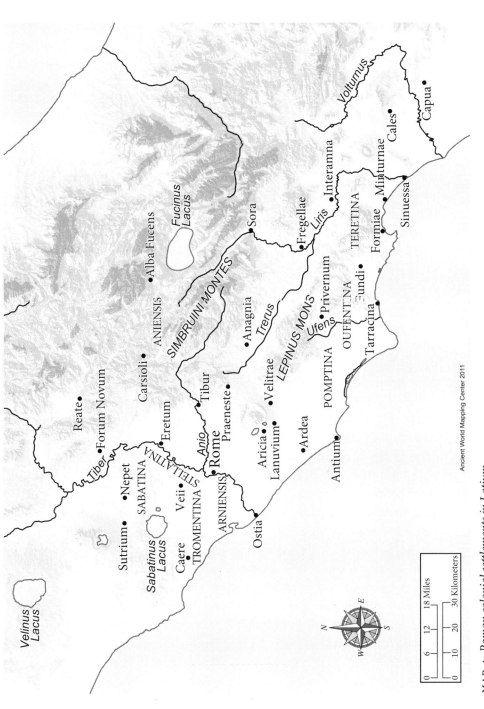

MAP 4. *Roman colonial settlements in Latium*

Velinus Lacus

Tiber

Reate

Forum Novum

Sutrium

Nepet

SABATINA

Sabatinus Lacus

Caere

Veii

TROMENTINA

Eretum

STELLATINA

ARNIENSIS

Anio

Rome

Praeneste

Tibur

Carsioli

ANIENSIS

SIMBRUINI MONTES

Alba Fucens

Fucinus Lacus

Sora

Anagnia

Trerus

Fregellae

Liris

Interamna

Volturnus

Cales

Capua

Minturnae

Formiae

Sinuessa

TERETINA

Privernum

Fundi

OUFENTINA

Tarracina

LEPINUS MONS

Ufens

POMPTINA

Velitrae

Aricia

Lanuvium

Ardea

Antium

Ostia

N
E
S
W

0   6   12   18 Miles

0   10   20   30 Kilometers

Samnites regarded its foundation as a sufficient reason to go to war two years later. In 313 Suessa Aurunca was founded in a lofty position controlling the lower Liris valley and Saticula high in the Volturnus valley. In the next year the Romans founded Interamna on the Liris south of Fregellae, at the confluence with the Rapido, which was important for access and perhaps also of cultural and psychological significance. In 303 Sora was set up, on a hill in the upper valley, within a bend of the river as it emerged from the Val Roveto gorge, on the route to Alba Fucens. The maritime citizen colony of Minturnae was established in 295 to control the mouth of the Liris and the crossing point for the *via Appia*. Settlements tended to be located near rather than at river mouths since there were dangers in the shallow waters of the river estuary.[49]

As the Romans took a firmer grip on Campania, they aimed to move against the Hirpini Samnites and occupied the site at Malventum, renaming it Beneventum (268). This was a crucial position, a road junction that controlled several river crossings of the Tamarus and also was adjacent to the river Calor. Aesernia (263) in the Upper valley of the Volturnus, was well protected by rivers and ravines and confirmed the final eclipse of the Samnites. Furthermore, Venusia (291) from a hilltop location dominated the valley of the Aufidus, perhaps the greatest of the rivers of southern Italy, and separated the Hirpini Samnites from the Lucani.

After the war with Hannibal, Rome was suspicious of the Campanian cities, and in 194 B.C. land was taken for the creation of three colonies (Puteoli, Liternum, and Volturnum), which Livy said guarded river mouths. This had the effect of cutting the important city of Capua off from the sea. So, Rome controlled the coast, but in the cases of Liternum and Volturnum (named after the river Volturnus) the colonies at the mouth of a river also controlled access to the interior. A further stage was the centuriation of the Campanian plain (the *ager Campanus*) by L. Postumius Albinus in 173. This amounted to about 110,000 *iugera*, and was a striking demonstration of the Roman control of the physical environment. The water meadows of the Volturnus and the marshes of the Clanius were excluded but they could be exploited as *subseciva*.[50]

North of Rome in Etruria, the approaches were guarded by two large citizen colonies, Saturnia and Heba, controlling the valley of the river Albinia, a route of communications from the Tyrrhenian coast to central Etruria. In northeast Italy, against the Gallic threat a colony had been founded in 268 at Ariminum, which dominated the eastern approaches to Cisalpine Gaul between the sea and the Apennines. At the mouth of the river Ariminus, Ariminum was potentially a sea and river port and an important part of the east coast road network. Further down the east coast dominating the valley of the Matrinus and hemming in Picenum was Hatria, founded in 289. Along the valley of the Po, Placentia was founded in 218 B.C. on the south bank of the river near its confluence with the Trebia; it was simultaneously a river fort and cog in the highway network. Cremona was established in 218 as the first outpost on the north bank of the Po; it was also a river fort and communications center. In 181 Aquileia (the last of the Latin colonies) was an important port on the Adriatic with good road and river connections to the interior.[51]

After the Gracchi, colonies served a variety of social and economic functions, in providing for the landless and the urban poor and developing trading and commercial opportunities. This, of course, could be combined with a strategic motive. For example, Narbo Martius (c. 114) had a strategically important site in southern Gaul on the road from Italy to Spain. Later settlements are generally described as "military" colonies, in that they frequently served the needs of discharged soldiers; they did not necessarily have a military function as garrison towns in certain areas, though some were useful in this way. For example, among the many colonies founded by Julius Caesar, three in Lusitania—Norba (in the upper valley of the Tagus), Metellinum (at a river crossing of the Anas), and Scallabis/Praesidium Iulium (in the lower reaches of the Tagus)—certainly served as fortress towns, keeping the tribes north of the Tagus under surveillance.[52] In 43 B.C. Lugdunum was founded at a significant site at the confluence of the Rhône and Saône, controlling communications along the river to central Gaul and to the east.[53]

Augustus also engaged in extensive foundations, both in Italy (twenty-eight colonies) and in the provinces, where he spent 260 million sesterces in buying land (doubtless a great deal of land also came into his hands as booty). The peaceful and orderly settlement of veterans was crucial for Augustus's regime, but his colonies frequently had a strategic objective, to guard routes of communication and to watch over potentially troublesome areas. For example, Pliny describes two foundations in the Transpadana: "Augusta Taurinorum in the foothills of the Alps, where the Po becomes navigable, and next Augusta Praetoria Salassorum, near the twin Alpine passes, the Graian and the Poeninan" (Little and Great St. Bernard passes).[54] Augusta Taurinorum was situated at the confluence of the Duria and the Po, Augusta Praetoria Salassorum on the river Duria (Bautica); the latter was established in 25 B.C. on the site of his camp by Terentius Varro, who had just defeated the Salassi. It was settled by veterans from the Praetorian Guard.[55] Both these towns were set up on captured land and controlled the passes through the western Alps. Similarly, in Spain in 25 B.C., P. Carisius founded Augusta Emerita with veterans who had fought against the Cantabri in northern Spain. The settlement was located at the confluence of the Anas and the Albarregas, an important route junction, and was destined to be a center of Roman influence in the area.

Just as the location of colonies was sometimes dictated wholly or partly by the need to control the riverine environment or seek its protection, so too the sites of military camps (*castra*) and forts were carefully chosen. Many camps were in origin temporary structures but developed into permanent bases during the first century A.D. onward. The author of a work on the laying out of a military camp gives advice on a suitable location:

> Furthermore, whatever position the camp has, it will need a river or a source of water on one side or other. Unsuitable locations, which earlier writers called "stepmothers," should entirely be avoided. So, a mountain should not loom over the camp, by which the enemy might get into a superior position or spy from a distance on what is going on in the camp. A wood that might conceal the enemy should not be close, or a ditch or a valley by means of which the enemy might secretly creep up on the camp. Also, it is essential that the camp should not be flooded and destroyed by a neighboring river, in flood because of a sudden storm.[56]

Although a wide variety of factors must have influenced the positioning of military camps, we are poorly informed about this by writers on stratagems, since their theme was specifically that of military campaigns. In fact, we need to take account of the entire context of a frontier zone, including relations with peoples beyond the Roman provinces. In the imperial period, many military bases were located in close proximity to rivers such as the Rhine and the Danube, and a riverine location of a military camp would facilitate lateral movement along a line of control and also have potential for good internal communications, especially when a camp was situated at a river confluence. Forts were often located in order to protect river crossing points and fords and secure communications along the road system.[57] The presence of a river also ensured a good water supply and might provide adequate supplies for bathing establishments. Along large rivers such as the Rhine and the Danube, military supplies could also be brought in by water. Furthermore, riverine communications assisted trade and commerce in the area of the camp, which in time could become an administrative center. Many military camps, and the civilian settlements (*canabae*) that grew up around them, assisted by good riverine communications, developed into substantial and wealthy communities (see maps 5–7).[58]

Therefore, along the Rhine and the Danube, Roman military camps embraced the great rivers and their tributaries, dominating strategic locations at

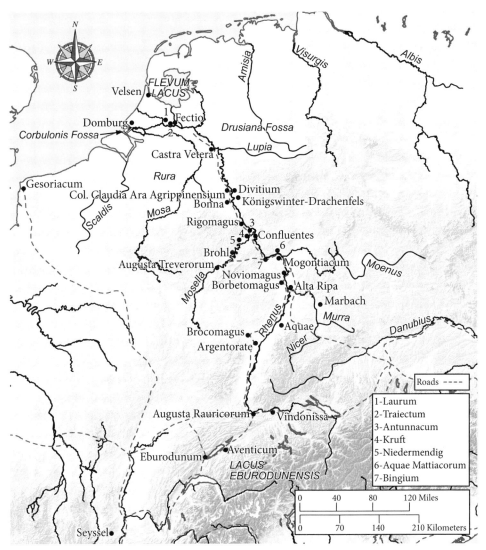

MAP 5. *Roman settlements and camps on the Rhine*

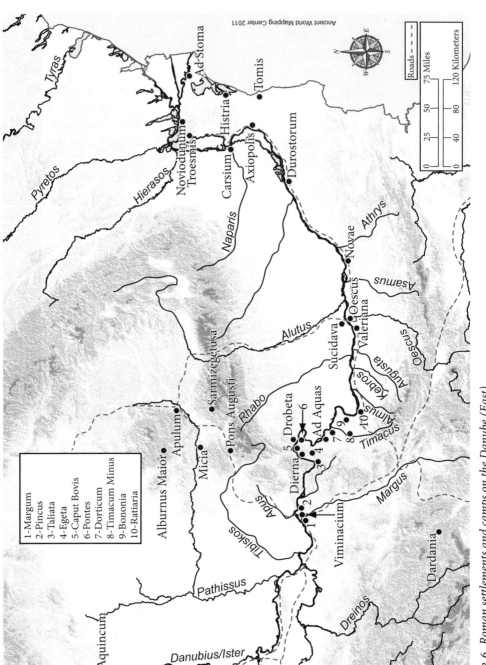

1-Margum
2-Pincus
3-Taliata
4-Egeta
5-Caput Bovis
6-Pontes
7-Dorticum
8-Timacum Minus
9-Bononia
10-Ratiaria

MAP 6. *Roman settlements and camps on the Danube (East)*

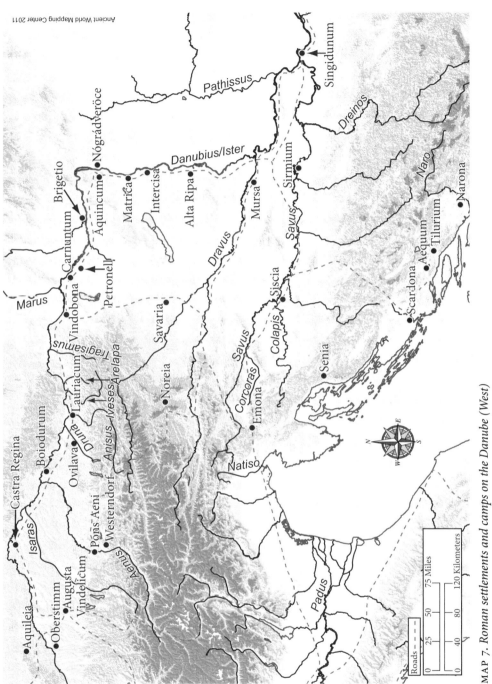

MAP 7. *Roman settlements and camps on the Danube (West)*

Singidunum

Pathissus

Dreinos

Danubius/Ister

Nógrádverőce

Brigetio

Aquincum

Matrica

Intercisa

Alta Ripa

Sirmium

Mursa

Savus

Naro

Narona

Carnuntum

Petronell

Vindobona

Dravus

Siscia

Scardona

Aequum

Tilurium

Marus

Savaria

Colapis

Tragisamus

Noreia

Savus

Senia

Laurlacum

Arelapa

Iveses

Anisus

Corcoras

Drnua

Emona

Ovilava

Boiodurum

Pons Aeni

Westerndorf

Vindelicum

Natiso

Castra Regina

Isaras

Aerius

Augusta

Oberstimm

Padus

Aquileia

Roads

0   25   50   75 Miles

0   40   80   120 Kilometers

N

E

S

W

the heart of the empire over a long expanse of time. Legions based here often remained for centuries, becoming assimilated into the local riverine environment and attracting in their wake the traders and merchants who were to extend the Roman presence and influence. On the Rhine the early bases of the legions were placed to control invasion routes, while the *auxilia* were spread out along the river. Military bases stood at Noviomagus (Nijmegen), Vetera (Xanten) at the mouth of the Lippe, Novaesium (Neuss), Bonna (Bonn), Mogontiacum (Mainz) at the confluence of the Rhine and the Main, the site of a Rhine bridge and the seat of the governor of Upper Germany, Confluentes (Koblenz) at the confluence of the Moselle and the Rhine, Argentorate (Strasbourg), and Ara Ubiorum (Cologne). Agrippa in 38 B.C. had moved the German tribe the Ubii to the west bank of the Rhine, and its principal town was to be the site of the altar (*ara Romae et Augusti*) for the imperial cult, from which the town took its name; it was also a legionary base and subsequently the seat of the governor of Lower Germany. Claudius set up a veteran colony here, Colonia Claudia Ara Agrippinensium, and some distance upstream at Köln-Alteburg the Romans built a naval base. Strung along the Danube was another group of large military settlements, notably: Castra Regina (Regensburg), Vindobona (Vienna), Carnuntum (Petronell), Brigetio (Szöny), Aquincum (Budapest), Singidunum (Belgrade), Viminacium (Kostolac), Oescus (Ghighen), Novae (Swisjtow), Durostorum (Silistra), and Troesmis. It is possible that military deployment along the Danube was "related to changes in topography and to the location of potentially hostile populations." On this view, forts along the river were placed at the start and end of large floodplains and the start and end of mountainous regions, allowing them to control traffic and cross the river, and therefore to protect communications and exchange.[59] In the east, Melitene and Satala in Cappadocia lay close to the Euphrates, and in Syria, Zeugma, Samosata, and Dura-Europus were important crossing points on the Euphrates.[60] In Britain, there were Roman legionary bases at Deva (Chester) on the river Deva (Dee), at Eburacum (York) on the Abus (Ouse), and at Isca (Caerleon) on the river Isca. In Spain, Legio (Léon), the base of the legion VII Gemina, was located at the confluence of the Bernesga and its tributary the Torio, and was strategically positioned with good communications to all parts of the peninsula.[61]

Whatever view might be held of how the Romans operated in frontier zones and their ideology of dealing with foreign peoples, it is inescapable that much of Rome's military disposition was located around major rivers, often linked into river systems through the exploitation of river junctions and tributaries. The riverine environment was inextricably part of army life and the settlements around the military camps. In fact, the army helped to foster vibrant local communities around the rivers, as can be seen from the independent importance of some of these communities in trade, commerce, and administration. Although the Roman army usually marched to wherever it wanted to go, geographically it was an army of rivers. The thinking of generals and emperors was at least partly conditioned by geographical and topographical awareness of watery areas, waterways, and rivers. Of course, the watery environment was not necessarily a barrier but more often perhaps an opportunity.

3   MILITARY SUPPLY

In the imperial period, the Roman army had become a static army based around its permanent camps. Expeditionary forces were assembled when necessary with detachments from various locations. This was less true in the republic, although by the last century B.C. legions were increasingly stationed in provinces for long periods. In any case, at all times the transportation of men and supplies was an important consideration in military planning. The availability of food supplies and ways of getting them to the troops could in some cases have a decisive impact on overall strategy, the nature and conduct of a military campaign, the length of the campaigning season, and the number of soldiers committed in the field.[62] The logistics of military supply naturally depended on the type of campaign and the nature of the terrain. An army on the march in hostile country could attempt to live off the land. Alternatively the troops could carry basic supplies with them, in normal circumstances probably enough for no more than two weeks. Outside the campaigning season an army would need a permanent station or secure winter quarters; when not living off the land, it had to have a supply dump or magazine to store provisions. This in turn presented two problems. First, supplies had to be conveyed to the magazine from other sources, possibly from a coastal port. Second, the supplies then had to be transferred from the magazine to the army in the field or in winter quarters.[63]

Rivers had potentially an important part to play in this process. There was a good reason for locating marching camps, forts, and winter quarters close to naturally navigable rivers, and also for establishing magazines in river valleys, so as to take advantage either of river transport or of the roads that often ran along the upper edges of the river valley. Our scattered sources may suggest a limited role for riverine military transport in the republic, although it is very difficult to estimate the extent of this.[64] Mediterranean rivers, as we have seen, tended to be turbulent and torrential, with unpredictable flow. In particular, some were greatly reduced, or dried up all together, in the summer months, precisely during the campaigning season; heavy rains in late winter and melting snow in early spring could cause rivers to burst their banks and flood land and interrupt road communications. The number of navigable rivers was limited, and campaigns must often have taken place in areas where there was no good waterway, so that road transport had to be used, whatever the difficulties.

Nevertheless, from the anecdotes in the military writers and scattered comments in historians, we do get a suggestion of a significant though uneven role for rivers in military campaigns. For example, as the Romans tried to defend against Hannibal's invasion of Cisalpine Gaul in 218 B.C., they established a supply base at Clastidium, from which provisions could be transported along the Po. This became crucial to Hannibal, who was seriously short of supplies, and when the prefect of the garrison betrayed the place to him, he used it as a magazine from which to supply his troops encamped on the Trebia.[65] Later, in 212 B.C. during the Roman siege of Capua, which had deserted to Hannibal, they established a supply center at Casilinum just north of Capua on the *via Appia*. Importantly Casilinum was on the navigable river Volturnus, along which supplies were brought from the coast.[66] The Tagus was essential to Brutus during his war to subjugate the Lusitanians in 136 B.C., and he fortified Olisipo to command the mouth of the river and bring in supplies.[67] The Rhône featured prominently in Gaius Marius's preparations for resisting the Gallic invaders, the Teutones and the Ambrones, in 102 B.C. He built a fortified camp on the bank, intending to bring supplies along the river. Since transport ships found it difficult to enter the Rhône mouth because of the shoals and mud, he had the soldiers construct a canal and diverted the river.[68] Crassus, during his ill-fated invasion of Parthia in 53, received advice to follow the route along the river Euphrates to Seleukeia, since this would not only prevent his army from being surrounded but also help the delivery of supplies by rivercraft.[69] The most explicit evidence for Roman concern for the transport of military supplies and the logistical importance of rivers is found in Appian's description of Octavian's campaign in Illyricum in 35 B.C. When Octavian encountered the Segestani, his primary objective was to seize a fortified stronghold (Segestica/Siscia) on the river Savus as a magazine suitable for supplying the projected war against the Dacians and Bastarnae on the other side of the Danube. Since the Savus was a tributary of the Danube, Octavian had ships built especially in order to transport supplies down the river to the Danube. Siscia was outstandingly important: "It is at the confluence of several rivers, all navigable, and is naturally suited to be a base in a war against the Dacians. . . . And to it flow rivers that bring a large amount of merchandise from other areas and from Italy."[70]

Caesar's commentaries on the Gallic campaigns and the civil wars (particularly the former) are once again an exceptionally valuable source for their exposition of a commander's view of a military campaign. It is generally agreed that Caesar wrote his commentaries to ensure that his actions were favorably received in Rome and that his version of events would be accepted. However, it must be admitted that he very rarely mentions supplies or military logistics, though he sometimes emphasizes the difficulties of acquiring grain in particular circumstances.[71] It is likely that the acquisition of supplies by one means or another was a routine duty of a Roman commander and not particularly noteworthy, even though it was vital to the soldiers. This theme does not feature strongly among famous stratagems collected by Frontinus and Polyaenus. Caesar does want to write about his strategic overview to protect Roman interests and about his tactics, which were in line with traditional Roman military practice. He is not afraid to record brutal operations against the Gallic peoples and list the numbers killed, since this was presumably acceptable in Rome. He also makes clear the role of his senatorial officers and his own diplomatic prowess and clemency, when it suited Roman interests. To sum up, although Caesar's account of his supply routes is rather unsatisfactory, it is valuable because he at least describes one geographical area during a series of campaigns.

Therefore, despite Caesar's comparative silence about supplies, it is worth speculating if he could have achieved such a speedy conquest of Gaul in ten years' campaigning without extensive use of the rivers of Gaul. The conquest and subsequent maintenance of Roman domination were facilitated by control of the great north-south route of communication along the river Rhône and its tributary the Saône, and routes to the west via the Loire and the Seine. Furthermore, the valleys of the Meuse and the Moselle provided access to the zone around the river Rhine.[72] Although the legions seem to get around the country by marches or forced marches, it is plausible to suppose that supplies were often brought by river. We may judge the importance of riverine transport of goods from the fact that the Gallic chieftain Dumnorix had amassed a fortune by intimidating others out of bidding for the right to collect the river tolls among the Aedui, which he then bought at a cheap price.[73] In a rare explicit reference, Caesar relates that during the campaign against the Helvetii in 58 B.C. the grain supplies that he was bringing by ship up the river Saône became less use to him because the Helvetii veered away from the river, and Caesar did not want to lose contact with them. So he had to press the Aedui to supply additional grain.[74] In 57 B.C., while campaigning against the Belgae in the territory of the Remi, Caesar pitched camp by the Axona (Aisne) so that the river protected one flank. An additional benefit was the ease with which his allies could send in supplies, and the context suggests that at least some of these came by river.[75] Caesar's lieutenant Labienus, campaigning near Lutetia (Paris) in 52 B.C., certainly had a large number of boats at his disposal, some of which were used to carry his heavy baggage upstream, while others were used to create a diversion.[76] Caesar noted that the town of Vesontio (Besançon) was strategically important precisely because of its position on the Dubis and was packed with all the supplies necessary for war.[77]

The Gauls too made use of rivers to move supplies of grain. When rebels captured the stronghold of Noviodunum on the Liger, which contained Caesar's baggage and reserves of grain, they took away as much grain as possible in boats along the river.[78] Indeed, this town on the Liger was one of Caesar's magazines in 53–52 B.C., along with Cenabum, also in an important position on the same river. In the previous year Caesar had located one of his magazines with grain and other valuables at Samarobriva on the river Samara (Somme).[79] Perhaps on many occasions the possibility of transporting supplies by river was in Caesar's mind. For example, early in his command, in 57 B.C., he left Labienus in charge of the legions in winter quarters in the land of the Sequani; this location would have been suitable for conveying supplies along the Rhône and Saône. It is worth noting that after the defeat of Vercingetorix when the legions were distributed to winter quarters, two officers were quartered in the land of the Aedui, at Cabilonnum (Chalon-sur-Saône) and Matisco (Mâcon) on the river Saône, to collect grain; this was again on the Rhône-Saône axis on a major route of communication and distribution.[80]

There is therefore some indication that rivers featured strongly in the thinking of commanders on military logistics in the republic, however vague the overall picture remains. This can hardly have changed in the imperial period, though in general we are not particularly well informed by historians about the supplying of armies on campaign; there is, however, additional evidence from inscriptions and imperial monuments such as the great columns recording the campaigns of Trajan and Marcus Aurelius. Furthermore, the establishment of the imperial fleets added a new dimension to the transport of men and supplies, and offered the possibility of military support to armies on campaign.

4 RIVER FLEETS OF THE IMPERIAL PERIOD

Roman writers take little interest in fleets and naval operations. This may reflect military reality, in that naval warfare contributed little to the military glory of Rome.[81] Traditionally, interest centered on the legions, and the command of the fleets, even the praetorian fleets stationed in Italy at Misenum and Ravenna, was left to men of equestrian rank; the provincial and river fleets were commanded by *equites* of junior standing.[82] In fact, throughout the history of the empire there are no major naval battles on record. This is probably not an accident of the evidence; the Romans controlled the Mediterranean Sea because they maintained a military presence of legions and auxiliaries in the lands on its periphery. Tacitus shrewdly observed, after discussing the organization of the Italian fleets and the presence of a detachment at Forum Iulii in Gaul, that "our greatest strength was on the Rhine, in the eight legions that offered protection against Germans or Gauls."[83] Nevertheless, the presence of rivers and river fleets offered the Romans an alternative means of transport and allowed them to keep an eye on restive peoples on both sides of a river without creating more military bases. Notably, although there is much evidence for bandits in the Roman world, there is little sign of piracy on seas or rivers in the imperial period. River fleets were a visible, mobile deterrent and also were ready to assist in major campaigns, in which they could provide another option, though we do not know what went on in imperial military councils.

It is clear that the river fleets, notably the *classis Moesica*, the *classis Pannonica*, and the *classis Germanica*, did have an important role in various military activities in the frontier zones. This included the supply of garrisons and larger armies, the movement of troops and animals, and surveillance and scouting. The fleets also served to control movement along and across major navigable rivers and to deter river crossing by hostile bands. Along the Danube, forts or camps were maintained on or close to the riverbank, and the fleet helped to maintain lateral communications.[84] Some naval presence on the Danube will have been required from the time of the first Roman involvement there. After the creation of the provinces of Pannonia and Moesia, two fleets were maintained, since it was difficult to sail along the entire course of the river past the rapids at the Iron Gates. Eventually the *classis Moesica* operated along the lower Danube bordering on Upper and Lower Moesia, while the *classis Pannonica* operated in Upper and Lower Pannonia. Such extensive naval provision was expensive, which indicates that the Romans recognized the value of the river patrols and that it was not merely a matter of imperial bravado. The title "Flavia" granted to both these fleets, probably by Vespasian,[85] suggests that they played a significant part in the effort to repel Sarmatians marauding across the Danube during A.D. 69 when legions were engaged elsewhere.

From the reign of Domitian, the *classis Moesica* was based in Lower Moesia under the control of the governor, and was also responsible for communications through the Euxine and toward the Bosporus. During Trajan's two wars against the Dacians, this fleet acted in a support role, as is vividly though vaguely illustrated by the sculptures on Trajan's column, which depict the progress of the campaign from the initial crossing of the Danube on a bridge of boats. Several scenes show ships carrying soldiers' packs and equipment, and there are also horse transporters. Trajan himself travels by boat along the Danube,[86] and the theme of moving supplies by rivercraft appears again.[87] The military record of the first mounted cohort of Spanish auxiliaries based at Stobi shows that some soldiers of the unit were working in the dockyards of *classis Moesica*.[88]

The Dacian wars brought changes to Roman military dispositions in the lower Danube. The Moesian fleet, however, continued to be based at Noviodunum and was responsible for patrolling the stretch of river upstream as far as the fortress of Novae and downstream to the Euxine. Marcus Arruntius Claudianus is described in an inscription as "prefect of the Moesian fleet and the bank of the Danube."[89] Probably during the Dacian wars in A.D. 103–4, new legionary bases were established at Durostorum, an important river crossing point, and at Troesmis; these supported additional auxiliary forts and, with the fortress at Novae, provided three legions to supervise the Danube through Lower Moesia. It seems likely that there was a naval station at Ghergina on the left bank of the Danube, near the junction with the river Hierasus, and that the fleet linked forts on these two rivers. Nevertheless, it is significant that Trajan's response to the perceived strategic problem of the lower Danube frontier zone lay in stationing more legions rather than developing the scope and role of the fleet.

During the campaigns of the 30s B.C., Octavian had used the river port base at Siscia; later, when fully in control of the resources of Rome, he launched campaigns from 15 to 12 B.C. to establish control of Pannonia, and the rivers Savus and Dravus served as valuable lines of communication. Certainly by the reign of Claudius, the *classis Pannonica* was patrolling the upper course of the Danube as far as Carnuntum, and we find this fleet transporting Vannius, the fugitive king of the Suebi across the river.[90] Trajan split the province of Pannonia into two, but the fleet, though based in Lower Pannonia, continued to patrol along the river in Upper Pannonia.[91] Its main base was at Taurunum, near Singidunum, three miles north of the junction of the Savus and the Danube.[92]

The carvings on the column of Marcus Aurelius may be artistically derivative from Trajan's column, but vaguely indicate that the *classis Pannonica* assisted the army during Marcomannic Wars along the lateral supply route of the Danube. More specifically, an experienced equestrian officer, Valerius Maximianus, was specially chosen by Marcus Aurelius and sent "on active service in the German campaign to bring down the Danube supplies for both armies in Pannonia." To help in the execution of this task, he was placed in charge of detachments of the fleets from Misenum, Ravenna, and Britain and also had command of African and Moorish horsemen on a scouting mission along the riverbank.[93] Subsequently, there is little evidence for the activities of the fleet during the second and third centuries, but it is interesting that Commodus in 185 built a series of forts along the bank of the Danube "to prevent the stealthy crossing of bandits."[94] Once again we see that fortified positions with soldiers seem to be more central to military planning than naval operations. However, the fleet was still operating at least in the reign of Septimius Severus, when the prefect, L. Cornelius Restitutus, set up an inscription.[95]

Although we have better evidence for the *classis Germanica*, our view of the role of the river fleets in Roman policy remains obscure.[96] Initially, during Augustus's early campaigns across the Rhine, ships were part of the overall strategy. The elder Drusus constructed a German fleet and sailed down the Rhine and, by building the *fossa Drusiana*, was able to sail into the North Sea. However, land operations were the key to the Roman conquest of the peoples between the Rhine and the Elbe, though the eastward advance could be profitably pursued along the main river valleys. In particular, the fleet assisted by bringing men and supplies along the Rhine and up the rivers Lupia (Lippe) and Moenus (Main). Germanicus in his campaigns of A.D. 15–16 again exploited Roman sea power, transporting part of his army by ship to the Amisia (Ems) and then down the river; this was also a return route for some of the troops.[97] In A.D. 16 he had a huge fleet of 1,000 ships built in order to transport his army along the North Sea coast and then upriver to the interior of Germany. The ships were specially designed to be adaptable with a capability for riverine operations; some were short but broad, lacking a clearly defined bow or stern, and very seaworthy; others were flat-bottomed so as to run aground easily on a beach or presumably to make headway along a navigable river; many had rudders at each end so that the steersman could quickly reverse direction and ground them on either side of a river; others were designed to carry catapults and had space for horses and supplies. In Tacitus's view the fleet was superbly suited for fast sailing or rowing.[98]

Setting out from the Batavian Island, Germanicus sailed down the *fossa Drusiana* though the *lacus Flevum* and into the North Sea, eventually reaching the mouth of the Ems. After successful fighting, part of the army embarked with Germanicus on the Ems for the voyage downstream to the sea. But this ended in disaster when a huge storm wrecked the fleet.[99] This marked the end of Germanicus's offensive operations, and thereafter, although Corbulo built a canal from the Meuse to the Rhine so as to avoid the North Sea,[100] the fleet did not have a decisive military role in Rome's more limited operations in Germany.

The scaled-down Rhine fleet proved militarily ineffective during the revolt of Civilis and the Batavians in A.D. 69. The Romans could muster only twenty-four ships in the lower Rhine, some of the sailors were disloyal, and they were effectively chased off the river. Eventually it was the reappearance of a competent legionary presence under the command of Petillius Cerialis that reasserted Roman control. Even so, the commander was severely embarrassed when the Germans made a night attack on his own squadron returning from Novaesium and towed away all the ships, including the flagship. When Civilis was defeated at the *insula Batavorum*, the Roman fleet, although ordered to intervene, failed to cut off his escape, through a combination of cowardly ineptitude and infirmity because of the dispatch of the crews on other military duties.[101] Subsequently, the closest to a naval engagement came when Civilis's native fleet and the Roman sailed past one another on the lower Rhine with a desultory exchange of weapons.[102] Therefore, for a time Civilis had virtually controlled the region from Novaesium downstream and aimed to intercept convoys from Gaul.[103]

From the time of the Flavians, the *classis Germanica*, commanded by an equestrian prefect, settled down to largely routine duties, based at Colonia Claudia Ara Agrippinensium, which was the capital of Lower Germany. The base here was occupied at least until the middle of the third century. There were smaller naval stations downstream at Novaesium, Vetera, and Noviomagus, and forts in the Rhine delta maintained by the fleet.[104] There was no fleet on the upper Rhine, though small naval dockyards constructed ships used by the legion XXII Primigenia at Mogontiacum for its own purposes.[105]

Although the Rhine fleet was not involved in fighting, it had to transport supplies and ordnance along the Rhine and its navigable tributaries to military camps, though it is difficult to gauge how consistently important this was.[106] Some of the oared ships found near waterways in the German frontier zone were unsuitable for rapid maneuvering and fighting and were probably intended for transporting soldiers along the rivers and routine patrolling.[107] Part of the fleet's military role was to discourage German incursions and to deny use of the river to those of whom the Romans disapproved. There were other routine duties, for example, the quarrying and transport of stone for building projects along the Rhine.[108] Some of the commercial possibilities associated with the operations of the fleet might be hinted at in an inscription from the Severan era, which shows how after service a sailor became a *negotiator cervesarius* (a beer salesman).[109] It is possible only to guess at the military activities of the *classis Germanica* during the wars of Marcus Aurelius and the later campaigns of Caracalla, Severus Alexander, and Maximinus in 235.

Finally, in the East, although the *classis Syriaca* is not securely attested before the reign of Hadrian, it may have existed in some form from the time of Augustus. Its base was probably at Seleukeia, which lay on the coast some twenty-five kilometers from Antioch and acted as its port. The presence of a naval station might explain the substantial efforts expended by Vespasian and other emperors to prevent silting in the harbor.[110] The Syrian fleet operated mainly along the coast of Syria and Judaea and played no direct part in Roman military operations against Parthia. Both Trajan and Septimius Severus did make use of ships on the Euphrates and Tigris, but these had to be specially built. In A.D. 115 Trajan constructed boats from trees around Nisibis and brought them to the river on wagons; the ships were so constructed as to be easily dismantled and reconstructed, and they were intended to serve as a boat bridge. Trajan's later plans for building a canal between the Euphrates and Tigris imply that he was using some ships on the Euphrates, perhaps to carry supplies along the navigable stretches.[111] In 197 Severus ordered the construction of a fleet, with which he sailed down the Euphrates before crossing to the Tigris on the King's Canal on his way to Seleukeia; according to Dio, some of the invading force made its way though Mesopotamia by marching alongside the Euphrates; the return journey was by boat and by land.[112] But there is no sign here of an integrated land and river campaign.

What happened to the character of the riverine fleets in the later empire? In the late third century and afterward, the naval resources of the empire did not escape the military reorganization that transformed the legions into the late Roman army. Much of the third- and fourth-century reorganization affected the Danube fleets, and naval units were grouped in the *classis Histrica*, the *classis Pannonica* I and II, the *classis Flavia* I and II, and numerous smaller units attached to particular towns, for example the *classis Ratianensis* at Ratiaria.[113] Naval resources were now more scattered, and the deployment was uneven, with concentrations at crucial points, such as Carnuntum, the junction of the Danube and Dravus and Savus Rivers, and the Iron Gates pass. Although bases were retained along the Danube, by the fourth century they were maintained by small independent squadrons of the *classis Moesica*. Small warships (*lusoriae*) were now employed.[114] From the *classis Pannonica*, *milites liburnarii* attached to the frontier troops operated on the Danube, and there were bases on both the Savus and the Danube.[115] It may be that this represents two stages of a developing reorganization, the first by Diocletian when he created substantial river fleets out of the remnants of previous naval forces. Then, probably in the time of Constantine, there was a move to split up existing units and locate smaller detachments in certain frontier locations.[116] However, these moves help to confirm the importance of the Danube as a frontier zone. The object was still to maintain naval forces on the river in order to deny its use to hostile peoples and to make it more difficult to cross.

The German fleet became less important, and many of its bases were abandoned in the third century, although *lusoriae* continued to patrol the river in 280.[117] This may suggest that there was a less sophisticated overall command and that responsibilities were devolved to smaller, self-contained units responsible for a part of the river in a small-scale operation; they were probably attached to the local military units. The *Notitia Dignitatum* shows a curious arrangement in Gaul, in the military district of Gallia Riparensis (apparently obsolete by the fourth century), including a prefect of the fleet of the Rhône and a prefect of the fleet of the Saône.[118] This perhaps had something to do with Diocletian's moves to suppress the rebellion of the Bagaudae in Gaul in 286.

We get a glimpse of the use of ships to transport an army in the later empire when Constantine moved to suppress the revolt of Maximian, who had assumed the purple at Arles before moving to Marseilles. Constantine marched his army from Cologne southeast along the Rhine and then southward to the Saône where he had arranged for a fleet to meet them at Chalon. From there, they sailed down the river to Lyon and the junction with the Rhône and then down the Rhône to Arles. The author of the panegyric to Constantine imagines the soldiers chaffing at the slowness of the river transport: "That sluggish and dilatory river (Saône) never seemed slower; the keels glided along silently and the banks receded so slowly that they shouted that they were not moving at all but standing still." The soldiers rushed to man the oars and "conquer the river's character by driving forward."[119]

5   FRONTIERS

In the wider area of strategic thinking, rivers often seem to have an appeal as psychological, diplomatic, or military frontiers or barriers. However, the very word "frontier" has in recent years engendered considerable controversy. A challenging analysis by Edward Luttwak of the changing pattern of imperial policy for managing relations with peoples outside Rome's direct control argued that in the first century A.D. up to the Flavians, the Romans maintained no formal defense line but kept large concentrations of troops close to the frontier areas, which were moved to deal with incursions and were supported by the efforts and forces of friendly rulers in the peripheral areas. Then, from the Flavian dynasty up to the end of the second century, a system of linear frontier defense developed, based on what Luttwak described as "scientific" frontiers. This preclusive defense dealt with all threats outside this ideal frontier line, thus protecting the inhabitants of Roman territory. In the critical phase of the third century, up to the military reforms of Diocletian and Constantine, a system of defense in depth emerged. The Rhine, the Danube, and, to a lesser extent, the Euphrates featured as part of the garrisoned defense lines of the second and third stages.[120] The Romans tried to maintain their control by the exercise of power, that is, their influence over other peoples, and the threat of force. Force was available through the presence of the legions, but if force were to be used, then, unlike power, it was expended and reduced.

These ideas inspired considerable debate, particularly concerning the Roman view of how to deal with peripheral areas.[121] There is, in fact, no Latin word that exactly expresses the modern meaning of "frontier" as a line on a map formally demarcating areas of control, and perhaps no clear concept of where official Roman administration ended and other means of influence prevailed. The idea of a formal frontier line appears only in the nineteenth century with the emergence of nation-states. At no point in time could it be said that imperial expansion was at an end, since the Romans set no formal limits to their power or their ability to annex and exploit, even though they might use other means when it suited, including diplomacy and vassal rulers operating in their interests. From the time of Augustus, conquest of the known world was on the agenda, encouraged by his desire for military renown, his determination to enhance his reputation, and the limitations of geographical knowledge, which made the idea of a program of large-scale conquest seem practicable.[122]

In this context it is also relevant to consider the factors that may have contributed to the ending of Roman advance, and the differences in the various parts of the empire. In some areas the Romans may simply have lost their impetus through a perceived shortage of troops or resources. But such negative reasons are not sufficient, and perhaps it is preferable to think in terms of frontier zones, where a complex of social, economic, and cultural factors may have contributed to Roman policy. In general, the Romans ceased forward movement when the equation was no longer in their favor, for example, in areas of ecological marginality where it was not profitable to occupy land or feasible in terms of providing supplies.[123] Local conditions around frontier zones therefore contributed significantly to the Roman response.

In this debate over whether frontier lines are merely convenient, or mark exhaustion, or indicate a more complex relationship with the surrounding lands, the role of natural or artificial barriers is particularly significant. Those who advocate the idea of no fixed linear frontier, generally contend that rivers were not intended as barriers to protect Roman territory and, in any case, would have been inefficient in this capacity. In fact, rivers tended to be obstacles to Roman offensive operations and were principally valuable as lateral supply lines. Consequently, the argument goes, it is unconvincing to define "scientific" frontiers along rivers such as the Rhine, the Elbe, the Danube, and the Euphrates. Furthermore, rivers should not necessarily be viewed as some kind of dividing line between cultures; for example, it can be argued that similar cultures and peoples existed on both sides of the Rhine. Consequently, Alföldi's idea of the "moral barrier" presented to the Romans by the Rhine and the Danube is cast in doubt.[124]

The Romans did, of course, make sophisticated distinctions between various types of boundary. The land surveyors distinguished between administered and unadministered land, namely measured and allocated land, and land beyond the surveyed boundary described as *arcifinius* or *occupatorius*, which might be occupied informally by ambitious settlers. This could have some resonance with Roman frontier policy.[125] But surveyors were concerned mainly with the measurement of lands within the state remit, either *ager publicus* or private allocations, and it is appropriate to emphasize here the great concern in their writings for formal, fixed boundaries and boundary marking techniques. In fact, rivers did perform an important function as boundaries of private lands or territories or provinces. There is absolutely no reason why a river could not form a natural boundary line, marking a territorial and political boundary, and in a sense serve as a barrier.[126]

If we examine what a variety of ancient writers say about rivers, we get a complex picture about Roman power and the role of rivers. Augustus, in his *Res Gestae*, describes the conquest of the Pannonians in 12–9 B.C. by Tiberius, noting that he brought them into the empire of the Roman people, and continues: "I extended the territory of Illyricum to the banks of the Danube." Augustus at this point clearly sees this riverbank as the limit and demarcation of Roman conquest. Yet in the next sentence he mentions that, in response to a Dacian raid, his army crossed the Danube and "made the Dacian peoples submit to the orders of the Roman people."[127] Therefore, to Augustus's way of thinking the river simultaneously acted as a dividing line between Rome and potentially hostile peoples and served as a line of control or a resource from which further wars of punishment or conquest were launched. Seneca, who was one of Nero's advisers at a time when a serious war threatened in the East, and presumably knew the vagaries of foreign policy and the layout of the empire, observed on the course of the Danube and the Rhine: "From this side flow the river Danube and the Rhine separating conquered lands and hostile lands, the one restraining the attacks of the Sarmatians, and dividing Europe from Asia, the other repelling the Germans, a nation bent on war."[128] Seneca explicitly asserts the value of great rivers in keeping back hostile peoples. The inscription honoring Tiberius Plautius Silvanus Aelianus, who was governor of Moesia also in the reign of Nero, celebrates among his achievements that "he brought across more than 100,000 people beyond the Danube (Transdanuviani) including their wives and children, and chiefs or kings to pay tribute. . . . he brought kings previously unknown or hostile to the Roman people to pay their respect to the Roman standards on the riverbank, which he was guarding."[129] Plautius not only defines one people by their position on the other side of the river but also directly confirms that his military role was to protect vigilantly the Roman side of the riverbank. Therefore, although Roman forces might expect to operate freely across the Danube, the river itself was certainly a possible defensive line. Since high-ranking and experienced Romans made these comments, they can hardly be dismissed as merely the embellishment of a well-known literary *topos*. And so we must take proper account of Josephus, who in his version of a speech to the Jews by Agrippa, arguing for the futility of war with Rome in A.D. 66, has the king speak of the savage Germans tamed by eight legions but also observe that the river Rhine keeps in check their ferocity.[130]

Tacitus, in his famously brief survey of the military achievements of Augustus, comments that the empire was now hemmed in by the Ocean or distant rivers. Here, rivers are seen as possibly some kind of physical barrier but certainly as a symbolic demarcation of the Roman Empire, and something in the service of Rome itself.[131] However, in the *Histories* Tacitus had been more explicit in his description of the revolt of Civilis and the Batavians during the civil war in A.D. 69 and the real threat to the legions in Germany, some of whom actually went over to the enemy. In this perilous situation, the Rhine seemed to be the last barrier. When a drought caused the river level to fall, extra patrols had to be posted to prevent the Germans from fording it: "The ignorant ascribed supernatural significance to the shortage of water, as if the very rivers, which had so long provided the empire's defense, were now deserting us."[132] Of course, as Josephus had recognized, it was the combination of the river and the legions and auxiliaries that was effective. During the mutiny of the German legions in A.D. 14, the Germans across the river knew of the sedition on the Roman side, and "if the riverbank was abandoned the enemy would invade."[133] Tacitus was bitterly critical of the military failures of Domitian's reign, especially in relation to the supposed slight to his father-in-law Agricola, who had been withdrawn from the governorship of Britain, prematurely in Tacitus's view, and not given another command. The situation was desperate, and the battle was not for the imperial frontier and the riverbank (in this case the Danube), but the winter quarters of the legions and the very provinces.[134] Therefore (even with Tacitus's exaggeration), the riverbank appears as an advance line of defense, before the legions are involved.

From a different perspective, Tacitus, in his long account of Rome's relations with the Parthians under the Julio-Claudians, had observed the diplomatic and military significance of the Euphrates as a dividing line and effective barrier between the empires.[135] The treaty established by Augustus in A.D. 1 actually recognized the river as a frontier line; it was unique for the Romans to accept this idea, and it is notable that the agreed boundary was a major river. After this, Roman generals were reluctant to cross the Euphrates even when relations deteriorated, though they did so or threatened to do so for limited objectives. In A.D. 35 Lucius Vitellius escorted Tiridates III, contender for the Parthian throne, to the bank of the Euphrates and, after religious ceremonies to placate the river, led his army across for a brief foray into Mesopotamia before returning to Syria.[136] However, Domitius Corbulo in A.D. 61, when conflict with Parthia threatened, did no more than guard the bank of the Euphrates vigilantly.[137]

We find the same combination of the symbolic and actual role of the Euphrates in a striking personal observation of Velleius Paterculus, recalling his service as a young military officer with Gaius Caesar in 1 B.C. Gaius met the Parthian king to discuss diplomatic relations between the two powers and the status of Armenia. They first met on an island in the middle of the Euphrates with equal retinues on each side; later the Parthian king dined with Gaius on the Roman side of the river, and then Gaius had dinner on the Parthian side. Velleius sees the river as the dividing line between two great empires, with a symbolic and almost mystical status of demarcation.[138] Similarly, in A.D. 18 the Parthian king offered to pay Germanicus the compliment of coming to the bank of the Euphrates to meet him.[139] In a different context on the Danube, when the Romans were in a more defensive position after Marcus Aurelius's campaigns against the Marcomanni in 173, the emperor prohibited this people from attending markets on the south bank of the river and compelled them to evacuate a band of land fifteen kilometers wide (later reduced to half that distance). Later, in 175 the Iazyges were also forced to move out of an area fifteen kilometers wide opposite the Danube bend.[140] In these dealings with hostile tribes, the river Danube served as defensible base, demarcating Roman interests and anchoring the system, and did not impede Roman intervention beyond the river. Arrian, who had been governor of Cappadocia and commanded soldiers under Hadrian, in his history of the campaigns of Alexander, commented that the greatest river in Europe was the Danube, which covered the greatest expanse of country and also acted as a barrier against the most warlike tribes. Was he perhaps thinking of the military situation along the river in his own day?[141]

It is clear that the idea that a river might constitute a physical barrier, protecting vulnerable Roman territory or marking a limit of established control, was at least one strand of thinking, whether wise or unwise, about frontiers, military dispositions, and diplomacy. The idea of a river as a barrier in real or psychological terms was taken up by other writers, who were less analytical but probably reflected contemporary thinking. Lucan, imagining a world at war, surmises that the Danube will be unable to hold back the Massagetae.[142] Suetonius, commenting on Augustus's rare employment of freedmen as soldiers, cites as one example the defense of the bank of the Rhine after the defeat of Quinctilius Varus in A.D. 9.[143] It is interesting that once again in a time of crisis a major river was seen as the first line of stable, organized defense. Florus, writing in the second century A.D. with a generally enthusiastic imperialistic view, laments the loss of Germany after Varus's defeat. Previously, the campaigns of the elder Drusus had secured Roman domination by taking control of rivers, garrisoning their banks, including the Rhine, the Meuse, and the Elbe, and constructing forts and bridges protected by fleets. But after the defeat of Varus, "the empire, which had not stopped on the shores of the Ocean, now came to rest on the bank of the Rhine."[144] Florus is disappointed precisely because the Rhine bank, which previously was merely a base and one stage in Roman military advance, now had a largely defensive purpose. The famous story of Germanicus's wife, Agrippina, who, as her husband's legions retreated from Germany, prevented panicking officers from breaking down the bridge over the Rhine at Vetera, shows that they at least thought that, with the bridge gone, the river was a good and necessary line of defense.[145] Much later, Hadrian removed the superstructure of Trajan's famous bridge over the Danube, to protect against invasion by hostiles who might overwhelm the garrisons on the north bank. It was still in this condition in Dio's day.[146] In common perception in the second century, direct Roman control was thought to stop on the Rhine, though this was described as "our bank."[147] The *Historia Augusta*, in a summary of Roman frontiers in the time of Hadrian, mentions that in many places the barbarians were divided off not by rivers but by frontier barriers and goes on to describe how Hadrian built large palisades to fence off potentially hostile peoples.[148] However much this account may have misunderstood Hadrian's work, the implication is that frontier policy, at least from the mid-second century, could on occasion consist in keeping potentially dangerous peoples in check by some fixed barrier, either a natural one, in the case of a river, or man-made.[149]

The admittedly scattered comments of ancient writers suggest that Roman thinking on rivers was by no means clear-cut. The Romans aggressively crossed rivers or occupied riverine areas, claimed them as their own, and represented them in imperial iconography as conquered men who now served as Rome's ally. In the Romans' seemingly inexorable advance, rivers served to facilitate movement, supply, control, and administration. Furthermore, it is important not to underestimate the cultural and psychological importance of mastery of a river (even if it was not a natural cultural barrier). Conquest was never ruled out, and it is doubtful if the Romans would have understood the concept of frontier zones or carefully considered the profit and loss account. The benefits or drawbacks of a particular area presumably emerged after advance and conquest had stopped for a variety of reasons. It is important to remember that decisions were taken ultimately by an autocrat and might indicate a passing whim rather than reasoned analysis. It will not have been obvious that Britain would be a profitable addition to the Roman provinces, but Claudius needed military glory, and all the problems could be sorted out later.

At all times, natural phenomena were arranged as far as possible to suit imperial self-interest. There were many reasons why a river valley or mountain or forest might be a desirable military objective; a river could mark off areas of control, offer cover or a breathing space, and, if necessary, as the Romans themselves said, serve to defend and protect until appropriate military measures were taken. Of course, just because the Romans stopped their advance at a river did not mean that they did not operate beyond it. The strength-return of the first mounted veteran cohort of Spanish, which was part of the army of Lower Moesia though stationed at Stobi in Macedonia in A.D. 105 or 106, shows that some soldiers were on active service north of the Danube or in a detachment at Buridava or on guard duty at Piroboridava.[150] These troops are described as "within the province," though Buridava is about sixty miles north of the river. This river was not a frontier but served as a line of military control in a wider system.

When it suited an emperor, a river was employed to make some aspects of imperial policy easier. Sometimes it did serve as a barrier, though always in conjunction with other factors, such as climatic conditions, riverine characteristics and topography, and, most importantly, troop dispositions. First, the width and depth of the river, its strength of current, and regularity of flow determined if it was possible for soldiers to swim or wade across. Second, seasonal factors might intervene; most dramatically, the Danube could freeze over in winter, allowing battles to be fought on the ice, as actually happened in the reign of Marcus Aurelius: "Therefore, some (of the Iazyges) charged straight at them while others rode around to attack from the flanks, for their horses had been trained to charge safely even over a surface like this (ice). The Romans were not afraid when they saw this, but drew together into a compact mass and faced all the enemy simultaneously; most of them put their shields on the ground and placed one foot on them so as to avoid slipping, and in this way received the enemy's attack."[151] Heavy rains and melting snows tended to produce torrential rivers, which were impossible to cross by any means. Floods in river valleys or deltas made communications and normal military operations problematic.

Third, the riverine terrain was important, since open country might make it difficult for large enemy forces to approach the river unseen and therefore give time for organizing resistance; on the other hand, thick woods or adjacent hills would make it easier to make a surprise approach to the river and undermine its value as a defensive line. Therefore, for various reasons the riverine environment was not fully predictable or controllable, and a river could rarely provide a consistently reliable strategic line. Troops might well be deployed differently along stretches of the same river. Furthermore, military planning would have to take account of the nature and likely hostility of local peoples; small numbers of guerrillas or raiding bands could probably cross even a large river quite easily, while for a large army a bridge of some kind was the most effective way of crossing safely. But bridge construction took time and a degree of technical skill and would significantly delay an attack. Florus believed that barbarians were too stupid to work out a proper method of river crossing. For example, the Cimbri tried to cross the Athesis (Adige) not by a bridge or boats, but first by swimming and then by using their hands and shields in a hopeless attempt to stem the current. Finally they blocked the stream by hurling in trees and crossed in this way.[152] Another factor in military dispositions was the sustainability of a frontier area; the maintenance of military garrisons in the vicinity of a river depended on the economic standing of the local region, particularly the availability of supplies, diplomatic contacts, and relations with the local population on both sides of the river.[153] In other words, a river by itself was a doubtful military objective. In the absence of a Ministry of Defense or an Institute of Strategic Planning, to find the best line of military control was an ad hoc question for the emperor, taking any advice he could get from governors and commanders on the spot.

Consequently, for a variety of reasons the nature and disposition of military forces were crucial. Only if legions and cavalry units were available in sufficient numbers to repel incursions or go on the attack using a river as a supply route, line of control, or assembly point could a river be part of strategic planning. Around A.D. 200, in the reign of Septimius Severus, there were eight provincial governorships along the northern riverine boundaries of the empire: Lower Germany (two legions), Upper Germany (two legions), Raetia (one legion), Noricum (one legion), Upper Pannonia (three legions), Lower Pannonia (one legion), Upper Moesia (two legions), Lower Moesia (two legions). Therefore, fourteen out of thirty-three legions in service were stationed along the banks of the Rhine and Danube, with a further two beyond the Danube in Dacia; in addition, there were more than one hundred units of auxiliary infantry and cavalry. It is interesting that when the Romans occupied the Agri Decumates around the headwaters of the Rhine, Danube, and Neckar, the new line of control, consisting of small forts and palisades, was firmly based on rivers; it ran from Regensberg on the Danube via Lorch to Miltenberg-Altstadt on the Main. Needless to say, in all these military arrangements the roads that ran along the riverbank were crucial to planning and communications.

There were also six legions along the Euphrates, including two in Cappadocia and two between the Euphrates and the Tigris in Mesopotamia. In addition, in the second century there were at least seven cavalry *alae* and twenty-two auxiliary cohorts in Syria. In the Euphrates frontier zone, after the annexation of the kingdom of Commagene to the province of Syria in A.D. 72 or 73, Samosata, the leading city of the area, stood right on the river directly opposite the Parthian controlled district of Osrhoene with its capital at Edessa. There is evidence of Roman activity in the construction of a water screw to raise water from the river between Samosata and Zeugma and also of road building in the hinterland west of the Euphrates. But there were no bridges over the river, and a legion was based at the fordable crossing point at Zeugma.[154] Here the river Euphrates formed part of a crucial frontier zone within sight of a potentially hostile empire. On any analysis, these three great rivers, the Danube, the Rhine, and the Euphrates, though not providing decisive boundaries, were nevertheless at the heart of Roman military dispositions, with the troops often based right on the riverbank or close to it in a series of camps and forts.

How far did the strategic overview change in the disposition of military forces in the late empire, and how did the riverine topography fit in? In some respects there was continuity in deployment along rivers. While the Danube and the eastern frontier zone, partly along the Euphrates, remained pivotal areas, there was a move away from the Rhine, although a large force was maintained in Gaul. There was a substantial concentration of legions, cavalry, and auxiliary cohorts in Moesia, Pannonia, Dacia (now centered on the Danube), Raetia, and also in Syria, Palestine, and Mesopotamia. In the Pannonias, there were 47,000 *limitanei* (see below), with 34,000 in the two Moesias, 16,000 in Dacia, 23,000 in Valeria, and 11,000 in Raetia.[155] There were 18,000 in Syria Phoenice, 11,000 in Syria, 18,500 in Palestine, 13,500 in Mesopotamia, and 22,000 in Armenia. As the Romans struggled to regain the military initiative while facing a greater need to ward off attacks, it is worth emphasizing that they still tended to concentrate their military dispositions along rivers.

What is more, strategic lines often appear to run along rivers. For example, the Danube-Iller-Rhine *limes* consisted of a protected road running from Lake Constance along the valley of the Iller to Piniana on the Danube, while another road ran from the lake through the valley of the Inn to Salzburg and Linz; a line of forts was constructed southward along the Aare to meet the Rhône at Geneva. Several of the commands in the later empire, in which a *dux* took military responsibility for a group of provinces, specifically included a riverine element: *dux Syriae et Euphratensis*; *dux Daciae Ripensis*; *dux Pannoniae II Ripariensis et Saviae*; *dux Valeriae Ripensis*; *dux Pannoniae I et Norici Ripensis*, the last four being along the Danube.[156]

Perhaps the most obvious change in the late empire was the appearance of static, permanent frontier and riverbank troops (*ripenses* or *limitanei*), as opposed to the field army (*comitatenses*), which was more prestigious, was not linked to an individual province, and was ready for deployment wherever required, generally under the command of the emperor. Despite their apparently lower status, the *limitanei* or *ripenses* probably remained good-quality troops at least into the fifth century. The *ripenses* were so named because the frontier zone (*limes*) included a riverbank, though it has been argued that *limitanei* and *ripenses* were two separate grades of soldier.[157] It does seem that in the fourth century and after, the emphasis was much more on defense rather than on the use of rivers as a basis for attack or aggressive exploration. The very name of *limitanei* or *ripenses* suggests a permanent location connected to the *limes* or the riverbank, not a remit to roam far and wide in search of new conquests.

Of course, all troops in frontier regions could operate across a river or beyond a *limes*, and it is certainly true the Romans never lost the urge to intervene and negotiate with or attack and disrupt peoples beyond the Rhine and the Danube.[158] Constantine aggressively maintained contact with the opposite bank of the Rhine by building the fortified bridgehead at Divitium (Deutz) opposite Cologne; "After the defeat and control of the Franks through the fortitude of Constantine, the fort of the Divitienses was built in their land in the presence of the emperor himself."[159] There was another similar fort at Mainz Kastel. On the Danube, the same emperor constructed a new bridge at Transmarisca-Daphne, which was enthusiastically celebrated on his coinage.[160]

Nevertheless, although imperial ideology and propaganda still insisted on Roman invincibility and extension of the empire, the language of other foundations and the emphasis on fortifications tell a different story and may have served to undermine the traditionally offensive strategy of Roman armies. The sometimes desperate defense of Roman territory against incursions, which often involved guarding a riverbank, is reflected in a late third- or early fourth-century dedication from Tropaeum Traiani by Iulius Valerius, a veteran among the soldiers who manned frontier forts (*burgi*), to Hercules Protector of the bank of the Danube (Hercules Ripensis).[161] Diocletian and the Tetrarchy celebrated the building of "a defense of the state for the future and forever" at Zanes, near the Iron Gates camp.[162] In 316 Constantine and Licinius carried out repairs at Tropaeum Traiani (Adamklissi) in the frontier zone some distance behind the Danube, "to strengthen the protection of the frontier."[163] The importance of the actual riverbank in the third and fourth centuries is also illustrated by several other inscriptions from the Danube area, which refer to one Hermogenius. He had been "placed in command of the bank, of legion VII Claudia, lower section."[164] An inscription from Moesia found near Singidunum, which refers to "legio IV Flavia par(s) sup(erior)," suggests that the legion was responsible for a stretch of the Danube riverbank around Singidunum.[165] This evidence indicates the permanent presence of soldiers along the Danube bank in an organized military structure in which they were responsible for particular stretches of bank. This is a clear sign of the development of the *milites ripenses*. The formulas used in these inscriptions hint strongly at defense and also suggest that rivers were pivotal, even though the frontier zone might cover a wide area.

Therefore, when Ammianus Marcellinus spoke of camps, forts, and towers along the Rhine, he was surely thinking of the river as providing a kind of defensive sanctuary, even though the Romans controlled both banks.[166] Similarly, Eumenius in his Panegyric delivered in 297 or 298, mentioned the "forts of cavalry and infantry rebuilt along the entire length (*limes*) of the Rhine, Danube, and Euphrates."[167] Mamertinus, in his Panegyric of Maximianus, breathes life into traditional Roman sentiments by praising the emperor because he set no limit to Roman power save what his arms could conquer. However, he describes the previous situation, where the Rhine seemed the natural demarcation line separating the Roman provinces from barbarian savagery. Consequently, with an echo of the situation during the revolt of Civilis, there was consternation in Rome when the volume of the river's flow declined, yet when in full spate it brought Rome security. Here Mamertinus seems to articulate a common view that the Rhine could act as a defensive barrier for Roman interests. By contrast, the claim that whatever can be seen beyond the Rhine is Roman is surely some wishful thinking.[168] In 369 Valens negotiated a treaty with the Goths on a boat in the middle of the Danube; religious restrictions on Athanaric, the leader of the Goths, prevented him from leaving Gothic territory. This certainly indicates a change in the balance of power—Augustus would not have held such a meeting in person—and also surely shows that the Romans considered the bank of the Danube the limit of their current ambitions.[169] Furthermore the author of the fourth-century manual on military devices, *De Rebus Bellicis*, apparently a man well informed about Roman government, observed that many native tribes on the periphery of the empire were protected by barriers such as forests, mountains, snows, deserts, marshes, or rivers. He rather wistfully notes the importance of such natural barriers, and of course the argument could be turned around, so that the Romans too could exploit this kind of obstacle.[170]

As Rome developed more complex relationships with transriverine peoples, it is likely that frontier-zone politics became more important and rivers declined in significance as physical obstacles. The *barbari*, and particularly the Goths, came to have a close part in Roman life. After 332 and the treaty agreement with Constantine, the Goths provided troops for the Roman army, and an interesting diplomatic connection ensued. After the disastrous Roman defeat at the hands of the Goths at Adrianople in 378, new circumstances prevailed, and thereafter at various times groups of Goths and other peoples were invited across the Danube to serve in the army as foreign peoples fighting as allies of the empire; they might then settle in Roman territory. The great northern rivers were now part of a complicated cultural and military interchange, which made long-established Roman and non-Roman distinctions less significant. By the late fourth century and early fifth, foreign chieftains and kings tended to control access to the river crossings previously dominated by Roman forces.

6   CONCLUSION: RIVERS IN THE SERVICE OF ROME

The place of rivers in Roman policy for the periphery of the empire cannot be assessed merely in terms of military technicalities of defense and attack. The psychology of boundaries and the riverine environment is also important, and we need to see things through Roman eyes. For a start, the numerous references to rivers in ancient literature often testify to the special place held by rivers in the affections of riverine communities.[171] Furthermore, as we see in chapter 9, rivers and springs were often credited with beneficent healing powers, which were also in the control of Rome. Rivers frequently acted as boundaries and literally and symbolically marked an end. This often involved the boundaries of private land but also included provincial boundaries, and rivers were considered to demarcate entire local regions, including provinces of the empire. In this role of geographical definition and limitation, rivers were so important that they sometimes gave their name to whole areas. Rivers also served as vital routes of communication, serving a military as well as a commercial purpose. It may be right that the Romans conquered peoples not land.[172] However, the acquisition of land often came with the subjugation of a people, and the monuments, natural features, and resources of that land with all their emotional connotations passed into the hands of the conquerors.

Furthermore, springs and rivers in the popular imagination usually had a divine or quasi-divine status, and frequently a long mythological pedigree and a culturally strong identification with local areas. To cross a river had religious significance, which involved negotiation with the riverine deity. So the formal crossing of a river was often a ceremonial occasion with offerings or sacrifices, as we see in Alexander the Great's observances to the river-god of the Danube for permitting him to cross.[173] Similarly, it may well be that Trajan's religious ceremonies on the banks of the Danube sanctified the approval of the river-god.[174] In this context, the idea of the "moral barrier" of great rivers such as the Rhine and the Danube has real meaning. The larger the river, the stronger was its regional meaning and identity. Consequently, the intellectual and cultural parameters associated with riverine communities had a role to play in the execution of imperial decisions. The long diplomatic wrangling between Rome and Parthia over the Euphrates in northern Syria reflects some of these ideas. Because both the Romans and the Parthians were able to cross the river, it cannot be seen as a physical barrier. Nor was it a cultural dividing line; instead it was the emblem and marker of the control of territory between the two empires, and mastery of its environment showed who had the upper hand. It is significant that after the defeat of Caesennius Paetus, the Parthian king made the Romans construct a bridge over the river Arsanias as a kind of "demonstration of victory."[175]

The Romans had no empire-wide strategy or policy for using rivers consistently as some kind of military control. But they exploited the riverine environment as and how it suited them, just like the other natural resources they encountered. Therefore, their opinion of the value of rivers changed according to the local conditions and the prevailing military situation. Rivers were very useful for moving goods and people, supplying troops, and monitoring and controlling the local population, which had to cross at particular fords or bridges. They also helped to identify in popular consciousness the extent and location of imperial conquests and the superiority of Roman arms; great rivers seemed to be important allies for further imperial advance. Later, as the political and military climate changed, rivers, which had always to some extent been a bulwark against non-Romanized and potentially threatening peoples, now increasingly became a kind of anchor for a more defensive military arrangement, though the Romans never really came to think entirely in terms of defense.

A fragmentary inscription from Aphrodisias in Caria illustrates some of these issues; it celebrates a legion, probably the I Parthica, in the following terms: "This legion is in Singara, of Mesopotamia, near the river Tigris."[176] Here we find geographical and administrative precision, in a statement of military presence in the vicinity of a great river. This describes the situation after Septimius Severus had annexed a new province, definitively moving Roman power beyond the Euphrates; but occupation was immediately delimited by another great river. In Dio's view the conquest of Mesopotamia was a serious mistake, involving Rome in enormous expenditure, endless fighting, and the quarrels of other peoples.[177] But Severus had argued that the new province was a protection for Syria, tacitly recognizing that the Euphrates could not be a decisive military line. In fact, the motives for the Parthian War had much to do with political pressure and the emperor's need for military glory against a traditional enemy of Rome. This episode is a rare insight into a foreign policy debate and the complex motivation for warfare, conducted against a backdrop of great rivers that had long fascinated historians, poets, and scholars in Rome.

six

EXPLOITING RIVERS

Pliny describes the Rhône as "by far the most fertile of the rivers of the Gallic provinces."[1] What did he mean? In all probability he had in mind not only the river's rich hinterland but also the bounty enjoyed by riverine communities that used the river as a conduit for merchandise on the way to and from the Mediterranean, central Gaul, and the Rhine. For ancient writers this was an important theme. Cato in the second century B.C. had set out criteria for the location of a property; it must have a substantial town nearby, or the sea, or a navigable river, or a good and well-frequented road.[2] Two centuries later Columella also affirmed that a farm should be not far from the sea or a navigable river, "so that produce can be transported out and purchases brought in."[3] More generally, ancient writers recognized the significance of river navigation, and although they gave a varied and uneven picture, we have an impression of pervasive and significant travel connections by navigable waterway in various parts of the empire. Rivers as routes of communication, the ways in which they benefited directly or indirectly local regions and linked more distant regions, and how people interacted with the watery environment were relevant issues. This was particularly important at the local level in small communities spread across a region in which the river provided continuity and connections. A major river's tributaries were often part of the framework of communication, widening access and economic opportunities.

However, ancient writers place the role of rivers as thoroughfares firmly in the context of other watery benefits of the riverine environment. Not only did they contain all kinds of fish; they provided drinking water for people and animals, a fertile environment for crops and riverine plants, and materials particularly for pottery making. Furthermore, as people mastered rivers and learned how to control their flow, they developed irrigation to put unpromising land under cultivation and to drain waterlogged areas, managing and maintaining profitable wetlands, and exploited water power to drive mills. Therefore, an important point about this watery environment was the serious competition for water resources. Water taken out of a river or diverted elsewhere could lessen the flow and adversely affect navigation. Competing usages for water often brought communities into conflict. In the Alps, the Salassi exploited the Duria by digging channels to draw off water to wash the gold from their mining activities and severely reduced the volume of water. This infuriated their farming neighbors further down the valley since they needed the water for irrigation.[4]

In this chapter, I begin by examining the general characteristics and problems of navigable rivers, the nature of ancient writing about such rivers, types of riverboat, the cost of river transport compared to road transport, possible connections between rivers and roads, and attempts to regulate river flow by canals and dams. I then consider how the Romans exploited other aspects of the fertile riverine environment, including the control and management of wetlands and the collecting and channeling of rivers and springs to secure a water supply.

1   NAVIGABLE RIVERS: CHARACTERISTICS AND PROBLEMS

In the watery environment, navigable rivers were a very important boon to communities in that they assisted both communications and the transport of goods and people, offering a natural highway to and from the sea. The layout of the river network could determine the location of important towns and centers of communication.[5] Local communities, manufacturers, producers, and traders could move goods and become more accessible without needing the construction of roads suitable for the passage of heavy, wheeled vehicles pulled by horses or oxen, for riverboats more easily transported heavy loads. In the upper reaches of rivers where navigation was impossible, heavy timber could be floated downstream. In summer, when smaller rivers dried up, their beds could be used as a makeshift road. Transport by river would not be disrupted by the kind of bad weather that made roads impassable or subject to other impediments of land travel or even, up to a point, to the threat of bandits. Furthermore, the construction of canals might facilitate a connected river network, allowing the movement of goods over a wider area. Ideally riverine transport should be integrated with local road networks.[6] In some cases paths and roads grew up alongside a river, especially on the earthworks that were sometimes built to keep a river within its banks.

In normal river morphology, since the land surface is never entirely flat, runoff flows downward by the most direct and steepest route, eventually deepening its bed. As it approaches its base level the gradient declines and the river valley widens as the river expands its channel on either side and deposits silt before reaching sea level. It is in the lower river valleys that the densest population occurs and where river navigation is of most value in providing travel routes and movement of goods. The value of navigable rivers was enhanced by the number of usable tributaries, which might open up a route of communication to the hills surrounding the main river valley.

On the other hand, river navigation was uncertain. Apart from insufficient flow due to seasonal variation, strong currents might make self-propelled navigation difficult and require the boat to be towed. Rapids, narrows, and waterfalls meant that the boat had to be taken out of the water and carried. In northern areas, rivers such as the Danube froze over in winter. Silting also caused problems and in many rivers will have reduced the draft of the boats that could be used. In modern times, dredging is often necessary to increase the depth of the channel, or other operations to narrow it. Tidal rivers produce their own problems, because at times of slack water silt is deposited speedily and is not always removed by the incoming tide, which has to contend against the downstream flow of fresh water. The ebb tide, however, increased by the freshwater flow (held up by the rising tide) is most effective in removing the accumulations of silt. The effective operation of this process depends in part on the shape and layout of the estuary.

The movement of large amounts of goods by river implies the construction or presence of ports to organize commerce and trade. Such ports are in general terms of two kinds. First, the port at the seaward end of the river acts as a center for the movement of goods. Merchandise brought by large seagoing ships can if necessary be stored here and then transferred to ships of shallower draft for movement along the river. This combined sea and river port also receives goods transported downstream from inland sites for on-shipment and therefore serves as a kind of clearing center. Second, the river port acts as a reception point for produce and manufactured items from inland areas, which are then moved downstream for sale in other regions or for export to more remote destinations. The river port also acts as a distribution center for imports brought upstream. A river with a populous hinterland could be very busy and the riverine ports correspondingly crowded, though, since a river is theoretically accessible to anyone who can get his produce to the bank and onto some kind of craft, there will have been many small-scale transactions, which will nevertheless have been vital to local people.[7]

It is worth noting that there were probably many more navigable rivers than our sources know about. Of the rivers cited in the *Barrington Atlas*, only a small proportion are recorded as having been navigable. There will have been many small and little-known rivers where limited navigation was carried on by local people for the benefit of riverine communities. In the main we know about the more significant rivers or rivers that happened to come to public attention. Therefore, there was probably a great deal of local river navigation, and in this context people took readily to exploring and exploiting rivers more extensively wherever possible, according to terrain and availability of other modes of transport. Some navigable rivers were extremely long and could be navigable over most of their course. This would offer some continuity in planning and arranging methods of moving goods and perhaps reduce expense. On the other hand, long rivers were sometimes navigable only for part of their course or even in several different parts. Shorter rivers navigable for most of their length offered access to remoter areas, especially, for example, in Bruttium where a series of parallel rivers ran down from the mountains to the coast.

2   ANCIENT WRITING ON NAVIGABLE RIVERS

"The river Atax A(ude) descends from the Pyrenees and, where it depends on waters from its own source, is a meager and shallow stream; otherwise, when it occupies a broader bed, it is nowhere navigable, except when it passes Narbo, but when it is swollen by winter rains, it normally rises to the extent that it cannot keep itself within its banks."[8] This description shows the importance of recording the navigability even of lesser rivers, and also some of the problems, including local geography, a bed that was too narrow for ships, and inconsistent and inadequate flow. The Atax was subject to seasonal flooding, which could bring disaster to prosperous and settled communities. Writers such as Strabo and Pliny and, to a lesser extent, Pomponius Mela had a broad interest in geography, topography, and anthropology. For them, local society was important with its trade and commercial activities, methods of transport, and movement. Therefore, to their mind rivers had relevance beyond their role in geographical measurement, direction finding, and demarcating boundaries.[9] Our writers, as well as commenting on some individual rivers, raise some interesting general points and show a high degree of interest in navigability. Some of their information is pretty basic, for example, that a river was *navigabilis*, or *capax navigiorum*, but sometimes they have details of the exact extent of navigability, the type of ships used, the nature of cargoes, and also the navigation season. This information even extends to India, and some must have come from traders or professional sailors who used the rivers. Strabo and Pliny also consider features that assisted or hindered the navigability of rivers. Small river volume could make navigation difficult, while silt also caused problems; navigation at a river mouth might need experienced sailors.[10] Polybius had also noted the difficulty of bringing in supplies by river because of the small volume and sluggish current.[11] Ideally, rivers should be wide and deep with navigable tributaries since water from tributaries increased river volume.[12] It was also possible to exploit the flood tide at estuaries, while artificial measures could help to control rivers and make them navigable.[13] In particular, the upper course of the Tiber needed dams and sluices, while for navigability other rivers required showers of rain to increase the volume.[14] As noted, the value of riverine navigation could also be increased by links between rivers, a good relationship with the road network, and a system of canals.[15]

Consequently bridges, fords, and river tolls were important and form part of Strabo's narrative,[16] and he has memorable descriptions of riverine communities where these factors worked well together.[17] In describing the area of southern Gaul around Tolosa (Toulouse), he is enthusiastic about how its various characteristics complemented one another:

> But above all it is important to raise a point that I made before, namely the harmonious conformity of the countryside in relation to the rivers and the sea, both the outer (the ocean) and the inner. If someone applied himself to this, he could well find that this is not the least important part of the quality of the region. I mean that everyone can easily exchange with everyone else the requirements of daily life and that the benefits of this are available to all in common.

He goes on to give his famous account of the Rhône and other Gallic rivers.[18] These routes of communication also benefited the Romans, and Rome itself was sustained by the transport of materials on the Tiber and its tributaries.[19] In a way, this fits Strabo's geographical vision, which was based on the centrality of the Mediterranean Sea, Italy, and Rome, and particularly those rivers that flowed into the Mediterranean and contributed to the economic vitality of the region.

Pliny also collects extraordinarily precise detail, for example, that the river Alpheios in Elis was navigable for six miles, or what type of ships could operate on rivers in Arabia; the Hyperis was navigable for merchant ships, the Phrystimus was generally navigable, the Granis for ships of moderate size.[20] Pliny is always interested in rivers that supported shipping, even as far away as India.[21] It is, of course, easy to associate these descriptions with Pliny's interest in trade and commerce and his researches into tolls and customs revenues, especially between Rome and the East. But this can hardly apply to many of the rivers that he mentions, where tolls cannot have been important. I think that part of Pliny's interest lies in the appearance of rivers; he likes them to be vibrant and active waterways. Furthermore, he is concerned about how small communities operated within the framework of river communications. So, access to main thoroughfares or major rivers was important, and it is notable that Pliny talks about navigable tributaries. For Pliny, the ideal was a river that combined commerce, access, and beauty in congenial surroundings. So, the river Baetis glided smoothly along a beautiful channel between numerous towns situated on the banks. At Colonia Patricia (Corduba), the river became navigable and also had numerous tributaries such as the Singilis and the Maenuba, which were navigable and provided access to the interior. As Pliny says, the Baetis "absorbed many rivers from which it took their glory as well as their waters."[22]

There is no doubt that Pliny believed that rivers were at the heart of many local communities and provided vital contacts where roads were inadequate or nonexistent.[23] In his opinion, rivers, while having a watery dimension, were more akin to land than to the sea, since they were surrounded by the more stable land. They therefore offered reliable thoroughfares.[24] It may be significant that some of his evidence came by word of mouth from Roman merchants.[25] Rivers facilitated the transport of materials and the exchange of goods, and river harbors such as those on the rivers Fertur in Apulia and Trinius in Samnium, provided the venue for much commercial activity as well as employment;[26] in Africa, the river Asana although tidal was well known for its harbor.[27] The Tiber itself of course was the chosen route for many of Rome's imports and was a "most gentle trader in all the earth's produce."[28] It is in the context of its vast navigable length, its constant water flow, its mighty tributaries, and the wealthy cities dotted along its banks, that we can understand Pliny's description of the Padus as the "richest" of all Italian rivers. A position near the confluence of rivers gave some cities a boost for trade. The famous Indian city of Automula stood on the coast at the confluence of five rivers and was well known for its market.[29] Laodicea was a very distinguished city in Caria, which gained from its position on the river Lycus and was also washed by the rivers Asopos and Kapros.[30] Pliny's description of barter in Sri Lanka, where traders left goods on the bank of a river alongside commodities deposited by local residents, who, if they were satisfied with the exchange went off with the goods, may not be out of place for some remoter parts of Italy or the provinces accessed by rivers.[31]

Therefore, ancient writers discussing geography and topography certainly offer a substantial amount of seemingly important evidence, especially since we can identify most of the rivers they mention. But how reliable is their evidence? Only rarely do they give a precise indication of their sources, as, for example, when Strabo refers to the increase of information after the campaigns of Alexander the Great in the East, and when Pliny mentions the investigations of Domitius Corbulo and Licinius Mucianus while on campaign. Yet Strabo, Pliny, and other geographical writers seem to have at their disposal sometimes quite detailed information. Was there some kind of inventory of navigable rivers, and what was the source of their information? We might guess at customs posts for traffic, or perhaps local knowledge passed on to boatmen and shippers. On the other hand, there may have been a more formal record in a kind of itinerary for river travelers similar to the itineraries for those using the road network.[32] Although ancient maps invariably depicted rivers, there is no clear evidence for river navigation charts. But Salway has suggested that in the Peutinger Map the red line markings added to certain rivers in northern Italy and in central and southern Germany indicate that an *itinerarium fluviale* had been consulted to identify navigable stretches.[33] This is interesting, but it is more plausible to suppose that the copyist simply adopted this as a decorative ploy.[34]

In fact, it is very difficult to evaluate our evidence for riverine navigation. Our writers might simply be in error or have been misled by efforts to promote the honor and standing of the local river. Furthermore, the course and characteristics of rivers changed over time, and what was true in Pliny's time may not have been true earlier or in the third century A.D. However, given the importance that Strabo and Pliny attach to river navigation and the development of local riverine communities, and their general interest in rivers, we should be encouraged to accept that they had at least made careful inquiries. There may be some help in river nomenclature, which perhaps carried a trace of the river's character as perceived by early settlers. For example, in Britain river names derived from Trisantona, such as the Arun in Sussex and the Trent in Staffordshire, might convey the idea of "great wayfarer"—a long wandering river that provided a significant route for traveling. However, this is uncertain because it is also possible that the root of the name combined the meaning "trespasser" in the sense of a river in flood.[35] Apart from this, we rely heavily on archaeology.

The ancient evidence must be viewed in the context of changes in the hydrological conditions in southern Europe. Although it is true that climatic conditions and other factors such as vegetation and the amount of forestation have changed since Roman times, it is likely that in overall terms there was broad similarity between modern and ancient hydrological conditions but that the factors supporting navigation were better in the ancient world. Recent investigation has suggested that many small rivers contained a greater volume of water in earlier times. For example, the yearly average flow of water in central Europe as a percentage of its volume in the late twentieth century was, for the period 100 B.C.–A.D. 0, about 120 percent and for A.D. 0–900, about 95 percent. It seems a reasonable conjecture that in the Roman world the necessary water flow would have been available for many rivers, even smaller, shallow ones, and that they were navigable, though it some cases passage will have been restricted to flat-bottomed vessels.[36]

This raises the point that, because successful navigation depends on certain riverine qualities, it might be useful to consider recorded river conditions and volume in recent times. Favorable conditions are a stable and constant rate of water flow and a wide riverbed; a gentle slope is better than a fast-moving river with rapids and a bed encumbered by rocks or silt. For example, the Baetis has a gentle decline—between Corduba and Seville, it is 0.5 meters per kilometer. The Anas has two sections of gentle slope divided by a steeper section; in upper reaches it is 0.66 meters per kilometer, but 1–2 meters per kilometer in the steeper section, and very slight in the lower reaches.[37] In modern times the flow of the Guadalquivir, Genil, and Guadiana has been regularly monitored. The Guadalquivir has an irregular and rather weak flow, with an annual median of 183.5 cubic meters per second at Seville. Its tributary the Genil, which rises in the Sierra Nevada, has an annual flow of 33.60 cubic meters per second at Puente Genil. The Guadiana has a modest flow, achieving 78.81 cubic meters per second at Puente de Palmas. All the rivers suffer from great variations in seasonal flow. For example, the Guadiana's flow from June to September falls to less than 10 cubic meters per second.[38] However, the tide in the Anas and Baetis could greatly assist movement upstream, and the ebb tide was also valuable. When water flow was reduced in the height of summer, some rivers would still be navigable for flat-bottomed boats and barges.

What is the minimum flow to permit navigation by even the smallest ships? It is interesting to consider the Ouvèze (Ovidis), which was a tributary of the Rhône and navigable in antiquity.[39] It has an average annual flow of 6.71 cubic meters per second, with less than 6 in June to November, although in February it has 12. So perhaps we can say that 10–12 cubic meters per second was very approximately the lower limit for navigation of very light ships. Wider rivers required a bigger flow of water of perhaps 40–60 cubic meters per second. Many rivers were probably navigable at least for part of the year. Sillières speculates that up to thirteen rivers in southern Spain were potentially suitable for navigation, at least for small craft: Sucro (Júcar), Tader (Segura), Salduba (Guadalhorce), Barbesula (Guadiaro), Guadalete, Río Vélez, Urius (Tinto), Luxia (Odiel), Río Piedra, and tributaries of the Baetis—Guadalimar, Guadajoz, Corbones, and Ribera de Huelva.[40] It is possible here to suggest a network of navigable rivers.[41] And some support comes from the continuing use of such rivers in later periods, especially the sixteenth and seventeenth centuries. For example, ships of 200–250 tons could get to Seville, while smaller ships sailed between Seville and Ilipa; the smallest were barges perhaps carrying several tons.[42]

3   RIVERBOATS

The evidence for craft used in river navigation is scattered and often difficult to interpret. In particular, there is a problem of definition and identification of craft specifically used on rivers, because many small vessels could be used for a variety of purposes, and also because some rivers were navigable for a certain distance by large merchant vessels. Our evidence consists in the first place of descriptions in ancient authors, from whom we can try to establish the Latin and Greek words defining different types of boats and the nature of boats used in river travel. Given the fragmentary nature of the ancient source material, our knowledge is unlikely to be complete, though inscriptions and papyrus documents referring to ships usefully supplement the literary sources. For example, the importance of rivercraft is seen in the archaeological traces left by river boatmen, who grouped together in prestigious corporations. Individual and group memorials celebrate the activities of the men who moved goods along inland waterways, and the number and location of the many inscriptions can help show the extent and provenance of river-borne trade. In addition, underwater archaeology is producing an increasing range of evidence about ancient shipwrecks and their cargoes, though most major finds have been in the ocean. Pictures carved on tombstones and other memorials and mosaics and paintings decorating private villas provide the most striking evidence for ancient ships and riverine navigation.[43] For example, several frescoes from Pompeii depict craft propelled by oars or punting poles.[44]

Especially important is the famous mosaic of Althiburus (Medeina) in Africa dating from the third or fourth century A.D., which covered the floor of the *frigidarium* in a private villa. At one end of the mosaic, Oceanus is depicted surrounded by fishes and Cupids riding on dolphins, while at the other end a river-god reclines on a rock surrounded by reeds and holding the branch of a tree in his left hand. The waters between the two figures are occupied by different types of ship, many of which are named and occasionally accompanied by a relevant excerpt of Latin poetry, and they clearly represent both seagoing and river-going vessels. It is not necessary to think that the ships closest to Oceanus or the river-god must be specifically sea or river craft. The only designation that precisely refers to a river is attached to the *stlatta*: "from here the legion had now moved across on boats on the river." Instead, the mosaic presents a generally colorful scene containing various boats for the owner's enjoyment. What is interesting is that the designer gave equal prominence to the ocean and to rivers, suggesting that in popular perception riverine navigation was a significant factor in everyday life, and that ships both large and small were a frequent sight along rivers. The many Celtic and Italian names for boats in the mosaic suggest that it was compiled in Italy by someone, perhaps from a Hellenistic background, who knew sailing practices in both Italy and Gaul.[45]

The main types of boats (and their operators) particularly suitable for use on rivers, including smaller rivers and the upper reaches of large rivers, are as follows.[46]

> *Caudicaria* or *codicaria* (*navis*): a kind of barge or lighter vessel that was towed upriver using a towing mast; some of these vessels were equipped with a sail and could travel under their own power.[47]
>
> *Codicarii*: men who took charge of craft operated by towing for the transport of goods along the Tiber.
>
> *Lenunculus*: a small boat or skiff often used in harbors to carry unloaded goods from large ships to a warehouse, or upstream.[48] *Lenuncularii tabularii auxiliarii* probably took bigger boats in tow to their berth in harbor and made sure that their papers were in order. *Lenuncularii pleromarii auxiliarii* operated lighters and small barges for loading and reloading ships that could not make it into harbor.[49]
>
> *Linter*: a small, light boat, which could be propelled by oars or sail, or by both; ancient writers refer to their use on the Tiber and on rivers in Gaul.[50]
>
> *Ratiaria*: a very small boat; the *ratiarius* used rafts or possibly operated ferries across rivers.[51]
>
> *Ratis*: a general term for a craft, propelled by oars but sometimes by sail; in Gaul it seems particularly to have been used on rivers.[52]
>
> *Scapha*: skiff or light boat that could be used for moving cargoes upstream or operate in harbors.[53]
>
> *Utricularius* or *utriclarius*: a person who probably used smaller rafts supported on skins stuffed with straw, and operated in smaller rivers and estuaries or perhaps occasionally ferried goods out to ships.[54]
>
> *Stlatta*: a small riverboat. Ausonius refers to them in use on the Tarn and Garonne; a *stlatta* is depicted in the Althiburus mosaic as a small rowboat.[55]
>
> Small boats of various types such as *cumba*, *lembus*, and *placida* are difficult to define but were probably propelled by oars; *actuarius* was

a merchant vessel using oars, though equipped with one sail.[56] *Lusoria* originally referred to river houseboats used for pleasure but was subsequently used of working vessels. By the fourth century, the *lusoria* referred to the light galleys used by the Roman navy on the Rhine and the Danube.[57] It is worth noting Tacitus's description of the huge 1,000-ship fleet that Germanicus constructed in A.D. 16, which contained a variety of specially designed ships, including some with two rudders so that the steersman could reverse direction and bring them ashore on either bank of a river.[58]

Navicularius: a shipper or shipowner, who could sail the ship himself or employ a captain.[59] He might also own more than one ship. The *nauta* or *marinus* was in general terms a sailor or boatman.

Many Greek terms were in use for small craft, which generally appeared on the Nile but were probably used on other navigable streams. Notable are: *kontoton* (poled boat—a kind of punt); *polykopon* (many oared; used for transporting grain, army supplies, and personnel with a capacity of 12½–25 tonnes); *platypegion* ("wide-built"; probably a barge); *halias* (an oared coastal craft that appears on the Nile as a dispatch boat in the Roman government service); *ploion zeugmatikon* (possibly a catamaran or several small boats yoked together).[60]

Finally, various types of coastal craft could also be used in estuaries and rivers. Here the different geographical types possibly indicate the small craft used by locals on many rivers for short journeys.[61] For example, the small boat (21 meters long and 5.6 wide) found at Comacchio in the delta of the Padus, which dates from the time of Augustus, was suitable for work on rivers, lagoons, and general cabotage.[62] The great variety of small craft perhaps suggests widespread use of rivers, though not all riverine navigation would have been important commercially; there will have been private transport of small quantities for local use, or perhaps for local trade or barter. Unusual variations in design may suggest that in the variegated nature of river transport precise definitions are not always helpful. For example, a relief of the second or third century A.D. found near Trier depicts a riverboat, which was probably used on the rivers Moselle or Sarre. It has an unusual design, being short and shallow with a tall, oblong sail. The craft resembles a raft, yet has the traditional ship component of a post carved in the shape of a goose head.[63] It is also important to note that larger ships could be sailed upstream for part of the course of some rivers, as Strabo says was the case in Spain.[64] Ships like the *corbita* and *ponto* were merchantmen, the second being native to the south coast of France.

Although there is no evidence that they had any particular role on rivers, it has been suggested that both these vessels could navigate some Spanish rivers in the right circumstances.[65] Both vessels appear in the mosaic of Althiburus.

Given the wide variety of craft using rivers, methods of propulsion were equally variegated.[66] Where estuaries and rivers of sufficient volume allowed larger cargo vessels to travel upstream, sails were used with the support of onshore winds. A ship of 240 tonnes with a beam of ten meters and length of thirty meters would have needed a depth of little more than three meters of water.[67] It was then possible to drift downstream using the river's current. Herodotus describes a method for exploiting the Nile current; the boatmen had a wooden device like a door frame, over which was lashed a reed matting, which they floated on a line in front of the boat; as this was taken up by the current it drifted and pulled the boat; a stone of about 120 pounds weight, was attached to the boat by a rope and dragged along well beneath the surface so as to keep it on course.[68] In the case of tidal rivers, boats could drift upstream on the flood tide and then use the ebb to return, as described by Ausonius.[69] In Roman times, a second oar was added at the prow to help with steering since in a slow current there might be little impetus on the main steering oar.[70]

But river navigation was more often accomplished by oars, and a long-established method of rowing in Gaul and Germany used push oars, which were tied to the sides of craft; the oarsman faced forward and pushed the oar away from him, thereby pulling the oar blade back and moving the craft forward. By turning the oar blade in the stroke, it was possible for the rower also to steer the boat. The pull oar (*remus*) was also used in Roman times. These oars were positioned in tholes in the gunwale and the rowers, who normally had their backs to the prow, pulled the oars toward themselves, propelling the craft forward. This method required a separate helmsman. Possibly oars were not permanently fixed on rivercraft, but could be reversed as circumstances demanded. Tacitus refers to movable oars on the boats of the Suiones, and he probably means that the rowlocks were secured by ropes and could be reversed for rowing in the opposite direction. It is also possible that the steering oar could be moved from the bow to the stern of the vessel.[71] Smaller craft could be propelled by a paddle, but in general oars were more effective.

Many illustrations of ships on reliefs depict them with rowers in operation. For example, a funeral monument at Neumagen shows a vessel with no mast propelled by six oarsmen and possibly six on the other side (though curiously twenty-two oars are displayed), with a steersman and one man who marks time by clapping his hands. The vessel carried four large casks, presumably of wine.[72] On the other hand, it is possible that this is in fact a warship used to transport wine for the army with twenty-two oars on each side and therefore forty-four oarsmen, or double this if there were two men to an oar. On this view, the merchant was not portraying his own ship on the tombstone but was celebrating that he was supplier of wine to the military.[73]

The use of a pole like a punt on small craft had the advantage of taking up less room than oars and also provided strong propulsion from riverbeds that were sufficiently shallow. This method was also valuable where there was no riverside path for towing. The pole was long, often had an iron tip, and could also be used for steering.[74] The punter could be permanently positioned at one end of the boat and propelled it by sliding the pole down onto the riverbed, pushing on it, and slowly withdrawing it. The punting pole is sometimes depicted with a handle like an old-fashioned crutch, and as the punter pushed the pole into the riverbed, he put the handle under his arm walked along the boat in the direction of travel. For this method the punter needed a gangplank running the entire length of the ship and also a separate helmsman. Some craft resembling punts have been discovered in Germany:[75] near Zwammerdam at a Roman auxiliary fort on the south bank of the Rhine, several dugouts, barges, and a steering oar (dating c. A.D. 150–225) have been uncovered.[76] The dugouts could be used on the river as far upstream as Switzerland; the barges were to transport heavy goods and may have been mainly for use downstream. Possibly the usual crew on a cargo vessel without oars in the Roman period was three men—that is, one helmsman and one man on either side using the punting pole as a crutch.[77]

Towing of rivercraft, by either mules, horses, or men, features strongly; towing was essential in certain rivers or certain parts of rivers and in getting past bridges with low clearance. The *navis caudicaria* had a mast of a sprit-rig type, which is set forward of amidships and could serve as a towing mast, since such a mast must be ahead of the center of gravity. A line was run from the team on the bank over a block on the tip of the mast and then down to the stern, where it was secured. Possibly some ships had a capstan on the afterdeck so that, where the going was difficult for the towing team, the ship could be winched upstream by attaching the rope to a solid fixture on land.[78] The mast was a stout pole and had to be retractable, consequently having no ladder and little running rigging; it could be fitted with cleats so that the crew could go aloft. Alternatively the towrope could be attached to the prow of the ship. A helmsman was required to keep the ship away from the banks and other obstacles. A relief from Igel on the river Moselle near Trier shows at least two men hauling a ship, which contains two large bales (possibly of cloth) and has a steersman on board.[79] A similar operation can be seen on a relief now in Avignon. The funeral monument of

FIGURE 8. *Mosaic, circa* A.D. *200, from the Piazzale delle Corporazioni in Ostia showing a small boat* (codicaria) *with winch, two steering oars, a cleated mast, and a man going on board carrying an amphora (JRS 1965, plate II.3). Copyright © 1965 The Roman Society. Image reprinted with permission of Cambridge University Press.*

the boatman Blussus from near Mainz shows a rivercraft on the Rhine or the Moselle in the mid-first century A.D.; it has a sprit rig and four-man crew, including a steersman at the stern and one man at the bow with oar, which can be moved from one side to the other as necessary.[80] There are at least two rowers, and it carries a large packing case. The mast indicates that the boat could be towed. It is particularly interesting that this vessel was equipped for several modes of propulsion.[81] A mosaic form Ostia shows a small craft, probably a *codicaria*, with a cleated mast, two steering oars, and a winch; an amphora is being loaded (figure 8). A relief found at Salerno cathedral depicts a riverboat (*codicaria*) in the process of unloading; it has a collapsible mast with cleats for climbing (figure 9).[82] An interesting mosaic from Mérida shows a small boat with sails and no oars being pulled by two men using a rope over their shoulders. This may be a representation of fluvial transportation on the Baetis.[83]

There is not much evidence for the men who did the towing since this was an unskilled, low-prestige activity, and they have left little record. The towing rope

FIGURE 9. *Relief from the third century* A.D. *in Salerno cathedral showing two men unloading a* codicaria *with one steering oar and a lowered, cleated mast; two crewmen work on the boat* (JRS 1965, plate V.1). Copyright © 1965 The Roman Society. Image reprinted with permission of Cambridge University Press.

was *helcium, funis,* or *remulcrum,* and the man who towed boats with the rope was the *helciarius.* Martial, referring to the idyllic situation of a friend's villa, rejoices that sleep cannot be interrupted by the shout of the boatswain giving the time for the rowers of craft on the Tiber or the uproar of the men towing boats.[84] The *helciarii* could work in the water if the bank was obstructed. It is impossible to say how many men were employed in towing rivercraft; to take fifteenth-century France as a general comparison, between 250 and 400 are recorded downstream from Lyon on the Rhône, which was a great thorough-fare but also a river where progress upstream was very difficult.[85] A helmsman and at least two men were needed for towing; towing by a gang of men would require enough space for them to walk well away from the river on a flat sur-face, though men should be able to deal with obstacles.[86] Towing by animals is not mentioned in respect of rivers in Gaul, though it might have been used.[87] Towing by animals requires more space on the banks, and a man towing a boat could make better progress over an uneven surface than an ox or a horse. How-ever, Procopius writing circa A.D. 550 refers to teams of oxen towing boats on the Tiber and it may be that animals were used in certain conditions for heavier loads.[88]

The government tried to ensure that rivers were kept open for navigation and that no action by any individual diminished or disrupted the water flow. Under the *Digest* heading "On rivers and the prevention of any action on a public river or riverbank that might interfere with navigation," the general rule is affirmed: "Therefore, if the water is drawn away so that the river becomes smaller and is less navigable, or if it is made wider and being spread out becomes shallower, or if it is made narrow and flows more rapidly, or if anything else is done that disturbs navigation, makes it more difficult or entirely prevents it, there will be a place for the interdict."[89] There was also some attempt to manage rivers and riverbanks in order to facilitate towing and the landing of cargo by keeping the area clear of obstacles. "The praetor does not prohibit every piece of work being done in a public river or on the bank of a public river, but only whatever is done that interferes with the landing of goods and navigation. Therefore, this interdict applies only to those public rivers that are navigable."[90] Aulus Gellius refers to a praetorian edict establishing contracts for clearing a river blocked by trees: "The word *retae* is used to describe trees, which either overhang the stream from the banks of the river or actually stand in the riverbed itself, and which might impede passing ships."[91] In certain cases, riverbanks would also have to be firmed up for towing. Passage by oxen or horses could be destructive of the banks, and if the towrope were attached to the prow of the boat, then it might rub against the bank. Disputes here will have involved the boatmen and those who owned the bank, since ownership could extend right to the point where the bank sloped downward toward the water.[92]

4   ROAD AND RIVER TRANSPORT

It would be very helpful in the analysis of ancient riverine trade if we could clearly establish the comparative cost of land and fluvial transport. The evidence is largely contained in Diocletian's Price Edict of A.D. 301, which aimed to curb price speculation and to produce relatively stable prices in the empire, though it was apparently promulgated only in the eastern part. Analysis suggests that sea transport was the cheapest way of moving goods but that transport by inland waterway was substantially cheaper than road transport by wagon or pack animals. Based on a calculation for moving wheat, the cost of land transport by wagon would be between 36.7 and 73.4 percent of the value of the wheat for every 100 Roman miles. On the basis of an Egyptian papyrus, which describes the transport of wheat by water about 13.6 miles from Arsinoe to Ptolemais Hormou, the cost would be 6.38 percent of the value of the wheat per 100 miles. If we take the figures from the edict for sea and road transport and compare them with the papyrus, the cost ratios are: sea, 1; inland waterway, 4.9; and road, 28–56.[93]

However, this calculation is not as straightforward as it seems. Diocletian's Price Edict is not concerned with regional variations or differences between wholesale and retail prices and may give theoretical figures. The prices are possibly based on those prevailing in large eastern towns such as Nicomedia, whereas prices in smaller communities may have been cheaper. The Egyptian papyrus dates from A.D. 42, and a comparison between prices in the early imperial period and the estimate of prices from the early fourth century A.D. may not be valid. Furthermore, longer-distance transport arrangements were often based on a river network (as within Gaul and also the connection between Gallic rivers and the Rhine), and merchandise would have to be transported by land between rivers. Many rivers were linked to the road network. So, the cost of transport of goods would often be a combination of road and river or sea, road, and river, and no direct comparison is possible. In some places even in a riverine environment, movement of heavy goods by river was impractical because of problems of river volume and seasonal variation. Despite these complications, river travel in straight competition was probably considerably cheaper than road travel. And Pliny in a letter to Trajan sums up the value of water transport. He pointed out that marble and farm produce were ferried across Lake Sophon (near Nicomedia) as far as the main road but that the onward travel to the sea by road was difficult and expensive. He recommended the construction of a canal to facilitate the onward transit of the merchandise.[94]

We might assume that travel by sea or river was quicker than by land, but it is very difficult to estimate the comparative speed of river and road transport. The Romans constructed an impressive road network, but moving along them was not always easy, especially in the case of the transport of heavy loads. Pack animals were common, most commonly mules or donkeys, though horses were used and camels in Egypt. A camel could carry up to 360 kilograms, at least over a short distance, while on flat ground a horse could carry about 170 kilograms, but only 100 kilograms on rough terrain. Mules in the right conditions could possibly carry almost as much as a camel. But they used panniers, which restricted the kind of load they could carry. Donkeys were sure-footed and relatively easy to maintain and could carry up to 150 kilograms.[95] Heavy or very bulky loads could most effectively be carried on wagons pulled by oxen, which could cope with greater weights and were more placid than horses. This method of haulage was very slow and the animals moved at about 1.5–3 kilometers per hour; in hilly country or with other obstacles they might manage only 9.5 kilometers a day.[96] However, in desert regions of Egypt the caravans may have managed to average about 30 kilometers a day.

At sea, merchant ships under sail might average two knots with a following wind on the trip from Rome to Alexandria. A smaller, fast sailing ship could manage four and a half to five knots. A small merchantman had cargo capacity of about 120–150 tonnes; many could carry from 400 to just over 500 tonnes and a few over 1,000 tonnes; however, many ships were in the 20–40 tonne category.[97] On inland waterways, it is very difficult to calculate the speed achieved by ships sailing or being rowed or towed upstream. Much would depend on the speed of the current and the morphology of the river.[98] In respect of towing, we hear that on the Tigris and Euphrates in the early period crews of two to eighteen men moved boats varying in size from 1 to 11 tonnes; a boat of average size of about 6 tonnes could achieve nine to ten kilometers upstream every day, whereas eighteen men could probably manage twenty kilometers; downstream it was possible to achieve thirty to thirty-five kilometers.[99] It has been suggested (on the basis of nineteenth-century figures for a canal) that in Roman times two men could pull 80–100 tonnes fourteen kilometers in a day; two horses could double the distance.[100] Others have argued that on rivers and canals it might be possible to achieve up to fifty or sixty kilometers a day.[101] However, normally towing along the banks of a river was much more difficult; for example, towing upstream on the Rhône in the fourteenth century could sometimes cover only five kilometers a day. In Roman times a distance of eleven kilometers a day for the trip from Ostia to Rome has been suggested.[102] Roman riverboats could carry up to 34 tonnes. But there were great variations, and a boat recovered from Britain probably had a capacity of only 9 tons. Nevertheless, even this could carry the same load as eighteen wagons or seventy-two pack animals. A single horse hitched to a barge can pull 250 times the load it can carry on its back.[103]

In general, it was often cheaper and faster to move goods to the interior by river than by road, but this was not invariably or consistently true in different areas. Rivers were more convenient and suited certain types of cargo, such as wine amphorae. But there were many variable factors, such as the nature of the river, seasonal changes in river volume, and onward transport connections. Furthermore, to move goods by river, you would need to invest in a boat, or hire suitable craft and crew and, if necessary, men or animals for towing. River transport was never likely to be an easy option and usually did not offer a complete route to the destination. In other words, most people probably used a combination of routes and means of transport which would change from time to time according to season and convenience and geographical location.

River valleys offered road builders routes provided by nature, which fitted in with the lie of the land and the movement of people. Rivers tend to run from the mountains down to the coast, and roads tended to run alongside rivers in the valleys, often on terraces beyond the likely reach of floodwaters. Roads in a sense followed rivers and emphasized the highway of communication provided by rivers and other inland waterways. In some locations, this was enormously convenient, and the Rhine and Danube provided excellent lateral communications; in Spain the Baetis and Anas similarly offered routes across the central-southern areas. However, there were limitations. The direction of a river did not always suit the provincial layout, and roads would not always need or be able to go to the head of valleys in the mountains. Hence, the crossing and bridging points were very important; the road could exploit a valley and then cross the river to move in another direction, for example, to make use of the valley of a tributary. The traveler then could benefit from such lateral communications. Routes and river crossings that sustained political, cultural, or commercial ties over long distances were particularly important. Therefore, a crossing point, be it bridge, ferry, or ford, could often be a major junction, which would serve both local and long-distance needs, depending on the location, and be a center for worship, meeting, trading, and ultimately settlement. Amphipolis on the river Strymon in Thrace was originally called Ennea Hodoi ("nine ways")[104] and was important because it was a center of communications and trade down the Strymon valley and along the coastal route to the Hellespont. Zeugma strikingly took its name ("junction") from its position at the chief crossing point of the Euphrates about 112 kilometers south of Samosata where four roads converged, linking Mesopotamia and Commagene; originally Seleukos I Nikator had founded two colonies—Seleukeia on the right bank and Apamea on the left bank. Where settlements grew up around bridges and fords, the importance of the river and bridge in urban development can be seen sometimes in the layout of the town. Streets or buildings might be aligned with the bridge, and in Arelate the amphitheater was aligned at a 45 percent angle with the pontoon bridge and linked by a road to the main road crossing the bridge, which then went on to Nemausus.[105] At Narbonne, the *via Domitia* crossed the river Atax and led straight to the forum and capitol of the town.[106]

If we imagine a typical river course, obviously the limit of navigation was a crucial point for crossing, since from here goods would have to be taken on by land in various directions. Elsewhere, a road might cross the river at the top of the valley before the increasing steepness of the valley sides made construction more difficult. But if a bridge was essential it might be built at the narrow point of the valley to facilitate construction. The confluence of two major rivers, or the point where a tributary joined the major river, would be important for river and road communications and would require a bridge. As the river descended through a deep ravine which its course had created, it would offer few crossing opportunities until it emerged onto the plain, which was a vital spot for access and the control of usable land. Of course, a bridge could impede navigation, especially if it had bulky piers in the water, unless there was room under the central arch for ships to pass; it is also true that the supports would tend to make the current run faster under the bridge.[107]

Now, most of our evidence concerns permanent bridges and depends on literary references, though archaeology can sometimes identify the remains of bridges and bridge supports.[108] Occasionally a bridge survives intact, as, for example, the bridge of Tiberius still in place at Ariminum (Rimini) carrying the *via Aemilia* over the river Ariminus (Marecchia), and the bridge of Augustus over the Tormes at Salmantica (Salamanca), which was on the main north-south route from Brigaecium to Augusta Emerita. But all trace of innumerable bridges will have been lost, and there will have been many local crossing points, both fords and ferries, unknown to us. So, our knowledge of fluvial crossing points is limited, and our understanding of road and river interrelation defective. Nevertheless, this is likely to have been an important factor in local and regional communication, just as the movement of goods and people by inland waterways was facilitated in some areas by a network of navigable rivers, between which they could move by road or track, with merchandise carried on by portage. Arguably one definition of a Roman road is "the shortest distance between two prominent seamarks or navigable rivers."[109]

It is worth emphasizing again that traders and travelers, official or otherwise, would make best progress by using a combination of roads and rivers. Tacitus vividly describes how one Roman official, the disgraced Calpurnius Piso, on his way back from the East, sailed across the Adriatic to Ancona, and then, making his way to the *via Flaminia*, joined a legion that was marching through Italy to Rome. But he incurred the suspicion of being too familiar with the troops, and at Narnia, where the road crossed the river Nar, he took ship and sailed down the river to its junction with the Tiber, along which he continued to Rome.[110]

6   REGULATING THE FLOW: CANALS AND DAMS

Given the importance of river travel in the Roman world, the contribution to trade and local economies by the movement of goods by fluvial routes and river valleys, and the overall seriousness of apportioning water in the riverine environment, it is worth asking about the ways in which the Roman government or local communities managed rivers in order to develop their use as thoroughfares by controlling or enhancing water flow.[111] This might involve the maintenance of towpaths and the construction of canals, dams, or weirs, which, apart from the capital outlay on them, would also require regular maintenance. This kind of provision was likely to increase the overall cost of fluvial transport.[112] Evidence for canals is very patchy, as we rely on occasional descriptions in literary sources and some archaeological remains.[113] It is possible that canals were sometimes built with a dual purpose, namely navigation and drainage (though it may be that a canal built for one purpose subsequently came to be used for another), and that they were intended to link rivers or extend riverine navigation. How far can we say that canals in Italy and elsewhere were built for economic reasons and improved communications? In Italy itself, most striking, though ultimately a failure, was Nero's plan to construct a canal about 257 kilometers long from Lake Avernus near Puteoli to Rome.[114] The primary objective was to ensure the safe shipment of grain to the capital for distribution to the populace. It would cut out the hazardous last part of the sea journey between Puteoli, which provided a safe anchorage, and Ostia, the normal entry port for Rome. Claudius had built a new harbor here, but a violent storm in A.D. 62 had destroyed no fewer than 200 grain ships in the harbor. The canal was to be wide enough for large, oared ships to pass, and convicted felons were to be conveyed to Italy to labor on the project. The first excavations were carried out in the hills near the lake.[115] Tacitus had doubts about the viability of the undertaking, which he ascribed to Nero's megalomania. But the canal on its route through the Pomptine marshes could have taken water from them and improved local drainage; water would also have been available from the rivers Volturnus and Liris. Of course, there were major technical difficulties further north, and tunnels would have been required though hilly areas. The expense of this may have been why, after order was restored following the civil wars of A.D. 68–69, the entire project was abandoned. But it should not necessarily be dismissed as foolish.[116] Soon after, further measures had to be taken to improve communications in this area and to safeguard grain supplies. Domitian incurred a large capital outlay to build the *via Domitiana* between Sinuessa and Puteoli,[117] and Trajan constructed another harbor at Portus for the grain fleet.[118]

As early as the third century B.C. there were attempts to improve navigation in the lower Tiber valley and regulate the flow of the river by digging a canal between the Veline Lake and the Nar, a tributary of the Tiber.[119] Later, under Tiberius, more elaborate plans had to be dropped because of local opposition.[120] There is some archaeological evidence for the building of dams or sluices in the upper course near Rocca di Montedoglio (Sanssepolcro), at Ponte di Fòrmole (Pieve San Stefano), and at Ponte di Valsavignone.[121] Under Augustus there were possibly attempts to strengthen the banks near Crustumerium about thirty-two kilometers north of Rome.[122]

Elsewhere in Italy canals were built to good effect around the mouth of the Padus. Pliny, commenting on the enormous volume of water in the river, tells us that a series of streams and canals controlled the water flow over a distance of 120 miles between Ravenna and Altinum.[123] The Canal of Augustus (*fossa Augusta*) brought the river to Ravenna via the town of Augusta. The *fossa Flavia*, a canal originally begun by the Etruscans, joined two arms of the Padus from Ostium Sagis to Ostium Volane via the town of Neronia. The name suggests that it was built by one of the Flavian emperors, though it has been claimed that it was in fact begun by Nero.[124] Further to the north the *fossa Clodia* probably linked the Ostium Philistina, Portus Edronis, and the two rivers Meduacus Maior and Meduacus Minor (map 8).[125] Claudius constructed this canal and probably made use of it during his triumphal return from Britain, when he made an excursion from Ravenna into the Adriatic on a vast ship. The emperor had perhaps crossed the Alps on his way from Gaul, or possibly traveled from Pannonia.[126] According to Strabo, Patavium was connected to the Adriatic by inland waterways.[127] Furthermore, a series of canals based on the Adige between Ferrara and Padua has been identified; they were for drainage and possibly for navigation.[128]

Therefore, in the Po delta and the surrounding area the Roman government seems to have sponsored initiatives to improve navigation. To some extent this contributed to the movement of military supplies and troops to Altinum, and then by the *via Claudia Augusta*, which ran through the valley of the Adige past Tridentum and over the Alps and eventually on to the Danube provinces. Claudius had completed this road, begun by his father Drusus Caesar in 15–14 B.C. However, about one hundred years before this, Aemilius Scaurus, as either consul in 115 or censor in 109 B.C., had been active in constructing navigable canals between the Roman colony at Parma and the Padus. Since he also built a military road (*via Aemilia Scauri*) from Vada Sabatia on the Ligurian coast to Dertona, his work on the waterways may have been part of a plan to assist the shipment of military supplies. Gallia Cisalpina was to remain a supply base for the armies north of the Alps.[129] On the other hand, canal construction will have helped fluvial trade and connections with the road network and should be considered as a possible contributor to the economic development of the area.

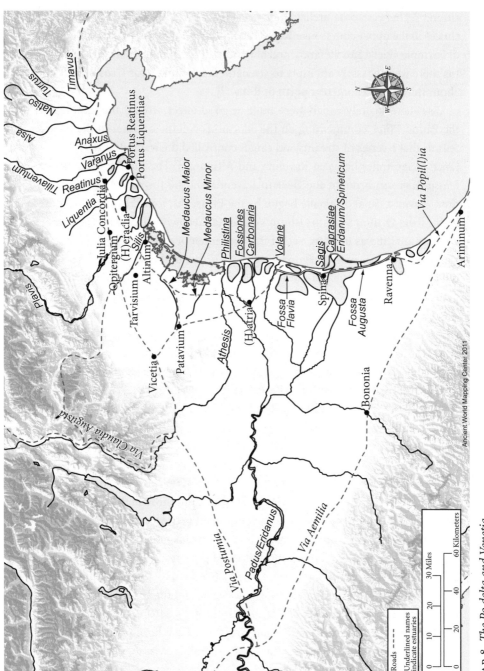

MAP 8. *The Po delta and Venetia*

Timavus
Turrus
Natiso
Alsa
Anaxus
Tilaventum
Varanus
Reatinus
Portus Reatinus
Portus Liquentiae
Liquentia
Julia Concordia
Opitergium
(H)eraclia
Silis
Plavis
Tarvisium
Altinum
Medaucus Maior
Medaucus Minor
Philistina
Fossiones
Carbonaria
Volane
Caprasiae
Eridanum/Spineticum
Via Popil(l)ia
Vicetia
Patavium
Athesis
(H)atria
Fossa Flavia
Sagis
Spina
Fossa Augusta
Ravenna
Ariminum
Via Claudia Augusta
Bononia
Via Postumia
Padus/Eridanus
Via Aemilia

Ancient World Mapping Center 2011

Roads ---
Underlined names
indicate estuaries

0   10   20   30 Miles
0   20   40   60 Kilometers

Outside Italy there is some limited and rather tantalizing evidence for canals in Britain. The famous Car Dyke, which ran from the environs of Cambridge to Lindum (Lincoln) around the edge of the Fens, may have been primarily intended as part of a land drainage system, though it was possibly also used for transport.[130] More clearly established as a transport route is the Foss Dyke, connecting Lincoln on the river Witham with the river Trent and the Ouse, and thence with the Humber estuary and the North Sea. Barges could use these inland waterways to bring farm produce from Norfolk to the military base at Eburacum (York).

It has been suggested that there is some evidence for work to regulate river flow and navigation in southern Spain on the river Baetis. This amounts to a dike or wall to divert or break the current and a rectangular structure near the river, which may be part of a river management system; there is insufficient evidence to identify any locks on the Baetis, which in any case would not have been necessary because of the river dynamics.[131]

Tacitus's description of the activities of Roman commanders in Germany certainly suggests varied motives in canal building. The elder Drusus had built a canal (*fossa Drusiana*) linking the northern arm of the Rhine to the river Ijssel, allowing passage down the river, through the canal to the Rhine and thence to the North Sea.[132] The original purpose was primarily military, though presumably it was available for other uses. In A.D. 47 Domitius Corbulo, as a substitute for military action (forbidden to him by Claudius) and to keep the troops active, built a canal twenty-three miles long between the Rhine and the Meuse (*fossa Corbulonis*). According to Tacitus, this was to facilitate travel by avoiding the trip by sea along the North Sea coast.[133] It is worth asking if Corbulo acted on his own initiative or was following the emperor's orders, which were possibly aimed at achieving more efficient riverine travel not just for military purposes. In A.D. 58 the governor of Lower Germany, Pompeius Paulinus, again aiming to keep the legionaries occupied, completed the embankment begun by the elder Drusus sixty-three years earlier to control the Rhine. At the same time Antistius Vetus, governor of Upper Germany, planned to link the Moselle and Saône rivers with a canal, so that sea-borne merchandise from the Mediterranean could be shipped along the Rhône and Saône and then by canal via the Moselle into the Rhine and thence to the North Sea. In Tacitus's view, this internal waterway would have solved some difficulties of land transport by linking the western Mediterranean with the northern seaboard.[134] The governor of the neighboring province of Belgica apparently objected on the grounds that he did not want troops in his province, which would upset the locals, and that the emperor might not approve. The governor, of course, had no right of veto, and one wonders if this was scouted as a possible plan with Nero's approval (he was keen on building canals), which was subsequently dropped for a variety of reasons including the expense.

Therefore, the motives explored by Tacitus range from the military and strategic, in order to facilitate the movement of troops and supplies and provide exercise for the troops, to the personal, in the desire of commanders to impress the emperor and win a reputation. But he also notes the possible economic benefits of a good fluvial network. Furthermore, since the construction of a canal was expensive, the motive may often have been to make some kind of imperial demonstration. Similarly, among the rivers of Gaul, the Rhône was outstanding as a waterway with significant inland cities such as Lugdunum, Vienna, and Arelate. The *fossa Mariana* ran southeast from Arelate to the Mediterranean, avoiding the delta with its uncertain navigation, and originally had a military purpose in permitting the import of supplies for Marius in his war against the Cimbri in 101 B.C.[135] Subsequently, Arelate became a vibrant sea and river port for merchandise passing along the Gallic river system.[136]

Pausanias describes how a Roman emperor attempted to make the river Orontes in Syria navigable from the sea up to the city of Antioch, a distance of about fifteen miles. In fact, the river followed a meandering course and at one point fell over a cliff. At great expense and with an enormous amount of labor he built a navigable canal and diverted the river into it.[137] It is likely that the emperor in question was Vespasian, whose governor M. Ulpius Traianus was active in several canal-building projects in the area.[138] Since Antioch was an important trading center, it is likely that the intention was partly at least to assist the movement of goods. More clear-cut evidence comes in the exchange of letters between Pliny as governor of Bithynia and Trajan about Lake Sophon (Sabanja), which lay about eighteen miles to the east of Nicomedia, which drained northeast through a tributary of the Sangarius.[139] He proposed to connect the lake to the sea by building a canal from its upper end to a river flowing into the sea. Nicomedia was an important entrepôt for the area, and a rich export trade in timber and marble and farm produce came across the lake and then had to be taken twenty miles by road to the city. Pliny, emphasizing that this land transport was more expensive than movement by water, cleverly flattered Trajan in order to arouse his interest in magnificent projects that would bring honor to his name. Trajan in reply expressed concern that the lake might be drained if it were given direct access to the sea via the canal and river. Pliny in his subsequent letter countered this by suggesting that the canal from the lake should not be brought right into the river but that an embankment should be built to keep them apart; goods could easily be carried across the embankment to the river. In any case, he thought that this would not be necessary because the river flowing out of the opposite end of the lake could be dammed so as to ensure that water loss was restricted. Pliny also examined the possibility of taking the canal directly to the sea. In this case, the counter pressure from the sea would prevent an excessive outflow of water, and other streams could be tapped to keep up the supply of water. Finally, he proposed the regulation of the flow of water by sluices (*catarracta*). This raises the question of locks, since Moore has argued that this refers to a modern "pound" lock with double gates. But this and the other evidence he cites do not prove his case, and it is more likely that Pliny refers to a single gate that could be lifted to admit craft and raise the water level over a long stretch. The canal lock (pound lock with set of gates) seems to have been first introduced in the fourteenth century A.D.[140]

In any case, Trajan considers the plan on its technical merits and does not mention the likely capital investment and its value against improved trading conditions in the neighborhood. He seems to give his approval if the survey is satisfactory. It is, however, likely that at least part of the outlay would be recouped from the local communities that were going to benefit, just as Pliny expects that they will provide the labor. We do not know if the plan went ahead, but the detailed discussion suggests serious intent.

In A.D. 101 the same emperor initiated a series of measures to prepare the way for the invasion of Dacia. These included the building of the famous fortified bridge at the traditional fording point at Pontes (Kostol), linking up with Drobeta on the northern bank, and the improvement of the towing path running along the river. West of Orshova, the Danube runs between lofty cliffs that compress the stream into a channel that is sometimes only 600 feet wide. The currents here were too strong for ships to travel upstream, and there was no scope to cut a canal. As early as Tiberius, a path was constructed on the southern bank to allow for towing. Claudius and Domitian maintained or extended this path, which was accomplished by drilling holes in the rock, placing wooden beams in them at right angles to the stream, and laying wooden planks on top. Trajan appears to have ordered the path to be cut deeper back into the rock walls.[141] In addition at the notorious rapids at the Iron Gate pass, Trajan built a canal. "Emperor Caesar Nerva Trajan Augustus Germanicus, son of the divine Nerva, chief priest, holding the tribunician power for the fifth time, father of the fatherland, consul for the fourth time, because of the danger of the rapids drew off the stream and made the Danube safe for navigation." The canal stretched for at least three and a half kilometers from the river Kasanja, a tributary of the Danube, crossed the Trstenica and the Kosovica, possibly continuing for another three and a half kilometers to Karataš.[142] Flat-bottomed barges could be towed along the canal, and it is significant that the auxiliary fort at Karataš was called *Caput Bovis*, literally "Head of the Ox," surely indicating the place where harnessed oxen began to tow the boats. Trajan's measures were, of course, intended to facilitate the supply of his armies, but improvement of navigation along the Danube and the increasing Roman presence will certainly have benefited all those communities that had access to the river or its tributaries.[143] Overall, even though on grounds of expense there was probably no general plan to develop canals to improve river communications; nevertheless, there is some evidence of significant government involvement, and there may well have been many more canals in use than we can now recover.

Another potentially important aspect of river management is the construction of dams.[144] However, there is a lack of evidence since many dams have disappeared or been significantly altered, while modern dams have been built on the site of others. The earliest known dam was built about 2950 B.C. in Egypt, but in the early period they were most commonly employed in the Middle East, especially in Mesopotamia, where the Euphrates and the Tigris played a vital role in the irrigation of the Fertile Crescent. These rivers flooded annually when the level increased after the melting of the winter snows, and in the height of summer the volume of water decreased; water was conducted to the fields by a network of canals, which were controlled by dams. These canals between the Tigris and Euphrates presumably also assisted movement and communications since some were navigable. The Persians were responsible for much of the development of this system, and Alexander during his campaigns in the area built the King's Canal between the two rivers and developed an artificial waterway to the west of the Euphrates.[145] Since, according to Strabo, both the Tigris and the Euphrates were navigable, the canals might also have been used for the movement of goods and people between the rivers.[146]

Early dam building was largely to meet the needs of irrigation. Romans will have encountered dams in the territories they conquered and doubtless absorbed and adapted the techniques of building as well as devising their own. Roman dam builders generally favored the gravity dam, which was a straight wall built across the river valley; it consisted of masonry with an earth or masonry filling, and the water side was of dressed stone blocks fitted together with hydraulic mortar. The wall held back the water by its sheer weight and by the strength of its foundations. The air face of the dam was stepped and was sometimes supported by additional buttresses. The arched dam had a curved shape and was also built to counter the pressure of the water by its weight and foundations. An arch dam (of which no clear example has been found in the ancient world) consisted of a relatively thin curved wall built across a gorge;

the structure contained an arching section that transferred the water pressure to the sidewalls and so away from the dam's foundations.[147]

Construction required a large labor force, and a strong central organizing authority to exercise initiative and control. This was provided by the Roman government, and its stable rule allowed the operation and maintenance of dams. Maintenance is very important because the river flow produces large quantities of silt. The nature and purpose of dams depended on local conditions and the needs of communities. It is not clear from our evidence that the Romans constructed dams primarily to facilitate river travel by controlling the water flow. However, attempts to control the Tiber show a relatively sophisticated hydrological knowledge. The river had a notoriously uneven flow. In its upper reaches, it often dried up in high summer. Pliny describes the course of the river through his estate at Tifernum Tiberinum: "It is navigable so that all my produce is transported down it to Rome, though only in winter and spring. During the summer the volume of water declines, and with its dry bed it abandons any claim to the name of a great river but takes it up again in the autumn."[148] After the junction of Tiber and its tributary the Clanis, there was much greater volume of water, improving navigability in the lower reaches but also threatening floods in and around the city. According to the Elder Pliny, in its upper course the Tiber "is a narrow stream, navigable only when its water is dammed up and then emitted, just as in the case of its tributaries, the Tinia and Clanis, whose waters have to be penned up for nine days unless rain showers have increased them."[149] This implies some kind of system of dams and sluices. Furthermore, in the famous senatorial debate concerning measures to control flooding in Rome, one proposal was to dam the river (Nera) Nar and also the Veline Lake near its outlet into the Nera.[150] Some archaeological remains of dams in the Tiber valley have been found, apparently controlling the flow of water to aqueducts.[151]

Elsewhere in Italy near Sublaqueum (Subiaco) Nero built a villa on the banks of the Anio and apparently had three dams constructed to provide artificial lakes. Debate continues about the exact site of the dams, but the important points for our purpose are the scale of the work undertaken, with the biggest dam being in all probability the highest the Romans ever built.[152] Furthermore, the dams were intended to create water features for decorative and recreational purposes. Given the ambition and technical accomplishment here, it may well be that the Romans built many other dams for more utilitarian purposes.

There is useful evidence from Glanum in Gallia Narbonensis, many sites in Africa (notably Kasserine, Leptis Magna), on the river Orontes near Homs in Syria, and near Mérida in Spain.[153] The purpose of these dams was not to improve river navigation but to provide a variety of other utilitarian services: to help irrigation by retaining a supply of water, to control excess flood and run-off water, and to preserve soil. In Africa, south of Leptis, the dam in the Wadi Lebda was designed to catch muddy flood water and silt and divert them away from the harbor. The city's water supply was guaranteed by the dam in the Wadi Caam, which collected the water from several springs and fed the aqueduct. Above the aqueduct was a huge dam 900 meters long, designed apparently to catch the silt from floodwater and protect the city's water supply. It had the additional effect of creating an area of fertile agricultural land.[154] Flood zone farming occurred where floodwater or runoff water could be directed over neighboring fields. Here, water control devices were used on the hillsides to trap soil and water in certain zones, permitting cultivation. Another benefit of this method was that the soil removed from the hillsides could not impede future runoff.[155] This was important since, in the absence of a sufficient source of running water, farmers had to find a way to sustain agriculture. Dry farming was possible, for example, in the Maghreb, since rainfall above 400 millimeters per annum can support some kinds of agriculture, provided that farmers can cope with the uneven rainfall throughout the year and the need to conserve water for the dry season and avoid runoff. Below 300 millimeters of rainfall per annum, dry farming of cereals was not possible. Full irrigation technology can deal with only a small area of land, and was usually impracticable because of the cost. Therefore, what worked best was probably a combination of methods according to local climatic and topographical conditions. In some locations terrace agriculture was the norm; here stone walls were built at right angles across the wadis, with the result that layers of silt were trapped between each of these dams. This produced a series of steps or terraces of cultivable soil, which also acted as a kind of water storage basin. It is possible, as Shaw argues, that Roman engineers took over systems that they found in operation but built on a greater scale. There seems to be a combination of local initiatives, sometimes under pressing need, to set up basic schemes for preserving or sharing water, which were supported or endowed by rich men, sometimes with community intervention. In some cases the Roman administration intervened, for example by sending a military surveyor to organize the pipeline at Saldae,[156] or sponsoring the water distribution scheme at Lamasba.[157]

In Spain, the important dam at Alcantarilla, south of Toledo, which was of less sophisticated construction than other dams in the province and probably dates from the second century B.C., was intended to store water for the public supply of Toledo. It is one of the earliest examples of a reservoir dam.[158] At Mérida, the two Roman dams are well preserved and have been kept for hydraulic use into the modern age. The dam at Cornalvo about 16 kilometers northeast of the town was designed to collect water from the Albarregas river. The dam is 220 meters long and 20 meters high with an earth and masonry structure with large stone blocks in a series of steps on the water side; there was a spillway channel to take away surplus water. A hollow tower (originally connected by an arch to the dam's crest) with a series of openings provided the low-level outlet. The water from the reservoir was taken in a covered channel to Mérida. The Proserpina dam 6.4 kilometers north of the town also collects the water of a small river to form a reservoir. This is a buttress dam about 430 meters long and about 12 meters high at the center, with a spillway channel on the left-hand side, to protect the crest from erosion; it is not entirely straight, because it follows the most suitable foundation line. The core of the dam wall was concrete, faced with large stone blocks in a series of steps on the water side; the downstream face was vertical, supported by an enormous earth mound that sloped from the crest to ground level. This put tremendous weight on the dam wall and nine stone buttresses were built on the water side to prevent the wall from collapsing when the reservoir was empty. There were two water outlets let into the dam's wall and sluices presumably controlled water flow. The Proserpina dam probably belongs to the early second century A.D., while the dam at Cornalvo, which seems to have a more advanced design, is likely to be later.[159]

Dams therefore served many functions; they regulated flow in rivers and canals and assisted in flood control, irrigation, and soil retention. Very importantly, reservoir dams stored the waters of rivers and streams to provide a public water supply. Although as far as we can tell dams were rarely built specifically to improve navigation (except perhaps in the upper Tiber valley), they did contribute to the management of the fluvial network for the benefit of local communities. But canals and dams were expensive, and their construction might affect the hydrology of the rivers and, by interfering with drainage, change the character of agricultural land in adjacent areas. The initiative in capital outlay would probably have to be undertaken by the central government, and it would not be financially viable for local communities to invest in order to benefit small-scale trade.

7   THE RIVERINE ENVIRONMENT: WATER MILLS,
      IRRIGATION, DRAINAGE, AND WETLANDS

Ancient writers readily recognized the variegated delights of the fertile river valley. For example, Strabo sings the praises of the river Iris in Cappadocia; it flowed past his native city, Amaseia, and then went on to water the plain of Themiskyra, which consequently was always "moist and rich in grass, capable of feeding herds of cattle and also horses, and allows the sowing of very large, indeed inexhaustible amounts of millet and sorghum seeds. It is so well-watered that it overcomes any drought and never does famine afflict any of the inhabitants." Through his geography, Strabo emphasizes that rivers were a source of fertility for the land through which they flowed, ideally producing deep flower-filled meadows and good pasture.[160] In river valleys, industries and activities flourished that required water, such as the manufacture of pottery, fulling (water was essential in this process),[161] and dyeing, as well as the growing of reeds, rushes, and medicinal herbs.[162] According to Pliny, the whole riverine environment produced usable materials such as glass-making sand, building stones, and all kinds of plants that were valuable for medicinal, culinary, or commercial exploitation.[163] For example, the Niger in Numidia was noted for reeds and papyrus, while the Rhine produced reeds suitable for manufacturing arrows.[164] Rivers also produced a variety of fish,[165] while others carried deposits of salt and, of course, provided watering holes for animals.[166] In addition, the waters of some rivers such as the Nile brought down either gold or precious stones.[167] The Padus, the Tagus, and the Hiberus were renowned as gold bearing, and this was thought to be the purest kind of gold, washed bright by the current.[168]

This theme of rivers and local prosperity was taken up by Pausanias, who pointed out the variety of watery benefits. So, the Maeander in Asia was famous for its tamarisks, and the Nile for avocado. In Boeotia, the river Asopos had the deepest reed beds; the Alpheios, wild olive; the Acheron, white poplar trees; and the river Po, the black poplar.[169] For Pausanias it seems that the value of living near to a river, for drinking water, washing, and good health, as well as the potential fertility of the land, outweighed any disadvantages, although he knew about the problem of alluviation, the persistent silting up of river mouths, and the dangers of flooding.[170]

Our writers are thinking of a kind of fertile, sylvan ideal, but it was necessary to make the river work, and although it is difficult to trace water installations, it is clear that river water provided the essential power to operate mills for grinding grain. The extent of this remains problematic, even though we are well informed about waterwheels, of which there were two types. The horizontal wheel, in which water was directed from the side onto paddles or blades mounted horizontally, turned the millstone directly by means of its vertical shaft. The vertical wheel, as described by Vitruvius, had two possible designs: the undershot or overshot wheel. The undershot wheel rested in the river and was turned by the force of the current. Therefore, the strength and consistency of the current were important, but even so this system could achieve only something in the order of 22 percent efficiency. It did, however, require little capital investment, merely a riverine location and a wall to support the wheel. The overshot wheel required water directed along a channel (a strong source of running water) from which it poured down onto the wheel's boxes and turned the wheel with its own momentum and weight. This system might achieve efficiency in the order of 65–70 percent but was more expensive to set up, requiring some hydraulic engineering to raise the water supply to the right level and a pit to catch runoff from the wheel. Both designs of vertical wheel operated on a horizontal axle and required right-angled gearing to transmit power to the millstone above on a vertical axle. More archaeological evidence for water mills is now coming to light and demonstrates their widespread adoption through the first and second centuries A.D.[171] Several sites had multiple mills, most notably Barbegal near Arelate, where sixteen wheels were in operation.[172] We can perhaps speculate that grain grown in a river valley could be ground into grain using the power of the river and then transported by the same river for sale elsewhere, or exported from a river and seaport.

Irrigation and drainage were often crucial to farming, and Varro had advised on the location of a farmstead that "the best thing is to have a spring on site, or, failing that, a perennial stream."[173] But copious, perennial streams were in short supply in the Mediterranean region, and large-scale summer irrigation was not feasible except in smaller local areas. On the assumption that a field of 1 hectare (2.47 acres) requires 20 millimeters of water for effective irrigation, an area of 100 hectares would require the daily output of a medium-sized city aqueduct.[174] Mechanical irrigation to produce such a huge amount was not often feasible since it was too expensive, too labor intensive, and too difficult to lift sufficient quantities of water to the required height.[175] The bucket wheel or a system of buckets on chains (scooping up water as it turned) was more effective, especially if a waterwheel could harness the power of a river to operate a bucket chain. This might serve to raise water from a river to a reservoir at a higher level, from which it could be conducted by sloping conduits to irrigate more distant fields. It is unlikely though that the benefits of this will have often outweighed the expense of installing and maintaining the system.[176] Most irrigation therefore probably consisted of water from a local spring or stream brought under gravity through small channels that have left little archaeological trace or at least have not been discovered.[177] Gravity-led irrigation would require a river with a clearly defined course and a pronounced downward slope. Aqueducts, in addition to their primary purpose of providing drinking water for large towns could also have a subsidiary part to play in irrigation. It might be possible to tap into an aqueduct's channels or to use the overflow to water crops or gardens.[178] In Rome, the *aqua Anio Vetus*, which was of inferior quality, was employed "for watering gardens and for the less edifying uses of Rome itself."[179] Near Lugdunum at the Gier aqueduct, it seems that when the aqueduct's channels were full, the siphons along its course could not cope with the volume of water. This overflow may have been diverted to agricultural use.[180]

In many places there was a close connection between irrigation and drainage, and in places in Italy drainage was more important.[181] Drainage channels constructed in one area could help to provide irrigation water for another and serve to manage rainfall, runoff, and flash floods. An important part of controlling the watery environment was the ability to ensure that naturally damp areas retained their moisture and to enhance the value of wetlands and meadows for pasturing animals. The Romans took fully into their remit peripheral areas, particularly marshy land and wetlands, which were too difficult for normal agriculture. Their activity here was significant, though less spectacularly visible than some of their other watery management. Throughout the ancient world the use of water meadows and the cultivation of floodplains continued to be important. Floodplains, with perhaps a mythical significance, may have been preferentially settled.[182]

In many cases the reclamation of marginal land was on a small scale, involving individual holdings or communities. The *agrimensores*, meticulous in their analysis of landholding, provide invaluable evidence on the exploitation of *subseciuum* and *compascuus*. *Subseciuum* was land left out of the original survey and distribution because it was at the time deemed unsuitable for cultivation. This land could be located either in the middle of allocated *centuriae* or on the periphery and might consist of scrubland, forest, stony, or waterlogged areas. The constant aim of landholders was to absorb this into their allocation and, where appropriate, to drain or clear it and work it profitably. This process was reckoned as valuable, and where possible the state sought to encourage and manage it. Hyginus advised surveyors to make a ledger of *subseciua*, "so that whenever the emperor wishes he can find out how many men can be settled in that area."[183] Vespasian famously intervened and tried to reclaim *subseciua* for the state and encouraged local communities to reclaim those areas for which they were responsible. There was an uproar from discomfited landholders, and Domitian by an edict granted *subseciua* throughout the whole of Italy to those in possession of them.[184] Evidence from imperial estates in Africa shows how Hadrian attempted to implement the series of regulations known as the Mancian Law to encourage the tenants of the estates to bring marginal land into cultivation.[185]

Private enterprise was important in the reclamation of land, and an interesting inscription from Parma confirms the importance of these ideas at the local level: "C. Praeconius, son of Publius, Ventidius Magnus, Roman *eques*, bequeathed in perpetuity these 35 *iugera* so that the return on them should be expended on festivities there for his companions, 'whosoever should have survived from them.' . . . Whatever you see, visitor, beside the spring, was previously disgusting bog and turgid water and a great cause of legal disputes."[186] It seems that this piece of land made waterlogged by a neighboring spring was potentially valuable if reclaimed for cultivation and, hence, brought about disputes over possession.

Marshy land once reclaimed and water meadows were a valuable resource and will have featured in the allocation in communities of land for common use or for pasture (*compascuus*). The surveyors had to record that landholders received this land "over and above their personal allocation but on the condition that they should hold it in common. In many places farms also received common pasture from land that was granted in the allocation. They hold this by favor of the colony, and on the map the words 'public common pasture land of the colony of the Julienses' ought to be written."[187] Such land could produce a rent, and in this case the marginal land was managed for profit by the local community supervised by the Roman state.

On a bigger scale, the Roman state was prepared to drain lakes and marshes and restore flooded land. The Fucine Lake in the Apennines near Alba Fucens in Italy and Lake Kopais in Boeotia provide outstanding examples of a managed watery environment with a combination of drainage and irrigation to preserve farmland and maintain meadows.[188] Suetonius describes Claudius's attempt to drain the Fucine Lake as one of his most notable enterprises. The Marsians, in whose territory it was, had often approached Augustus, but he declined to intervene. Claudius employed 30,000 men to dig an outlet canal over three miles long from the lake to the river Liris, tunneling or leveling a mountain. The task took eleven years, and according to Dio was not entirely successful.[189] The emperor was not just after the glory of a spectacular project but genuinely intended the reclamation of land; he secured private capital to fund some of the work on the basis that the investors would receive the reclaimed land. It has been calculated that Claudius drained about 50 of the lake's 140 square kilometers; further work by Hadrian drained another 30 square kilometers.[190] Reclaimed lands on the periphery of the lake will have been fertile, and the lakeside town of Marruvium had lands (possibly reclaimed) demarcated by "mountain" and "maritime" *limites*.[191] However, farming in this reclaimed, peripheral area was risky, and in 117 the lake took back some of its domain, requiring emergency intervention, as we see from a dedication "for the recovery of the fields and the reestablishment of the landholders whom the violence of the Fucine Lake had driven out."[192]

Lake Kopais in Boeotia was an inland drainage system into which flowed several rivers from the west, especially the Kephisos, several from the vicinity of the lake itself, the river Melas from the northwest, and other streams from Mount Helicon. It was hemmed in by mountains, broken only by the valley of the Kephisos. The lake has odd qualities and can change in character depending on the season and the silting up of the swallow holes that contribute to its drainage. It stood out as the dominant geographic and economic factor in the life and history of the settlements clustered around it, since cities derived support and income from the lake's produce, particularly fish and eels at Kopai, flute reeds from the southwest section, unguents from Khaironeia, and various other lake plants producing food, especially for animals. In the varied economy of the region agriculture was also important. Several efforts were made to control the lake by channeling some of the rivers to prevent the flooding of arable land or to reclaim damaged land. An inscription set up by the city of Koroneia records an intervention by Hadrian in A.D. 125, who wrote concerning the establishment of dikes to channel the rivers flowing into the southwest part of the lake. Hadrian specifically named the Kephisos and the Erkynne among other rivers: "Work will commence as soon as possible, so that they flow within their banks and do not turn aside from their course and, as happens now, flood much of the agricultural land. I shall also bring you a water supply. I shall provide the money, a sum of 65,000 denarii, which the experts in these matters say will be necessary. You should choose those who are to supervise (the project)."[193]

The emperor's continuing interest appears in a subsequent letter about the Phalaros River, noting the beneficial effects of work done on it, and advising the city to make sure that outsiders who had acquired land took proper care of the dikes. "It is essential [that those along the banks] place their embankments and supports into the river, but [. . .] should not cause a blockage in it."[194] Then in A.D. 135 Hadrian again wrote to the magistrates and people of Koroneia, apparently about further problems with the river Phalaros, and indicates that they had had a personal meeting with him; "I have written to the distinguished Aemilius Juncus, my friend, to go to the Phalaros River and do whatever he thinks is necessary. You should make clear to him what you said in my presence."[195] These documents, along with several others concerning a land dispute between Koroneia and Thisbe, were carved on a wall in Koroneia, and together show not only imperial interest in local affairs but also determination to control the environment and its use by subject communities.

According to recent investigations in Britain, the Wentlooge Level in the estuary of the river Severn was drained and probably also embanked in the Roman period. The important evidence here consists of the drainage ditches, which are of two types; those of inconsistent direction are likely to be natural drainage channels, but others are usually straight, shallow, and sharp edged, though of varying widths, and are man-made. Some run parallel to the coastline, while some run at right angles to it. Because a considerable amount of work was involved in this undertaking, it is probably right to assume that soldiers, perhaps of legion II Augusta at Caerleon, were employed. In consequence the reclaimed land would then become imperial property administered by a procurator. In fact, large tracts of tidal wetlands amounting to about 325 square kilometers were drained on the left bank of the estuary of the Severn. Although the evidence is somewhat ambiguous, it seems likely that the reclaimed land was partly used for arable cultivation, with also sheep and cattle husbandry, and possibly the raising of horses for the Roman army; there was in addition some iron working.[196]

Reclamation and drainage remained a subject of imperial interest, and in the late fifth century, Theodoric, the Gothic king of Rome, is found undertaking beneficial activity near Tarracina and implicitly criticizing his predecessors: "King Theodoric . . . with divine approval and splendid good fortune restored, for public use and the safety of travelers, the Decennovium of the *via Appia*, that is, the road and locations from Tripontium to Tarracina, which had been flooded by marshes converging from both sides, under all previous emperors."[197]

Furthermore, through the ongoing process of alluviation, rivers renewed and extended areas of fertile land in their deltas. The Romans clearly understood the potential value of alluvial land—that landholders could profit from the addition of valuable soil and that land in the river valley could be extremely fertile. However, the process of alluvial action needed to be carefully managed, since river action changed the configuration of the land, altered boundaries, and inflicted loss on landholders. The intervention of the government in the Maeander delta clearly shows imperial concern from Augustus onward.[198]

8   AQUEDUCTS

Important as the entire watery environment was, the most striking benefit of running water enjoyed by the Romans was of course a constant supply for drinking and other purposes.[199] The clearest demonstration of Roman aquatic domination was their ability to control the sources of running water and, in particular, to transport water to communities and cities far away from those sources. This watery aggrandizement began with the provision of water for Rome itself and involved great capital investment by the state, starting in 312 B.C., when the censors Appius Claudius and C. Plautius had the *Appia Claudia* aqueduct constructed, which was fed by springs in the *ager Lucullanus* between the seventh and eighth milestones on the *via Praenestina* to the east of the city. After this exploit, C. Plautius was nicknamed Venox or "Hunter" because he had hunted out the springs of water, providing a vivid illustration of the crucial role of sources of clean drinking water in the early city.[200] Yet the aqueduct was to be named after his colleague, who skillfully remained in office after Plautius had resigned.

In general, the Romans preferred not to use stored water and favored a source of running water, either a river or a spring, which was copious enough to provide a continuous stream.[201] Normally a riverine city would not use its own river because the water was polluted by city waste and might be too difficult to raise to the required level, so it looked for sources in the neighboring hills, and although river water contained suspended pollutant material, this could be partly removed by the use of settling tanks. Furthermore, careful observation and exploitation of river characteristics and currents are apparent, for example, in the arrangements for the aqueduct at Side in Pamphylia; this was supplied from the river Manavgat, but the intake was positioned at its confluence with the buoyant waters of the Dumanli spring, so as to draw off water that mainly consisted of the purer spring waters.[202] Although spring water was purer, it tended to have certain chemical characteristics, which for example produced hard water and consequent encrustation of pipes.[203]

In his historical account of the development of Rome's aqueducts, Frontinus carefully explains the sources of the water, both springs and rivers, with their different characteristics and qualities.[204] The names of some of the aqueducts reveal their origin, like the *aqua Anio Vetus* (272 B.C.) and the *aqua Anio Novus* (begun in A.D. 38), which had their source in the river Anio; the former was muddy colored because of its river origins, while the latter also tended to be cloudy in winter and after summer rainstorms. The *aqua Marcia* was built in 144 B.C. by Q. Marcius Rex, the urban praetor. The *aqua Tepula* (125 B.C.) took its name from its traditionally tepid and rather unpleasant water, though its quality was improved by Augustus. Frontinus found it hard to understand why Augustus introduced the *aqua Alsietina*, named from its source, the *lacus Alsietinus*, to the west of the Tiber, which was of such poor quality that it could be used only to supply the Naumachia and the surrounding water gardens. By contrast, the *aqua Marcia* from the *fons Pitonia* was thought to have some of the best water in Rome, renowned for its frigidity and purity.[205] Nero created a public outcry by bathing in its springs. The Claudia, which was begun by Gaius and completed by Claudius in A.D. 52, was fed by two springs, the Curtius and the Caeruleus, and the latter's name suggests its sparkling purity. The *aqua Virgo* (19 B.C.) was named in honor of the young girl who pointed out the source of springs to soldiers who were searching for water; thereafter, there was a small temple on the site with a painting depicting this incident.[206] The disposition of the aqueducts shows a spreading outreach around the city to take control of available water sources in the Tiber floodplain, in the hills to east as far as Tibur, and at Mount Simbruinus in the valley of the Anio, encompassing rivers and springs. Trajan introduced the *aqua Traiana*, which had its source at the northwest tip of *lacus Sabatinus*, near the Aquae Apollinares Novae, and entered the west of the city at the crest of the Janiculum. Then in the third century, Severus Alexander used springs near Gabii to supply his baths complex, through the *aqua Alexandriana*.[207]

From the early period, the men responsible for building aqueducts were important and prominent public figures, often censors or consuls. The provision of a spectacular public service would often be politically useful, and it is significant that between the *aqua Tepula* (125 B.C.) and the *aqua Julia* (33 B.C.) no major aqueducts were constructed in Rome, as the senate aimed to prevent the self-aggrandizement of individual powerful men.[208] The tradition of high-level state intervention was resumed by Augustus and his henchman Agrippa, who built three aqueducts; Augustus also did much to restore, repair, or augment existing aqueducts. Thereafter, the provision of a clean and copious water supply for the various requirements of the city was an imperial prerogative, and, as noted, Gaius, Claudius, Trajan, Caracalla, and Severus Alexander all built new aqueducts or added new sources, while many emperors took on responsibility for essential maintenance. Augustus had been happy to claim credit, on the arch conveying the *aqua Marcia*, for mundane repair work: "Imperator Caesar Augustus . . . repaired the channels of all the aqueducts."[209] Caracalla in 212/13 carried on the work more expansively: "Imperator Caesar M. Aurellius Antoninus Pius Felix Augustus . . . arranged for the *aqua Marcia*, which had been blocked by various impediments, to be brought into his very own revered city, by clearing out the source, cutting and digging through hills, restoring the channel, and even adding a new source, the Antoniniana."[210]

Originally public funds, including war booty, were used to pay for aqueducts. Augustus recognized that the whole process of providing and maintaining the city's water supply was a permanent obligation, and created a sophisticated administrative structure to be carried on by senators; a senatorial decree instructed the curators of aqueducts (appointed by the senate on the emperor's recommendation) to see to it "that the public fountains gush forth water as unstintingly as possible day and night for the use of the people."[211] The most famous of the curators was Sextus Julius Frontinus, who thought it worthy of his position to write a handbook expounding the curator's duties and exulting in the technical marvels of the aqueduct system. After a lengthy review of the extent and building techniques both above and below ground of the aqueducts, he affirms the superiority of Roman achievements: "With these essential structures supporting so many waters, you might of course compare the indolent pyramids or other pointless though famous works of the Greeks."[212] Increasingly emperors paid from their own pocket, and the superb feats of engineering that rose on great arches not only demonstrated mastery of the natural world but also provided a spectacular imperial display. Furthermore, ornamental *nymphaea* at several parts of the city where water was released, for example, the *aqua Julia*, celebrated the end product of the aquatic process.[213]

Although the aqueducts had pride of place, Augustus's Naumachia in the Transtiberim was another watery benefaction. It was a huge basin used for displays of naval warfare and was first associated with the temple of Mars Ultor, dedicated in 2 B.C. The grubby water from the new *aqua Alsietina* supplied the basin, and a nearby park brought well-watered sylvan peace. In later times, the park remained as a reminder of imperial generosity (*nemus Caesarum*). Augustus had taken a new watery source and used it for imperial display and the gratification of the people.[214] Agrippa did not lag behind in similar generosity. As well as his imposing bath complex, nearby he constructed the *stagnum Agrippae*, apparently a park and artificial lake, which was drained by an artificial channel (the Euripus).[215] Agrippa's villa, also situated in Regio IX, was left in his will to the people of Rome as another green, open space (*horti Agrippae*); opposite the villa was Agrippa's bridge, located between the modern Ponte Mazzini and Ponte Sisto.[216] This part of the Campus Martius was now dominated by water-inspired investment, as the great men of the new order set about commanding and controlling the watery resources at the heart of Rome. Furthermore, it was not only concerned with display and relaxation; the water supplies of the Tiber valley were to be marshaled to strengthen and enhance the imperial city, and the work on the riverine embankments would keep the Tiber in its place, for the safety of the Roman people.

However, the profusion of fresh water did not lead to improved urban hygiene. Drinking, washing, and irrigation ideally required clean water from a running source, but it was inevitable that in large towns all forms of human waste were likely to be deposited in the nearby river. Rome, for example, while larger than other cities, was relatively carefully managed, but sewage disposal was not well organized, and although surplus water from the aqueducts was used to flush out drainage channels, street drains, and gullies, much of this detritus certainly found its way into the Cloaca Maxima, which flowed directly into the Tiber.[217] The river must have been seriously polluted and frequently malodorous. What is more, corpses were sometimes deposited in the river. The Romans had no method for measuring and monitoring river pollution, except by sight and smell.

9   ROME AND THE DISTRIBUTION OF WATER

Roman mastery of water and water technology showed the power of the conqueror. But that power was also revealed in the ability of the government to dispense watery benefits at will. This was particularly true of the imperial period when the emperor presided over all benefactions, from which he derived honor and respect, and consolidated his own power and that of Rome. Naturally, a consistent supply of drinking water was a top priority of local communities, not least because in the more arid parts of the Mediterranean, where many rivers dry up in summer, control of perennial springs or rivers was of paramount importance. There was a two-way process here in that the Romans often had to invest resources to make the best use of running water, and this opened the way for imperial generosity, which was often copied at the local level. Aelius Aristides, in his Panegyric of Rome, observed that gifts never stopped flowing from the Romans to the cities,[218] and it is in the urban life of the Roman world that the benefits of their technology, administrative experience, and aquatic control were most apparent. It is possible, however, that through this very process farmers may often have been deprived of some of the water they needed for irrigation.[219]

Imperial aquatic benefactions were generous, although our evidence (mainly through inscriptions) is uneven.[220] A dedication from Nicopolis in Syria during the reign of Tiberius shows the due solemnity of the process and the operation of delegated authority: "Tiberius Caesar Imperator Augustus, son of the divine Augustus, grandson of the divine Julius, chief priest, consul on four occasions, with tribunician power, arranged for the aqua Augusta to be brought to Nicopolis under the direction of Gnaeus Saturninus, legate of Caesar Augustus."[221] Augustus under his auspices had provided grand projects to favored communities in Italy and the provinces. In Campania, he undertook an ambitious and expensive plan to construct a water channel, the aqua Augusta, from the springs at Serino near Abellinum (Avellino); it ran for ninety-six kilometers via Sarnum (Sarno) around the north side of Vesuvius to serve Naples, Baiae, and Misenum, while a spur branched off to Pompeii.[222] In Egypt, in A.D. 10/11 Augustus diverted the river Sebaston from Schedia because it had caused a flood.[223] In Gallia Narbonensis, the aqueduct to supply Colonia Augusta Nemausus (Nîmes), which was probably begun in 19 B.C., brought water from the most suitable source in a difficult hydrological area, Uzès about fifty kilometers away; it crossed the river Gardon on the spectacular Pont du Gard, over fifty meters in height on a series of three superimposed arches. Nemausus was named after the spirit of the sacred spring, which had a sanctuary predating the Roman occupation. The fountain sanctuary was in the northwest area of the city, where the spring flowed from a hall near the theater, served the baths and then fed a large pool surrounded by porticos, with a *nymphaeum*. In 26/25 an altar was built near the water shrine to serve the imperial cult, providing an important emotional and psychological link for locals with the tradition of the origins of the city and its watery patron.[224]

In the neighboring province, Lugdunum was generously provisioned with water; its four aqueducts (two built under Augustus, one under Claudius, and one under Hadrian), with a discharge of about 76,000 cubic meters every twenty-four hours, helped to mark it out as a major community.[225] At Tarraco (Tarragona), the most important city in the large province of Hispania Tarraconensis, the local aqueduct, also attributed to Augustus, was visually striking, being thirty-five kilometers long, with a bridge twenty-nine meters high on its way into the city. At Segovia, the aqueduct built by Claudius took its water from the Rio Acebeda, a small river about twelve kilometers south of the city, where a carefully engineered weir built across the river course diverted water to the aqueduct channel.[226] Elsewhere at important sites in Spain, such as Toletum (Toledo) and Augusta Emerita (Mérida), dams engineered with Roman skill served the cities' aqueduct system to deliver stored water.[227] An inscription from Soloi celebrates Nero because he brought water to the town over a number of miles.[228]

A striking monument to Roman aquatic engineering is the inscription from Lambaesis celebrating the achievements of Nonius Datus, veteran of the legion III Augusta, who designed and supervised the construction of a water channel to the town of Saldae (Bejaia or Bougie) in Mauretania Caesariensis in A.D. 152. This was part of the Toudja aqueduct, which brought water to the town over about twenty-one kilometers. The local community found it impossible to overcome the technical problems of tunneling, and Datus returned at their invitation to rescue matters. The inscription honors Endurance, Courage, and Hope (all personified with carved figures) and highlights the moment when "the work was completed and the water was sent through the channel." The procurator dedicated the channel, confirming the watchful interest and approval of the Roman government and its officials, and the quantity of water is proudly recorded.[229] Although this was not one of the great civic centers of the Roman world, there was a genuine interest in making the water supply work. We may compare the provision of water for Kremna in Pisidia, which, because of its position, did not have a good natural water supply. The large public cisterns had to be filled by an aqueduct, which brought water from a spring about two kilometers to the southwest; the necessary route was circuitous, and since the spring was below the level of the city, the water had to be raised mechanically. Here substantial efforts were made to supply a relatively small amount of water, probably for the city baths. It is not clear if the Romans paid for or organized this project.[230]

Wherever the Romans founded settlements and established an administrative structure, they sought to manage water resources. Apart from the planning and construction of aqueducts, this appears most clearly in the setting up of a legal framework for controlling rivers and dealing with disputes and in the rules for new settlements.[231] For example, the law that established the Colonia Genetiva at Urso (Osuna) in Baetica under the direction of Julius Caesar, made specific provision to safeguard the continuity of water rights and access to watery assets: "Whatever rivers, streams, fountains, pools, waters, ponds, or marshes there are within the land, which shall have been divided among the colonists of this colony, there is to be passage to men and animals to those streams, fountains, or pools and to those waters, ponds, or marshes and access to water for those who shall hold or shall possess that land, in the same way as there was for those who held or possessed that land."[232]

It is reasonable to ask if water was one of the agents of Romanization and assimilation, as communities became dependent on Rome's aquatic generosity and engineering know-how.[233] The dissemination of its practices permeated the urban structure of communities in Italy and in the provinces of the empire. Towns and cities copied the increasingly elaborate water collection and distribution, and local communities, always aware of the benefits of rivers and springs, extended and celebrated their use for the advantage of the urban community. This was part of the process by which they attempted to adopt the Roman way of life and technical mastery of the natural environment. However, although Rome had a monopoly of major projects, generous imperial subventions could stimulate local initiatives, which replicated Rome's procedures but allowed the local elite to have prestige. Rivers and springs were at the center of a social and patronage culture both for the emperor and for local dignitaries. Consequently, water benefactions by provincial and municipal grandees followed the imperial lead, and there was sometimes competition between cities to have the best water supply.

Even in the case of long-established Greek cities, the Roman government intervened to ensure the proper management of water resources, though not necessarily providing funding. Pliny investigated the plans for an aqueduct at Nicomedia, which twice had had to be demolished, inspecting the source of running water and construction methods. Though concerned about the administrative incompetence, Trajan insists: "We must ensure that the community of Nicomedia is provided with a water supply." It is likely that the cost of this would be borne by the local population. Sinope also lacked a water supply, and Pliny appealed to Trajan, pointing out that there were good supplies of water sixteen miles away: "Under my management, there will be no shortage of funds, Sir, if you will give your approval for this kind of scheme that is so beneficial to the health and ambiance of this very thirsty community." Trajan agreed on the benefits of a good water supply, as long as the community could meet the expense.[234] In general, Rome allowed local communities to get on with managing their water supplies, provided that the expense was kept within acceptable limits.

The evidence from inscriptions shows widespread activity by local communities in water management of rivers and springs, as well as great public interest.[235] Problems arose with the supply of running water because of insufficient sources, or because the supply had been disrupted by natural disaster, neglect, or a lack of money, which prevented water collection and distribution. Therefore, communities searched for new sources or restored old ones, cleared out or rebuilt channels and pipes, and constructed new outlets. The inhabitants of Cora south of Rome on the lower slopes of the Lepinus Mountain managed a fairly accurate description of the phenomenon of runoff as they recorded the collection in a channel of "water that came from heaven and then rolled down the mountainside."[236] In the management of watery sources, the particular value of drinking water is a priority, with an emphasis on water purity and public utility to sustain human life, though a splendid water supply is also an ornament to the community, while lack of water causes real hardship and challenges its status.

The idea of using local public funds to support the channeling of rivers and springs to secure a water supply went back to the republic. For example, an inscription of the late second century B.C. celebrates L. Betilienus Vaarus, who implemented decisions of the senate of Aletrium and established various facilities in the town, including a pool for bathing, a pool at the town gate, and a water supply for the community. The local office of censor was voted to him twice, which may suggest that he used some of his own money to carry out this work.[237] Interestingly, combined with these watery amenities Vaarus also provided "a plain (*campus*) where they play"; such grassy and well-watered areas were also very important in urban life.[238] In the imperial period, "the community and people of Corfinium repaired the channel of their aqueduct decayed with age"; it apparently passed though the territory of neighboring Superaequum.[239] At Urvinum a local magistrate undertook the search for a new water source, building a conduit and a nymphaeum, all at public expense.[240]

But this was also an arena suitable for the expenditure of moneys by private individuals who reaped the benefits of public acclaim and commemoration for their altruism. Local magistrates or distinguished local people were generous in their benefactions, sometimes leaving money in their wills.[241] The idea of personal generosity is well brought out by an inscription from Teate Marrucinorum: "In honor of the imperial house, Dusmia Numisilla, daughter of Marcus, in her own name and that of her husband L. Trebius Secundus, restored at her own expense the water supply, which had been brought through by C. Asinius Gallus and had failed, by tracing it from its source, in addition building a conduit and wells, and augmenting it by new branches."[242] The process of bringing water from a spring was not always straightforward, and Faianius Plebeius went to great lengths to overcome various difficulties to supply water to his community of Forum Novum for a variety of uses: "P. Faianius Plebeius, member of the Board of Two, at his own expense brought water from his own land to the community of Forum Novum, and made all the fountains and ensured that the water gushed into the pool, which is in the *campus*, and checked that it was operational. And since the vendor of the land, in which the bathing establishment was situated, had not taken sufficient steps to reach agreement with the purchaser about the water, to ensure that it could flow into the bath, P. Faianius Plebeius offered his own water supply for that bath, so that the members of the community should not lack the amenity."[243]

In Ephesus, the senator C. Laecanius Bassus Caecina Paetus was a great benefactor of the city "who had provided both for the construction of a water tank and for the bringing the water into it." In 74 Paetus held the post of curator of the banks and bed of the Tiber.[244] At Albingaunum (Albenga), a local notable, C. Valerius Severus, who was consul in 124, arranged for a water supply to be taken "from his own springs" in order to combat fires.[245] The significance of rivers and springs in local life and the goodwill to be gained can be seen in the enthusiasm with which new water arrangements were welcomed; in an inscription from Castulo in Hispania Tarraconensis, Annia Victorina celebrated with a formal dedication and banquet her establishment of a water supply and elaborate accessories.[246] Some of the excitement that accompanied the dedication and inauguration of a new aqueduct comes down to us in a dedicatory epigram from the fifth century A.D. celebrating a water supply at Antioch: "He alone succeeded in bringing the stream of the Anantas(?) from the mountains to land that had previously been parched."[247]

10   CONCLUSION: "A MOST GENTLE TRADER
      IN ALL THE EARTH'S PRODUCE"

Pliny's encomium on the Tiber helps to show how rivers were considered crucial to the Roman Empire despite the perennial problems of Mediterranean waterways. The ancient writers can give us a lesson on routes of communication by their treatment of navigable rivers, in that they recognized a wide range of waterways and substantial variations across different areas; there was no connected system, although the movement of goods along a river valley could be a unifying force. The Roman government attempted to manage the watery environment, control natural forces, and minimize disruption, through the supervision of rivers and ports and the exploitation of river navigation. The Romans also appreciated the potential of the entire riverine environment within the territories they controlled and exploited it for irrigation, distinctive wetland cultivation, and the provision of fresh running water. They built aqueducts; used canals, dams, and irrigation techniques; and, as far as possible, regulated rivers. Though uneven and often inadequate, this process was nevertheless part of government response to the environment.

Furthermore, the Romans grasped the importance of understanding the geographical and topographical context of the riverine environment and accepted that river travel and other activities needed to be analyzed against a background of change: the river might become unruly and navigability decline; its flow might have to be regulated; or the regular deposition of silt might alter the outline of the land. But despite changes in morphology, rivers connected communities, localities, and regions and assisted cultural contacts, movement, and trade on both a small and large scale. As riverine dwellers learned to devise and build suitable rivercraft and, with ingenuity and hard work, to propel ships upstream, they opened up enormous opportunities, especially since in the ancient world it is likely that many more rivers than nowadays were navigable and over a greater distance. The Mediterranean Sea was Mare Nostrum and sea travel connected disparate regions of the empire. However, much social, political, and economic activity occurred at the regional and parochial level in fragments of territory at the periphery of the Mediterranean or in the hinterland, where navigable rivers and river valleys provided essential connections and opportunities.

seven

MOVEMENT OF GOODS BY RIVER (1)

SPAIN, GAUL, THE RHINE, AND BRITAIN

Navigable rivers served as thoroughfares, contributing to trade and the local economy in regions where, for various reasons, waterways, riverine commerce, and other river qualities were seemingly important. What is the evidence for the movement of goods by rivercraft along navigable waterways, and how can we estimate rivers' importance in relation to other trading routes?

We are heavily dependent on archaeological investigation of the distribution of amphorae that carried oil and wine, and other artifacts. Amphorae are particularly important because their provenance and date can often be established by their type and design. Therefore, it is possible to monitor the import and export of oil and wine to and from certain regions and to relate areas of olive and vine production to likely means of transportation. Furthermore, if pottery works manufacturing amphorae can be identified in river valleys, they may have been located there because they were close to the source of oil or wine, suitable clay, and potential transport along the river. On the other hand, we cannot always tell how and why pots got to their find spot. For example, a large concentration of amphorae-making facilities along a river valley may mean that the pots were associated with riverine trade; but it may simply suggest that, when communities tended to cluster in the fertile land of river valleys, many potential users of pots in the area encouraged pottery production. In some cases it may be possible to plot finds of imported materials across a province, showing the role of river valleys in the movement of goods. River ports can be valuable indicators of riverine activity; their layout and extent, and the number of wharves, storehouses, and other facilities might also give an idea of the extent of trade entering the port. Underwater archaeological investigation of ships that sank in the ocean can help to show trade routes from which we can occasionally extrapolate the importance of internal routes along rivers. Although there is little evidence for shipwrecks in rivers, identification of artifacts lost or thrown into rivers can be helpful. Finally, inscriptions can shed light on river boatmen and help to show the kind of cargoes being carried by boat.

This kind of evidence, when taken with the observations of commentators such as Strabo and Pliny and what we know of local road networks, can give a picture of the economic and cultural context in which rivers were exploited by local communities. Even so, the result is sketchy, and we are often dealing with possibilities rather than facts. In many provinces there was no framework of navigable rivers, and instead smallish areas were served by limited, probably seasonal navigability over relatively short distances.

1   THE SPANISH PROVINCES

In the view of ancient commentators, there was no doubt that the Spanish and Gallic provinces were preeminent for their navigable rivers serving as routes of communication and transport (map 9). Strabo writes that in Spain many major rivers had tributaries that were themselves navigable, though he does not name all of them. In the main his enthusiasm seems to be justified. The Anas (816 km long) and the Baetis (560 km long), flow from east to west, before turning south to enter the Atlantic west of Gades (Cadiz);[1] according to Pliny, the Baetis has among its navigable tributaries the Singilis and the Maenuba, and was navigable at least as far as Corduba.[2] The lower course of the Anas was navigable for seagoing ships up to Myrtilis, and lighter craft could get to the rapids at Salto del Lobo; the limit of its navigability was about twenty kilometers south of Badajoz.[3]

Both rivers provided a transport route from the Sierra Morena through their valleys to the coast and the important ports and estuaries. Further north, the Durius (760 km long, but no longer navigable) and the Tagus (936 km long) also flow from east to west into the Atlantic Ocean.[4] They offer a route of communication from the high Sierra de Gredos and the Sierra de Guadarrana. The smaller river Minius flows from the Cantabrian Mountains to the Atlantic coast. In Strabo's view, this river (called Blaenis by some) was the greatest of the rivers of Lusitania and was navigable for ninety miles from the coast. Also, flowing parallel to the Tagus, are the Mundas and the Vacua, both navigable for a short distance. All these rivers were tidal but had high banks and could accommodate the high tide without flooding the surrounding land.[5] The Hiberus (920 km long) is the principal river of Spain, flowing from northwest to southeast between the Iberian Mountains and the Pyrenees to the Mediterranean 128 kilometers south of Barcelona. It offers a route of communication

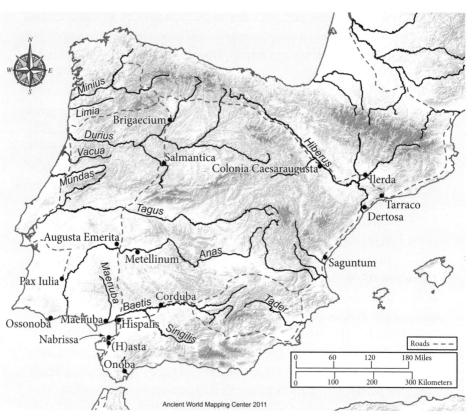

MAP 9. *Navigable rivers in Spain according to Strabo, Pliny, and Mela*

from the Mediterranean coast to the interior and to northern Spain. Its tributaries flow east, giving access to the Meseta, and west (toward Gaul).[6] There are several fairly short, navigable rivers in Lusitania flowing to the west coast and the Atlantic and providing access to the interior of the northwest. The Limia flows from the Sierra de Mamed, the Mundas from the Serra da Estrela past Conimbriga, and the Vacua from the Sierra da Lapa. It is possible that seasonal navigation was common in Spain, even if our sources do not make this clear.

In addition, according to Strabo, who alone deals with this in any detail and concentrates on Spain, there were many estuaries and coastal channels made navigable by the tide. The importance of this is very difficult to estimate because of changes in sea level and alterations in the coastline.[7] Referring to the estuary of Asta and Nabrissa, Strabo defines estuary (*anachrusis*) as "hollows covered by the sea at high tide, which like rivers afford a sailing passage to the interior and the cities on their shores."[8] In Baetica the major cities were on the rivers, on the sea, and on the estuaries because of the importance of trade, and

Baetica's wealth was enhanced by the ease with which goods were exported using these assets; Strabo emphasizes that the estuaries are like rivers and are navigable inland even for large vessels. It is even better because there is no opposing current and the sea sweeps you on because of the flood tide. In Strabo's view this was particularly important on the south coast of Spain because of the weight of water pressing through the Straits of Gibraltar. There were so many of these estuaries, navigable inland for a considerable distance, that "virtually the whole country is conveniently navigable for the export and import of goods." The main difficulty was the corresponding violence and speed of the ebb tide, which could leave a ship grounded.[9] In the lower reaches of the Baetis, great variations occurred in the tides so that water backed up as far as Ilipa, some 130 kilometers from the coast, and coastal plains flooded as far as eight kilometers inland.[10] Local people, recognizing the potential value of the estuaries, built settlements nearby, such as (H)Asta, Nabrissa, Onoba, Ossonoba, and Maenuba. Canals were also used to improve navigation and sometimes the flood tide produced more opportunities by flooding low-lying land separating isthmuses and creating a watery expanse across which travel was possible from estuary to river and river to estuary.[11]

Useful estuaries existed also on the west coast of Spain, around the Kal(l)ipous, which was navigable as far as Salacia. The estuary of the Tagus was very deep and over two miles wide at its mouth and large merchant ships could navigate it. When the flood tide came the land was flooded for a distance of about twenty-seven kilometers and the whole plain above the estuary was navigable for big ships for some ninety kilometers to the city of Moron (possibly Alto do Castelo, Alpiarça), and thereafter by rivercraft. Decimus Junius Brutus in 136 B.C. had fortified a post at Olisipo at the mouth of the river to safeguard inland navigation and the bringing in of supplies.[12] Thereafter, the Tagus continued to be navigable for a distance.

According to Strabo, among the rivers of western Iberia the Baetis ranked in size between the Tagus and the Anas and was navigable for large merchant craft for about 90 kilometers up to Hispalis (Seville); further upstream the river was navigable as far as Ilipa for smaller merchant vessels. For small rivercraft (specially built rather than the dugouts used in earlier times) it was possible to travel for approximately 219 kilometers to the area just beyond Corduba (Córdoba), though beyond this point toward Castulo the Baetis was not navigable.[13] This roughly corresponds with more modern times. The riverine districts of the Baetis were heavily populated, very fertile, and well cultivated, with delightful farms and gardens. On the other hand, at Ilipa silver was mined and there were deposits of copper and gold in the vicinity. Strabo believed that the produce of the land and the mined ore were shipped to the coast along the river. It was the large number of merchant vessels operating on the Baetis that ensured the wonderful prosperity of Turdetania.

The Baetis basin covers an area of 56,362 square kilometers and had the densest urban and rural settlement in Spain in the imperial period.[14] The area between Hispalis and Corduba was particularly fertile, with a combination of irrigated and dry-farmed land suitable for a great variety of crops. The basin was also drained by important tributaries of the Baetis, particularly the navigable Singilis. To the west of Hispalis, there was a large fertile area drained by the Río Tinto and the navigable Maenuba (Guadiamar River), which probably joined the Baetis downstream from Seville, while to the west of Corduba was land suitable for olives and other arboriculture. The area between Hispalis and Corduba was largely given over to the cultivation of olive trees, which were also grown on the river Singilis below Astigi (Ecija). The main olive-growing areas were in a triangle between Hispalis, Corduba, and Astigi and also between Corduba and Jaén (map 10). To the north, the river basin was bordered by the Sierra Morena, which was suitable for nonagricultural and mixed economies and also harbored a large range of metals. In the context of the Spanish provinces, Baetica was heavily populated, especially on the banks of the river Baetis in the area bordered by the Roman administrative centers of Hispalis, Corduba, and Astigi.[15]

Large Roman villas and *latifundia* were located within this zone,[16] and these communities speedily developed rapidly into important centers for trade and commerce or centers of communication. Hispalis was an entrepôt for the movement of goods to and from southern Spain and a hub of a communications network leading to the important market of Rome; it was to continue as an important trading port, becoming the center for trade with America.[17] Corduba was in a strategic position, originally controlling an important ford and later a bridge over the Baetis and the network of communication in southern Spain. It had valuable mineral deposits in the mountains of its hinterland and was a center for river traffic on the way to Hispalis and thence to Rome.

Baetican olive oil was exported in enormous quantities to Rome in amphorae. Huge numbers of amphorae were dumped at Monte Testaccio, a repository behind the warehouses of Rome's main river port, and deliberately broken, and it has been calculated that the hill contains fragments of about 24,750,000 amphorae, suggesting about 7 million kilograms of olive oil a year. It is possible that Spanish oil imports may have amounted to 4 million kilograms a year in about 55,000 containers.[18] Olive oil was very important in the ancient world, providing a relatively inexpensive source for cooking and light, and also being

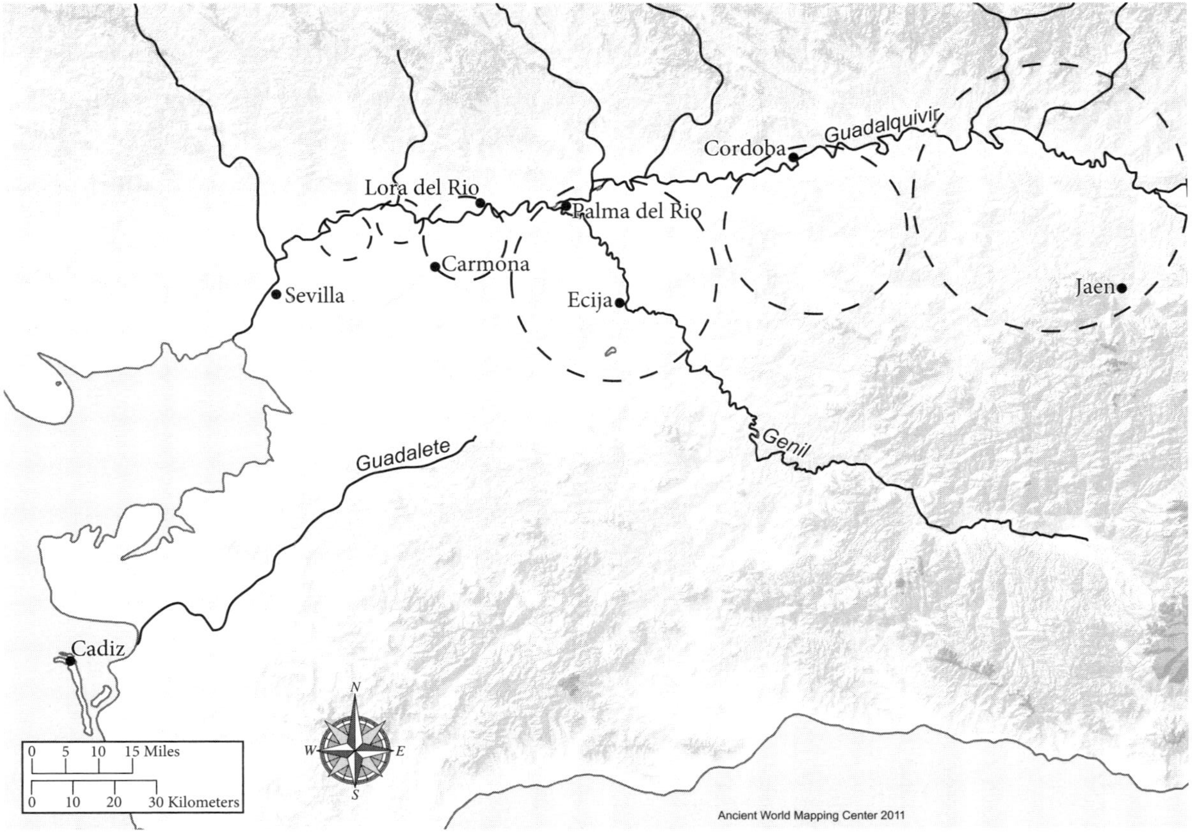

MAP 10. Areas of olive cultivation along the Baetis valley. Adapted from Michel Ponsich, "The Rural Economy of Western Baetica," in S. Keay (ed.), The Archaeology of Early Roman Baetica, Journal of Roman Archaeology Supplementary Series 29 (Portsmouth, Rhode Island, 1998), 174, with permission.

Ancient World Mapping Center 2011

part of some medicines and perfumes.[19] This helps to establish the context of the huge trade in olive oil from Baetica; presumably it could be sold at an affordable price and make a profit, despite the distance of 2,000 kilometers from Hispalis to Ostia. This raises the interesting question of transport networks, and suggests that cheaper riverine transport played a large part. Other exports such as wine, fish products, some grain, metals, and pottery to North Africa were also important.

It is significant that the manufacture of Spanish amphorae was concentrated in the area along the Baetis notable for olive cultivation, and many pottery kilns have been identified. Arguably the potteries were based here because of the proximity of the oil-producing areas, and because they were close to embarkation ports for shipment of the oil to Hispalis, though the management of the potteries was apparently unrelated to the production of the olive oil itself.[20] Of course, the fact that potters need clay and water might in itself be a sufficient reason for their location close to a river. However, usable clay was available well away from the rivers, as the location of brick and tile kilns shows (map 11).[21]

Rivers may have been the preferred method of transporting amphorae, which were breakable but also heavy; an empty amphora weighs 28–30 kilograms, with 65–70 liters it would weigh 80–100 kilograms.[22] The point furthest along the Baetis where pottery is found is fifteen kilometers south of Corduba. The absence of bridges as far as Corduba facilitated traffic, and apart from Corduba and Hispalis, there were eight ports (of which seven were *municipia*) on the right bank (Italica, Ilipa Magna, Naeva, Canama, Arva, Axati, Detumo, Carbula) and four on the left bank (Brenes, Tocina, Guadajoz, Palma del Río). Furthermore, we find important centers for the manufacture of amphorae close to these ports. Oil could be transported to the markets in temporary containers and then put in amphorae for onward transport by river.[23]

The presence of a large number of potteries and pots in the Baetis valley is reasonably associated with the importance of fluvial transport, though it is true that from pre-Roman times the valley attracted large numbers of settlers, and with a relatively high density of population in a rich farming environment there will have been a great need for pots. And it is worth pointing out that several of the great amphorae-producing workshops also produced other ceramics, tiles, and household pottery. Part of their profit came from supplying the local population with essential wares.[24] It must also be agreed that a very important area for olive production, west of Corduba around Jaén, extended a considerable distance away from the river. It may be that in this area, since centers for the production of olive-oil amphorae have yet to be found, the oil was carried in skins by pack animals along transhumance routes.[25]

Nevertheless, it seems likely that the great amphorae were manufactured as close as possible to the oil-producing land and the available network of communication. So, oil from the estates would be brought on mules possibly in skin containers, or down the Singilis tributary, and placed in the amphorae close to the point of manufacture, and then loaded onto flat-bottomed barges for the trip down the upper reaches of the Baetis to Hispalis. The usual harvesting time of the olives (December–February) would coincide with the time of highest water volume in the rivers. The olives would be ready for transport on the river from February to April and would presumably arrive in Hispalis for onward shipment to Gades by merchant vessels just as the winter period of closed sailing came to an end. It may be that to some extent oil production was conditioned by proximity to the river. Larger producers tended to occupy the land closest to the river, since this would make transport cheaper. Oil producers further away from the river could satisfy local needs.[26] The amphorae for Baetican oil (Dressel 20 amphorae) were spherical in shape, and were particularly suitable for flat-bottomed barges, being more stable than taller, slender amphorae, which might need some additional support or a hold for storage. A barge ten by three meters could contain seventy or eighty amphorae.[27]

Among other Spanish exports, wine was particularly important. There were extensive vineyards along the valley of the Baetis in the area from Corduba to Gades and also along the Mediterranean coastal area. Wine was exported in amphorae from Baetica, though not in such large quantities as oil; transport was by river to Hispalis, on to Gades, and then by sea (map 12).[28] The fertility of Baetica also appeared in the production of grain, which, although not nearly as important to Rome as that from Africa and Egypt, was so valuable that it could make a profit even if transported by land. For transport by river, the grain would have to be stored after the harvest and its river transport delayed until autumn (when there was sufficient water flow in the tributaries of the Baetis), with the result that the barges would arrive in Seville toward the end of the period of maritime navigation. Local needs in Baetica could be met by land transport but bigger population centers such as Hispalis, Gades, and Corduba could be supplied by river transport in winter.[29]

Strabo praised the variety and quality of fish from the Baetican seaboard,[30] and there was a thriving industry in salting fish in southern Baetica, with more than 100 centers.[31] The installations for manufacturing amphorae along the southern coast were probably closely linked to the production of salt fish. In addition, fish sauce (*garum*) was a valuable by-product and high-profit export of the fishing industry, since it was an important and expensive ingredient in Roman cooking.[32] River fishing was also important along the Baetis, and the

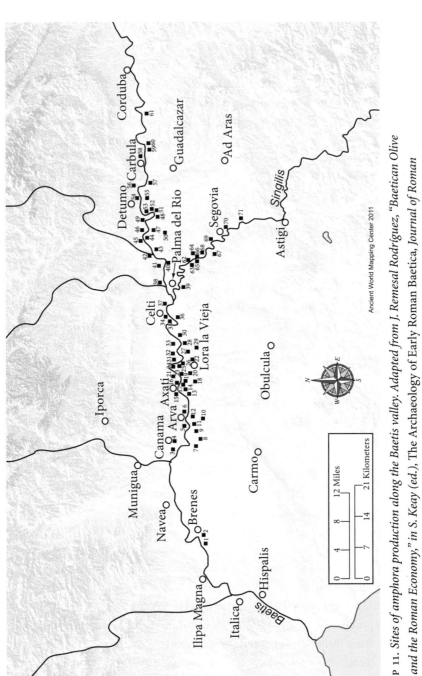

MAP 11. *Sites of amphora production along the Baetis valley. Adapted from J. Remesal Rodríguez, "Baetican Olive Oil and the Roman Economy," in S. Keay (ed.), The Archaeology of Early Roman Baetica, Journal of Roman Archaeology Supplementary Series 29 (Portsmouth, Rhode Island, 1998), 187, with permission.*

Ancient World Mapping Center 2011

1. Cruz Verde
2. Villar de Brenes
3. Huertas de Alcolea
4. Alcolea del Río
5. El Tejarillo
6. Arva
7. Guardajoz
8. Adelfa
9. Juan Barba
10. El Tesoro
11. Mejía
12. Tostoneras
13. Azanque-Castillejo
14. El Judío
15. La Estacada de Herrera
16. Lora del Río
17. Alamo Alto
18. Cortijo de Mochales

19. La Catria
20. Catria Alta
21. Huertas del Río
22. Lora la Vieja
23. Cortijo del Guerra
24. Haza del Olivo
25. Manuel Nieto
26. El Acebuchal
27. La Ramblilla
28. Madre Vieja I and II
29. El Marchante
30. Las Sesenta
31. La Mayena
32. La María
33. El Berro
34. El Tesoro
35. La Botica
36. Calonje Bajo

37. Peñaflor
38. Huertas de Belén
39. Casas de Pisón
40. Cortijo de Romero
41. Isla de la Jurada
42. Cerro de los Vuelos
43. Villacisneros
44. Casa de Encinarejo
45. La Umbría de Moratella
46. Casa del Guarda
47. La Correjidora
48. Soto del Rey
49. Haza de los Laticos
50. Cortijo de Bramadero
51. Barranco del Picacho
52. La Dehesilla
53. La Estrella
54. Dehesa de Arriba

55. Mingaobez
56. Guadiato
57. Villaseca
58. Almodóvar
59. El Temple
60. El Temple (Este)
61. Cortijo de la Reina
62. Malpica Sur
63. Tierras del Judío
64. Maplica
65. Cortijo del Judío
66. Cortijo de Villalata
67. Tarancón
68. Las Valbuenas
69. Isla Grande
70. Alcotrista
71. Las Delicias

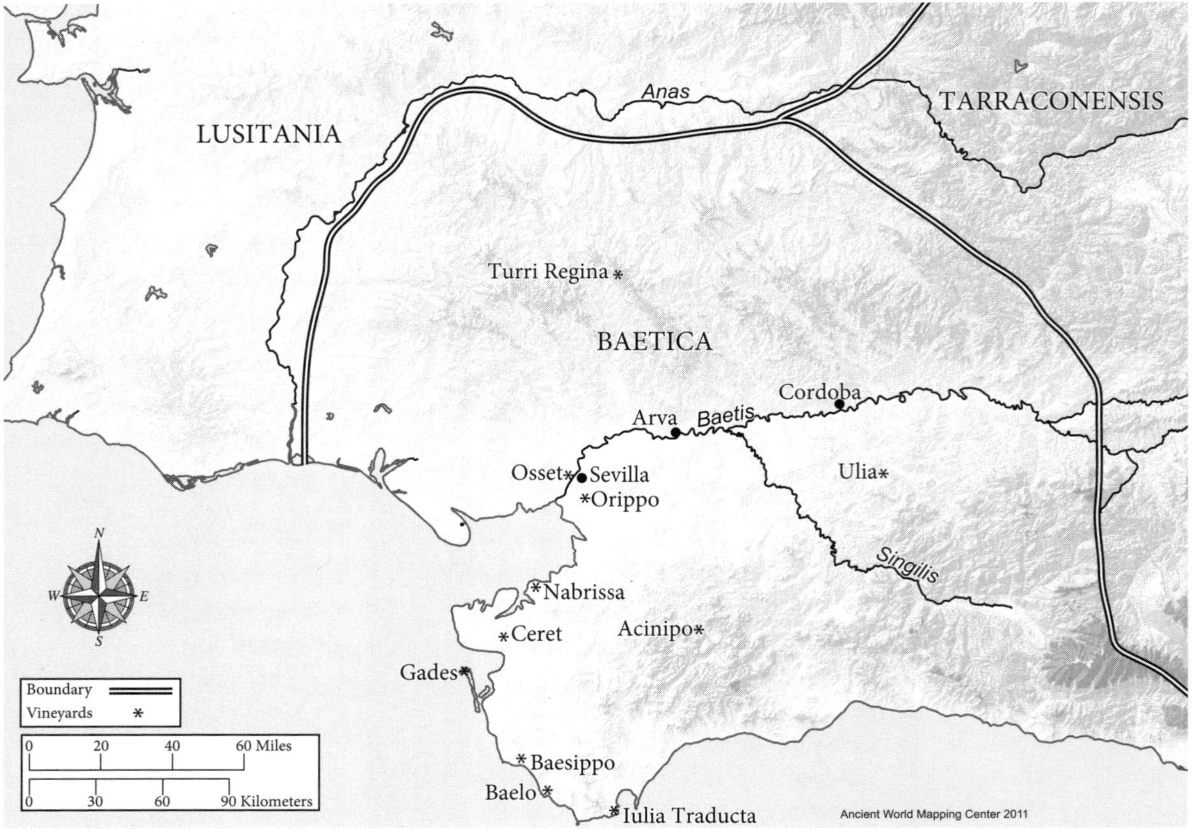

MAP 12. *Vineyards in the Baetis valley and vicinity. Adapted from Michel Ponsich, "The Rural Economy of Western Baetica," in S. Keay (ed.), The Archaeology of Early Roman Baetica, Journal of Roman Archaeology Supplementary Series 29 (Portsmouth, Rhode Island, 1998), 177, with permission.*

Baetis sturgeon was especially renowned. The fish were caught as they migrated up and down the river. This kind of fishing was lucrative, at least in the local context, and notably several towns on the river, Ilipa, Caura, and Cunbaria, celebrated shad on their coinage.[33]

The northern hinterland of Corduba in the Sierra Morena was a fruitful source of metals. These mining products were very expensive, and the usually prohibitive cost of land transport would be overcome by the innate cost of the product. It may be significant that some road-building activity took place on routes crossing mining areas. However, many mining regions of Sierra Morena were some distance from Hispalis, and it will have made sense to transport the loads of ingots as cheaply as possible by using the Baetis. Mules were employed to bring the ingots to the river, then small barges and rafts, and to keep the load steady the lead ingots were nailed to the floor of the boats. Along the Baetis several ports were suitable for loading ingots onto barges for shipment downstream, and on the right bank of the Guadalimar, a tributary of the Baetis, near Castulo large blocks of stone have been discovered and tentatively identified as a quay serving rivercraft.[34] From Hispalis, larger ships would take the ingots on by sea, mainly to Italy (map 13).[35]

It has also been suggested that the important supply of metals from Spain to the Roman market had a wider influence.[36] The shipments may have encouraged the oil trade, in that shippers sought part cargoes to go with the metals, which being very expensive could subsidize the transport of the other goods. In respect of stone quarries, there is no clear evidence for the export of marble from Baetica, although decorative stone was used locally (map 14).[37] However, pottery from Andújar was used extensively in southern Spain, and some was exported to north Africa. Hispalis was the center of a business in which pots in easily portable shapes were transported along the Baetis by barge in large numbers, and then distributed by roads leaving ports bordering the river.[38]

Among the Spanish provinces, Baetica was unquestionably the most famous and the wealthiest, because of the combination of easy communications, productive mines, and enormous olive and wine production.[39] The Romans obviously had a considerable interest in the area, but how far they controlled river routes for profit or for any other purpose is difficult to answer from the available evidence. On the whole, it is likely that they largely left the local communities to their own devices. There is no clear sign that the government intervened in the oil trade despite the presence in Rome of the mysterious *portus olearius* from the first century B.C.[40] There will, of course, have been much work for *navicularii* (ship operators) and *negotiatores* (merchants). An interesting inscription set up in Rome in the A.D. 140s by the businessmen in olive oil from

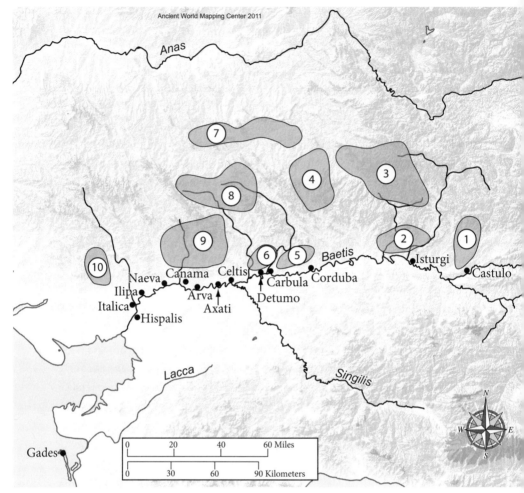

1. Linares–La Carolina (lead/silver)   6. Posadas (lead/silver)
2. Andújar-Montoro (copper)   7. La Serena (lead/silver)
3. Alcudia (lead/silver)   8. Azuaga-Fuenteovejuna (lead/silver, copper)
4. Pedroches (copper, lead/silver)   9. Seville (lead/silver, copper, iron)
5. Córdoba (copper)   10. Aznalcóllar (copper)

MAP 13. *Metal exports from the Baetis valley. Adapted from Claude Domergue, "A View of Baetica's External Commerce in the 1st C. A.D. based on Its Trade in Metals," in S. Keay (ed.),* The Archaeology of Early Roman Baetica, *Journal of Roman Archaeology Supplementary Series 29 (Portsmouth, Rhode Island, 1998), 205, with permission.*

MAP 14. *Sites of marble quarries in Spain. Adapted from M. Mayer and I. Rodà,*
"The Use of Marble and Decorative Stone in Roman Baetica," in S. Keay (ed.),
The Archaeology of Early Roman Baetica, *Journal of Roman Archaeology*
Supplementary Series 29 (Portsmouth, Rhode Island, 1998), 225, with permission.

Baetica celebrates their patron, M. Petronius Honoratus, who had been prefect of the grain supply.[41] But what is the connection? It is unclear if they were hoping for some business advantage from an official who had a direct interest in their activities, or if he was simply a generally influential patron.

Inscriptions on amphorae offer a hint of some form of control. They were stamped with their empty weight and also with the weight of the oil they contained. The monitoring of this seems to be connected with the *conventus* districts associated with the three towns of Corduba, Astigi, and Hispalis.[42] This may have been a local control against fraud or perhaps was part of local account keeping for the *portoria* tax.[43] The direct intervention of the government at this stage may have been limited to making sure that the needs of the army were satisfied, since there was a demand for Baetican oil in the army camps of northern Europe and in also in Britain.[44] It is not clear if this was by requisition or if the Romans simply encouraged normal trade, which was assisted by the existing trade in metals. In any case, we find a hint of the importance of the oil trade in an inscription from Astigi mentioning a *diffusor olearius*.[45]

It is not until the reign of Marcus Aurelius that we have clear evidence of some measure of deliberate intervention, in the inscription set up at Hispalis in honor of Sextus Julius Possessor.[46] This equestrian official, after holding the position of military tribune, served as assistant to the prefect of the grain supply, "with the task of keeping account of Spanish and African oil, of transporting supplies and paying the expenses of the shippers." The inscription was erected by the boatmen of Hispalis (*scapharii Hispalenses*) "because of his honesty and outstanding integrity." This may suggest some business dealings, but as Possessor (who was of African origin) was also responsible for African oil, it is more likely that he was based in Rome than in Hispalis. It is possible that the boatmen encountered Possessor in his subsequent post as "procurator on the bank of the Baetis," in which he will have been responsible for maintaining the channel for the passage of rivercraft, maintaining the towpath, and also perhaps for facilitating river use in general. Other inscriptions show the importance of the boatmen of the river at Hispalis.[47]

However, although Possessor may not have been an agent of the office of the prefect permanently based in Baetica, his role does indicate the state's involvement in encouraging if not directing the shipment of oil to Rome by underwriting the cost of shipment. Inscriptions also reveal a "procurator Baetis," and the "procurator of the emperor of the river bank of the province of Baetica."[48] Among other things, they may have been in charge of river navigation. A rescript from Marcus Aurelius and Lucius Verus confirmed, with safeguards, the incentive of immunity from civic obligations in their communities for those shipping grain or oil to Rome.[49] Furthermore, in Marcus's reign there was a procurator at Ostia to receive oil.[50] Since oil was so important in Mediterranean life, its transportation will have been economically worthwhile and perhaps only limited intervention by the government was required. In general, it is fair to say that by the late second century a structure was in place for the transport of oil to Rome, although it is not clear if the government aimed at subsidized oil distribution or simply at making oil available in sufficient quantities at a reasonable price. However, an inscription from Rome celebrating Titus Aelius Faustus shows that oil was at least occasionally distributed to the people in the time of Marcus Aurelius and Commodus.[51] Under the Severan dynasty, a regular daily oil distribution was introduced to go with the grain distribution for some of the population of Rome.[52]

Baetica was particularly wealthy, and if other areas were less prosperous we cannot say that this was due to the presence or otherwise of navigable rivers. Of course, other regions in Spain did have good riverine connections, even if on a lesser scale. The peninsula had a wide variety of river navigation including direct routes to the interior, connection with the coast and river ports involved in cabotage, and smaller rivers navigable for short distances, which flat-bottomed boats could use for local traffic. Therefore, although there was no river network comparable to that in Gaul, fluvial connections in Spain outside Baetica also had the potential to assist economic development. For example, a fine pottery, *terra sigillata Hispanica*, was produced at Tritium Magallum (Tricio) in the upper valley of the Hiberus (Ebro) and exported to many places in Spain.[53] It is likely that the pottery was taken by road across the Iberian mountain fringe to the headwaters of the Durius and Tagus and thus transported to the Meseta. The Hiberus valley was also important for viticulture and the wine could be brought down the river for export to Rome or Africa.[54] A road ran down the valley to Celsa before branching off to Ilerda, and important tributaries may have provided some access to the hinterland. There were important Roman centers on the river—Dertosa (a river port near the coast), Colonia Caesaraugusta, Illurcis, Calagurris (Nassica) Iulia, and Ilerda on the Sicoris, a tributary of the Hiberus. Dertosa, at the junction of the great coast road and the Hiberus, served as the center of the wine trade, other agricultural produce, and the export of ceramics.[55] Imports also came this way and the Hiberus served as a significant commercial route for the whole region, with some possible signs of Roman intervention to create river ports.[56] At the town of Valentia (Valencia) in Tarraconensis on the river Turia about two kilometers from the sea, the installations of a small river harbor and a large granary have been identified, with substantial deposits of broken amphorae from Italy.[57] Small-draft boats probably transported goods from the coast along the river to Valentia, from which they could be moved on by road.

In Lusitania, the Tagus flowed from the interior to the west coast and was perhaps navigable for twenty to thirty kilometers beyond Olisipo (Lisbon); its tributary, the Zêzere, was also a potential route in Roman times. In this region there was an economic connection between salting factories and Roman ceramic production and the course of the Tagus, along which transport will have been by barge.[58] The principal ports on the Tagus were situated close to fords on the north to southwest routes. The fish sauce (*garum*), which was so important in Baetica, was also produced in Lusitania, especially at Tróia at the mouth of the river Sado (one of the estuaries of the Tagus) from which the sauce could be exported.[59] North of the Tagus valley at Conimbriga, amphora production may be connected with the fact that the river Mundas (Mondego) was perhaps navigable for ships of limited size.[60]

The role of the river Anas was to some extent limited to local traffic because there were problems of water volume and seasonality, and particularly because of the sixty-meter waterfall at Pulo do Lobo (near Serpa), which prevented access to the river mouth, although this could have been bypassed by using pack animals. The Colony of Augusta Emerita occupied an important position on the river for traffic downstream to Badajoz. Near the bridge, remains have been identified as port installations, though they may have been walls to control water flow. Nevertheless, supplies probably came to Emerita by water along the east-west axis using small boats.[61] Setúbal must have had port facilities, and there will have been smaller ports at the mouth of the Mondego. In any case the river port of Myrtilis was an important center for the export of minerals from southern Lusitania.[62] *Codicarii* ships, which operated on rivers, could additionally convey goods along the coast to Gades. The Durius also shows the dynamic of Atlantic commerce; there was ceramic production in the valley, and the fluvial route was used for distribution of wine and oil and fish salting, produced around Olisipo. Throughout this valley, there was a relation between farm estates and watercourses as a means of transporting produce.[63]

Rivers of north and northeast Spain were not so important in commercial terms. Here the river dynamic was different with less volume of water. Nevertheless, rivers in the area provided a kind of interaction between the coast and the sea, since their mouths could serve as anchorages, ports, bases of Roman cabotage, and watering places on a dangerous coast. The wine amphorae, salt, and ceramics found in northern Spain were part of a trading network, in which rivers could combine with land routes, along and from the coast, since interior roads ran along river valleys.[64]

Our ancient writers point out that in Gaul a remarkable network of navigable rivers extended from Narbonensis with the Rhône and its many tributaries, right up to northeast Gaul, from which there were connections with the German provinces; westward river routes extended into central Gaul through the Loire and the Seine, while the Garonne provided access to the southwest (map 15). In the 1980s France still had about 7,360 kilometers of navigable rivers, allowing goods to be transported from the Mediterranean to the Atlantic or English Channel, with only a limited amount of movement needed by road.[65] King among the rivers of Gaul was the Rhône. It is true that its course was swift and turbulent, making it difficult to sail upstream, and this was exacerbated by a high gradient at certain points where the valley narrowed. Nevertheless, because of its volume of water it was navigable for at least 150 Roman miles to the confluence with the Isère, and more than 25 miles beyond this to the confluence with the Saône at Lugdunum.[66] The Rhône originates in the Rhône glacier at the Saint Gotthard massif and, flowing through Lake Geneva continues to the Mediterranean, over a distance of about 800 kilometers. It is the fastest and most powerful river in France, with an output of 1,800 cubic meters per second at the delta; its drainage basin extends to about 100,000 square kilometers.[67] This great river dominated the province of Gallia Narbonensis, flowing through Cabilonnum (Chalon-sur-Saône), Lugdunum (the provincial capital), Vienna (Vienne), Valentia (Valence), Arausio (Orange), Avennio (Avignon), and Arelate (Arles).[68] Its straight course offered direct access and a route of communication to central Gaul. Furthermore, it had important tributaries, navigable in the ancient world: the Arar (Saône), the Isara (Isère), and the Druentia (Durance). The Saône rising at Vioménil in the Vosges Mountains and joining the Rhône at Lyon is 480 kilometers long with an average flow of 410 cubic meters per second, and it provides access to central Gaul, bringing northern communication within reach of the Seine and the Marne. The Isère rises in the French Alps near Val d'Isère and flows westward for 290 kilometers to join the Rhône just north of Valence (it is now unnavigable). The Durance rises near the Col du Galibier, flowing through Brigantio (Briançon), Emburodunum (Embrun), Segustero (Sisteron), and Cabellio (Cavaillon) to join the Rhône south of Avennio. Also important is the Dubis (Doubs), which joins the Saône north of Cabilonnum; it is 435 kilometers long and encloses in a loop the city of Vesontio (Besançon).[69]

Outstanding among the great navigable rivers of northern France is the Sequana (Seine), which rises in the Langres plateau and flows for 770 kilometers generally in a northwesterly direction before emptying into the English

Rotomagus

Lutetia

Mosa

Rhenus

Mosella

Civitas Namnetum

Caesarodunum

Liger

Sequana

Autessiodurum

Divodurum

Andematunnum

Massava

Vesontio

Augustodunum

Dubis

Arar

Lacus
Lemannus

Burdigala

Forum Segusiavorum

Lugdunum

Genava

Acaunum

Vienna

Garunna

Isara

Culuro

Valentia

Rhodanus

Tolosa

Arelate

Druentia

Atax

Narbo
Martius

Massilia

Roads - - -

0	50	100	150 Miles
0	75	150	225 Kilometers

Ancient World Mapping Center 2011

MAP 15. *Navigable rivers in Gaul*

Channel. It remains one of the most easily navigable rivers in France and has been a great commercial route to the heart of the country, since large vessels can sail up the river as far as Rouen. Among its many tributaries, of particular interest is the Matrona (Marne), which is 520 kilometers long and joins the Seine near Paris; it provides a route to eastern France and Germany. In eastern France, navigable rivers were the Mosella (Moselle) and Mosa (Meuse). The former rises in the Vosges Mountains and is 515 kilometers long, flowing north into Germany between the Eifel and Hunsrük mountain ranges; it washes Tullum (Toul), Divodurum (Metz), and Augusta Treverorum (Trier) before joining the Rhine at Confluentes (Koblenz). In the present day, the Moselle (known as Mosel in Germany) has a canal to facilitate the movement of heavy barges between Metz and Koblenz. The Meuse rises in the Langres plateau near Noviomagus (Nijon) and flows north for 900 kilometers, going past Sedan (the head of the navigation) into Belgium, and past Atuatuca (Tongeren); it is joined by the Sabis (Sambre) at Namur. After this, it goes eastward before turning north and going on to form a common delta with the river Rhine. In modern times a series of canals helps to make it a major commercial waterway of Europe. In Roman times, the Mosa, with possible connections to other rivers in Gaul, offered a route of communication and transport from the southern Rhône valley to the German provinces and transfer of goods to the Rhine, as it flowed within 50 kilometers of the legionary base at Vetera (Xanten) on the Rhine and within 25 kilometers of Noviomagus (Nijmegen).

The Liger (Loire) is the longest river in France, rising in the Cevennes and flowing northwest to Orléans before turning west and eventually emptying into the Atlantic south of the Brittany peninsula. It is about 1,000 kilometers long, and its basin drains an area of 117,000 square kilometers. In its long course, the Liger washed the important settlements of Forum Segusiavorum (Feurs), Decetia (Decize), Cenabum (Orléans), Caesarodunum (Tours), Iuliomagus (Angers), and Portus Namnetum (Nantes), which saw the convergence of four roads that ran both north and south along the coast and to the interior.[70] This river continued an important communications route to the province of Lugdunensis and the west coast. If the Elaver (Allier), which rises in the Massif Centrale and flows north for about 410 kilometers, passing Gergovia (Gergovie), Augustonemetum (Clermont-Ferrand), and Vorogio (Vouroux),[71] before flowing into the Liger near Nevers, were navigable in Roman times, it would be an important extension of the potential of the Loire as a route of communication into central and southern Gaul.

In southwest France, the Garumna (Garonne) rises in the Pyrenees and flows for about 647 kilometers, emptying into the Atlantic about 26 kilometers north of Bordeaux (Burdigala).[72] Today it remains navigable in its lower course though it suffers from uneven water flow and steep gradients. In Roman times, it washed Tolosa (Toulouse, where the modern Canal du Midi begins), Viriodunum (Verdun), and Aginnum (Agen). It is possible that the Garumna was linked by portage to the Atax (Aude), which flowed into the Mediterranean near Narbo (Narbonne) and had its headwaters near Sostomagus, just over 30 kilometers from Tolosa and the Garumna. This could have been an effective communications route in southwest Gaul, the Mediterranean, and the Bay of Biscay.

Among these river systems, the Rhône, as Strabo pointed out, had good connections with other rivers to both the west and the east, and in particular land transport carried merchandise to the river Sequana (Seine), along which it was carried to the coast, and thence to Britain.[73] The overland route from Lugdunum to the Sequana was about 200 kilometers.[74] Because of the river currents, traffic headed west toward the Arvernians and the Liger (Loire) found the road route from Lugdunum easier, since it crossed level ground and was only about 160 kilometers long. Once the Loire was reached, then goods could be moved on by river.[75] There was also the trade route along the Mediterranean coast, via the mouth of the Rhône.[76] The rhythms and style of navigation would vary from river basin to river basin, as sailors used whatever form of propulsion suited the conditions—the natural current, sails, or towing by man or animal.[77] Navigation might be seasonal, with autumn and spring the times for heaviest traffic. As already discussed, a combination of road and river transport was often most effective.[78]

The Roman authorities made use of the river network as they found it, and there is little evidence that they attempted to regulate the flow of rivers to improve navigation; for example, no program of works advanced commercial objectives, and no attempt was made to construct canals linking the main rivers by cutting through the mountains that separated the river valleys. The technological problems and expense may have been too great, or the links between the river network and the road system may have seemed adequate. The *fossa Mariana* in the Rhône delta was the only obvious intervention.[79] In fact, at the Rhône delta self-help was the order of the day; since the low coastline made it difficult to see the river mouth in bad weather, the Massilians set up towers with beacons to guide the mariners.[80]

Strabo gives only one specific example of long distance trade from Gaul, in the shipment of hog meat from the Sequani apparently down the Gallic rivers and onward to Rome.[81] However, to some extent his view of the importance of river transport in Gaul is supported by inscriptions showing the activities of shippers and boatmen on the rivers and by archaeological evidence relating to river ports and the movement of goods. The associations of shippers (*navicularii*) and boatmen (*nautae*) who plied their trade on the rivers were very important socially and economically. Ships owned by the *navicularii* could, of course, be seagoing, but they might often operate in river estuaries and could be enticed upstream for commercial profit. Therefore, many Gallic shipowners traded along the river network of Gaul and also through the Mediterranean to Italy and Spain. The corporations of shipowners in Gaul had offices at Narbo, Arelate, and Lugdunum, and the last two in particular suggest the importance of their river-based activities. Some individual *navicularii* were men of wealth and status in their community. Indeed, one side of the memorial stele of the boatman Blussus from Mainz depicts him carrying a full purse in his left hand; on his right is his wife, richly dressed and carrying a small dog on her lap, and behind them is their son, Primus.[82] The other side of the stele shows Blussus's boat in operation on a river, presumably the Rhine. Similarly, Julia Nice set up a funeral monument for her husband, Marcus Frontonius Euporus, magistrate of the Colony Julia Augusta Aquae Sextiae and *navicularius marinus* at Arelate, "curator of the same corporation and patron of the sailors of the Druentia and the corporation of the *utricularii* of Ernaginum."[83] Shippers probably enriched by the river Sequana (Seine) showed their gratitude by dedicating offerings at Blessey about two kilometers from the source of the Seine; one shows a man rowing a boat, the other a statue of the goddess Sequana on a boat.[84]

The corporations (*corpora* or *collegia*) of shipowners represented the gathering together of people who had similar business or trade interests.[85] Certainly, the economic significance of these bodies is marked by the fact that there were large numbers of them in Gaul, even though the Roman government was not keen to see societies formed that could perhaps disrupt public order in a province or become another source of authority or influence outside the provincial administration. But, among other things, these organizations were very valuable for the transport of military supplies for the army of the Rhine.[86]

Lower down the social scale, the boatmen (*nautae*) of the Gallic rivers made a fundamental contribution to the wealth and economy of the provinces where they operated.[87] There was also a religious aspect to the *collegia* of boatmen, since religious statues stood on riverbanks and in harbors to offer protection to mariners and travelers.[88] The geographical distribution of the corporations of boatmen is significant, and in Gaul they are found on the Rhône, Saône, Loire, Seine basin, Moselle, Durance, Ardèche, Ouvèze, and Lake Léman. The boatmen were associated with rivers rather than particular towns,[89] and the location of the inscriptions marks out the major trade and transport routes through Gaul. The important role of the boatmen can be judged from the relatively large number of inscriptions and from the status of the corporation of boatmen on the Rhône and Saône (the most important rivers with the biggest concentration of corporations), which was described as *splendidissimum corpus*.[90] We find a sailor on the Saône holding the responsible public office of supervisor of public funds (*curator peculi rei publicae*) at Glanum.[91]

Sailors from the Rhône and the Saône appear together or individually, but it seems that normally some boatmen would specialize in operating on one particular river. So, from the area between Valentia and Vienna, the Rhône boatmen made an offering to "the most generous emperor Hadrian."[92] Similarly, we have the corporation of "Rhône boatmen operating on the Rhône."[93] And from Lugdunum there is a dedication set up by Gaius Julius Sabinianus, Rhône boatman, "in honor of the Rhône boatmen. . . . For the dedication of this gift he gave 13,000 sesterces for all those who sail."[94] The significant presence of the Rhône boatmen can also be seen in an inscription found on the right bank of the river at Géligneux, set up by M. Rufius Catullus, who was apparently "curator of the sailors of the Rhône."[95] This is unlikely to be an official position of the Roman state, and Catullus was presumably holding a position in the corporations of boatmen.

The Saône too had its own boatmen, for example, recorded in a memorial from Castrum Divionense (Dijon),[96] and at Lugdunum Matrona set up a memorial to "a boatman of the Saône and honored raftman at Lugdunum, a dear husband with whom she lived for sixteen years, three months, and fifteen days without any emotional disagreement."[97] On the other hand, some operated on both rivers,[98] and at Lugdunum a man was celebrated as the patron of the Rhône boatmen who sailed on the Saône and also of the raft operators at Lugdunum.[99] Again, an inscription from Aventicum celebrates Otacilius Cerialis, who was patron of the boatmen of the Saône and Rhône.[100] In the amphitheater at Nemausus, the boatmen of the Rhône and Saône had forty seats reserved for them, as well as twenty-five for those operating on the Ardèche and Ouvèze. This shows first the status of the boatmen, since it was "granted by decree of the town council," and also something of their relative numbers. Presumably this was a gesture to the boatmen that was perhaps followed in other communities and was not intended to include every boatman who might work the route. Therefore, this may represent a proportion of their total numbers. Another dedication at Lugdunum celebrates the boatmen of the Saône, the Loire, Condate (at the confluence of the Rhône and Saône), and the Arecarii boatmen.[101] The inscription from the amphitheater at Nemausus shows that boatmen were operating on the Ouvèze and probably the Ardèche (if that can be identified as the Atrica), both tributaries of the Rhône.[102] Therefore, even if the Rhone was the main artery of transport, other rivers also contributed to the distribution of goods.

The Druentia, which joined the lower Rhône just south of Avennio, also had its corporation of boatmen.[103] Further south in the delta, Ernaginum stood at an important road junction, and an inscription indicates that a usable stream did once flow past here to the Rhône, though it was probably not a branch of the Druentia.[104] In the western Rhône valley, boats were operating on the small rivers—the *nautae Aruranci* (Arauris) Aramici set up a dedication "in honor of the divine house."[105] Away from the Rhône valley, we have boatmen from the Liger (Loire),[106] the Moselle,[107] and the Seine near Paris.[108] At Portus Namnetum (Nantes) an offering was made to *Deus Volcanus* "for the welfare of the inhabitants of the *vicus* of the Port and the boatmen of the Loire," and it has been suggested that this close relationship perhaps indicates an independent socioeconomic unit separate from the surrounding area.[109] On *lacus Lemannus*, there were two ports, one for the use of *ratiarii superiores* (ferrymen in the upper reaches), and the other for the *nautae Lacus Lemanni*.[110]

Although relatively few river ports have been discovered, the evidence is suggestive, and it seems that, in the movement of goods based on river networks and river ports, both river ports and seaports at the mouths of rivers and those upstream had an important role to play.[111] Ideally, river ports should be on a stretch of river that was navigable upstream and downstream and preferably have connections to other rivers. They should also have good links with the local road network and be at the intersection of road and fluvial transport.[112] Depending on the volume of flow, ports might have to provide for the transfer of merchandise from oceangoing craft to riverboats. Port facilities could be pretty rudimentary, perhaps only wooden piers that have left no trace. But eventually business dealings could lead to the appearance of quays, warehouses, and offices. Whereas some river ports would principally serve a relatively small local area (and any riverside town was potentially a river port as long as it had a suitable landing site), others served an entire region.

Among the most important in Gaul were Arelate and Lugdunum. The former, on the estuary of the Rhône, was a river and marine port, the head of river navigation on the way to further river connections, and a base for sea and coastal travel. Here two important roads converged, and a famous bridge over the Rhône, originally constructed of boats and strikingly depicted on a mosaic at Ostia, ensured communications.[113] Access to the sea was provided by either the river or the *fossa Mariana*. Large seagoing ships could transship their cargo onto river-going craft. It was a great commercial center for Gaul, with port facilities on the right bank of the river at Trinquetaille.[114] It was the base for corporations of shippers and shipwrights, professions connected with navigation, and various types of boatmen.[115] The *navicularii* of Arelate also had an office in Ostia, as we see from the mosaic depicting the port of Arelate and its pontoon bridge.[116] For a time at least Arelate was the flourishing center for the export of Gallic grain, a substantial cash crop. Its importance to the Roman state can be seen in the petition of complaint shippers addressed in A.D. 201 to Septimius Severus about the problems and improper exactions they were facing in carrying out their service for the state.[117]

Lugdunum, at the confluence of the Rhône and Saône, was chosen by Agrippa and Augustus as the nodal point for their road system, at the center of six converging roads. These radiated to Aquitania, to the Rhine, to the northern coast, and to Narbonne and the Massilian coast; there was also a road east to Lake Léman.[118] Therefore, while Lugdunum was partly turned toward Italy and the Mediterranean, it also encouraged many routes of communication and, with its combination of road and river transport was a river port, was a great commercial and administrative center and attracted traders from all over the Mediterranean. Workshops of potters, bronze founders, and glassmakers were located on both banks of the Saône, while on the island of the *canabae* in the center of the river stood storehouses and docks for the merchants plying their trade on the Rhône and Saône. In fact, many potters seem to have worked on the river's edge, perhaps suggesting the convenience of the shipment of goods by the river.[119] Lugdunum's prime position in Gallic river navigation enhanced its connections with all of Gaul, and two large corporations of sailors of the Rhône and the Saône, who sailed equally on both rivers, had their *schola* on the banks of the Saône.[120] Other corporations were based in the environs of Lugdunum, such as the *nautae Arecarii* from Condate at the confluence of the Rhône and the Saône.[121] Interestingly, one Attalus, who was a *sevir Augustalis* at Lugdunum and a dealer in perfume, was also a boatman and possibly a member of the corporation of Rhône boatmen.[122] There were also associations with the boatmen of the Liger (Loire), and ferrymen were based at Lugdunum and further down the river at Montmélian.[123]

In addition, Lugdunum was the crucial city in military supply routes that assisted the development of a route of communication along the Rhône, Saône, Moselle, and Rhine valleys as the main economic axis of Gaul and Germany. This was the richest and most important part of Gaul, and military spending was an important part of the economy.[124] By the mid-first century A.D. the Roman military presence on the Rhine was centered in the provinces of Upper and Lower Germany, with the legions based in camps along the west bank of the Rhine, notably Bona (Bonn), Mogontiacum (Mainz), Vetera (Xanten), Novaesium (Neuss), Colonia Agrippinensis (Cologne), Vindonissa (Windisch), and Argentorate (Strasbourg). The needs of the army in these bases offered many opportunities to the Gallic communities and were a stimulus to trade. Providing supplies for the army (wheat, wine, metals) had economic possibilities, since at least some of this depended on normal trading conditions and not taxation in kind. Lugdunum was the place at which goods were transshipped and traded by the large community of merchants in the city, for distribution by either the river or the road network.[125] North of Lugdunum, the route continued along the river Saône to Chalon-sur-Saône, where cargoes were unloaded for the overland journey to the head of the Moselle valley. Important towns were spread out along this route, particularly Divodurum (Metz), Augusta Treverorum (Trier), Colonia Agrippinensis (Cologne), and Mogontiacum (Mainz), all of which had large communities of merchants. These towns served as centers for trade and the transshipment of merchandise in the region. Both Cologne and Mainz were river ports on the Rhine, which was itself a major route of communication.[126] The Rhône-Rhine axis had three branches: first the Rhône to Seyssel (Condate), on to Geneva and to the Rhine by the lakes of Neuchâtel and Morat, and by the Aar; second by the Saône and Doubs, then on to Belfort, joining the Rhine near Basel; third by the Saône and the plateau of Langres, joining the Moselle and from there to the Rhine at Confluentes. This seems to be the principal route. All these routes were in use in the Augustan era on the evidence of amphorae discoveries at Chalons, Avenches, Augst, Besançon, Titelberg, and Xanten.[127]

In the network of Gallic river routes, apart from famous cities such as Arelate and Lugdunum, many smaller river ports nevertheless had a vital function in serving local areas and offering lines of communication for farmers and craftsmen. River ports have been identified, admittedly sometimes tentatively on the basis of remains interpreted as quays, at Angers, Bordeaux, Chalon-sur-Saône, Creil, Corbilo, Lazenay, Orléans, Nantes, Narbonne, Paris, Roanne, and Tours.[128] In addition, a site at Pommeroeul between Mons and Tournai in Gallia Belgica has revealed particularly valuable evidence. Here there was a Roman settlement on the Roman road from Bavai to the north, where the river Haine had a tributary, on which was a small river harbor, opposite an island in the stream.[129] A quay has been identified, as well as a platform dating from the second century A.D., which seems to have been a landing stage, necessary because of silting in the channel. Five boats were also discovered, dating from the first or second century A.D. One of the barge-type boats had a gangplank stretching the length of the ship; it was probably useful to punt the boat on meandering rivers with marshy banks like the Haine.[130] Finds in the area suggest the type of freight carried on the river: leather, peat, coal, building materials from nearby quarries, pottery, and agricultural produce from the numerous villas dotted around the countryside. One of the boats at Pommeroeul was filled with pottery. The village was favored by its position at the intersection of two routes. By road it was connected to the coastal area and, through Bavai, to the whole network of roads in northern Gaul.[131] By waterway, the boats of shallow draft could go much further up river, while downstream the current would carry craft to the Scheldt, which was an important outlet for goods to and from the Rhineland, and to the mouths of the Meuse and Rhine.[132] These chance finds suggest lively trading and commercial activities carried on at the local level with connections to more distant areas (maps 16 and 17).

How do we estimate the quantity of river traffic, and the nature of traded goods? Large numbers of lead customs seals found in the Saône bed near the ports of Lugdunum are good evidence for vigorous river traffic.[133] In respect of the Gallic wine trade, the principal wine route in Gaul before the significant development of local viticulture was the Aude-Garonne axis, bringing wine from Narbonne to Bordeaux via Toulouse. Subsequently, the Rhône-Saône axis became the significant route and its extension along the Moselle and Rhine. Many wine merchants were established at Lugdunum, and it is suggestive of the connections in the wine trade that some of them came from the Moselle region. So we find a dedication of a statue at Lugdunum "in honour of Apronius Raptor . . . , from Trier, a magistrate of the same community, boatman on the Saône, patron of that corporation, the wine merchants based at Lugdunum (set this up) for their deserving patron."[134] Then there is Murranius Verus, a citizen of Augusta Treverorum, who dealt in wine and pottery at Lugdunum.[135] This trade would have mainly been concerned with the import of wine into Gaul for consumption there or onward shipment to the Rhine, though it has been suggested that vintages from the three Gauls were to become an easily salable commodity.[136]

As in Spain, amphorae were used to carry wine and olive oil, and their remains can give an indication of substantial river traffic. Large finds of fragments of amphorae have occurred at the first river ports upstream and at the limits of the navigation where goods were transferred to land carriers, for example, at Cavillonum (Chalon-sur-Saône), at Rodumna (Roanne) on the Loire, and on the same river at Ratiatum (Rézé).[137] However, it is difficult to estimate the scale of this trade as there are some indications that liquids were transported in barrels, which only rarely leave any trace in the archaeological

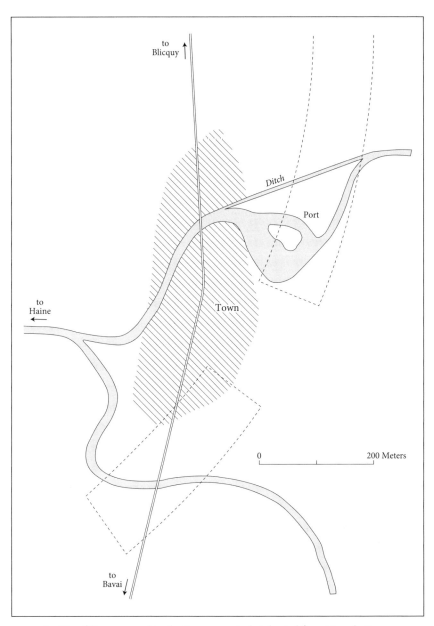

MAP 16. *Site of Pommeroeul in the Roman period. Adapted from Guy de Boe,*
"Roman Boats from a Small River Harbour at Pommeroeul, Belgium," in J. Du
Plat Taylor and H. Cleere (eds.), Roman Shipping and Trade: Britain and the
Rhine Provinces, *Council for British Archaeology Research Report, no. 24*
(London, 1978), 23, with permission.

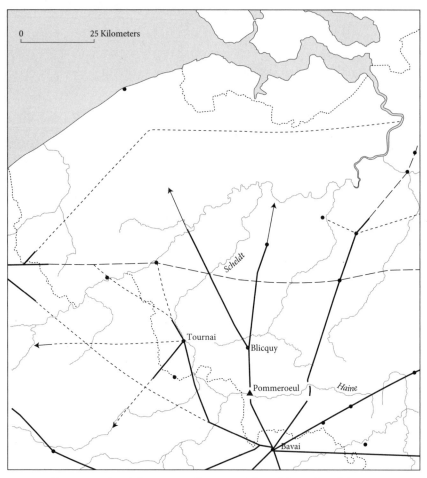

MAP 17. *Pommeroeul and the surrounding area. Adapted from Guy de Boe,*
"Roman Boats from a Small River Harbour at Pommeroeul, Belgium," in J. Du
Plat Taylor and H. Cleere, (eds.), Roman Shipping and Trade: Britain and the
Rhine Provinces, *Council for British Archaeology Research Report, no. 24*
(London, 1978), 29, with permission.

record. Diodorus Siculus with irritating vagueness comments that Italian merchants imported wine into Gaul, where the inhabitants were notorious drinkers. They used craft on navigable rivers and then carts over flat areas; the wine was carried in amphorae and the traders got slaves in return.[138] He presumably refers to his own time, though this is not clear.

Gaul seemingly was a link in an even wider distribution of merchandise across the northern parts of the empire. For the presence of Mediterranean amphorae in Britain opens the question of how they got there. One possible route is that by direct voyage via Narbonne or Bordeaux. But an alternative is that they were shipped up the Rhône, unloaded at Lugdunum and then transferred overland to Roanne, whence they could be taken along the Loire to Nantes for export to Britain. Another possibility was to continue with riverine transport along the Saône, then across the Langres plateau to the river Seine.

What was the relative cost of these routes? The evidence does not permit a clear answer, and it is also true that such routes might not be in direct competition with one another since some places could be reached only by water. However, in view of the fact that the Atlantic sea route from Narbonne or Bordeaux was seemingly the cheapest, it is odd that Gallic wine amphorae are found in large quantities at the mouth of the Rhône and along river routes to the Rhine. It may be that the Rhineland (with its heavy military presence) was the main market and that a system was established to deal with this lucrative trade; it then made sense to use this to supply the (less important) British market.[139]

Eastward, the Dubis provided an important connection, from which the overland route crossed Col de Montbéliard on the way to the Rhine. From the Saône, it was also possible to reach the Moselle by road. There was also an important route from Gaul to Noricum and Lake Lausanne, where lakeside port facilities were situated.[140] Lausanne was a significant *vicus* and a stopping point on the road between Italy and Germany. Of the five recorded inscriptions relating to shipping in Switzerland, four were found at Geneva and Lausanne; three mention *nautae* and one *ratiarii*. The fifth was discovered at Avenches and refers to *nautae Aruranci Aramici*. Small harbors have also been discovered at Geneva and Lausanne-Vidy.[141]

Much of the fluvial transport noted above involved agricultural produce, but naturally the Gallic rivers carried a wide range of merchandise. It is believed that the pottery industry in Gaul, which produced the famous *terra sigillata* ware, must have used a distribution network partly based on rivers. A branch of the Italian arretine pottery manufacture was established in Lugdunum circa 10 B.C. and then at La Graufesenque (Aveyron) in western Gaul about A.D. 30, and subsequently circa A.D. 130 at Ledosus (Lezoux), near Clermont-Ferrand on the river Allier, a tributary of the Loire.[142] By the end of the second century, manufacture was based in eastern Gaul. Since pottery was frequently traded and exported in large amounts throughout the western provinces, its movements can help show trade routes in Gaul. Pottery is easily broken, and river transport was probably less likely to damage it than land transport, making the shippers the essential middlemen between the potters and the retailers. Wherever and however pots were transported, other goods will have followed.[143] To base pottery manufacture at Lugdunum and Ledosus would make sense if river transport was important for distribution, since both had access to important riverine communications. But the site at La Graufesenque does not so easily fit into this picture. Although situated on the river Tarn, it is not really very convenient to any major river network, except possibly the Garonne. In fact, it has been argued that the goods, which were exported as far away as Britain and the Rhine, were not shipped down the river Tarn, which was probably not navigable beyond Gaillac, but taken overland by road to Narbo, about eighty kilometers away.[144] This may suggest that river transport, though convenient for pottery production, was not necessarily decisive, and helps to emphasize that land transport linked to the river network was also very effective for trade.

Water transport where feasible will have been most suitable for the movement of heavy metal or stone objects since it was expensive and slow to move large weights by teams of oxen. Consequently ingots of precious metal from Limoges and Séronais and iron ore were transported along the main river valley routes.[145] Gallic metal was shipped to Germany for the manufacture of weapons for the Roman army, and ingots and also south Gaul Samian pottery used the Narbonne-Rhône route for northward transport.[146] It is a reasonable assumption that quarried stone for the many building projects in Gallic towns must have been carried by ship.[147] Some support appears in the presence of a significant number of quarries near major rivers, or on the tributaries of major rivers.[148] The fine, white stone of Seyssel was extracted from the quarry at Sainte-Foy, about twelve kilometers north of Seyssel. The quarries, which had been first exploited a little before the Roman period, were organized so that the blocks of stone could be lowered directly without elaborate arrangements into barges waiting on the river Rhône below.[149] Builders at Lugdunum probably used blocks brought upstream along the Rhône from Glanum, and sometimes red granite from Flacé, brought along the Saône. It has been calculated (on the basis of a journey from the quarries at Villebois to Lyon in 1747) that it would take eight days for a return journey on the Rhône, two downstream and six upstream. A boat with a cargo of stone could probably go down the river at a rate of about thirty kilometers a day.[150] Rafts were also used, benefiting from periods of high water, as for example in moving stones from Bellèze (embarked at Boussens) and marble from Saint-Béat (embarked at the port of Rapp) down the Garonne to Toulouse.[151] There are other examples where quarries were organized for fluvial transport. Near the Charente, not far from Saintes, the ships moored at the entrance to the galleries and received their cargo of stone, which had been extracted about ten meters away under the hills that bordered the river.[152] South of Bourges at Lazenay, a port installation in a side arm of the river Cher was probably a stone depot for barges with a small displacement of water. It was constructed with a rubble fill and brick facing and vertical beams and was probably in operation in the first century A.D.[153]

It is difficult to estimate the importance of the transport of textiles, since in normal conditions cloth does not survive in ancient deposits. However, we have depictions on various monuments of river traffic. In particular, from Igel near Augusta Treverorum (Trier) a column with bas-reliefs shows at least two men hauling a barge loaded with two bales of cloth on the Moselle.[154] Transit from river barge to wagons would have been relatively easy.[155]

The combination of evidence for riverine transport is uneven and relates mainly to the first three centuries A.D. What we have in fact is an impression of lively maritime and riverine trade, which cannot be fully demonstrated by epigraphy and iconography.[156] In respect of the relationship between rivers, and between rivers and roads, there were certainly numerous connections between the river basins, and goods could be moved long distances by different types of boat, by towing, and by road haulage. This, however, was not a consolidated network and was not directly managed. So, goods could be moved either to or from the Mediterranean by a combination of river transport and roads in a series of stages. But those who received merchandise, say in northern Gaul on the river Sequana, would not necessarily have had any connection with, or knowledge of, those who had begun the shipment on the lower Rhône.

In this context it is difficult to assess the general benefits brought by rivers to whole regions of Gaul, or to produce specific evidence on how exactly rivers may have made local communities more prosperous, or how far they were integrated into local economic life. It is interesting that many agricultural centers (villas) are scattered along river valleys. Of course, this might be expected in any case, given the advantages conferred by running water, the possibilities for irrigation, and a pleasant riverine location. However, in the Moselle valley, a distinctive group of such sites lies concentrated along the banks of the river. Most are situated in the Trier region, where many rich agricultural centers faced onto the river. It is reasonable speculation that here the river was used for transporting agricultural produce from the villa mode of production and encouraged investment.[157] There were also ancillary trades in shipbuilding and ship maintenance.

Some exciting evidence shows in one instance the integration of river power and waterpower into a local economic setup. The famous flour mill at Barbegal near Arelate offers a fascinating glimpse of the use of river power to sustain and develop economic activity and local agricultural production. This was a mass-production unit driven by waterpower, and water for the mill (and the aqueduct of Arelate) was brought from sources in the Alpilles and led by a water channel over a series of steps in two descending millraces, with eight water-wheels on each side; the millhouses and their millstones were situated between the millraces. It was capable of producing nine tons of flour every twenty-four hours.[158] What was the purpose of a mill on this scale? The original excavator thought that grain was imported by river to Arelate for grinding at the mill, but more recent investigations have suggested that grain was probably grown in the valley of Les Baux, partly on land reclaimed from the wetland, and not brought in along the river. Since there is no river near the mill, the transport of grain to and from the site must have been by land. It is possible that the mill was a municipal construction dating from the early second century intended to supply Arelate with flour. Alternatively it may have been built privately by a company (*societas*) of estate owners in the valley of Les Baux (this would explain the sixteen separate millhouses); there is certainly a link between the mill and the many agricultural establishments in the valley.

Routes of communication of course came at a price, and river tolls offered an easy form of economic exploitation of the presence of rivers and river transport. The people of Massilia had grown rich on the tolls they exacted on the river traffic using the new canal built by Marius linking the coast to the Rhône. It is not clear how long this generous concession granted by Marius himself was maintained.[159] In any case the Roman government collected *portoria*, a tax levied on goods in transit within the empire and also in some places those moving into zones outside Roman control. For the administration of *portoria* the empire was divided into circumscriptions, which sometimes but not always coincided with provincial boundaries, for example, the three Spanish provinces made up one circumscription. *Portoria* were collected at stations at circumscription boundaries. The tax was levied as a percentage of the value of the goods carried, and the Quadragesima Galliarium ("the 2½ percent of the Gauls") comprised the four Gallic provinces, the two Germanies, the small provinces in the western Alps, and most of Raetia.[160] Were the collecting posts in the Gallic provinces at ports or river ports? What role did the rivers play?

In respect of *portoria* in the western and central Alps, there were two branches of the Mont Genèvre route over the Cottian Alps into Gaul; one led through the valley of the river Druentia,[161] the other through the valley of the Isara to Cularo (Grenoble), where a collecting station was located.[162] The route by the Petit-St.-Bernard followed the Duria valley and then the route down into Gaul by the Isara valley; one collecting station was at Genava (Geneva).[163] The route via the Grand-St.-Bernard continued northward to the collecting station at Acaunum on the Rhône south of Lacus Lemannus.[164] On the Mediterranean coast Arelate was the most important port for access to southern Gaul, and an office for the *portorium* tax on transported goods may have been situated here. The presence of an office of the Gallic *portoria* at Ostia emphasizes the importance of the trade between Rome and the western provinces along the Mediterranean coast.[165] There was possibly also a collecting station at Massane near Fos, the start of Marius's canal, probably because the *portoria* had incorporated the old tax on navigation on the canal, and at Marseilles.[166]

There was certainly an office at Lugdunum for the collection of the Gallic *portoria*, and the town may have been a center for the administration of the tax. Here more than 4,000 lead customs seals were found on both sides of the river; they had originally been attached to crates of merchandise and presumably indicated that the tax had been paid or that the goods were exempt.[167] Andematunnum (Langres), an important road junction of five routes, also served as a collecting station.[168] Furthermore, there will have been at least one station controlling traffic on the Saône; previously the Aedui and Sequani had been at loggerheads over the river that divided them, both claiming ownership and the right to collect the transit tolls from those sailing on it. "Now everything is under the control of the Romans."[169] However, the number and location of these stations are unknown. It is a plausible conjecture that the internal collecting stations dealt with supplementary transit taxes, which depended on the administrative system of the *portoria*, for example, for the use of a bridge, or ford, or certain waterways and entry into a town. They may also have checked that the payment on the outer circumscription boundary had been paid.[170]

3   ALONG THE RHINE

The provinces of Upper and Lower Germany were dominated by the Rhenus (Rhine), which is about 1,320 kilometers long, flowing generally northward, and emptying into the North Sea. Its highest source, the Hinter Rhine, rises in the Rheinwaldhorn Glacier in the Swiss Alps and joins the Voder Rhine, which flows from Lake Tuma, forming the Rhine proper at Reichenau. The river has important tributaries such as the Neckar, Main, and Moselle and a series of canals linking it with the Maas, the Rhône-Saône, the Marne, and the Danube. Strabo implies that the Rhine was navigable but does not specify any part of its course.[171] From 12 B.C. the Romans maintained a fleet on it that helped to supply the army and also made the river available as a route of commerce. Although the Rhine in Roman times was probably wider and shallower than nowadays, its course meant that it served the two Germanys and had contact with Raetia and access to Illyria and the Danubian provinces, as well as Gaul, through its tributary connections and portage. The river Ems flowing eastward was also navigable. The Albis (Elbe) is about 1,170 kilometers long and rises in Bohemia, eventually entering Germany and flowing northwest past Dresden, Wittenberg and Magdeburg, and thence to the north German plain, finally emptying into the North Sea at Cuxhaven. Its estuary stretches for 97 kilometers, and nowadays it is navigable for about 845 kilometers. Strabo implies that it was navigable.[172] It was presumably a north-south route for Roman and other traders as well as a local route of communication.

As noted earlier, the Rhine could be reached by the eastward extension of the Rhône valley. The great river had come dramatically to the Romans' attention during Caesar's conquest of Gaul. In one sense it divided peoples, separating Gallic tribes from those on the other side of the river — *transrheni* and *cisrheni*; the Gauls were distinct from the Germans "who lived across the Rhine."[173] However, when the Belgae plotted rebellion against Caesar in 57 B.C., they were joined by Germans living on the Gallic side of the Rhine, and it was recalled that most of the Belgae were in fact descended from Germans, who long ago had settled in Gaul because of the richness of the land.[174] Caesar professed concern that German tribes might cross the Rhine in search of good land, and once settled in Gaul might be a danger to Italy.[175] So, the river served to define the position and character of local communities.

The Romans had an ambivalent attitude to the river after its appearance in the *Gallic War*. Subsequently, the Rhine became an important artery of communication, providing a route through the German provinces and excellent lateral penetration via its tributaries to the east on the route toward the Elbe. The Rhine also became a kind of boundary of the provinces of Germany and part of a frontier zone, though in the Agri Decumates the Romans controlled territory beyond the river. Therefore, although the Rhine served as kind of boundary, it was in addition a springboard for military action on the east bank when necessary. There were many bridgeheads, from which contact, both hostile and friendly, could be maintained with German peoples. There will also have been fairly primitive ferries.[176] Probably the early Roman view of the river was largely military, not commercial, but the qualities of the Rhine that endeared it to military men as a means of moving troops and supplies, could also be important for trade and commerce, especially in relation to Gaul, and to a lesser extent Britain.

What did the Romans think about the course and characteristics of the Rhine?[177] Caesar commented on its fast-flowing current, its breadth and depth, its various mouths and tributaries, and its length as it flowed through the territories of many peoples.[178] Cicero vividly described the Rhine surging and foaming between its banks,[179] and others too noted the rapid flow of the river, though Strabo commented on its even slope.[180] Everyone recognized that the Rhine was navigable and normally enjoyed a perpetual and steady volume of water.[181] Obviously it served as a route of communication especially between the military bases along its bank.

The Rhine as great waterway for the transport of goods is, of course, a familiar modern concept. With the help of extensive canalization, the river has steadily realized its natural potential as a major trade route passing through northern and central Europe. Between 1900 and 1970, Rhine traffic rose from 20 to 190 million tons.[182] Its breadth, steady volume of water, and even flow without major obstacles in its central and lower course contribute to its continuing economic importance. Although in Roman times we sense the Rhine's economic significance, it is difficult to trace in detail the nature and extent of its role. It is a plausible assumption that the Roman military presence along the river in the provinces of Upper and Lower Germany and the occupation of the Agri Decumates provided opportunities for civilian commercial traffic, though it may not have been as secure or as lucrative as the Rhône. The movement of supplies from Gaul and Italy to military bases positioned along the banks of the Rhine must have benefited the civilian *canabae* and possibly communities further away from the banks; other goods could be shipped along with the military supplies. As we have seen, there is also some evidence for a supply route further afield to Britain and possibly, in addition, a link with Danube traffic. Once again we must emphasize that the important opportunity for communications is provided by the whole river valley, with its road network and connections with bridges and fords.

The evidence for nonmilitary river traffic falls into several categories. First, river boatmen were present on the Rhine and its tributaries, though the evidence is much less compelling than that for the Gallic rivers. Nevertheless, an inscription from Fectio (Vechten) in Lower Germany near the mouth of the river refers to "the boatmen who reside at Fectio," suggesting a fairly substantial group.[183] Similarly, in Upper Germany at Ettlingen near the Rhine, northeast of Argentorate, a group of boatmen (*contubernium nautarum*) set up an inscription.[184] From the same area came a boatman from Marbach in Upper

Germany near the confluence of the Nicer (Neckar) and Murra (Murr), close to Stuttgart; C. Julius Urbicus set up a dedication on behalf of the well-being of the emperor to the "spirit of the sailors" (*genius nautarum*).[185] This again would imply a group of sailors in the vicinity. Most striking is the memorial inscription of Blussus from Mogontiacum in Upper Germany.[186] Whether Blussus was a *nauta* (boatman) or a *navicularius* (boat owner), this is still good evidence for the importance of riverine trade on the Rhine, since he seems to be very wealthy and Mogontiacum was an important center on the Rhine, with a bridge over the river. Furthermore, in Aventicum (Avenches) the *nautae* of the Arara and Aramcius set up a dedication at their own expense. The Arara is probably the river Aar east of Lacus Eburodunensis (Lake Neuchâtel) and seems to have been a navigable tributary of the Rhine.[187] Today it is the largest river in Switzerland, draining most of the country and taking its water to the Rhine between Basel and Lake Constance. The inscription is important since it shows a measure of organization and the grouping of boatmen into some kind of corporation that we encountered on the Gallic rivers. Although boatmen are found operating in both Upper and Lower Germany, with most in Upper Germany near Argentorate, it may be that much of the activity consisted in moving smallish cargoes locally. Larger cargoes may have been tacked onto military convoys. In this case there would be less need for large numbers of independent boatmen.

Second, as noted, there were clear connections between the river systems of Gaul and the Rhine.[188] For example, river voyages on the Rhône could be interrupted at Condate and also at Seyssel, from which you could reach Geneva forty kilometers away by land, and here the sailors of Lake Léman took over. From Geneva by the lakes and then tributaries and some land sections, the traveler could arrive on the Rhine at Augusta Raurica (Augst), a little upstream from Basel.[189] Furthermore, along the Rhine there were important sites where tributaries met the river—Novaesium near the river Rura; Mogontiacum and the river Moenus; Castra Vetera and the river Lupia; Argentorate near the river Nicer, perhaps providing a route further east to the Danube. Also there was a route from the mouth of the Rhine to Britain, via Boulogne. Marine and river transport to some extent lay in the hands of the same people, and in many cases the same kind of craft could be used on Rhine-Maas river systems.[190]

Third, although it may be optimistic to say that "groups of shippers controlled the navigable waterways of central Europe and traded via their branch offices in London, Bordeaux, Lugdunum, Trier, Cologne, and the mouth of the Rhône,"[191] there is definitely some evidence to suggest substantial trading activity by way of the Rhine. First, several inscriptions in honor of the goddess

Nehalennia found at the Eastern Scheldt estuary off Colijnsplaat show the activities of *negotiatores* (merchants), who moved their goods down the Rhine.[192] Val(erius) Mar[. . .], who honored the goddess for the excellent protection of his goods, was seemingly trading with Kent and the area around Boulogne. Publius Arisenius Marius, who was a merchant trading with Britain, similarly celebrated the goddess.[193] Another merchant trading with Britain was C. Aurelius Verus, who (it has been plausibly argued) was identical with the homonymous trader who made a dedication to Apollo at Cologne. This certainly suggests the importance of the Rhine as a conduit for trade.[194] The goddess Nehalennia is here depicted with a basket of fruit, rudder, and cornucopia, suggesting an association with bounteous prosperity. She is sometimes depicted with a ship, and "Nehalennia" may be partly connected with "ship."[195] An inscription found at York and dated to A.D. 221 shows Lucius Viducius from Rotomagus (Rouen) on the river Sequana, who was possibly a merchant trading with Britain.[196] We also have evidence of a merchant in grain from Nijmegen, who presumably conducted his business along the river.[197] Altars at the Roman sanctuary at Domburg on the southern channel of the Scheldt and at the sanctuary of Nehalennia were dedicated by sailors, merchants, and shipowners, showing the importance of the Scheldt as a trade route in pottery, fish-sauce, salt, and wine.[198]

What other evidence is there for the details of this river-borne trade along the Rhine? Amphorae from Spain found at Cologne and Mainz suggest wine imports by the river. At Woerden in a branch of the Old Rhine, the remains of a riverboat have been discovered; it was normally used to carry spelt wheat, and it seems that the crew lived on board.[199] In the case of pottery, there were pottery centers near navigable rivers and the development in Germany of an industry in high-class pots.[200] In east Gaul there were many small potteries, but the pottery at Rheinzabern near Karlsruhe dating to the mid-second century was on the same kind of scale as the large workshop at La Graufesenque. This ware was *terra sigillata*, and the east Gaul potteries exported to Britain, shipping the goods along the Rhine and across the channel.[201] There is also interesting evidence in the distribution of *terra nigra* cups, with a large number along the Rhine valley and its tributaries and in the area between the Rhine and the Ems (map 18).[202] Furthermore, we have evidence of trade in glassware from Cologne carried on by *nautae*, and there is a significant distribution of cups along the Rhine valley.[203]

Like other rivers, the Rhine provided a convenient means for transporting stones.[204] Stone was a valuable asset, being prized for building work in various Roman centers along the Rhine valley and beyond. For example, the stone

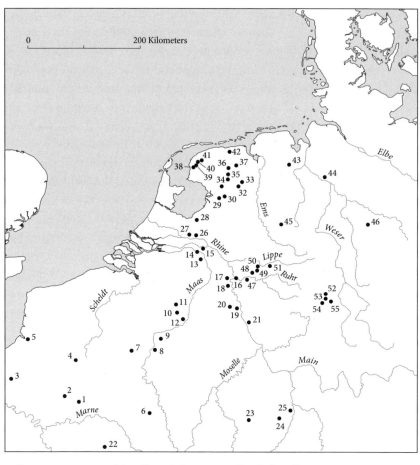

1. Chouy	20. Cologne-Mungersdorf	39. Tzum–De Botertobbe
2. Champlieu	21. Schwarzrheindorf	40. Tzum–De Parel
3. Rouen	22. Troyes	41. Dronrijp
4. Vermand	23. Zweibrücken-Niederauerbach	42. Brillerij
5. Abbeville-Homblières	24. Gommersheim	43. Gristede
6. Lavoye	25. Altrip	44. Mahndorf
7. Jamiolle	26. Wageningen	45. Atter
8. Furfooz	27. Rhenen	46. Meerdorf
9. Samson	28. Garderen	47. Essen-Hinsel
10. Tongeren	29. Dalfsen	48. Bochum-Harpen
11. Bilzen	30. Varsen	49. Castrop-Rauxel, Zeche Erin
12. Herstal	31. Rhee	50. Castrop-Rauxel, Habinghorst
13. Cuyk	32. Aalden	51. Westick
14. Heumensoord	33. Zweelo	52. Kirchberg
15. Nijmegen	34. Wijster (with Looveen)	53. Gleichen
16. Duisburg	35. Hooghalen	54. Geismar
17. Moers-Asberg	36. Peelo	55. Obervorschütz
18. Krefeld-Gellep	37. Zuidlaren-Midlaren	
19. Cologne	38. Arum	

MAP 18. *Finds of* Terra nigra *pottery in Gaul and Germany. Adapted from J. H. F. Bloemers, "Acculturation in the Rhine/Meuse Basin in the Roman Period," in R. Brandt and J. Slofstra (eds.),* Roman and Native in the Low Countries: Spheres of Interaction, *BAR International Series 184 (Oxford, 1983), 194, with permission.*

quarry at Drachenfels Mountain near Bonna produced a particularly attractive kind of stone. Here a Roman harbor has been identified, with two harbor basins, a loading station, and moles constructed for protection against the river current. A road led from the mountain to the loading basin. It was probably the ships of the *classis Germanica* that transported the stone, and the findspots of this kind of stone show that distribution was closely based on the Rhine valley.[205] The great millstones of Niedermendig (Eifel) were transported on the Rhine on barges at least until the end of the third century. The kind of barge may be similar to the one that sank at Wantzenau near Argentorate, with a cargo weighing just over one tonne. The wreck probably dates from the third century A.D. and the cargo consisted of millstones and basalt from the quarries at Niedermendig.[206] At Trier the bridge was constructed from great blocks of volcanic stone, which were cut out near a river harbor at Antunnacum (Andernach), about 200 kilometers along the Moselle and Rhine; the quarry is only 1 kilometer from the Rhine and therefore well suited for the transport of heavy loads of stone by river. From the harbor the route would be about 20 kilometers upstream to the junction with the Moselle and from there another 180 kilometers to Trier.[207]

If there were no barges, large stones could be floated on rafts, which could be broken up or sold after use. Larger rafts made from beams were sometimes constructed, and the remains of two have been discovered near Argentorate. They had steering oars and were adapted for use on the river Bruche, a tributary of the Rhine. With their narrow, elongated shape, they could carry a cargo of 3,500–4,000 kilograms through rapids, narrows, and other obstacles on the river, exploiting periods of high water in the spring, which would fit in with the seasonal work of the quarries. The river port at Montagne-Verte, which was in operation from the mid-first to the second half of the second century, had installations that were at least partly intended for the unloading of construction stones and blocks for funeral monuments on their way to Argentorate.[208] There were other quarries on the left bank at Brohl and Kruft, and in some cases the *classis Germanica* was in charge of transporting the stones, since we find dedications to "Hercules of the Rocks" (Hercules Saxans) by soldiers of the fleet.[209]

Finally, we return to river ports. The German fleet operated from ports along the Rhine. But if the location was suitable, it made sense to provide facilities for other commercial traffic, and trade for the civilian population, not least in the *canabae* at the military camps, would come in the wake of the fleet. At Argentorate, port installations have been identified, and it has been argued that there was a sanctuary dedicated to Rhenus Pater in the neighborhood of the river port and that this was frequented by boatmen.[210] At Mogontiacum, the river harbor was situated about two kilometers downstream from the legionary base at Dimesser Ort, beyond the confluence of the Main and the Rhine. This was a great base for Roman warships patrolling the river, but there was also a civil harbor.[211] This was also the case at Castra Vetera (Xanten), where the first quays may have been built circa A.D. 80 and were later extended and improved as the community developed. Laden ships would need at least one meter of water, and silting up of the branch of the Rhine took place, as in the long term the river level changed near Vetera. Some dredging was necessary, and between 160 and 170 the quay fell out of use.[212] On a smaller scale, the Romans established a fort at Velsen on the Oer-IJ, a northern branch of the Rhine circa A.D. 15, possibly during Germanicus's campaigns. Close by, a second fort was established circa A.D. 40. The first fort had a harbor complex, which was presumably used for importing supplies for the garrison.[213] In many cases there will have been small landing stages along the river that will have left little trace, although three quays have been identified on the banks of the lower Rhine near Woerden, dating from the first to the late second century A.D.; it seems that they were built by soldiers of the XV *cohors voluntariorum*.[214]

A good indication of civilian traffic on the river is the presence of collecting stations for *portoria*.[215] An inscription from Bonn mentions a collector "XXXX Galliarum et Portus Lirensis." De Laet argued that the *portus Lirensis* referred to a district along the Rhine established in the first century A.D., which was eventually incorporated in the circumscription of the four Gallic provinces, and stretched along the middle and lower courses of the river.[216] He identified seven *portoria* collecting stations on the riverbank, which would illustrate normal commercial activity along the river, since *portoria* were not paid on military traffic: Colonia Claudia Ara Agrippinensium (Cologne), the most important city of Lower Germany, the site of a bridge across the Rhine built by Constantine in 310, and a center for trade with free Germany; *Bonna* (Bonn); *Confluentes* (Koblenz), at the confluence of the Rhine and Moselle, where the road along the left bank of the Rhine ran through the town and presumably was carried on a bridge over the Moselle (figures 10 and 11);[217] *Bingium* (Bingen), at the confluence of Rhine and Nava (Nahe) near an important bridge; *Mogontiacum* (Mainz), situated on the west bank on a site about forty meters above the Rhine and almost opposite the confluence with the Moenus (Main);[218] *Alta Ripa* (High Bank), which had a splendid position near the confluence of the Rhine and Nicer (Neckar), whose valley was another important avenue of penetration into Germany; and *Ellelum*, a large settlement on the Rhine south of Argentorate.

However, the documentary evidence for associating these locations with

FIGURE 10. *The confluence of the Rhine and Moselle at Koblenz.*
Author's photograph.

portoria is debatable, and the *portus Lirensis* may refer to a district or small circumscription for *portoria* based on some now unidentifiable location, possibly situated between Bonn and Cologne.[219] Nevertheless, although there is a lack of clear evidence for customs collecting along the Rhine on a large scale, it is surely the case (although naturally it cannot be a conclusive argument) that these seven locations are ideally suited for collecting a transit tax, levied in the first instance on goods being taken across the Rhine toward unconquered Germany. Merchandise had to get to these centers, and was presumably being shipped along the Rhine, and also via the Gallic rivers, as described above. It would be reasonable to impose a tariff on goods being brought along the river, perhaps for onward shipment, and it is worth speculating that there was a collecting station for a *portorium* tax on goods leaving Germany for Britain. In any case, the evidence overall suggests that the Rhine was important for the movement of goods, despite the possible impediments to trade such as the presence of potentially hostile tribes on the east bank, lack of goods for exchange, or military traffic on the river.

FIGURE 11. *The Deutsches Eck in Koblenz at the confluence of the Rhine and Moselle, with statue of Kaiser Wilhelm I. Author's photograph.*

The riverine communities of the Rhine valley often owed their existence to military bases. These were busy centers, with a lot of movement to and fro, and many people involved in supplying the army and providing for military requirements. The local population met with Romans in the *canabae* and *vici*, civilian settlements that grew up around military camps. The Rhine and its tributaries were at the center of this activity. The names of riverine communities directly recall the river or watery sources: Aquae near Argentorate, Aquae Mattiacorum, and Alta Ripa and Confluentes. At Noviomagus, the original legionary base was built on an escarpment on the edge of the Waal floodplain on a small branch of the main stream.[220]

Unfortunately, we are relatively poorly informed about the civilian population and its activities in these centers of river valley life. Because of modern building, it is often impossible to reconstruct the plans of the main riverine towns and examine the shape and growth of the community around the river. We would like to know what was the significance of the Rhine for riverside communities, and in what ways they were defined by the presence of the river and its tributaries. We know, for example, that the Rhine produced fish and that the Main bore a large fish that allegedly had to be extracted by oxen.[221] But we do not know if men made a livelihood by fishing in the river, though at the port at Velsen there were many fish remains, which must have come from local sources.[222] We also assume that river-borne trade brought wealth, but we are ignorant of the precise economic benefits derived from the presence of the river, although traders were present in the riverine communities.[223] However, an inscription from the area of the Rhine and Moselle offers an interesting insight into local psychology. It is a funeral monument referring to the *genius vici* (spirit of the *vicus*), possibly in honor of the *ripani* (riverbank people), and gives us a hint of local identity and pride in the concept of being a member of a small community and a riverbank dweller along the Rhine and Moselle.[224]

4   BRITAIN

Some of the problems in clearly identifying the movement of goods by rivers are typified by Britain, where the use of rivers remains mysterious. It seems that many rivers were navigable in Roman times for a considerable distance inland and were undoubtedly used for transportation and communication. The main east-west watershed lies toward the west of the island, and the principal rivers to the east of the watershed, notably the Thames, Nene, Trent, Ouse, Tyne, and Forth tend to have broad valleys providing crucial routes of communication. Camulodunum (Colchester) was the crossing point of the river Colne, which was navigable from the estuary to the settlement, and from here roads went to Venta (Caister), Branodunum (Brancaster), and London.[225] Similarly, the military base of Eburacum (York) was located on the Abus (Ouse), and the crossing point here took roads to the north and east and west. With a few exceptions the rivers to the west tend to be smaller or less penetrative. However, Glevum (Gloucester) was located on the Sabrina (Severn), and from it roads radiated to north and south Britain, to Wales, and to central Britain and London.[226]

It is of course likely that many smaller rivers will have been navigable for some distance by small craft.[227] R. Selkirk has argued that the Romans used rivers much more than has previously been supposed to transport goods and, in particular, to supply forts. They not only sailed along naturally navigable rivers but also exploited rivers beyond the tidal mark and smaller rivers unrecorded by any source. They accomplished this by direct intervention, using a series of dams, flash locks, and even pound locks.[228] Much of Selkirk's research was directed at northeast England, taking Piercebridge as the exemplar, and the typical aspects of his system are fort, *vicus*, river (large or small), a road with possibly a bridge, remains of a dam, and old waterways, which may have been reused.[229] Therefore, in this view forts were built beside rivers not to protect crossings but for ease of supply by barge, and this form of transport would have been more efficient than the roads of northeast Britain. He also argued that this transport pattern could be extended to the rest of the empire. However, this interesting thesis has been seriously undermined.[230] Rivers in northeast England are in the main not suitable for extensive boat transport, because they are subject to torrential floods in winter and are also prone to extensive siltation. This would have made the use of dams difficult, and in particular they would have needed a disproportionate amount of maintenance. Also, it is possible that the sea level was slightly lower in the Roman period, which, if true, means that the tidal marks would also have been lower. There is no provable archaeological evidence for pound locks, and flash locks, which did exist in the Roman period, are inefficient and at risk from torrential rivers.[231] This argument reaffirms, therefore, that forts were generally located to protect river crossings for the important road system. It is best to conclude that in Britain, as elsewhere in the empire, naturally navigable rivers were used wherever possible by the Romans to supplement the road system; there was only limited technical intervention by the government; on small rivers or in the upper reaches of larger rivers, local contacts were often carried on in small craft; and, in many areas, the movement of goods was accomplished by a combination of road and river transport.

Eight

MOVEMENT OF GOODS BY RIVER (2)

THE DANUBE, ITALY, AND THE EAST

To continue our theme of the exploitation of navigable rivers, we turn first to the role of the Danube and its tributaries and the more shadowy, remoter rivers flowing into Black Sea. The kind of riverine activity in these regions can be contrasted with that in Greece, where rivers served only rarely as routes of communication. In Italy there was limited navigation, and we are poorly informed about seemingly important rivers such as the Arnus in Etruria and the Liris and Volturnus in Campania. However, the Padus and Tiber stand out as vital thoroughfares. In the eastern part of the empire, the evidence is uneven; the Tigris and Euphrates were great rivers on the periphery of Roman control often at the center of military and diplomatic activity, but other rivers such as the Orontes and Maeander attracted significant local interest. The enigmatic Nile dominated the province of Egypt, though ancient writers concentrated on the miraculous impact of the annual inundation.

1   THE DANUBE AND ITS ENVIRONS

The Danube caught the imagination of ancient writers and, with the exception of the Volga, is the longest European river, unusually flowing from west to east. It is about 2,850 kilometers and has a drainage basin of 512,000 square kilometers. Rising in the Black Forest, it flows northeast across south Germany to Castra Regina (Regensberg), where it turns southeast; later the river turns south across the great plain of central Hungary and, after Singidunum (Belgrade), falls into an upper and a lower basin, and its course between the basins is obstructed by many gorges for a distance of about 130 kilometers with whirlpools and dangerous currents, culminating in the Iron Gate, where a wall of rock sweeps across the riverbed. In some respects, the upper and lower courses were treated as separate rivers. After the Iron Gate gorge, its course broadens and eventually expands into a large delta before entering the Black Sea through seven mouths. In the present day the Danube has more than 300 recognized tributaries, including the Inn, Drava, Sava, Tisza and Prut, and is navigable by barge from Ulm and by larger vessels from Regensberg. However, navigation is impeded by ice in winter and by a significant variation in water level according to season.[1] A canal links the Danube to the Main and Rhine, and other canals link it to the Oder and Tisza Rivers. In the ancient world, it was a great natural route of communication and transportation, extending through seven Roman provinces crucial for communication between west and east: Raetia, Noricum, Upper Pannonia, Lower Pannonia, Upper Moesia, Lower Moesia, and Dacia. It emptied into the Black Sea with its numerous ports and trading contacts to Asia and the East. Furthermore, its many tributaries opened up connections with the interior of the provinces. These routes were used to transport the produce of remote mines to the Danube.[2] The Danubian rivers, as well as assisting the movement of troops and military supplies, seem significant in cultural, military, and economic terms.

Among the tributaries of the Danube, the Sava rises in the Julian Alps in Slovenia and flows for about 930 kilometers southeast past Zagreb, finally reaching the Danube at Belgrade (Singidunum). Its major tributary is the Drina, and nowadays it is navigable as far as Sisak (Siscia). The river and its valley were an important route of communication between Upper and Lower Pannonia and thence link up with the Danube. There was also a route from the Dalmatian coast port of Senia through the Alpes Delmaticae to the Sava River valley and the interior. The Drava was navigable and equally important; rising in the Carnic Alps in the Alto Adige in Italy, it flows east, then southeast for 720 kilometers before joining the Danube. There are two other rivers rising in the Alpes Delmaticae: the Corcoras was a navigable tributary of the Sava opening up another interconnecting route to the main valley, and the Colapis (Kulpa) joined the Sava at Siscia. They provided links to the south of the river and possibly to the coast. The navigable Titius flowed from the Dalmatian uplands to the sea at Scardona. The Naro had a broad mouth, and apparently both triremes and merchant ships could sail upstream to a trading station (*emporion*), which was situated eighty stades from the sea. This was presumably Narona, from which goods could be moved inland and along the road to Novae and Tilurium. The river Drilon (Drin), which according to Strabo was navigable east toward Dardania, rose at *lacus Lychnidus* (Lake Ohrid) in Macedonia, finally emptying into the Adriatic near Lissus.[3]

The Danube was famous among Greek and Roman writers, not least for its tributaries; Pliny spoke of sixty, half of which were navigable.[4] It was a natural route of communication and transport for local riverine communities, and traditionally small craft constructed from single, hollowed-out logs were sailed on the river. Alexander the Great discovered that riverine dwellers along the Danube used such craft for fishing, for moving along the river, and sometimes even for banditry.[5] For much of the imperial period, of course, the Danube was a river frontier, except during the occupation of Dacia from the reign of Trajan to Aurelian (A.D. 106–275). The Romans maintained a strong military presence along the river, based on a string of military camps and the deployment of warships. Military operations and the requirements of army supply would also facilitate trade by keeping the river clear of bandits and other obstructions. After the conquest of Dacia, communication with the new province north of the river became important. Naturally, river valley communications did not depend on the rivers alone. A great road ran along the south bank of the Danube from Castra Regina in Raetia to the estuary at Ad Stoma in Lower Moesia. From Dierna there was also a road along the north bank passing though Drobeta, where Trajan's famous bridge was located. We know that on at least one occasion the Romans intervened to improve navigation on the river. In A.D. 101 in preparation for the invasion of Dacia, Trajan reconstructed the towpath beside the river and built navigable canals beside dangerous rapids at the notorious Iron Gates pass.[6]

There is insufficient evidence to give a coherent account of the extent of civilian navigation along the length of the Danube. However, the ancients clearly assumed that it was navigable, and it is significant that Trajan's inscription, from one of the most difficult parts of the river, talks of how the new canal makes river navigation "safe," implying that before there had been well-established river traffic here.[7] Furthermore, Claudius Aelianus, writing in the early third century, refers to cargo boats on the deep bay of the Danube.[8] A fragmentary inscription from Axiopolis (Hinok) on the bank of the Danube in Lower Moesia mentions boatmen of "all the Danube," implying perhaps that boatmen operated along the whole river.[9] And at Viminacium we have a *nauclerus* who made an offering to Mithras.[10] Then, an inscription from Apulum in Dacia in honor of the equestrian P. Aelius Strenuus, priest of the altar of Augustus, notes that he was augur and magistrate of the Colony of Sarmizegetusa, augur of the Colony of Apulum, magistrate of the Colony of Drobeta, patron of the *collegia* of the workmen, ragmen, and boatmen, contractor for the pastureland, salt pans, and supplies.[11] Finally, the remains of a boat have been found at Oberstimm, by a tributary of the Danube near Manching, apparently abandoned in a military harbor.[12]

This is not much to go on, but we can ask about the routes that trade followed, the approach routes to the Danube, and the traders. Strabo, as so often, has useful observations. Aquileia was an entrepôt for goods transported to and from the Danube area; the river Natiso was navigable by merchant ships for about eight miles inland from Aquileia, and the Illyrians living near the Danube traded slaves, cattle, and hides for sea produce, wine stored in large wooden containers, and olive oil, which they transported on wagons, presumably when the Natiso ceased to be navigable. Strabo also mentions another river flowing from the Alps which was navigable inland for more than 140 miles, and which offered a route to Noreia (Neumarkt).[13] This river cannot be identified, but there is no reason to doubt that river transport was important in Aquileia's prosperity. The Savus (Sava) valley provided another important trade route to Aquileia from Noricum and further east. Indeed, "water transport was just as important as road transport for supplying the needs of the province."[14] Both the Savus and Dravus (Drava) were significant routes of communication to the Danube valley and contributed to making the Danube a highway from Raetia, Noricum, and Italy to the Pannonian and Moesian provinces, and thence to the Black Sea and Asia. Goods could also come in the opposite direction.[15] It is, however, important not to exaggerate the connectivity of the area; traders will have had to use a combination of river and road, and the roads from the Natiso to the Savus or Dravus through the Carnic Alps offered no easy route.

Oil and wine were needed for military camps and *canabae*, and were imported through Aquileia; the majority of amphorae were found in southern Pannonia near the confluence with the Savus, and there is good evidence for the import of Baetican olive oil.[16] Amphorae have been found in northeast Pannonia, which was one of the most distant parts that this oil reached, though they tend to be concentrated in the frontier zone of the Danube near the military camps at Aquincum, Brigetio, Ad Stationes, or the civilian settlements close to them. It is possible that loads of Baetican oil came by sea to ports in the east Adriatic or to Aquileia and thence by road to the valley of the Savus. Having reached the Savus, the oil was perhaps transported by river to its mouth and thence by the Danube. Baetican oil eventually came to supplement local supplies from Istria. How would a Spanish oil merchant make a significant profit by exporting from Baetica through Hispalis to Pannonia and pay customs tariffs? Perhaps they were exempt from *portoria* if the oil was mainly for the military.

In the commerce of the region, the manufacture and transport of pottery were particularly important. Pottery from Noricum was exported along the Danube; there were Samian potteries on the Aenus (Inn) at Westerndorf and near *pons Aeni*.[17] Products were sent along the Inn and then further east along the Danube.[18] The finds indicate that this route for pottery was to supply soldiers in forts at Boiodurum, Lauriacum, Vindobona, Carnuntum, Brigetio, Aquincum, Intercisa, and Mursa, though some pottery has been found in civilian contexts. It is likely that the production area was placed to ensure good river connections to the Danube because of the difficulty of moving the pottery by road. Also in the first century A.D. *terra sigillata* pottery arrived in Pannonia along the Danube; from Carnuntum it could be distributed southward by land.[19]

Aquincum (Budapest) in Lower Pannonia became a center for the manufacture of pottery, with a large pottery quarter in the town. The work of the potter Pacatus has been found at Mursa and near Singidunum, which suggests that the pottery was being transported along the Danube valley as far away as Moesia. Pottery makers could compete for a time with imported wares at least on the lower Danube because transport costs to convey imports this far would be high. Manufacturers came and settled here in Carnuntum and Brigetio. Amber was another important trading commodity along the banks of the river.[20]

From Flavian times, Italian traders arrived in greater numbers in the Danube area, and by A.D. 100 Gallic-German trade was thriving along the Danube, bringing supplies to military bases and cities.[21] Although river valley roads were also important, gradually there was a shift to increased river transport and a change in the pattern of transport, with less use for the Savaria-Mursa and Poetovio-Aquincum roads. We find *collegia* of traders in Aquincum who had come from the Rhine as well as Roman citizens.[22] An inscription on an altar to Jupiter Optimus Maximus, Neptune, and Mars in honor of the *collegium negotiantium* may suggest prosperity that was attributable to shipping and the military.[23] The founding of colonies at Siscia and Sirmium under the Flavian dynasty will have helped commerce and river traffic along the Savus to the Danube. We can see signs of trading activities toward the head of the Savus valley, at the town of Emona on the river of the same name, where a group of merchants set up an inscription.[24] The creation of the province of Dacia by Trajan in A.D. 106 opened up more trading and commercial opportunities. An inscription from Aquileia celebrates a "trader from Dacia whose home community was Cologne."[25] At least twelve new towns were established including the important colonies at Sarmizegetusa and Apulum, and lucrative gold mines were located at Alburnus Maior.[26] Sucidava on the north bank of the Danube in Dacia was at the end of a commercial route and a point of transit between two provinces. There was a local pottery industry here, though luxury pots were imported. There was also a river bridge in use before that built by Constantine at Valeriana.[27]

East-west trade was carried along the Savus and the Danube as far as Dierna and Drobeta. Roman citizens with a curator in charge are attested from Margum at the mouth of the river Margus (Morava), an area important for internal trade with the Balkans along the river valley.[28] At the eastern end of the Danube valley the vigorous life of riverine communities can be seen in the dispute between Histria and the local *portoria* collector. The Histrians won their case not to pay tax on the fish they caught and the pinewood they brought in; pickling fish was the city's main source of revenue. Coins produced in local mints of communities at the eastern end of the Danube depict the river, showing pride and perhaps recognition of its value.[29]

In the negotiations between Marcus Aurelius and the tribes north of the Danube in the late second century, one of the items on the agenda was the right to attend Roman markets. This was initially denied to the Quadi in case the Iazyges and the Marcomanni mingled with them, bought provisions, and spied on Roman installations. Later the Marcomanni secured terms that permitted them to dwell within a distance of five miles of the Danube, and the Romans allotted places and days when they could visit the markets.[30] This suggests well-established trading activities along the Danube with formal markets, which the natives also found lucrative. In the fourth century, regular trade on the banks of the Danube is attested not only by late Roman small coinage but also by the inscription from the time of Valentinian reporting that a fort (*burgus*) was erected to facilitate trade (*commercium*).[31]

One further indication of commercial activity, as in other regions, is the presence of *portoria* stations. The Publicum Portorii Illyrici contained all the Danubian provinces and eventually also the Thracian riverbank.[32] The position of *portoria* collecting stations was dominated by great routes of communication along which commercial traffic traveled. In the Illyrian circumscription this was the Danube, its tributaries, and other rivers that fed into the Danube drainage basin. There was also much activity around the valleys of the Savus and Dravus, from the movement of goods and people across from Noricum and Raetia to the Danube, and from the Adriatic ports, especially Aquileia.[33] For example, Siscia in Upper Pannonia, situated at the confluence of the Savus and Colapis, was well placed to collect tolls on merchandise transported by ship down the Savus and for the crossing of these rivers. An internal collecting station was located here.[34]

Other stations were dotted along the south bank of the Danube not only to levy tolls on goods entering or leaving the Roman provinces across the river but also to exploit the Danube's role as a great route stretching from west to east from the Alps to the Black Sea.[35] Although the roads running along the main river valleys were a vital part of the communication network, as usual it is impossible to say what volume of traffic they carried compared to the rivers. Many of the *stationes* were situated at the confluence of the Danube and important tributaries.[36] Towns here were often important centers for communications and a nodal point for roads and river communications, which could bring merchandise from the Danubian provinces to the Danube for onward shipment, or vice versa. For example, the legionary camp at Brigetio (Szöny), at the meeting of land and water routes, became an important community it its own right, eventually attaining the rank of colony. It is also the case that *stationes* on the northern bank of the Danube often had a close association with tributaries of the Danube; for example, the collecting post at Dierna, at the confluence of the Czerna and the Danube, raised tolls on goods being taken across the river or being transported up the tributary.[37] Other posts within Dacia, such as Szeged, were at a river confluence, whereas *pons Augusti* was at the crossing of a road and river, and Micia was situated on the river Marisos, one of the principal routes for bringing merchandise into Dacia.[38] Drobeta, located at the Danube bridge at the end of the Iron Gate pass, was on the main route from Dacia to sites south of the Danube; goods were embarked at the town's port for shipment via the Danube and the Sava to Italy.

The location of customs posts on some of the smaller rivers may well suggest that there was a great deal of small-scale local traffic. The control of river junctions was always important, and lucrative. In this context, it is significant that many of the internal collecting posts within the circumscription were associated with rivers. In Raetia, *pons Aeni*, at the confluence of the Inn and Mangfall, most likely collected a toll for use of the bridge. In Dalmatia, Aequum presumably collected tolls on the river Tilurius, while Timacum Minus in Upper Moesia was an important nodal point for routes and for the passage of the river Timacus.[39] Much of the collecting of *portoria* was based on the idea of a transit toll for movement along a river or for crossing a river at a particular location. It is also clear that routes for travelers usually passed along the valleys of rivers. So, with a small charge the government could exploit the natural movement of goods and people without harming trade and riverine commerce or encouraging smuggling.

In general, many riverine communities along the Danube, whether involved in the collection of *portoria* or not, were linked into the complex of military, civilian, and commercial enterprises. Military bases and their civilian settlements, which were often strategically important by position, became great centers of communications, trade, and movement. In many cases, river towns have preserved their leading role and have become leading cities or capitals across central Europe, for example Regensburg, where three rivers joined the Danube, Vienna, Belgrade, Budapest, and Szöny. The Roman military presence, the roads they built, and the river Danube and its tributaries sustained this development. For example, Carnuntum (which was not destined to be one of the great cities of Europe, being now the Austrian village of Petronell) was an important Roman settlement, which became the seat of the governor of Upper Pannonia. It had a splendid position on the Danube, located at the intersection of two major directions—south-north from Italy via Aquileia, and east-west from the Alps to the Black Sea. Opposite, across the Danube, the valley of the river Marus (March) provided an avenue for people and merchandise coming from the north. The town was regarded as chief entrepôt for external trade from Pannonia.[40] It began life as a military camp in the time of Tiberius and from the reign of Trajan the legion XIV Gemina was the garrison. Soon civilian settlers flowed in, and *canabae* grew up around the camp on the banks of the Danube. A permanent, well-appointed civilian settlement eventually developed to the west of the camp, and to this Hadrian granted municipal status. Septimius Severus, governor of Upper Pannonia, in 193 launched from his residence at Carnuntum his successful bid to become emperor. In 194 he granted colonial status to the community. Other smaller settlements also depended on their position and the movement of men and supplies to the Roman army. Ovilava (Wels) sat on the road across the Alps from Aquileia, which went on to intersect the road through the Danube valley to Lauriacum; it was also a crossing point of the Druna, a tributary of the Danube. Hadrian granted municipal status to the community, and it became a colony under Caracalla. Later, in the provincial reorganization of Diocletian, it became the capital of Noricum Ripense.[41]

Our sources' knowledge of riverine navigation beyond the mouth of the Danube is very uneven. For example, the Tyras (Dniester), after a course of about 1,370 kilometers, enters the Black Sea through an estuary. It is tempting to suppose that the river was a route inland for Roman traders, but Strabo merely speaks of sailing around the Sea from the mouth of the Danube to the Tyras.[42] Further to the east the Borythenes (Dnieper) is one of the longest rivers in Europe, extending some 2,300 kilometers, and with the assistance of a dam it is now navigable for virtually its entire course. In the ancient world, according to Strabo, it was navigable for over a hundred kilometers, but Pomponius Mela was more optimistic, claiming that it was navigable over its entire distance.[43] In the estuary of the Borysthenes and the Hypanis lay the great trading city of Olbia. Dio Chrysostomos gives a vivid picture of the land between the mouths of the Borysthenes and Hypanis, a muddy shore overgrown with reeds and trees, and a marsh. "And it is here too that there is a huge number of salt-works from which most of the barbarians buy their salt, as do the Greeks and Scythians who inhabit the Tauric Chersonese."[44]

Furthermore, the river Phasis, circa 310 kilometers long, was navigable as far as the city of Sarapanis, from which people and merchandise could transfer in a four-day wagon ride to the river Kyros (Kura).[45] This river rose in Armenia (northeast Turkey near Kars) and flows northeast and then southeast for about 1,530 kilometers to the Caspian Sea. It is still navigable for 480 kilometers upstream. Strabo notes that it has many navigable tributaries (only the Alazonius can be securely identified) and implies that it is navigable far into the Armenian uplands, with links to other rivers.[46] Again this whole area must have been penetrated by Roman traders.

Another major river was the Tanais (Don), flowing into Lake Maiotis in the northeast corner of the Black Sea. This river, 1,930 kilometers long, is now navigable for 1,370 kilometers and for seagoing vessels as far as Rostov-on-Don. It was an important trading route to the interior from Scythia. On the southern coast of the Black Sea, the Sangarius (Sakarya) flowed through Bithynia in a meandering course for about 790 kilometers and, according to Strabo, was navigable after its junction with the Gallos, which if true suggests that it offered a significant route to the interior from the Black Sea coast; previously it had apparently not been navigable.[47] Perhaps there had been a change in river morphology, or a process of trial and error in navigation by local people.

Greece with its great mountain ranges and small plains and precipitate rivers is not well suited for riverine communication. Rivers made little substantial contribution as routes of communication and transport, which depended on movement of goods by road, track, or sea around the coasts. However, there was some riverine navigation. For example, the river Loudias reaches the sea a few miles west of the Axios and was said to be navigable as far as Pella on the Loudias Lacus.[48] The river rose in the *mons Barnous*, flowing southeast through the plain of Almopia and then through a gorge into the Macedonian plain. In Thrace, the river Hebros, which rose in the Haemus mountain range, flowed southeast, eventually turning south and inclining southwest before emptying into the sea at Ainos.[49] It was navigable for about 22 kilometers inland as far as Kypsela on the *via Egnatia*, where there was a bridge over the river. Goods could be distributed by road east and west.[50] Pausanias mentions that the Pamisos was navigable for about 2 kilometers from the sea, and the Neda in Arcadia close to the sea, though only for small boats; it had a particularly twisting course.[51] Other interesting rivers famous in mythology are the Acheloüs and Alpheios. The former was navigable in its lower course as far as Stratos about

33 kilometers upstream. Was this a route of communication for settlements in the Acarnanian peninsula? The latter according to Pliny was navigable for only six Roman miles, though in its lower course it had important tributaries, including the Ladon, Kladeos, Kytherios, and Enipeus. The river Peneios with its source in the Pindus Mountains flows generally east for about 216 kilometers; Pliny claims that it was navigable for half its length, which he gives as sixty-two and a half miles (about 92.5 km). This would provide access from the coast to the Thessalian plain, though there is no independent evidence for the claim. Also in western Greece the river Arachthos (Arta), which rose at *mons Lakmon* in Paroraia, flowed southward through a steep valley past the city of Ambracia before entering the Ambracian Gulf. It was navigable at least as far as the city and could therefore facilitate imports.[52]

2   ITALY: ARNUS, LIRIS, VOLTURNUS

In Italy the torrential nature of many rivers meant that there was little scope for them to serve as large-scale routes of communication, moving large numbers of people and goods, and navigable rivers do not feature prominently in our sources. The well-developed road system was seemingly more significant for communications, and the Apennines were both a watershed and a barrier to river travel. However, in northern Etruria, two rivers dominated the landscape, the Auser (Serchio) and the Arnus (Arno). The Arnus rises in the Apennines on Monte Falterona, and its course of about 240 kilometers covers a catchment area of around 8,247 square kilometers, as it flows south toward Arretium (Arezzo) before turning west and continuing past Florentia (Florence) and Pisae (Pisa, south of Monte Pisano) and emptying into the Ligurian Sea. Both rivers because of volume of water and strong current provided a limited route of communication to Liguria and central Etruria.[53]

Pisae stood at the junction of the Arnus and the Auser rivers, about six kilometers from the ancient coastline. Excavations of the river port of Pisae have revealed the remains of ships and smaller craft (dating from the second century A.D. to the fourth or fifth century A.D.), suitable for coastal and inland navigation on the Arnus; there were also wooden and stone docks dating from the fifth century B.C. to the first century A.D. The remains of the ship cargoes suggest a wide-ranging trade in pottery, artifacts, fruit, and agricultural produce.[54] Kilns for the manufacture of amphorae have been discovered in the lower Arnus valley (first century A.D.); raw materials could be brought in by river and the finished product moved for sale.[55] Imports and exports of the entire Arnus valley would have passed through Pisae, and wine continued to be an important export into the fourth century. From the second century B.C.

amphorae were also made in the lower valley of the Caecina and exported through the coastal port at Vada Volaterrana.[56]

The river Liris (Garigliano) in Campania is one of the longest in Italy; nourished by many small tributaries in the Abruzzi, it has a catchment area of about 5,020 square kilometers and flows for about 158 kilometers from north of Antinum, with a current in summer nowadays of about 2.30 kilometers per hour and reaching an average depth of 7–10 meters, though this can be dramatically altered by thunderstorms. Although the river has constant flow, heavy spring and winter rains can turn it into a torrent, which can flood the plain around Minturnae; the ancient town is covered by an alluvial deposit up to 2 meters thick. In the lower course of the river, below the Roman town, the hydrology may be largely unchanged from ancient times.[57] In recent times the Garigliano has been navigable for about 10 kilometers from its mouth, and the Liris was possibly even more suitable for river traffic. A text from the *Digest* shows that in the time of Tiberius the river was navigable, at least for some ships. The problem concerned a shipowner who was responsible for bringing a cargo to Minturnae but found that his ship was unable to sail up the river; he transferred the cargo to another vessel, which foundered at the entrance to the river, raising questions of who was responsible for the loss.[58] Some ships therefore were expected to sail upstream to the river harbor at Minturnae, about 2 kilometers from the coast. Other vessels that were presumably too big to navigate the river had to transfer their cargo at the river mouth, where there was no suitable harbor, and goods were then transported upstream by barges. Although there is no epigraphic record of boatmen, corporations of maritime shipowners and ship's carpenters, and of men who processed pitch, had their base at Minturnae.[59]

Minturnae was a Roman maritime colony founded in 296/295 B.C. at a stopping-station on the *via Appia*; it was an important road junction because of the river crossing and also had direct access to the coast. It was destined to be a communications center, and there was an important bridge carrying the *via Appia* over the Liris; the river bridge was first built at least as early as the third century B.C. and subsequently repaired. There were also roads leading off up the river valley to the important spa at Aquae Vescinae fifteen kilometers inland, where there was a hot spring and bathing. Minturnae was a busy Italian town with a substantial river-borne trade. From the second century B.C., the Romans built wharves and quays along the river, downstream from the location on the west bank of the river now identified as the site of the ancient bridge in the town. The river may have been canalized between the quays and its mouth. It is not clear, however, how extensive the port installations were. The port was very busy from the republic to the end of the first century–second century A.D. and then declined somewhat; or possibly the port began to spread downriver. Minturnae imported marble, iron, copper, lead, wine, *garum*, and preserved fruits, and may even have had a local shipbuilding industry. It exported local pottery, wine, salt, and timber.[60] Kilns for pottery manufacture have been discovered along the lower course of the Liris.[61] It is possible that tufa was brought from local deposits and then transported to Minturnae first by road and then downstream on barges.

The active river port at Minturnae can help give us an idea of how smaller riverine communities exploited the possibilities of a navigable river. Elsewhere evidence is more limited. Although it has been suggested that the Clanius (Regi Lagni) and Savo (Savone) were important, with the latter being navigable, the Volturnus (Volturno) was the most significant with its drainage basin of 5,677 square kilometers. Volturnum (founded as a colony in 194 B.C.) had an important position on its river.[62] It is likely that the ancient Volturnus, which has a course of about 175 kilometers and a catchment area of 5,455 square kilometers, was navigable, possibly as far as Capua for light barges, and that Capua had a river port.[63] The region was very productive, partly through the rich soil deposited over the years by the river, and the area at the river delta was potentially very rich in deposits of sand for the manufacture of glass.[64] It is a plausible suggestion that the navigable river was the principal way of transporting farm produce (wine, olives, and cereals). Although the only evidence is that villas were distributed close to the banks of the river, there were probably embankments where goods could be speedily disembarked, and the overall situation may be compared to that at Minturnae.[65]

3   ITALY: THE PADUS AND CISALPINA

Among ancient writers and also modern commentators, it is the Padus (Po) and the Tiber than claim most attention. The Padus was outstanding because of its length and width; rising in the Cottian Alps, it is the longest river in Italy, flowing generally eastward for 650 kilometers through a broad valley before emptying into the Adriatic through several mouths. It is a route of communication from east to west across northern Italy.[66] The Padus passed the important settlements of Augusta Taurinorum, Placentia, Cremona, Parma, Brixellum, and Patavium in the Delta. It was, and still is, navigable for small vessels about 480 kilometers upstream, but subject to seasonal variations. The river also had a large number of tributaries, which in Pliny's view were also navigable. Among these the most important were the Tanarus (Tanaro), rising in the Maritime Alps and flowing northward past Hasta (Asti) to join the Po, and the Trebia, flowing northward from the Ligurian Apennines for 110 kilometers to join the Po at Placentia (Piacenza). There were other significant rivers flowing from the Ligurian Alps to the Po: Tarus (Taro), Secia (Secchia), Incia (Enza), Scultenna (Panaro), and Rhenus (Reno).[67] From the Alps there are the following tributaries, generally stated by Pliny to be navigable: Stura, Orgus, Duria (Bautica) flowing through Aosta (the Dora Baltea), Duria (Dora Riparia) flowing into Augusta Taurinorum, Sesites (Sesia) flowing past Vercellae, the Ticinus (Ticino) rising in the St. Gotthard Massif and flowing for about 285 kilometers through Lake Maggiore (*lacus Verbanus*), the Lambrus (Lambro) reaching the Po near Placentia, Addua (Adda) near Cremona, the Ollius (Oglio) flowing past Bedriacum, and the Mincius (Mincio, 76 kilometers long) rising at the southern end of lake Garda and washing Mantua.[68] The Natiso (Natisone) near Aquileia also provided limited navigation to the interior, though its lower course has now changed.[69]

Cassiodorus vividly brings to life river travel in the valley of the Padus in the sixth century A.D., in a letter to the maritime tribune of Venetia.[70] "For you another route opens up, which is peaceful and always safe. When the seas have been closed off by furious storms, a route is disclosed to you through the most delightful of rivers. Your ships do not fear savage winds; they put into land with the greatest pleasure and have no thought of foundering when they frequently hit the bank. From a distance it seems that the ships are borne though meadows, since you cannot see their hulls. They walk forward hauled by ropes." Cassiodorus notes how the boatmen did not trouble with sails but walked along the bank towing the ships. In fact, the Padus had a different character from that of other Italian rivers in the number of its tributaries, the cities along its course, changes in volume from winter snow melt, and its extensive delta and lagoons.

The Etruscans had been busy in the Padana. Atria flourished in the sixth and fifth centuries B.C. under Etruscan influence, though it is not clear if they founded it; the Etruscans built a canal from the river Sagis, taking the waters of the Padus into the marshes of the Atriani and apparently linking up through this navigable canal with Spina, which was also a prosperous town under Etruscan influence.[71] There were two systems of navigation: rivers were extended by cuttings and channels that ran at right angles to the coast, and artificial canals ran parallel to the coast. In this way the riverine and lagoon communities could maintain their connections with the open sea and also along the coast between the rivers. At Spina, for example, a channel about fifteen meters wide joined the branch of the Padus with the sea.[72]

In the early period, these ports were prosperous because of the importation of Greek artifacts, especially pottery, into the Padus valley. The Roman conquests and subsequent settlements opened the way for further economic development, large-scale land division and field systems, and the establishment of communications stretching across north Italy through the valley to the Adriatic and the important ports of Aquileia and Ravenna; from the time of Augustus the latter was an important naval base.[73]

Cisalpine Gaul was a kind of hinge between the Mediterranean and northern Europe.[74] The ancient writers tell us that certainly from the early empire the Padus valley was the main arterial route of commercial penetration and fluvial communications in northern Italy. For Strabo, the Padus was the largest river in Europe apart from the Danube, dividing almost in the middle the great north Italian plain, where wheat, barley, other cereal crops, and vines were grown in large quantities.[75] It began swift flowing and brimming with water, later becoming wider and more languid as it progressed toward the Adriatic, absorbing the water from many tributaries. More precisely, Strabo noted that the journey via the Padus from Placentia to Ravenna took two days and nights.[76] According to Polybius, the Padus was navigable in his day for 2,000 stades (about 356 km) as far as the river Tanarus. He also comments that it had a larger volume of water than any other Italian river because of the number of its tributaries from the Alps (augmented by melting snow) and the Apennines.[77] In Pliny's view, the Padus was navigable as far as Augusta Taurinorum (Turin), about twenty-five kilometers further west of the Tanarus, perhaps indicating increased need to use the river as more settlements were made upstream. Along the bountiful course of this famous river were carried the products of all the seas.[78] The Padus probably had a greater volume in antiquity because less water was removed for industrial and agricultural purposes.

The tradition of movement by canals along the delta was maintained. The towns of Opitergium, Concordia, Atria, and Vicetia, which were partly hemmed in by marshes, were nevertheless connected to the sea by small canals.[79] Patavium was connected by a canal about thirty-nine kilometers long to a harbor at Meduacus on the river of the same name. Streams and canals between Ravenna and Altinum were intended to cope with flooding. Many small channels in this area served as drainage ditches for the swollen river; when heavy seas drove seawater back through the ditches into the swamps, the salinity killed harmful swamp life and made the areas more salubrious.[80] Major engineering works were developed, designed to assist communication between Ravenna and the Padus, and along the lagoons of the coast as far north as the mouth of the Meduacus Maior.[81] The work of M. Aemilius Scaurus in building canals had probably been for the movement of military supplies;[82] but canals could be used for other traffic, and better drainage made more land habitable, and so more settlements could be established.

While it is true that the valley of the Padus dominated the road system and the valleys of its many tributaries provided a ready route for the road builders, other roads cut across river valleys in the interests of direct access.[83] Across the Padana region it is reasonable to say that in the moving of goods and people, rivers supplemented roads but were not part of an integrated system; perhaps they became more important if and when roads deteriorated. The Antonine Itinerary refers to the route of the public post from Ravenna to Altinum, comprising travel partly by road and partly by lagoon.[84] The dynamic relation between roads and rivers is revealed by the language of formal inscriptions set up to honor the work of emperors in building or repairing roads and bridges. Claudius celebrated the completion of his father Drusus's road through the Alps, which ran "from the river Po to the river Danube." He defined another branch of the road as running "from Altinum to the river Danube."[85] In Picenum the same emperor arranged the construction of the new *via Claudia* for about forty-eight miles "from Foruli to the confluence of the Aternus and the Tirinus."[86] Similarly, Augustus had repaired the *via Aemilia* "from Ariminum to the river Trebia."[87] The river seemingly provided a readily recognizable location, even though Placentia was the large adjacent settlement. Maximinus, who at the siege of Aquileia in 237, styled himself "restorer and founder" of the city, boasted that his recruits had repaired the road from the gate right up to the bridge, which was probably the *pons Sonti* over the river Aesontius.[88] Rivers, bridges, and roads were all a concern to emperors and constituted the elements of a transport system that depended in the Cisalpina on substantial fluvial navigation and an extensive road network. The various elements had to work together; roads had to get across rivers, but boatmen did not want badly positioned bridges; rivers sometimes needed the assistance of canals to extend their navigability. The pattern of imperial assistance was presumably based on the local knowledge of surveyors.

No ancient source describes the type of ship in use on the Padus or its tributaries. Given the winding course of the river, smaller sailing ships may have been most suitable. Pliny speaks of sailing ships on the Padus with sails made from rushes.[89] Catullus apparently sailed his yacht from the Adriatic along the Padus and then up the river Mincius to Sirmio on Lake Garda. It is interesting that a painting from a villa at Sirmio shows a rowing boat and a sailing boat.[90] As noted above, in the sixth century Cassiodorus spoke of boatmen hauling ships along by ropes. Sidonius Apollinaris traveled from Patavium to Ravenna in a *cursoria* (seemingly a fast boat of the imperial post), propelled by oars. Lucan speaks of boats made of reeds and oxhides on the river Padus.[91] All these seem to be light, small craft, and Livy describes how in 302 B.C. a Greek fleet penetrated the river Meduacus on a raiding mission; however, the river would not support the heavier ships and the soldiers had to be transferred to lighter, flat-bottomed vessels.[92]

There is some archaeological evidence specifically for craft in use in the Padana area.[93] Clearly many different craft were in operation, depending on their function and the condition of the riverbed. Rafts (*rates*) were used for floating down heavy loads, such as wood and stones. The *linter* had various forms but was basically like a dugout canoe. About ten examples of this type of boat have been found in the region of Patavium and about twenty in the delta area.[94] Dimensions vary between eight and eighteen meters in length, seventy and ninety centimeters in breadth, and thirty and sixty centimeters in the depth of the sides; the stern was cut off with a fitted bulkhead. A *pontonium* was probably a flat-bottomed craft made of planking.[95] Insofar as we can draw any conclusions from this scanty evidence, the Padus and its tributaries bore a substantial traffic, but people and merchandise were carried in many small ships, with comparatively small loads; these craft were voyaging along small distances serving local people; longer voyages along the Padus will have been made in a series of stages.

Other evidence for the extent of riverine activity depends on scattered indications of the presence of boatmen in various locations, river ports and port installations, and the range and type of goods traded. Some evidence for navigation within the region comes from the presence of a *collegium* of boatmen (*nautae*) or possibly owners (*navicularii*) at Ticinum (Pavia), on the river Ticinus not far from its junction with the Padus, which was also an important road junction.[96] We also have evidence for boatmen at Ari(o)lica (Peschiera) on the Mincius at Benacus Lacus.[97] Furthermore, boatmen from Verona were staying at Peschiera,[98] and this suggests that there was possibly a river route along the Mincius.[99] In the Transpadana, the lakes came into play, and the Mincius and Athesis were important thoroughfares. The Athesis (Adige) entered the Alps into Raetia and permitted access to the valley of the Inn. In the lower Padus, some evidence suggests a pattern of navigation, in which Ravenna was a center of internal connections; we also find boatmen or traders from Brixia,[100] Comum,[101] Mantua,[102] Adria,[103] and Ravenna;[104] Sidonius Apollinaris refers to boatmen from Cremona and Brixellum.[105] There is also an indication of Cisalpine trade in the inscription from Augusta Raurica (Augst) celebrating the "coll[egium negotiatorum] Cisal[pin(orum) et transalpine(orum). . .]."[106] Traders are also attested at Lugdunum, Mediolanum, and Aventicum, suggesting a range of commercial contacts in which Cisalpine traders participated.

Ideally, ports would be located to control points of convergence of river, lagoon, and maritime routes—for example, at Cremona, which had excellent road and river communications, suitable for its fair.[107] Placentia, Brixellum, and Hostilia were also well placed. At Patavium remains have been discovered of quays of a river port, with shops and a road for carts alongside the river. Similarly, at Altinum there were quays bordering the navigable canal, while at Corte Cavanella on the Athesis a dock has been uncovered. There were also some port installations at Sirmio on Lake Garda.[108] Ravenna, a great naval base and combined sea and river port, naturally provided access to the interior. Aquileia, as noted above, was an important seaport with river connections. Although the physical evidence is scanty, much local trade will have been small scale with small craft drawing up to a bank or perhaps to a wooden pier, which has left no trace.

The Padana was, of course, an area of Italy rich in agricultural produce, including cereals, wax, honey, resin, pitch, and salt. It was also famous for its wool and certain types of wine, which were stored in huge wooden casks. Unfortunately there is little clear evidence for how these goods were transported, although we may surmise the importance of river transport.[109] However, the Padana was also the source of many highly prized building stones and marble, and perhaps such heavy goods could best be floated down rivers on rafts, as happened in Gaul and on the Rhine. Similarly, bricks, because of their fragility as well as their weight, were best transported by water. Heavy logs could certainly have been moved by raft, and in the case of larch—which was fire-resistant, greatly sought after for building, and grew along the banks of the Padus—Vitruvius notes that it was shipped by raft down the river to Ravenna.[110]

However, even if merchandise was carried along the inland fluvial highways of the Padana, it is doubtful if the region had good access to the rest of Italy. The mouth of the Padus was far distant from most Mediterranean markets, and this is the best explanation of why no great port developed at the mouth of the river.[111] Cereal products of the Padana would not be able to complete with producers closer to Rome in Campania and Latium, and imports from Sicily. Even the valuable larch, which was moved by river, would incur substantial transport costs if transported onward to Rome or elsewhere. It is possible that grain, as well as woolen goods, which were rather easier to transport, could be transported along the Padus and then from Dertona to Genua, from which they could be shipped to Ostia. But the cost of the overland trip of fifty Roman miles from Dertona to Genua and the onward shipping would surely have been prohibitive.[112] Much of the movement of goods by river and road, apart from important export items, may have been internal trade.

Nevertheless, as noted, there was an important trade route to Raetia and the northeast through Aquileia;[113] from the late republic the area had been a supply base for campaigns in Illyricum, and later it was to supply Roman military bases along the Danube. Hostilia (originally the port of Verona) became an important nodal point in its own right, as a crossing point of the river and the starting point of the *via Claudia Augusta* begun by the Elder Drusus in 15 B.C. Travelers coming by the road from the north through Verona would at Hostilia continue their journey by canal to Ravenna.[114] It was intended to link Augusta Vindeliciorum (Augsburg) and the Danube basin in Raetia with the Padus delta; the road forked at Tridentum with one branch going to Altinum,[115] the other to Hostilia. We know from inscriptions at Ostia that shippers "of the Adriatic Sea" had offices there.[116]

Sidonius Apollinaris writing in the fifth century gives the most compelling description of navigating the Padus from Ticinum to Ravenna, revealing the excitement of rapid travel downstream with changes of rowers, the surging tributaries of the Padus, the pleasant wooded scenery, and the great port of Ravenna, but also the problems of the waterways through the lagoons fringing the coast:

> At Ticinum I boarded a *cursoria* (this is the name of the craft), and was rapidly brought down to the Po; I laughed at our drinking songs about Phaethon's sisters and the fanciful tears of the trees. I saw the reed-covered Lambrus, the blue Addua, the rapid Athesis, and the languid Mincius, which arose in the Ligustican and Euganean mountains, as I was carried past their mouths, helped on my way by their surging water. Their banks and edges were cloaked everywhere in groves of oak and maple trees. Here harmonious birdsong delightfully echoed and the nests of birds constructed on hollow reeds and on prickly rushes and on smooth bulrushes swayed gently. All this riot of plants sustained by the moisture of the spongy ground put out their roots along the riverbanks. Then going on my way I arrived at Cremona whose environs were once deeply breathed in by Tityrus from Mantua. Next I entered Brixellum, leaving it almost immediately as soon as our rowers from Venetia were replaced by boatmen from Aemilia. A little later with a favorable voyage I reached Ravenna. . . . Here everything is very favorable for trade, and large quantities of foodstuffs were being landed. But the sea surges in on one side, while on the other was the sewerlike dirt of the channels, which was stirred up by the poles of the boatmen, a sticky,

slimy mess from the depths moved by the progress of the ship. Therefore, in the midst of water we were thirsty, because nowhere was there any fresh water from an aqueduct, or a clean storage tank, or a flowing fountain, or a well free from slime.[117]

4   ITALY: THE TIBER VALLEY

The Tiber rises in the Apennines of Tuscany north of Pieve Santo Stefano at Mount Fumaiolo and flows for 406 kilometers through north-central Italy, draining a basin of around 18,000 square kilometers and emptying into the Mediterranean at Ostia, the port of Rome. The river was certainly navigable north of Rome as far as Ocriculum, and probably further by small craft. However, it has an irregular flow; for example, the average annual discharge is 220–45 cubic meters per second at Rome, but it varies from more than 300 cubic meters in March–April to around 120 cubic meters in August.[118] The time of greatest flow is usually from March to April because of the combination of high rainfall and snowmelt.

The Tiber's tributaries, the Nar (Nera) and the Anio (Aniene), substantially increase its flow, for example, from a discharge of 68.8 cubic meters per second to 178 cubic meters per second.[119] The Nar, flowed from the *mons Tetricus*, washing Interamna Nahars and Narnia with its bridge over the Nar and meeting the Tiber just south of Horta. This offered a route into Umbria. The Nera has abundant flow because it is fed by high rainfall and flows through permeable rock from its limestone springs in the Abruzzi, so that much of the water is retained for the river. The difference in the upper Tiber valley can be seen by the fact that at Barca di Torgiano south of Perusia, at the entry to the valley, the monthly average in January is 40 cubic meters while at Passo San Francesco downstream of the confluence with the Nera it is nearly 240 cubic meters. So, the river in the upper valley has the qualities of an unpredictable Mediterranean mountain torrent and can be reduced to a trickle in summer because of seasonal or uncertain rainfall and limited areas of permeable rock.[120] The Anio, which flows into the river north of Rome, arises in the Simbruini Mountains near Subiaco, southeast of Rome and then flows though the valley adjacent to Tibur (Tivoli); about 108 kilometers long, it provides a route to central Italy. The Tinia (Topino), which flowed down from Hispellum, was navigable when water was collected for nine days and then released. The Clasius, another tributary of the Tiber, was possibly navigable. The Clanis (Chiani) joined the Tiber near Volsinii Veteres (Orvieto) after flowing through the territory of Clusium in Etruria.[121]

Another feature of the Tiber's hydrology is that it is liable to sudden and violent floods especially in the lower valley and in Rome. In the flood in Rome in 1900, the discharge achieved 3,367 cubic meters per second, that is, about fifteen times the average. In fact, the floods are relatively moderate in comparison with some other rivers, though capable of causing great destruction and loss of life. They also tend to concentrate in November and December, and so could probably be predicted by regular users of the rivers and river traffic. In December 2008, two days of continuous heavy rain in northern Italy created the threat of flooding in Rome, despite the embankments, and damage to the bridges. On 13 December the water level recorded at the Ponte Milvio reached 13.5 meters, about 5 meters above the normal seasonal level. In 1878 the water level reached more than 18 meters. In ancient Rome, floods were frequent, and damage and loss of life will have been considerable, though we are poorly informed on the details. For example, in 23 B.C. the Tiber destroyed the wooden *pons Sublicius* and flooded all the low-lying parts of Rome making it navigable for boats for several days.[122] The final characteristic property of the Tiber was the enormous quantity of silt brought down by the river, which produced its characteristic tawny color, often remarked on by ancient authors.[123] This helped the creation of a substantial alluvial flood plain, though the river did not greatly extend its delta. The coast has advanced at each river mouth about three kilometers since Roman times. The reason is that strong currents flowing north at the mouth and the steeply shelving shore have prevented silting up.

The length and position of the Tiber made it important, since with its tributaries it opened up routes of communication from the central spine of the Apennines down to Rome and Ostia and into Umbria, Tuscany, and the Sabine territory. Although Cicero praised Romulus's choice of the site of Rome because the city was on the bank of a "constantly flowing river whose wide stream flows into the sea with a steady current,"[124] the Tiber is a troublesome and at times tumultuous river, and its hydrology can cause major problems. Nevertheless, ancient commentators tend to assert enthusiastically the qualities and navigability of the Tiber. Dionysius Periegetes commends the Tiber as the "most kingly of rivers" with a wide, pure flow.[125] Strabo commented on the transport of marble and wood and other produce down the upper course of the river and its tributaries, as well as the traffic from Ostia to Rome.[126] Dionysius of Halicarnassus, although observing the lack of a safe anchorage where the Tiber flowed into the sea, mentions that seagoing ships could reach Rome along the river and that it was navigable by riverboats of reasonable size right up to its source.[127] The Elder Pliny, though eloquent about the Tiber's contribution to Roman commerce after its junction with the Clanis, was much more circumspect about the upper course, which was a only a narrow stream with a rocky and uneven channel, which permitted only rafts or even logs of wood.[128] The Younger Pliny, however, praises his estate at Tifernum Tiberinum in the upper Tiber valley north of Arna. The river cut through the estate and drained away all surplus water. Although it transported his crops to Rome, he complained that in summer it virtually dried up.[129] Other writers add admittedly rather vague detail to the picture. Juvenal talks of flagons of indifferent wine "brought down the Tiber," while Martial, describing the panoramic view of Rome from the villa of Julius Martialis on the Janiculum Hill, picks out the vibrant river activity near the *pons Milvius* as ships flitted about, though the onlooker could not hear the shouts of the sailors or the uproar of the men hauling ships.[130] The Milvian Bridge is north of Rome and suggests traffic from upstream.

The fact that we do not have evidence for boatmen or guilds of boatmen in the upper Tiber valley is not surprising because boats will have been small and probably independently operated by individuals who owned their own boats. Movement of goods and people will have been in short local stages. In addition, two inscriptions referring to the "codicarii naviculari infernates" (lower) and "codicari nav(iculari) infra pontem S(ublicium?)," by making this distinction of ships on the lower course of the Tiber, suggest strongly that that there were *codicarii* operating on the upper course.[131] Efforts and proposals to modify the Tiber's course and characteristics confirm the importance attached to regular use of the river as a route of communication for the movement of people and goods. Much attention was given to improving navigation in the upper course of the Tiber, including damming and releasing the water after nine days.[132] It has even been suggested that this nine-day period was timed so as to coincide with the *nundinae* or markets that were held from time to time, where agricultural produce moved by boat would be sold along the Tiber valley and in Rome.[133]

Although there is no specific evidence for the type of boat used on the Tiber upstream of Rome, we may surmise that they were smaller craft propelled by oars or a small sail and that towing was required in some localities. Ships traveling downstream could use the current, though this would be seasonal; presumably certain agricultural produce that did not need processing and was not speedily perishable could be stored on site and transported downstream to Rome when riverine conditions permitted. Travel downstream from Ocriculum to Rome could have taken up to five days depending on the volume of water.[134] Although travel upstream would have been expensive, nevertheless, in the nineteenth century it was still apparently profitable to haul ships by oxen or buffalo upstream even north of Orte.[135]

The importance of the city of Rome and its influence on the Tiber valley in terms of settlement and agricultural practice are being more fully investigated in the Tiber Valley Project.[136] The evidence suggests an increase over the first two centuries A.D. in the number of occupied sites, expansion into previously uncultivated areas, and a variety of settlement patterns depending on proximity to Rome; areas furthest away were occupied less intensively or later in time. In the third century A.D., as settlement contracted, the more distant areas were the first to feel the effect. It is more difficult to establish what crops were being planted, though the evidence suggests that in the Tiber valley and floodplain horticulture was widespread, with the production of legumes, olives, vines, some grain, and also transhumant pastoralism.[137] There was also to some extent an interrelation of agriculture, brick production, and other activities such as quarrying. Towns and numerous rural settlements were located on both sides of the Tiber, and it has been suggested that units of habitation were positioned in direct rapport with the hydrographic system of the region; people originally settled on the neighboring hills for protection, within sight of the Tiber valley, in a position to control the confluence of the tributaries that flowed into the Tiber.[138] Ferries and travel by boat will have helped the connections between riverine communities along the Tiber valley, the exploitation of agricultural production, and the promotion of trade with local markets as well as with Rome and a wider market. For example, Forum Novum in the Sabine hills northeast of Rome had good communications by road, and also by river to the Tiber.[139] Links with the *via Salaria* on the east and the *via Flaminia* on the west were satisfactory, and by the early first century A.D. it was a *municipium*. By contrast, at Iguvium (Gubbio) in the Apennines away from the Tiber valley, constraints were imposed on trade partly because of the lack of water transport.[140]

In addition, *nundinae*, which were mentioned above, may be relevant. *Nundinae* were days organized "so that country people could meet in order to trade and sell goods."[141] Lists of market days (*indices nundinarii*) preserved in inscriptions offer a list of towns with an indication of the days on which the *nundinae* took place.[142] Although it is not entirely clear according to what rule, geographical or temporal, the *indices* were drawn up, it is possible that because the *nundinae* of the various towns are distributed on different days, to avoid coincidence, the *indices* served both the farmers of the area and the urban workers, as well as traveling merchants.[143] The *indices* are grouped in central Latium and Campania, areas that are characterized by farms and intense cultivation. The communities furthest away on the list are Rome, Luceria, and Saepinum, and the last two had important markets for animals. It is worth considering if the location of towns where *nundinae* were held is connected with their position on, or close to, navigable rivers. This would, in some circumstances, facilitate access for traveling merchants, sellers of agricultural produce, and possibly other townspeople.

The Campanian towns listed with *nundinae* include Aquinum on a tributary of the Liris, Interamna Lirenas in the Liris valley, Minturnae at the mouth of the Liris, Casinum in the valley of the river Scatebra, Fabrateria Vetus on the Trerus/Tolerus, Telesia in the upper valley of the Calor, Beneventum on the Calor and Tamarus, Nuceria in the plain of the Sarnus, Cales on a minor tributary of the Volturnus, and Allifae on a tributary in the upper valley of the Volturnus; even Suessa in its lofty position on an outcrop of the Roccamonfina had the Liris in the valley below. This is suggestive but not conclusive since we cannot be sure how far these rivers were navigable and for what kind of craft. However, the important point as so often is that a combination of routes would be in use, in which rivers provided access, along with roads and tracks that ran along river valleys. Often the main users would be local merchants traveling over short distances. For example, someone traveling from Interamna Lirenas to Beneventum could use the river or valley of the Liris to reach Minturnae, from which an onward journey by road would reach the Volturnus; then travel by boat and the river valley would bring the traveler to the valley of the Calor and thence to Beneventum.

It is also worth recalling that Cremona's great annual fair toward the end of October owed much to its position on the navigable river Po.[144] Another renowned fair took place at Campi Macri near Mutina on the *via Aemilia*, which was also near the river Scultenna, a tributary of the Po. Furthermore, the fair held near Consilinum, was at a locality now significantly called S. Giovanni alla Fonte; the original fair was at the Temple of Leucothea, a divinity connected with water. Subsequent Christian celebration was a continuation of this, in some way connected with baptismal rites. The fair perhaps went back into earlier Roman times and took place at a famous local spring.[145] In these examples, there is certainly an interesting connection with water. However, some of the towns are well beyond the point to which the rivers were likely to be navigable, and it may be that the riverine environment contributed to the movement of goods that was completed by road or track along the valleys.

Although many questions remain unanswered about the relationship between communities in the Tiber valley, it is clear that a wide range of goods was traded along the valley.[146] Wine seems to have been especially important. There is some evidence that installations for the handling of wine were in the northern part of Rome and that these depots were designed to cater for wine coming down the Tiber. Production of lower-quality wine was expanded to cater for the large local urban population in Rome and the surrounding area, once the need to grow grain locally was reduced by grain supplies from overseas. It is also possible that after the eruption of Vesuvius in A.D. 79 the volume of Campanian wine available for export was considerably reduced. We hear that in the third century *fiscalia vina* were stored and distributed at Aurelian's Temple of the Sun, close to the *via Flaminia*, and that wine barrels were transported to here from the port depot called "The Storks" (Ciconiae), which was possibly on the Campus Martius, though the exact location of this installation is disputed.[147] It seems that wine was unloaded here from riverboats, and centers of the wine business, the *portus vinarius* and *forum vinarium*, were adjacent.[148] An inscription honors Fulvius Charetes, a debt collector operating in the "upstream *portus vinarius*." The inscription was found in the territory of Falerii in the Tiber valley, which may suggest that Charetes was involved in the financing of the wine trading upstream along the valley.[149] An indication of the extent of this trade is found in the presence of the so-called Spello amphorae. These were containers smaller than other amphorae, with a flat base probably specially designed for river transport. They have been discovered in several places in the upper and middle Tiber valley, notably at a kiln near Hispellum. Remains of amphorae of this type make up about a quarter of the wine amphorae discovered in several buildings in Rome and are datable between circa A.D. 90 and 150. This suggests an extensive trade, though not all the amphorae necessarily came directly from the Tiber valley, and some may have been transported down the *via Flaminia*.[150] Another pottery kiln at Scoppieto served the Umbrian towns and Rome along the Tiber route.[151]

The Tiber valley also produced large amounts of heavy items essential for the building work in Rome. Strabo noted the need for timber and stones for the building of houses or for their repair, since they frequently collapsed or burned down. In the Tiber valley, many mines and forests produced a copious supply of wood, which was ferried on the Tiber and down the valleys of its tributaries, the Anio, the Nar, the Tinia, and the Clanis.[152] Logs of wood could be floated or brought down on rafts or barges. The quarries along the Tiber valley and its tributaries provided a wide range of excellent building stone: tufa from Fidenae near Castel Giubileto and Grottaoscura; *lapis Tiburtina* (travertine) from the Anio area, near Salone and Tor Cervara; *lapis Gabinus* from near Gabii; and *lapis ruber* from the Anio. Stone blocks were loaded on barges and brought down to the confluence with the Tiber and thence to Rome.[153] The plentiful supplies of clay along the river valley offered the opportunity for ceramic manufacture, and large quantities of fragile material could be transported along the Tiber.[154]

Several ancient writers comment on the value of lands on the banks of the river Tiber, which remained highly desirable from the republic into the imperial period. Annius Milo had an estate at Ocriculum, to which weapons had allegedly been conveyed along the Tiber. Sextus Roscius in the time of Sulla was held to be seriously wealthy precisely because he owned thirteen splendid estates, most of which were on the banks of the Tiber.[155] Columella, as we have seen before, particularly recommended the qualities of a riverside farm because its produce could easily be transported.[156] Pliny's estate in the upper Tiber valley seems to be a case in point, with grainfields and vineyards. A rural estate has recently been identified on the river Anio with a river landing.[157]

The presence of imperial property in the Tiber valley also indicates the potential economic importance of the region. A bronze plaque, discovered in the river during the building of the Ponte Vittorio Emanuele, refers to three imperial estates on the banks of the Tiber north of Rome: "belonging to M. Ulpius Diadumenus, freedman of the emperor, procurator of the sacred domain at Fidenae, Saxa Rubra, and ad Gallinas Rubras, utilized in the service of our emperor."[158] The three estates were linked by the river, and it is likely that their produce was brought by special boat for sale in Rome. In this context we have an intriguing inscription from the mid-first century A.D. referring to a "procurator Caesaris ad ripas Tiberis."[159] This man held the post early in his equestrian career and was perhaps responsible for ensuring that transport along the Tiber went smoothly without interruption, and that banks were kept clear of possible obstacles to towing ships.

Port installations in the Tiber valley confirm the importance of riverine trade, although once again the evidence is poor since many have been destroyed and buried by alluvial activity.[160] Furthermore, landing places and moorings could have been very simple with small-scale wooden structures.[161] Since people and products came down from both sides of the valley to the Tiber, there were certainly more ports than we can know about. We do have evidence for some kind of port installations just north of Rome, in the territory of Cures on the east bank opposite Lucus Feroniae, at Badia di Ponzano near Capena, at the mouth of the river Treia at Falerii, at Ocriculum, near Horta at Piscinale Amelia ed Orte, also at Castiglioni near Horta, and at the confluence of the river Pallia (Paglia) and the Tiber near Velzna or Volsinii Veteres (Orvieto).[162] We may speak of a pattern of port facilities in the middle Tiber valley offering access on both sides of the river and possibly also serving as ferry bases for transport across the river. The port at Ocriculum seems to have been particularly important and well appointed.[163] In Rome at Ponte Milvio about three miles north of Rome, some traces remain of quays and a carriageway for towing ships. These port installations seem to be more suitable for rivercraft coming from the north down the Tiber.[164] It was precisely in this area that the wine depots were concentrated to collect and distribute wine.

The lower Tiber valley and the route of communication from Ostia to Rome add another dimension. This seems to be a different world from life upstream. Here, amid the lower floodplain and salt marshes, there are few large settlements. The factors influencing the use of the river between Ostia and Rome were very different. The river was supplier of the capital with vast amounts of produce from all over the empire, which flowed into Ostia, Rome's port, and was transported to Rome along the Tiber and by road. Furthermore, the state intervened to ensure the delivery of certain foodstuffs in bulk, particularly grain for distribution to about 200,000 citizens, and olive oil from the time of Septimius Severus.[165] The center of much of this activity was Ostia, built at the mouth of the Tiber about 24 kilometers from Rome. Florus reports the tradition that Ostia had been founded by King Ancus Marcius and emphasizes the importance of the geographical location by making the king foresee that Ostia would be a kind of maritime receptacle for Rome of the wealth and produce of the whole world.[166] The colony at Ostia probably dates from the fourth century B.C., though its exact relation to the river is uncertain because the lower course of the Tiber changed significantly after a flood in the fifteenth century.[167] The main problem at Ostia was the lack of a harbor; the only moorings were at the docks along the riverbank. Smaller cargo ships could dock at Ostia's riverside quays, but larger craft had to unload at sea to smaller river-going vessels. Large granaries and storage facilities at Ostia allowed huge quantities of goods to be stored there until riverboat transport became available. The largest cargo ships normally sailed to the Campanian port of Puteoli, where goods were offloaded and transferred to smaller coastal craft, which sailed up to the quays at Ostia. Claudius built a new harbor two miles north of Ostia linked by canal to the Tiber. This was a safer anchorage, but proved to be vulnerable to silting and also to storms because of its size. Trajan subsequently improved the installation by building an internal, hexagonal harbor. After goods had been safely unloaded, an enormous logistical exercise was still required to transport them upstream to Rome. Because of the strong current, it would be difficult to row up the river, and its meandering character made the use of sails problematical.[168] Meiggs suggests a combination of sails, oars, and haulage. It was common practice to move the cargo in special barges (*naves codicariae*), which were probably towed by men or, in later times, oxen.[169] Seneca in discussing the origin of the name *naves codicariae*, mentions specifically that they carried merchandise along the Tiber.[170] This was a cumbersome process and the journey could take three days.[171] Propertius speaks of lying on the banks of the Tiber and watching ships moving slowly past pulled by ropes.[172] It was certainly quicker though more expensive to travel to Rome by either the *via Ostiensis* (south of the river) or the *via Portuensis* (north of the river).

The Tiber south of Rome must have been thronged with river traffic at certain times. The city may have required approximately 237,000 metric tons of grain each year in the early empire, and along with oil and wine imports, more than 6,000 boatloads on the Tiber would be needed.[173] There will also have been huge imports of many other traded goods.[174] How was this organized? There is no clear evidence of a river master or harbormaster. It is possible that the *procurator ripae Tiberis* was responsible, though in that case we might expect to hear more about his duties. On the other hand, overall charge may have rested with the office of the *praefectus annonae*, or perhaps the curators of the beds and banks of the Tiber. A fragmentary dedication (found in Ostia) in honor of Hadrian between A.D. 126 and 138 seems to refer to certain shipowners and dealers receiving permission to sail along the Tiber, which possibly indicates some kind of control of riverine activities.[175]

In Rome the first and earliest port was the *portus Tiberinus* near the *pons Aemilius*, south of the Tiber Island, making use of the loop in the river. Later, as this proved increasingly inadequate, the main port facility developed in the late third or early second century B.C. The *porticus Aemilia* was a large, roofed construction for the storage of goods; these were unloaded at stone wharves, which were built circa 174 B.C. and stretched out over one kilometer. The riverbank quays were raised and rebuilt in the second century A.D. and spread over three levels.[176] These impressive stone and brick embankments had solid travertine stone blocks for mooring, equipped with apertures for the insertion of ropes. However, ships will have had to draw up lengthwise and not at right angles at the quays, because of the force of the Tiber's current. This greatly restricted the number of ships that could be unloaded simultaneously.[177] There may also have been landing stages along the Tiber between Ostia and Rome.[178] Substantial evidence from inscriptions reveals the activities of the boatmen and shippers on the Tiber using various kinds of transport vessels.[179] Some shippers specified that they operated below the Sublician Bridge, at the port of Rome.[180] The port area had a number of *collegia* showing the range of its fluvial activity.[181]

Although for most of the rivers and waterways in the territories of their empire the Romans had no policy of consistent intervention or management to control their flow, it might be thought that the Tiber was different, given its role as a commercial thoroughfare and route for feeding the city, not to mention its place in the watery traditions of Rome. The government certainly tried to master the riverine characteristics, prevent flooding, and preserve the public utility of the river. Augustus apparently took the first steps, but as so often in the management of the city's amenities, he moved cautiously.[182] After the serious flood of A.D. 15, the initial suggestion from Asinius Gallus was to consult the Sibylline Books. Tiberius, however, entrusted the job of controlling the river to two senators, whose subsequent suggestions about modifying the tributaries of the Tiber were eventually rejected.[183] Their appointment was obviously an ad hoc solution, which was followed up by the formal institution of a permanent board of five curators, chosen by lot by the senate, responsible for the bed and banks of the Tiber, "so that the river would not overflow in winter or dry up in summer, but should always as far as possible flow at the same level."[184] These were the *curatores riparum et alvei Tiberis*, and the office was still in existence in the time of Constantine in the fourth century. At the start, the five senators acted as a college, the head of which was always of consular rank. This continued at least to the reign of Claudius,[185] but from the time of Vespasian the position was apparently held by one man, usually of consular rank.[186] It was a mark of the status attributed to the watery security of the city that senior senators held this position. For example, the younger Pliny served as curator after his consulship and before his governorship of Bithynia; in a letter, he suggests the importance of the duties of this and similar public offices.[187] Pliny's predecessor, Ti. Julius Ferox, is the first curator known to have held the additional responsibility for the sewers of the city, which is henceforth added to the office's title—"curator alvei Tiberis et riparum et cloacarum urbis."[188] There was now a more obvious degree of personal involvement by the emperor; all references to selection by lot have disappeared, and inscriptions note that curators are appointed "by authority of the emperor."

Although the details of the operation of the curatorship of the Tiber are obscure, several other officials are mentioned in inscriptions. In A.D. 41–44 an equestrian, Sp. Turranius Proculus Gellianus, served as "prefect of the curators of the bed of the Tiber"; this position was of junior status in terms of equestrian office holding, and Gellianus may have acted as a kind of administrative assistant.[189] Probably from the second century there appears another equestrian official, the *adiutor curatoris alvei Tiberis et cloacarum*. For example, circa A.D. 184 Q. Petronius Melior held this position before serving as procurator of the grain supply.[190] The change in title may derive from the change to a single curator. It is possible that the assistant normally remained in Ostia, where the curator had an office, as well as headquarters in Rome.[191] There will also have been secretarial assistants, such as Aurelius Faustinus, the imperial freedman *commentariensis albei (alvei) Tiberis*, whom we happen to hear about in an inscription from Tarraco.[192]

The job of the curators was to control the water level in the river and prevent flooding, though the inundations of the city persisted.[193] This will have involved some work on the banks and monitoring of the situation upstream, although there is no archaeological evidence.[194] Even more important was the Tiber's course between Rome and Ostia, because of the amount of commercial traffic, including the vital grain barges using the river; the curators needed to ensure navigability and also keep the towpaths passable. Some evidence vaguely suggests that the curator dealt with boatmen using the river; an inscription records how the boatmen of the ferry crossing of Lucullus had paid to restore a monument in honor of the imperial house "with the permission of Ti. Julius Ferox, curator alvei Tiberis et riparum."[195] However, it is not clear if the curator supervised the port of Rome; in such a busy area, responsibility probably lay with a number of officials, including the prefect of the grain supply and the curators of the buildings of the city.

In general, the curator of the Tiber had to look after the public interest in respect of the river and prevent any interference or blockage of it. This will have included supervising repair of the bank where necessary. An inscription set up in Rome circa A.D. 300 records how Diocletian and Maximianus "restored to its previous state, over a distance of one hundred and ten feet, the bank, which had collapsed through the passage of time, under the supervision of the curator Manius Acilius Balbus Sabinus."[196] Very importantly, the curator was responsible for marking off the public area of the river from neighboring private property; the riverine zone was then at the state's disposal, and certainly in the case of land survey, this zone was partly intended to isolate that land most vulnerable to flooding. In this capacity the curator would authorize any use of the public area, as we see in an inscription dated to 244, which refers to the assignment of a particular location by the curator.[197]

In fact, much of our archaeological evidence relates to the demarcation of the formal width of the riverine zone, by the erection of boundary stones (*cippi*) at the direction of the appropriate magistrates.[198] The consuls of 8 B.C. were at work, and Augustus himself also appears as the initiating authority; the wording on these *cippi* shows the formal, precise procedure involved: "Imperator Caesar, son of a god, Augustus, chief priest, in the 17th year of his tribunician power, demarcated the boundary, in accordance with the decree of the senate, in a straight line, the next stone is 206 feet; (*on the side*) in a straight line the next stone is 205 feet."[199] A similar formula continued throughout the imperial period: "On the authority of Imperator Caesar Trajan Hadrian Augustus. . . . L. Messius Rusticus curator riparum et alvei Tiberis et cloacarum urbis restored the boundary in a straight line in accordance with the previous demarcation, the next stone being 107 feet (away)."[200] Imperial supervision, the application of a consistent policy, and the following up of previous work are revealed in another inscription from Rome, recording that Antoninus Pius, "when A. Platorius Nepos was curator of the bed and banks of the Tiber and the sewers of the city, built up and restored the boundary markers, which had collapsed through age, in a straight line, which had been positioned . . . feet from the next stone on the authority of Imperator Caesar Trajanus Augustus . . . under Julius Ferox, curator of the bed and banks of the Tiber and the sewers of the city."[201]

It remains an interesting point that the Romans never succeeded in preventing extensive flooding in low-lying parts of Rome.[202] This failure can hardly be attributed to a lack of will or resources, since the government undertook other large projects for drainage and conveying water. One factor may have been an underlying respect for the water and its traditional association with the divine, and the idea that floods were an expression of the gods' anger or future intentions. However, this is extremely unlikely since the Romans systematically and enthusiastically exploited and controlled watery sources throughout the empire. On the other hand, the effects of floods may have been limited, with upper-class householders and major public buildings avoiding the worst of them.[203] In any case, for ordinary Romans life expectancy was limited and daily existence was precarious among the many threats in Rome, including above all fires. Temporary and relatively infrequent inundations may not have seemed quite such a disaster as they do in the modern world.

5   THE EASTERN PROVINCES

In Asia notable rivers assisting communication from the Mediterranean to the interior were the Scamander, flowing into the Troad, and the Kalbis, rising near Mount Tarbelos, flowing southwest to the Mediterranean coast at Caunus and being sufficiently deep to sustain cargo-carrying vessels.[204] The Xanthos in Lycia (formerly the Sirbis) was navigable at least by rowboat, and after 1.8 kilometers came the Temple of Leto and about eleven kilometers beyond that the city of Xanthus. Strabo had apparently made this journey himself.[205] Patara nearby had a harbor, from which goods could be imported and exported. When discussing Limyra and the river Limyros, Strabo noted that you had to move inland to the town on foot, confirming that he was alert to the navigability or otherwise of rivers in the vicinity.[206] The Kestros, which according to Mela was easily navigable, rose in the Taurus Mountains in Pisidia and flowed south through the Pamphylian plain, washing Perge and emptying into the Mediterranean. It was about seven miles upstream to Perge and the road network, providing a good route of communication and transport in Pamphylia.[207] Further east along the coast was the river Eurymedon, which also rose in the Taurus range and flowed south for about 160 kilometers, through Aspendos to the Mediterranean. Pliny provides a snippet about the Eurymedon, which was navigable as far as Aspendos, where there was a river port, from which salt, wheat, wool, and oil were exported; Aspendos also commanded the coastal road traffic with a bridge over the river.[208] The river Calycadnus (Gosku Nehri) rising in the mountains of Lycaonia flowed southeast, passing Claudiopolis and Seleukeia ad Calycadnum on its way to the coast. It was navigable upstream at least as far as Seleukeia, opening up trade routes along the coast and also to the interior of Isauria.[209]

The Orontes has its source in the Bekaa valley in Syria Coele near Baalbek, and in a course of about 400 kilometers flows northward through Syria before swinging west at Gephyra and then flowing southwest past Antioch to the sea near Seleukeia Pieria, the port of Antioch. Strabo thought that the river was navigable at least as far as Antioch in a day's journey. The port city of Seleukeia was also connected by road to Antioch, and it is unclear how easily the river was navigable. Pausanias mentions a plan by an unnamed Roman emperor to cut a canal between the river mouth and Antioch because of the Orontes' uneven course.[210] Furthermore, a milestone found on the left bank of the river and dated to A.D. 75 records the construction in the Dipotamia of a canal three miles long with bridges by soldiers of four legions and twenty auxiliary cohorts under the command of the governor, M. Ulpius Traianus.[211] This canal will have assisted navigation on the Orontes and trade between Syria and the Mediterranean; goods transported by river could be exported from Seleukeia. Another inscription found on the west bank of the river in Antioch celebrates the construction of a canal to assist the work of fullers, who needed large quantities of water to process the wool. Barriers were constructed to divert the river, and the canal stretched for about a mile and a half toward the foot of Mount Amanus. Once again M. Ulpius Traianus authorized the construction, and the work was organized by the people of the city, each city block taking responsibility for a designated stretch.[212] Presumably the work of the fullers and the export of wool were important enough to the city to justify the building of the canal.

The Maeander was the most famous eastern river in antiquity (apart from the Nile). It rose near Kelainai in Phrygia and flowed about 380 kilometers in a west-southwest direction, first passing though a deep canyon before its confluence with the Lycus, and then through a wide, fertile valley before entering the Latmic Gulf (Bafa gölü) near Miletus. The importance of the course of the river in the region is shown by Strabo's practice of calculating the distance from the river to important towns.[213] The Maeander was famous for its smooth flow as well as its winding course and its ability to spread fertilizing mud.[214] The enormous growth of the Maeander delta is shown by the southeast part of Bafa gölü, which is still brackish, and the total integration of the former islands of Hybanda and Lade into the floodplain. In Strabo's day, Priene, originally founded as a coastal city, was about 7.8 kilometers from the sea. The delta progressed rapidly in late classical and Hellenistic times until about A.D. 100 and then slowed down. The most intense period of alluvial activity at Miletus was probably in Roman imperial times. By the fourth century A.D., the lower Latmic Gulf was closed, and by the sixth century the area around Miletus was silted up.[215] The speed of delta progression was influenced by a variety of factors, including changes in sea level or climate throughout the Mediterranean or further afield, soil characteristics and erosion, topographical changes, coastal currents, and also possibly careless land use and deforestation. When most available soil has been eroded, the delta growth slows because there is little left for the river to carry and soil formation is too slow to compensate.[216]

Although Strabo and Pliny do not comment on the navigability of the Maeander, a graffito on the wall of the slave quarters at Delos, which celebrates Antioch because of its figs and abundance of water, continues: "Maeander the savior, provide salvation and grant water." On the stucco of the wall of the quarters, there is what seems to be a drawing of a ship, possibly on the river Maeander. The most likely interpretation is that this slave was pining for his homeland; therefore the crude drawing of a ship with sails and oars may indicate river transport on the Maeander.[217] But it is unlikely that any such transport was extensive; the winding course of the river, for which it was famous, would have made progress slow and the use of sails difficult.

It is more likely that the main route of communication was the road, which ran southward from Ephesus though a pass before turning eastward and proceeding along the Maeander valley on the northern side of the river via Tralles, from which a branch went south along the valley of the Marsyas (a tributary of the Maeander) to Alabanda, and on to Antioch on the Maeander, where there was a bridge. The road crossed the bridge and then ran on the southern side to Karoura, before continuing through the valley of the Lycus to Laodicea ad Lycum, and then eastward to Apamea and Metropolis. Here another road ran north to Synnada, Prymnessos, and Dokimeion, the site of important quarries. There was also a route from Laodicea to Hierapolis and Tripolis ad Maeandrum, and a further stage of the highway leading southeast to Philomelium and Tyriaion.

Specific evidence for local commerce and trade in riverine communities along the Maeander valley is limited, though the operation of river ferries might indicate the importance of the river valley traffic.[218] The mines mentioned above at Dokimeion in Phrygia beyond the end of the valley were famous for marble, some of which has been found in Rome, though it is unclear how the marble was transported from the interior to the coast. The Maeander valley was renowned for its fertility, especially in the production of olives and figs, and according to Strabo, the lake at the source of the Maeander produced a reed that was suitable for the mouthpiece of the flute.[219] Another source of income was provided by the village of Karoura, which had hot springs (some in the river, some outside) and a large number of inns, including perhaps one run by a brothel keeper.[220] Karoura marked the border of Lydia and Phrygia and was probably an important meeting point. The economic value of living in the lower Maeander valley and the delta appeared in small commercial activities. Notably, the sea bass and various types of mullet found in the lagoons near Miletus and the Maeander delta were famous, and fishermen were able to exploit the variegated wetland environments in the delta including freshwater river fishing.[221] The lagoons were protected by sandbanks, which had been part of a dispute between Miletus and Priene in the time of Augustus, when Epikrates had intervened to gain concessions for Miletus from the emperor.[222] In the second century A.D. Magnesia ad Maeandrum had a specialized salt fish market to distribute the produce of its neighbors in the Maeander delta.[223] This fits in neatly with the important salt pans in the vicinity.[224]

It is difficult to put a definite value on the economic significance of the exploitation of these natural assets, but an inscription of the early first century B.C. from Priene describes a long dispute between Priene and Roman tax collectors over revenue from salt pans on the north side of Maeander delta.[225] The Hellenistic monarchies, the Seleukids and the Attalids, had aimed to control at least some of the salt pans in their dominions, and the senate in the late republic seems to have pursued this as a source of substantial public revenue. The people of Priene had cleverly established new salt pans, which were dedicated to Athena Polias, and therefore exempt from government taxation. They initiated the process of asking the senate to recognize the holy status of the salt pans and were in dispute with the tax collectors, who attempted to exact the taxes pending the senate's decision, and even went so far as to use force. The outcome of the case is uncertain, but the inscription is good evidence for the value of the income from salt and the high emotions roused by threats to it.[226]

The nature of the evidence makes it impossible to estimate the extent to which economic activity was encouraged by the route of communication along the river valley or along the river itself. The Roman government certainly recognized that the river delta area was an asset and attempted to control and manage it. Along with local people, it appreciated the environmental impact of the Maeander and its capacity to change the landscape. This interest went back at least to the time of Augustus.[227] Furthermore, the acquisition of new farming land was placed firmly among the advantages brought by the river. In the fourth century A.D. the orator Himerios, praising Scylacius, probably *vicarius Asiae* in A.D. 343, marveled at the accretion of new land by the Maeander's action, comparing it favorably to the gift of the Nile. The Maeander's action is direct, almost visible. "But the Maeander, having stolen the sea from its sailors, has given furrows to the laborers to till with their ploughs, in place of the waves."[228] However, Himerios congratulates Scylacius because of his canal building to ensure that the internal lake adjacent to Miletus did not dry up. He is aware that the river was unstable and potentially dangerous and would continually disturb the existing environment, and in particular bring about the silting up of harbors. The Maeander's advantages for ordinary people probably outweighed the moral outrage of Himerios at the river's interference with nature. But there was a combination here of local politics and environmental issues, in that river valley communities sought to exploit the natural workings of the river while hoping that the imperial government would ward off the harmful consequences. Evidence shows that there were many subsequent attempts by government officials to deal with the riverine activity in the delta. In the fifth century the proconsul Vitianus is found constructing what seems to be some kind of causeway in the territory of Miletus.[229] The purpose was presumably to help access from Miletus to other locations when the river flooded the delta during the winter. An inscription on the statue base of one Hesychius at Miletus seems to celebrate among other things the provision by the Roman government of "channels of beautiful flowing waters," which may refer to canals to control the excess of water in the Maeander flood plain.[230]

Many coins minted by cities in the Maeander valley over a long period from at least the third century B.C. to the third century A.D. pay respects to the river. It is notable that the famous meandering pattern was replicated on coins in a formulaic way like a geometrical figure. The river was often mentioned by name on coins, and symbols including reeds and cornucopiae celebrated its flowing streams and its watery bounteousness. The coins of Antioch ad Maeandrum depict the famous river bridge, with a statue of the river-god reclining holding a reed and cornucopia. Other riverine communities in the Maeander valley honored the river on their coinage in the traditional way: Tralles, Tripolis, Priene, Magnesia ad Maeandrum, Apamea, Dionysopolis, and Hyrgaleis.[231] Apamea has an unusual coin showing the Ephesian goddess (with a small temple on her head) standing in the middle of the four rivers associated with the city—the Maeander, Marsyas, Orgas, and Thermon.[232] Although the Maeander is particularly well represented in city coins, other cities in Asia identified themselves with their rivers, emphasizing fertility and sometimes local fish.[233] A coin of Laodicea is particularly expressive; it depicts the city goddess Laodicea enthroned with two river-gods at her feet, the Lycus and Kapros, recumbent against water urns. Kapros holds a cornucopia and a reed.[234] In other coins the Lycus and Kapros are symbolized by a wolf and a boar respectively.[235] At Hierapolis in Phrygia, the river-god Chrysoroas holds two ears of grain and a poppy.[236]

This numismatic evidence shows how Greek cities had respect for their rivers, and this was associated with the tradition of minting coins that expressed elements of local topography, recognizing the role of rivers in navigation, trade, and agriculture. The Maeander certainly stands out among the rivers of Asia; local people identified with it and celebrated certain attributes, including its contribution to fertility and its distinctive winding course; they had perhaps a greater sense of shared common identity with the river valley than was usual in parochial Greek city-states. The river name was a significant source of identification for local communities, as well as the name of the city-state. It is also worth noting that the numismatic evidence persists through the imperial period; civic identity associated with the river was preserved.

This particular devotion or attachment to the Maeander does suggest that the river featured significantly in the lives of local riverine communities, as a route of communication, a source of fertility, and a focus of cultural identity. It may be that in western Asia Minor the great river valleys, which provided routes of communication for hundreds of kilometers into the interior, encouraged a greater sense of regional identity than in mainland Greece. Especially in the more heavily urbanized Hellenistic and imperial periods, geographical networks were important, and one of the most important elements in Asiatic regional identity was the river, and in this the most developed network was the middle and lower Maeander valley. In this context the prominence of river names in the onomastics of Ionia is striking. In particular, among potamophoric names there was a strong devotion to the Maeander name and its derivatives. Indeed, the Magnesians in some respects conceived of themselves as "Maeander dwellers" as well as the inhabitants of a particular city.[237] The river again provided a strong element of regional identity, which remained unaffected by the Roman presence.

Further east some rivers were well known, although they were on the periphery of Roman influence. The Euphrates rises in the Armenian mountains and is 2,740 kilometers long; eventually one channel passes through Babylon while the other joins the Tigris to flow into the Persian Gulf in a vast alluvial delta. In Strabo's day the Euphrates was navigable as far as Babylon, about 545 kilometers. There was a system of canals to deal with the excess of water during the river's flood tide in the spring and early summer, and there were problems for river navigation if these were not properly maintained.[238] As Strabo says, there were many advantages of the Euphrates as a route from the Persian Gulf to Mesopotamia. Pliny, relying apparently on information from Domitius Corbulo and Licinius Mucianus, thought that the upper course of the Euphrates was navigable in places: from Dascusa to Sartona for fifty miles, to Melitene for twenty-four miles, and to Elegeia for ten miles. After passing through the Taurus range, the river became navigable again, for forty miles to Samosata. Pliny then speaks of a ten-day voyage between the Parthian town of Philiscum and Seleukeia and also Babylon.[239]

The Tigris rises in the eastern part of the Taurus range and flows southeast passing Ctesiphon and Seleukeia where it is only about eighteen miles apart from the Euphrates; it splits into two channels, one of which joins the Euphrates south of Seleukeia; the other flowed further east and was called the Pasitigris. The Tigris was navigable upstream as far as Seleukeia/Opis according to Strabo. Alexander had apparently voyaged up the Pasitigris in the direction of Susa.[240] It is not clear how much navigation was possible in the river's upper reaches. The river Oxus (Amu Darya) rises in the Pamir Mountains of Central Asia and flows generally northwest for about 2,580 kilometers. According to Strabo (on the authority of Aristobulus), it was navigable and was part of a riverine transportation route that brought large quantities of merchandise from India along the Oxus to the Hyrcanian/Caspian Sea; it was transported across the sea and was carried thence by the river Kyros, eventually to the Black Sea.[241]

Arguably the Nile was the most spectacular example of a river at the heart of an entire province. The Nile has its sources among the headwaters of Lake Victoria and the White Nile flows for 3,700 kilometers to Khartoum, where it joins the Blue Nile and the Atbara to form the Nile. The river has a total length of 6,656 kilometers and, as well as providing irrigation and depositing fertile silt, acted as a great channel of communication throughout Egypt from Alexandria to the cataracts, where portage was possible. The Nile valley also provided the main route for road communications within and throughout Egypt and connected communities along the valley.[242] However, it is difficult to take the Nile as a good case study since in many ways it was unique or at least entirely atypical, in the extent of the inundation and its absolutely essential contribution to the fertility of the valley. The Nile valley was also strikingly different in the degree of government intervention and exploitation. Furthermore, the river followed an unusually straight course with no significant tributaries. In particular it was unusual in providing an important route for the transport of state-organized grain to Alexandria and the export of luxury goods to Ethiopia, and facilitating the transit trade to and from the Far East. Journeys downstream were assisted by the tide, while the prevailing wind from the north allowed ships to sail upstream.

Presumably as a result of an accident of the evidence, our knowledge of river transport in Egypt is limited. There is some evidence for approved harbors and stopping places and the use of canals. Grain could be moved by barge along navigable canals to a port on the Nile.[243] Apart from the movement of goods required by the state, there is not much evidence for commercial traffic or the operation of boatmen,[244] although some private fluvial transport was available along with passage in cargo ships.[245] Problems were caused by the annual inundation from June to September, and movement of grain along the river was organized to take account of its navigability. For example, in A.D. 165 a local official requested more animals for transport in the Arsinoite nome, "so that while the river is still navigable, transportation may be carried out, as the water is already imperceptibly falling (?) and there is urgent need that grain be brought down quickly."[246] At the height of the inundation, river travel will have been very difficult because of the removal of the usual landmarks, though local people using the small Nile craft made from papyrus may have been able to travel further by water.[247] Diodorus comments that travel upstream was impossible during the flood.[248]

The important point is that by itself the Nile could not sustain transport within Egypt. River navigation was combined with movement of goods by road or track using various pack animals. Goods had to be transported to the river and not all areas were equally served by canals or water channels. For example, the Fayum was up to 100 kilometers from the river. Therefore, it is correct to emphasize the road network in Egypt. A major road ran along the Nile valley from the Mediterranean coast to Syene, although all signs have been removed by the annual inundation and changes in the river's course. Other important roads linked Koptos on the Nile with the ports of Berenike and Myos Hormos on the Red Sea coast. The *via Hadriana* linked Hadrian's new city of Antinoopolis on the Nile to the coast and continued to Berenike.[249] The link between river and land transport can be seen in the import of luxury goods from the Far East; they were brought by ship along the Red Sea to the two important ports, Berenike and Myos Hormos, from which they were taken by road to Koptos and thence by the river Nile to Alexandria for reexport to the empire. In terms of the history of the Nile, most attention concentrates on the annual inundation and its impact on the economic prosperity of Egypt and the culture and society of the province.

There were seemingly few navigable rivers in the provinces of Africa and Mauretania to interest our sources. However, in Mauretania Tingitana, the Sububus (Sebou) from its source in the Atlas range flowed northwest and then southwest, washing the Colony of Banasa on its way to the Atlantic, a distance of about 450 kilometers. Pliny called it "splendid and navigable," and it offered a route of communication and transport to the interior in an area with few Roman roads.[250] On the Mediterranean side of the province, the rivers Tamuda and Laud flowed parallel to each another from the mountains to the coast of the Mediterranean.[251] All were navigable for ships and, in an area with virtually no good roads, must have served to keep small communities of the interior in contact with the outside world. In fact, the town of Tamuda was situated on the river of the same name.

6   CONCLUSION: RIVER CONNECTIONS

The enthusiasm of the ancient commentators for recounting the navigability of rivers seems to be well founded, although we might think that occasional details on the exact extent of navigability derive from local tales and experience rather than precise measurement or records. Riverine transport of merchandise, both officially and through private enterprise was a significant feature of ancient economic activity. Much of this was doubtless on a very small scale, with local operators traveling along a limited stretch of water, utilizing tributaries of bigger rivers, and leaving little or no trace. On major riverine thoroughfares, the Romans exploited what was available and made only limited attempts to control or improve navigation. Although military supply and communications were important along the Rhine and Danube (suggesting the potential role of rivers in military strategy), commercial traffic was also substantial. The route along the Rhône valley was partly aimed at supplying the military, but the extensive use of other rivers in Gaul and in Spain shows that military supply was not the sole or even predominant motive in the use of rivers in the movement of goods. Partly because of geographical factors and river direction, waterborne trade in Spain and Gaul was particularly extensive and probably not typical of other areas, where small-scale local transport was often more important. Nevertheless, despite differences in scale, examples of riverine navigation from various parts of the empire suggest roughly similar activities, with the same types of rivercraft, infrastructure, facilities, and local experience. This helps to produce a reasonably convincing if impressionistic picture of the use of rivers, even when precise evidence is scarce. Descriptions of rivers in ancient writers and the riverine qualities celebrated on coins and in other artistic media suggest that often there was no mechanical calculation of navigability, but a general recognition of a river's capacity to confer prosperity. Rivers were celebrated as part of the life of local communities, in which their role as a guide and a connection to other communities along the river valley and beyond was one of many characteristics and benefits.

Nine

HEALING WATERS

RIVERS, SPRINGS, RELAXATION, AND HEALTH

"Let the earth shake and spread far and wide the path of rivers. Let the Rhine and the Rhône flood these fields, and let the rivers make their huge springs change course."[1] Thus, Lucan, lamenting the impact of Caesar's campaigns in Spain, imagines the cleansing power of rivers, which will sweep away the calamity of civil war from the land. This appeal is set within a precise geographical description, which emphasizes the importance of rivers in the military maneuvering. The poet cleverly merges riverine qualities, including the practical and the mystical and symbolic.

This introduces our theme of rivers as healers, where the cleansing power of running water could be seen as both real and psychological. Early settlers naturally tended to gravitate to the vicinity of riverbanks. Running water offered a source of clean drinking water and possibly a ready supply of food, because wild animals also came to the riverbank to drink. Once man had mastered the art of fishing, the river became a plentiful source of available food in its own right. Riverine dwellers could wash themselves and their clothes in the river, and the watery environment produced potentially useful aquatic plants and herbs. In the Mediterranean summer water had a cooling and refreshing effect, which might have helped the sick, for whom no more sophisticated treatment was available. In more general terms rivers provided a pleasant environment in which to live.

As we have seen before, ancient writers in their river descriptions dwell on the sound and sights of rural life in river valleys. Exaggerated as some of this will have been, nevertheless we have here an authentic statement of traditional appreciation of watery, sylvan tranquility. Local people in river valley communities not only had access to a valuable resource but also had an excellent means of leisure and amusement that did not cost much and for which they did not have to travel long distances. Furthermore, the divine spirit thought to be inherent in rivers and the associated legendary stories of supernatural power and riverine curiosities, which underpinned the belief in their ability to interfere in human affairs, help to explain the extensive interest in the Roman world in springs and rivers with curative properties. In addition, the developing empire came in contact with other peoples, especially in Gaul and Germany, and among Greek communities, who believed in the special qualities of springs and rivers. Many of these people would have appreciated phenomena and the veneration of the sources of hot springs.[2] It is also the case that Roman use of rivers and springs and particularly of spa centers is an example of their control of the natural environment and exploitation of watery resources no less significant than their economic, commercial, political, and military exploitation of riverine resources. The Romans were not constrained by concerns about protecting the environment and were conspicuous consumers and dispensers of water, often casually using water resources as a plaything to decorate gardens and city centers with fountain displays, and even to provide aquatic sports and battles in the arena.[3]

This chapter considers the leisure activities associated with running water, rivers, and springs as cleansing and health-giving agents, aquatic curative properties, oddities of nature associated with running water, and finally spas (*aquae*) as organized centers of exploitation of the healing properties of springs.

1   RELAXING WATERS

In the Old Testament rivers appear frequently as a source of purity and power, but sometimes of restorative comfort, as in the twenty-third Psalm: "He maketh me lie down in green pastures: he leadeth me beside the still waters." Even a mighty river can also be a bringer of peace: "Behold, I will extend peace to her (Jerusalem) like a river, and the glory of the Gentiles like a flowing stream."[4] In the Roman world it seems that in everyone's view the watery environment was conducive to pleasant recreation and tranquility: the seductive burbling of the river or stream, the lush vegetation and elegant trees, the striking vistas, and even the noise of birdsong.[5] In the *De Legibus* Cicero affirmed the restorative qualities of a natural riverine setting, which was far better than artificially constructed streams in elaborate gardens.[6] And he vividly describes the pleasures of taking a dip in the cool waters at his villa near Arpinum at the confluence of the rivers Liris and Fibrenus.[7] In the ancient world, just as in the modern, a river view was popular among property owners. Pliny in his emotional panegyric on the Tiber mentions that the river is not offended by the villas crowding right up to its banks.[8] The notoriously sumptuous gardens of Regulus on the right bank of the Tiber had porticos with statues of the owner right along the bank.[9] Varro, referring to his villa near Casinum, mentions that a stream ran through the property, "fifty-seven feet wide, clear and deep, with stone borders." There were bridges across the stream, and along its banks ran a ten-foot-wide open walkway. It was here that Varro kept his aviary.[10] Similarly, Statius celebrates the villa of Manilius Vopiscus at Tibur, which straddled the river Anio gently flowing between the buildings on either side.[11] Rich Romans in their estates liked to combine natural features and buildings and, where necessary, subdued natural phenomena to their own ends.[12] Arguably the gardens of greatest taste were those that exploited watery sources, and when water sources did not exist, rivers, waterways, and waterfalls had to be created. Emperors often gave the lead; Nero's *domus aurea* had an artificial river and lake;[13] in Hadrian's Villa at Tibur, water was a crucial part of the design, with a visual, aural, and psychological importance. We find pools, fountains, water features, dining rooms with water, the artificial creation of a riverine vista in the villa environment—in fact, the creation of the moral purity of the countryside in a built environment. This sheds some light on how the Romans thought about rivers, leisure, and the landscape.[14] After all, the aquatic pleasures of emperors included visits to sacred rivers and springs such as the Clitumnus.

2   BOATING, SWIMMING, AND FISHING

Given the respect for the scenic beauty of rivers and the diverting pleasures of running water, we might expect boating on rivers and lakes to have been a popular form of relaxation, although there is little explicit evidence for it. Rivers were a focal point for riverine dwellers and those in surrounding valleys and could draw people together in communal pleasures and festivals, not least because rivers also served as thoroughfares. There is some evidence for the pleasurable use of rivercraft. Pliny mentions boating on the river Clitumnus near the sacred shrine, and we hear of sailing on the Lucrine Lake and on Lake Como.[15] Rivers therefore could offer a pleasant aspect with many people out in small boats. Propertius imagines how Cynthia will enjoy herself at Baiae. "May some safe inlet keep you close, I pray, / where yielding water gives the swimmer way; / some tiny boat trusting to minute oars, take / its pleasure with you on the Lucrine lake."[16] Rich men who lived adjacent to water will have owned a sailboat or rowboat, and poorer people could probably hire a small boat. We can note Pliny's casual reference to Hippo in North Africa, where people of all ages enjoyed fishing, boating, and swimming.[17]

Ordinary river dwellers will often have used rivers to get around on day-today business and personal trips, though we should not expect much evidence of this.[18] Frequent references in travel writers to the navigability of rivers may suggest not only an interest in commercial transport but also the importance of rivers for daily travel. But is there any sign that people, particularly the well-off, traveled by river for pleasure? In Egypt, which, of course, may not be typical, the Nile provided a viable means of transport, of both goods and people, partly because numerous canals linked the river to remoter parts of the valley.[19] In general, in normal circumstances it is possible that because of the Nile waterway there was a reasonable degree of mobility even for poorer people, at least within a limited radius.[20] There were, of course, certain special occasions for revelry, including the notorious processions from Alexandria to Canopus for the public festivals in honor of Serapis, when boats crowded with musicians and dancers went up and down the canal.[21] A fragmentary papyrus of the first century A.D. describes a journey by a party of people from Alexandria probably to Oxyrhynchus. They traveled by canal and river to Memphis and then by canal and the Bahr Yusuf to Oxyrhynchus. The journey took nine days and they stopped at Memphis on the west bank and Babylon and Aphrodito on the east bank. The leisurely nature of the trip suggests that they were using water transport for pleasure, and they went bathing on at least five days of the journey.[22]

You could travel by river or by canal in order to avoid unpleasant roads or roads that were inadequate or dangerous. Horace famously describes what was intended to be a pleasurable journey with several companions to Brundisium in 37 B.C., during which he met up with other friends, including Maecenas and Virgil.[23] At Forum Appii, where the Appian Way was particularly difficult, they traveled by night barge on the canal through the Pomptine marshes as far as Lucus Feroniae, where Horace and his friend could wash in the holy spring of Feronia.[24] This part of the trip, according to Horace, was very unpleasant, because of the mosquitoes, the frogs, and the uproarious conduct of the bargeman and another traveler. It was also very slow. Resuming the road, they crawled on to Anxur, "loftily poised on its limestone cliffs." Horace needed to apply salve to his enflamed eyes. So, this was not a good advertisement for travel by water for pleasure. On the other hand, Ausonius, in his poem in praise of the river Mosella (Moselle), notes that you could travel either by drifting with the current in a rowboat or by having men pull a barge. Ausonius's description of the river's beautiful appearance, clear waters, and splendid vistas, as well as the pleasures of river bathing after a hot bath (comparable to Cumae) and the skills of fishermen, suggest a personal experience of journeying on the river for pleasure.[25]

Of course, emperors organized sumptuous river travel, though this was frowned upon by their critics. When Nero slowly traveled down the Tiber from Rome to Ostia, or cruised in the Bay of Naples, he had cubicles erected at intervals along the shore decked out for every kind of amusement and equipped with women enticing him ashore; his friends were expected to provide dinners.[26] During his triumphal advance on Rome in A.D. 69, Vitellius used to sail along the rivers of northern Italy on elaborate ships decorated with various garlands and provided with luxurious amusements.[27]

Virgil in book IV of the *Aeneid* famously described a race at sea between the leading sailors of Aeneas's fleet. Was he thinking of scenes from Roman life that he had witnessed? It is interesting to speculate on the possibility of regattas, races for small boats, and other forms of aquatic competition as a celebration and center of communal activity for riverine communities. On a large scale, we might think of the events later staged at the Naumachia at Rome. Catullus described his seagoing yacht, in which he claimed to have sailed from Asia Minor to Sirmio on Lake Garda, as the fastest ship afloat, powered by either oars or sail, which may suggest some kind of racing.[28] There were trireme races at Athens in the Panathenaic festival, and a regatta is mentioned in an inscription of the second century B.C. from Cyzicus, though this also probably took place at sea.[29] Augustus apparently staged boat races at the festival in honor of his naval victory at Actium.[30] At Hermione in the Peloponnese, the local community observed a festival in honor of Dionysos, which included a boat race, which was apparently still being held in Pausanias's day.[31] Just as nowadays rowing competitions and regattas have an important social side, Baiae was notorious in Roman times for its drunken boating parties.[32] Aelian by contrast paints an idyllic picture of the pleasures of the river Peneios, which, gentle and smooth as olive oil, offered opportunity for pleasant recreational sailing in the shade of the trees along its banks.[33]

Suetonius when recounting Caligula's many curious abilities in the arena and on stage mentions that despite these skills he was unable to swim.[34] The implication is that that many Romans knew how to swim, and the evidence suggests that they were fond of swimming. On the medical side, Galen believed that swimming was beneficial, and Aelius Aristides frequently swam in rivers even in winter for the sake of his health.[35] In the army, as Vegetius points out, recruits were trained to swim during the summer, "because rivers cannot always be crossed on bridges and an army in retreat or on the advance is often compelled to swim."[36] The Romans of old, taught by military campaigns and endless crises to develop the art of war to a high level, had selected the Campus Martius beside the river Tiber "in which the young men after their military training could wash off the sweat and dust and overcome tiredness resulting from their exercises by vigorous swimming."[37] The Elder Cato taught his son military skills of javelin throwing and fencing, riding and boxing, but also to swim in the fastest and roughest parts of the river.[38]

In Cicero's day, young men still came to bathe in the Tiber, though perhaps now mainly for pleasure. Certainly Clodia, according to Cicero, had fun in watching them from the gardens of her villa by the Tiber, which she had purchased for this purpose.[39] Julius Caesar of course famously demonstrated his swimming ability during his campaign in Egypt, by swimming for about 200 yards while holding important papers above his head in his left hand (presumably a kind of side stroke), and dragging his cloak after him with his teeth.[40] In the early empire it was possible still to think of the river Tiber being used to exercise the body, at least in Horace's poetic imagination—"Watch out in case Enipeus, who lives next door, attracts you more than is proper . . . no one can swim more swiftly than he down the Tiber."[41] For Ovid, typical male pursuits were exercising in the Campus Martius, bathing in the freezing water of the *aqua Virgo*, or swimming in the gentle waters of the Tiber, although the level of sewerage pollution will not have made this very alluring.[42] Certainly Augustus taught his grandchildren not only their letters and other basic skills but also swimming.[43]

For aquatic pleasure combined with a kind of religious significance, we have Pliny's description of the upper course of the river Clitumnus, where bathing was permitted outside the sacred part of the river. Here the community of Hispellum maintained a bathing establishment and an inn on the river for the use of visitors to what was clearly a popular location.[44] The German soldiers who accompanied Vitellius's army to Rome in A.D. 69 were keen swimmers and enthusiastically swam in the Tiber, though with disastrous results for their health, from either overexertion or the effect of the polluted water in an already unhealthy environment.[45] The Batavians were especially renowned for their swimming skills, and cavalry regiments impressed Hadrian by swimming the Danube fully armed.[46]

Fishing was another riverine activity. Pliny noted that one of the pastimes at the seaside town of Hippo was fishing. He meant presumably from rocks by the shore. But river fishing we must assume was a pleasure to be enjoyed by all those who lived in a riverine environment. There is little direct evidence, which is not surprising since this was probably a commonplace local activity. However, the jurist Marcianus confirmed that no one could be prevented from coming down to the shore to fish in the sea and also noted that nearly all rivers were held to be public. Gaius observed that there was free public use of riverbanks just as of the river itself, according to the "law of nations" (*ius gentium*).[47]

Elsewhere we find: "All rivers and harbors are public, and therefore there is a communal right of fishing for everyone in harbors and rivers."[48] Individual fishing rights could be established, and if someone had fished in a particular location for many years, he excluded another from the same right.[49]

Although Pausanias nowhere explicitly recognizes a responsibility of local communities to keep rivers pure, he points out that rivers could bring many benefits, depending on the quality of the water. Most importantly, rivers provided plentiful fish, whose texture and taste depended on water purity; they could be caught for food or sold for profit. The river Pamisos in Messenia had fish of a particular quality because its waters were so clean. Fish that enjoy mud, like the gray mullet, preferred more sluggish waters. The Pamisos and the Acheloüs also had sea fish, which swam upstream especially during the spring. Pausanias goes on to write an enthusiastic reference for Greek rivers, which do not produce enormous fish that attack men, unlike the Indus, which had crocodiles, and the Nile with crocodiles and hippopotamus. Even the Rhine and Danube contain dangerous fish. By contrast, "Greek rivers are not at all terrifying as far as monsters are concerned."[50]

Of course, fishing could also have a commercial aspect. In fact, most evidence deals with fishing for the elite and the creation of fisheries. Subsistence fishing, fishing for recreation, or small-scale enterprises did not attract the attention of our sources. River fish were originally important in Roman cuisine, and already by the second century B.C. a pike caught "between the two bridges at Rome," that is, the *pons Aemilius* and the *pons Sublicius*, just south of the Tiber Island and below the influx of the Cloaca Maxima, was a speciality.[51] Great value was placed on fresh fish.[52] However, by the first century B.C. sophisticated Roman taste came increasingly to reject freshwater fish in favor of sea fish. Marcius Philippus, consul in 56 B.C., on being served a river pike at Casinum, spat it out, saying "I'll be damned if I did not think that it was fish."[53] With these sentiments came the development of luxurious fish ponds filled with seawater, like those of Lucullus.[54] However, fresh fish from the city of Rome remained a delicacy.[55] And while it is true that in Diocletian's price edict sea fish cost twice as much as best river fish, it is notable that river fish are still worth listing.[56] Many types of fish flourished in the rivers of the western provinces. We can see the local interest from the way in which writers can relate the kinds of fish found in some rivers. For example, in the fourth century Ausonius expatiated on the best fish found in the Moselle, including trout and salmon,[57] and vividly described fishing in the river — "But where the shores can be easily reached / no fish is safe from the fisherman's skill." The type of fishing varied; some used individual hooks, while another "out on a sandbar" used nets buoyed up on corks to catch large shoals, and boys tried to catch fish from the banks. "These scenes are enacted along shores and banks / within the sight of old country estates perched / high on crumbling cliffs which overlook / a quiet valley and a rolling stream."[58]

3   HEALING WATERS AND AELIUS ARISTIDES

The river as an agent of cleansing and healing had a long history. In the Old Testament, the prophet Elisha instructed Naaman, the military commander of the king of Syria, to bathe in the Jordan to cure his leprosy. He at first declined, showing respect for local river rivalry by arguing that Damascus had plenty of rivers. However, he eventually relented, dipped himself seven times in the Jordan, and was cured.[59] In the second century A.D., Aelian was expressing similar sentiments by recording the common view that the river Peneios in Greece was beneficial for those who bathed in it and brought good health.[60] The dynamic qualities of running water allowed virtually any river to serve as a medium for healing by either drinking, swimming, or immersion. Springs too were regarded as particularly efficacious in promoting health; their sudden emergence from the ground was impressive, and thermal springs that bubbled had a demonstrably special quality. Cicero expressed what was probably the traditional Roman view by quoting an old proverb on the value of taking the waters: "As long as a man is at the waters he is never dead."[61] Varro, referring to the spring Juturna, noted that the name came from the idea of helping (*iuvare*), "and so many sick people are in the habit of coming to this water because of its name." In his mind, the different qualities of water were connected with the prevalence of river spirits. The Younger Pliny, burdened with affairs of state, thought wistfully of fishing and hunting as a sick man longs for wine, and of baths and springs as part of a relaxing watery environment.[62] People regularly thank the spirits of the waters for their relief and medicinal qualities.[63] The longevity of this respect for springs is splendidly demonstrated by the story of how the wild Goths in the seventh century took pleasure in the hot waters near Anchialus in Moesia: "Amid the other sites of innumerable hot springs in the whole world, these were outstanding and the most effective for the cure of the sick."[64]

The distinguished Greek sophist Aelius Aristides had the wealth and leisure to explore both rivers and springs in a search for good health; he was an assiduous visitor at curative hot springs and a keen river bather. In the *Sacred Tales*, he tells us about his various bouts of ill health between circa A.D. 143 and 170, and this is exceptionally detailed evidence for aquatic treatment. He was taken ill on a trip to Rome in 143, and returned to his home at Smyrna, where he was advised to attend the warm springs southwest of the city.[65] The regime of treatment he followed seems to have been recommended by doctors and was also under the divine guidance of Asclepius (in Roman form Aesculapius), revealed in a series of dreams.[66] He mentions fifteen occasions on which he visited either hot springs or a river. River bathing was an important part of his treatment; this consisted of washing or bathing and sometimes swimming in a river, usually specifically designated; this was a treatment in cold, running water—in one case the water was so cold that it was frozen—and might consist of total immersion, after which the body was allowed to dry naturally.[67] At Smyrna, although there were warm springs in the area, Aelius took his treatment in the river that flowed by.[68] He seems to set greater store by immersion in running water than in hot springs. On one occasion, at Pergamum, going upstream to avoid the contaminated water in the city, Aelius dived into the river when it was in full spate, roaring and carrying rocks and logs.[69] He also bathed in a river near the estate at which he was staying at Cyzicus.[70] However, he continued his warm spring treatments at Cyzicus and at a cold spring near Pergamum.[71] Although Aelius, if he did have a fragile constitution, was probably lucky to have survived bathing in icy water in the middle of winter, he is convinced that all these treatments were beneficial. What also comes across strongly is the piety of Aelius, who seems to believe in the efficacy of Asclepius and offers homage to the river Aisepos, the Nymphs, and Artemis Thermaea, who looked after the warm springs at the river.

4   HEALING WATERS: VITRUVIUS, PLINY, AND PAUSANIAS

While Romans and Greeks were happy to bathe in rivers and lounge around the hot springs (Aelius says that the springs at Cyzicus were packed with a noisy crowd),[72] the explanation of what effect the waters had was more complex. The Romans seem to have believed that visits to the normal public baths promoted health.[73] Aelius, an intelligent and educated man, clearly felt that immersion in water of various kinds was good for him in some way. However, attempts to account for water's special qualities ranged from the scientific to the merely superstitious. It is appropriate to start with Vitruvius and Pliny the Elder, who manage to combine both approaches, but nevertheless took a great interest in the watery environment and convey something of the importance of rivers and springs in the Roman world and their place in the thinking of doctors, the ill, riverine dwellers, believers and unbelievers.

Vitruvius in his architectural writings has a long excursus on the properties of watery cures.[74] He believed that water was the most valuable of all things for practical use, since without it no living thing could be born, sustained, or provided. "Therefore, we must with assiduous and painstaking care seek out and choose water sources to enhance human health." He goes on to set out procedures for testing the quality of spring water, which in turn illustrate an obscure aspect of ancient ecology.[75] First you should examine the physical qualities of the people living nearby; good signs were a clear complexion and few eye complaints. Wholesome water should leave no trace on a copper vessel, and if water was boiled in a copper jug, allowed to cool and then drained off, it should leave no deposit of mud or sand. Similarly, it was a good indicator if vegetables boiled in the water cooked quickly. Salubrious water should also be limpid and transparent and have no reeds growing in it.

Vitruvius correctly interprets the variety in the qualities of rivers and springs as due to the different regions, rocks, and soils that they flowed across, or through which they made their way to the surface, and the type of underground volcanic activity.[76] In this way the distinctive taste and smell of certain waters emerged, for example, the sulfurous smell of the Albula at Tibur.[77] He observes that rivers could taste sweet or salty depending on the land they passed through, and in some cases the prevailing character of one river could be altered by another river flowing into it; some waters were poisonous, presumably because of the heavy mineral and chemical content.[78] He is also aware that polluted drinking water caused health problems, for example, at Tarracina.[79] Vitruvius seems to assume that most treatment came by immersion of the whole body or part of it in the waters, but he also notes that some water from hot springs could be drunk and had a fine taste, rivaling the finest water source in Rome, the *aqua Marcia*.

Therefore, as far as Vitruvius is concerned the curative properties of water are self-evidently explained by the qualities of the soil and rocks though which the water passed, especially when it was thoroughly heated. In general, hot water was thought in a rather obscure way to be beneficial. More specifically, he thought that particular ailments could be assisted by certain water treatments: sulfur springs assisted muscular weakness, alum springs parts of the body atrophied by paralysis or disease; bitumen springs assisted detoxification and healed internal complaints. Alkaline cold springs such as those at Pina Vestina and Cutili assisted purges and soothed scrofulous tumors in the intestines. On the other hand, springs associated with certain minerals such as gold, silver, iron, copper, and lead had many impurities and when taken internally might be harmful in causing cramps and gout. Yet, at the river Cydnus near Tarsus, people suffering from gout bathed in the river for relief. Some rivers and springs acquired an oily surface; at Soloi in Cilicia, the river Liparis coated with oil those swimming or washing in it, though it is not clear if this had any medicinal effect. There were springs well known for their ability to dissolve gallstones, as in Lyncestis, Velia, and Teanum in Campania.[80]

Like Vitruvius, Pliny emphasizes the importance of water as an element; rivers take up an enormous amount of space, can devour land, put out flames, and make plants grow. He too is interested in the type of water most useful to humans and quotes medical opinion that stagnant water should be avoided and that running water was best because of its movement and impact. Different rivers have different qualities and the standard of the water can be judged by various factors; the presence of a lot of mud is a bad sign, but an abundance of eels indicates good water quality; bitter or discolored water is bad, also water that leaves a deposit on cooking pots or in which vegetables cook slowly. In Pliny's view the coldest and most salubrious water is that of the *aqua Marcia*, the gift of the gods to the city of Rome.[81]

Water springs can be hot or cold or sometimes blended together, as at Tarbellicae in Aquitania and in the Pyrenees. Their appearance is benign and welcome to humans since they bring help in ill health, they increase the number of gods because they receive homage, and they are instrumental in the foundation of cities. The springs have various properties—sulfur, alum, salt, alkaline, bitumen, a mixture of acidic and salt—and treatment can be by drinking, bathing, or inhalation of fumes. Curative waters may help ailments of various parts of the body: muscles, joints, the feet, especially gout, broken bones, wounds, purging, stomach problems, head, ears, and eyes. Like Vitruvius, Pliny noted that some springs were thought to be efficacious for particular problems. So, the springs at Sinuessa benefited female infertility and (curiously) male insanity, while those on the island of Aenaria/Pithekoussai cured gallstones.[82] The spring at Thespiae helped pregnant women and that at Linos in Arcadia prevented miscarriages; on the other hand, the river Pyrrha allegedly made women infertile. The water at Lake Alphius assisted the treatment of skin disease, and a Roman man of praetorian rank, Titius, had erected a statue there in gratitude for his cure.[83] Among the Tungri in Germany, a spring tasting of iron acted as a detoxification agent and put an end to tertiary fevers.[84] Pliny is aware of the importance of the mineral content in the soil and also that the qualities of rivers and the water they bring change throughout the year and are affected by climatic features, such as the amount of rainfall. He also has commonsense advice against too long exposure to vapors or drinking too much of the water, and he warns that it is not necessarily a proof of curative properties if water causes metals to discolour.[85] He often returns to the salubrious effects of warm springs[86] and their potentially healing properties.[87]

It is clear that both Vitruvius and Pliny gathered a great deal of information about rivers and springs, containing much ancient tradition and lore, and attempted to analyze the benefits of the watery environment. This topic was clearly important in ancient society, and a student of the environment and natural history and a student of architecture, which relates to man and the environment, would naturally be interested in it. But a substantial part of their accounts is taken up by the fantastic and supernatural qualities of certain springs and rivers. For example, we hear of two springs with the capacity to make sheep black or white or a mixture of both. The springs Krathis and Sybaris had the same effect on humans—those drinking from the Sybaris became darker and harder with curly hair, while those drinking from the Krathis became whiter and softer with straight hair. In Boeotia, two springs near the river Hercynnus alternately aided memory and brought oblivion. Some springs made people give up wine, others made them inebriates.[88] Some of these might be explicable, for example, the spring that improved the singing voice had perhaps helped to cure hoarseness. Water that was both bitter and sweet was possibly the result of deep currents. But many stories are pure fable.

Pliny does note specifically that the watery environment was responsible for numerous oddities of nature, many of them seemingly fantastic.[89] Why did our authors find it difficult to disregard the fabulous? Modern readers need to see this question though the eyes of the ancients. Rivers and springs were very important for human existence; there were many unexplained aspects, such as disappearing rivers, the sudden appearance of streams, underground rivers, flash floods, damaging and ultimately uncontrollable inundations in Rome, the annual miracle of the Nile inundation, and springs of bubbling hot water, many of which *did* bring about odd things. In fact, springs represented an unusual, even turbulent part of nature that man could sometimes not control, exploit, or defend against. What is more, many rivers and springs had from earliest times been worshiped as deities and represented in human form. A rigorously or exclusively rational approach was not appropriate. There were many inexplicable events, and our writers did not feel able to reject the accumulated weight of tradition. The intellectual context is of a prescientific, benevolent rationalism, in which intelligent and articulate inquirers accepted the cultural imperatives of their society, including many long-standing ideas and a whole nexus of inherited river lore. This reflects the times in which they lived and is an invaluable guide to the significance of the watery environment. People wanted to believe in the power of their rivers and springs, and the countless votive offerings tossed into them demonstrate popular faith. The many dramatic stories served to emphasize and proclaim the immense power of water, and consequently its potential ability to cure mundane or more severe ailments.

Pausanias, like Vitruvius and Pliny, also had an interest in the curative properties of water, and would certainly have approved of Aelius's health regime,
since he relates in a matter-of-fact way the benefits of certain rivers and springs
and precisely identifies their qualities. Clearly he expected his audience to value
such water sources and their potential to cure the physical ailments of humans.
Near the river Anigros in Eleia, there was a cave where sufferers from leprosy
prayed to the nymphs (daughters of the Anigros). They then wiped the dis-
eased parts of their body and swam across the river, "leaving their disgrace in
the water and emerging healthy and clear-skinned."[90] Here we have the age-old
tradition of the river as purifier. Also in Elis, at Herakleia, there was a sanctuary
of the nymphs where a water spring ran into the Alpheios. Those who washed
in this spring were cured of all types of aches and pains.[91]

Pausanias was fascinated by hot springs and gives a list of the more interesting ones, noting the "white water" across the river Anio, which flowed into
the Tiber north of Rome, where when you first went into the water you began
to shiver but soon felt very warm. On the other hand, in Pausanias's own day,
hot water had been discovered in Latium that was so acidic that within a few
years it consumed lead pipes. The pipes imply that a bathing station had been
established.[92] Near Kenchreai there was Helen's Bath, where a strong stream
of water ran into the sea from a rock and made it look as if the sea was beginning to boil.[93] Immersion in hot and salty water meant that you needed a swim
afterward, which was certainly part of Roman practice, and Pausanias in his
emphasis on hot springs and a pleasant warm bath may well be thinking of the
habits of the Roman upper classes.

But he was well aware of the curative properties of springs, noting that at
Kynaitha in Arcadia there was a spring that promised that those who drank it
would be cured of rabies.[94] On the route from Thouria to Arcadia, the springs
of the river Pamisos provided healing for little children.[95] Furthermore, the
springs and baths in southern Ionia were famous for promoting general well
being.[96] Most spectacularly, the river Selemnos in Achaea cured the wounds of
sexual passion. If men or women washed in it, they forgot their love. Pausanias gave a measured response. "If there is any truth in this legend, the water of
Selemnos is worth more to mankind that a great sum of money."[97] Pausanias
valued these stories because of their local interest and wider cultural relevance,
but he also remained aloof from judging their credibility.

There were also water springs that could predict the outcome of sickness.
Near Patrai, at the sanctuary of Demeter, the sick suspended a mirror tied on
a cord so that it just touched the water surface. Then after making an offering and praying to the goddess they looked in the mirror, which revealed the

sick person either alive or dead.[98] At Oropos in Attica at the shrine of Amphiaros, there was a tradition that when someone had been healed by following an oracular response, in gratitude silver and gold coins were dropped into the adjacent spring, from which Amphiaros was said to have risen as a god.[99] Occasionally, springs or wells allegedly imparted some kind of psychological change, leading to prophetic powers,[100] or hallucinations, enabling the person who imbibed to see sights in an area out of the line of sight.[101] All these stories closely associate running or welling water with the process of transformation and healing.[102]

5   HEALING WATERS: THE MEDICAL VIEW

Doctors, of course, had a professional and, one might say, a scientific interest in the possibilities of water cures; this was connected with the widespread belief in ancient medicine that bodily humors influenced health and disease. Hippocrates (c. 470 B.C.) had been concerned about the water quality in rivers. Men who drank from big rivers with tributaries rather than from smaller streams often suffered from gallstones, kidney problems, and hernias. But flowing rivers that drew off rainwater were healthy and clear and good to drink. In the absence of good river water, men might have to drink spring water or water from stagnant pools and swamps, which could lead to distended stomachs and problems with the spleen.[103] In the case of springs, Hippocrates did not approve of drinking water from hot water sources. The water was often hard and caustic because of the minerals that were inevitably present through the generation of the heat. It was better to seek water flowing from hilltops, which was usually sweet and clear.[104] Galen (court physician of Marcus Aurelius), in his commentary on Hippocrates' treatise *Airs, Waters, Places*, discussed the qualities of different types of water and was critical of some waters from soil containing iron and copper and other minerals, which could be harmful to those who drank them. But sometimes they were beneficial, as in the waters near Rome at *aqua Damnata*, which helped intestinal complaints when drunk in moderation. For Galen, the value of springs and thermal bathing was connected with the traditional ancient view of the need to manage the humors in the body.[105] Again, in his treatise *On Preserving Health*, Galen noted that naturally occurring hot water was not efficacious for certain diseases of the head. The implication is that some springs were useful for treating certain ailments, and he mentions springs at Prusias and at Lucetoi that had medicinal properties, and the Aquae Albulae, which were good for treating wounds.[106] Therefore, in Galen's view the merits of each spring had to be judged carefully and likely benefits assessed.[107]

Celsus, who wrote in the reign of Tiberius, in general approved of bathing in hot water to manage the bodily humors and believed that this could assist the treatment of skin ailments, muscular complaints, diseases of the joints (particularly gout), overexertion, wounds, digestive problems, fevers and diseases of the eyes, and urinary infections, as well as recovery from surgery.[108] In the case of paralysis of the limbs he recommended that the limbs should be moved about in pools supplied with mineral waters.[109] He also named individual spas for certain ailments, for example, the cold water at Aquae Cutiliae and Aquae Simbruinae for digestive problems, and the vapor bath at Baiae to induce sweating.[110] Celsus recognized the importance of immersion in warm salt water and brine.[111]

Soranus, the famous doctor of the second century A.D., prescribed swimming in natural medicinal waters, as long as the head was kept covered in the open air.[112] He also recommended bathing for gynecological disorders and suggested ten different spas for treatment of chronic conditions.[113] Furthermore, we should remember that the doctors treating Aelius Aristides seem to have encouraged him to seek remedies by bathing in both rivers and hot springs.[114] Another distinguished patient, Augustus, who always seemed to follow his doctor's orders, visited the Aquae Albulae, which flowed into the Anio between Rome and Tibur. He took hot salt water and sulfur baths for rheumatism, sitting on a wooden seat, which he called by the Spanish name *dureta*, and plunging his hands and feet into the water one after the other.[115] It seems that he also visited a healing spring in the Pyrenees.[116]

6   HEALING WATERS: THE POPULAR VIEW

Against this background of the interest of the wealthy and educated and the enthusiastic or cautious approval of doctors, it is not surprising that ordinary folk in the Roman world took a straightforward view of the possibility of finding a cure in rivers and springs. They prayed to watery spirits and to associated divinities. Asclepius (or Aesculapius) and Hygeia (or Hygia) and various other gods, who were instrumental in healing, appear at water centers. The importance of a supply of running water to health was often expressed in terms of divine support. So, an aqueduct at Aquincum included a dedication to Asclepius and Hygia, and the same divinities appear in the dedication of a swimming pool in Africa.[117] Religious fervor and homage to rivers were associated with the healing process. Horace was cynical about a woman who prayed to Jupiter to release her son from a fever, promising in gratitude to have him stand naked in the Tiber. The cold would kill him in Horace's view.[118] But many votive and ritual offerings, not to mention Aelius Aristides' willingness to plunge into freezing rivers, show the sincerity of belief that various gods acted through the medium of water.

We must try to imagine the excitement of a visit to a riverbank or curative springs, and the whole ambience of veneration and worship. Lucian in this satirical account of the charlatan Alexander of Abonouteichos describes how in this town a large pool of water had collected in the foundations of a new temple to Asclepius and Apollo. Alexander had hidden a goose egg here in which he had inserted a newly hatched snake, and by producing this spectacularly convinced the local population that Asclepius himself had arrived. The people excitedly wished themselves health and wealth, and within days the city was filled with crowds of pious people to see the god. Lucian thought that they were entirely deluded, but the attempted trick shows the importance in local communities of the presence of the god (in this case especially associated with healing), the excitement generated, and the expected commercial opportunities for the city. For Alexander then set up a business in oracles from the god, many of which dealt with questions of health.[119]

It is possible that most rivers were viewed as a source of healing. After all, running water traditionally cleansed away sins and impure elements. And in mythological tales, rivers often fathered numerous children, which could easily suggest that river water might assist in problems of female fertility and other gynecological questions. Poor people, who did not have the means or leisure to travel, would find rivers easier to get to than hot springs or spa towns, since they could walk to the nearest river valley and throw small offerings into the stream. Rivers were particularly accessible and could be approached anywhere along their banks, though certain parts might be more auspicious. In the Tiber just north of the Aventine about 200 small cups have been found; these seem to be offerings of drinking bowls used to drink the waters of the river for medicinal reasons.[120] The bed of the Tiber has also yielded a large number of other votive offerings dated from the third to the late first century B.C. There are many sculptures of parts of the body that were clearly deliberately thrown in—hands, feet (these two the most numerous), head, penis, intestines, uterus, a baby, female breast—and they represent an attempt to seek divine aid for the appropriate ailment through the medium of the river or to offer thanks for recovery. The largest number of the votive offerings was discovered on the left bank at the head of the *pons Fabricius*, at the *insula Tiberina*.[121] The Tiber Island contained the Temple of Aesculapius with a strong tradition of healing. The healing properties of the river also appear in the religious ritual of immersing women in its waters.[122] Persius describes a kind of purifying ritual, which consisted of plunging your head into the Tiber two or three times in the morning and purifying yourself with the river at night.[123]

We have already seen how in Pausanias's day the river Peneios retained a reputation for its healing and generally beneficent qualities.[124] Other scattered evidence confirms this picture for various rivers. For example, near Pouillé on the banks of the river Cher, there is a small sanctuary with a votive offering representing eyes and a reference to the river.[125] The source of the river Seine was also particularly venerated. Pre-Roman worship here was in honor of the Dea Sequana (the source of the Seine). In the vicinity have been found many dedications from people who were seeking cures or celebrating release from ill health; they consist of coins (dating from Augustus to Magnus Maximus), bronze plaques, statues, *ex voto* offerings of various limbs, typically in the form: "To the Goddess Sequana Clemency, Montiola willingly and deservedly fulfilled her vow."[126] This site was an object of frequent pilgrimage throughout the Roman period, and there were substantial buildings including a large swimming pool to which water was led from the river by a pipe. It is speculated that there were also warm baths and that hydrotherapy was available.[127] Other dedications to rivers may be connected to the cleansing and medicinal role of rivers associated with their divine attributes.[128] The site of the source of the Clitumnus was especially holy, as we have seen above, its waters were sacred, and people were not allowed to pollute it with their bodies. Pliny says that there were many inscriptions honoring the spring scribbled on pillars and walls, many of which were admirable and some amusing.[129] It is likely that some of these were votive offerings made to the spring for healing.

In general, the amount of evidence for rivers in a healing guise is limited, but that is not surprising since rivers did not attract as much attention as certain springs, particularly thermal water cures. There was, of course, a close relationship between rivers and springs; both had similar religious connotations and were associated with the same range of legends and miraculous qualities. Both served to enhance local honor and identity. A spring could go on to form a stream or river if not channeled, curtailed, or collected. So, rivers and springs were emotionally and psychologically linked. Springs differed from rivers in that they had in many cases a fairly sophisticated exploitation of the water source, the addition of sometimes elaborate buildings, the development of commercial opportunities, and a measure of organization. Rivers were not as fashionable and did not bring large numbers of people together in one place, though they offered wider and less expensive access. Worship and appeals for healing at river venues may have been commonplace but did not often come to the attention of ancient writers and commentators. However, study of springs can help our understanding of how the ancients viewed and exploited the watery environment.

7   SPAS (AQUAE): THE EVIDENCE

There is no word in Latin to convey the English equivalent of *spa* for a natural mineral water source and the buildings that grew up around it. The Romans normally employed *aquae* to describe such sites,[130] sometimes with the addition of *calidae* (hot). In this section, I employ the word spa to describe the use by the Romans of naturally occurring mineral or thermal waters and springs for medicinal or therapeutic purposes (map 19).[131] This normally pre-supposes a degree of organization at the site. Geographical locations are de-scribed using *aquae* and an adjectival construction, such as Aquae Mattiacae (Wiesbaden in Germany) or Aquae Helveticae (Baden in Switzerland). Occa-sionally *fons* (font; spring) is used to describe a mineral spring, as in Fons Aponi. This kind of terminology can reasonably securely identify the site of thermal establishments, though supporting evidence is important: literary ref-erences, iconographic representations, dedications to the springs or related divinities, and archaeological remains showing water conduits and facilities as-sociated with curative waters. At spa sites, pools can resemble those at ordinary baths but some have distinctive features, notably benches around the interior sides to allow people to sit and soak in the water; also several sets of stairs into the spa pool would allow easy entry for the infirm as well as providing some-where to sit; the depth of the main pool at a spa is typically about 1.5 meters, which allows full immersion or exercise in the water.[132]

Ethnohistory, namely the survival of ancient practices into later ages and be-liefs in the efficacy of certain springs for cures, is also relevant for the identifi-cation of ancient spas. Unfortunately the popularity of many ancient spa towns, which has continued right up to the present day, led to much subsequent build-ing, which has obscured any ancient remains. There is a further difficulty. It is certainly true that places called *aquae* were probably built at or near natural springs, which were believed to have healing properties and were often asso-ciated with a healing deity. But inscriptions referring to a healing divinity such as Asclepius or Hygia, or both, cannot without other evidence imply the pres-ence of curative springs. Some of the surveys of *aquae* in the Roman world have perhaps been overambitious in identifying curative watery sites.[133] Further-more, there are many inscriptions referring to *balnea* or *thermae*, which may indicate the presence of hot springs but, without other evidence, may refer to ordinary bath complexes with artificially heated water. Similarly, the site of

MAP 19. *Spas in the Roman world*

Ancient World Mapping Center 2011

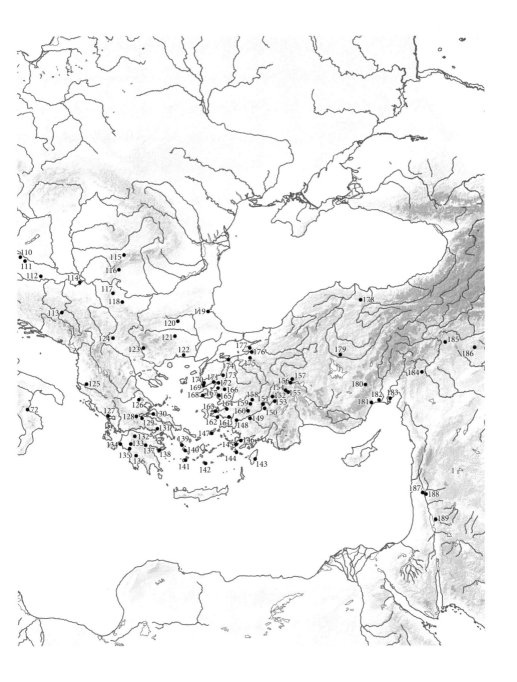

1. Aquae Arnemetiae
2. Aquae Sulis
3. Aquae Granni
4. Aquae Mattiacorum
5. Divodurum
6. Montbouy
7. Alesia
8. Balesmes-sur-Marne
9. Bourbonne-les-Bains
10. Aquae Aureliae
11. Badenweiler
12. Aquae Helveticae
13. Aquae Nisincii
14. Aquae Bormonis
15. Aquae Neri
16. Evaunum
17. Aquae Calidae
18. Aquae Segetae
19. Saint-Galmier
20. Aquae
21. Divonne-les-Bains
22. Menthon-Saint-Bernard
23. Brides-les-Bains
24. Salins-les-Thermes
25. Saint-Martin-d'Uriage
26. La Motte-Saint-Martin
27. Aix-en-Diois
28. Allan
29. Aquae Sextiae Salluviorum
30. Aquae Griselicae
31. Aquae Tarbellicae
32. Aquae Siccae
33. Aquae Convenarum
34. Vicus Aquensis
35. Aquae Onesiorum
36. Amélie-les-Bains
37. Aquae Voconiae
38. Aquae Calidae
39. Aquae Calidae
40. Aquae Bilbitanorum

41. Fons Tamarici
42. Aquae Quinti(n)ae
43. Aquae Calidae
44. Aquae Celenae
45. Aquae Quarquernae
46. Aquae Originae
47. Aquae Flaviae
48. Aquabona
49. Aquae Dacicae
50. Aquae Sirenses
51. Aquae Calidae
52. Aquae Herculis
53. Aquae
54. Aquae Tacapitanae
55. Aquae Regiae
56. Aquae Caesaris
57. Aquae Flavianae
58. Aquae Thibilitanae
59. Ad Aquas
60. Aquae Aptuccensium
61. Aquae Traianae
62. Aquae
63. Ad Aquas
64. Aquae Persianae/Naro
65. Aquae Carpitanae
66. Aquae Calidae
    Neapolitanum
67. Aquae Segestanae
68. Aquae Larodes/Thermae
    Selinuntae
69. Akragas
70. Thermae Himeraeae
71. Lipari Island
72. Krathis/Sybaris
73. Surrentum
74. Stabiae
75. Aquae Vescinae
76. Mons Dianae Tifatinae
77. Neapolis
78. Puteoli

79. Baiae
80. Aenaria
81. Aquae Sinuessanae
82. Teanum Sidicinum
83. Castelforte
84. Aquae Neptuniae
85. Ad Aquas Salvias
86. Aquae Albulae
87. Simbruinum
88. Aquae Septem
89. Aquae Cutiliae
90. Aquae Labanae
91. Aquae Tauri
92. Aquae Caeretanae
93. Aquae Apollinares
94. Aquae Apollinares Novae
95. Aqua Viva
96. Aquae Passeris
97. Ad Aquas
98. Fons Clitumni
99. Fontes Clusinae
100. Aquae Populoniae
101. Aquae Volaterranae
102. Aquae Senanae
103. Bagno di Romagna
104. Aquae Pisanae
105. Aquae Statiellae
106. Aquae Bormiae
107. Aquae Aponi
108. Fons Timavi
109. Aquae Pannoniae
110. Aqua Viva
111. Aquae Iasae
112. Aquae Balissae
113. Aquae S(. . .)
114. Aquae Bassianae
115. Aquae
116. Ad Mediam
117. Brestovacka Banja
118. Ad Aquas

119. Aquae Calidae
120. Augusta Traiana
121. Haskovo bani
122. Linos (?)
123. Scaptopara
124. Aquae
125. Nymphaion
126. Krannon
127. Actium/Nicopolis
128. Hypata
129. Thermopylae
130. Aidepsos
131. Thespiai
132. Kynaitha
133. Thelpousa
134. Kyllene
135. Alpheios river
136. Phigaleia
137. Kenchreai
138. Hermione
139. Kythnos
140. Seriphos
141. Melos
142. Thera

143. Lindos
144. Nisyros
145. Kos
146. Salmacis
147. Ikaros
148. Magnesia
149. Tralles
150. Colossae
151. Hierapolis (Pamukkale)
152. Sebaste
153. Apamea
154. Eukarpia
155. Hierapolis
156. Aquae Ger . . .
157. Leontos Kome
158. Thermae Theseos
159. Karoura
160. Philadelphia-Neocaesarea
161. Lebedos
162. Teos
163. Erythrae
164. Smyrna
165. Atarneus
166. Pergamum

167. Perperene
168. Mytilene on Lesbos
169. Larisa
170. Alexandria in Troad
171. Antandros
172. Thebe
173. Pionia
174. Cyzicus
175. Prusa ad Olympum
176. Kios
177. Pythia Therma
178. Thermae Phazemoniton
179. Aquae Saravenae
180. Tyana/Colonia
   AureliaAntoniniana
181. Soloi/Pompeiopolis
182. Tarsus
183. Aegae
184. Aquae
185. Abarne
186. Aquae Frigidae
187. Hammath/Ammathous
188. Hamat Gader
189. Kallirhoe

modern thermal establishments might be a guide but can offer no certainty.[134] In general, our evidence for spas is fragmentary and we probably hear only of the most celebrated; in some cases we depend on the chance survival of an inscription. Many thermal springs will have been small, catering for an entirely local audience and leaving little trace of their activities.

8   TYPES OF TREATMENT

Since it was widely recognized that springs had different qualities, different treatments were recommended, which might consist of drinking spring water, immersing yourself or swimming in the water, inhaling vapors, or sitting in hot, sulfurous air.[135] Among water-drinking cures, the water at Lugdunum was the most beautiful and very pleasant to drink, while hot springs at Autun had a good taste and no smell.[136] A combination of the warm springs and sulfurous air was employed at Vichy, which was said to help liver and chest complaints.[137] Among the hot springs in Campania, at Arco Felice and Leucogaei Fontes water was applied in drops to the eyes to repair weak vision.[138] By contrast, at Stabiae visitors drank the cold spring, which was useful for treating gallstones.[139] About four miles away from Teanum Sidicinum, a cold spring, the Aqua Acidula, was also drunk.[140] Combined treatments were popular, and Rutilius Namatianus, describing the spa at Aquae Tauri in Etruria near Centumcellae, says: "Its waters are not spoilt by a sour taste, nor are they hot and colored with smoking sulfur; their clean smell and pleasant taste confuse the visitor, who wonders whether they are better for drinking or for bathing!"[141] Similarly, at Aquae Vesevinae (on Mount Vesuvius) visitors could drink or swim in the waters.[142] At Agnano (specifically a thermal site since there was no town nearby) in Campania, the remains of buildings suggest arrangements designed partly to enable people to sit and inhale hot vapors; the natural hot air was also used in a system of underfloor heating. As noted, many pools at thermal sites were equipped with seats so that visitors could sit and soak in the water.[143]

Some treatments at thermal establishments were more complex. Soranus set out his procedure for dealing with patients who were suffering from paralysis of the legs. "You should ensure that the patient uses mineral waters, especially thermal springs . . . and you should prescribe swimming in the sea or in these thermal springs. First of all, attach an inflated bladder to the paralyzed limbs to reduce the efforts required in swimming. You should also send a stream of water . . . onto the paralyzed parts, for the impact of the water is very efficacious in changing the condition of the body."[144] In other cases of paralysis of the stomach, when it was incapable of retaining any food, Celsus warned against use of baths (in hot water) and recommended among other things that cold water should be poured over the patient, that jets of cold water should be directed at his stomach, and that he should bathe in cold medicinal springs, such as those at Cutilia near Rome and Simbruinum near Tivoli.[145]

We have a rare opportunity to examine the procedures at a curative spring from the scene depicted on the famous silver bowl (inscribed *Salus Umeritana*) from Otañes near Castro Urdiales in northern Spain. The site is unknown but apparently had medicinal waters (figure 12).[146] A personified female figure represents the spring, holding a reed and leaning on an urn from which flows a stream of water. This is channeled into a large tank from which a boy fills a container; elsewhere a man sits in a chair and receives a goblet of water from another boy; at this spring, visitors apparently drank the water for its restorative properties. A third boy fills a large barrel on a four-wheel truck pulled by two

FIGURE 12. *Silver and gilt bowl from Otañes, Castro Urdiales, in northern Spain, ornamented in low relief, depicting activities at a spa. Image reproduced with the kind permission of Dr. Ralph Jackson of the British Museum.*

mules; this intriguingly suggests that the water was exported from the site in the same way as in modern times bottled water is distributed far from source. However, high transport costs would have made long-distance distribution unlikely, and there is no clear evidence for amphorae containing mineral water. It is possible, though, that water was transported in barrels or animal skins. The religious aspects are expressed by the presence of two altars on site at which men make offerings; one at least seems to be a patient who has been cured, the other holds a walking stick and is perhaps making a vow to the healing waters. Possibly he has traveled a considerable distance. The bowl suggests a busy health resort with many people employed to provide its services, though no formal buildings are portrayed. It has been argued that images are commonplace if not banal,[147] but it would be helpful precisely if the practices portrayed were commonplace at most curative springs. Although no other source mentions Salus Umeritana, the site was important enough to be celebrated on this silver bowl, and it is likely that there were certainly many other similar sites about which we hear nothing.

We get another glimpse of curative waters on the broken silver handle of a pan, which was discovered at Capheaton in Northumberland, dating from the third century A.D. An interesting design depicts the goddess Minerva standing over a spring with her foot on an urn from which flows a stream of water. This makes its way between elegant structures, one of which is a temple. From the other, which might be a fountain house, a figure appears to take a goblet of

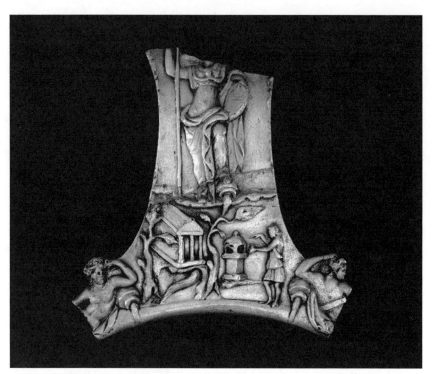

FIGURE 13. *Fragment of the handle of a silver vessel with gilded decoration showing the goddess Minerva above a temple near a spring at which a figure makes an offering. Dating from the second or third century A.D., it was found at Capheaton in 1747 and is now in the British Museum. Image copyright © Trustees of the British Museum, used by permission of the Trustees of the British Museum.*

water. This may or may not be intended to represent Aquae Sulis (Bath), but more generally portrays a sacred spring and the beneficent effects of the waters (figure 13).[148]

The mixture of treatments provided at spas and the other amusements available ensured that they remained popular venues. The many references in ancient writers, the inclusion of spas in the Peutinger Map, and the frequent inscriptions honoring local waters and their protecting divinities all testify to the continuing popularity of spas and the respect accorded to the curative properties of watery sources. Even smaller sites sometimes have elaborate buildings, suggesting popularity and investment. The extended treatment of *aquae* in the works of Vitruvius and Pliny confirm that they expected great interest among their audience.[149] In the context of our fragmentary source material stray pieces of information are very helpful. For example, Strabo tells us that whereas the city of Caere, once very distinguished, was now only a shadow of its former self, the hot springs nearby (now Bagni del Sasso) had a larger population because of people coming for the cure.[150] Commenting on the abundant hot springs in Etruria, he observes that because they were near Rome they were very well attended, just as much as Baiae though the springs there were the best known of all.[151] Of course, sites such as Baiae and Aidepsos on Euboea were famous and extremely popular. And Aelius Aristides had noted with some disapproval that the hot springs at Cyzicus were full of a noisy crowd of people.[152]

However, a packed house was not always a good thing. The village of Scaptopara in Thrace possessed the advantage of hot springs and was situated between two army camps. To make matters worse, two miles away from the village an important festival lasting fifteen days took place every year. These attractions should have brought commercial prosperity, but many visitors left the festival and descended on Scaptopara, forcing the inhabitants to provide hospitality of all kinds. What is more, soldiers and other official travelers left their appointed routes and came to the village, while senior officeholders, like the provincial governor or imperial procurator, who came to take the waters had to be entertained at local expense. Appeals to the governors of Thrace brought some relief, but the abuse soon broke out again. So, eventually the villagers threatened to leave their ancestral homes and in A.D. 238 appealed directly to the emperor.[153] This sad tale indirectly illustrates the popularity of the hot springs in the area. We may compare the community of Hippo in North Africa, where the appearance of a friendly dolphin was at first a boon to the town as people flocked to the spectacle; but later the constant arrival of officials and the expense to the local community became burdensome, and Hippo began to lose its reputation for peace and quiet. The dolphin had to be quietly eliminated.[154]

9   SPAS, ROUTES, AND ITINERARIES

If we use the basis of sites identified by the designation *aquae* or *fons*, there are more than 100 spas attested in Italy and across a large swath of the territory of the Roman Empire.[155] How does the location of springs and spa establishments relate in general terms to settlements, roads and rivers, and the framework of communications? Thermal springs, of course, occur naturally, and it is impossible to alter that location unless you are prepared to transport the water over long distances, which would be technically difficult and prohibitively expensive. Therefore, it is worth asking if the presence of a mineral spring led to the foundation of an adjacent settlement. Indeed, the Elder Pliny speculates that in the case of Aquae Sextiae in Narbonensis and Aquae Statiellae in Liguria the nearby thermal springs had contributed to the emergence of the settlements.[156] This is plausible but hard to demonstrate. It might be more realistic to ask if the existence of a thermal spring encouraged the development of a road, which might in due course have assisted the development of a town and connections to neighboring areas. The problem is that we rarely know when a spring was first recognized or exploited, and when it started to inspire greater interest and attract visitors. Most major building at spas seems to date from the first century A.D. onward (although the evidence is very patchy), when the route of most major roads had been well established. However, it is likely that existing roads, which had been built for a variety of reasons, helped in the expansion of the site of some curative springs. Then, because these spas served as way stations or as convenient stopping points on roads on rivers, buildings were gradually constructed for travelers and visitors.

For example, Aquae Thibilitanae near Thibilis in Numidia and Aquae Regiae in Africa Proconsularis, were located at important road junctions.[157] In central Gaul, thermal sites are often found along major roads and at crossroads.[158] In Aquitania Aquae Tarbellicae (Dax) commanded a prominent road junction, and in Lusitania Aquae Originae, Aquae Quarquernae, and Aquae Flaviae (Chaves) are found on two significant roads linking Asturica and Bracara Augusta.[159] The connecting road network was crucial for Aquae Mattiacae, across the Rhine from Mogontiacum.[160] At Fons Aponi in the Venetia, it seems that a network of minor roads facilitated communication between the spa and the cities of Patavium and Ateste.[161] In other cases, although the spa had good road connections there were other reasons for the development of the site. The well-known spring at Bagno di Romagna was at the center of a road network, and in the republic a great development took place with the construction of an elaborate complex of buildings. However, the reasons for this went beyond the enjoyment of a medicinal source; there were also religious and social factors of great consequence, connected with the development of Sarsina on the river Sapis as a local center.[162]

In some areas, rivers were at least as important as roads for communication. The spa at Evaunum, northwest of Augustonemetum (Clermont-Ferrand) in Aquitania, was an important river and road junction. Similarly, Aquae Calidae was well placed in the valley of the Elaris and had several roads, while another well-known spa, Aquae Bormonis, lay on a road running along the Liger valley. Some spa sites were more remote, and Aquae Convenarum and Aquae Onesiorum, the one north, the other south of Lugdunum Convenarum in Aquitania near the Pyrenees, had no road connections but were positioned in river valleys. In the area of the Rhône there are several sites in the vicinity of rivers but far from any road, such as Aix-en-Diois, Brides-les-Bains, Saint

Martin d'Uriage, Salins-les-Thermes.[163] Presumably at some sites people had to walk on minor tracks or travel as far as possible by rivercraft. Spas at such sites may have been enjoyed largely by local communities. In eastern Emilia between Piacenza and Parma, some small mineral water sources are not associated with the *via Aemilia* or any other road. The hydrological patterns of the landscape will have meant that these springs were often tied quite closely to local river networks; several are on the tributaries of the Po, while others lie between rivers.[164]

Ancient itineraries take account of spas, help to show how they were listed, and illustrate the geographical context. The most spectacular are the itineraries carved on four silver goblets found at Vicarello (near Lake Bracciano) showing a route from Cadiz to Rome with place names and distances.[165] Vicarello is usually identified with Aquae Apollinares Novae, a site of thermal springs.[166] Although Aquae Voconiae in Hispania Tarraconensis on the coastal road from Tarraco to Narbo is listed, the purpose of the goblets is unclear, and since Aquae Apollinares does not appear on the itinerary, they can hardly have been intended as a guide to help visitors find the spa, and their discovery at Vicarello may be coincidental. It is possible that the entries were copied from a list with a utilitarian purpose of guiding business travelers to Rome.

The Antonine Itinerary, probably dating the late third century A.D., which displays roads, towns, and staging posts throughout the provinces, mentions several spas.[167] So, in Spain we find: "Also by another route from Bracara to Asturica 25 miles as follows: to Salaniana, 21 miles; to Aquae Originae, 18 miles; to Aquae Querquernae, 14 miles; to Geminae, 16 miles; to Salientes, 18 miles; to Praesidium, 18 miles."[168] On the route from Spain to Aquitania, spas feature prominently: "Also from Aquae Tarbellicae to Tolosa, 130 miles as follows: to Benearnum, 19 miles; to Oppidum Novum, 18 miles; to Aquae Convenarum, 8 miles; to Lugdunum, 16 miles; to Calagurris, 26 miles; to Aquae Siccae, 16 miles; to Vernus Sol, 12 miles; to Tolosa, 15 miles."[169] The spas here are mentioned as convenient refreshment or relaxation points along a major route.

The most interesting evidence is the Peutinger Map, which was probably originally compiled in the fourth century A.D. though incorporating features of earlier work. It presents in pictorial form the details of an itinerary through the inhabited world from Spain to India and depicts the road networks with their posting stations and a variety of topographical features, including rivers and mountains. It is unclear if the map had an official function, but it certainly did serve as some kind of guide to travel in the empire, since it has mileage indications and also shows the kind of facilities and conditions that the traveler might meet along a particular route.

The map employs iconographic images, one of which shows a square building with open courtyard and pool sometimes colored blue, an entrance door flanked by towers, and possibly a representation of a colonnade. The most common version appears thirty-six times with several variations.[170] There have been many interpretations of these, and some have suggested that they were inns or baths, but recently scholars have argued convincingly that they represent thermal healing establishments.[171] Was one purpose of the map therefore to mark these for travelers? Several places with the building symbol on the map and the name *aquae* or *fons* are described in the literary texts as places for cures. For the illustrator, the main pool and courtyard were the most recognizable aspects of thermal spring sites, which seem to suggest they often had quite elaborate buildings.

If we accept the argument about the icons depicting spas, there are twenty-two spa symbols in Italy, eight in Gaul, seven in Africa, and ten in the eastern provinces; eight other named spas appear without the spa symbol. So there may be fifty-five designated spas on the Peutinger Map. This would tend to confirm that they were a significant feature in Roman life, at least in the fourth century, though it is very unlikely that established sites were not important in the earlier period. Furthermore, some of the spas are not positioned at an intermediate point along a route but at the end of a road. It is likely, therefore, that one purpose of the map was to act as a guide for those seeking to visit spas. How did interested people find their way to spas? In the absence of clear evidence, we might guess that poorer people found out by word of mouth and used traditional landmarks to find local spas (they can hardly have traveled far) and that the rich had friends or servants or agents to advise them and find the best route. But it is possible that the long-standing and continuing popularity of certain spas meant that they were formally entered on maps, for the guidance of imperial officials and other well-connected travelers who wished to visit them.[172] Of course, the Peutinger Map is a complex document with a variety of purposes. It has been argued that one objective was to demonstrate the civilized amenities of the empire, and in that case the thermal curative sites that so spectacularly exploited nature would be a useful addition.[173] In general, when the mapmaker set out to construct the topography of communications, he established the landscape with rivers, mountains, shorelines, and other natural features, into which roads could then be fitted, underpinned by various towns and other centers that served as landmarks, provided services, and helped to orientate the traveler.

Despite the evidential difficulties, the Peutinger Map raises an important point about the status of spas and travel to them. In some ways, spas resemble the great bathing establishments, common in the towns and cities of the empire, and in which the Roman interest in watery relaxation was most famously expressed. Spas could not match their scale but had certain common features; a supply of hot and cold running water, treatments, swimming, and a general concern for health, exercise, and increasing care of the body; baths like spas were also important social centers. The provision of baths was often supported by the local community with the help of rich citizens so that bathing was free or had only a nominal charge. Emperors also played a role in providing baths in Rome and some of the larger cities in the provinces.[174]

It is interesting that in Campania at sites that have more extensive remains, such as Agnano, Castelforte, and Teanum, the mineral and thermal waters seem to play a subordinate role to the bathing establishment, which operated in the traditional way. Ordinary hot water by itself was thought to be therapeutic, and normal baths were more often recommended by doctors as presumably being more available.[175] However, a combination of treatments might also be important.

It is likely that many hot springs had no permanent structures or elaborate buildings. Visitors drank or immersed themselves in the waters, and did not expect to spend the night. However, some spas were of outstanding importance, virtually served as a holiday destination, and attracted visitors from a long distance who will have expected elaborate provision, including inns, lodging, and dining facilities. It is true that some spas soon acquired a reputation as a playground for the rich and famous (particularly catching the eye of writers), and they became the haunt of the elegant elite in search of much more than a warm soak. Although we turn to these first, it is worth pointing out that the activities at thermal springs reflected many facets of Roman society, and their visitors, when we have evidence, seem to represent a reasonable cross section of the population.

10   FASHIONABLE SPA RESORTS

Campania was especially well known for its curative springs (Pliny sent his wife there to recover her health),[176] and of all the sites Baiae was the most famous. Strabo comments that the springs at Baiae were suited to the cure of ailments and also pleased the fastidious, while Pliny notes the enormous variety of the remedies available from the plentiful water supply.[177] The local topography as described by Cassius Dio produced fire and water combined; the locals collected the water in reservoirs and then took the steam from it through pipes into the upper rooms of bathing establishments, where it was used for vapor baths. They believed that this produced a dry heat. The mechanism for doing this was expensive but was very useful for routine daily heating and for effecting cures.[178] There was a considerable degree of organization here in controlling nature for profit and medicinal purposes.

In the eyes of Roman commentators, Baiae was particularly popular and stylish, and many of the Roman elite had villas in the vicinity.[179] There was, of course, other activity at the springs, including prostitution, and it is not surprising that in the Middle Ages the Christian Church was worried about some of the amusements at hot springs.[180] Horace wrote admiringly about the sulfur baths and hot springs at Baiae, which were famous for their power to drive off chronic rheumatic attacks. Horace had been such a regular visitor that his horse knew the route (this tells us how some visitors traveled). But now it seems that his doctor had prescribed a different regimen, namely cold-water showers at rival establishments at Clusium and also Gabii. With the insight of an entrepreneur, Horace speculates that the town of Baiae will be resentful if a prominent man goes elsewhere, possibly starting a move to a rival attraction and leaving the myrtle groves deserted; that would be a commercial disaster.[181] This is an important point since visitor revenue will have helped sustain the local economy. Round bottles have been discovered, made in the third and fourth centuries, which may be examples of tourist souvenirs sold to visitors. On the other hand, they may have been flasks for drinking the water.[182] The engraved sides show views of Baiae and Puteoli with the main sights, including baths, terraces, theaters, and temples.

It is difficult to recover the layout of Baiae partly because changes in sea level have altered the topography of the entire coastal region. However, some excavation has taken place in the volcanic slope above the gulf of Baiae; a large structure called the "Temple of Mercury" is a rotunda with windows in the top tier for ventilation and light, and a circular skylight in the top of the dome like the Pantheon. The building is, in fact, a large swimming pool, where, in grandiose surroundings, visitors could soak in the thermal waters. Other structures on the terrace provided more areas for immersion and an open-air swimming pool. Nearby at the "Baths of Venus" there is another structure, which is built on two levels with a large bathing pool occupying the lower story; this seems to be part of the hydrotherapy facilities.[183] An inscription from Pompeii was possibly an advertisement for a bathing establishment that combined a source of fresh water and thermal hot water: "Baths (thermae) of M. Crassus Frugi, with seawater and freshwater bathing. Januarius, freedman."[184] These may have been located on the seashore on the promontory to the west of the Sarno river mouth.[185]

One site in Greece almost matched Baiae for elegant relaxation. Plutarch's description of Aidepsos in Euboea in the province of Achaea neatly encapsulates many relevant themes. The springs are first mentioned in the fourth century B.C. but the site did not become popular for its curative properties until the Hellenistic period or the early imperial period. "It became a popular resort town for people from all over Greece, especially because of the place called Hot Springs, which possesses many natural properties for the splendid enjoyment of leisure, and is further enhanced by villas and elegant apartment houses. Game and fowl are abundantly caught there, and the sea is equally generous in supplying the market with provisions for the table. . . . This resort flourishes especially when spring is at its height, for many continue to come there all through that season. They gather together, free from every want, and being at leisure, endlessly engage in conversation."[186] The town was well appointed, having baths, colonnades, banqueting halls, and canals to draw water.[187] Plutarch shows that Aidepsos was crowded and very busy, that the springs had brought wealth and luxurious appointments to the town, that there were seasons for curative springs, and that presence of large numbers of people encouraged local commercial enterprises to supply the food market. Also people at the springs enjoyed other leisure activities.

It had important Roman visitors. Sulla came in 86 B.C. to treat his gout in the hot waters and took a holiday at the same time.[188] It was here in the early first century A.D. that Poppaeus Sabinus, governor of the combined province of Moesia, Macedonia, and Achaea, received a delegation from the Thessalian *koinon*, though it is not clear if he had come to take the waters. Inscriptions show the presence of groups of businessmen and imperial freedmen, and there are examples of donations from Roman emperors.[189] But a cross section of people attended the springs. The tomb inscription of Diogenianos from Nicomedia, who was a sea captain, records how he came to Aidepsos for the thermal spring and died there. "But now as navigator I remain at the hot springs of Aidepsos. So, bitter fate has laid it out for me to bathe by the road."[190] The community built on the springs flourished into the fourth century A.D. The thermal waters are still operative, and the modern town of Loutra Aidepsou has restricted the possibilities for excavation. However, the remains of a bathing establishment have been identified, dating perhaps to the second and third centuries A.D.[191]

Baiae and Aidepsos were probably atypical in size and importance, but other lesser-known spas had buildings and large numbers of guests, as everywhere the Romans set out to put their stamp on the natural environment.[192] Other sites mentioned by ancient writers have yielded archaeological remains and inscriptions showing sophisticated resorts offering specific cures, with some specially built facilities for curative bathing. In Italy, Aquae Sinuessanae near Sinuessa on the Campanian coast at the foot of Mount Massicus, was a stylish gathering place and famous not only for the restorative properties of the local waters but also for the mild climate. The rich and famous repaired there, such as Narcissus in A.D. 54, worn out by the intrigues of Claudius's court, and Tigellinus in the reign of Otho.[193] However, we cannot tell for what perceived benefit T. Caunius Priscus, legate of the emperor and consul designate, chose to set up an inscription in Lambaesis in honor of the Aquae Sinuessanae, along with his wife and his two children.[194]

Another site well known because of imperial patronage was Aquae Cutiliae, which was close to the birthplace of Vespasian in the Sabine country. Both Vespasian and Titus visited the cold springs here, though, as it happened, both of them died soon after. Vespasian used to spend every summer there and was judged to have used the cold waters too freely during his last illness.[195] This was an elegant and substantial bathing installation with a large pool (60 by 24 meters) and a depth of 1.80 meters; a sophisticated hydraulic system was probably intended to supply water to the pool as well as the nearby nymphaeum.[196]

Fons Aponi near Patavium was a long-established thermal site frequently mentioned by ancient writers and particularly important in the imperial period.[197] With its sulfurous vapors, it was a "public respite from illness" and a "communal support for doctors." It brought "unpaid healing," implying perhaps that the medicinal waters were provided free of charge. In the popular view the spring's curative properties were divinely inspired to help weak human bodies, and a draft of its water could heal many ills and restore lost energy without the need for surgery or other potions. In the fifth century, Cassiodorus still refers to it as a "bringer of healing" (*salutiferus*), and according to Ennodius (bishop of Pavia in the fifth century), it was "bringer of vapors" (*fumifer*) and healed bodies with a combination of heat and water and fumes.[198]

The whole site of Fons Aponi had a pleasant aspect with fertile land all around, and the natural hot water that bubbled out of the source was led to an elegant bathing establishment, where the temperature could be adjusted by addition of cold water.[199] The buildings were impressively decorated in the thermal spring zone, including a bath complex with a large bath probably dating from early first century A.D., a pipe to bring the hot water, and an *aedes publica*. There were also sacred buildings and many votive offerings including models of feet.[200] The visitors represented a cross section of Roman society, including Cassius Severus, a discharged praetorian and *speculator*; Proculus, a local magistrate; a freedman; and a soldier of legion XIII Gemina.[201]

Aquae Tauri near Civitavecchia, which is mentioned by Namatianus as notable for its sulfurous fumes, had a specially designed bathing establishment to suit thermal springs, with large pools, easy access, and benches to sit in the water. Lead pipes in the floor brought hot water from the spring.[202] The site of the springs Aquae Caeretanae, which has been identified at Piano della Carlotta (Cerveteri),[203] also had a large bathing complex with pools, dating from the first to the third century A.D.[204] At Teanum (Teano), excavations have revealed a Roman bathing establishment close to mineral springs some distance from the town; there were at least twenty-seven rooms with elegant decoration, mosaic floors, and many statues, including one river-god; there was also an inn nearby.[205] This is interesting because the site is little known from other sources, yet was clearly well equipped with facilities. Similarly, at Castelforte the bath buildings, which were not connected with any town, perhaps had associations with thermal springs, and it is possible that there was a kind of hospital (*valetudinarium*) for sick visitors, which implies an extensive infrastructure and emphasizes the curative role of the springs.[206]

Outside Italy, the Romans developed or tolerated spas they encountered in the territories they ruled and often identified local gods with a Greco-Roman counterpart.[207] When new buildings in the Roman style were added to spas, part of the effect if not the intention was to impress the local population. It is likely that the Roman army used the water of hot springs as a cure for soldiers, and that the army was involved in the development of spas along the upper Rhine.[208] At Aquae Mattiacorum (Wiesbaden) just north of the crucial juncture of the Main and the Rhine, the bath complex was extensive, including a swimming bath, four shallow baths, and private cubicles. The thermal medicinal bath and sanatorium were intended to serve not only the local garrison but also the soldiers and officers of legion XXII Primigenia stationed at nearby Mogontiacum. It probably also catered for the local population.[209] The goddess Diana in the form Diana Mattiaca was associated with the spring's healing powers, as was Apollo. Life at the spa is illustrated by an inscription erected by the wife of a legionary legate T. Porcius Rufianus giving thanks for the recovery of the health of their daughter Porcia Rufiana.[210] At Aquae Granni (Aachen) in Lower Germany, circa A.D. 80, the soldiers built baths above hot sulfur springs, which along with a large temple formed a health center seemingly for the use of the troops.[211]

There was also a strong military presence at Aquae Helveticae (Baden), near the legionary base at Vindonissa; the hot springs were situated on both sides of a sharp bend in the river Limmat, a tributary of the Rhine, and the military road from Augusta Raurica to Vindonissa and thence to Raetia passed through and crossed the river. In the bathing pool there were seats below water level, and no heating system was necessary. Many votive offerings have been unearthed, and a large building with many rooms in which medical instruments were discovered has been identified as a hospital for the legionaries. By A.D. 69 the spa had grown into a reasonably sized town, which attracted many visitors who came to take the waters in pleasant surroundings; it was sacked by Aulus Caecina in A.D. 69 but subsequently recovered.[212]

Bourbonne-les-Bains near Andematunnum (Langres) in Upper Germany is located on a minor road and is not an important traffic junction, but it has been argued that this was the earliest spa outside the Mediterranean provinces, possibly dating from the late first century B.C., and that it may have been established for soldiers at a nearby military base.[213] Among roughly 5,000 Roman coins mainly of low denominations discovered at the bottom of the installation to catch water from the thermal spring, there is an enormous proportion of Augustan coins. Perhaps the Romans introduced the practice of throwing coins into thermal springs and at Bourbonne soldiers threw in an offering on behalf of the emperor.

In Gaul communications were very important and spas were associated not only with roads but also with the watery framework of rivers and river crossings. Much work has been done in an attempt to identify potential thermal sites, their buildings, and links with divinities associated with water.[214] Several locations were clearly of great significance. For example, we may take the impressive group of sites grouped around the valley of the Elaver (Allier). Boubon-l'Archambault at a road junction near a tributary of the Elaver had two warm water sources, and one cold with high iron content; a substantial complex of buildings grew up. Aquae Neri (Néris-les-Bains) stood at a road junction from which a road led north to Bourbon and south to another thermal site at Evaunum; it also lay in a river valley of a tributary of the Cares, which in turn flowed into the Liger (Loire). Among the extensive remains, two swimming pools have been identified. Nerius was the local spirit. Aquae Calidae (Vichy) was located on the Elaver and close to other smaller tributaries; it was also on the road from Augustonemetum. Although the site was in use in pre-Roman times it was substantially developed in the imperial period and numerous *ex voto* offerings have been discovered.[215]

In Britain, at Aquae Sulis (Bath), an important ford of the river Abona (Avon) and the meeting point of several roads, there were three hot springs. The main spring was in the King's Bath; of the other two the Hetlin was the hotter with a temperature of 48°C. All three springs were a focus of religious activity in the Roman period and had probably been an object of reverence long before the Romans came. In the Celtic world watery places were endowed with especial religious significance; they represented locations where the under-world communicated with the real world. The Temple of Sulis Minerva stood immediately to the north of the bathing establishment, which was grandiose with a suite of heated rooms and thermal swimming baths, axially arranged and visually integrated with the spring.[216] Among the many votive offerings are several from soldiers "for the welfare of . . ." and others from a cross section of ordinary people, such as stonecutters and sculptors.[217]

There seems to have been a substantial concentration of thermal establish-ments in northern Spain, in many cases going back to pre-Roman times and partly associated with the Roman network of roads crossing the peninsula as well as river valleys.[218] Under Roman influence, indigenous divinities blended in with the cult of the nymphs, and there was a degree of acculturation. In northwest Spain, indigenous cults tended to prevail because of limited Ro-manization, whereas in the northeast divinities from the classical pantheon preside.[219] The most important sites in the area were at Aquae Celenae, Aquae Querquernae with a bathing establishment, and Aquae Flaviae, all of which are mentioned in the Antonine Itinerary.

There were different circumstances in Africa, where the Romans in the prov-ince and Romanized Africans frequented specially built centers around ther-mal springs.[220] These *aquae* sites are scattered and were usually associated with neighboring towns, and people had to travel to them, since it was too difficult to transport the water. Since these sites were associated with therapeutic quali-ties, they tended to develop facilities for the visitors,[221] and some sites were very significant, notably Aquae Dacicae in Mauretania Tingitana in the valley of the el Hamma River near a sulfurous spring, which was piped to several pools.[222] Other sites, especially in Numidia and Mauretania, were closely connected with the army. Most of the deities at African spas were Greco-Roman, such as Ascle-pius and Hygia, but although the development of spas had much to do with Romanization, many will have been known to locals before the Romans ar-rived.[223]

In the Near East, there has been an important investigation into the location of hot springs in Israel, which are particularly interesting because of rabbinic literature.[224] In Jewish ideology, an aura of mystery surrounded such springs, and in rabbinic texts it was recognized that hot springs were popular and im-portant to the local people and occasioned many questions for rabbis. The sages had to back down from banning the springs at Tiberias, where there were also non-Jewish visitors.[225] The hot springs at Hammat Gader near Tiberias, which are mentioned by Eunapius, were apparently of particular importance. An inscription ascribed to the empress Eudocia in the mid-fifth century praises the springs for their beauty, healing powers, and mixture of hot, cold, and tepid waters.[226]

Only in a small number of cases are we well informed about thermal and curative sites. Unfortunately more typical is the example of the curative springs at Scaptopara, which we hear about by accident, while a passing comment by Vitruvius on the spring of Salmacis in Greece, which was specially noted for its taste and clarity, is our only evidence that it had a nearby inn that attracted visitors.[227] Similarly, Aquae Hypsitanae in Sardinia is little known, but an inscription recording a vow from an important man, Q. Baebius Modestus, prefect of Sardinia, to the nymphs for his good health, gives a glimpse of the potential importance of the site.[228] Elsewhere in less fashionable areas in the Danube provinces, thermal springs were frequented at least by Roman officials, for example, at Aquae Balissae and Aquae S. near Sarajevo.[229]

11   MANAGEMENT OF SPAS

Our information about thermal and curative springs, even in cases of abundant archaeological evidence, is limited and particularly so in terms of the management and organization of establishments. The most important point is that the spas and attendant activities were sometimes run by private individuals and perhaps occasionally by local city governments, and that the Roman government intervened only if specifically approached or if there were problems. These local ventures received sporadic benefactions from important people and occasionally from emperors. At *mons Dianae Tifatinae*, Sulla dedicated springs to Diana (possibly associated with Mefitis) "well known for their wholesomeness and ability to heal," and all the surrounding land.[230] Later, Augustus constructed a map of the area, and the original lands were eventually restored by Vespasian.[231] Presumably the temple and its officials were responsible for managing the spring. We hear about one Velleius Urbanus, who was *magister* of the shrine of Diana Tifatina.[232] In the case of the famous source of the river Clitumnus, Pliny explains how Augustus presented the site to the community of Hispellum. The community maintained a bathing place "at the town's expense" and also an inn, which was presumably self-financing.[233]

An inscription from the area of Augusta Traiana in Thrace circa A.D. 162–63, in the governorship of Tullius Maximus, is very important for the light it sheds on the contribution of local people to the maintenance of hot springs and also their place in the community. "Ulpius Hieronymus from Nicomedia, high priest of the imperial cult, provided at his own expense for the holy nymphs and the glorious city of Augusta Traiana, a bathing establishment, two changing rooms, a cold room, and a nymphaeum from the foundations, with every kind of decoration for them and the statues, and a reservoir; and he also brought in cold water; his wife Valeria Frontonilla shared the priesthood with him, and he bestowed all the expenses during the time of his priesthood."[234] The building of the channel for cold water indicates that this was a thermal establishment where the natural temperature of the water was too hot for bathing. We see here civic pride, the importance of thermal bathing establishments as a way of enhancing a town's status (and perhaps economic position), and the role of rich individuals in sustaining the expenditure. It is not clear how maintenance costs were met, but perhaps there was a small charge for use. We may compare the management of other baths, which were often privately run for profit by individuals, or the subject of generous endowments by the wealthy. It is also possible that a town might lease its spa to a business manager (*conductor*), who would contract to run it and make it pay. We hear nothing of fees being charged at spas, and the ancient commentators assume that they are freely available. It is possible, however, that fees were charged at least at private spas.[235] A large factor in the cost of thermal spring establishments will have been the employment of staff. There is virtually no evidence for this, and we should probably not expect to find a record of staff since they will have been generally poor, often slaves or freedmen, and not likely to set up monuments that might record their presence. Many were presumably employed temporarily, for example as barbers, porters, or cloakroom attendants. The evidence of the Spanish silver bowl shows at least three attendants working at this site.[236] They seem to be young boys (perhaps slaves) and are engaged in looking after the visitors and filling water jugs or containers. This snapshot may give us an idea of how small spas were staffed.

12   CONCLUSION: "AS LONG AS A MAN IS
      AT THE WATERS HE IS NEVER DEAD"

Among ancient writers the idea of the cleansing force of running water was commonplace, and it was combined with recognition of aquatic healing power especially in thermal springs, neatly summed up in Cicero's proverb. That they were expressing a widely held view can be seen from the number of offerings to rivers and springs and the numerous locations designated *aquae* or *fons* throughout the territory of the Roman Empire. These sites highlight the geographical spread of Roman influence and activities, and also the detailed mapping of the topography of the assets of imperial rule. With their Roman names and religious associations, and Roman-designed buildings, they were in a sense an expression of the conqueror's exploitation of the natural environment. Certainly the presence of so many spas on a quasi-official source like the Peutinger Map suggests that these were important, easily recognizable landmarks in the Roman world and also perhaps of importance in cultural and social terms. If it is right to suggest that the map was not all entirely or mainly for practical purposes and had the purpose of boosting the educated reader's pride in the empire by creating a large attractive tableau of imperial geography,[237] then the appearance of spas again suggests that these were significant in the cultural and social life of the empire as part of sophisticated amenities now recognized as characteristically Roman. The interest they excited led to a genuine debate on the nature, value, and use of such resources and their preservation. Here there was an interface of scientific inquiry (into the curative properties of springs and rivers) and the miraculous events associated with the divine attributes of these great natural phenomena.

However, at a local level, the history of rivers and springs as healers once again shows the pride and honor in promoting the power of the nearby river or spring and providing good facilities. In parochial rivalry, to have a well-known watery source in your locality put you ahead of your neighbors. There was a range of connection, only vaguely discernible, between local communities when neighbors and those from further afield came to visit the springs and rivers, since they fitted into a pattern of road communication and also the watery framework of rivers and their tributaries and accessible river valleys. In this interchange there was also the possibility of real commercial advantage. The rich helped out in the provision, maintenance, and restoration of facilities, as in many other local ventures and amenities. There was also interaction and a channel of communications with the government as important people came to visit, and in some cases even the emperor arrived. However, the administration of thermal centers was largely carried on by local people, while the central government remained passive.

The long-standing belief in the divine inspiration for the healing power of thermal springs, mythology, the personal generosity of Roman officials, and the provision of sophisticated facilities, are all nicely illustrated in two verse epigrams (probably of the fourth century) from Havza (Thermae Phazimonitarum in Helenopontos), celebrating the restoration of the local baths by Jovinus, "best of governors"; one poem greets the nymphs, who are the guardians of the beautiful waters, and Hephaestus, who supplies the heat. And now Jovinus has provided a splendid crown, that is, a fitting building for the nymphs, who can mingle with the lovely graces (often associated with baths).[238]

Ten

ROME IN CONTROL OF THE WATERS

"I compelled the rivers to flow wherever I wanted, and I wanted them (to flow) wherever it was beneficial. I taught the barren land how to be cultivated for I touched it with my own rivers." This uplifting story in Polyaenus's *Strategemata* celebrates some of the exploits of Queen Semiramis, which equaled those of any man. The point of the story was the importance of tough, direct action by a leader, but there was also a kind of imperial moral, in that great kings and queens could exercise control over natural forces and use this power to bestow benefits, in this case with river water channeled into irrigation.[1] The idea of control over a river as a demonstration and confirmation of imperial power is splendidly illustrated by the story of how Alexander the Great found that the Persian kings had stored in their treasury at Susa water brought from the river Nile and the river Danube, in order to demonstrate the size of their empire and their dominion over the entire world.[2]

The Romans would certainly have approved of these stories and recognized their implications. As the Elder Pliny had observed, Rome was the master of the world, and it would befit the imperial people to ensure that the world's bounty was not wasted.[3] The steady acquisition of control over watery assets through the republic was followed by a more benevolent willingness to distribute them or to enhance opportunities for access to them. The Roman emperor, as Father of the Fatherland, was responsible for his people in Italy, and resources and manpower were expended in overcoming the climatic uncertainties of the Mediterranean area. The benefits of the watery environment could then be shared with provincial communities on the basis of need or imperial advantage. In any case it was not in Rome's interest to disturb the established place of rivers at the heart of local communities, where they reinforced identity and had strong cultural and religious associations. As Rome formally occupied riverine territory, so in a sense it inherited and absorbed the psychological support of the traditional sanction and alliance of the local river. This was one of the many complex factors linking rivers to the strategic disposition of the Roman army.

This chapter considers riverine symbolism in the conceits of Roman writers and imperial iconography on Rome's mastery of rivers, these same rivers as allies of the imperial administration, and the consequences for river ideology when people imagined the breakdown of Roman control. An epilogue presents some concluding comments.

1   RIVERS AS SYMBOLS: CONQUEST

The Greek sophist Aelius Aristides, in his famous speech in praise of Rome in the mid-second century A.D., made the point that natural obstacles never stopped the Romans: "You have surveyed the whole inhabited world, built bridges of all sorts across rivers, cut down mountains to make paths for carriages, filled the deserts with way stations, and civilized all with system and order."[4] More prosaically, an inscription of the fourth century from Sïresa (Huesca) in Spain celebrates how, on imperial instructions, the governor repaired a road "notorious for its boulders and subject to frequent flooding by river water, after it had been leveled, the ground pacified and the hostile river entirely tamed."[5] Pliny had put to Trajan the idea of the nobility of controlling the environment, as he tried to interest the emperor in a project to build a waterway to connect the lake near Nicomedia with the nearby river: "The project is worthy . . . of your outstanding position."[6] And in a letter to Caninius Rufus, who was planning to write a poem about Trajan's Dacian War, Pliny offered advice on worthy themes: "You will tell of new rivers sent flowing over the land, new bridges built across rivers, and military camps holding fast to lofty peaks."[7] To defeat a courageous enemy was a noble theme, but mastery over the natural environment was no less important, and it is notable that, in his list of "fabulosa material," he chooses to start with Roman feats of engineering in which Trajan overcame natural obstacles, mainly watery ones.

Emperors, as the embodiment of the res Romana, must overcome all obstacles of terrain and natural phenomena to advance the empire. But how were such ideas to be expressed or represented in public? On the one hand, Roman ideology was naturally aggressive, but on the other a more subtle approach could pay dividends in winning the support of local people. This had much to do with perceptions of space and the riverine environment, since rivers helped to provide a framework for the geographical and topographical space in the Roman world. Rivers also had long-standing religious and cultural associations, both regionally and across smaller areas, which did much to reinforce local identity. In addition, they facilitated movement and contact between communities and peoples, stood out as landmarks, and helped to measure distances and demarcate boundaries. As such, they were an integral part of all geographical writing and mapmaking. The ability to divide and assign land, draw up and adjudicate boundaries, keep records and maps, and allocate water resources was one symbol of the ruling authority. Therefore, the background to rivers and the power of Rome is complex.

The very act of crossing a river was not just a physical act but had religious and psychological implications. Hesiod's traveler washed his hands at a river and said a simple prayer,[8] but great peoples or kings on major ventures saw river crossings as a crucial and sometimes fraught undertaking. In the adventures of the Israelites, river boundaries and river crossings and other natural landmarks were at the heart of the search for land. So the Lord's instructions to Joshua were: "Arise, go over this Jordan, thou, and all this people, unto the land which I do give them, even to the children of Israel. . . . From the wilderness and this Lebanon even unto the great river, the river Euphrates, all the land of the Hittites, and unto the great sea toward the going down of the sun, shall be your coast."[9] Mystery and a new world lay beyond rivers, and new lands to conquer. A potentially hostile river-god would need to be placated. As Alexander the Great prepared to cross the Indus, which Arrian described as the greatest river of Asia and Europe except the Ganges, he sacrificed to the local gods, held athletic and equestrian games beside the river, and gained favorable omens for crossing.[10] It is no surprise, therefore, that Roman soldiers preparing to embark on the invasion of Britain in A.D. 43 mutinied, claiming that crossing Oceanus would mean a campaign beyond the limits of the known world.[11] There may have been other reasons for their reluctance, but their expression of this idea shows the strength of feeling about the natural barrier of water.

In the thought world of Roman writers, the generals or leaders of Rome gained control of rivers with all their cultural and mythological connotations and religious aura, and that emanation was then conferred on them. Yet, other peoples revered their own rivers; the Histri, for example, swore by the Danube before going into battle.[12] If rivers were seen as inspiring a national war effort, the warriors might despair at the loss of their river and its banks to the Romans, who had appeased or subdued the power of the river spirit. As early as the fourth century B.C., in the events allegedly leading up to the capture of Veii in 396 B.C., tradition had it that an old man of Veii mysteriously prophesied that the Romans would not take Veii until the waters of the Alban Lake had been drained. He then lectured them on the best method for extracting the water. The senate had already sent messengers to Delphi to inquire about the lake's abnormal height. The reply of the Pythian Apollo confirmed the old man's prophecy: "Roman, do not allow the Alban water to be confined within its own lake, do not allow it to flow to the sea in its own course. You will let it out and water your fields with it; you will disperse it in channels and extinguish its power. Then boldly attack the enemy walls."[13] It hardly matters that this story was one of the many fabulous tales associated with the fall of Veii, of which Livy was rather dismissive.[14] It indicates that, in popular imagination, the pre-ordained victory of the early Roman Republic, territorial encroachment, and nascent political control are closely linked with the mastery over watery resources; to extinguish the power of the water is tantamount to the conquest of a hostile people.

By the first century A.D. the watery interest of Rome had moved much further afield. Mighty rivers such as the Danube, Rhine, Euphrates, and Nile framed its horizons. For example, the Romans thought that the Rhine was a great river and took it into their own riverine ideology. Martial describes the Rhine as "father of nymphs and rivers," therefore emphasizing its place in the riverine hierarchy.[15] This as usual was the Roman viewpoint, though Tacitus makes an effort to give the German view. The rebel Civilis addressing his followers proclaimed: "The marshes are the Romans' enemy. Before your eyes are the Rhine, and the Gods of Germany. Join battle under their divine support."[16] Here the Rhine is part of the emotional and cultural leadership of Germany. Of course, once it was within Roman power, the Rhine could represent the defeat of the whole German nation.

Therefore, rivers were legitimate objects of conquest, and although they were powerful, destructive, and unpredictable, there was no doubt that they could and should be mastered, since control of the water or the waterway represented the next step in acquiring further territory beyond the water. In the Roman view, the gods assisted the operation of natural processes, and emperors represented themselves as having divine support in their service of the empire. Therefore, since rivers were often regarded as gods or at least as having some divine characteristics, it was reasonable that river-gods too, once won over by imperial might and justice, would lend their efforts to supporting the emperor. Tacitus recounts how a German tribe, the Ampsivarii, approached Rome seeking permission to settle on vacant land and appealing to the gods. But the Roman governor Duvius Avitus replied bluntly that they must obey the orders of their betters, for the gods they were imploring had given the decision to the Romans.[17] The ambitious first prefect of Egypt, Cornelius Gallus, in his grandiloquent inscription celebrating his military achievements beyond the cataracts of the Nile, included his native gods "and the supporting Nile."[18]

In fact, the very act of crossing or bridging a river indicated Roman superiority and suggested the diminishment of the opposition's geographical space, symbolized by its river's loss of status and even volume. To reach a mighty river and demonstrate your presence on the bank indicated an appropriation of surrounding territory, and we recall how Drusus optimistically set up trophies on the Elbe.[19] According to Statius, Domitian's bridge over the river Liris had an arch at its approach with triumphal statuary.[20] This kind of trophy, in friendly territory and involving no kind of military action, suggests real pride in crossing rivers and shows the value of celebrating triumph over the natural elements.[21] The theme of the Romans' domination of the riverine environment, which then becomes a potent symbol of Rome's ability to control not only natural phenomena but also other peoples, appears in the conceits of writers of the imperial period. The river was a kind of symbolic weapon in which its cultural and religious powers and influences were transferred to the Romans. Therefore, passage along a river was not just a matter of the occupation of territory, but amounted to control of a whole social and cultural nexus. This public articulation of triumph over nature and riverine domination introduced a psychological dimension, as against more practical manifestations of Roman control. The place of rivers in imperial ideology and their psychological and cultural significance, especially on riverbanks and at confluences, are most strikingly illustrated by ceremonies at Mogontiacum in honor of Germanicus, who died in A.D. 19.[22] These events combined military pageantry with honor for the imperial family and were held on the banks of the Rhine at its confluence with the Main, confirming the Roman presence and absorbing the local riverine community into the Roman ideology of commemoration.

The defeat of personified river figures is a recurrent theme in poets and other writers. Horace, proposing to sing of Augustus's new triumphs, speaks of the Euphrates as having been added to defeated peoples and flowing with diminished eddies, just as the Geloni (a Scythian tribe) now must ride their horses across a narrower plain within their assigned area.[23] Similarly, Virgil describes a long procession of conquered peoples among whom some are distinguished by peculiarities of dress or weaponry, others by geographical location or their neighboring river, which had been suitably chastened, in particular the two-horned Rhine, the Euphrates now flowing with reduced impetus, and the Araxes in Armenia, furious at being bridged.[24] The same idea of the active hostility of a river appears in Silius Italicus, who describes soldiers invading the surging waters of the river Rhône, which is hostile to bridges.[25] In the words of Ovid, victory in Germany and triumphal celebrations came as the Rhine offered up its waters to be Germanicus's slaves.[26] Statius in a poem addressed to Maecius Celer, describes how, on his return from the wars, he will tell stories about the rapid Euphrates and the famous crossing point at Zeugma, "the route of the Roman peace."[27] The poet imagines the way across the subdued river as part of the process of the imposition of Roman control. Rivers can have feelings, and mourn the defeat of their people at the hands of Rome. Propertius admits that he is a poet of soft themes and not of war, and therefore declines to describe how Rome drives back the German hordes, or how "the savage Rhine stained with German blood carries along the mangled bodies in its sad waters."[28] When the emperor Julian's army defeated the Germans in Strasbourg in 357, Ammianus similarly describes how the Rhine was amazed to see its waters augmented by floods of German blood.[29]

In the same way the Younger Pliny, in his Panegyric addressed to Trajan, gives the personified Rhine and Danube human emotions; they can recognize and delight in Roman disgrace, if the emperor fails to act decisively and courageously. Part of the emperor's duty is to maintain the riverbank as Roman property since rivers can become a danger because of weak emperors.[30] He sees Trajan's battle with the Danube in personal terms; when the river froze over and Rome's enemies seemed to be armed, not with weapons but the very climate, a strong emperor scared them away.[31] On the other hand, insolent kings who provoked Trajan would not be protected by seas, or large rivers, or high mountains; all these will give way to Trajan's *virtus*.[32] Rivers, therefore, even though majestic or aggressive, can never be an obstacle to Roman advance.

In this context, it was entirely appropriate to describe a general's conquests in terms of rivers added to the empire, as Cicero did with Caesar: "Future generations will certainly be astonished when they hear and read about your commands and the provinces you have gained—the Rhine, Ocean, the Nile, countless battles, amazing victories."[33] In the imagination of Lucan, Caesar's soldiers lamented the shedding of their blood in northern lands in conquering the Rhône and the Rhine, only to face the prospect of civil war.[34] Elsewhere he says that Caesar put chains on the Rhine.[35] In physical terms, images of conquered rivers were carried in Caesar's triumphal procession, the Rhine, the Rhône, and Ocean fashioned from gold.[36] This was the most effective riposte to the incident during the Gallic wars, when German tribes replied arrogantly to Caesar's demand for the return of men who had joined in attacks against the Romans: "The Rhine marked the limits of the power of the Roman people." Caesar had no right to interfere beyond it.[37]

Augustus and his family followed this practice of triumphal celebration. According to Tacitus, in Germanicus's triumph of A.D. 17, as well as booty and captives, images of mountains, rivers, and battles were carried.[38] Poets did not have to stick to what had been accomplished, and Ovid on several occasions speculates on future Augustan triumphal processions, in which the Euphrates and Tigris will appear with appropriate imagery, the former with reeds, the latter with blue-colored hair. Later he returns to the same theme; lakes, mountains, rivers, and forts will establish the context of remorseless Roman military conquest. Our writers understood about the traditional attributes of rivers and could vividly express a reversal of fortune by disordering those attributes.[39] The Rhine is depicted with horns (its typical attribute), but now broken; the river is covered in green slime and marred by the red German blood in the water, and no longer looks like a healthy stream.[40] So the sparkling river surrounded by flourishing reeds becomes grubby (*squalidus*) and disfigured and the reeds are crushed.[41] Propertius imagines the Nile (flowing weakly now) being brought to Rome with its seven captive streams for Augustus's triumph.[42]

In psychological terms, the ability of a government and its agents to draw and display maps in public places indicated imperial status. According to the size of the area depicted, be it region, province, empire, or the entire known world, the map would show areas controlled by your armies, or areas where you intended to go. And the ability to discover and record information and construct a map was tantamount to claiming domination over rivers and other natural features depicted in them, as well as the associated resources and peoples. In practical terms, once roads, rivers, mountains and other features had been mapped, the government could send its armies and administrators wherever it wished. Maps therefore expressed a kind of imperial ideology, as in the case of Agrippa's famous map in Rome.[43]

In the imaginative context of Roman writers, warfare sometimes was symbolically a contest between rival rivers. The Tiber, of course, reigned supreme; Ennius had established the tone with his description; "river that is the leader among all," and that was followed by Virgil's "lord of the waters," and in the rhetoric of the second century "the river Tiber, master and lord of the waters flowing around."[44] It was not difficult to predict that in Augustus's future conquest of Parthia the Euphrates would flow beneath the rule (*iura*) of the Tiber.[45] Defeat might mean a reduction in the power of the rival river, but ideally that would only be temporary, since the river, duly restored to full standing, would then be in the service of the Roman conquerors. To have the biggest or most revered rivers was part of world domination and brought other rivers and their peoples into your orbit, and a mighty territorial empire would bring dignity to your native rivers. So Virgil describes the Tiber as the most honored in heaven and lord of rivers, even though it was dwarfed by rivers such as the Rhine and

Danube.[46] Here the Tiber was a reflection of Rome's mighty empire. With military came cultural superiority, and into the fifth century the Tiber continued to represent the pinnacle of Latin culture to which outsiders might aspire. Sidonius Apollinaris recounts how Arbogastes, the Frankish count of Trier, had written an eloquent Latin letter to him asking for a theological work. Sidonius replied that, although Arbogastes lived among barbarians, he really was quite civilized, which he expressed as follows: "Though you now drink the waters of the Moselle, the words you utter are those of the Tiber."[47]

Since emperors came from the upper classes, understood their prejudices, and responded to their way of thinking in the treatment of foreign peoples, imperial iconography and the presentation of the emperor's role reflected senatorial expectations. In turn, the works of poets and other writers were partly a response to that iconography and the role of emperors in presiding over the natural world and mastering rivers and their peoples. All this fitted easily into the terminology used to describe the emperor and his subjects, in which he appeared as a noble savior and protector of the world. So Tiberius told the people of the Greek city of Gythium: "I consider it fitting that all men in general and your city in particular should reserve special honors befitting the gods in keeping with the greatness of my father's (Augustus's) services to the whole world."[48] Emperors, of course, frequently intervened to restore communities from natural disasters, offer help and guidance, and provide amenities. Emperors' public celebration of their mastery of the natural environment was more subtle (so it can be argued) than mere triumphalism. The production and display of maps and itineraries showing the known world, and Rome's ability to get anywhere in it by road, river, or sea, as well as expressing the power of the conqueror also showed Rome working with the natural environment and making areas more accessible. In Roman art, personification of the river spirit as a bearded man allowed imperial iconography, through the minting of coins and the creation of statues, monuments, and architectural tableaux, to place the emperor in imposing scenes where he enjoyed the benevolent support of a river-god and displayed his ability to overcome or win over the powers of nature for the benefit of Rome. In addition, the depiction of river-gods often showed them in turn as masters of the surrounding watery environment.[49] In formal presentations the Romans had one eye on the visual and emotional impact of well-known natural phenomena and the important position of rivers in the psychology of communities. This was the artistic expression of the ideology apparent in an inscription set up at Philae in the time of Augustus celebrating the deep eddies of the Nile, which ensure that Egypt will be forever prosperous

FIGURE 14. *Scene from Trajan's Column showing the bearded figure of the river Danube ushering the Roman army across the river on a bridge at the start of the invasion of Dacia (F. Lepper and S. Frere,* Trajan's Column *(Gloucester, 1988), plates VI–VII). Image reproduced with the kind permission of Professor Sheppard Frere.*

"for the good fortune of Caesar." In the writer's mind the power of the river peacefully enriches the province in the interests of the emperor.[50]

Nevertheless, river iconography does have a strong theme of physical domination. According to Statius, Domitian erected in the forum a colossal equestrian statue, with the emperor in military dress and his horse's right hoof on head of the river-god of the Rhine. The statue was also celebrated on the coinage.[51] This aggressive imagery may reflect Domitian's desire for military glory, witnessed by his many wars and triumphs and imperator acclamations. The coherent architectural context of the columns of Trajan and Marcus Aurelius offered the sculptors the opportunity to think about the great river Danube in the context of prolonged Roman military campaigns. Here too the crossing of the river, this time in a military context, predominates. By gesture and presence, the river-god who emerges from his river supports the Roman advance psychologically, and also physically, by seeming to usher the troops across the river; he willingly accepts the bridge over which the Romans cross by appearing underneath it, and the river, now a Roman river, provides a route of transport for the troops. In a sense, the river, along with the emperor, oversees the Roman advance (figure 14).[52] The bridge itself also seems to have celebratory trophies depicted on it.

The construction of great triumphal arches, which in part symbolized Rome's domination over important routes, was another element linking rivers to imperial triumphs. On the country side of the Arch of Trajan at Beneventum is depicted a kneeling female figure along with two river-deities; the most likely interpretation is that the figure represents Dacia, with the rivers Tisza and Alu-tus demarcating the boundaries of the province. On the same side of the arch in the spandrels are two half-naked figures; one, old and bearded, probably represents the Danube, the other, more youthful, is likely to be the Tisza.[53] The Arch of Septimius Severus in Rome also has important river iconography, referring to his defeat of the Parthians and the absorption of the Euphrates within Roman control in the new province of Mesopotamia.[54] Casual observers did not need to identify individual rivers. To them it would seem like a triumphal display of probably well-known river iconography.

It is worth emphasizing that the representation of the Euphrates in human form dates from Roman times.[55] An inscription circa A.D. 73 from Ayni on the banks of the Euphrates between Samosata and Zeugma celebrates the construction on the authority of Vespasian and Titus of a device to raise water from the river; the personified river is depicted on the inscription and is associated with another inscription referring to the legion III Gallica.[56] Imperial interest and control of the watery resources, the military presence, and the presiding river all come together to celebrate the pervasive power of Rome. Furthermore, it seems that there was a filtering down of iconography to the rest of the population. In a funeral monument probably of the early third century set up by a veteran of the legion XXX living at Lugdunum, the river Rhône and probably the Saône are depicted. This river was now a thoroughly Roman river and had a symbolic role to play in the triumph of the empire. The rivers could be interpreted as a triumphal emblem of Roman official art, which would be appropriate for a soldier's memorial.[57]

Certain riverine coin types particularly emphasize imperial ideology and the successes of imperial policy.[58] The ambience is often belligerent; rivers in frontier zones, such as the Rhine and the Danube, became part of the military establishment, assisted the war effort, and demonstrated the subjection of neighboring riverine areas. Therefore, they depict emperors, the watery environment, and Roman military victory. One particularly vivid image on the coinage of Trajan portrays the Danube in human form, standing upright, placing his right knee on the female figure of Dacia, or even grasping her by the throat (figure 15).[59] Trajan has recruited the local river into the service of Rome. In general rivers are associated with military victory and the humiliation of the enemy.[60] Occasionally the emperor takes a more obviously dominant role, and a vivid image on a commemorative medallion of Severus Alexander shows the emperor treading down the Tigris and Euphrates, a reference to his campaign against the Persians.[61]

FIGURE 15. *Sestertius of Trajan, A.D. 103–11, depicting Danube, standing and placing a knee on the sitting figure of Dacia, whom he grasps by the throat. Reverse legend:* SPQR OPTIMO PRINCIPI SC *(RIC II, p. 283, no. 556; the figure of the Danube was originally wrongly identified as the Tiber). Image reproduced by kind permission of Spink and Son, London.*

2 RIVERS AS SYMBOLS: COOPERATION

Despite the generally belligerent tone of Roman writers, many coins were struck depicting rivers as benevolent allies of the Romans. A coin of Domitian of A.D. 85 shows the emperor in military dress holding a spear, while the bearded figure of the river-god (Rhine) reclines at his feet.[62] Similarly, the Danube reclines on rocks, resting his arm and right hand on a ship's prow, suggesting the river's helpful role as an ally representing the watery environment (with aquatic plants) in Trajan's campaigns. The Tigris and Euphrates are summoned as friendly representatives of the riverine environment to assist Trajan's attempt to create Roman provinces in Armenia and Mesopotamia (figure 16). The Danube appears as an ally of Marcus Aurelius, who crosses a bridge over the river at the head of his soldiers.[63]

Roman mastery of rivers naturally brought great benefit and wealth to the empire, through riverine navigation, riverine products, and trade and commerce. Consequently, for those who designed the types in the Roman mint, rivers also flowed in a tranquil context, and emperors are peacefully identified with important waterways. Such themes appear throughout the imperial period. The role of rivers in sustaining Rome's colonies abroad is celebrated in coins minted at Augusta Emerita in Baetica in the reign of Augustus. As the priest plows the sacred furrow in the foundation of the city, the head of the river-deity of the Anas spits out water.[64] A coin minted under Hadrian shows

FIGURE 16. Sestertius *of Trajan, A.D. 114–17, showing Trajan in military dress standing in the forefront holding a spear and parazonium; the figures of Armenia, Euphrates, and Tigris recline on the ground. Reverse legend:* ARMENIA ET MESOPOTAMIA IN POTESTATEM P.R. REDACTAE SC *(RIC II, p. 289, no. 642). Image reproduced by kind permission of Spink and Son, London.*

Hercules of Gades, the great port of Baetica, with a ship's prow at his feet, and to the right the river Baetis, the main riverine thoroughfare of the province.[65] The Danube, now fully incorporated into the Roman world, appears in a coin of Trajan leaning on a ship and holding a water jug; emperor and river are joined in the legend: "Danube; consul for the fifth time, Father of the Fatherland, the Senate and People of Rome to the excellent Princeps."[66] Furthermore, Trajan chose to celebrate the introduction of a new source of fresh water for Rome, the *aqua Traiana*, by depicting the river-god. Representing the spirit of the freshwater source of the aqueduct, the god reclines on rocks from which water gushes under a pleasant arched grotto; in his right hand, he holds a reed and rests his left arm on an urn (figure 17).[67] Hadrian appears with the Nile (Nilus), who reclines, leaning on a rock, holding a reed in his right hand and a cornucopia in his left; there are two children playing, and there are reeds, a hippopotamus, and a crocodile in the water.[68] This fits in with the famous statue of the river in the round from Rome, which represents the river as a great benefactor in many areas of life associated with the watery environment.[69] Furthermore, river-gods appear in the coinage of Hadrian as benevolent bringers of richness and fertility, and in the case of Antioch on the Maeander, the river is intimately linked to the success of the local community; the female personification of Antioch, wearing a tower crown, sits on a rock holding ears of grain, while the bearded river-god swims or wades below (figure 18).[70] Coins issued by Pergamum under Marcus Aurelius show its rivers, the Selinos and the Keteios, which supplied the city's aqueducts, just as the Cayster and Kenchrios

FIGURE 17. Sestertius of Trajan, A.D. 103–11, showing the river-god reclining on the left under an arched grotto supported by two columns; his left arm rests on an urn, and he holds a reed in his right hand. Reverse legend: AQUA TRAIANA S.P.Q.R. OPTIMO PRINCIPI SC (RIC II, p. 278, no. 463). Image reproduced by kind permission of Spink and Son, London.

FIGURE 18. Bronze quadrans of Hadrian, A.D. 125–28, showing Antioch as a female figure with a towered crown sitting on the left holding ears of grain and resting her right elbow on a stork perched on a rock; the river-god swims in front. Reverse legend: COS III SC. Image reproduced by permission of the American Numismatic Society.

appear on the coinage of Ephesos under Antoninus Pius.[71] Fluvial abundance is linked to the technical brilliance of the water supply.

Other coins issued by Greek cities under the emperors showing local river-spirits demonstrate how those communities and their iconography had been assimilated into the ideological structure of imperial rule and dynastic politics. The city-state, once proudly independent, was now happy to show its river operating in the service of Rome. In a sense, this was a relaxed adjustment and artistically interesting; the Romans worked with the local watery environment and respected its attributes; but they were also ruthless in taking the limelight with local riverine deities and working them into the Roman way of doing things. For example, Hadrian is honored on coins of Apollonia, which also depict a young, unbearded river-god representing the Rhyndakos; Marcus Aurelius is linked with the Hebros at Plotinopolis; at Juliopolis, Caracalla appears with the bearded Sangarius and other figures; and Elagabalus is associated with the river-god of Marcianopolis.[72]

Rivers were present in imperial, dynastic, and frontier politics, sometimes appearing with imperial women. A coin issued by Amaseia celebrating Faustina the Younger, daughter of Antoninus Pius and wife of Marcus Aurelius, depicts the bearded river-god Iris holding on to a ship's prow with his right hand and clutching a reed in his right. Similarly, a coin of Germanicopolis/Gangra in honor of Julia Domna, wife of Septimius Severus, shows the river Halys.[73] Miletus celebrated the river-god of the Maeander on the reverse of a coin that displayed a bust of Faustina on the obverse.[74] Such coins ostentatiously link the identity of cities with imperial dynasties.

Coins from several cities of Asia Minor struck under the Severan dynasty have personifications of rivers that make allusion to political events. In particular, a coin minted by Cyzicus depicts the river Aisepos, along with Septimius Severus and a trophy, and seemingly commemorates the emperor's victory over Pescennius Niger at Byzantium during the civil war.[75] The political theme is vividly illustrated by coins issued by Constantine celebrating his appointment of Hannibalianus, son of his half brother Dalmatius, as ruler of the kingdoms of Pontus and Armenia. He ultimately intended to install him as king of Persia, and the reverse of the coins depicts the Euphrates, proclaiming imperial ambitions (figure 19).[76] Another coin minted in the reign of Constantine shows an attempt to link a mighty river, now subject to Rome, in wider public policy. We see the emperor in military dress holding a spear and shield advancing across a bridge preceded by Victory holding a trophy; below the Danube rests as a suppliant; the legend is "salus Reip Danubius," bringing the river together with the well-being of the state.[77] Other coins depict the Euphrates with vari-

FIGURE 19. *Silver coin of Constantine, A.D. 335, showing Euphrates reclining on the left with his elbow on a water jug; he holds a fish in his right hand and a rudder in his left hand, with reeds in the background. Obverse legend: FL ANNIBALIANO REGI; reverse legend: FELICITAS PUBLICA (RIC VII, p. 584, no. 100). Image reproduced by kind permission of Spink and Son, London.*

ous attributes of its watery environment including aquatic plants and a ship's prow, with the legends "securitas publica" and "felicitas publica," where the great river, so well known to Romans, helps to guarantee the safety and good fortune of the *res publica*. Because rivers were involved in imperial politics, they also became embroiled in Rome's civil wars, in which they took sides. The anonymous panegyrist of Constantine gloats over his defeat of Maxentius in 312 at the Milvian Bridge, where Maxentius was drowned in the Tiber. He sees this as a fitting end for the usurper and celebrates the Tiber, who once had advised Aeneas and saved Romulus: "You sustain your Rome by bringing in supplies, you protect it with your swirling walls, and you properly wanted to be part of Constantine's victory, so that he drove the enemy into you and you killed him."[78]

3   REVERSAL OF FORTUNE

The Roman claim to mastery of the elements and dominion over rivers was susceptible to reversal of fortune.[79] In all ages, the symbolism of the calm peace of benevolent streams giving way to the destructive power of great rivers and floods implied invasion and political collapse:

Forasmuch as this people refuseth the waters of Shiloah (a local Jerusalem stream) that go softly. . . . Now therefore, behold, the Lord bringeth up upon them the waters of the river, strong and many, even the king of Assyria, and all his glory; and he shall come up over all his channels and go over all his banks. And he shall pass through Judah; he shall overflow and go over, he shall reach even to the neck.[80]

In the Roman world rivers were closely tied to imperial rule and the breakdown of control meant that they were no longer necessarily the allies of Rome. Rutilius Claudius Namatianus, in a poem describing his return to his native Gaul in 416, poignantly mentions the impossibility of traveling by land because of barbarian incursions. The Goths have already cut the *via Aurelia* through Etruria: "It is best to trust the sea because the rivers are not bridged and the land has become wild again."[81] Disorder and decline are synonymous with inability to control the natural elements in Italy. A wider but related theme was that divine retribution and upsets in nature were often thought to accompany injustice, outrages, and disasters. The prophecy of Vegoia, who was allegedly an Etruscan nymph, demonstrates the consequences of disturbing land boundaries. Those who remove boundary stones will receive retribution on their families, but nature will also make war on them with storms, whirlwinds, heavy rain, and hail.[82]

This kind of story was partly conventional, since predictions of disaster and the overturn of government were frequently accompanied by weird riverine behavior, such as the idea that rivers ran backward at times of crisis. Nevertheless, they could be linked specifically to the fate of the Roman world. Some of the more observant enemies of Rome understood the import of the conquerors' propaganda about control of nature and generous provision of amenities and shrewdly turned it to their advantage. We have from the mid-second century A.D. a discussion between rabbis, one of whom praised the Romans for establishing marketplaces, bridges, and baths. But rabbi Simeon ben Yohai replied, "All that they have established they have established only for their own benefit. They have established market places to place prostitutes in them, baths for their own pleasure, bridges to collect tolls."[83] The rabbi was punished for his subversive critique of the usual Roman claim to use and channel nature's resources for the good of its subjects.

More dramatic is the book of Revelation, which belongs to a genre of Jewish and Christian apocalyptic literature, aiming to reveal the truth of God's purpose partly through prophecy. The author imagines the overthrow of the dominating economic and political power of Rome (Babylon). During the overturning of the existing world order, seven angels appear with seven plagues: "The third angel poured his bowl on rivers and springs, and they turned to blood." The sixth angel caused the "great river Euphrates" to dry up. Finally, an earthquake brings Babylon crashing down with the disappearance of islands and mountains.[84] Certainly this vision of the reversal of the normal order vividly emphasizes the end of Rome's calm and uncontested enjoyment of the natural world, and the contamination of its prized aquatic domination.

The pseudo-Sibylline Oracles collected in the fifth century A.D. and later, contain a mixture of Judeo-Christian and pagan ideology, with predictions of destruction for cities and communities in the Roman world. In the normal run of things the Creator God decked the world with plants and mingled the sea with rivers, bestowing air and watery clouds.[85] But the Tiber will come to lament for her city.[86] In Cilicia a city was to be destroyed by deep strong rivers, and earthquakes were to come.[87] In the turmoil that will come upon the Roman Empire, rivers and springs, the givers of life, will be burned up along with the cities. And hills will be set on fire, rivers burned and springs exhausted, while the disordered world comes to an end.[88]

Despite their claims to riverine domination, the Romans would have thought that the maledictions of the book of Revelation and the Oracles rather unjust. They realized that local river identities continued to inspire interest among communities and loyalty in the riverine area. Smaller rivers were nonetheless significant and sometimes served as tributaries to the great rivers that linked them to other regions. Most rivers had their divine associations and, endued with vigorous power of procreation, were often addressed as "father," as well as being associated with the foundation and culture of regions and peoples. With their normal respect for traditional practices, the Romans welcomed local riverine lore, which Pausanias happily recounted for his Greek audience. Arrian, during his governorship of Cappadocia, wrote to Hadrian describing his tour around the coast of the Black Sea and commenting on the qualities of the river Phasis. "It is not indeed customary for those arriving by ship to bring water to the river Phasis. When they enter the river's stream an announcement is made to pour overboard all the water held on the ships. If they do not do this, the story is that all who neglect this observance do not have a lucky voyage."[89] This is a striking indication of respect for local riverine custom, which Arrian considered important enough to include in his report for the emperor. A wise emperor would see that vibrant local communities were in the Romans' interests and would wish to associate himself with them, being inclusive of their riverine traditions.

4   EPILOGUE: "THE ROMANS ALWAYS WIN"

An anonymous graffito artist from the Roman province of Arabia comments vividly on the inexorable advance of Roman power.[90] It is unlikely that he had rivers in mind, but nevertheless Rome was a river city, founded at an important ford over the river Tiber, and enjoying traditional associations with watery themes and early foundation legends involving the Tiber. From this watery storytelling about a local and moderately sized river, Rome came to absorb the rivers of the world. Writers, commentators, and mapmakers, working from a new pinnacle of geographical knowledge achieved by imperial conquest, recognized the crucial significance of rivers as highly visible natural phenomena that helped to demarcate the parameters of their world. Rome's empire was based on control of the land adjacent to the Mediterranean Sea, whose place in the Roman domain was effectively expressed as *mare nostrum*. But the empire's structure was also linked to major rivers and river valley routes, which were preeminent for strategic, economic, and cultural reasons. The Romans took rivers into their service to further their military, political, and administrative interests; whatever rivers and their locality had to offer was at the disposal of Rome, and these benefits were exploited either directly or indirectly through taxation. In one sense, rivers held the empire together, since as great markers and connectors they provided one of the ethnographic and geographic reference points of the empire. The Romans ruled people, but people occupied land and that had to be defined. As the empire developed, with its unwavering control of territorial provinces, rivers became an important part of the administrative structure, demarcating community and provincial boundaries in terms of provinces, non-Roman lands, the territory of a colony or local city, and the land of settlers or veterans or of the original inhabitants. Rivers, with their quasi-divine status and their association with local traditions made excellent boundaries and featured prominently in the measurement and notation of distance in land records, maps, and itineraries.

The Roman government coveted the physical assets of nature and recognized the imperative of controlling and exploiting watery resources, including the economic possibilities of deltas and wetlands. In the early days, territorial aggrandizement was assisted by river valleys and riverine locations. Thereafter, running water remained crucial to the developing empire. In the shifting patterns of frontier zones and the ebb and flow of warfare, rivers remained as stable anchors for the military infrastructure; supported by military roads and numerous legionary bases and forts, rivers were at least a potential and temporary refuge behind which a response to threatening forces could be organized, or along which attacks could be launched. The Romans also controlled rivers as routes of communication and avenues for commercial traffic. Domination over river routes confirmed freedom to move about the empire, the totality of Roman influence, and the effect of the *pax Romana*. Control over the sources of running water secured drinking water for local communities and also (mediated through Roman engineering skill) for the cities with their increasing populations. In Rome and other cities, plentiful supplies of water contributed to health, hygiene, and safety. Therefore, to supply or withhold water was a means of controlling others and of winning favor. Furthermore, the riverine environment and the many spas that Rome fostered offered recreation and restoration of health in mind and body. Finally, the Romans controlled the intellectual, cultural, and religious background of the watery environment of river valleys since rivers were now Roman, even if they kept their traditional names. The emotional impact of rivers at the local level should not be under-estimated. People often knew the history and mythology of their rivers; genu-ine geographical interest and geopiety combined with superstition, anecdote, and healthy fun in tales of riverine sexual indiscretions. Consequently, power-ful ideas of community identity, prosperity, wealth, and connectivity were linked to riverine culture.

The way in which riverine resources were exploited was dictated by the powerful elite in Rome or in local cities, and in the use, management, and im-provement of watery or river-borne facilities, lesser people joined in, helped, or tried to keep out of the way. Those who opposed were on the other side of river psychology, sometimes literally "the other" on the far side of a river, whom the Romans were reluctant to tolerate. Therefore, building bridges had a psychological as well as a physical importance. The dominant people had to display their prowess by allowing no riverine rivals in the vicinity. Rivers were emphatically not regarded as limiters of Roman power but rather seen as enablers of expansion and warfare and supremacy over other peoples. Con-sequently, Caesar decided to cross the Rhine partly because of the psycho-logical impact on the Germans, when they saw that the army of the Roman people had the capacity and courage to cross. Furthermore, he elected not to cross on boats, not only for safety reasons but because he felt that this would not adequately reflect his standing or that of the Roman people. It was nec-essary to demonstrate complete mastery by building a bridge, whatever the difficulties.[91] In the end, it is not surprising that subject peoples saw the natu-ral environment as yet another of Rome's conquests, identified riverine health with the well-being of the empire, recognized the emotional and psychologi-cal significance of some rivers more than others, and equated the Tiber with Roman power and the city itself. Ammianus Marcellinus, although he came from Syrian Antioch and had a Greek educational background, was the out-standing Latin historian of the fourth century. He nostalgically evokes the spe-cial position of the river Tiber and the hold that it had on Roman minds in his comments on the emperor Julian, who died in 363 without ever having set eyes on Rome or the Tiber. Reflecting on the emperor's burial place near Tarsus in Cilicia, Ammianus laments: "If someone then had displayed proper judgment the river Cydnus should not see his ashes and remains, although it is a pleasant and limpid stream, but to preserve the glory of his fine deeds they should be washed by the Tiber, which cuts through the eternal city, lightly touching the monuments of the divine emperors of old."[92]

ABBREVIATIONS

AA	*Archäologischer Anzeiger*
AAAG	*Annals of the Association of American Geographers*
AArchSlov	*Acta Archaeologica (Arheoloski Vestnik)*
AC	*L'Antiquité Classique*
AE	R. Cagnat et al. (eds.), *L'Année épigraphique* (Paris, 1893–)
AEA	*Archivo Español de Arqueologia*
AJA	*American Journal of Archaeology*
AJAH	*American Journal of Ancient History*
AJP	*American Journal of Philology*
AJPh	*American Journal of Philology*
AL	*Archeologia Laziale*
Annales ESC	*Annales: économies, sociétiés, civilisations*
ANRW	H. Temporini et al. (eds.), *Aufstieg und Niedergang der römischen Welt* (Berlin, 1972–)
AnUCA	*Anales de la Universidad de Cádiz*
AS	*Anatolian Studies*
AW	*Antike Welt*
BAM	*Bulletin d'archéologie marocaine*
BAtlas	R. Talbert (ed.), *Barrington Atlas of the Greek and Roman World* (Princeton, 2000)
BCH	*Bulletin de Correspondance Hellénique*
BCTH	*Bulletin Archéologique du Comité des Traveaux Historiques*
BdA	*Bollettino d'Arte*
BGU	*Berliner Griechische Urkunden* (Berlin, 1895–)
BIDR	*Bullettino dell'Instituto di Diritto romano*
BJ	*Bonner Jahrbücher*
BMC	E. H. Mattingly et al. (eds.), *Coins of the Roman Empire in the British Museum*, vols. 1–6 (London, 1923–66)
BRGK	*Bericht der Römisch-Germanischen Kommission der Deutschen Archäologischen Instituts*
CAAH	*Cahiers alsaciens d'Archéologie, d'Art et d'Histoire*
CEFR	*Collection de l'École Française de Rome*
CIG	*Corpus Inscriptionum Graecarum* (Berlin, 1825–77)
CIL	Th. Mommsen et al. (eds.), *Corpus Inscriptionum Latinarum* (Berlin, 1863–)
CJ	P. Krueger, (ed.) *Codex Justinianus; Corpus Iuris Civilis*, vol. II (Berlin, 1877)

CQ	*Classical Quarterly*
Digest	Th. Mommsen (ed.), *Digesta; Corpus Iuris Civilis*, vol. I (Berlin, 1872)
EAA	*Enciclopedia dell'Arte Antica Classica e Orientale*
FGH	F. Jacoby (ed.), *Fragmente der griechischen Historiker* (Leiden, 1923–)
GRBS	*Greek, Roman and Byzantine Studies*
IEJ	*Israel Exploration Journal*
IG	*Inscriptiones Graecae* (Berlin, 1873–)
IGLS	L. Jalabert, R. Mouterde, J.-P. Rey-Coquais, M. Sarte, and P.-L. Gatier (eds.), *Inscriptions grecques et latines de la Syrie*, I–VII, XIII.1, XXI.2 (Paris, 1911–86)
IGRR	R. Cagnat et al. (eds.), *Inscriptiones Graecae ad res Romanas Pertinentes*, vols. 1, 3, 4. (Paris, 1906–27)
IJNA	*International Journal of Nautical Archaeology and Underwater Exploration*
ILAfr	R. Cagnat and A. Merlin (eds.), *Inscriptions latines d'Afrique* (Paris, 1852–1937)
ILGN	E. Espérandieu, *Inscriptions latines de Gaule (Narbonnaise)* (Paris, 1929)
ILLRP	A. Degrassi (ed.), *Inscriptiones Latinae Liberae Rei Publicae* (Florence, 1957–63)
ILS	H. Dessau (ed.), *Inscriptiones Latinae Selectae* (Berlin, 1892–1916)
JAS	*Journal of the Asiatic Society of Great Britain and Ireland*
JEA	*Journal of Egyptian Archaeology*
JHS	*Journal of Hellenic Studies*
JRA	*Journal of Roman Archaeology*
JRS	*Journal of Roman Studies*
JSav	*Journal des Savants*
LIMC	*Lexicon Iconographicum Mythologiae Classicae* (Zurich, 1981–)
MAAR	*Memoirs of the American Academy in Rome*
MBAH	*Münsterische Beiträge zur antiken Handelsgeschichte*
MedAnt	*Mediterraneo Antico*
MEFR	*Mélanges de l'École Française de Rome*
MEFRA	*Mélanges de d'Archéologie et d'Histoire de l'École Française de Rome*
NP	*Der Neue Pauly* (Stuttgart, 1996–)
O. Florida	R. S. Bagnall, (ed.), *The Florida Ostraka: Documents from the Roman Army in Upper Egypt*, Greek, Roman and Byzantine Monographs 7 (Durham, N.C., 1976)
OGIS	W. Dittenberger (ed.), *Orientis Graeci Inscriptiones Selectae* (Leipzig, 1903–5)
OJA	*Oxford Journal of Archaeology*
PBSR	*Papers of the British School at Rome*
P. Giss.	O. Eger, E. Kornemann, and P. M. Meyer (eds.), *Griechische Papyri*

	im Museum des oberhessischen Geschichtsvereins zu Giessen (Leipzig-Berlin, 1910–1912)
PLRE	A. H. M. Jones, J. R. Martindale, and J. Morris (eds.), *The Prosopography of the Later Roman Empire* (Cambridge, 1971–92)
P. Oxy.	B. P. Grenfell, A. S. Hunt, et al. (eds.), *The Oxyrhynchus Papyri* (London, 1898–)
PP	*La Parola del Passato*
RAE	*Revue archéologique de l'Est et du Centre-Est*
RAL	*Rendiconti della Classe di Scienze morali, storiche e filologiche dell'Accademia dei Lincei*
RAN	*Revue archéologique de Narbonnaise*
RE	G. Wissowa et al. (eds.), *Real-Encyclopädie der classischen Altertumswissenschaft* (Stuttgart,1893–)
RIB	R. G. Collingwood and R. P. Wright (eds.), *The Roman Inscriptions of Britain*, I: *Inscriptions on Stone* (Oxford, 1965)
RIC	E. H. Mattingly, A. Sydenham, et al. (eds.), *The Roman Imperial Coinage* (London, 1923–94)
RPAA	*Rendiconti della Pontificia Accademia romana di Archaeologia*
RPh	*Revue de Philologie*
RSL	*Rivista di Studi Liguri*
RSNum	*Revue Suisse de Numismatique*
Sammelbuch	F. Preisigke (ed.), *Sammelbuch griechischer Urkunden aus Ägypten* (Strasbourg, 1913–)
SEG	J. J. E. Hondius et al. (eds.), *Supplementum Epigraphicum Graecum* (Amsterdam, 1923–)
SHA	Scriptores Historiae Augustae
Sylloge	W. Dittenberger (ed.), *Sylloge Inscriptionum Graecarum*, 3rd ed. (Leipzig, 1915–24)
T	C. Thulin, *Corpus Agrimensorum Romanorum* I.1 (Leipzig, 1913; repr., Stuttgart, 1971)
TIB	*Tabula Imperii Byzantini*
TIR	*Tabula Imperii Romani*
WA	*World Archaeology*
WAS	*Die Wasserversorgung antiker Städte* (Mainz, 1981)
ZPE	*Zeitschrift für Papyrologie und Epigraphik*
ZSS	*Zeitschrift Savigny-Stiftung für Rechtsgeschichte, Romanistische Abteilung*

APPENDIX 1 SPAS IN THE ROMAN WORLD

Listed first are locations that reasonably clearly were thermal/curative centers. Evidence is based on designations usually as *aquae* or occasionally *fons*, citations by ancient writers, and archaeological surveys concerning the nature and design of bathing establishments. Listed second are sites lacking the designation *aquae* or *fons* but which can reasonably clearly be associated with thermal or healing qualities. It does not aim to include all possible sites, because some are extremely hypothetical. (See map 19; parenthetical numbers before sites listed below correspond to the numbers in the key to map 19.)

References works: *RE* II.294–307; *RE* suppl. I.113; III.136–37; *NP*, s.v. *Aquae*; *TIR*; *TIB*; *BAtlas*; *It. Ant.* = Cuntz (1929); *Tab. Peut.* = Levi and Levi (1967); Stillwell, MacDonald, and McAllister (1976); Gsell (1911); Grenier (1960); Croon (1961), (1967); de Caro and Greco (1981); Mora (1981), 51–57; Heinz (1983), 157–75; Dunbabin (1989); Jackson (1990), (1999); Chevallier (1992); Houston (1992); Yegül (1992); T. Allen (2003).

SITES ATTESTED AS *AQUAE* OR *FONS*

(59) Ad Aquas: Numidia, near Thuburnica, on road from Simitthu to Hippo Regius; *It. Ant.* 43.2; *Tab. Peut.* 4.5; *CIL* 8, p. 936; cf. p. 1428; Jouffroy (1992), 93; *BAtlas* 32B3

(63) Ad Aquas: Africa, c. 21 miles from Maxula (Ghades); *Tab. Peut.* 6.1; possibly identical with spring Aquae Carpitanae (see ad loc) near Carthage, *RE* II.295.27; Livy 30.24.9; Strabo 17.3.16 (834); Jouffroy (1992), 93; *CIL* 8, p. 131; *BAtlas* 32F3

(118) Ad Aquas: Upper Moesia in the Danube valley, near Dorticum; *TIR* L 34 (Amsterdam, 1968), Aquincum 23; *BAtlas* 21E5

(97) Ad Aquas (Aquasanta Terme): Italy, on river Truentus, near Asculum; *BAtlas* 42E3

Ad Aquas Caesaris: Numidia (see below, Aquae Caesaris)

(85) Ad Aquas Salvias (Tre Fontane): Italy, south of Rome; Ferrari (1957), 33–48; *BAtlas* 43B2

(116) Ad Mediam (Băile Herculane): Dacia, near Praetorium on the road from Dierna to Tibiscum; *CIL* 3.1566 ("Herculi genio loci fontibus calidis . . ."); *TIR* L 34 (Amsterdam, 1968), Aquincum 24; *BAtlas* 21E5

(48) Aquabona: Lusitania, between Caetobriga and the coast opposite Olisipo; de Alarcão (1988), vol. II.2, 127; *BAtlas* 26A3

Aqua Damnata: near Rome; Galen (see Wasserstein, 1982, G 36–37)

(110) Aqua Viva (Petrijanec): Upper Pannonia, southeast of Poetovio; *It. Ant.* 130.1; *Tab. Peut.* 4.4; *RE* II.307.97; *BAtlas* 20D3

(95) Acqua Viva (Acquaviva): Etruria on the Via Flaminia, south of Ocriculum; Potter (1979), 117–18; *BAtlas* 42C4

(115) Aquae (Calan): Dacia, on road from Sarmizegetusa to Apulum; *CIL* 3.1412; Ptolemy 3.8.4; Stillwell, MacDonald, and McAllister (1976), 75; Lepper and Frere (1988), 115–16; *BAtlas* 21E4

Aquae (Cioroiul Nou): Dacia; *AE* 1967.392; Stillwell, MacDonald, and McAllister (1976), 75

Aquae: Upper Moesia, on road from Viminacium to Durosturum; *It. Ant.*, 218.4

(62) Aquae: Africa, on road from Carthage to Agbia, near Coreva; *Tab Peut.* 4.3; Jouffroy (1992), 93; *BAtlas* 32D4

(53) Aquae (El Hamma du Djerid): Africa; Jouffroy (1992), 94

(124) Aquae (?) (Vranjska Banja): Macedonia; *TIR* K 34 (Ljubljana, 1976), Naissus 17; *BAtlas* 49E1

(184) Aquae (Yavuzeli): Commagene, north of Zeugma on river Marsyas, a tributary of the Euphrates; Archi, Pecorella, and Salvini (1971), 32–33; *BAtlas* 67F2

(20) Aquae (Aix-les-Bains): Gallia Narbonensis; *CIL* 12.2459–60; 5874–76; Grenier (1960), 404–9; Prieur (1976); Canal (1992); *BAtlas* 17F2 (Aquae Sextiae)

Aquae Albenses: Numidia, location not clearly established; *RE* II.295.9; Jouffroy (1992), 89

(86) Aquae Albulae (Adaquas Albulas): Italy, near Tibur; *Tab Peut.* 4.5; *CIL* 14, p. 435, 3908, 3909 (Aquae Albulae sanctissimae) = *ILS* 3892, 3910–18, 3534 = *ILS* 6227; Strabo 5.3.11 (238); Martial 1.12.2; Vitruvius, *De Arch.* 8.3.2; *BAtlas* 43C2

Aquae Angae (Lamezia Terme): Lucania on road from Consentia to Vibo Valentia; *Tab Peut.* 6.1; *RE* II.295.12

Aquae Ang[u]lanae (?) (Agnano): Campania, south of the crater of Agnano; Houston (1992), 359–60

(93) Aquae Apollinares (Bagni di Stigliano): Italy, near Forum Clodii; *It. Ant.* 300.3; Hodges (1995); *BAtlas* 42C4

(94) Aquae Apollinares Novae: Italy, (Vicarello) to north of Lacus Sabatinus; *Tab. Peut.* 4.3; *CIL* 11.3281–84; Künzl (1992); T. J. Allen (2003), 408; *BAtlas* 42C4

(107) Aquae Aponi /Fons Aponi (Montegrotto Terme): Italy, near Patavium; Lucan 7.193; Martial 6.42; Sil. Ital. 12.218; Pliny *NH* 2.227; *CIL* 5 p. 271, 2785; *ILS* 3894–3894a; Lazzaro (1981); *BAtlas* 40B2

(60) Aquae Aptuccensium (Hammam-Biadha): Africa, near Aptucca; Beschaouch (1974–75), 193–94; Jouffroy (1992), 93; *BAtlas* 32C4

(1) Aquae Arnemetiae (Buxton): Britain; Rivet and Smith (1979), 254–55; *BAtlas* 8F1

Aquae Auguriae: Italy, site uncertain; Caelius Aurelianus, *On Chronic Diseases* 5.4.77; *RE* II.295.15

(10) Aquae Aureliae or Aurelia Aquensis (Baden-Baden): Upper Germany, on the road on the east bank of the Rhine from Argentorate to Mogontiacum; *RE* II.2.2426; *NP*, s.v. *Aquae* III.6; Heinz (1983), 157; *BAtlas* 11I4 (Aquae)

(112) Aquae Balissae/Municipium Iasorum (Daruvar): Upper Pannonia, near the road from Mursa to Siscia; *It. Ant.* 265.7; *AE* 1964.11; 1965, p. 56; *NP*, s.v. *Aquae* III.9; *BAtlas* 20E4

(114) Aquae Bassianae: Dalmatia, Slatina (near Mitroviesa); *AE* 1952.192

(40) Aquae Bilbitanorum (Alhama de Aragón): Tarraconensis, near Bilbilis; *It. Ant.* 437.2; 438.14 *CIL* 2, p. 410; *TIR* K-30 (Madrid, 1993), Caesaraugusta 49; *BAtlas* 25D4

(106) Aquae Bormiae: Raetia; Pauli (1973), 105–20; *BAtlas* 19C3

(14) Aquae Bormonis (Bourbon L'Archambault): Lugdunensis, on the road between Decetia and Aquae Neri; *Tab. Peut.* 1.4; *RE* suppl. III.137.20; Grenier (1960), 442; Corrocher (1992), 178–79, argues that this site should be identified with Bourbon-Lancy; *BAtlas* 18A3

Aquae Briginnienses (Brignon): Gaul, near Nîmes; *RE* II.297.21; *CIL* 12.2913

(92) Aquae Caeretanae: Italy, north of Caere (Bagni del Sasso); Strabo 5.2.3 (220); Livy 22.1.10; *AE* 1989.305–6; Cosentino and Sabbatini Tumolesi (1989); Cosentino (1992); *BAtlas* 44B1

(56) Aquae Caesaris (Youks): Numidia, west of Theveste; *Tab. Peut* 3.4; *CIL* 8, p. 244; Gsell (1911), 28.253; Jouffroy (1992), 91; *BAtlas* 33A2 (Ad Aquas Caesaris)

(119) Aquae Calidae (Burgaski Mineralni Bani): Lower Moesia, between Anchialus and Deultum; Hoddinott (1975), 221; *BAtlas* 22E6

Aquae Calidae: Cappadocia in Taurus Mountains south of Tyana; *Tab. Peut.*9.2; *RE* II.298.25

(17) Aquae Calidae (Vichy): Aquitania, near Augustonemetum on the river Elaver; *Tab. Peut.* 1.4; Morlet (1957); Grenier (1960), 435–42; Corrocher (1992), 182–85; *BAtlas* 14I2

(51) Aquae Calidae (Hammam Righa): Mauretania Caesariensis, near Zucchabar; *It. Ant.* 31.4; Ptolemy 4.2.6; *CIL* 8.2.9599–605; Gsell (1911), 13.28; Jouffroy (1992), 90; *BAtlas* 30D4

Aquae Calidae: Africa between Thabraka and the river Bagrada; Ptolemy 4.3.33; *RE* II.298.29

(43) Aquae Calidae (Cuntis): Tarraconensis, near Iria Flavia; *TIR* K-29 (Madrid, 1991), Conimbriga 22; *BAtlas* 24C2

(39) Aquae Calidae (Caldes de Montbui): Tarraconensis, near Baetulo; *TIR* K/J-31 (Madrid, 1997), Tarraco 35–36; *BAtlas* 25H4

(38) Aquae Calidae (Caldes de Malavella): Tarraconensis, on the road from Blandae to Gerunda; Merino, Nolla, and Santos (1994); *BAtlas* 25H4

(66) Aquae Calidae Neapolitanorum (Sardara): Sardinia near Neapolis on the road from Othoca to Caralis; *It. Ant.* 82.6; Ptolemy 3.3.7; Rowland (1981), 117–18; *BAtlas* 48A3

(65) Aquae Carpitanae (Hammam Korbous): Africa, near Carpi; *CIL* 8, p. 132; 8.24106; *BAtlas* 32G3

(44) Aquae Celenae (Caldas de Reis): Tarraconensis on the road south of Iria Flavia; *It. Ant.* 423.8; 430.3; Ptolemy 2.6.24; Diez de Velasco (1992), 136; *TIR* K-29 (Madrid, 1991), Conimbriga 22–23; *BAtlas* 24C2

Aquae Cirnenses: Africa; *RE* II.299.35; location uncertain

(33) Aquae Convenarum (Capvern): Aquitania, close to the road from Aquae Tarbellicae to Tolosa; *It. Ant.* 457.7; *Tab. Peut.* 1.1; *CIL* 13, p. 25; *BAtlas* 25F2

Aquae Cumanae: Campania, near Baiae (?); Livy 41.16.3

(89) Aquae Cutiliae (near Paterno): Italy, on the river Avens east of Reate; *It. Ant.* 307.1; *Tab Peut.* 4.4; *CIL* 9.4663–71; Reggiani (1979); *BAtlas* 42E4

(49) Aquae Dacicae (Sidi Moulay Yakoub): Mauretania Tingitana, west of Volubilis, in valley of the el Hamma River; *It. Ant.* 23.3; Stillwell, MacDonald, and McAllister (1976), 75; Jouffroy (1992), 89–90; *BAtlas* 28C5

Aquae Eleteses (Retortillo): Lusitania, near Salamanca; Gómez Moreno (1967), 59

Aqua Ferentina: Italy, at foot of the Alban Mount; *RE* VI.2.2207; Livy 1.51.9.

(47) Aquae Flaviae (Chaves): Tarraconensis, on the road from Bracara Augusta to Asturica; *It. Ant.* 422.6; *CIL* 2.2474; Tovar (1989), 302–3; de Alarcão (1988), 2:6–7; Diez de Velasco (1992), 137–38; *BAtlas* 24D3

(57) Aquae Flavianae (Henchir el Hammam): Numidia, near Mascula Tiberia; *CIL* 8, p. 1681; 17722 ("tribunus curator . . . Aquis Flavianis praepositus"); 17725; 17727; *AE* 1960.96; Gsell (1911), 28.137; Jouffroy (1992), 91; *BAtlas* 34F2

(186) Aquae Frigidae/Meiacarire (Khan Sheikhan): Mesopotamia, northwest of Singara, near Sauras; *CIL* 8, p. 1906; 20215; Dillemann (1962), 157–58; *BAtlas* 89C3

(156) Aquae Ger(. . .) (Gecek): Asia, north of Prymnessos; *CIL* 3.14200; *RE* XX.1.816; *BAtlas* 62D4

(3) Aquae Granni (Aachen): Lower Germany, between Colonia Claudia Ara Agrippinensium and Atuatuca; Cüppers (1982); *NP*, s.v. *Aquae* III.3; *BAtlas* 11G2

(30) Aquae Griselicae (?) (Gréoux-les-Bains): Narbonensis; *AE* 1986.485; cf. *CIL* 12.361= *ILS* 1114; Grenier (1960), 526–27

(12) Aquae Helveticae (Baden bei Zurich): Upper Germany, near Vindonissa on river Limmat; Tacitus, *Histories* 1.67; Pauni (1992), 392; Koller and Doswald (1996); *NP*, s.v. *Aquae* III.2; *BAtlas* 18F2

(52) Aquae Herculis (Hammam Sidi el Hadj): Numidia, south of Lambaesis; *Tab Peut.* 3.1; *CIL* 8, p. 276; 279; Gsell (1911), 37.59; Baradaz (1949), 220–28; Jouffroy (1992), 91; *BAtlas* 34D2

Aquae Hypsitanae or Lesitanae: Sardinia; Ptolemy 3.3.7, with Müller (1883–91), p. 386; *AE* 1998.671

(111) Aquae Iasae (Varaždinske Toplice): Upper Pannonia in *ager Poetoviensis* south of the river Dravus; *CIL* 3.4121; *RE* II.301.49; *NP*, s.v. *Aquae* III.8; *BAtlas* 20D3

(90) Aquae Labanae (Bagni di Grotta Marozza): Latium, near Eretum; Strabo 5.3.11 (238); *RE* II.301.51

(68) Aquae Larodes/Thermae Selinuntae (Sciacca): Sicily, near Selinus; *It. Ant.* 89.4 has Larodes; *Tab. Peut.* 6.1 has Iabodes; Strabo 6.2.9 (275); R. J. A. Wilson (1990), 228; *BAtlas* 47C3

(4) Aquae Mattiacorum (Wiesbaden): Upper Germany, near Mogontiacum; *CIL* 13, pp. 406–7; 17.2626; Pliny, *NH* 31.20; Ammianus 29.4.3; Schoppa (1974); *NP*, s.v. *Aquae* III.4; *BAtlas* 11I2

Aquae Nepesinae: Italy, near Nepet; Caelius Aurelius, *On Chronic Diseases* 3.2.45; 5.4.77; *RE* II.302.57

(84) Aquae Neptuniae: Italy, near Tarracina; Livy 39.44.6; *RE* II.302.58

(15) Aquae Neri (Neris-les-Bains): Aquitania, on road from Augustonemetum south of Avaricum; *CIL* 13.1371; 1376–77; Grenier (1960), 430–35; Desnoyers (1978), (1985); Yegül (1992), 120–21; Corrocher (1992), 179–82; *BAtlas* 14H2

(13) Aquae Nisincii or Alisincii (Bourbon-Lancy?): Lugdunensis, between Augustodunum and Decetia; *Tab. Peut.* 1.4; *RE* II.303.61

Aquae Novae: Numidia; *Gesta* 1,198, 1.59 (A.D. 411); Jouffroy (1992), 91–92

(35) Aquae Onesiorum (Bagnères de Luchon): Aquitania, south of Lugdunum Convenarum; *CIL* 13.349–64; Strabo 4.2.1 (190); Grenier (1960), 411–13: *BAtlas* 25F3

(46) Aquae Originae (Riocaldo): Lusitania, between Bracara Augusta and Asturica; *It. Ant.* 428.1; *TIR* K-29 (Madrid, 1991), Conimbriga 23; *BAtlas* 24C3

Aquae Palmenses: Africa, Sukra near Carthage; *CIL* 8.24515

(109) Aquae Pannoniae (Baden bei Wien): Upper Pannonia, between Vindobona and Scarbantia; *It. Ant.*, 261.5; A. Neumann (1976–77), 144; *TIR* M 33 (Prague, 1986), Castra Regina 21; *BAtlas* 20D1 (Aquae)

(96) Aquae Passeris (Bagni Giasinelli): Italy, near Ferentium; Martial 6.42.6; *CIL* 11.3003 (Aquae Passerianae); *Tab Peut* 4.1; Esch (1990), 146; *BAtlas* 42C4

(64) Aquae Persianae/Naro (Hammam-Lif): Africa, in the bay of Carthage, between Tunes and Carpi; Apuleius, *Florides* 16; Jouffroy (1992), 93; *BAtlas* 32F3

Aquae Perticianenses: Sicily, between Lilybaeum and Drepanum; *It. Ant.* 97.10; *RE* II.303.69

(104) Aquae Pisanae (San Giuliano Terme): Italy, near Pisa; Pliny, *NH* 2.227

(100) Aquae Populoniae (Bagni della Leccia): Etruria, near Fufluna/Populonium; *Tab Peut.* 3.2; *RE* II.304.73

(45) Aquae Quarquernae (Baños de Bande): Tarraconensis, on the road from Bracara Augusta to Asturica; *It. Ant.* 428.2; Ptolemy 2.6.46; Tovar (1989), 296; Diez de Velasco (1992), 137; *BAtlas* 24D3

(42) Aquae Quinti(n)ae (Guntín): Tarraconsensis, south of Lucus Augusti; Tovar (1989), 303; *TIR* K-29 (Madrid, 1991), Conimbriga 23; *BAtlas* 24D2

(55) Aquae Regiae (Henchir Khatera): Byzacena, on road from Hadrumetum to Sufes; *It. Ant.* 53.2; 54.2; 55.2; 56.2; *ILS* 9452; Pliny, *NH* 4.4; Jouffroy (1992), 95; *BAtlas* 33E1

(113) Aquae S(. . .) (Ilidža): Dalmatia, near road to Narona; Wilkes (1969), 382–83; *BAtlas* 20F6

Aquae Sacaritanae: Africa; *CIL* 8.12286; *RE* II.304.78; location uncertain

(179) Aquae Saravenae (Kirsehir): Cappadocia, west of Caesarea; Ptolemy 5.6.2; *RE* II.304.79; *TIB* 2 *Kappadokien* (DenkWien, 1981), 143–44; *BAtlas* 63E2

(67) Aquae Segestanae (Terme Segestane): Sicily, just north of Segesta; *It Ant.* 91.2; Strabo 6.2.9 (275); Giustolisi (1976), 58–63; R. J. A. Wilson (1990), 392; *BAtlas* 47B3

(18) Aquae Segetae (Sceaux en Gâtinais?): Lugdunensis, in the valley of the Liger, west of Lugdunum; *Tab Peut.* 1.5; Grenier (1960), 726; Vallat (1981), 236–39; *BAtlas* 17C2

(102) Aquae Senanae: Italy near Sienna; Caelius Aurelianus, *On Chronic Diseases* 2.1.48

(88) Aquae Septem/Septem Aquae: Italy, near Amiternum; *RE* IIA 2.1550; *CIL* 9.4206–8

(29) Aquae Sextiae Salluviorum (Aix-en-Provence): Narbonensis; *It. Ant.* 298.5; *Tab. Peut.* 2.1; *CIL* 12, p. 65; 4414; Strabo 4.1.5 (180); Grenier (1960), 402–4; *NP, Aquae* III.5; *BAtlas* 15E2

(32) Aquae Siccae (St-Cizy): Aquitania, on the river Garumna, on the road from Lugdunum Convenarum to Tolosa; *It. Ant.* 458.1; Manière (1980); *BAtlas* 25G2

(81) Aquae Sinuessanae (San Rocco, near Mondragone): Italy, just south of Sinuessa on the Via Domitiana; Livy 22.13.10; Pliny, *NH* 31.8; Martial 6.42.5; *CIL* 10, pp. 463–64; 10.4734; *CIL* 8.2583 = *ILS* 3893; Pagano (1990), 32–33; *BAtlas* 44E3

(50) Aquae Sirenses (Hammam bou Hanifia): Mauretania Caesariensis, in valley of river Sira; *CIL* 8.9745 ("numen Aquarum Sirensium"); Gsell (1911), 32.18; Jouffroy (1992), 90; *BAtlas* 29E1

(105) Aquae Statiellae (Acqui Terme): Italy, in Liguria; *It. Ant.* 294.7; *Tab. Peut.* 2.4; *CIL* 13.6903; *CIL* 5, p. 850; 7504–31; *CIL* 8.502; 23294; Strabo 5.1.11 (217); Pliny, *NH* 3.49; Antico Gallina (1986), 98–124; *BAtlas* 39C4

(2) Aquae Sulis (Bath): Britain, on river Avon; *It. Ant.* 486.3; Ptolemy 2.3.13; *CIL* 7, p. 24; *AE* 1983.636; 1984.620; Cunliffe and Davenport (1985); Cunliffe (1988); Rivet and Smith (1979), 255–56; Burnham and Wacher (1990), 165–76; *BAtlas* 8E3

(54) Aquae Tacapitanae (el-Hamma): Tripolitania, near Tacape on the road to Capsa; *It. Ant.*, 74.1; 78.2; *CIL* 8, p. 9; Jouffroy (1992), 95; Mattingly (1994), 97; *BAtlas* 35B1

(91) Aquae Tauri (Bagni di Traiano): Italy, near Centum Cellae; *Tab Peut.* 4.3; Rutilius Namatianus, *De Reditu Suo* 250 ff.; Heinz (1986); *BAtlas* 42B4

(31) Aquae Tarbellicae or Terebellicae (Dax): Aquitania, at a junction, with important routes going on to Burdigala; *It. Ant.*, 455.10; 456.6; 457.3; Pliny, *NH* 31.4; Ptolemy 2.7.8; *CIL* 13.1, p. 53; Grenier (1960), 414–17; Gauthier (1981); *BAtlas* 25D2

(58) Aquae Thibilitanae (Hammam Meskoutine): Numidia, near Thibilis on the road from Cirta to Hippo Regius; *It. Ant.*, 42.5; *Tab. Peut.* 3.1; *CIL* 8, p. 539; 5495–503; Gsell (1911), 9.144; Jouffroy (1992), 92; *BAtlas* 31G4

(61) Aquae Traianae (Hammam Seiala): Africa, south of Vaga; *ILAfr* 440; *CIL* 8.14457; Jouffroy (1992), 94; *BAtlas* 32D3

(75) Aquae Vescinae (Terme di Suio): Italy, on the river Liris, north of Minturnae; *AE* 1914.217 (*genius Aquarum Vescinarum*); 1982.153; 1989.145; Coarelli (1982), 380–81; *BAtlas* 44E3

Aquae Vesevinae: near Mount Vesuvius; Caelius Aurelianus, *On Chronic Diseases*. 2.1.48; Houston (1992), 360

(37) Aquae Voconiae (west of Caldes de Malavella): Tarraconensis, on the road from Barcino to Narbo; *It. Ant.*, 398.1; *TIR* K/J-31 (Madrid, 1997), Tarraco 36; *BAtlas* 25H4

(101) Aquae Volaterranae: Italy, Monte Cerboli (?) near Volterra; *Tab Peut.* 3.2; *RE* II.307.100

Fons Aponi (see above, Aquae Aponi)

(98) Fons Clitumni (Pissignano): Italy, on the river Clitumnus between Fulginiae and Spoletium on the Via Flaminia; Pliny, *Epistulae* 8.8; *BAtlas* 42D3

(99) Fontes Clusinae (Chianciano Terme): Italy, near Clusium; Strabo 5.2.9 (226); Horace, *Epistualae* 1.15.1–11

Fontes Sequanae: Lugdunensis, at the source of the river Seine; *CIL* 13.2861–64; Grenier (1960), 617–39

(108) Fons Timavi (S. Giovanni di Duino): Italy, near Aquileia and the mouth of the river Timavus; *Tab. Peut.* 3.5; Bosio (1991), 213–23; Roberti (1992); *BAtlas* 19F4

(41) Fontes Tamarici (Velilla de Guardo or Velilla del Rio Carrión): Tarraconensis, near Palantia; Pliny *NH* 31.23–24; Fernández de Avilés (1961)

OTHER SITES LIKELY TO BE THERMAL OR CURATIVE CENTERS
Italy and Sicily

(80) Aenaria: island of Ischia; Pliny, *NH* 31.9; Strabo 5.4.9 (248); *CIL* 10.6786; Houston (1992), 359

(69) Akragas: Sicily; Strabo 6.2.9 (275); Crouch (1993), 209–10

Arco Felice: Campania, on the site of Cicero's villa near Puteoli; Pliny, *NH* 31.6

(103) Bagno di Romagna: Umbria, near Sarsina; Ortalli (1992)

(79) Baiae: Campania; Dunbabin (1989); *NP*, s.v. *Baiae*

(83) Castelforte: Campania; *Notizie degli Scavi* (1887): 406–10 (L. Fulvio); Houston (1992), 360–61

(72) Krathis/Sybaris: Thurii; Pliny *NH* 31.13

Leucogaei Fontes: Campania, between Puteoli and Naples; Pliny, *NH* 31.12; Houston (1992), 361

(71) Lipari Island: Diodorus Siculus 5.10.1

(76) Mons Dianae Tifatinae (S. Angelo in Formis): Campania, north of Capua; Velleius 2.25.4; *CIL* 10.3811

(77) Neapolis (Naples): Campania; Strabo 5.4.7 (246)

Patavium (Padua): Po valley; Pliny, *NH* 31.61

Pina Vestina: Picenum; Vitruvius, *De Architectura* 8.3.5

(78) Puteoli (Pozzuoli): Campania; Pausanias 4.35.12; 8.7.3; Houston (1992), 362

(87) Simbruinum: near Tibur; Celsus, *De Medicina* 4.12.7

(74) Stabiae (Castellamare di Stabia): Campania, south of Pompeii; Pliny, *NH* 31.9; Columella 10.133; Houston (1992), 363

(73) Surrentum (Sorrento): Campania, private spa described by Statius, *Silvae* 2.2.18–19

(82) Teanum Sidicinum (Teano): near Teanum was the Aqua Acidula; Pliny, *NH* 31.9; de Caro and Greco (1981), 235–37; Houston (1992), 363–64

(70) Thermae Himeraeae, Sicily on river Thermos; R. J. A. Wilson (1990), 166–7; *BAtlas* 47D3

Note also possible sites in the Po valley combining mineral sources and (slight) evidence of a water-related cult; Calvani (1992)

Spain

See in general Diez de Velasco (1987); and, by the same author, a survey of northwest Spain and Lusitania (1992); note also the useful studies by Almagro Moltó (1992) and Dupré and Pérex Agorreta (1992). The evidence is sometimes too slight to bear a firm identification of a thermal site. The following list contains only the more likely locations.

Aurium (Orense, Las Burgas): Tarraconensis; *CIL* 2.2527

Baños de Molgas (near Aurium): Tarraconsensis; can possibly be identified with Salientibus; *It. Ant.* 428.4; Diez de Velasco (1992), 137

Baños de Montemayor: Lusitania, near Colonia Norbensis Caesarina (Cáceres); *CIL* 2.883–89; 891

Caldas de Cuntis (Pontevedra): Lusitania, near Ad Duos Pontes; *CIL* 2.2546; Filgueira and D'Ors (1955), 40–42

Caldas de Vizela: Lusitania, near Bracara Augusta; *CIL* 2.2402–3 = *ILS* 4514a and b

Caldellas: Lusitania, near Amares in Portugal; *CIL* 2.5572

La Calda: Tarraconensis, near Legio; Diego (1986), 76–77

Gaul/Germany

Grenier (1960), 401–955, made a thorough study of watery locations in the Gallic provinces, though he may be rather too optimistic in his identification of thermal and curative sites. The difficulty is in distinguishing between sanctuaries that included water deities, and specifically thermal/curative centers. The following list contains only the more likely locations.

(27) Aix-en-Diois (Les Fontanelles): Narbonensis; *CIL* 12.1561; Rémy and Buisson (1992), 233; *BAtlas* 17E4

(7) Alesia (Alise, Sanctuary of Moritasgus): Lugdunensis; Grenier (1960), 655–60

(28) Allan: Lugdunensis, near Valentia (Valence); Rémy and Buisson (1992), 233–34

(36) Amélie-les-Bains: Aquitania; Grenier (1960), 409–10

(11) Badenweiler: Upper Germany, near Fribourg; Grenier (1960), 460–68; Yegül (1992), 119; Heinz (1999), 185, and fig. 174

(8) Balesmes-sur-Marne: Lugdunensis, south of Andematunnum; Thévenard (1996), 52.036; *BAtlas* 18C2

(9) Bourbonne-les-Bains: Lugdunensis, east of Andematunnum; Grenier (1960), 445–49; *BAtlas* 18C2

(23) Brides-les-Bains: Upper Germany, near Darantasia on the river Isara; Gimard (1992), 209–10; Rémy and Buisson (1992), 234; *BAtlas* 17H3

Deneuve (sanctuary of Hercules): Belgica; Moitrieux (1992), 71–72; *BAtlas* 11G4

(5) Divodurum (Metz, Nymphaeum de Sablon): Belgica; *CIL* 13.4292; Grenier (1960), 824–25; *BAtlas* 11G3

(21) Divonne-les-Bains: Upper Germany, near Colonia Iulia Equestris/Noviodunum; Rémy and Buisson (1992), 235–36

(16) Evaunum (Evaux-les-Bains): Aquitania; Grenier (1960), 417–23; Dussot (1989), 162; *BAtlas* 14H2

(22) Menthon-Saint-Bernard: Narbonensis, near Boutae (Annecy); Rémy and Buisson (1992), 236–37

(26) La Motte-Saint-Martin: Narbonensis, near Cularo (Grenoble); Rémy and Buisson (1992), 238–39

Les Bolards: Lugdunensis, near Nuits-Saint-Georges; *CIL* 13.2846; Thevenot (1948); Grenier (1960), 648–54; Deyts (1992), 59

Les Fontaines Salées: Lugdunensis, on banks of river Cure, near Saint-Père-sous-Vézelay; Grenier (1960), 449–60; Martin (1960), (1962); Lacroix (1964)

Massingy-les-Vitteaux: Lugdunensis, near Alesia; Grenier (1960), 667–68

(6) Montbouy: Lugdunensis, on the route from Cenabum (Orléans) to Autessiodurum (Auxerre); Grenier (1960), 730–33; Fauduet (1992), 199–200

(19) Saint-Galmier: Lugdunensis, on the banks of the river Croise, near Montbrison; Rémy and Buisson (1992), 240

(25) Saint-Martin-D'Uriage: Narbonensis, near Grenoble; Rémy and Buisson (1992), 241; Rivet (1988), 323 and map at fig. 42

Saint-Vulbas: Lugdunensis, near Belley; *CIL* 13.2452 (Bormana Augusta); Rémy and Buisson (1992), 241

(24) Salins-les-Thermes: Upper Germany, near Darantasia on the river Isara; *AE* 1939.34; Gimard (1992), 208–9

(34) Vicus Aquensis (Bagnères-de-Bigorre): Aquitania, west of Lugdunum Convenarum; *CIL* 13.389; Grenier (1960), 413–14; Lussault (1997), 105–6; see *BAtlas* 25F2

Danube Area

(120) Augusta Traiana: Lower Moesia, west of Stara Zagora; Hoddinott (1975), 201–5; Yegül (1992), 111; *BAtlas* 22C6

(117) Brestovacka Banja: Upper Moesia, north of Romuliana; *TIR* L 34 (Amsterdam, 1968), Aquincum 40; *BAtlas* 21E5

(121) Haskovo bani: Lower Moesia, southeast of Philippopolis/Trimontium; Hoddinott (1975), 212–15; *BAtlas* 22C7

(125) Nymphaion (Selenicë): Macedonia, near Apollonia; Strabo 7.5.8 (316); Dio 41.45; Aelian, *Varia Historia* 13.16; Hammond (1967), 231–34; *BAtlas* 49B3

(123) Scaptopara: Thrace, in the valley of the river Strymon; *CIL* 3.12336

Greece

For Greece, the islands, and Greek communities in Asia, see in particular the extensive work of Croon (1952), (1953), (1956), (1961), (1967)

(127) Actium/Nicopolis: Epirus; Croon (1967), 240

(130) Aidepsos: Achaea, northern Euboea; Plutarch, *Quaestiones Conviviales* 667C–D; Gregory (1979)

(135) Alpheios river: Achaea, near Heraea; Pausanias 8.26.1

(138) Hermione (Ermione): Achaea, in the Argolid; Lauffer (1989), 267–68

(128) Hypata (Hypati); Loutra Hypatis: Achaea, in the Spercheios valley; *Archaeological Reports* 24 (1977–78): 38–39; *BAtlas* 55C3

(137) Kenchreai (Baths of Helena): Achaea, on south side of Isthmus of Corinth; Pausanias 2.2.3

(126) Krannon: Macedonia; Pliny, *NH* 31.20; Lauffer (1989), 251–52

(134) Kyllene: port of Elis; Croon (1967), 230

(132) Kynaitha: Achaea, in Arkadia; Pausanias 8.19.2

(122) Linos: Thrace (?); Pliny, *NH* 31.10 locates a Linus fons in Arkadia

(136) Phigaleia: Achaea, in Arkadia; Pausanias 8.41.4–5

(133) Thelpousa: Achaea, in Arkadia; Pausanias 8.25.3

(129) Thermopylae: Macedonia, Croon (1956), 211

(131) Thespiai: Achaea, in Boeotia; Pliny, *NH* 31.10

Islands

(147) Ikaros (Therma/Asklepieis); Robert (1969), 549–68; *BAtlas* 61C2

(145) Kos; Croon (1967), 230–31

(139) Kythnos; *RE* XII.220

(143) Lindos (on Rhodes); Croon (1953), 288

(141) Melos; Athenaeus 2.42; Pliny, *NH* 31.61

(168) Mytilene (on Lesbos); Croon (1956), 196–97

(144) Nisyros; Croon (1967), 231

(140) Seriphos; Croon (1967), 232

(142) Thera; Croon (1967), 231

Asia and the East

(183) Aegae: Cilicia; Athenaeus 2.42; Croon (1967), 239, n. 3

(170) Alexandria in Troad: Asia; *RE* I.1.1396.16

(171) Antandros: Asia, in Troad; Croon (1967), 234

(153) Apamea: on the Maeander in Phrygia; Croon (1956), 200; *TIB* 7 Phrygien und Pisidien (Vienna, 1990), 188–89

(165) Atarneus: Asia; Pausanias 4.35.10; *RE* II.2.1896

(150) Colossae: Asia; Croon (1967), 238

(174) Cyzicus: Bithynia; Aelius Aristides, *Or.* 51.13; Croon (1967), 235

(163) Erythrae: Asia; *RE* VI.1.580

(154) Eukarpia: Asia; Croon (1967), 237; *TIB* 7 Phrygien und Pisidien (Vienna, 1990), 250–51

(155) Hierapolis: Asia (Phrygia); Croon (1953), 296–97; see *BAtlas* 62D5

(151) Hierapolis (Pamukkale): Asia, in the Maeander valley; Croon (1967), 238; Belke and Mersich (1990), 268–72; *BAtlas* 65B2

(159) Karoura: Asia, between Phrygia and Caria, in the Maeander valley; Strabo 12.8.17 (578)

(176) Kios: Bithynia; Croon (1967), 236

(169) Larisa in the Troad: Asia; Pliny, *NH* 31.61

(161) Lebedos: Asia; Pausanias 7.5.5

(157) Leontos Kome: Phrygia, to west of Dokimeion; Robert (1980), 277; *BAtlas* 62E4

(148) Magnesia: Athenaeus, *Deipnosophistae* 2.43a; Croon (1967), 237–38

(166) Pergamum: Asia; Aelius Aristides *Or.* 39.4–6; 53 (referring to a well and receptacle for spring water); Croon (1967), 228

(167) Perperene: Asia; Croon (1967), 235

(160) Philadelphia-Neocaesarea: Asia, near Sardis; *RE* XIX.2.2091; Croon (1967), 237

(173) Pionia: Asia; Robert (1962), 364; Croon (1967), 235

(175) Prusa ad Olympum: Bithynia; Athenaeus, *Deipnosophistae* 2.43a; *RE* XXIII.1.1082–83

(177) Pythia Therma: Bithynia; Croon (1967), 236; Robert (1979), 276

(146) Salmacis: Asia, near Halicarnassus; Vitruvius, *De Architectura* 2.8.11–12

(152) Sebaste: district of in Phrygia; Croon (1967), 236–37; Belke and Mersich (1990), 376–78

(164) Smyrna (Agamemnoniai Thermai): Asia; Aelius Aristides, *Or.* 48.7, 50, 69; Pausanias 7.5.6; Croon (1967), 237; *BAtlas* 56E5

(181) Soloi/Pompeiopolis: Cilicia; Pliny, *NH* 31.17; *RE* IIIA 1.935

(182) Tarsus: Cilicia; *RE* IVA 2.2413.3; Croon (1967), 239

(162) Teos: Asia; Pausanias 7.5.5; *RE* VA 1.552

(172) Thebe: Asia; *RE* VA 2.1595.5

(178) Thermae Phazemoniton: Cappadocia; Robert (1948), 75–87; Magie (1950), 1067–68; Croon (1967), 236, n. 3; *BAtlas* 87A4

(158) Thermae Theseos: Asia; *Tituli Asiae Minoris* 5.1,26; *RE* VA 2.2388.4; *BAtlas* 62A4

(149) Tralles: Asia; Athenaeus, *Deipnosophistae* 2.43a; *RE* VIA 2.2093.2

(180) Tyana/Colonia Aurelia Antoniniana: Cappadocia; Croon (1952), 120–23

Judaea

(187) Hammath/Ammathous (el Hzammam): Judaea, at Tiberias; Pliny, *NH* 5.71; Dvorjetski (1999), 118–19; *BAtlas* 69C4

(188) Hamat Gader: Judaea, south of the Sea of Galilee in valley of river Yarmouk; Eunapius, *VS* 459; Hirschfeld and Solar (1981); Yegül (1992), 121–24; Hirschfeld (1997), 1–14; Dvorjetski (1999), 119

(189) Kallirhoe: Judaea, on the eastern shore of the Dead Sea, a series of springs, most importantly Hammam Ez-Zara; Josephus, *BJ* 1.657; Ant., *Iud.* 17.171–72; Avi-Yonah (1984), 167; Dvorjetski (1999), 121–22; *BAtlas* 71B2; note also the related thermal site at Hammei-Ba'arah, close to Machaerus; Josephus, *BJ* 7.186–89

Mesopotamia

(185) Abarne: region of Gumathene; Ammianus 18.9.2; *BAtlas* 89B2

Africa

Djebel Oust: Africa, in valley of the Katadas between Uthina and Thuburbo Maior; Jouffroy (1992), 94.

Hammam Berda: Numidia, north of Calama; Gsell (1911), 9.92; Jouffroy (1992), 92

APPENDIX 2 NAVIGABLE RIVERS
ACCORDING TO ANCIENT AUTHORS

D = *Digest*   PM = Pomponius Mela, *Chorographia*
P = Pliny, *Natural History*   PP = *Periplous Ponti Euxini*
Pa = Pausanias   S = Strabo

ITALY CISALPINA
Aquileia—unnamed river near (S 5.1.8)
Padus (Po) (S 5.1.5; 5.1.11; P 3.117)
Navigable tributaries of the Po (P 3.118):
    Addua (Adda)
    Duria (two rivers) (Dora)
    Gabellus (Secchia)
    Incia (Enza)
    Jactum
    Lambrus (Lambro)
    Mincius (Mincio)
    Natiso (Natisone) (S 5.1.8)
    Ollius (Oglio)
    Orgus (Orco)
    Rhenus (Reno)
    Scultenna (Panaro)
    Sesites (Sesia)
    Stura (Stura)
    Tanarus (Tanaro)
    Tarus (Taro)
    Ticinus (Ticino)
    Trebia (Trebbia)

ETRURIA AND TIBER VALLEY
Anio (Aniene) (S 5.3.7; 5.3.11; P 3.54)
Arnus (Arno) (S 5.2.5)
Auser (Serchio) (S 5.2.5)
Clanis (Chiani) (S 5.3.7; P 3.53)
Nar (Nera) (S 5.2.10; 5.3.7; P 3.54)
Tiber (Tevere) (S 5.2.5; 5.3.5; P 3.53–54); navigability of Tiber tributaries (S 5.2.9)
Tinia (Topino) (S 5.2.10; 5.3.7; P 3.53)
Umbro (Ambra) (P 3.51)

SOUTHERN ITALY

Arocas (Crocchio) (P 3.96)

Carcinus (Corace) (P 3.96)

Crotalus (Alli) (P 3.96)

Liris (Garigliano) (D 19.2.13)

Salapia and Sipous—river between (S 6.3.9)

Sarnus (Sarno) (S 5.4.8)

Semirus (Simeri) (P 3.96)

Thagines (Tacina) (P 3.96)

APULIA

Fertur (Fortore) (P 3.103)

SPAIN

Anas (Guadiana) (S 3.1.9; 3.2.3)

Baetis (Guadalquivir) (S 3.2.3; P 3.9–10)

Durius (Douro) (S 3.3.4)

Hiberus (Ebro) (S 3.4.10; P 3.21)

Limia (Limia) (S 3.3.4)

Maenuba (Guadiamar) (P 3.12)

Minius (Miño) (S 3.3.4; P 4.112)

Mundas (Mondego) (S 3.3.4)

Singilis (Genil) (P 3.12)

Tagus (Tajo) (S 3.3.1)

Vacua (Vouga) (S 3.3.4)

Navigable estuaries:

    (H)Asta and Nabrissa (S 3.1.9; 2.4–5)

    Maenuba (S 3.2.5)

    Onoba (S 3.2.5)

    Ossonoba (S 3.2.5)

    Tagus (S 3.3.1)

GAUL

Arar (Saône) (S 4.1.11)

Atax (Aude) (S 4.1.14; PM 2.81)

Druentia (Durance) (S 4.1.11);

Dubis (Doubs) (S 4.1.11)

Garumna (Garonne) (S 4.1.14; PM 3.21)

Isara (Isère) (S 4.1.11; P 3.33)

Liger (Loire) (S 4.1.14)

Mosa (Meuse) (P 4.100–101)

Rhodanus (Rhône) (S 4.1.11, 14)
Sequana (Seine) (S 4.1.14)

GERMANY
Albis (Elbe) (S 7.1.3)
Amisia (Ems) and other unnamed navigable rivers (S 7.1.3)
Rhenus (Rhine) (S 7.1.3)

DALMATIA, PANNONIA, AND MOESIA
Colapis (Kolpa) (S 4.6.10; 7.5.2; P 3.148)
Corcoras (Krka) (S 4.6.10)
Danubius, Danuvius, Istros, Hister (Danube) (S 7.3.13; P 4.79, with
    thirty navigable tributaries)
Dravus (Drava) (S 7.5.2; P 3.147)
Drilon (Drin) (S 7.5.7)
Naro (Neretva) (Pseudo-Scylax 24). See Wilkes (1969), 8
Savus (Sava) (S 4.6.10; 7.5.2 [confused]; P 3.147)
Titius (Krka) (S 7.5.4)

MACEDONIA, ACHAEA, AND THRACE
Acheloüs (Acheloos) (S 10.2.2)
Alpheios (Alpheios) (P 4.14)
Arachthos (Arachthos) (S 7.7.6)
Hebros (Evros) (S 7 frag. 47)
Loudias (Loudias) (S 7frag. 20)
Peneios (Peneios) (P 4.31)

SCYTHIA, COLCHIS, AND HYRCANIA
Borythenes (Dnieper) (S 7.3.17; PM 2.6; *PP* 59)
Kyros (Kura) (S 11.3.2); its tributaries:
    Alazonius (Alazani)
    Chanes
    Rhoetaces
    Sandobanes
Ochus (Sangalak) (S11.7.3 S 11.7.3)
Oxus (Amu Darya) (S 2.1.15; 11.7.3)
Parthenios (Bartin Su) (PP 14)
Phasis (Rioni) (S 11.2.17; 11.3.4; P 6.13)
Tanaïs (Don) (S 11.2.2–3)
Tyras (Dniester) (S 7.3.15)

EASTERN PROVINCES AND EGYPT

Calycadnus (Göksu Nehri) (S 14.5.4)
Eurymedon (Köprü Çay) (S 14.4.2; PM 1.78)
Halys (Kizil Irmak) (PP 24; cf. S 12.3.12)
Kalbis (Dalyan Çay) (S 14.2.2)
Kestros (Asku) (S 14.4.2)
Melas (Manavgat Çay) (S 14.4.2; PM 1.78)
Neilos (Nile) (S 11.11.5; 17.1.24; P 5.59; PM 1.50)
Orontes (Nahr el-Asi) (S 16.2.7; Pa 8.29.3)
Pyramos (Ceyhan Nehri) (S 12.2.4)
Sangarius (Sakarya) (S 12.3.7; PP 7)
Scamander (Menderes Çay) (P 5.124)
Xanthos (Esen Çay) (S 14.3.6)

MESOPOTAMIA AND THE FAR EAST

Euphrates (S 16.1.9; P 5.83–84; 6.124–6; PM 3.76–77)
Tigris (S 15.3.5; 16.1.9; P 6.127–30)

AFRICA

Laud (Oued Laou) (P 5.18)
Malva = Mulucha (Oued Moulouia) (?) (P 5.19)
Sububus (Oued Sebou) (P 5.5)
Tamuda (Oued Martil) (P 5.19)

INDIA

Acesinus (Chenab) (P 6.71)
Arbium (P 6.97)
Cabirus (P 6.94)
Cainnas (P 6.64)
Casuagus (P 6.65)
Cophes (Kabul) and its navigable tributaries (P 6.94)
Crenacca (P 6.65)
Ganges (Ganges) (P 6.65)
Granis (P 6.99)
Hydaspes (Jhelum) (S 15.1.17)
Hypasis (Beas) (P 6.71)
Hyperis (P 6.99)
Indus (Indus) (S 15.1.32; P 6.71–72)
Parospus (P 6.94)
Phrystimus (P 6.99)
Pomanus (P 6.94)

Prinas (P 6.64)

Rhamnumbova (P 6.65)

Saddaros (P 6.94)

Sitioganus (P 6.99)

Sodamus (P 6.94)

Sonus (P 6.65)

Tonberum (P 6.97)

Zarotis (P 6.99)

NOTES

CHAPTER 1

1. *FGH* 90F 134.

2. Note Cosgrove and Petts (1990), 1–4, on the value of watery resources, especially fluvial. Humans appropriate the fluvial and invest it with meaning so that it becomes a metaphor mapped onto other dimensions of human life.

3. The inscription reads "qui nasce il Tevere sacro ai destini di Roma." Mussolini, who had been born in Emilia Romagna, arranged for the boundary between Tuscany and Emilia Romagna to be changed so that the source of the Tiber would be in the region of his birthplace.

4. Strabo 3.2.1 (141); see in more detail chapter 2.

5. Cf. Haslam (1997), 225–26. Cosgrove and Petts (1990), 13–34, note that river corridors originally tended to be heavily forested and with abundant vegetation. Much of this has now been lost. The removal of riparian vegetation can reduce marginal habitats and affect birds and other wild life.

6. Petts and Foster (1985), 11.

7. Here I follow the analysis of Petts (1989), 3.

8. For a classic statement of this idea, Petts (1989), 211: "They change because it is in their nature to do so: flowing water is changing water, and flowing water changes the land (and bed) through which it flows."

9. Petts (1989), 1.

10. See Vita-Finzi (1969), 3. We should note, however, how complex are the factors that determined the richness and longevity of site distribution, including soil, topography, communications, social structures, and economic climate; these ideas are expounded by Wightman (1982).

11. Newson (1987), 6–8; Petts (1989), 41–53; Petts and Foster (1985), 9–10.

12. Petts and Foster (1985), 20–34.

13. Newson (1987), 2. For the ancient view, see chapter 2, section 5; in the Middle Ages, it was held that there were two simultaneous cycles—the atmospheric and the subterranean (Squatriti, 1998, 160–64).

14. Brown (1997), 38, on factors in floodplain flooding.

15. Brown (1997), 104–15.

16. See Butzer (1972), 178–79; and see further below, section 2.

17. In the case of floodplains, see Brown (1997); nature and process, 17–44; dating, 45–62; alluviation in the Mediterranean, 237–48; also Renfrew and Bahn (1991).

18. Vita-Finzi (1969), especially 91–92, 116–20.

19. See Cherkauer (1976), 106–8, 118–19.

20. See Brown (1997), 225–27.

21. See the discussion in Horden and Purcell (2000), 314–20. Bintliff (1992) argues that

Vita-Finzi's view of Mediterranean erosional history as one of "punctuated equilibrium" has some value. Climate has some role to play in such changes, but the anthropogenic may be more important.

22. Rackham (1996), 25–26.

23. Butzer (1972), 184, 216–19.

24. See Rickman (1988a), 106–8. Note also Rivet (1988), 7, for the lack of change in the coastline of southern France in classical times; for the Rhône, Delano Smith (1979), 328–30. See also Le Gall (1977), arguing that there was little significant change in sea level from the age of glaciation.

25. Fleming (1969), (1978); Schmiedt (1972), 120–23; 309–16; useful discussion in Pirazzoli (1976), (1988). For the effect of generally minor sea level changes in Greece, note Rackham (1996), 25–26.

26. Frederiksen (1984), 14.

27. Frederiksen (1984), 17. A useful discussion of the geological background of the Mediterranean is found in Ager (1980).

28. Delano Smith (1979), 331.

29. Note the valuable comments by B. D. Shaw (1976) on the difficulties of measuring past climates in the prehistoric period.

30. B. D. Shaw (1981a), 383.

31. See Neumann (1985) and (1992), arguing that temperature conditions in the third century B.C. were much the same as in the twentieth century; Sallares (1991), 390–96; Horden and Purcell (2000), 318; Stoddart (2006), 103, 113, for the similarity of the climate of republican Italy to the climate of the Mediterranean today.

32. Delano Smith (1979), 314.

33. On difficulties of the evidence and ability of societies to adapt, see Wigley, Ingram, and Farmer (1981), 6–16, 26–27, 162–64; on stability of climate, Semple (1932), 99–100.

34. B. D. Shaw (1981a), especially 385–96. Theories of climate change often center on the Maghrib partly because of its reputation for extensive cereal production in Roman times, which can be contrasted with more recent desiccation. Furthermore, cities like Timgad and extensive Roman villa complexes seemed to nineteenth-century explorers and colonizers to be in the middle of desolate areas. One argument to explain this was that of climatic change, namely that there had been higher rainfall in the Roman period. Shaw critically examined the evidence for climate change based on the traditional emphasis on the disappearance of certain animal species from the Maghrib, the decline of groundwater sources to the extent that they could no longer support agriculture, and the tradition that North Africa was a major exporter of grain in the Roman world. He observed that the disappearance of large mammalian fauna cannot simply be ascribed to climate change, because man played a large part in destroying animals or their habitats. The idea of a loss of groundwater resources seems to have been greatly exaggerated, and the reasons for desertification are imperfectly understood. Africa in the Roman period did export large quantities of grain, but it continued to be a substantial cereal exporter in subsequent periods, and its continuing productivity may be ascribed to the arid environment, relatively

low population levels, and an imperial presence that could command exports of grain whatever the local conditions. In terms of ecological change, in the Maghrib it seems that, for example, the loss of forest occurred most seriously in the twentieth century through human activities and cannot certainly be taken as indicating climate change. Finally, historical geology (Shaw, 1981a, 393–96) suggests that the Romans exploited Africa in climatic conditions that resembled the present more than medieval times.

35. Livy 5.54.4. For a useful survey of the geological characteristics of the site of Rome, see Ventriglia (1971); a particularly interesting and evocative account of the geology of the site can be found in Heiken, Funiciello, and de Rita (2005); for other comments on the location of Rome, see chapter 8, section 4. For topography's role in making sense of the past in the case of Rome, see, briefly, Edwards (1996), 42–43.

36. Livy 1.3.10–11; Dionysius Halicarnassus, *Antiquitates Romanae* 1.76.2; Plutarch, *Romulus* 3–4. For this story, see also chapter 4, section 6. See, in general, Bremmer, in Bremmer and Horsfall (1987), 25–48, especially 27–34; this myth probably dates at least from the early third century B.C., but Bremmer argues for the sixth century. See also Malissard (1994), 14–15, for the psychological association between the Romans and water in respect of the foundation of Rome. See Wiseman (1995), especially 1–17, 103–28, 160–68, for the multiplicity of myths about the origins of Rome, the role of Romulus and Remus and possible associations with plebeian power sharing in the fourth century B.C. For the development of the foundation legends, see also Wiseman (2004), 138–48.

37. *BMC* II, p. 187, no. 774; legend: *Roma*; see chapter 4, n. 245.

38. Horsfall, in Bremmer and Horsfall (1987), 12–24, discusses the Aeneas legend.

39. *Aeneid* 7.25–36; Horsfall (2000), 65–66.

40. *Aeneid* 7.531–37.

41. *Aeneid* 8.31–78.

42. *Aeneid* 8.86–101.

43. See further chapter 4.

44. Strabo 5.3.8 (236).

45. *NH* 3.53–55; see chapter 8, section 4.

46. *De Aquis* 1.4. For a survey of the watery topography of Rome, see Holland (1961), 21–49. Heiken, Funiciello, and de Rita (2005), 85–109, discuss the Tiber's small tributaries within the city and show how they relate to subsequent building activities and earthquake damage over the years.

47. Servius, *Ad Aeneidam* 12.139.

48. Ovid, *Fasti* 1.705–8; Dionysius Halicarnassus, *Antiquitates Romanae* 6.13.4.

49. Florus 1.28.15; Valerius Maximus 1.8.1.

50. See Platner Ashby (1926), 311–13; L. Richardson (1992), 230–31; Claridge (1998), 95–97; Steinby (1993–99), 3:168–70. The original shrine was restored in A.D. 283 but retained the original inscription: "Iuturna(i) S(acrum); or possibly S(PQR)."

51. Note the *fons Lollianus* and *fons Scaurianus*; see Steinby (1993–99), 2:258–59.

52. Cicero, *De Legibus* 2.56; Solinus 1.21.

53. Cicero, *De Natura Deorum* 3.52; *CIL* 6.32493; Festus 75 L; See Steinby (1993–99),

2:255–57. Malissard (1994), 246–49, argues that early aqueducts in Rome were associated with conquest and booty.

54. But note L. Richardson (1992), 153, who disputes this, arguing that the motive for dedicating the shrine may have come from the name of the gate.

55. Steinby (1993–99), 2:257–58.

56. For the quality of the water, see Frontinus, *De Aquis* 1.4; Vitruvius, *De Architectura* 8.3.1. The *vicus* was a subdivision of a city *regio*.

57. Pliny, *NH* 34.19; Plutarch, *Numa* 13.2; Festus 152 L; Steinby (1993–99), 1:216.

58. It may have been in the Forum Boarium, though this is disputed by L. Richardson (1992), 153; *muscosi fontes*, Virgil, *Eclogues* 7.45.

59. Livy 23.32.4; Festus 232 L; L. Richardson (1992), 292; Steinby (1993–99), 4:93–99.

60. *CIL* 6.975 = *ILS* 6073; *CIL* 6.167 = *ILS* 3682a. Fourth-century Regionary Catalogs identify Regio XII as *Piscina publica*. For a survey of springs in the city, see Heiken, Funiciello, and de Rita (2005), 133–36 (with map on p. 134).

61. Festus 39 L, 296L, 284L; Cicero, *De Natura Deorum* 2.9. *Peremnis* is formed by combining *per* and *amnis*. See also Holland (1961), 18–20; L. Richardson (1992), 289–90; Steinby (1993–99), 4:81–82.

62. See chapter 5 at n. 1. For rituals associated with boundaries in space and time, and related to the riverbank, see Purcell (1996a), 186–87.

63. *CIL* 6.154 = *ILS* 3888 (A.D. 123).

64. *CIL* 6.164 = *ILS* 3889 (A.D. 165); cf. *CIL* 6.163, 165. L. Richardson (1992), 153, thinks that the *magistri* might be officials overseeing the *Piscina publica*; but referring to the *fons Scaurianus*, he talks of a "sacred college." Steinby (1993–99), 4:93–94 and 2:258–59, also speaks of people concerned with administration of springs and fountains. There is a suggestion that some of these inscriptions may be false. Note the "cultores Urae (Eure) fontis" (*CIL* 12.3076).

65. See chapter 9 at n. 37.

66. Livy 1.16.1; Ovid, *Fasti* 2.491–96; Steinby (1993–99), 1:234. For the ninth region, see Muzzioli (1992).

67. Livy 6.5.8. See Cornell (1989), 403–4; Cornell (1995), 320; Mommsen (1963), III.1, p. 171 and n. 6; L. Taylor (1960), 48. Note also Purcell (1996a), 201, though he mistakenly writes Aniensis instead of Arniensis. The river name is not known in antiquity.

68. Festus 464 L; 505; L. Taylor (1960), 47–49.

69. Frontinus, *De Aquis* 1.6; L. Taylor (1960), 55–56; L. Richardson (1992), 11. In A.D. 38 the New Anio was brought to the city, though it had poor-quality water (Frontinus, *De Aquis* 1.14–15).

70. See Livy 9.20.6; Festus 263 L; L. Taylor (1960), 50.

71. Festus 498 L. Mommsen identified the Teres with the Trerus (Sacco), but L. Taylor (1960), 57–59, argues persuasively that the tribe's territory belongs to the coastal region from the Liris to the Volturnus in the land of the Aurunci. The Teres must remain an unknown tributary of the Liris, perhaps north of Minturnae.

72. See Cornell (1995), 177–78. He observes that some toponyms derive from the name

of a tribe, not the other way round. But I think that this is unlikely in the cases of the rivers discussed above.

73. For this argument, see L. Taylor (1960), 63–64; on *lacus Velinus*, see chapter 4.

74. Livy 1.33.6; Plutarch, *Numa* 9; Festus 374 L. For the *pontifices*, see Holland (1961), 332–42; Beard, North, and Price (1998), 24–26.

75. Dionysius Halicarnassus, *Antiquitates Romanae* 1.38.3; Ovid, *Fasti* 5.621–22; Dumézil (1966), 435–37.

76. See the interesting comments by J. G. Frazer (Loeb edition of Ovid's *Fasti*, 1931), 425–29, especially 428–29. For a good survey of the evidence emphasizing a ceremony of purgation and the role of the Vestal Virgins, see Holland (1961), 313–31. Further discussion in chapter 4 at n. 164.

77. Crawford (1992), 33.

78. *CIL* 6.9847.

79. Platner and Ashby (1926), 374; *CIL* 1².1000, 1001 = 6.2219, 2220.

80. Cicero, *De Lege Agraria* 2.96.

81. L. Richardson (1992), 405.

82. *CIL* 6.31547 = *ILS* 5928; *CIL* 6.31548b = *ILS* 5929a; *CIL* 6.31555 = *ILS* 5934. For the curators, see chapter 8 at n. 184.

83. See above for the *prata Quinctia* and *prata Mucia*.

84. See chapter 4.

85. See Purcell (1996a), 190; Mocchegiani Carpano (1984), 21–22; Le Gall (1953a), 264; Segre (1990), especially 14–15, for the early configuration of the Tiber mouth.

86. For the Ebro, note Petts (1989), 233; see further chapter 7, section 1. For an excellent survey of the geography of Spain in its historical context, see Schulten (1955–57).

87. See in general Curchin (1991), 12–14.

88. See chapter 7; also Rivet (1988), 3–9.

89. See, e.g., de Izarra (1993); Parodi Álvarez (2001). For a valuable description of the valley of the Guadalquivir, see Abad Casal (1975), 26–31.

90. See, e.g., Salway (1981), 4–5; B. Jones and Mattingly (1990), 1–5.

91. Frere (1987), 292.

92. See Salway (1981), 563–64.

93. B. Jones and Mattingly (1990), 200; see also chapter 6 at n. 130.

94. B. Jones and Mattingly (1990), 198–99. For the so-called Piercebridge formula and its difficulties, see chapter 7 at n. 228.

95. See Crouch (1993), 67–78, for geology of Greece.

96. See in more detail chapter 7, section 3; chapter 8, section 1.

97. See the Danube Commission Web site: www.danubecom-intern.org.

98. See the Web site of the Central Commission for Navigation on the Rhine: www .ccr-zkr.org. Demangeon and Febvre (1935) is still valuable; Commission Centrale pour la Navigation du Rhin, *Rapport Annuel* (1937).

99. See chapter 4 at n. 146.

100. *Res Gestae* 26.

101. Strabo 7.1.3–4 (291).

102. See the summary in Alföldy (1974), 9–11.

103. See Wilkes (1969), xxiv–vii.

104. See Mitchell (1982), 95–100; (1993), 5–7, for a survey of the topography of Anatolia. Some riverbeds can be dry and stony in summer and autumn but become torrential after winter snowmelt and heavy spring rains. For a study of the Maeander valley, see Thonemann (2011).

105. Velleius 2.101.

106. Campbell (2000), 47.

107. See chapter 6, section 6.

108. For a good general survey of the benefits brought by the Nile, see Braudel (2001), 66–68; also Bowman (1986), 11–20.

109. Braudel (2001), 92–93.

110. Above all, see Bonneau (1964), (1981), (1993), (1994).

111. See, in general, Walker (1967), 86–87; Traina (1990), 14–22, has a useful geographical description of Italy; Stoddard (2006) deals with the geography and environment of republican Italy, but his comments are relevant to the imperial period.

112. Delano Smith (1978).

113. Walker (1967), 87, provides a summary; excellent analysis of the nature and development of the river in Petts (1989), 113–25.

114. Le Gall (1953a), (1953b). For the Tiber valley survey, see below at n. 130.

115. See Braudel (2001), 19–21, on the important role of rivers in Mediterranean history.

116. See further chapter 4, section 1.

117. Ecclesiastes 1.7.

118. See Bell and Boardman (1992), 2–6, for a summary of the methodology. In some respects there is, however, a clear connection; for example, terrace systems continue to be an important response to farming steep slopes, and so here perhaps the present can be carefully used as a key to the past.

119. Haslam (1991), 303.

120. Brittain (1958), 17.

121. Ulpian in *Digest* 43.20.1.26. *Rivalis* also meant "rival"; see *Oxford Latin Dictionary*, s.v. rivalis².

122. Mann (1973), 14.

123. Talbert (2000).

124. Information in the *Rapport annuel* of the Commission Centrale pour la Navigation du Rhin (see n. 98).

125. *Dioptra* 31; Lewis (2001), 281.

126. See above, n. 89; and below, n. 130.

127. Surveyors distinguish various types of running water: river, public river, riverbank, riverbank forming a boundary, watersheds, and rainwater, which had different characteristics from river water: *Flumen* (T74.11), *flumina non mediocria* (T43.12), *amnis*

publicus (T42.25; 44.19), *fluvius* (T88.7), *rivus* (e.g., T66.6; cf. 74.12; 102.17; see Campbell (2000), 548, s.v. *rivus*), *naturalis rivus* (T102.17), *rivus rectus* (T114.25), *divergia aquarum* (T76.18), *aquae pluviae* (T9.21).

128. See chapter 3, section 4.

129. Chapter 3 at n. 20.

130. H. Patterson (2004), especially 2. For work on the Maeander valley, see above, n. 104.

131. Note the comments of Rackham (1996), 17, warning about pseudo-ecology derived from ancient sources.

132. Herodotus 2.10–11; Thucydides 2.102.

133. Strabo 1.3.7(52). See also chapter 2, section 5.

134. *Anabasis* 5.6.4–8.

135. *NH* 3.16.

136. Pausanias 8.24.11. Alcock (1993), 81, notes that there is insufficient evidence to confirm or deny Pausanias's contention.

137. See chapter 3, section 5.

138. In the *Origines*, Campbell (2000), 272.8.

139. Strabo 1.3.7 (53). The date of the oracle is unclear.

140. *Metamorphoses* 15.259–72; Bömer (1986), 324–26.

141. For these themes, see chapters 2 and 4.

142. See Horden and Purcell (2000), 322–28, on these themes, especially 323–24; also 337–41.

143. Petts and Foster (1985), 15.

144. Braudel (2001), 60–66, makes a good point concerning the development of early civilization in the river valleys in Mesopotamia and the importance of the domestication of the rivers; notably, the Sumerians settled on unpromising land but by irrigation made it very fertile.

CHAPTER 2

1. Terras (1965), 55.

2. For useful discussion of the tradition of ancient geography, see Prontera (1983); Sordi (1988); Cordano (1992).

3. Müller (1861), xv–xl, 103–76; Garzyra (1963). For some late geographical texts, see Riese (1878), 21–55 (*Cosmographia Julii Caesaris* before A.D. 376) and 71–103 (*Cosmographia Pseudo-Aethicus*, which gives a lot of attention to rivers); see also Nicolet (1991), 95–96. For the beginnings of a technical interest in rivers among the ancients, see Brittain (1958), 200–218.

4. Dionysios Perigetes: Danube (line 330); Don (line 679).

5. Dionysios Perigetes, lines 990, 1146, 228 (the Nile).

6. Dionysios Perigetes, lines 351–56.

7. Berger (1880); Berggren and Jones (2000). The translation of Stevenson (1932) is unreliable in places. For a translation into German, see now Stückelberger and Graßhoff

(2006). Ptolemy wrote a number of astronomical treatises as well as his *Geography*, which set out to map the known world. A separate development was in the work of the so-called bematists ("pacers"), surveyors who accompanied the campaigns of Alexander the Great, measuring distances along important routes.

8. This was an outstanding accomplishment, although he distorted the Mediterranean with excessive elongation from east to west and extended the continent of Africa to connect with China; see Dilke (1985), 71–86.

9. Ptolemy, *Geographia* 1.1–2.

10. See Maddoli (1988); Clarke (1999), with an excellent bibliography. Strabo was a compiler of information and does not emphasize his personal travels and visits. He did visit Rome several times and journeyed in Egypt.

11. Strabo 1.2.1 (14).

12. Strabo 1.1.23 (13). Strabo thought that a serious work could be entertaining, though the usefulness of the material employed had to come first (1.19).

13. For example, in Strabo's account of Sicily, 6.2.1 (266). See 10.3.5 (465), for his discussion of Polybius's definition of the function of chorography.

14. Strabo 17.3.25 (840).

15. Clarke (1999), 210–28, emphasizes the Romanocentric nature of Strabo's geographical description.

16. Strabo 1.1.1 (2).

17. Strabo 1.1.16 (9).

18. Strabo 1.1.17 (10). This possibly refers to the campaigns of the elder Drusus on which he was engaged at the time of his death in 9 B.C. But if the text was subsequently revised, it may be a reference to Varus in A.D. 9.

19. Strabo 12.8.7 (574). Note the valuable discussion in Clarke (1999), 81–97, on the combination of geography and history in Polybius. Strabo also wrote a history, most of which is now lost; Clarke (1999), 193–94.

20. See Clarke (1999), 32, who debates whether in Strabo the natural world is described as a static phenomenon or plays an active role in the historical narrative. See also pp. 88 and 295–99 for helpful comments on the question of geographical determinism and the initiative of peoples.

21. Strabo 5.3.7 (235).

22. See Clarke (1999), 198–99, 205–6, 210–28. Strabo also did not base his spatial view specifically on continents or latitudinal zones. Of course, even a description based on the *periplous* can give rise to wider visions and descriptions in which rivers can play a part.

23. For the role of the past in Strabo's descriptions, see Clarke (1999), 252, 275.

24. Caesar, *BG* 1.1.

25. *NH*, *pref.* 13. For Pliny's career, see Syme (1969); Beagon (1992), 1–25.

26. *NH* 2.166.

27. *NH* 1, at book III; use of *clarus* for rivers, 4.82, 107.

28. *NH* 27.3.

29. River flow could be associated with lakes, *NH* 3.109; 4.38.

30. *NH* 3.39–41. See in general Beagon (1992); Murphy (2004), especially 138–48.

31. Silberman (1988); Brodersen (1994); Gómez Fraile (2002), for Pomponius Mela and the Elder Pliny on Spain.

32. Text, Rocha-Pereira (1973–81); text and translation, H. L. Jones (1918–35).

33. Habicht (1985), 4, on writing from personal observation; 13, his home; Bearzot (1992); Elsner (1992); Arafat (1996); Lafond (2001); Alcock, Cherry, and Elsner (2001). See further chapter 4. Habicht (1985) generally supports the accuracy of Pausanias; see also Rackham (1996), 22.

34. Pausanias 2.1.5.

35. Pausanias 8.41.10.

36. Scylax: Müller (1854), xxxiii–li, 15–96; Menippus: Diller (1952); the anonymous *Stadiasmus* or *Periplous maris magni*: Bauer (1955); *Periplous of the Red Sea*: Huntingford (1980); Casson (1989); Arrian's *Periplous of the Black Sea*: Silberman (1995).

37. Nicolet (1991), 92.

38. E.g., Scylax, section 33, a town on the river Peneios.

39. Scylax, 17, sailing time upstream.

40. Scylax, 24.

41. *Periplous Pontis Euxini*, 13; 23.

42. *Periplous of the Red Sea*, e.g., 11, 15, 35, 40, 44, 54–55, 63.

43. Stadiasmus 136, 213, 217, 247.

44. Texts: *Itinerarium Antonini* and *Itinerarium Burdigalense*; Cuntz (1929).

45. In the same document is an *Itinerarium Maritimum*; see Dilke (1985), 112–29; Arnaud (1993); R. W. B. Salway (2004), 68–85. The sources for the compilation were probably officially recorded routes, local guides, and records of the journeys of individuals. See Talbert (2007), 263–67, who also speculates that the work was put together for his own amusement by someone with minor administrative responsibility in the Roman state; Löhberg (2006) offers an extensive commentary.

46. Müller (1854), lxxx–xcv, 244–54.

47. Cuntz (1929), 86–102; Hunt (1982), 55–58; pilgrim routes in general, Hunt (1982), 50–82; Elsner (2000).

48. Text: Weber (1976); see further below at n. 236.

49. See Dilke (1971); Hinrichs (1974), Clavel-Lévêque et al. (1993), (1996); Guillaumin (1996); Campbell (1996), (2000); Behrends et al. (1998), (2000).

50. See Nicolet (1991), 89–92; Janni (1984). For a general survey of the Roman view of space, see Whittaker (2004), 63–87.

51. Arrian, *Periplous* 7.1–3. On a wider scale, the Don was the boundary of Asia and Europe (19.1). Not all Arrian's rivers can be clearly identified, but in the cases of known rivers, the relative distances between them seem fairly accurate, despite the fact that they are all multiples of 30 stades. A stade is 600 feet or 182.88 meters; a Roman mile equals $8\frac{1}{3}$ stades.

52. Cuntz (1929), 11.1–12.2. For river mouths, see 431.8; 446.10.

53. Cuntz (1929), 416.4–418.5.

54. Cuntz (1929), 549.7–9. Talbert (2007) points out that knowledge of distance between places is essential in the construction of the Antonine Itinerary, although a hodological approach was not the only way to define space.

55. See, e.g., Strabo 11.6.1–2 (507); 12.2.9–10 (539).

56. See Clarke (1999), 201.

57. For example, the Danube could be described as the greatest of rivers; Strabo 12.3.26 (553).

58. For scale in Polybius, see Clarke (1999), 110.

59. As observed by Janni (1984), 61–62. Note also 120–30: the world is a net of one-dimensional routes.

60. See Janni (1984), 156.

61. Pliny, *NH* 3.49, 51, 56, 70, 74.

62. *NH* 3.132.

63. *NH* 4.115. For the measurement of distance from river mouth to river mouth round the Black Sea, see 4.77–78; 6.3–4. Note also the Kyros near the Caspian Sea (6.45).

64. *NH* 4.122.

65. See Strabo, e.g., 2.4.7 (108); 2.5.31 (129); 7.4.5 (310); 15.1.26 (696–97).

66. Strabo 1.2.1 (14). Claudius Ptolemy notes the impressive impact of the Rhine and the Danube, by the length of their course, the bends and changes of direction, the countries and peoples they delimited, and their sheer expanse through a large geographical area (2.11).

67. Appian, *Preface* 4; Josephus, *BJ* 3.107; Cassius Dio 39.49 and 53.12.6, on the Rhine as a boundary; Herodian 6.7.2.

68. Strabo 2.1.26 (80), quoting Eratosthenes.

69. Strabo 17.3.24 (839).

70. *Annales* 1.9.

71. Pliny, *NH* 7.12. Murphy (2003), 313–21, emphasizes that Pliny's description of river characteristics is related to his background in Roman government.

72. Mela 1.7–8, 15; 2.1.

73. Mela 3.16.

74. Mela 1.25, 29.

75. Caesar, *BG* 4.10.

76. *BG* 16.

77. Tacitus, *Annales* 2.6; *Germania* 3.3; 23.1; 29; 32; 34; 37; 41. Note also how the followers of Maroboduus and Catualda were settled "beyond the Danube between the rivers Marus (Morava) and Cusus (Váh)"—*Annales* 2.63. Note the use of rivers in geographical descriptions in Livy 21.2.7; 24.6.7; 45.29.7.

78. *Germania* 41.2. Tacitus is apparently referring to the Roman advance to the Elbe in the time of Augustus, and the subsequent withdrawal to the confines of the Rhine after the defeat of Quinctilius Varus in A.D. 9.

79. *ILS* 986; cf. 985. Note also how Dionysius of Halicarnassus celebrates the Danube as the biggest river in Europe, which traveled across all the northern area to the Pontic

Sea (*Antiquitates Romanae* 14.1.1); Aulus Gellius, citing Sallust and Varro as authorities, also has the Danube as the biggest river, though some regarded the Rhône as a possible rival (*Attic Nights* 10.7; quoted in preface).

80. Pliny, *NH* 3.31.

81. This is cleverly argued by Janni (1984), 132, referring to Pliny, *NH* 3.31.

82. See Janni (1984), 106–7, for characteristic markers to be crossed, for example, on Alexander's march eastward.

83. Strabo 2.1.30 (83). For other examples of riverine boundaries, see 1.4.8 (66); 2.1.23 (79); 2.5.17 (120); 2.5.26 (126); 4.2.1–2 (189–90); 4.3.1 (191–92); 4.4.2–3 (195–96); 4.5.1 (199); 5.3.10 (237); 6.4.2 (287–88); 7.1.1 (289); 12.3.27 (553–54).

84. As with the Maeander, which also had a curving course; Strabo 13.4.12 (628–29).

85. Strabo 15.1.26 (696–97).

86. E.g., Strabo 7.4.8 (312). For this theme, see Janni (1984), 108.

87. Strabo 7.7.4 (322–23). We have the same use of rivers in Claudius Ptolemy; in Upper Pannonia, he divides the major towns into those below the Danube and those remote from the river; elsewhere he uses the phrase "below the Danube," "on the Danube," "below the bend of the Tanais," and again those communities "close to" or "remote from the Danube" (2.14; 3.5; 3.10).

88. Strabo 16.2.5 (750).

89. Strabo 7.7.1 (320–21), tribes demarcated by rivers and mountains.

90. Strabo 4.3.4 (193).

91. Strabo 13.1.21 (590).

92. Strabo 12.8.16 (578).

93. Strabo 3.1.6 (139). Cf. 7. frag. 23, which also shows the use of rivers in geographical descriptions to establish location and relativity.

94. Cf. Strabo's description of the Euphrates and Tigris, which might allow the reader to form an overview of the whole area; 11.12.3 (521).

95. Note the altars at the confluence of Euphrates and Tigris (Ptolemy, *Geographia* 5.18). Dilke (1985), 81, says that rivers are given coordinates only at their mouths. But Ptolemy also gives coordinates for water sources and where rivers meet boundaries, tributaries, and river junctions.

96. *Geographia* 2.10.3–7.

97. *Geographia* 2.6.1–2; see also 2.11 on the coastline of Germany. Note also Mela's description of the coastline of Lusitania north of the river Durius (3.10).

98. *Geographia* 2.15.1.

99. *Geographia* 3.5; note also Asia, 5.2; Cappadocia, 5.6. In the case of Lower Moesia, Ptolemy uses a combination of rivers, mountains, and sea (3.10.1).

100. Noted by Dilke (1985), 85, in respect of the Po valley. Ptolemy does not give the coordinates for roads.

101. Chevallier (1989), 36. See also chapter 7, section 2.

102. Ptolemy, *Geographia* 3.1.53 (Umbria); 3.1.48–50 (Etruria).

103. Pliny, *NH* 3.126.

104. See *BAtlas* 40; map 8.

105. See *NH* 3.112–14; *BAtlas* 42; see also map 3.

106. See above, n. 81.

107. *NH* 3.19–24; see *BAtlas* 27 and 25. Along the coast, we have Urci on the modern river Andarra, Baria on the modern river Almanzora, New Carthage, the river Tader, Ilici on the modern river Vinalopá, Lucentum, Dianium, Sucro on the river Sucro, Valentia on the river Turia, Saguntum on the river Udiva, the river Hiberus, the river Subi, Tarraco on the river Tulcis, Subur, the river Rubicatum, Barcino, Baetulo, Iluro, the river Arnum, Blandae, the river Alba, Emporiae, the river Ticis. See Hoyos (1979), 454, for the idea that one of Pliny's sources for his account of Spain was a *periplous*, possibly by Varro.

108. For Pliny's comments on navigable rivers, see below at n. 200 and in general chapters 6–8.

109. For an introduction to the significance of internal boundaries within the Roman Empire, see the important paper by Talbert (2005); also (2004a).

110. Cicero, *Philip.* 6.5.

111. Strabo 3.4.20 (166).

112. *CIL* 2.4697 = *CIL*² 2/5.1280; *RE* suppl. VI, s.v. Ianus Augusti; Haley (2003), 35–37.

113. Strabo 2.5.30 (128–29).

114. Strabo 4.2.2 (190).

115. Strabo 4.4.2–3 (196).

116. Ptolemy, *Geographia* 2.7.3–5.

117. *Geographia* 2.13.1.

118. Varro, *Lingua Latina* 5.28.

119. For the time theme in Strabo, see Clarke (1999), 245–93, especially 277.

120. Pliny, *NH* 3.21. Another possible Spanish river name in a provincial context has appeared in an edict of Augustus (dated to 15 B.C.) recently discovered in Spain, which refers to "my legates who were in control *transdurianae provinciae.*" It is possible that the *transduriana provincia* was for a time a third province (along with Hispania Ulterior and Citerior), encompassing northwest Spain with Asturia and Callaecia; it was subsequently absorbed into the other provincial territory. Lucius Sestius Quirinalis (consul in 23 B.C.), who is referred to in the edict as governor of the province, seems to be the proper governor of Hispania Ulterior; discussion in Alföldy (2000b), especially 203–5.

121. Strabo 2.1.26 (80).

122. Strabo 5.1.4 (212).

123. *ILS* 1396.

124. Pliny, *NH* 3.127.

125. Pliny, *NH* 5.119.

126. *NH* 6.9; 3.27.

127. Ptolemy, *Geographia* 6.14.10.

128. Strabo 5.4.2 (241). Elea was named after a spring, 6.1.1 (252); Sybaris, 6.1.12 (263). For the naming of Sybaris after the nearby river, see also Dionysius Halicarnassus, *Antiquitates Romanae* 19.1.1; Adrias, 7.5.9 (317).

129. *NH* 3.114. Dio Chrysostomos notes a city Borythenes/Olbia named after the river Borsythenes because of its size and beauty (*Orationes* 36.1). Note Haslam (1997), 244–47, on English place-names and the prevalence of riverine themes.

130. *NH* 4.106.

131. *Geographia* 2.9.11.

132. Mela 3.15.

133. Mela 2.63–65.

134. Mela 2.51.

135. Mela 1.82; 2.65.

136. See chapter 4.

137. See Clarke (1999), 264–76, on the importance of the foundation and foundation legends in a city's history.

138. Strabo 7.7.7 (326).

139. Pausanias 8.6.6. For rivers used as territorial markers, see also, for example, 1.4.5 (Sangarius); 1.9.7 (Danube); 1.11.2 (Thyamis); 1.30.3 (Rhine); 2.7.4 (Asopos); 2.38.7 (Tanaos); 6.21.4 (Diagon); 8.27.17 (Oxeater); 8.54.1 (Alpheios).

140. Pausanias 8.3.6–7 (339). For the Tiber and the foundation stories of Rome, see chapter 1, section 3.

141. Pausanias 3.1.1.

142. Pausanias 9.1.1; cf. 8.28.7, Brenthe.

143. Pausanias 8.28.2, Lousios (the Wash) and the Gortys in Arcadia.

144. Pausanias 2.5.2. The Phliasians and Sikyonians claimed that the Asopos was not local but the continuation of the Maeander.

145. Strabo 7.7.9 (327).

146. See below at n. 153.

147. This theme is developed further in chapter 4.

148. Mela 2.54; 1.93.

149. Strabo 7, frag. 14.

150. Pausanias 9.4.3; cf. 8.23.2, his description of the Kaphyan plain; 8.25.11: "The Ladon leaves the sanctuary of the Fury behind on the left and flows past the shrine of Onkaian Apollo on the left and the sanctuary of Child Asklepios on the right, where the tomb of Trygon is, who they say was Asklepios's nurse."

151. Pliny, *NH* 3.122. For the nomenclature of Padus and Bodincus, see now Peretti (1994), 87–89; for Pliny's description of the river, see Murphy (2003), 319–21.

152. Pausanias 5.5.6; cf. 6.21.8.

153. Pausanias 8.7.4.

154. Strabo 11.11.5 (518).

155. Strabo 4.1.11 (185–86).

156. Strabo 12.4.6 (565).

157. Aulus Gellius, *Attic Nights* 10.7.2.

158. I am indebted to James Adams for advice on this section.

159. Rivet and Smith (1979), 18–22; quotation, 22. See also 427: "But it is safest by far

to assume that rivers universally had British names even if unconscious Latinisation has affected their recorded forms."

160. Caesar, *BG* 1.12.

161. See the interesting ideas of Janni (1984), 41–43, who argues that the ancients perhaps preferred a verbal description (rather than a map), which was dignified and gave a visualization of the nature of the lands. It is important to view ancient geographical conceptualization on their terms, without modern preconceptions.

162. Pausanias 9.34.3.

163. Pausanias 8.23.2 (Tragos); 8.25.13 (despite its beauty, the river Ladon was not big enough to produce islands like the Danube and the Po). For Pausanias's audience, see Habicht (1985), 24–26.

164. Pausanias 2.31.14.

165. Pausanias 7.25.7. Note also the Hagno spring on Mount Lycaeon in Arcadia, which was said to produce, like the Danube, the same volume of water in winter and summer (8.38.3).

166. Pausanias 2.36.7.

167. Pausanias 9.39.4.

168. Pausanias 7.21.1.

169. See further chapter 4, section 4.

170. Pausanias 7.24.2.

171. Pausanias 7.27.1; 5.5.9 (Anigros).

172. Pausanias 4.35.8–10.

173. Pausanias 8.28.2.

174. Pausanias 8.20.1.

175. Pausanias 8.25.13.

176. Pausanias 10.32.7, 33.3.

177. Pausanias 10.35.4; cf. 35.5. By contrast Belemina was marked out as the wettest place in all of Laconia (3.21.3) with many natural springs and the river Eurotas running through it.

178. Pausanias 10.33.4. The quotation is from Homer, *Iliad* 2.522–23; see 10.34.1 for bird life (bustards) along the Kephisos.

179. Strabo 1.1.7 (4), originally applied to Oceanus, which flowed like a river.

180. Strabo 3.3.1 (151) (Tagus); 3.3.4 (153) (other Spanish rivers); 9.3.16 (424) (Kephissos); 4.3.3 (193) (Rhine); 4.6.5 (203) (Padus); 7, frag. 20 (Axios); 8.3.19 (346) (Anigros); 8.6.7 (370) (Inachos); 9.1.24 (400) (Kephissos); 11.3.4 (500) (Phasis); 14.4.1 (667) (Katarraktes); 7.7.5 (324) (Acheron); 9.5.20 (441) (Peneios).

181. Strabo 3.4.12 (162).

182. In the case of the Eridanus at Athens, see Strabo 9.1.19 (397).

183. Strabo 12.2.4 (536), the Pyramus.

184. This is ignored by Nicolet (1988), 92–94.

185. Strabo 9.1.24 (400).

186. Strabo 9.4.4 (426).

187. Strabo 7.1.5 (292). Note that Strabo is in error for the sources of the Rhine (see Janni, 1984, 153) and also in respect of the Tigris (see Syme, 1995, 28 ff.). He is however correct on the sources of the Danube, though he gets distances wrong: Janni (1984), 151. For the comments of Eumenius on the sources and mouths of rivers, see below at n. 235.

188. See, e.g., Strabo 1.3.8 (53); 13.4.7–8 (627); 13.4.15 (630); especially 15.1.16 (691); 15.2.14 (726); 15.3.6 (729).

189. Strabo 15.1.16 (691); see also 15.1.23 (695). Natives always wanted to talk about the Nile first, 1.2.29 (36); see chapter 1 at n. 108.

190. Strabo 1.3.4 (50). Sailors called these "the breasts"; see, in general, chapter 1 at n. 133. Note also the silting up of Ephesus 14.1.24 (641); the Scamander and Simoeis 13.1.31 (595), 34 (597); the special impact of the Menander 12.8.17 (578); silt brought down by the Kyros in Albania, which contributed to the formation of dangerous shoals at its mouth 11.4.2 (501).

191. Strabo 9.2.16 (406). He is here referring to Lake Kopais in Boeotia.

192. Cf. Strabo 8.8.4 (389).

193. The river Erasinos, Strabo 8.6.8 (371). See also, e.g., 12.2.4 (536) (Pyramos); 12.8.16 (578) (Lykos).

194. Strabo 10.1.14 (449).

195. See further chapter 4, sections 3 and 4.

196. Strabo 1.2.30 (36); and see chapter 1 for the hydrological cycle.

197. Strabo 1.3.4–7 (49–52); he also held that the seabed of the Atlantic and of the Mediterranean were at different levels.

198. Arrian, *Periplous* 8.1 ff. Furthermore, river qualities certainly have their part to play in Arrian's assessment of the character, accessibility, and perhaps the economic value of an area. He notes navigable rivers (9.5; 10.1) and also the interrelation between river mouths and harbors (12.4–13). For those sailing along the coast, the early morning breezes blowing from the rivers were of some assistance though the oars were also needed (3.2).

Elsewhere in his writings, Arrian compared the European and Asian and Indian rivers. The greatest river in Europe was the Danube, which covered the greatest expanse of country and also acted as a barrier against the most warlike tribes. However, even the Danube could not match the rivers of India. He measured their superiority by the volume of water, their breadth, their size at source, speed of flow, and the number of tributaries (*Anabasis* 5.6.8; *Indica* 3.9, 4.14). Arrian's idea of the status of rivers is also based on their navigability and their geographical and topographical impact. Rivers by bringing down vast quantities of silt could create plains near the sea (*Anabasis* 5.6.3–4). But rivers were also unpredictable and subject to climate, seasonal variation, and other factors. For example, in India after the summer solstice, the effect of heavy rains and melting snow is that the rivers flow fast and deep. In the winter the volume of water is reduced, the water is clearer, and some rivers become fordable (*Anabasis* 5.9.4). Also mountains with heavy rainfall tended to produce turbulent rivers (*Indica* 6.4).

199. For these themes, see in detail chapters 7 and 8.

200. *NH* 5.5.

201. *NH* 3.95–96.

202. Strabo 9.5.19 (439–40); 12.2.8 (538).

203. Strabo 3.5.9 (175). See also 7, frag. 43 (44); access, 9.4.14 (428); flooding, 11.8.6 (512–13).

204. Strabo 15.1.19 (693).

205. Strabo 5.4.13 (250–51).

206. Strabo 8.8.4 (389) "deadly water."

207. See chapter 9, section 4.

208. Note *torrens* as a river synonym, *NH* 27.55. Harmful effects of rivers' ability to change landscape, 6.136; 138–39; 140; river flooding and marshes, 5.90; 36.73; 36.105. For the potential violence of rivers, see the vivid description of the *dimicatio naturae* of the Euphrates, 5.84. Note the famous tributaries of the Danube (3.149); the Indus (5. 103).

209. *NH* 5.118 (Smyrna).

210. As in Pliny's description of the Baetis, where the numerous adjacent towns and the river's navigability suggest commercial activity (3.9–10). Beagon (1992), 194–200, concentrates on the significance of *amoenus*.

211. *NH* 3.54; 15.137.

212. *NH* 4.30–31.

213. *NH* 5.71; for the famous winding course of the Maeander, see 5.113.

214. *NH* 3.49.

215. For mud and increased fertility, see Beagon (1992), 196.

216. *NH* 3.117–19.

217. Polybius 2.16.6–12.

218. *NH* 3.54–55.

219. See chapter 4, section 7, for the representation of rivers.

220. Mela 1.68.

221. Mela 3.40. For the Padus, see 2.60–62.

222. Mela 2.6. Note also the Rhine (3.24) and the "clari amnes," the Tigris and the Euphrates (3.76–78).

223. For the surveying texts, see chapter 3, section 1.

224. Only the late writer Agennius Urbicus mentions rivers as imposing symbols in the bigger picture of world geography; the rivers Tanais and Nile appear as great natural phenomena dividing continents (T22.30; T = Thulin, 1913).

225. T43.12–24.

226. See Campbell (2000), 232–39.

227. T122.5 (Siculus Flaccus).

228. T88.4–13.

229. E.g., T102.17; 114.7; Campbell (2000), 269.15–18. For the *Liber Coloniarum*, see Campbell (2000), 164–203; also chapter 3, section 3.

230. For the keeping of archives, see Moatti (1993).

231. We might compare the government purpose of river mapping in France from the fifteenth century onward; see Petts (1989), 96–97.

232. For a summary, see Campbell (2000), xxiii–vi.

233. Campbell (2000), 389–90, with illustration 91.

234. Sáez Fernández (1990); Dilke (1985), 108–10; Rodríguez-Almeida (1981).

235. *Panegyrici Latini* IX (IV) 20.2.

236. See A. Levi and Levi (1967); R. W. B. Salway (2004), 86–92; Talbert (2004c); and see now Talbert (2010).

237. Codex Vaticanus Urbinas graecus 82. See Fischer (1932); Buonocore (1996), 238–41, 355–59, 372–75, for color reproductions of the maps in this and other manuscripts.

238. Dilke (1985), 80–81.

239. *CIL* 3.6418 = *ILS* 2259; cf. Pliny *NH* 3.139 for the Varvarini. Note also similar cases. A soldier of legion I Minervia serving on the Danube presumably in a Dacian war made an offering to local deities and identified the location partly by the nearby river: "ad Alutum flumen secus monte Caucasi" (*ILS* 4795; the reference to the mountain is obscure). Amazaspos, an Iberian prince in alliance with Trajan against the Parthians, recorded his burial spot "by the holy city that Nikator built, near the olive-nurturing waters of Mygdon" (*IG* 14.1374; *IGRR* 1.192). This refers to the city of Nisibis, which Seleukos I Nikator had originally called Antiochia Mygdonia.

CHAPTER 3

1. Agennius Urbicus, *Land Disputes* T42.18–25.

2. Fitch (1907).

3. *Digest* 43.21.4.

4. *Digest* 43.12, 13, 14, 15, 20, 21, 22, 39.3.

5. For the problem of interpolation, see the useful summary by Robinson (1997), 102–30.

6. For variability in natural phenomena and response to risk, the mechanisms to protect against scarcity and damage, and their important role in human societies, see in general Halstead and O'Shea (1989), 1–7.

7. See Dilke (1971); Hinrichs (1974); Clavel-Lévêque et al. (1993), (1996); Guillaumin (1996); Behrends et al. (1998), (2000); Campbell (1996), (2000).

8. For a detailed examination of land disputes, see Burton (2000); Campbell (2005b).

9. See further chapter 10.

10. For basic linguistic definitions, see chapter 1, section 5.

11. E.g., *infestatio fluminum* (T6.15); *inundatio camporum* (T38.3); *inrumpere* (T42.21); *vis aquae abstulerit* (T64.4); *torrens violentior excedit* (T83.11); *flumen torrens violentum decurrit . . . mutet, transferat, insulas efficiat* (T87.12); *aqua lambiscendo abstulerit, amittat . . . maiore vi decurrens . . . mutasset* (87.17); *violentia tempestatis abreptum* (T88.1); *tempestas concitasset, excedens, vagaretur, iniuria, defluere* (T88.7); *maiores imbres, excedere aquam, inundare* (T88.11); *abstrahat . . . relinquat* (T114.27–78); *subitis violentisque*

imbribus excedens ripas defluet ultra modum . . . egrediatur . . . vexet terras . . . incommo-dum patiantur adsiduitate tempestatum contentoque flumine alveo ripisque suis; iniuria (T122.9–14); *nives inmodicae* (T43.6); *relegatio subita*, sudden change in a river's charac-ter because of a thaw and subsequent flooding (T43.7). Part of this section was previously published in somewhat different form in Campbell (2009) and is reproduced here by permission.

12. *Institutes of Justinian* 1.1.

13. *Digest* 1.8.5.

14. *Digest* 43.12.3.2.

15. *CIL* 14.4704(2) a–c: "sine praeiudic(io) publico aut privatorum"; the translation is based on the interpretation of Le Gall (1953a), 156–57 (date: A.D. 23–41).

16. *CIL* 14.4702 = *ILS* 9376: "de sen(atus) sent(entia) poplic(om) ioudic(avit)."

17. *CIL* 14.4703: "privatum ad Tiberim usque ad aquam." See *Notizie degli Scavi* (1910), 232–33 (G. Mancini); *Notizie degli Scavi* (1921), 258–62 (G. Calza).

18. For this interpretation, see Meiggs (1960), 32, 471–72, pl. II. The lettering on the stones suggests a date approximately between 150 and 80 B.C. Note also Le Gall (1953a), 166–67; Robinson (1992), 90–91.

19. Tuccillo (2010) argues that the inscription probably refers to a right of passage from a possessor's holding to the river, to secure the use of the water. Decision of Pius, *Digest* 1.8.4.

20. *Digest* 43.12.1.1–3.

21. *Digest* 43.13.1.

22. *Digest* 43.12.1.15.

23. *Digest* 2.11.2.6–7.

24. *Digest* 43.13.1.8.

25. González (1986), 175, chapter 82; cf. the *Lex Tarentina* (Crawford, 1996, 1:304–5, lines 39–42).

26. *Digest* 7.4.24 (Iavolenus, quoting Labeo). See also below, section 4. Usufruct was the right to use someone's property without impairing it.

27. See chapter 10.

28. *Digest* 39.3.10.2; cf. also 43.12.1f; 43.14. Aulus Gellius, *Attic Nights* 11.17, has an inter-esting discussion about the wording of an old edict of a praetor, and the interpretation of the words *flumina retanda*. He thought that it referred to attempts to keep rivers clear from trees growing on riverbanks or inclining over a river; nets attached to them (pre-sumably to dry) could impede shipping. For river navigation, see chapter 6.

29. *Digest* 8.3.3.3; 43.20.3.3–6; 43.22; cf. 8.3.15; 8.3.35; 8.4.11.1; 8.6.16; 8.6.19.

30. *Digest* 43.14.9.

31. *Digest* 43.20.3.

32. *Digest* 8.3.35.

33. T110.14–21.

34. *Digest* 8.3; *CJ* 3.34. See the excellent discussion by Capogrossi Colognesi (1966).

35. *Digest* 43.20.

36. *CJ* 3.34.6 (A.D. 269). Cf. in general *Digest* 43.22 "Concerning Springs" for protection of access to springs.

37. See Hodge (2002), 249–50; Frontinus, *De Aqueductis* 1.9; *CIL* 14.7696. On water-sharing provisions outside Italy, see B. D. Shaw (1982) (Lamasba); F. Beltrán Lloris (2006) (Ebro).

38. *CIL* 6.10250.

39. There has been a considerable debate. See principally de Robertis (1936; 1945–46) arguing for the exercise of *imperium* as against the civil law to enforce expropriation by the state; also Robinson (1992), 26–32. R. Taylor (2000), 93–127 (with full bibliography), holds that the Roman government had no right of compulsory expropriation/purchase and compensation. He thinks that there is no clear evidence for expropriation for public utility and that this would not be consistent with principles of Roman law with its emphasis on the rights of property owners.

40. Campbell (2000), 362–63.

41. *De Legibus* 3.8: "salus populi suprema lex esto."

42. *ILS* 244 = Ehrenberg and Jones (1976), no. 364. Note, however, that in Crawford (1996), 1: 549–50, it is suggested that the phrase "ex usu rei publicae" means "according to the custom of the *res publica*." However, even on this interpretation, the check on the emperor's exercise of power is limited.

43. Frontinus, *De Aquis* 104, referring to the senatorial decree of 11 B.C. R. Taylor (2000), 112, curiously seems to doubt that emperors ultimately controlled water supply and distribution.

44. Dio 49.14.5; Velleius 2.81.2; Strabo 10.4.9 (477); *AE* 1969/70.635; Ducrey (1969).

45. *Digest* 43.8.2.21.

46. *Digest* 19.2.33 (Africanus): "Si fundus quem mihi locaveris publicatus sit, teneri te actione ex conducto, ut mihi frui liceat, quamvis per te non stet, quo minus id praestes. . . . nam et si colonus tuus fundo frui a te aut ab eo prohibetur, quem tu prohibere ne id faciat possis, tantum ei praestabis, quanti eius interfuerit frui, in quo etiam lucrum eius continebitur; sin vero ab eo interpellabitur, quem tu prohibere propter vim maiorem aut potentiam eius non poteris, nihil amplius ei quam mercedem remittere aut reddere debebis."

47. For discussion, see Ankum (1980). R. Taylor (2000), 101–2, attempts to downplay the significance of this passage as evidence for expropriation by the government. He also argues that that Africanus is not interested in the act of *publicatio* but only in the current contract; but in Africanus's presentation, the lack of culpability of the seller is closely connected with fact that the farm has been made public. Robinson (1992), 31, also cites *Digest* 6.1.15.2, where Ulpian seems to refer to lands assigned to soldiers with a small sum paid to the possessor as compensation. At 21.2.11 pr., Paul refers to the purchase of lands in Germany beyond the Rhine. The purchaser paid part of the price, and when his heir was approached for the balance, he claimed that these holdings had partly been sold and partly

distributed to veterans as discharge payment on the orders of the emperor. The question was: is this the vendor's responsibility? The view was that the purchaser had to pay because what happened after the contract of sale was completed was his responsibility.

48. Frontinus, *De Aquis* 125: "uti cum ei rivi, specus, fornices, quos Augustus Caesar se refecturum impensa sua pollicitus senatui est, reficerentur, ex agris privatorum terra, limus, lapides, testa, harena, ligna ceteraque quibus ad eam rem opus esset, unde quaeque eorum proxime sine iniuria privatorum tolli, sumi, portari possint, viri boni arbitratu aestimata darentur, tollerentur, sumerentur, exportarentur; et ad eas res omnes exportandas earumque rerum reficiendarum causa, quotiens opus esset, per agros privatorum sine iniuria eorum itinera, actus paterent, darentur."

49. I can see no justification for thinking that this refers to exemption from taxes designed to pay for the maintenance of aqueducts, as suggested by R. Taylor (2000), 95–96.

50. *De Aquis* 128: "Posset hoc S.C. aequissimum videri, etiam si ex re tantum publicae utilitatis ea spatia vindicarentur. Multo magis autem maiores nostri admirabili aequitate ne ea quidem eripuerunt privatis quae ad modum publicum pertinebant, sed cum aquas perducerent, si difficilior possessor in parte vendunda fuerat, pro toto agro pecuniam intulerunt et post determinata necessaria loca rursus eum agrum vendiderunt, ut in suis finibus proprium ius res publica privatique haberent."

51. R. Taylor (2000), 116. His argument is that the possessors were occupying public land claimed by the city of Rome.

52. For discussion of the identity of the Julius Frontinus in the *Corpus Agrimensorum Romanorum*, see Campbell (2000), xxvii–xxxi.

53. T23.18: "vindicant tamen inter se non minus fines ex aequo ac si privatorum agrorum" (Nevertheless, they lay claim to boundaries among themselves just as if they were (the boundaries) of private lands); T39.7: "Proprietas non uno genere vindicatur" (Ownership is claimed in more than one way).

54. Cf. the inscription in the time of Hadrian from Chagnon in Lugdunensis near the Roman aqueduct forbidding plowing, sowing, or planting "within that space of land that is set aside for the protection of the aqueduct" (*CIL* 13.1623 = *ILS* 5749).

55. *CIL* 10.4842 = *ILS* 5743 = Ehrenberg and Jones (1976), no. 282; see also Capini (1999), 21–23: "Edict of Imperator Caesar Augustus. . . . Furthermore, in respect of that piece of land in the estate which is, or is said to be, that of Quintius Sirinius, son of Lucius, of the tribe Teretina, and in the estate which is, or is said to be, that of Lucius Pompeius Sulla, son of Marcus of the tribe Teretina, and which is closed off by a wall, though which place or under which place the conduit of that aqueduct runs, let not that wall nor any part of that wall be pulled down or destroyed for any purpose other than repairing or inspecting the conduit; and let there be nothing private there to prevent the water traveling, flowing, and being brought. . . . It is resolved that on the right and left of that conduit and around those structures which were established for bringing that water, eight feet of land should be left clear, and it is to be right and proper for the people of Venafrum or anyone acting in the name of the people of Venafrum to pass through this place for the purpose

of bringing that water or of building or repairing the structure of the aqueduct, provided that this is done with no malicious intention."

56. See Capini (1999), 28–34; also, e.g., *CIL* 10.4843 = *ILS* 5744; *AE* 1962.91.

57. As was argued by Robinson (1992), 30; *contra* R. Taylor (2000), 126. However, he misrepresents her arguments. The point is not that magistrates had a right to commit *iniuria*, but that they were empowered to take certain actions on behalf of their community while causing the minimum disruption to private interests.

58. Crawford (1996), 1:408 and 427.

59. I disagree with R. Taylor (2000), 118.

60. See J. S. Richardson (1983); Birks, Rodger, and Richardson (1984). "Let those same people who are written above be the judges. . . . In the place where the Salluienses most recently and officially put in stakes, which matter is the subject of this action, if it would be permissible for the Salluienses within their rights to make a canal through the public land of the Sosinestani within those stakes; or if it would be permissible for the Salluienses within their rights to make a canal through the private land of the Sosinestani in the place where it would be proper for a canal to be made so long as the Salluienses paid the money which is the value which would have been placed on the land where the canal might be brought"; translation from Birks, Rodger, and Richardson (1984), 46.

61. *CIL* 11.3003a = *ILS* 5771.

62. Livy 40.51.

63. Cicero, *De Lege Agraria* 1.5.14–15; see R. Taylor (2000), 98–99.

64. Dio 38.1.4.

65. Discussed by R. Taylor (2000), 103–6.

66. Suetonius, *Augustus* 56.2.

67. See Kockel (1985); also H. Bauer (1985); Vodret and Bauer (1985).

68. *AE* 1988.1119.

69. See T102.17; 114.7; Campbell (2000), 227.13, 23, 27; 230.34–35; 231.37; 248.18; 249.6, 26; 260.32; 261.33; cf. 41; 264.28; 265.27; 267.13, 22–23.

70. Campbell (2000), 266.35–268.1 (a late anonymous writer in the *Corpus Agrimensorum Romanorum*).

71. T114.7–15.

72. T128.8–11; 76.18.

73. *CIL* 9.5570; cf. *AE* 2000.488 (Tolentinum).

74. Campbell (2000), 190.30; 192.23; 194.30; 196.6; 198.3.

75. T142.14–19. An Egyptian papyrus describes how the river Tomis was used to establish part of the boundary of one property, *P. Oxy.* LI.3638, line 12 (A.D. 220); cf. XLIV.3184a, line 21, for river guards of the boundaries among a group of village liturgists (A.D. 296).

76. Translation in Campbell (2000), 232–39. Congès (2005), 76, discusses the importance of rivers and springs in the *Casae Litterarum*. Her detailed and sympathetic analysis tries to make sense of these difficult texts. She may, however, be too optimistic in trying

to relate the descriptions to real locations in the Tiber valley. They are simply not precise enough, and why do they not make the location explicit if this was intended?

77. T74.10–19.

78. *SEG* 1.329; 18.294; 24.1109.

79. *CIL* 3.586 = *ILS* 5947a. Note also the decision of the Minucii brothers in 117 B.C. relating to the landscape and boundaries inland from Genua, in which rivers and streams play an important part: *CIL* 1².584 = 5.7749 = *ILS* 5946; *ILLRP* 517; Johnston, Coleman-Norton, and Bourne (1961), no. 46. Crawford (2003) makes an interesting attempt to compare the description of this landscape in antiquity with its current interpretation.

80. Among modern discussions, note in particular: Brugi (1897), (1930); Sargenti (1965); Capogrossi Colognesi (1966); Maddalena (1970); Pavese (2004). See Hermon (2008a) for a brief survey of the land surveyors' writings on the management of water. The important study of Maganzani (2010) appeared too late for me to take detailed account of it. Part of this section was previously published in Hermon (2010), 317–26, and is reproduced by permission of the editor and publishers.

81. Campbell (2000), xlvii–liii.

82. T48.8–11.

83. See below at n. 142.

84. Note the observations of Sargenti (1965), 238–39, on possible differences of approach between land surveyors and jurists.

85. T43.4–8.

86. T69.6–8.

87. *Digest* 10.1.8.

88. *Digest* 41.2.3.17.

89. See below at n. 112.

90. *Digest* 7.4.10.2 (Ulpian); he refers to a permanent change in the land's character.

91. *Digest* 8.6.14.1.

92. *Digest* 2.11.2.6.

93. *Digest* 39.2.24.11.

94. *Digest* 13.7.30.

95. *Digest* 19.2.15.2–5.

96. Summary in Robinson (1992), 86–91; see now Aldrete (2006). For the curators of the bed and banks of the Tiber, see chapter 8 at n. 184.

97. T24.5–12.

98. *Digest* 39.3.1.

99. See the discussion by Rodger (1970).

100. *Digest* 43.15.1; 39.3.23.2; T43.9–11; 87.6–8.

101. T114.29–115.2.

102. *CJ* 7.41.1, Gordian III in 239.

103. For official archives relating to land distribution, see Moatti (1993).

104. Translation and commentary by Bouma (1993).

105. T83.7–9; 122.5–6; see also chapter 2, n. 227.

106. T88.4–13. This land was effectively treated as *subseciuum*—land not officially occupied, which could be exploited by neighboring landholders.

107. T44.20–23; 88.15–18.

108. T43.17–24; see further chapter 2 at n. 225.

109. T63.1–2.

110. T44.3–23.

111. Hyginus (T87.12–15) may refer to this process; however, it is more likely that he is talking about the movement of large pieces of land by the river.

112. T37.21–38.2. The author goes on to cite Africa, where the huge area and the flooding of the plains led to confusion in the identification of sites. Cf. the description of the action of the Nile in Strabo 17.1.3 (787): "The Nile removes and adds soil and changes the shape of land and obliterates the other markers by which your own land is demarcated from another's. It is essential, therefore, that the lands are remeasured again and again."

113. As happened in *ager occupatorius*, T102.9–15. For a discussion of the meaning of *alluvio* and its relevance to the designation of boundaries, see Lewis (1983), and below, n. 135.

114. *Digest* 7.4.23. Cf. 41.1.38 from the work of the jurist Alfenus Varus (consul 39 B.C.) preserved in the Digest of Paul, with the rather speculative discussion in Sargenti (1965), especially 204–15.

115. He is referring to a short-lived flood in which the water receded in the same incident and did not change the character of the land.

116. As argued by Sargenti (1965), 223.

117. *Digest* 7.4.24 (Javolenus quoting Labeo). Javolenus comments: "I agree that this is true if the river occupied the garden with a temporary inundation. For, if the river changed its bed and began to flow from there, I think that the usufruct is lost, because the location of the riverbed has become public property and cannot be restored to its previous legal condition."

118. See diagram 1, where B represents a landholder for whose property the original course of the river indicated by the arrows marked the boundary; the river then changes course and flows through his property, but its original bed should still mark the boundary between the property of B and A; when the river returns to its old course, landowner B can naturally occupy its temporary bed; cf. *CJ* 7.41.1.

119. T8.15. See Campbell (2000), illustration 20 (= diagram 2 in this volume) and 323–24. The diagram that accompanies the Frontinus passage does not clearly fit the text; it seems to illustrate a situation where a river has changed course and flowed through the farm of Septicius. If the section marked AB is meant to show a dried-up bed, then the question is: does this now belong to the farm? But, if AB represents a flowing offshoot from the main stream, the question will concern the section of land now cut off (*insula Septiciani*): what is its status?

120. T42.23.

121. T42.16.

122. See below, section 5.

123. Note particularly the discussion in Sargenti (1965); Maddalena (1970), especially 1–37; Pavese (2004), 43–124; cf. Buckland (1975), 211–12, who argues that at least by the early second century lawyers tended to support the interests of the riparian possessors.

124. *Institutes of Justinian* 2.1.23–24; cf. *Digest* 41.1.7.5. It may be of course that lawyers in pleading their client's case helped to influence the development of the law.

125. *Digest* 41.1.30.3. He describes a case where, as the water recedes, it deposits a layer of soil on the land that had previously been flooded.

126. *Digest* 43.12.1.7.

127. *Digest* 41.1.7.5. See above at n. 118 for discussion of this issue.

128. *Digest* 41.1.7.5. Maddalena (1970), 115–16, interprets the final phrase—"sed vix est, ut id optineat"—to mean that in practice, in the circumstances described, the original owner could not easily recover his land. The next section (41.1.7.6) continues: "It is a different matter if a man's entire land has been inundated; for the inundation does not change the shape of the farm, and therefore, when the water recedes, it is obvious that it belongs to the person in whose possession it was." This seems to contradict what he has just said, but he may be referring to a temporary inundation and not a change in the river's course; cf. *Institutes of Justinian* 2.1.24.

129. Strabo 12.8.19 (578). The language is rather vague and the Loeb translation (H. L. Jones, 1918–35, 5:517) unhelpful, but Strabo seems to have in mind that the river widened its course or shifted its channel and pushed aside or smoothed out a curve in its course, sweeping the land away and permanently occupying the area. The landholder on one side of the river would suffer loss as the river now flowed through part of his land, but the landholder on the other side did not profit in any way. Therefore, there were few options for redress and hence the idea, presumably by local custom, of suing the river itself. In Italy, a landholder could perhaps sue the local community through whose territory the offending river flowed (we may compare the case of the river Pisaurus discussed previously). Of course, landholders had the responsibility of looking after the bank to prevent erosion, but they were not to blame if the river action was violent.

130. T6.15. For a discussion of the category of "land carried by the river" in Egypt under the Ptolemies and Romans, see Blouin (2010).

131. *Digest* 41.1.7.1–2; Gaius, *Institutes* 2.70–72; T87.12–88.3. Hyginus is here probably referring to a situation where the force of the current actually removes a large chunk of land—hence, the words "carries across its bank . . . the land of many people" and "land swept away (abreptum)." This is not just a case of land being submerged by the flood (cf. Sargenti, 1965, 238–40). Because measurements have been taken, the landholder could define and recognize the portion of land that he had lost and get compensation for it. The fact of the river's changes in course may be mentioned mainly to show the violence of this disruptive phenomenon.

132. *Digest* 41.1.7.2.

133. T42.5–15; 87.4–11. A papyrus from Oxyrhynchus (*P. Oxy.* III.486, lines 14–16, A.D. 131) describes how one Dionysia involved in a land dispute seeks permission to re-

turn to her land because the time for sowing and "the repair of land swept away by the river" required her presence.

134. For land exchanges in the *agrimensores*, see, for example, Siculus Flaccus (T119.21–27.). A rescript from Gordian in A.D. 239 confirmed that land removed gradually and deposited on the land of another landowner was acquired by him (*CJ* 7.41.1).

135. *CIL* 11.1147, 6.83–88. This most likely refers to the recording of alluvial land established after the last census registration; see Veyne (1957), 116; Pavese (2004), 46, 111–13.

136. *Digest* 41.1.56.

137. *Digest* 41.1.16. Maddalena (1970), 46–69, argues that the *ius alluvionis* was confined to cases in which a river left its bed or an island appeared in the stream, and that it was excluded in *ager limitatus* because on the banks of a river in this land there was an area set aside (*exceptus*) for the river. This he claims remained in the ownership of the Roman people (see especially 57–58). I agree with the general direction of this approach, though it has difficulties, partly because the problem of alluviation is not confined to the proximity of the banks but might extend far beyond, as indeed Hyginus points out (T87.12–15: "carries across its bank the land of many people over a wide area"). Maddalena also ascribes too precise a meaning to *ius alluvionis* and forgets that it is rarely mentioned in the legal sources and not at all by the surveying writers. Lewis (1983), 92–93, argues that *alluvio* normally refers to a flood and that the meaning attached to it of depositing land is just a special case or consequence of *alluvio*. As the water of the flood retreated, so the edge of the stream shifted progressively and revealed the land that it had originally covered. On this basis, the *ius alluvionis* preserves the utility of the river as a boundary marker by guaranteeing the continuation of the original boundary line as the water recedes. But this meaning certainly does not emerge from the legal texts. At 41.1.16, the second part of passage ascribed to Trebatius does not cohere with the first. It may be that he was referring to another case, based on *limites*, but not directly related to *ius alluvionis*.

138. *Digest* 41.1.12 pr. There was no *ius alluvionis* in these circumstances.

139. *De Oratore* 1.173.

140. *Digest* 18.6.7 pr.

141. *Digest* 19.1.13.14. See also 18.6.11; an action for recovery of land could not be brought by the purchaser when some of the land was destroyed by a flood, earthquake, or other accident before any measurement had been taken (Scaevola).

142. Quoted with approval by Hyginus, T87.12–88.3.

143. *Digest* 41.1.30.2; see diagram 3.

144. *Digest* 41.1.7.3–4.

145. *Digest* 41.1.56.1; see diagram 4.

146. See *Digest* 41.1.65.1–4.

147. Discussion in Feissel (2004). Quotations from lines 10–14 and 61–62.

148. Theod., *Nov.* 20.2 = *CJ* 7.41.3 (A.D. 440).

149. As argued by Feissel (2004), 321–22.

150. I am much indebted to Peter Thonemann for discussion on this topic and for access to his research on the Maeander before publication; see chapter 1, n. 104.

151. *SEG* 44 (1994).938 (set up c. A.D. 50); cf. Hermann (1994), 211–13.

152. See Campbell (2000), xlviii–xlix.

153. *Pro Balbo* 45.

154. See further chapter 6, section 6.

155. *CIL* 12.107 = *ILS* 5868; this perhaps refers principally to the river Isara (Isère).

CHAPTER 4

1. *Annales* 1.79. M' Curius Dentatus (censor in 272 B.C.) had constructed a channel though the mountains to connect Lake Velinus with the Nar (Cicero, *Ad Att.* 4.15.5). The local peoples now apparently regarded this work as part of the natural setting.

2. For the importance of tributaries, see chapter 2, e.g., at nn. 60, 208.

3. See Brittain (1958), 115–40, for discussion of man's analysis of the significance of running water.

4. Herodotus, 1.138, 188.

5. Philostratus, *Vita Apollonii* 1.20.

6. C. L. Roth (1875), 304. Suetonius's work on *De naturis rerum* apparently took account of the characteristics of rivers, according to Reifferscheid (1860), 240–44. Callimachus had written "Concerning Rivers"; see Pfeiffer (1949–53), frags. 457–59.

7. Müller (1861), 637–65. Pseudo-Plutarch concentrates on how rivers were named, but much of the information is fanciful, and we cannot be sure that authors such as Chrysermos of Corinth are genuine (sec. 20). He also examines local geography and vegetation near the rivers and associated riverine legends.

8. *De Rerum Natura* 5.261–72; translation by R. Latham (Penguin, 1951), pp. 178–79.

9. *De Architectura* 8.1.7; 2.5–6; see Biswas (1970), 57–71; Aristotle, *Metereologica* II.2.356a; 350a, discussed the origins of springs and rivers, arguing for the importance of rainfall but also the subterranean condensation of air into water. Seneca in the *Quaestiones Naturales* was skeptical about the importance of rainfall in the origins of rivers, because he thought that rain would be unable to penetrate more than ten feet of the surface. He followed the Aristotelian view that there was moisture confined within the earth itself that was forced out and explored the possibility that there were large underground reservoirs supplying rivers (3.4–9).

Agrippa's map of the empire had been constructed from his geographical commentary and was displayed after his death on the *porticus Vipsaniae*.

10. 4.43. Horace, *Epistulae* 1.2.41–43, also comments on the endless flow of rivers.

11. Marcus Aurelius 5.23; 2.17.

12. Marcus Aurelius 6.15; 7.19.

13. Seneca, *Epistulae Morales* 58.22–23.

14. *Epistulae Morales* 41.3.

15. *Gnomologium* 3.1. We might compare Callimachus's comparison of two rivers in the *Hymn to Apollo* 108–12, metaphorically representing epic poetry and his own kind of

poetry. The stream of the Assyrian river is great but it carries a great deal of earth and refuse; not every kind of water pleases the gods, and a small stream might satisfy them if it were pure and undefiled. See F. Williams (1978), 87–96. Note also Callimachus poem 95; Brink (1963), 159–60.

16. From the Septuagint, Psalms 104(105).41: God struck the rock and water flowed in waterless places; 23(24).2: God established the earth, sea and rivers; Wisdom of Solomon 5.22; 11.6: rivers involved in vengeance on the unjust. Cf. Exodus 7.20–21; Ezekiel 29.3; Job 28.10–11: God's control over the natural world is fundamental. Also Eusebius, *Demonstratio Evangelica* 2.2.6; 2.3.19; and 6.7.2; cf. *Preparatio Evangelica* 8.8.26.

17. See Schama (1995), 247.

18. Eurotas and Padus, Ovid, *Amores* 2.17.32; Tagus, *Amores* 1.15.34, McKeown (1987–89), 415–16; Maeander, Strabo 12.8.15 (577); Pseudo-Plutarch 9, "turning back on itself"; Anio, Strabo 5.37.4; Marsyas, Ovid, *Metamorphoses* 6.400; Baetis, Lucan, *Pharsalia* 2.589; Nar, Martial, *Epigrammata* 7.93.1; Tiber, Virgil, *Aeneid* 7.30–31; 8.64. For descriptions in Strabo, Pausanias, and other geographical writers, see chapter 2. For the adjective *flavus*, see Nisbet and Hubbard (1970), 25, who describe it as a "conventional euphemism."

19. Horace, *Carmina* 1.9.4; 4.7.4; 12.3; cf. Virgil, *Georgics* 1.310.

20. Horace, *Carmina* 4.2.5; cf. 3.29.33–41.

21. Lucretius 1.280–89 (translation by Latham, 35, n. 8 above). Note Livy 21.31.10 for the difficulty of crossing the Alpinus in flood.

22. *Quaestiones Naturales* 3.10.2, 16.1; 4a.2.19–20. And see further chapter 1.

23. Pliny, *Epistulae* 8.8. See McKay (1972), 154–55, on the river Clitumnus.

24. Virgil, *Georgics* 2.146; Propertius 2.19.25–26; 3.22.23; Statius, *Silvae* 1.4.128–29; Silius Italicus 4.545–46; Claudian, *vi cons. Hon.* 500–514. Caligula paid a visit to the river (Suetonius, *Caligula* 43.1).

25. Horace, *Carmina* 3.13. for the context and structure of the poem, see G. Williams (1968), 148–52; (1969), 87–90. Aelius Aristides addresses a speech of praise to a source of water at Pergamum (*Or.* 53), but C. P. Jones (1991) contends that this refers to the inauguration of an aqueduct under Marcus Aurelius, rather than a spring.

26. Aelian, *Varia Historia* 3.1.37.

27. *De Rerum Natura* 2.29–31.

28. Catullus, 68.57–62; cf. Virgil, *Georgics* 2.199–202; *Eclogues* 5.47; Calpurnius Siculus 2.58; Ovid, *Metamorphoses* 3.407–12, on the ideal position for a spring and pool. According to Horace, the Liris was a peaceful river gently nibbling the land (*Carmina* 1.31.7–8). For the Liris in literature, see Nisbet and Hubbard (1970), 352. For "nibbling," see Nisbet and Hubbard (1970), 353, though this interpretation is not certain.

29. Cicero, *Ad Atticum* 13.16.

30. Statius, *Silvae* 1.3.

31. Silius Italicus, *Punica* 4.643–48. Cf. Horace, *Carmina* 2.9.21–22, where *vertices* may suggest personification; see Nisbet and Hubbard (1978), 150.

32. Ovid, *Amores* 3.6.

33. Statius, *Silvae* 4.3.67–94, with Coleman (1988), 120–27. For the idea of a river re-

senting a bridge, see Virgil, *Aeneid* 8.728 (in the Araxes). See also Catullus 17 (Thomson, 1978). Silius Italicus (*Punica* 3.455) has the vivid idea that men invade the river (Rhine), which is hostile to bridges.

34. Note the useful observations of Bedon (2010).

35. Fortunatus, 10.9 (*De Navigio suo*); 3.13.1–10; translation by George (1995). See also George (1992).

36. See in general Tuan (1974), (1976); Livingstone (1995); also chapter 2.

37. Dio Chrysostomos 33.2.

38. See chapter 2, section 4.

39. *Pharsalia* 1.399–401; cf. 6.371–77, on rivers that give their waters to the Peneios. Silius Italicus, *Punica* 3.442–65, vividly describes the tumultuous course of the Rhône, emphasizing how it swallows up the waters of the Arar. Note also Tacitus's comments on the Rhine, which broke into two branches: "The channel bordering Germany keeps its name and turbulent course until it meets the sea. On the Gallic bank, the course is broader and slower (the inhabitants call it by a different name, the Vahalis); then further down this too changes its name and flows into the same sea as the Mosa in the great estuary of that river" (*Annales* 2.6).

40. Herodotus 4.90–91. Note Schama (1995), 264, for the Jordan as a site for redemption and deliverance, in contrast to the Nile, which symbolized Jewish captivity.

41. *Georgics* 1.509.

42. Propertius 3.3.44–45.

43. Virgil, *Eclogues* 1.62; Horace, *Carmina* 2.20.20. Nisbet and Hubbard (1978), 347, cite examples of poets who identify the people of a country by the river they drank. For the Danube and the Don, see *Carmina* 4.15.25–28.

44. Juvenal 3.62. See Courtney (1980), 164.

45. *Georgics* 2. 155–57: "adde tot egregias urbes operumque laborem, / tot congesta manu praeruptis oppida saxis, / fluminaque antiquos subter labentia muros." See McKay (1972), 158. See also Putnam (1975) on Georgics II, especially 173 on line 157.

46. For a useful summary of Virgil and the rivers of northern Italy, see Goodfellow (1981).

47. *Pharsalia* 2.394–420.

48. *Pharsalia* 421–27. Compare Lucan's description of the rivers of Greece (6.361–80) with their various qualities including a mixture of legend.

49. See also Silius Italicus, *Punica* 8.446–55, describing the arrival of the Umbrians to join the Roman army before Cannae. Each group is associated with its local river: the Aesis and Sapis and Metaurus (noisy, fast-flowing, rocky), the Clitumnus (with its sacred waters), Nar (with pale waters rushing to join the Tiber), the Tinia (inglorious), Clanis, Rubico, Sena (named after the Senones), and the assembled force of the gentle Sarnus.

50. *Res Gestae* 26.2; 26.4; 30; 31.2.

51. Nicolet (1988), 103–24; Vitruvius, *De Architectura* 8.2.6. For this theme of Roman power, see chapter 10.

52. *Ad Aeneidam* 7.87. In what follows I use Haslam's definition of a spring (1991), 41: "A spring is the place of rising, the source, of a well, stream or river, a flow of water rising naturally out of the earth."

53. See Beard, North, and Price (1998), 1:13–14, 30–31. Edlund-Berry (1987), 54–62, argues for the importance of sacred places in nature. The availability of good water at the right time for the Greek colonists in Italy was an important factor in religious observances; rivers were seen as offering divine protection.

54. *Onirocritica* 2.27 (Pack, 1963).

55. See below, section 7. For the mystic qualities of water, see Thevenot (1968), 200–207; on the qualities of springs and their religious ambiance, see Buxton (1994), 109–13.

56. Suetonius notably included among Claudius's essential public works the provision of cool and generous supplies of water though the Claudian and new Anio aqueducts (*Claudius* 20.1).

57. *Metamorphoses* 6.349–51 with Bömer (1976), 101.

58. See below, section 4; for the significance of living water, see Holland (1961), 8–20.

59. Notably in the story of Narcissus (*Metamorphoses* 3.407–12).

60. Seneca, *Quaestiones Naturales* 3.26.3; 5.13.1, whirlpool; see also 3.19.4; 6.8.1–3. As we have seen, rivers often caught the attention because they had, or were believed to have, special qualities and powers.

61. Chapter 2, section 4. Note also the famous story told in Chios about the river of pain and the river of pleasure. Those who drank the first were overcome by grief and died weeping; those who drank the second had a joyful resurgence of youth until they got back to childhood (Aelian, *Varia Historia* 3.18, regarding this as incredible).

62. R. Parker (2000); Thonemann (2006), with particular reference to the Maeander. Thonemann argues that the common personal names in Mandro- and -mandros are directly derived from the name of the river; in mainland Greece, the two Kephisos rivers in Attica and the Kephisos in Boeotia produced many personal names. Curbera (1998) notes that many Sicilian cities were named after rivers but argues against overvaluing the worship of rivers in Sicily based on coin evidence, since the frequency of river images on coins may be due to the eponymous character of the rivers.

63. See Ninck (1921); Edlund-Berry (1987), 58–61. See also below at n. 71 for the position of temples at river crossings.

64. Carter (1994), 177–83, on the location of rural sanctuaries in fifth-century Greece along river valleys; Cole (1994), 204–5. Note also Horace, *Carmina* 1.21.5, worship of Diana who delights in rivers; for this concept in literature, see Nisbet and Hubbard (1970), 256.

65. *Amores* 3.1.1–4.

66. *Metamorphoses* 1.276–80; Ovid imagines all rivers congregating underground before they flow out.

67. Peneios, *Georgics* 4.319–24; Tiber, *Aeneid* 7.137–38. For the theme of the Tiber welcoming the Trojans, see Benario (1978), 5–10.

68. See n. 3 above.

69. Pliny, *Epistulae* 8.8. Cf. 8.20.5: boats were prohibited on the sacred waters of Lake Vadimon. See also Tacitus, *Annales* 14.22, Nero bathing in the source of the *aqua Marcia*.

70. See further chapter 9, n. 233.

71. *De Architectura* 4.5.2.

72. *Anabasis* 1.4.5. Note also the contrasting episodes of Lucullus and Crassus at the Euphrates: for the former, the river level fell, and it was claimed that the river-god had intervened in his favor (Plutarch, *Lucullus* 24); for the latter, there were unfavorable omens (Plutarch, *Crassus* 19). On campaign in Greece, Sulla sacrificed on the banks of the Kephisos (Plutarch, *Sulla* 17). For the religious significance of river crossings, see in general Toutain (1926), especially 4–6.

73. 1.41.2; for representations of rivers see below, section 7. For the popularity of the Acheloüs as a deity, see Macrobius, *Saturnalia* 5.18.6, quoting Ephorus. For Greek religious ritual in Pausanias, see Pirenne-Delforge (2001).

74. Pausanias 5.14.5–6.

75. Pausanias 5.13.11.

76. Pausanias 5.10.7; 15.7.

77. Pausanias 8.24.12. Cf. Pliny, *NH* 36.58, on Vespasian's erection of a statue of the Nile in black basalt in the temple of Peace in Rome.

78. At Potniai, Pausanias 9.8.1.

79. Pausanias 1.37.2; 8.41.3.

80. Pausanias 1.37.2.

81. Pausanias 2.17.2. Garlands woven from the herb asterion picked on the bank of the river Asterion were offered to Hera.

82. Pausanias 4.3.10.

83. Pausanias 10.8.5.

84. Pausanias 10.34.4.

85. Servius, *Ad Aeneidam* 1.259; the waters of the river were traditionally used in observances to Vesta (7.150).

86. As suggested by Dumézil (1966), 379–81.

87. For this theme, see chapter 9.

88. No attempt is made to record every inscription; particularly important examples are discussed in what follows.

89. *CIL* 5.3915 = *ILS* 6706; cf. *ILS* 3913; *AE* 1962.261: "Nymphis et genio loci," set up by the prefect of the first cohort of Batavians at Housesteads; *AE* 1987.1069: "Neptuno [Ny]mphiis et genio loci," set up by an equestrian official and others.

90. *AE* 1983.711; for Silvanus, see Dorcey (1992).

91. *AE* 1974.390 (from Tarraconensis): "Nymphis fontis Amevi," or perhaps Ameucn(i). Cf. *CIL* 2.5726 from Astures Transmontani, a dedication to a named spring, fonti Sagin[i]es(i).

92. *AE* 1989.306; *ILS* 3913; *ILS* 3894a; *CIL* 9.4644 = *ILS* 3857; *CIL* 11.1162 = *ILS* 3870; *CIL* 8.17722 = *ILS* 3879. Malissard (1992), 98–99, makes the point that statues at fountains in towns recall the origins of water.

93. *CIL* 7.171; cf. 1104, a dedication to the *nymphae* by a detachment of legion VI Victrix.

94. *CIL* 2.5084 = *ILS* 3880; *CIL* 8.2583 = *ILS* 3893; cf. *CIL* 3.10893 = *ILS* 3865 and *CIL* 3.1129 = *ILS* 3867; *CIL* 3.1566 = *ILS* 3891.

95. *ILS* 5741; cf. *SEG* 36.1399.

96. *AE* 1983.395.

97. *CIL* 8.5884 = *ILS* 3906.

98. *CIL* 10.6071 = *ILS* 3884.

99. *CIL* 6.143 = *ILS* 3896.

100. *CIL* 12.3076.

101. *CIL* 10.4734 = *ILS* 3868; *CIL* 11.3287 = *ILS* 3876a; *CIL* 2.150 = *ILS* 3883; *CIL* 8.2583 = *ILS* 3893 (wife and daughters of governor; see above, n. 93); *AE* 1983.474 from Lusitania. Slave, *AE* 1964.259.

102. *CIL* 9.4644 = *ILS* 3857; *CIL* 5.3106 = *ILS* 3859; *CIL* 10.5163 = *ILS* 3863; *CIL* 3.1129 = *ILS* 3867; *CIL* 3.3116 = *ILS* 3869. See also *AE* 1969-70.691, for a fifth-century poem celebrating the return of waters at Thibilis in Numidia. *CIL* 3.1129: "Nymphae novae," 3382: "Nymphae perennes," 10462: "fonti perenni"; 6.150, 8718, 31564; 5.3106: "ob reditum aquarum"; 13.11759: "Nymphae perennes."

103. *CIL* 6.154 = *ILS* 3888.

104. The *corpus fontanorum* at Ostia consisted of fullers; *CIL* 14. 4573. See Meiggs (1960), 313; cf. *CIL* 12.3337, *collegium fontanorum* at Nemausus.

105. *CIL* 2.2005 = *ILS* 3885 (*Fonti divino*); *CIL* 5.4938 = *ILS* 3890 (*Fontibus divinis*); *CIL* 2²/7, 224 (*fonti sacro* from Corduba); *ILS* 9262 (*deabus Nymfabus*); *CIL* 14.46a (*divinae*); 3.1396; 10.7860 (*sanctissimae*); *ILS* 4725 (*deae Coventinae*); 4726 (*deae Nimfae Coventine*); below at n. 153; *CIL* 7.875 = *ILS* 9317 (*deae Nymphae Brigantiae*); *CIL* 13.6265 = *ILS* 7075 (*deabus Nymphis vicani Altiaienses*); *CIL* 3.5861: "Apollo Grannus et Nymphae"; *CIL* 10.6787-89; 11.3286-88 = *ILS* 3873-77 (Apollo); *CIL* 6.536 = *ILS* 3284 (Neptune); *CIL* 8.4322 = *ILS* 2484: "IOM et nymphae." There are also frequent references to *nymphae Augustae*, perhaps acquiring extra dignity from association with the imperial name. See, e.g., *CIL* 3.1957, 3047, 3116, 4043, 4117, 4119, 5146-48, 5678, 8419, 10892, 11155, 11688.

106. *CIL* 2.3786.

107. *CIL* 8.2662 = *ILS* 3895.

108. *CIL* 11.1823 = *ILS* 8748.

109. *CIL* 14.2 = *ILS* 3339.

110. *AE* 1982.661.

111. *CIL* 6.29195 = *ILS* 8482. However, nymphs were vaguely associated with the realms of the blessed (cf. *AE* 1974.327, a memorial to a man's wife, Daphne, "who has gone to the Nymphs"). The boy had "betrayed" his parents by dying young.

112. Varro, *Lingua Latina* 6.22; *ILS* 8744 (Fasti Maffeiani ad loc.); *AE* 1988.625 (calendar from Tauromenium).

113. Cicero, *De Legibus* 2.56. Festus mentions religious observances for *fontes* outside the *porta Fontinalis* (75 L); this may refer to a shrine dedicated in 231 B.C. by C. Papirius Maso (Platner and Ashby, 1926, 210; L. Richardson, 1992, 153).

114. Plutarch, *Numa* 13.2; Festus 152 L.

115. *CIL* 2.150; cf. 6277.

116. Horace, *Carmina* 3.13.2–8.

117. A range of examples: Acheloüs, *AE* 1987.897; Adsalluta, *CIL* 3.5134; Ampsaga, *CIL* 8.5884 = *ILS* 3906; Arar and Rhône, *AE* 1992.1240; Arrabo, *AE* 1999.771 and *CIL* 5.6629; Baetis, *CIL* 2.1163 = *ILS* 3905; Cydnus, *SEG* 12.511(25); Danube, *CIL* 3. 5863 = *ILS* 3912; Durius, *CIL* 2.2370 = *ILS* 3904; Euphrates and Tigris, *SEG* 30.1479, 1787; 31.1454, 1472B (A.D. 663); 35.1084 (late second century A.D.), 1475 (c. A.D. 591); 44.1410 (A.D. 762); 45.1905A (A.D. 442); 46.1470; 47.2080; Eurotas, *IG* V.1.538 and *SEG* 42.314, lines 20–26 (referring to a bridge on the Eurotas); cf. *SEG* 45.279; 35.1026; Halys, *AE* 1999.234, new reading of *CIL* 6.35612; 1993.912; Hermos, *IGR* 2.1388 (third century A.D.); Hiberus, *AE* 1999.1043 (referring to an irrigation canal supplied by the Hiberus); Kalykadnos, *SEG* 44.1228 (second/third century A.D.); Lygus, *SEG* 15.380 (second century A.D.); Maeander, *IG* 14.1848; *SEG* 14.459 (fourth/third century B.C.); Melas, *SEG* 20.75, 14–15 (second century A.D.); Meles at Smyrna, *SEG* 18.495; Rhine, *AE* 1969–70.434; 1993.1227; *ILS* 3913; *CIL* 13.5255, 7790, 7791, 8810, 8811; Rhône, *AE* 1997.748; 1992.1240; Sangarius, *SEG* 32.1273, 1274 (second/third century A.D.); Savus, *CIL* 3.40098 = *ILS* 3908/9; Sequana, *CIL* 13.11575; Synnada (river southeast of), *SEG* 40.1225; Timavus, *ILS* 3900. cf. *CIL* 5, p. 75; *CIL* 1².652 = *ILS* 8885; Vidasus and Tiana (?), *CIL* 3.10819 = *ILS* 3910.

118. Suetonius, *De Rhetoribus* 4; Statius, *Silvae* 1.2.263–65; Virgil, *Aeneid* 7.734; *CIL* 10.1480; Frederiksen (1984), 19.

119. *ILS* 3903.

120. *AE* 1969–70.434, set up by Oppius Severus, a legionary legate. See Vollkommen (1994), 5 with fig. 2; cf. also n. 117, Rhine; *CIL* 13.5255 = *ILS* 9267 from Burg: "flum. Rheno pro salute." Cf. *CIL* 3.3416 = *ILS* 3911, the Danube at Aquincum "flows down."

121. *AE* 1977.762; cf. 1987.897.

122. *CIL* 6.20674.

123. See Bonneau (1964), 29–131.

124. Bonneau (1964), 135–214.

125. Bonneau (1964), 254–314.

126. Bonneau (1964), 315–60. For later views of the Nile's properties, see Schama (1995), 256–63; for representations of the river, see below, section 7.

127. Tibullus 1.7.23, with Murgatroyd (1980), 219–20. In papyrus documents, it is routinely described as "great river" from the Ptolemaic to the Roman period; see, e.g., *P. Teb.* 25, line 23 (117 B.C.); 92, line 3 (second century B.C.); *P. Oxy.* XVII.2125, lines 17–18 (A.D. 220–21); XXXVIII.2876, line 10 (early third century); *Sammelbuch* 10889, line 9 (A.D. 135); 11272, line 11 (A.D. 211).

128. *P. Oxy.* XI.1380, lines 121–26.; cf. a hymn to Isis from Ptolemaic times, *Sammelbuch* 8138, line 11.

129. As summed up by Bonneau (1964), 356.

130. *Panegyricus* 31, 32.3.

131. *P. Oxy.* IX.1211 = *Select Papyri* (ed. A. S. Hunt and C. C. Edgar, Loeb vol. 2), no. 403; see in general Bonneau (1964), 361–420.

132. Seneca, *Quaestiones Naturales* 4a.2.7; Pliny, *NH* 5.57.

133. Bonneau (1964), 421–39.

134. *P. Oxy.* XVI.1830, lines 5–6.

135. *CIL* 2.4075. Only the god's right foot and water flowing from an urn remain; and see below at n. 261.

136. *SEG* 35.1409 (c. A.D. 150).

137. *CIL* 3.10395, 11894.

138. *CIL* 2.1163 = *ILS* 3905; see Abad Casal (1975), 101. For dedications to other rivers, see *CIL* 2.2370 = *ILS* 3904; *CIL* 8.5884; 3.5138; 3.4009; 3.10819; 3.3416; 3.5863 = *ILS* 3906–13.

139. *ILS* 3900 and 8885 (see n. 117). The first inscription is on an altar on the banks of the river Celina, far from the location of the Timavus, near Aquileia. Note also *Notizie degli Scavi* (1925), 20: "Aesontio (Isonzo) sacr. L. Barbius Montan(us) p(rimi) p(ilaris) v.s.l.m."

140. *SEG* 32.1273: "Poseidon Sangarios"; cf. 1274: "to Sangarios lord" (second/third century A.D.).

141. *CIL* 3.5863 = *ILS* 3912; *ILS* 3913.

142. *ILS* 9266. Cf. also *CIL* 13.7791, 8811.

143. *CIL* 3.5138 = *ILS* 3907; cf. *CIL* 3.5134 and 5138. Note also inscriptions honoring the "Savus Augustus" (*CIL* 3.3896; 4009).

144. *CIL* 13.1036, 1042–45, 1541 = *ILS* 7041; 1605; *CIL* 13.1674 = *ILS* 7013; 1675; 1702; 1710; 1712; *CIL* 13.1714 = *ILS* 7014; 1716; 1719; *CIL* 13.2940 = *ILS* 7050; 3144; *AE* 1992.1240. See also and with more examples, Thevenot (1968), 208–10.

145. Crawford (1996), 1:528; González and Arce (1988); Millar (1988).

146. Cassius Dio 55.2. Note also the importance of Ad Confluentes (Koblenz) at the confluence of the Moselle and Rhine; see chapter 7, section 3.

147. *CIL* 12.3070, 3098; see Grenier (1960), 493–506; Gros (1987), 347, on the altar of Augustus at the water shrine. Grénier in his magisterial compilation assembles the archaeological evidence for shrines and other constructions in Gaul that can plausibly or possibly be associated with baths and water sources of any kind; see also Thevenot (1968), 117–32, and Pascal (1964) 91–97, for a general survey of water deities in Cisalpine Gaul.

148. See also chapter 9.

149. De Izarra (1993), 230. On small water-divinities, see Grenier (1960): Narbonese Gaul, 493–535; Matrebo Namausikabo at Nîmes, 493, n. 1; Matres Almahae at Aups and Matres Ubelnae at Saint-Zacharie, 523; local divinities of water sources in Aquitania, 537; local healing god Vindonnus at Essarois, associated with hot springs, 639; Segomo, water-

god of the Sequani, also associated with the sun, 679; *Icovellauna*, water-deity near Metz, 824; *CIL* 13.4292; *Sirona* at Sainte-Fontaine near Merlebach, 828–29; *CIL* 13.4498; Matronae Aufaniae at Nettersheim, common in Gaul, though probably not exclusively deities of water sources, 902–7; Nehalennia at Domburg, 944–45; river-divinity Aciona at Augusta Suessionum (Soissons), Guillerme (1983), 24; dedication identifying local deities as belonging to the region Arurensis (named from river Arar), *CIL* 13.5161 = *ILS* 4707. An altar found at Bourdigala (Bordeaux) has a dedication to Bourdiga, protecting goddess of Bordeaux, and the river Garonne is perhaps represented; *AE* 1922.116; Keppie (1991), 93 with fig. 56.

150. De Izarra (1993), 230; Grenier (1960), 608–39; Thevenot (1968), 211–15; see also chapter 9.

151. Grenier (1960), 685–94 (with figs. 204–7).

152. *AE* 1976.454. This kind of *ex voto* offering could also contain elements of native religious procedure.

153. *ILS* 4726 = *RIB* 1526; note also *RIB* 1522–25, 1527–35. Cf. *ILS* 9317: "deae Nymphae Brig(antiae)" in the reign of Caracalla, from near Hadrian's wall.

154. See P. Salway (1981), 691.

155. See the survey by Bel Faïda (2002).

156. *Genius numinis caput Ampsagae, CIL* 8.5884 (Sila); *genius fluminis, CIL* 8. 9749 9 (Saint-Denis de Sig).

157. *CIL* 8.4673 = *ILS* 4480.

158. See Grenier (1960), 947–55.

159. Le Gall (1953b), 66–73; see also chapter 9 at n. 121.

160. Festus 274L; cf. 232L; Ovid, *Fasti* 6.235–40.

161. I agree here with Le Gall (1953b), 46–50.

162. *CIL* 6.2298/27; I², p. 327; Le Gall (1953b), 56, the name Volturnus perhaps had an Etruscan origin. For the *Fasti Vallenses*, see *CIL* I², p. 240.

163. Discussion in Le Gall (1953b), 83–95. Toutain (1926), 6–7, argues that this ritual was originally linked to purificatory rites for crossing the river and establishing the first bridge; hence, he attaches significance to the word *pontifex* ("bridge maker") as a title for the most important body of priests in the Roman state. See also Holland (1961), 332–42. Varro, *Lingua Latina* 5.83–84 linked the origin of *pontifices* to a bridge across the Tiber because rites were conducted on both sides of the river.

164. Varro, *Lingua Latina* 5.45; 7.44; Ovid, *Fasti* 3.791–92; Dionysius of Halicarnassus, *Antiquitates Romanae* 1.38.

165. Ovid, *Fasti* 6.713–14.

166. *Contra* Le Gall (1953b), 90–93, who argues that there was a purificatory element in these actions.

167. Le Gall (1953b), 96–110.

168. L. Richardson (1992), 428, thinks that there was a *sacellum* dedicated to the god of the river in the *vicus Tiberini*, but the precise location of this area is uncertain; see Steinby (1999), V:194.

169. Livy 10.47. An embassy had been sent to Epidaurus to bring back the god's statue; it brought a snake instead, which left its ship in the Tiber and swam to the island.

170. For the Tiber Island, see Platner and Ashby (1926), 281–82; L. Richardson (1992), 209–10; Steinby (1996), 99–101. For the festival of Tiberinus, *Fast Amit.* Ad vi Id. Dec., *CIL* I², pp. 245, 336.

171. Le Gall (1953b), 59–60; dedication to Tiberinus between Ameria and Tuder, *CIL* 11.4644 = *ILS* 3902.

172. *CIL* 11.3057 = *ILS* 2152.

173. Dio 80.1. And see above, n. 166. A type of Tiber fish was also called Tiberinus; it cruised close to the banks, between the Aemilian and Sublician bridges, consuming dung from the sewers. Lucilius 1174–76M = E. H. Warmington (Loeb, 1938) 601–3 (Macrobius, *Saturnalia* 3.16, 17).

174. *De Natura Deorum* 3.52. For discussion of the name, see Momigliano (1938). On one story Janus took as his partner Camasene, who bore him Tiberis, a warrior figure who allegedly gave his name to the Tiber (Wiseman, 2004, 162).

175. Livy 1.3.8; cf. Ovid, *Metamorphosis* 14.613; Varro, *Lingua Latina* 5.29–30. Albula might, in fact, be connected with the nymph of the sulfur springs at Tibur (Virgil, *Aeneid* 7.83–84; Servius, ad loc. 8.332).

176. See, e.g., Virgil, *Georgics* 4.369. For artistic representations of the reclining Tiber based on Greek cultural images taken over by Rome, see below, section 7.

177. Livy 1.3–4, with Ogilvie (1965), 46–48; cf. Plutarch, *Romulus* 3–4; Ovid, *Fasti* 2.381–424; Varro, *Lingua Latina* 5.54. For foundation myths, see chapter 1, section 3 and n. 36.

178. Martial, *Epigrammata* 4.64.24.

179. *Aeneid* 8.31–78.

180. *Aeneid* 8.69. For the theme of the Tiber in the *Aeneid*, see *Enciclopedia Virgiliana*, s.v. Tiberis; Benario (1978).

181. See above at n. 1; cf. also Silius Italicus (1.606–7), where Father Tiber is enriched by the waters of the Anio as he descends in a tawny stream.

182. Mars Ultor, Le Gall (1953b), 24 with pl. VII. The hypothetical pediment design is based on the identification of a relief on the facade of the Villa Medici; for coins, see below, section 7. For the symbolism of the forum of Augustus and the temple, see Zanker (1988), 113–14, 194–96; Rich (1998), 91–97.

183. *Silvae* 3.5.111–12. For these themes, see chapter 10, sections 1 and 2.

184. Ovid, *Epistulae ex Ponto* 4.10.57–58: the Danube refuses to yield first place to the Nile. See André (1977), 142, 174–76, for Ovid's treatment of rivers.

185. Horace, *Carmina* 4.4.38, the Metaurus witnessing the defeat of Hasdrubal; Virgil, *Aeneid* 6.873, on the Tiber as a witness to Rome's struggles. See Tibullus 1.7.9–13, with Murgatroyd (1980), 215–16, 318; Maltby (2002), 285. Does the idea of witnessing have special resonance for the Romans because of the convention of depicting rivers and other natural phenomena at triumphs? The depiction of the conquered river perhaps validates

the triumph. Either one can testify to something via autopsy or one can say the river witnessed the event. Tibullus makes the river testify to his own autopsy.

186. Silius Italicus, *Punica* 4.638 ff.

187. See n. 33 above.

188. *Panegyrici Latini* XII.17–18.

189. Horace, *Carmina* 2.9.21.

190. Juvenal 3.62.

191. See Habicht (1985), 20, 64–68, for the importance of myth and history in Pausanias's thinking; for discussion of methodology in the analysis of myths, see Dowden (1992), 22–38. Buxton (1994), 4, notes the importance of interpreting myths in context, since stories were often located in peasant communities. Lafond (2001) examines how Greeks tried to define their role with reference to the past, which connected with their cultural identity. Ostrowski (1991), 10–14, offers an overview of the legendary actions of rivers and their cult in ancient writers.

192. Pausanias 5.7.1–3.

193. Pausanias 2.5.1–2; 12.5; 9.1.2.

194. Pausanias 5.7.1–2. The energetic Alpheios also had designs on Artemis, 6.22.9. For elaboration of the Arethusa story, see below at n. 227.

195. Pausanias 2.15.4, 17.2; 6.6.4; 7.4.2; 9.34.5.

196. Pausanias 8.24.4.

197. Pausanias 1.38.5; another river locality for the abduction, 2.36.7.

198. Pausanias 2.3.3.

199. Pausanias 7.23.1–2.

200. Pausanias 1.4.1 (Po); 2.15.4 (Inachos); 4.35.9 (Joppe); 9.38.6 (Kephisos). Note also the smell of the Anigros (5.5.10).

201. Pausanias 5.17.11.

202. Lucian, *De Syria Dea* 8; J. L. Lightfoot (2002), 327–28, collects other evidence of a color phenomenon.

203. Pausanias 1.32.5; cf. 9.33.3, naming of river Lophis.

204. Pausanias 5.3.2.

205. Pausanias 4.33.3; cf. also 2.3.5 (after Glauke); 6.21.7 (named after horse); 10.8.5 (Kastalia).

206. Pausanias 7.19.2–20.1.

207. Pausanias 5.1.9.

208. Pausanias 8.41.1; 8.28.2. See Dowden (1992), 121.

209. Pausanias 9.39.4.

210. Pausanias 2.38.2; 5.5.10.

211. Pausanias 9.30.4.

212. For example the spring Kassotis in Phokis, see Pausanias 10.24.5.

213. *IG* XII.5.569 (possibly third century B.C.).

214. Virgil, *Aeneid* 2.719.

215. Virgil, *Aeneid* 4.635.

216. Valerius Maximus 7.3.1.

217. Cf. Schama (1995), 264–65; for the continuation of ritual washing in rivers in the Middle Ages, 265–66. Note also *CIL* 9.4130 = *ILS* 5775 (Aequiculi), which refers to the bringing of a supply of water to a shrine.

218. Pausanias 8.18.1; *LIMC* VII.1, 818–20; Brewster (1997), 69–71.

219. Lucan, *Pharsalia* 9.355; Ovid, *Metamorphoses* 11.603–4 (Lethe); Plutarch, *De Superstitione* 167a, rivers of the underworld flaming with fire. For place-names and mythology, see Bell (1989).

220. E.g., Pausanias 7.23.1–2; 9.31.6 (the story of Narcissus). Note that Alcock (1993), 258, argues that Pausanias's account of religious practice in Greece was not overly distorted by nostalgia: "he was an observant participant in contemporary religious practice."

221. See further chapter 10.

222. *NH* 3.102, Iapyx; 3.127, naming of Istria; 4.115, Minius as river of forgetfulness; 5.106, Marsyas; 8.166, miraculous horses in Spain; 37.31, the Padus and the daughters of Phaëthon.

223. *NH* 5.4, 31.

224. *NH* 2.232.

225. Notably the Peneios and his daughter, Daphne; Inachus and his daughter Io; Syrinx and Ladon; Kephisos and Liriope; the spring Salmakis; Limnaee, nymph of the Ganges; Alpheios and Arethusa; Acheloüs entertaining Theseus; Acheloüs and Hercules; the creation of Acis; the Ausonian water nymphs.

226. Ovid, *Metamorphoses* 8.549–59.

227. Ovid, *Metamorphoses* 5.577–641, with Bömer (1976), 374–86.

228. Lucian, less concerned with day-to-day survival, turned a cynical eye on such stories. *Dialogi Marini* 3.1. contains a humorous exchange between Poseidon and Alpheios about watery love affairs.

229. C. P. Jones (2006). Note also Livy 1, preface 7: "It is a privilege granted to antiquity to make the origins of cities more distinguished by mixing divine things with human."

230. Ostrowski (1991), 8–9, notes that personification is a modern term and raises the question if in this case there is personification of the river or merely the image of the river-god. This issue cannot be resolved on available evidence but does not affect the significance of how the ancients chose to give artistic vigor and reality to rivers. For the personification of running water as a theme in ancient literature, see also de Saint-Denis (1981), 547–50.

231. *De Architectura* 7.5.2.

232. Dio Chrysostomos, *Orationes* 4.85.

233. Aelian, *Varia Historia* 2.33. Cf. Maximus of Tyre 8.1.

234. For a general survey of the early development of images of rivers, see Ostrowski (1991), 15–25; Klementa (1993), 4–6.

235. De Izarra (1993), 231–32, improbably speculates that bulls were chosen because they roamed riverbanks. Presumably many other animals also roamed there.

236. Ostrowski (1991), 19 with figure 18.

237. Ostrowski (1991), 23–24. Zoomorphic images continued in some Greek representations of Acheloüs. See, above all, Klementa (1993) for an important compilation of examples of the portrayal of reclining river-gods in statues and on coins.

238. Klementa (1993), 106; the Tigris is sometimes unbearded. The earliest example of the portrayal of a young river-god is the Kladeos on the western pediment of the temple of Olympian Zeus. Klementa (1993), 205; Ashmole (1972), 175–77, pls. 33–35. See also Ostrowski (1991), 30, n. 24.

239. For portrayal of nymphs, see *LIMC* VIII.1, 891–902; for detailed consideration of images of nymphs and marine deities, with which I am not directly concerned, see Becatti (1971).

240. A standing river figure appears only on coins and a seated figure is rare; for a survey, see Ostrowski (1991), 26–59.

241. Klementa (1993), 9–134, cites the evidence for twenty-three reclining river-gods represented in sculpture, statues, or mosaics: Nile, Tiber, Ocean, Euphrates, Tigris, Jordan, Maeander, Eridanos, Scamandros, Ladon, Pyramos, Peneios, Eurotas, Orontes, Acheron, Kokytos, Anio, Arno, Adige, Sarno, Numicus, Rhine, Moselle.

242. *LIMC* I.1, 12–36; I.2, 19–54.

243. See in general Klementa (1993), 194–226.

244. Discussion of Oceanos in the imperial period in *LIMC* VIII.1, 907–15; see also Voute (1972).

245. Le Gall (1953b), 23–34; Klementa (1993), 68–71; *BMC* II, p. 187, no. 774, A.D. 71; legend: *Roma*. Cf. *RIC* II, p. 217, nos. 17–18, with bearded head of Tiber crowned with reeds; on the reverse: she-wolf and twins.

246. See J. M. C. Toynbee (1934), 113.

247. Klementa (1993), 52–71; *LIMC* VIII.1, 25–27, VIII.2, 16–20.

248. Klementa (1993), 66–67.

249. Bonneau (1964), 348–49; Nile symbols, Klementa (1993), 9–51.

250. Bonneau (1964), 315–36; Ostrowski (1991), 23; Klementa(1993), 45–48.

251. Bonneau (1964), 337–42. In Egypt, Nile continued to be god of the inundation, while in Rome it was treated as the river of Egypt with traditional attributes (356). The Nile is rarely represented with other gods, but at *BMC* IV, p. 1167, he holds hands with the Tiber (see below, n. 266). *LIMC* VI.1 720–26; VI.2 424–29.

252. Dunbabin (1999), 49–52.

253. Cf. also *SEG* 45.448, possible personification (figure holding a hydria) of water sources on a mosaic of a Nilotic landscape, from a church at Sobata (sixth century A.D.).

254. Note *SEG* 23.451 from the first century A.D.: "you have seen the boundaries of the wide Ister."

255. Lepper and Frere (1988), 50 and pl. VI; see also chapter 10. The river was named Danuvius in its upper course up to the cataracts at the Iron Gates, and Istros in its lower course; Strabo 7.3.13 (305). For representations of the Danube, see *LIMC* III.1, 343–44; III.2, 255.

256. See Vollkommen (1994). His cautious survey discusses the difficulty of making

a clear identification of representations of the Rhine, and he concluded that only three coins types and possibly three or four other representations can be securely identified as the Rhine, although the river played an important role in the ancient sources. For the theme of Roman control (mainly expressed on the coinage), see chapter 10. General survey in *LIMC* VII.1, 632–35; see also VII.2, pls. 5, 6, 12, 13; *EAA* VI (1965), 600, s.v. *Rhenos* (A. Bisi); *Der Kleine Pauly IV* (1972), 1394–95, s.v. Rhenus (H. Cüppers).

257. Klementa (1993), 102–7; *LIMC* IV.1, 70–74; IV.2. 30–31; *RE* VI.1, 1215–16 (K. Tümpel); Tigris, *LIMC* VIII.1, 27–28. For the personification of the four rivers of paradise (Phison, Geon, Tigris, Euphrates) in a mosaic, see *SEG* 31.1454; for the role of the Euphrates as one of these rivers, see *LIMC* IV.1, 74. For the interpretation of the river-deities on the arch of Trajan at Beneventum, see chapter 10 at n. 53.

258. See Klementa (1993), 109–13, Maeander (as a bearded man); Eurymedon (*SEG* 35.1409, marble statue of river-god c. 150 A.D.; the city paid for it from its own resources). See Klementa (1993), 113–34, for a review of the evidence for other rivers. Note that there is no ancient authority for identifying some statues (138).

259. De Izarra (1993), 230.

260. *LIMC* VII.1, 636; A. Bisi, *EAA* VI (1965), 670, s.v. *Rhodanos*.

261. *LIMC* V.1, 421; V.2, 298; *EAA* IV (1961), 23–24, s.v. *Hiberus*; *RE* IX.1, 807, s.v. Iberus 1, 2 (A. Schulten). Inscription, Alföldy (1975), 13 no. 22, with pl. 11; *CIL* 2.4075.

262. So *LIMC* III.1, 821–22; III.2, 594; *RE* VI.1, 446–48 (J. Escher). Note also Klementa (1993), 113–17. Peretti (1994), 265–93, has an interesting survey of the presentation of the Padus by historians and poets. Zanker (1988), 174–75, speaks only of a female figure representing winds on land, riding on a goose over a stream, depicted by an upended water jar and reeds growing thickly along the bank.

263. See Ostrowski (1991), 33.

264. *BMC* II, p. 187, no. 774; *sestertius* A.D. 71; reverse: Roma seated on rock with the seven hills represented by rock, she-wolf and twins, and Tiber reclining holding a reed; legend: Roma; *RIC* III, p. 118, no. 706 (A.D. 140–44) = J. M. C. Toynbee (1934), pl. 16.3 = fig. 5; p. 303, no. 1142 (A.D. 174–75). *BMC* IV, p. 638, no. 1498; p. 210, no. 1313 with legend: Tiberis.

265. Imhoof-Blumer (1923), no. 551 = Cohen (1880–92), II², p. 271, no. 17; Ostrowski (1991), 45, though erroneously mentioning the Nile.

266. J. M. C. Toynbee (1934), 113–15; bronze issue from Alexandria, A.D. 155. Toynbee (139) discusses a controversial coin of Nero representing the harbor of Ostia. The bearded figure holding a rudder and dolphin is often said to be Tiber where it flows into the sea; but she argues that it is Ocean, as a dolphin is not a normal attribute of a river.

267. See further chapter 10 at n. 68.

268. The classic collection of these coins is that of Imhoof-Blumer (1923); note also Burnett, Amandry, and Ripollès (1992). There is a brief but valuable survey of the portrayal of rivers on coins by Klementa (1993), 189–93. In chapter 10, sections 1 and 2, I discuss the depiction on coins of rivers and the success of imperial military policy, and the exploitation of, or association with, riverine resource.

269. Imhoof-Blumer (1923), no. 141.

270. There is a useful summary in Head (1911); note especially his discussion of: Ephesus (577), Erythrae (579), Phocaea (590), Smyrna (594), Aezanis (664), Eumenia (674), Cadi (668), Cibyra (670), Hadrianopolis-Sebaste (675), Themisonium (687), Acmoneia (663), Appia (668), Dorylaëum (672), Midaëum (681); see also chapter 8, n. 231. Imhoof-Blumer (1923): Prusias, 233; cf. also 238; Imbrasos at Samos, 283; Caicus of Stratonicea, 332; Anthios at Antioch, 407. Other important coins depicting rivers: 145 (river-god of Markianopolis); 156 (Deultum); 167 (Nikopolis ad Mestos); 168 (Strymon; 185 (Plotinopolis; Marcus Aurelius with the Hebros); 186 (Serdica); 195 (Traianopolis and Hebros); 204 (Elis and Alpheios); 210 (Amasia and river Iris); 218 (Germanikopolis and river Halys); 220 (Juliopolis and river Sangarius); 238 (Apollonia and river Rhyndakos); 246 (Pergamum and river Kaikos); 264 (Ephesos with river Kaystros); 267 (Erythrae and river Aleon); 269 (Magnesia and the river Maeander); 278 (Smyrna and river Hermos); 285 (Antioch and the river Maeander); 290 (Aphrodisias and river Morsynos); 297 (Akrasos and river Kaikos); 339 (Tralles and river Maeander); 340 (Tripolis and river Maeander); 351 (Apamea and river Maeander); 358 (Dionysopolis and river Maeander); 367 (Hierapolis and river Chrysoras); 368 (Hyrgaleis and river Maeander); 384 (Laodicea and river Lykos); 415 (Sagalassos and river Kestros); 435 (Diokaisareia and river Kalykadnos); 438 (Hierapolis and river Pyramos); 471 (Antiocheia and river Orontes); 543 (Siscia and river Savus); Imhoof-Blumer (1923), 373 (Edessa and swimming river-god Skirtos; Nisibis with river-god Mygdonios).

See also Burnett, Amandry, and Ripollès (1992), p. 178, no. 665, for local river-god Crusas of Assorus in Sicily (first century B.C.); p. 640, 4465A, for river-god Chrysoras at Balanea/Leukas in Syria; p. 596, no. 4062, Anazarbus-Caesarea in Syria (time of Nero); pp. 417–21, nos. 2483–84, Smyrna (Julio-Claudian); no. 2490 (A.D. 68/69).

271. Ostrowski (1991), 24–25; *LIMC* I.1, 840–51, especially 843; I.2, 668–77; Burnett, Amandry, and Ripollès (1992). 1:614, no. 4152; tetradrachm 5/4 B.C.; obverse: head of Caesar Augustus; reverse: Tyche of Antioch seated with palm branch; river-god Orontes in front.

272. *SEG* 17.200 (A.D. 221–24); Imhoof-Blumer (1923), no. 285. For the importance of coins as symbols of cities, see Temporini (1982), on Miletus and the Maeander; also Klementa (1993), 109–13. The importance of the Maeander in popular feeling and the ubiquity of the original river spirit can be seen in local nomenclature, where Mandrodorus is very common. For potamophoric names, see above at n. 62, and chapter 8 at n. 237.

273. See Curbera (1998).

274. Beltrán Martínez (1950), 349, 367, with figs. 471, 486.

275. See further chapter 10, section 2.

276. Cf. *BMC* III, p. 390, no. 1078 (Hadrian, A.D. 134–38), with reed and gushing water; p. 258, no. 132 (A.D. 119–38); here the river-god holds a rudder, representing river traffic; water gushes from an urn.

CHAPTER 5

1. Livy 2.10, with Ogilvie (1965), 258–61.

2. Gnecchi (1912), 2:9, no. 5. It was part of a series of types minted between 140 and 144 celebrating ancient Roman traditions, mythology and religion; legend: "Cocles." Horatius is depicted swimming the river while the Etruscans bombard him and the Romans cut down the bridge.

3. See in more detail chapter 10.

4. See Campbell (1987).

5. Frontinus, *Stratagemata* 1. *prooem.*

6. For military maps, see Sherk (1974).

7. *How to Survive under Siege* 8.1; see Whitehead (1990), 114. Presumably Aeneas meant by building dams and dikes.

8. *Hellenica* 5.2.7 (385 B.C.).

9. Frontinus, *Stratagemata* 3.7.

10. *Stratagemata* 3.4 (Alexander); 3.5 (Semiramis).

11. *Strategemata* 1.3.5, Herakles and the Kephisos.

12. *Stratagemata* 3.7.3. Note Onasander's advice against camping on marshy or damp ground (8.2).

13. Tacitus, *Annales* 1.64.

14. Polyaenus 4.3.28; 8.13.

15. Frontinus, *Stratagemata* 3.7.1, 2; see Caesar, *BG* 8.40. Note also Pausanias 10.18.2 on the siege of Phana by the Achaians, when an oracle revealed the importance of cutting off the water supply.

16. Frontinus, *Stratagemata* 3.7.6; attributed to others by Polyaenus and Pausanias.

17. Caesar, *BG* 8.40–43. See also *BC* 3.97 for Caesar's efforts to prevent the Pompeians from having access to river water; cf. 1.73; 1.83–84, the campaign against Afranius and Petreius.

18. Frontinus, *Stratagemata* 3.14.2–4.

19. *Stratagemata* 2.2.7.

20. *Stratagemata* 1.6.2.

21. Caesar, *BG* 1.8.

22. *BG* 1.12. This incident is also described by Polyaenus 8.23.3. Cf. 1.1.3; 1.43.2; 2.1.27; 3.9.2 for stratagems involving river crossings.

23. *BG* 2.9; cf. 23.

24. *BG* 8.27.

25. *BG* 6.7–8.

26. Frontinus, *Stratagemata* 1.5.3; cf. 1.4.8; 9;10; Polyaenus 1.49.4, Xenophon forces a river crossing; 3.9.61; 8.23.9, Caesar effects an opposed crossing. See also 4.4.2; 6.4.2; 7.21.3; 8.23.5; cf. Caesar, *BG* 5.18 (below, n. 31). It was agreed that good discipline made it easier for troops to bridge a river; see Frontinus, *Stratagemata* 4.2.1; and Aeneas Tacticus 1.2, who advised that soldiers needed to be drawn up properly in order to cross a river.

27. Frontinus, *Stratagemata* 1.5.1, 5.2; cf. 4.7.28.

28. Cicero, *Ad Familiares* 10.23.2–3.

29. Polyaenus 2.2.1. This ploy was used by the Greek mercenary commander Clearchus.

30. Polyaenus 4.7.12.

31. *BG* 5.18.

32. *Epitome of Military Science* 1.10.

33. See chapter 9, section 2, for swimming in rivers.

34. Dio 69.9.6; *CIL* 3.3676 = *ILS* 2558 = Campbell (1994), no. 47.

35. See further below, section 5.

36. *BG* 1.13.

37. *BC* 1.48–55. For the crossing of the river Sicoris, see *BC* 1.62–64. Pack animals were stationed upstream to break the current, and the infantrymen (with light equipment) crossed almost up to their necks in water.

38. *BG* 7.34–35. For clever exploitation of the river Sequana by Labienus, see 7.57–58.

39. *BG* 4.17.

40. *Anabasis* 5.7.3–5.

41. Dio 68.13.

42. T78.10–17; translation in Campbell (2000), 83.21–28. Hyginus was writing probably in the early second century A.D.

43. T143.8–11; translation in Campbell (2000), 143.24–27 (Hyginus Gromaticus).

44. T43.17–22; translation in Campbell (2000), 41.12–20. See chapter 3 at n. 108.

45. As appreciated by Caesar, *BG* 1.38. Cf. also Avaricum (7.15); Gergovia (7.34); Uxellodunum (8.40).

46. Cornell (1995), 310–11. See chapter 10 at n. 13 for the story of draining the Alban lake. For colonies, see map 4.

47. Salmon (1969), 43.

48. For the site, see Crawford and Keppie (1984), 21–22. For the development of the *via Latina* in the Liris valley, see Coarelli (1988b), 41–42.

49. See Purcell (1996b), 274–75. He argues that Italy has many river mouths but few harbors. In Italy, river mouths provided sites and/or names for *coloniae* such as Volturnum, Luni, Minturnae, Liternum, and perhaps the first settlement at Ostia. These were forts on the coast, but they also served as gates, as is explicit in the toponym Ostia; therefore, the river is more important than its mouth. For a good summary of early colonial foundations, see Salmon (1969), 40–81. However, the idea embraced by Salmon that colonies were entirely state-organized and closely controlled uniform ventures, in fact virtual replicas of Rome, has been effectively challenged by Bispham (2006), who argues for the diversity and difference of colonies founded in the middle republic. This should not affect the military and strategic context of the foundations discussed in the text. For the colonies at Alba Fucens and Minturnae, see Bispham, 105–8, 111–13. For concepts of the colonial process in terms of Roman historiography, see the useful discussion by J. R. Patterson (2006).

50. Livy 32.29.3; Frederiksen (1984), 270–75; Campania in the *Liber Coloniarum*, Campbell (2000), 413–27.

51. For discussion of the link between colonies and roads in the early republic, see Coarelli (1988b).

52. Salmon (1969), 135.

53. Dio 46.50.3–6; *CIL* 10.6087 = *ILS* 886; Tacitus, *Historiae* 1.65. Caesar seems to have been responsible for planning this colony. For its subsequent importance, see chapter 7 at n. 118.

54. *NH* 3.123; for Augustus's colonial foundations, see in general Keppie (1983).

55. Dio 53.25.3–5.

56. *On Camp Fortifications* 57–58. Authorship was mistakenly attributed to Hyginus Gromaticus. For an example of local water conditions and Roman military establishments in Africa, see Hilali (2010).

57. This is a matter of debate; Selkirk (1983) in presenting his Piercebridge Formula argued that forts were positioned on rivers in northeast Britain because military supplies were moved by barge. See chapter 7 at n. 228.

58. See chapter 7, section 3.

59. For an excellent survey of riverine frontiers, camps, forts, and fortified landing places, see Breeze (2011), 92–117. Breeze emphasizes that along the Rhine, early legionary bases were placed astride main invasion routes moving along tributaries of the river, while later bases were often located at a confluence, providing excellent communications and a good place for a harbor. See also Gerlach (2008). For a good discussion of Köln-Alteburg, see Doppelfeld (1975). For the comments on deployment along the Danube, see Sommer (2009), especially 108, 111–12.

60. For the location and role of Samosata and Dura-Europos and Rome's developing interest, see Millar (1993), 82–83, 114–15; for Zeugma, see Tacitus, *Annales* 12.12.

61. Curchin (1991), 74–76.

62. Erdkamp (1998), 141–55.

63. Erdkamp (1998), 46–83; J. Roth (1999), 206, on the payload of pack animals.

64. For the importance of river transport in military supply and the capacity of river-boats, see in general J. Roth (1999), 196–97. See in general chapter 6 for carrying capacity and speed of transport on rivers.

65. Livy 21.48.8–9; Polybius 3.69.

66. Livy 25.20.2–3; 22.5–6.

67. Strabo 3.3.1 (152).

68. Plutarch, *Marius* 15; see also chapter 6 at n. 135.

69. Plutarch *Crassus* 20.

70. Strabo 7.5.2 (313); Appian, *Illyrian Wars* 22.

71. For example, *BG* 7.11. Cf. 7.14, 17; 8.7.

72. See chapter 7, sections 2 and 3.

73. *BG* 1.18.

74. *BG* 1.16.

75. *BG* 2.5.

76. *BG* 7.60.

77. *BG* 1.38. See in general Labisch (1975), 77–78, 91, 121–24.

78. *BG* 7.55–56.

79. *BG* 5.47.

80. *BG* 7.90.

81. In the republic, naval warfare had intermittently played a role, especially in the first war against Carthage, and part of the Roman seagoing fleet was housed on the river Tiber at Rome in the *navalia* (ship sheds), originally in the lower part of the Campus Martius, opposite the Prata Quinctia; see chapter 8, section 4.

82. SHA, *Vit. Pert.* 2.2. Pertinax commanded the German fleet early in his equestrian career. For river fleets, see Starr (1960), 129–66; Reddé (1986), 288–308; Konen (2000); Saddington (2007), 213–17.

83. *Annales* 4.5.

84. Reddé (1986), 298–306.

85. *CIL* 16.37, *classis Flavia Moesica*; Starr (1960), 132.

86. Lepper and Frere (1988), pls. 5–6, 25–26.

87. Lepper and Frere (1988), pl. 35.

88. See Fink (1971), no. 63.

89. *AE* 1972.572: "praef(ectus) class(is) [Moesicae et ripae Dan]uuii." Claudianus subsequently was promoted to senatorial rank. See Reddé (1986), 303–6, for other possible bases.

90. Tacitus, *Annales* 2.63; 12.29–30.

91. Inscriptions from Emona close to the source of the Savus (*CIL* 3.14354⁹) and from Sirmium (*CIL* 3.3223 with p. 2277) may suggest that the fleet operated on this river; but they might simply indicate the presence of individual sailors not that the fleet was operating regularly here. Note also an inscription from Poetovio on the Dravus (*CIL* 3.4025).

92. Reddé (1986), 300.

93. *AE* 1956.124; Pflaum (1960), no. 181 bis, and pp. 481–83. Note also Lucius Aburnius Torquatus, equestrian officer, who was in charge of the supplies for the Parthian War (114–17) on the banks of the Euphrates (*ILS* 9471).

94. *CIL* 3.3385 = *ILS* 395, discovered not far from Aquincum on the Danube.

95. *CIL* 8.7977 = *ILS* 1146.

96. For an attempt to make the most out of the evidence for the role of the Rhine squadron, see Starr (1960), 141–52; Reddé (1986), 290–98, 356–61; Konen (2000); (2002), 327–40.

97. Tacitus, *Annales* 1.56–71.

98. Tacitus, *Annales* 2.6.

99. Tacitus, *Annales* 2.7–26.

100. Tacitus, *Annales* 11.20. See also chapter 6, sect. 6.

101. Tacitus, *Historiae* 5.18; 21.

102. Tacitus, *Historiae* 5.23.

103. Tacitus, *Historiae*.

104. Starr (1960), 147–48; Reddé (1986), 290–98. At Cologne the base was at Alteburg, three kilometers south of the military base. There may have been a naval base at Arentsburg between the two arms of the Rhine on the *fossa Corbulonis* (Reddé, 1986, 293–95). There was possibly some liaison between the Rhine fleet and the *classis Britannica*, which had its principal base at Gesoriacum (Boulogne-sur-Mer) and was active transporting men and supplies between Gaul and Britain. For the British fleet, see Starr (1960), 152–56; Konen (2002), 319–27.

105. Starr (1960), 148.

106. Tacitus, *Historiae* 4.26–27; see in general Reddé (1986), 370–86.

107. For ships found at Oberstimm dating from the early second century, see Bockius (2002). Ships found near Mainz date from the fourth century and had thirty to thirty-two oars; see Höckmann (1993); Pferdehirt (1995).

108. *AE* 1923.32, 33 (Brohl): "Sacred to Hercules of the rocks, Celsus, centurion of the infantry *singulares*, and his fellow soldiers of the *singulares* to Licinius Sura, legate, willingly and properly fulfilled their vow." See also *CIL* 13.7697, 7715, 7719; 13.8036; 10027[226]; on the quarries at Bonna in 160, see Starr (1960), 151; and Konen (2002), 311, 333–37. For transport of stone by boat along the Rhine, see chapter 7, section 3.

109. *AE* 1928.183; Konen (2002), 339.

110. Starr (1960), 114–16. See chapter 6 at n. 137 and chapter 8 at n. 211.

111. Dio 68.26–28. His plans to link the two rivers were thwarted because they were at different elevations. See also Lightfoot (1990), 118–21.

112. Dio 75.9; Ammianus 24.6.1.

113. See Reddé (1986), 628–35, especially 632.

114. See *Notitia Dignitatum Occ.* 39–42; *CTh.* 7.17 (A.D. 412) on establishing maintenance for a fleet of *lusoriae*.

115. *Notitia Dignitatum Occ.* 32–34. For example, on the Dravus the *classis Histrica* was based at Mursa; on the Savus the *classis Aegetensium* was at Siscia, while other units were based at Servitium and Sirmium; see Reddé (1986), 318, for a convenient map.

116. Reddé (1986), 635.

117. Ammianus 17.2.3; see Starr (1960), 151–52.

118. *Notitia Dignitatum Occ.* 42.17, 20–23; A. H. M. Jones (1964), 99.

119. *Panegyrici Latini* VI (VII).18.3–4. See Nixon and Rodgers (1994), 211–53, especially 244, for the historical context.

120. Luttwak (1976). For the role of friendly kings in frontier zones, see Braund (1984), 91–103.

121. The most useful discussions are by J. C. Mann (1974), (1979); Isaac (1992), 387–418; Whittaker (1989), (1994), (1996), (2000), (2004); Mattern (1999), 81–122; summary with full bibliography in Wilkes (2005).

122. For discussion of Augustus's policy, see Brunt (1963); Wells (1972); Gruen (1996). Augustus left for Tiberius the famous "concilium coercendi imperii intra terminos" (Tacitus, *Annales* 1.11). This should, I think, be construed as vague guidance to keep the em-

pire within reasonable limits, which were left to the experienced Tiberius's judgment. Whittaker's (1994, 25) interpretation of this passage as a reference to the civil provincial boundaries is unlikely. This is certainly not what Tacitus thought Augustus meant. In fact one of his explanations was that Augustus was jealous, clearly of further military conquest. For the likelihood that the Romans thought that the world was much smaller than in reality and that consequently widespread conquest was feasible, see now Moynihan (1985).

123. J. C. Mann (1974) speculated on lack of steam; criticized by Whittaker (1994), 85–97; (2000), 311–17. Wheeler (1993) contains an entirely unconvincing critique of Whittaker (1989).

124. Alföldi (1952); Whittaker (1994), 73–78.

125. As pointed out by Whittaker (1994), 19–20.

126. Austin and Rankov (1995), 173–80, believe that the Romans did tend to view rivers as military barriers and particularly argue that they were suspicious of building bridges into hostile or unoccupied territory, in case they provided a line of attack. I do not, however, find this part of the argument entirely convincing. The absence of bridges may reflect lack of perceived need if there were no economic or communication advantages in having a bridge. Braund (1996) highlights modern doubts about the validity of rivers as effective barriers, noting that they were means of lateral communication, that it is an accident that northern frontiers are attached to rivers, and that the same kinds of people were on both sides of the rivers. He does, however, believe that some of this is in conflict with what the Romans thought or expressed in their writings. His main argument has been effectively challenged by Rankov (2005), with whom I am in general agreement.

127. *Res Gestae* 30.1–2.

128. Seneca, *Naturales Quaestiones* 6.7.1.

129. *CIL* 14.3608 = *ILS* 986.

130. Josephus, *BJ* 2.377.

131. Tacitus, *Annales* 1.9.

132. Tacitus, *Historia* 4.26.

133. *Annales* 1.36. See also *Historia* 3.46: the Dacians gain control of both banks of the Danube.

134. Tacitus, *Agricola* 41.2.

135. For the diplomatic relations between Rome and Parthia, see Campbell (1993).

136. Tacitus, *Annales* 6.37; cf. 12.11.

137. Tacitus, *Annales* 15.3, 9, 17.

138. Velleius 2.101.2–3. Velleius also describes an incident during Tiberius's campaigns in Germany when a barbarian chieftain crossed the Elbe to midstream in a canoe, before asking permission to approach the Roman bank and pay his respects to Tiberius (2.107).

139. Tacitus, *Annales* 2.58.

140. Dio 71.15; 72.3.2; 71.16.1. See Austin and Rankov (1995), 180.

141. Arrian, *Anabasis* 1.3.1. He refers to tribes active in his day, the Quadi and Marcomanni.

142. Lucan, *Pharsalia* 2.50.

143. Suetonius, *Divus Augustus* 25.2.

144. Florus 2.30.38–39.

145. Tacitus, *Annales* 1.69.

146. Dio 68.13.5–6. Trajan had taken the opposite view that the bridge would enable help to arrive quickly if the garrisons on the other side were attacked.

147. Martial, *Epigrammata* 5.3.1.

148. *Life of Hadrian* 12.6. This collection of biographies was probably written by a single author in the fourth century.

149. It is, however, possible that the author of the *Historia Augusta* was reflecting on developments in the fourth century; see Whittaker (1994), 82.

150. Fink (1971), no. 63; discussion in Lepper and Frere (1988), 244–59.

151. Dio 71.7.

152. Florus 1.38.12.

153. See Whittaker (1994), 98–131; note also Konen (2002) on the economic significance of provincial fleets.

154. See the useful summary in Millar (1993), 80–82; French (1994), 41–43. In A.D. 49 Cassius Longinus, governor of Syria, had encamped at Zeugma to protect the crossing (Tacitus, *Annales* 12.12). On the water screw at Ayni, see Jalabert, Mouterde, et al. (1929–), I, nos. 65–66 (*IGLS*).

155. A. H. M. Jones (1964), 1450. See also Wilkes (2005), 724–67, for a summary of frontier deployment from A.D. 197 to 337.

156. See Southern and Dixon (1996), 25, 43 with fig. 7; Whittaker (1994), 169. For the commands in the later empire, see *Notitia Dignitatum Or.* 33; *Or.* 42; *Occ.* 32; *Occ.* 33; *Occ.* 41.

157. J. C. Mann (1977), 11; cf. Isaac (1988), 142–43; Whittaker (1994), 203. For *ripenses* in general, see Berchem (1952), 83–87.

158. Whittaker (1994), 192–242, calls in question the idea of a complete collapse of the frontiers and the adoption of a defensive ideology; he argues (203) that Roman strategy on the Danube was never intended to be defensive. However, while it is true that all substantial military units have a capacity for attack as well as defense, this cannot tell us much about overall strategy based on the rivers. Wilkes (2005), 252–68 (especially 258–59), takes a more defensive view of later empire frontiers.

159. *CIL* 13.8502.

160. Demougeot (1983); fortifications, F. Johnson (1983), 245–57.

161. *AE* 1976.626.

162. See Petrović (1977). For similar language in Lower Moesia, see *CIL* 3.6151; 7487. Whittaker (1994), 184, thought that the language was "formulaic," but in my view it is more likely to reflect common thoughts and practices of the time.

163. *CIL* 3.13734.

164. *AE* 1976.587 a), from Svinita, north of the Danube. Cf. *AE* 1976.595; also 1972.495, where "Hermogeni p(rae) p(ositus) [- - -]," can be restored as "ri(pae) leg(io) VII Cl(audia) Parce" on the basis of *CIL* 3.13814 a), found south of the Danube and datable to the late third or fourth century. Legion VII Claudia was stationed at Parce.

165. *AE* 1978.701 (from the early fourth century); the abbreviation *p s* in other similar inscriptions could be interpreted this way.

166. Ammianus 28.2.1: "to prevent the enemy from ever being able to attack our territory without being seen."

167. *Panegyrici Latini* (ed. R. A. B. Mynors, 1964) 9(4).18.4.

168. *Panegyrici Latini* 10(2).7.

169. Ammianus 31.4.13; cf. 30.3.3–6: Valentinian negotiated peace with the king of the Alamanni on a ship in the middle of the Rhine.

170. Ireland (1984), vi. For the context of this work, see Astin (1983).

171. See chapter 4.

172. Isaac (1992), 395.

173. Arrian, *Anabasis* 1.4.5.

174. See chapter 10 at n. 10.

175. Tacitus, *Annales* 15.15.

176. *ILS* 9477.

177. Dio 75.3.3.

CHAPTER 6

1. Pliny, *NH* 3.33: "multo Galliarum fertilissimus."

2. Cato, *De Agricultura* 1.3.

3. Columella 1.2.3.

4. Strabo 4.6.7 (205).

5. Indeed, Gabba (1975), 147, perhaps rather extravagantly argues that in antiquity, because of the difficulty of transport, large towns or cities could exist only on a seacoast or beside navigable rivers. For the general benefit of rivers to ancient peoples as routes of communication, see Brittain (1958), 72, 97–99.

6. For a useful general assessment of the importance of the combination of road and river transport in Egypt, see Adams (2007), 3–16.

7. See Rickman (1996), 282–83, on the general importance of river ports in the Roman world; for a survey of harbors in general, see Blackman (2008), 638–54.

8. Mela 2.81.

9. See chapter 2, section 2, for Ptolemy and Pausanias, who for different reasons were less concerned with the relationship of geography and topography to local peoples.

10. Pliny, *NH* 6.99 (on the Zarotis in the East).

11. Polybius 9.43.6, referring to the Euphrates; see Walbank (1967), 187.

12. Strabo 4.1.2 (177) (Rhône); Pliny, *NH* 4.79 (Danube).

13. Strabo 3.2.5 (143).

14. Pliny, *NH* 3.53–54.

15. See Strabo 3.2.5 (143) and 16.1.10–12 (740) on rivers in the East and the system of canals between the Euphrates and Tigris.

16. See Strabo 3.3.2 (152) on the crossing point on the Duris; also 3.4.6 (158–59) (Sucro) and, for bridges, 3.4.10 (161).

17. For Strabo's attention to the economic geography of Italy, see Foraboschi (1988); useful discussion also in Tozzi (1988); Pasquinucci (1988).

18. Strabo 4.1.14 (189); cf. his description of the Baetis at 3.2.3 (142); see further chapter 7.

19. Strabo 5.3.7 (234).

20. Pliny, *NH* 4.14; 6.99.

21. E.g., *NH* 6.64–65, 71–72.

22. *NH* 3.9–12.

23. See Murphy (2003) 315–22, for rivers as routes of communication in Pliny's *Natural History*.

24. See Beagon (1992), 200.

25. *NH* 6.146 in respect of the valley of the Euphrates.

26. *NH* 3.103, 106.

27. *NH* 5.13; cf. Pomanus with a good harbor at its mouth (6.94).

28. *NH* 3.54.

29. *NH* 6.75.

30. *NH* 5.105.

31. *NH* 6.88 (information again supplied by Roman traders).

32. See chapter 2, section 1.

33. In Adams and Laurence (2001), 44.

34. As argued by Talbert (2002), 532, in his review of Adams and Laurence (2001).

35. Ekwall (1928), 417–18; Rivet and Smith (1979), 476–78; Coles (1994).

36. Eckoldt (1980), 11–15, reviewing the arguments for navigation on small rivers (a small river is defined as one with a volume of less that 20 cubic meters per second). See Eckoldt (1984), 5, for river volumes; see below for the enhancement of shallow streams by artificial means; and see de Izarra (1993), 34, on the fact that probably only small changes have occurred in the disposition of French rivers from ancient times. Note that archaeological evidence confirms that the Rhône-Saône-Seine and the Aude-Garonne routes were the most important in the late Iron Age. These routes brought raw material from the interior to the Mediterranean; manufactured luxury goods moved in the other direction. See King (1990), 117.

37. Sillières (1990), 712–17.

38. Sillières (1990), 708–10; Fornell Muñoz (1997), 135–36.

39. See Burand (1971). There are two rivers of this name in the Rhône area. The more northern is a tributary on the right bank of the Rhône that joins the river at Pouzin. The other is 95 kilometers long and a tributary on the left bank of the Rhône. The Ovidis is probably the left bank river since the other is very short. Also the left bank river has some

traces at Vaison of quays possibly for unloading boats; there was a corporation of *utriclarii* at Vaison (*CIL* 12.1387).

40. Sillières (1990), 712–16. In his view, their hydrological characteristics allow us to speculate that they may have been navigable in antiquity.

41. Sillières (1990), 724–29, fig. 17; García y Bellido (1945).

42. Sillières (1990), 740–44.

43. Discussion in Casson (1965); (1971), 331–37.

44. See Baldassare (1990–), 1:597, no. 15; 6:687, nos. 7–8; 8:815, no. 173. The last three seem to have a Nilotic context.

45. See Dunbabin (1978), 127, 136. The drawing for the mosaic may have been copied from an illustrated manual; Rostovtzeff (1957), 2:616, pl. 29; Casson (1971), fig. 137; de Izarra (1993), 109. *CIL* 8.27790 = *ILS* 9456.18(19): "hinc legio stlattis iam transportaverat amne."

46. In general, see Casson (1965), (1971); Rougé (1975); Greene (1986) 31–34; de Izarra (1993), 104–19; Parodi Álvarez (2001), 21–37; Schneider (2007), 77–81. For types of boat, see also Sillières (1990), 735–38; for a summary of ships and navigation in the ancient world with bibliography, see now McGrail (2008); and for boatmen operating in ports, see Rougé (1966), 192–201.

47. See Casson (1965), 37 and pls. I–V. See further below at n. 82.

48. Casson (1971), 336 and fig. 190; *CIL* 14.252 = *ILS* 6176.

49. Casson (1965), 34–36; (1971) 335–37.

50. Propertius 1.14.3–4 refers to these craft on the Tiber, Caesar on the Saône (*BG* 1.12) and Seine (*BG* 7.60), Livy on the Rhône (21.26.8); see de Izarra (1993), 113–14.

51. Casson (1971), 330.

52. De Izarra (1993), 116–18.

53. Cf. Strabo 5.3.5 (232); *Digest* 14.2.4 pr. The man in charge of a small boat was a *scapharius*; see *CIL* 2.1168.

54. Rougé (1966), 200–201; Kneissl (1981); Deman (1987), especially 91–95. Two other interpretations of *utriclarii* are possible: makers of skins, and road transporters of wine and oil carried in skins on mules or horses. These seem particularly unlikely since it requires the word to carry too much implied meaning, and the context of most of the evidence suggests a riverine connection.

55. Ausonius, *Epistulae* 26.31; de Izarra (1993), 118–19.

56. See Casson (1971), 330, 338; de Izarra (1993), 106–8; Parodi Álvarez (2001), 35.

57. See *P. Oxy.* VII.1048 (fourth–fifth century A.D.); XVI.905.21 (fourth–fifth century A.D.); *Sammelbuch* 9563.15 (fourth century A.D.).

58. Tacitus, *Annales* 2.6; see chapter 5 at n. 98.

59. See Rougé (1966), 233–34.

60. Casson (1971), 334.

61. Summary in Casson (1971), 338–43; see also Houston (1988a), 553–60, arguing that there were many small ships trading and many therefore could navigate rivers. Also, there

were numerous small coastal ports with very few facilities; we may surmise that this might also be the case on rivers.

62. Discussion in Berti (1985); also Zerbini (2002). Its cargo consisted of lead, amphorae probably for wine, and pottery.

63. See Casson (1971), 335 and fig. 195.

64. Strabo 3.2.3 (142).

65. Parodi Álvarez (2001), 27. See Rougé (1966), 66–73, on the tonnage of commercial ships.

66. Summary by de Izarra (1993), 157–72.

67. Rickman, (1985), 108.

68. Herodotus 2.96.

69. De Izarra (1993), 163.

70. Ellmers (1978), 11.

71. De Izarra (1993), 159; Tacitus, *Germania* 44.1, with J. G. C. Anderson (1938), 205. For ships with two rudders, see Tacitus, *Annales* 2.6.

72. Rostovtzeff (1957), 1: 224, pl. 39.1; de Izarra (1993), 129–32.

73. Ellmers (1978), 7–8 and fig. 12.

74. De Izarra (1993), 159–61.

75. See Ellmers (1978), 3–4.

76. De Weerd (1978). For a survey of river wrecks discovered between Gaul and Germany, see Bockius (2004), 105–9. A general characteristic is a flat bottom with vertical or sloping sides, with ramplike ends; these craft could carry heavy loads in relatively shallow waters. See also chapter 7.

77. Ellmers (1978), 11.

78. Casson (1965), 38.

79. See Rostovtzeff (1957), 224, pl. 39.5.

80. Casson (1971) pl. 189; de Izarra (1993), 128–29.

81. Ellmers (1978), 3, thinks that this ship is a version of the native German barge.

82. Casson (1965), pl. V.1.

83. San Nicolás Pedraz (2002), 279, tav. V.2.

84. Martial, *Epigrammata* 4.64.22.

85. De Izarra (1993), 165.

86. See Haslam (1991), 124.

87. De Izarra (1993), 165–66.

88. *History of the Wars* 1.26.10–13; Casson (1965), 39, argues for the use of animal power, against Le Gall (1953a), 257, 325–26.

89. *Digest* 43.12.15; see also chapter 3.

90. *Digest* 43.12.12.

91. *Attic Nights* 11.17. *OLD*, s.v. *retae*; *reto*; see also chapter 3, n. 28.

92. See chapter 3, section 1.

93. *BGU* III 802; for the context of the papyrus, see Adams (2007), 191, Note also

P. Oxy. XLIII.3111 (A.D. 257), a freight contract involving the movement by boat of 800 *keramia* of wine to the II *Traiana Fortis* legion at a charge of 80 *drachmae* per 100 *kermaia*. For discussion of the price edict, see A. H. M. Jones (1964), 841–42; Duncan-Jones (1974), 366–69; Hopkins (1982), 86, who has a ratio of 1:6:55; Greene (1986), 39–43; Sillières (1990), 749–52. Laurence (1999), 95–108, argues cogently that although water transport was cheaper, the difficulty and cost of land transport have been overestimated, because water transport would often complement movement by land: "to discuss water and land transport as competing systems according to price is to misunderstand the economics of transport in the Roman world" (105); see also 109–22 and Laurence (1998). It is inaccurate, however, for Laurence (1999), 109, to claim that Peter Brunt dismissed river transport as "unimportant for the most part"; Brunt (1971), 180, argued that river transport was cheaper and more comfortable than land transport but that the Mediterranean rivers imposed certain limitations. Note also Deman (1987), 81–87, for a useful survey of the comparative value of river transport.

94. Pliny, *Epistulae* 10.41. And see further below at n. 139.

95. Adams (2007), 52–64, 77–81. Le Gall (1994), 70, suggests that donkeys could carry from 75–200 kilograms depending on the terrain. Raepsaet (2008), 589, argues that a horse walking can carry a load of 100/120 kilograms for 40 kilometers in the course of a day at 4 kilometers per hour, a European mule 150/180 kilograms for 20–24 kilometers in a day at 3–5 kilometers per hour.

96. On the basis of *CTh.* 8.5.8, a freight wagon was limited to 429 kilograms.

97. Casson (1971), 170–73, 183–90; Houston (1988a), 553–60. A ship of 200–250 tonnes could proceed up the river Baetis as far as Seville; see Sillières (1990), 740.

98. For the speed of travel by water or road, see Casson (1971), 22–23, 29; Chevallier (1976), 178–97; Landels (1978), 159, 171; Duncan-Jones (1990), 7–29 (on sea travel); Laurence (1999), 81–94.

99. Casson (1971), 22–23, 29.

100. De Izarra (1993), 166.

101. Calzolari (1992), 86.

102. Le Gall (1953a), 256–57.

103. See Roth (1999), 197; White (1984), 128–30, 153; J. D. Anderson (1992), 3, comparing an eighteenth-century British packhorse pulling a barge upstream.

104. Herodotus 7.114.

105. Zeugma, Pliny, *NH* 5.86; Arelate, Chevallier (1976), 200; Burnand (1977), 302–3; Rivet (1988), 192.

106. Rivet (1988), 132.

107. See Mesqui (1986), 95–96, referring to France in the fifteenth century.

108. For an excellent survey of bridges, see Gazzola (1963); O'Connor (1993); also Quilici (2008), 569–73. For traces of three ancient bridges near Fregellae, see Coarelli (1979); for bridges and ferries in Gaul, see de Izarra (1993), 70–74.

109. Horden and Purcell (2000), 126.

110. Tacitus, *Annales* 3.9. Cf. 5.10 for Poppaeus Sabinus, governor of Macedonia, using

sea and road travel from the Gulf of Torone in northeastern Greece to Actium on the west coast, via the Isthmus of Corinth.

111. As discussed, one avenue was through legal enactment to control water use and to protect watery sources; see chapter 3.

112. There are other methods of briefly increasing river flow that will have left no trace, for example, deploying a herd of cattle to block the current and then rapidly moving them out of the way so as to release a flood of water that might free a grounded barge, as suggested by Haslam (1991), 121.

113. For discussion, see Moore (1950); N. A. F. Smith (1977-78); also Greene (1986), 34-35; de Izarra (1993), 51-54.

114. See Johannowsky (1994), 161.

115. Suetonius, *Nero* 31.3; Tacitus, *Annales* 15.42.

116. See the comments of Laurence (1999), 114-15.

117. Statius, *Silvae* 4.3.40-55.

118. Meiggs (1960), 161-66; Keay et al. (2005).

119. Livy, *Epitomae* 11; see White (1970), 160-69; Laurence (1999), 111-14. For navigation on the Tiber, see also chapter 8, section 4.

120. See chapter 4 at n. 1. Note also Forbes (1965), 46-49, on Roman drainage projects.

121. Quilici (1985-86), 214-15. About these sites Le Gall (1953), 124, n. 5, had expressed skepticism after a visit in 1947. See also G. D. B. Jones (1962), 197-201, for a dam at Lucus Feroniae.

122. *Historia Pseudo-Isidoriana* 5; Quilici (1985-86), 204-5.

123. Pliny, *NH* 3.119-22.

124. Laurence (1999), 118.

125. For canals, see Laurence (1999), 116-22; at the Po delta, see Uggeri (1987), (1990).

126. Pliny, *NH* 3.119; Levick (1990), 143; Laurence (1999), 120.

127. Strabo, 5.1.7 (213).

128. N. A. F. Smith (1977-78), 77; White (1970), 170 and n. 57.

129. Strabo 5.1.11 (217); Uggeri (1987). Scaurus was censor in 109; but his activity may be dated to his consulship in 115.

130. N. A. F. Smith (1977-78), 77; Frere (1987), 267-68. Haslam (1991), 117 and 192-93, points out that the town pattern of modern Lincoln is partly determined by the old Roman waterway.

131. Sillières (1990), 722-24.

132. Tacitus, *Annales* 2.8. Germanicus traveled down the river, via the canal to the Rhine, through the North Sea and the Zuiderzee to the mouth of the Amisia (Ems); N. A. F. Smith (1977-78), 78.

133. *Annales* 11.20; N. A. F. Smith (1977-78).

134. *Annales* 13.53.

135. Plutarch, *Marius* 15.

136. See chapter 7, section 2.

137. Pausanias, 8.29.3.

138. See chapter 8 at n. 212.

139. Pliny, *Epistulae* 10.41–42; 61–62; Laurence (1999), 119–20.

140. In a pound lock two guillotine gates are established a distance apart on the river forming a chamber. The boatman traveling upstream opens the lower gate and lets water drain out of the chamber and then drags his boat inside and closes the gate. Water is allowed into the chamber from the upper gate until the water level in the chamber is equal to that beyond the upper gate. The gate is now lifted, and the boat dragged through. The gate is then closed again. The procedure is repeated in reverse for boats going downstream. Flash locks consist of one lifting-gate or set of horizontal boards across a canal or a river. The boatman traveling upstream has to remove the horizontal boards one by one or open the gate slowly. Water pours through equalizing the water level, and the boat can be dragged through; the gate is closed again, and the boatman must then wait for the water level above the gate to rise again. This might take some considerable time. See Moore (1950); Sherwin-White (1966), 647–48. N. A. F. Smith (1977–78), 81–83, does not rule out the pound lock, but sluices and stanch or flash locks may be more likely. Selkirk (1983), 89–93, argues strongly that the Romans did use pound locks; the technology was then lost until the fourteenth century. For cogent criticism of this view, see Anderson (1992).

141. See *ILS* 5863 = Smallwood (1966), no. 413. The interpretation of "anco(ni)bus sublat(i)s" is disputed; it might refer to the placing of supporting brackets under the wooden pathway or possibly to the removal of the brackets so that efforts could be concentrated on cutting into the rock face and widening the path that way. See discussion in Lepper and Frere (1988), 287–89; Petrović (1990).

142. Šašel (1973); Lepper and Frere (1988), 286–87. There may have been other canals in the vicinity; see Procopius, *De Aedificiis* 4.6.

143. In Egypt, a navigable canal from the Nile to the Gulf of Suez perhaps excavated in the reign of the Pharaoh Sesostris was rebuilt by Trajan and called Trajan's Canal or Trajan's River; Pliny, *NH* 6.165; Adams (2007), 33–34; *P. Oxy.* XII.1426. It was still called Trajan's Canal in the fourth century; cf. *P. Oxy.* LV.3814.

144. See, in general, Brittain (1958), 53–79; N. A. F. Smith (1971); Schnitter (1983); Malissard (1994), 158–60.

145. See N. A. F. Smith (1971), 1–14.

146. Strabo, 16.1.10–12 (740–41).

147. N. A. F. Smith (1971), 33–35. It is possible that the dam at Glanum in Narbonensis was of the arch type.

148. Pliny, *Epistulae* 5.6.12.

149. *NH* 3.53.

150. Tacitus, *Annales* 1.79; see chapter 4 at n. 1. For water management by canal in the Tiber Valley, see above at n. 119.

151. G. D. B. Jones (1962), 197–201. See G. D. B. Jones (1963) for the north Ager Capenas, especially 102, fig. 1, for the route of the Tiber.

152. N. A. F. Smith (1971), 26–32; (1991), 124.

153. N. A. F. Smith (1971), 32–49.

154. N. A. F. Smith (1971); Cifani and Munzi (2002), 1915–18.

155. For the following summary, I am much indebted to the detailed discussions by B. D. Shaw (1982), (1984), (1991). For water management in Tunisia, see Slim (1992).

156. Saldae, *CIL* 8.2728 = *ILS* 5795 A.D. 152; translation in Campbell (1994), 125–26.

157. Lamasba, in Numidia, about 100 kilometers south of Cirta and 40 kilometers north-west of Lambaesis, in the semiarid lands of the Maghrib, had a large territory amounting to about 300 square kilometers, and the town had an important position between the mountains and the plain, close to a perennial spring. The irrigation decree was issued by the local municipality in the time of Elagabalus. It may have been unusual for water distribution arrangements to be organized by a formally recorded written agreement, but possibly there had been a dispute here (*CIL* 8.18587 = *ILS* 5793). The source was the Aqua Claudiana, presumably a perennial spring, since water is provided over six months. The scheme worked by time units, and the water was provided to landholders in order of sequence from a main channel to properties arranged in sections on either side of it. For detailed discussion, see B. D. Shaw (1982). The inscription is in Latin, and the emperor is mentioned, which suggests some degree of nurturing concern by the Roman authorities.

158. N. A. F. Smith (1971), 48.

159. N. A. F. Smith (1971), 43–48.

160. Strabo, 8.6.7 (370), Argos is fertile and well-watered; cf. 8.5.6 (368), quoting Euripides' description of Messenia; 7, frag. 36. Cf. 8.4.5 (360), "deep-meadowed"; 12.3.8 (543), name of Parthenius, flowery districts; 16.4.14 (773) and 18 (776–77), even in mythology "river-lands" are associated with fertility; 17.1.3–5 (787–88), effect of the Nile on land; 17.1.48 (817), Nilometer; 12.3.15 (547), Iris and rich plain of Amaseia. Rivers, as well as bringing down in their stream precious stones and gold, encouraged the production of rushes, helped form productive marshes, and even acted as rubbish removers. The presence of good fish was a particular boon, as in the Greater Rhombites, "where the greatest catches are made of fish suitable for salting" and the local inhabitants used small islands as bases from which to fish; 11.2.4 (493–94). For discussion of modern river usage, see Haslam (1991).

161. See Forbes (1965), 81–89; Bradley (2002), with response by A. I. Wilson (2003). See A. I. Wilson (2003), 444, for the water supply for fulling; the fullers' guild in Rome was known as the *conlegium aquae* (*CIL* 6.10298). See also Frontinus, *De Aquis* 2.94; 98.

162. Note also that the mining industry required large amounts of water, though in a different way from other industries. Large reservoirs were needed to collect water and then release it to clear away the overburden. See Landels (1978), 25–26; for mining practice in Spain, see P. R. Lewis and Jones (1969); (1970); G. D. B. Jones (1980).

163. *NH* 5.75; 25.75–76; 36.174.

164. *NH* 5.44; 16.161. For reed plantations on the Nile, see *P. Oxy.* XIV.1671 (third century A.D.).

165. *NH* 9.44. For the bass in the Tiber at Rome, see 9.169; for fishing, see chapter 9, section 2.

166. *NH* 31.75. For salt deposits, see Healy (1999), 118.

167. *NH* 37.114.

168. *NH* 33.66.

169. Pausanias 5.14.3.

170. Pausanias 8.24.11; 8.22.8, on flooding at Stymphalos in Pausanias's own day.

171. Landels (1978), 16–26; Wikander (1979), (1991), 142–45, and (2000); Horden and Purcell (2000), 255–76; A. I. Wilson (1995), on development of the horizontal waterwheel, (2001), and (2002), 9–17; R. J. A. Wilson (1996), 20, on the increasing discovery of water mills; Hodge (2002), 254–57. The earliest datable waterwheel of which some traces remain is at Avenche (A.D. 57/58); see Castella (1994). Horizontal and vertical wheels may have been in use contemporaneously; see N. A. F. Smith (1983–84). Vitruvius, *De Architectura* 10.5; cf. Ausonius, *Mosella* 362–64, who may refer to a water-driven marble cutting saw. The technical details of the use of waterpower are beyond the scope of this study.

172. Sellin (1983); Leveau (1996); Bellamy and Hitchner (1996); Hodge (2002), 257–61. For the mills on the Janiculum, see Van Buren and Stevens (1915–16), (1927); for mills in the baths of Caracalla, see Schiøler and Wikander (1983). For Barbegal, see further chapter 7 at n. 158.

173. Varro, *De Re Rustica* 1.11.2.

174. See Hodge (2002), 247. In modern analysis, 1 millimeter in depth of water = 1 liter applied to 1 square meter. To supply 20 millimeters of water to a field of 1 hectare (= 2.47 acres) requires 200 cubic meters. To supply 100 hectares with 20 millimeters would require 20,000 cubic meters, or the output of a medium-sized Roman city aqueduct.

175. Water-raising devices were the screw pump, the *tolleno* or *shaduf*, and the drum, which could not raise water to a great height. The screw pump was operated like a kind of treadmill; see Landels (1978), 59–63. The *tolleno* consists of two wooden pillars about five feet high with a cross beam over which is placed a long, narrow pole. This acts as a pivot and has a bucket at one end and a counterweight at the other; the weight lifts the filled bucket to waist height, and the operator can then operate the pole to direct the water to an irrigation reservoir. These devices would leave no trace in the archaeological record.

176. For water pumps in general, see Landels (1978), 58–75; and Oleson (1984), 291–301 (screw), 325–50 (compartmented wheel). See Hodge (2002), 249, for some estimates on how much water could be provided by mechanical devices. See also Wikander (1979).

177. However, note, for example, the channels in the floodplain of the river Herakleia in southern Italy (*IG* 14.645, 13–15). For limited schemes to organize the distribution of water, see above at n. 156.

178. Discussion in White (1970), 151–72; Hodge (2002), 246–53. And see further below, section 8. Of course, illegal tapping of aqueducts seems to have been common. Frontinus notes this in Rome, and in rural areas it must have been very difficult to police miles of water channel.

179. Frontinus, *De Aquis* 2.92.

180. As argued by Hodge (2002), 249.

181. Delano Smith (1979), 177, summarizes the benefits of irrigation; for the pattern of irrigation in the Mediterranean, see Horden and Purcell (2002), 238–55.

182. See Brown (1997), 254–56, 279–92; also Semple (1932), 108, for use of alluvial areas and wetlands; Delano Smith (1979) 339, on famous European wetlands; Traina (1988).

183. T165.5.

184. T96.21.

185. *CIL* 8.2561; A. C. Johnson, Coleman-Norton, and Bourne (1961), no. 229.

186. *AE* 1960.249.

187. T165.1.

188. Horden and Purcell (2000), 245–47; Leveau (1993). See Argoud et al. (1987), 17–123, for the theme of hydraulics in the ancient world. See Thomas and Wilson (1994) at n. 96 for evidence of irrigation of meadows in the *ager Faliscus* and pp. 168–69, on the role of water mills in Italy. Virgil, *Eclogues* 3.111 ("close the stream now, boys, the meadows have drunk enough"), expresses the bucolic ideal of well-watered farmland. For the geographical setting of the Marsi and the Fucine Lake, see Letta (1972), 9–22, especially 11–12.

189. Suetonius, *Claudius* 20; Dio 60.11. Dio thought that part of the plan was to make the Liris more navigable.

190. Discussion in Leveau (1993).

191. For such lands, see Traina (1988); Marruvium: the *Liber Coloniarum* refers to "limitibus maritimis et montanis"; Campbell (2000), 196.16–19.

192. *CIL* 9.3915 (Alba Fucens): "ob reciperatos agros et possessores [reductos] quos lacus Fucini violent[ia exturbarat]"; discussion in Letta (1972), 133–35.

193. See Fossey (1979), 569; J. H. Oliver (1989), nos. 108–9. For exploitation of wetlands, lagoons, and freshwater lakes, note also Strabo's description of Calydon in Greece in a plain watered by the river Euenos, where there was a large lake rich in fish, the fruits of which were enjoyed by "the Romans at Patrae" (10.2.21 [460]). It seems that the Roman colony set up by Augustus at Patrae had been awarded control over the lake as part of its revenues.

194. J. H. Oliver (1989), 110.

195. J. H. Oliver (1989), 112.

196. I rely here on the work of J. R. L. Allen and Fulford (1986), (1990), and J. R. L. Allen, Fulford, and Rippin (1994).

197. *CIL* 10.6850/1 = *ILS* 827.

198. For alluvial action, see chapter 3, section 5.

199. Guillerme (1983), referring mainly to the medieval period, has some interesting comments on the importance of controlling the watery environment, since rivers were an integral part of the life and psychology of the city and part of the hydrographic framework.

200. Frontinus, *De Aquis* 1.5; Richardson (1992), 15–16; Steinby (1993–99), 1:61–62.

201. For the theme of the sources supplying aqueducts, see Hodge (2002), 67–92. See Malissard (1994), 155–60, on the importance of a source of pure water for aqueducts.

202. Hodge (2002), 69–70.

203. Hodge (2002), 73–79, 227–32.

204. For the aquatic management system in Rome in the context of watery environment, see in general Wolodkiewicz (2005).

205. Frontinus, *De Aquis* 1.11; see also Pliny, *NH* 31.41–42.

206. Frontinus, *De Aquis* 1.10.

207. Richardson (1992), 15–19; Steinby (1993–99), 1:60–61. For a brief survey of Rome's aqueducts, see Heiken, Funiciello, and de Rita (2005), 141–47.

208. As pointed out by W. V. Harris (1979), 159.

209. *CIL* 6.1244 = *ILS* 98 (5–4 B.C.).

210. *CIL* 5.1245 = *ILS* 98. Cf. *CIL* 5.1246 = *ILS* 98, Titus's repair of the *aqua Marcia*.

211. A decree of the senate, reported by Frontinus, *De Aquis* 2.104.

212. Frontinus, *De Aquis* 1.16.

213. Note the comments of Venuleius on the vital importance of water (*Digest* 43.21.4); see chapter 3 at n 3.

214. Vell. Pat. 2.100.2; *Res Gestae* 23; Dio 66.25.3; Tacitus, *Annales* 14.15; Suetonius, *Augustus* 43.1; *Tiberius* 72.1.

215. Tacitus, *Annales* 15.37; Strabo 13.1.19 (590); Richardson (1992), 146–47.

216. Dio 54.29.4; *CIL* 6.31545 = *ILS* 5926.

217. See Scobie (1986), for problems of waste disposal.

218. Aristides, *To Rome* 98–99.

219. On the other hand, A. I. Wilson (1999) argues that, although aqueducts served primarily urban needs, they had a wider utility and had a potential role in rural life through branch channels; he examines evidence from the Roman Campagna, North Africa, southern Gaul, and sites at Aquincum, Catania, and Caesarea Maritima. Therefore, the Romans did not merely impose their view of aquatic civilization based on the cities; the rural population could also benefit to some extent.

220. See, in general, Hodge (2002), especially chaps. 6 and 10.

221. *CIL* 3.6703.

222. Potenza (1996); Hodge (2002), 282–83. For a survey of aqueducts in Campania, see Pagano (1996).

223. *Sammelbuch* 401.

224. See Grenier (1960), 493–506; Rivet (1988), 162–81; *CIL* 12.3070, 3098.

225. Hodge (2002), 24.

226. Hodge (2002), 69, 129–34.

227. Hodge (2002), 87–90; and see above, section 6.

228. *SEG* 31.1363.

229. *CIL* 8.2728 = *ILS* 5795. For imperial involvement, see also *CIL* 13.11757 (A.D. 187): "Pro salute Commodi . . . iussu Clementis Dextriani leg. Aug. pr. pr. quod aqua non

esset induxit per Iul. Demetrianum cent. Leg VIII Aug . . . per pedes . . . (Raetia, Castella Oehringen)."

230. See the discussion by Owens (1992). The methods for raising the water are unclear.

231. See in detail chapter 3.

232. Crawford (1996), 393–454, clause 79.

233. See Malissard (1994), chap. 4 and especially 132–33, for baths as agents of Romanization. Dvorjetski (1999), 124–26, has some interesting comments on the significance of the Roman provision of baths and other facilities in Judaea.

234. Pliny, *Epistulae*, 10.37–38, 90–91; Sherwin-White (1966), 613–14.

235. See, e.g., *ILS* 5743–98, and other material cited in this chapter.

236. *CIL* 10.6526 = *ILS* 5772.

237. *CIL* 1².1529 = 10.5807 = *ILS* 5348 = *ILLRP* 528.

238. For Italian towns, see Devijver and van Wonterghem (1981). Cf. also Blake, Bishop, and Bishop (1973), who usefully catalog building activity in Italy from Nerva to Antonines. The large number of water features is notable: aqueducts, cisterns, storage areas, water pipes, fountains and nymphaea, large and small bathing facilities; see now Jouffroy (1986), especially 66–71, 110–14, 146–47; for baths, 93–96, 125–29, 148–50.

239. *CIL* 9.3308 = *ILS* 5760.

240. Urvinum, *CIL* 11.6068 = *ILS* 5782. See in general Corbier (1984), who considers municipal provision of water in Italy, where there continued to be opportunities for local euergetism. In some cases individuals operated under the order of the local council. In at least one case, the curatorship of water (Puteoli) was permanent. Curators were from the upper tier of the local *ordo*, and the official curator could make a financial contribution; there was a combination of municipal finances and private support. Note also a *tribunus aquarum* at Tibur.

241. *CIL* 5.3402 = *ILS* 5757.

242. *CIL* 9.3018 = *ILS* 5761.

243. *CIL* 9.4786 = *ILS* 5767. For discussion of the inscription, see Coarelli (2005), especially 85–94; he attempts to identify sites mentioned in the inscription with discoveries at the site of the town (see p. 89, fig. 3), the route of the ancient aqueduct at Forum Novum and a bath building. The springs that supplied the baths still rise in Laia valley north of Vescovio; a villa identified between the springs and the bath building is likely to be that of Plebeius. Coarelli (94–98) makes an interesting case for identifying this Faianius Plebeius with the *eques* Faianius, who escaped a treason charge on the intervention of Tiberius (Tacitus, *Annales* 1.73).

244. *AE* 1977.794.

245. *AE* 1975.403.

246. *CIL* 2.3240 = *ILS* 5764.

247. *SEG* 30.1505. Cf. *CIG* 2782 with *SEG* 29.1068 (late second century A.D.), indicating a substantial celebration at Aphrodisias on the installation of a new water system exploiting the river Teilemes.

CHAPTER 7

1. For evidence supporting navigation on the Baetis, Ana, Singilis, and Maenuba, including modern hydrology and the later history of river use, see Sillières (1990), 703–21. See also Abad Casal (1975), 59–74; Parodi Álvarez (2001), 163–86. For navigable rivers in Spain according to ancient writers, see map 9.

2. Pliny, *NH* 3.9–12; Sillières (1990), 712–16; Fornell Muñoz (1997).

3. Sillières (1990), 728.

4. See Petts (1989), 221.

5. Strabo 3.3.4 (153).

6. Petts (1989), 233–36.

7. Discussion in Sillières (1990), 729–34, who distinguishes between estuaries and smaller channels resembling shore valleys. See also Parodi Álvarez (2001), 59–66.

8. Strabo 3.1.9 (140).

9. Strabo 3.2.4 (143). The manuscript has navigable inland for 8 stadia, which cannot be correct. Suggestions have been 800 or 100. A stade is 600 feet.

10. Strabo 3.5.9 (174). Outside Spain, Strabo describes the seven mouths of the Danube, along the largest of which ("Sacred") it was possible to sail for about twenty-one kilometers to the island of Peuce in the estuary (7.3.15 (305)). See Sillières (1990), 729; on the question of sea level, 733–35.

11. Strabo 3.2.5 (143).

12. Strabo 3.3.1 (151); Curchin (1991), 36–38.

13. Strabo 3.2.3 (142); cf. Pliny, *NH* 3.10. For navigation on the Baetis, see in general Fornell Muñoz (1997), 137–43. See Sillières (1990), 705–6, for discussion of Strabo's precise meaning in respect of the stretch of river above Corduba as far as Castulo, which some have held was navigable. For an interesting study of water management in Spain in Roman and later times, see Martín-Bueno (2008).

14. See Keay (1998a), 13; for urban density, 85.

15. See Ponsich (1974–91); also (1998), 174 and fig. 1 = map 10 in this volume. For the general importance of Baetis as a route of commerce, see Abad Casal (1975); López Monteagudo (2002), especially 597–605.

16. Strabo 3.2.3 (141); Keay (1998a and b).

17. In general, see Rickman (1985), 109; for trade with America, see Chaunu (1959).

18. Rodríguez-Almeida (1984); Remesal Rodríguez (1998), 197. Note that many redundant containers will have been dumped elsewhere. Remesal Rodríguez (1998), 195, points out that amphorae produced in one location in Baetica apparently traveled together and were thrown away together. For the olive oil trade, see also Haley (2003), especially 25, 40, 57–59, 83–91. For a comprehensive survey of the finds at Monte Testaccio, see Blázquez Martínez and Remesal Rodríguez (1999–2007).

19. Mattingly (1988), 33–34. Mattingly also has some cautionary comments (54–56) on using the evidence of pottery remains at Monte Testaccio to extrapolate the proportion of Spanish as opposed to African olive oil imported into Rome. On the importance of oil production, see also Blázquez Martínez and Remesal Rodríguez (1980), (1983).

20. For a general survey, see M. Beltrán Lloris (1970); Peacock and Williams (1986); also Mattingly (1988), 38–44; Remesal Rodríguez (1998), 185–90 and 187, fig. 1, for production sites of amphorae along the Baetis and the Singilis; map 11 in this volume. See also Haley (2003), 83–91.

21. Ponsich (1983b), 106.

22. Ponsich (1983b), 106.

23. Ponsich (1998), 173–75. Note *CIL* 2. 1182, boatmen, for example, *lyntarii cananienses*, *oducienses*, and *naevenses*, referring to Canama (Alcolea de Río), Oducia (Tocina), Naeva (Cantillana).

24. Haley (2003), 95–96. Cf. Barker and Lloyd (1991), especially 238, on the large number of scattered units of rural habitation and the role of towns and large villages in trade and manufacture and the implications for local and regional transport and distribution.

25. Suggested by Ponsich (1998), 175; (1983b), 108–9.

26. Sillières (1990), 754–56.

27. Sillières (1990), 744. *CIL* 15.4233: "devect(um) Hispalem" (scratched on part of an amphora). For further discussion of the importance of the mechanisms for oil export to Rome and elsewhere, see Colls et al. (1977), 23–40; Chic García (1984), (1988); Remesal Rodriguez (1998).

28. See Ponsich (1998), 177, fig. 3; Sillières (1990), 756–57; Haley (2003), especially 26, 41, 59–60, 91–92; map 12 in this volume.

29. See Sillières (1990), 757–58; Haley (2003), 40, thought that grain from the Baetis valley came to Corduba along the road network, but it is likely that river transport also played a part. For the importance of Gades as a port and the role of Hispalis, see Rougé (1966), 143–44.

30. Strabo 3.2.7 (145).

31. Ponsich (1988), 28–29 and fig. 6.

32. Spanish fish sauce was much appreciated. See Dalby (2000), 103–4; Edmondson (1987).

33. Ponsich (1998), 179, 181, fig. 5.

34. Sillières (1990), 758–60. For Castulo, Sillières (1990), 719–20; Haley (2003), 65–68.

35. Domergue (1998), 203–6, with fig. 3.

36. By Mattingly (1988), 52.

37. Mayer and Rodà (1998), 217, 225, fig. 4. See also Sillières (1990), 761–63. Sites of some quarries in Spain have an interesting correlation to rivers; in south/southwest Spain out of about twenty quarries, at least eight are close to or on navigable rivers. This may suggest that in some cases exploitation and development were connected with routes of transportation, either by barge or by road along river valleys.

38. Sillières (1990), 763–65.

39. For the wealth of Baetica in the Roman period, see Haley (2003), 186–90; Curchin (1991), 130–53; Richardson (1996), 157–68, 225–30; Chic García (1997).

40. *AE* 1980.84.

41. *CIL* 6.1625b = *ILS* 1340.

42. Mattingly (1988), 43–44.

43. For this tax in Spain, see de Laet (1949), 286–94; Chic García (1984), 44.

44. Gaul: Le Gall (1983); military and civilian sites in Britain: Williams and Peacock (1983). But see the comments of Mattingly (1988), 53, n. 101, doubting the quantity of oil exported to Britain.

45. *CIL* 2.1481; Chic García (1984), 41.

46. *CIL* 2.1180 = *ILS* 1403; Pflaum (1960–61), 504–7; Tchernia (1980), 155–56; Rickman (1980), 224.

47. Chic García (1984), 37; *CIL* 2.1168–69; 1183.

48. *CIL* 2.2129 = *ILS* 1404 = $2^2/7$, 97; *AE* 2003.930 (from Obulco (Porcuna)).

49. *Digest* 50.6.6.6.

50. *CIL* 14.20 = *ILS* 372.

51. *CIL* 6.34001 = *ILS* 9022.

52. *SHA*, *Vita Severus* 18.3.

53. See M. Beltrán Lloris (1990), 111–34. Similar pottery was also produced at Andújar and was widely used in Baetica and southern Lusitania.

54. Curchin (1991) 150.

55. Parodi Álvarez (2001), 68–69. And see below for the position of Dertosa.

56. Parodi Álvarez (2001), 70–82; for port installations, 83. For Caesaraugusta, see Dupré (1983), 402.

57. Alberich, Ribera i Lacomba, and Marco (2004).

58. Parodi Álvarez (2001), 212–13.

59. See Edmondson (1987), 122–34, 152–57, for ports on the Mondego and also Scallabis on the Tagus; Parodi Álvarez (2001), 197–201.

60. Parodi Álvarez (2001), 213–14.

61. Sillières (1990), 720–22. For the characteristics of the Anas, see above at n. 3. For navigability on Anas in general; see also Edmondson (1987), 152–57.

62. Curchin (1991), 134; Parodi Álvarez (2001), 194–95; see also Edmondson (1987), 152–57.

63. Parodi Álvarez (2001), 223–25.

64. Parodi Álvarez (2001), 227–37.

65. Haslam (1991), 127. For an excellent survey of ancient evidence on Gallic rivers and a bibliography, see Chavallier (1975). See also map 15 in this volume.

66. Strabo 4.1.2–11 (178); Ammianus 15.11.16–18. For the characteristics of Gallic rivers, see chapter 1, section 4. Note Strabo 4.3.3 (193) where the distance from the mouths of the Rhône to Lugdunum is given as somewhat less than 250 miles. The correct total is about 160 miles; see also Pliny, *NH* 3.33; cf. 2.224. For the importance of the Rhône as a route of communication, see Dufournet (1968), and above all Leveau et al. (1999). For a general survey of the Rhône in Greek and Roman literature and its role as a route of commerce, see de Saint-Denis (1981), especially 564–70. For how Caesar understood the trade possibilities along the Rhône, see Martin (1980). For a valuable collection of ancient evidence and modern discussions, see Chavallier (1975).

67. See in more detail Petts (1989), 57–70.

68. *BAtlas* 17D2–5; 15D1–2.

69. *BAtlas* 17H4, F5; 15E2, D2; 18B3.

70. *BAtlas* 17C2; 14I2, G1, F1, E1, D1.

71. *BAtlas* 14I2, 3.

72. Petts (1989), 249–59.

73. Note Christol and Fiches (1999), 141–55, arguing that road and river transport were complementary on the Rhône; movement upstream was difficult, and evidence is scarce.

74. See chapter 6, section 5, for a review of river connections.

75. Strabo 4.1.14 (189). For overland connections between Saône, Loire, and Seine, see Fustier (1967); Jalmain (1972).

76. A. J. Parker (1984). For the importance of the Saône, see Schlippshuh (1974), 98–99. Note A. J. Parker (1992), 75, on a wreck dating from A.D. 161 in the Garonne at Cadaujac.

77. A. J. Parker (1992), 37–38, 77.

78. For this theme in Gaul, see Braemer (1989). He cites *CIL* 13.5489 from Dijon—a sailor's tomb depicting a man unloading a wagon—as an indication of the importance of transhipment and the role of river ports.

79. See chapter 6, section 6. See Ager (1980), 262, for a good description of the Rhône delta. In some places, fairly simple dikes may have served to control water flow, for example, on the Durentia, where a similar system to that employed on the upper Tiber was possibly in use. De Izarra (1993), 66–70, especially 67. The last 70 kilometers of its navigable course has a slope of 212 meters.

80. Strabo 4.1.8 (184).

81. Strabo 4.3.2 (192).

82. De Izarra (1993), 127–29. Rostovtzeff (1957), 2:613, thinks that Blussus is wearing half-national dress. See also chapter 6 at n. 80, and below, n. 186.

83. *CIL* 12.982 = *ILS* 6986. Note the *navicularius marinus* from Narbo who was also a magistrate of the colony and the conductor of the iron mines on the right bank (probably of the Rhône); *CIL* 12.4398 = *ILS* 6971.

84. Statue, Grenier (1960), 620, with fig. 189. The man apparently rowing a boat is depicted in color on the cover of de Izarra (1993).

85. See in general Meiggs (1960), 311–36.

86. See below, section 3.

87. For the nature of the boats they operated, see chapter 6, section 3.

88. See de Izarra (1993), 232–35. He argues that before a voyage the sailors invoked various deities for protection and after a safe voyage gave thanks to those deities. We also hear about Eusus, guardian against dangerous waters.

89. *Utriclarii* by contrast were linked to towns, presumably because they carried or ferried goods over short distances at a particular location. Alba, *AE* 1965.144; Arles, *CIL* 12.700, 729, 731, 733, 4107; Cavaillon, *CIL* 12.136; Cimiez, *AE* 1967.281; Ernaginum, *CIL* 12.982; Lattes, *AE* 1966.247; Lyon, *CIL* 12.1742; 13.1954, 1960, 1985, 1998 (= *ILS* 7035). This

last interesting though enigmatic inscription celebrates Illiomarus Aper, who died aged eighty-five after an untroubled life. He was a linen trader or linen weaver who was inscribed in the corporation of *utriclarii* based at Lyon; either this position was honorary, or he had adopted a new occupation. The various possibilities are discussed by Deman (1987), 91–95; *CIL* 2009; 2023 (= *ILS* 7034); 2039. Narbonne, *CIL* 12.283; Nemausus, *CIL* 12.3351; Riez, *CIL* 12.360; 372; St-Gabriel, *CIL* 12.982; Vaison, *CIL* 12.1387; Vienne, *CIL* 12.1815. Note the view of Kneissl (1981), supported by Deman (1987), 87–105, that *utriclarii* were involved in transport by land; this seems unlikely, as previously discussed, chapter 6, section 3.

90. *CIL* 13.1695; there is doubtless an element of conventional self-praise in the inscription. See in general Frank (1959), 476–86; 513.

91. *CIL* 12.1005; see also 3316 and 3317.

92. *CIL* 12.1797.

93. *CIL* 13.1996 = *ILS* 7031.

94. *CIL* 13.2002 = *ILS* 7032. On other Rhône boatmen, see *AE* 1995.1141.

95. *CIL* 13.2494 = *ILS* 9439, curator n. R[hod].

96. *CIL* 13.5489; cf. 1911; 1954; 1972; 2020; 2028; 2041; 5161 = *ILS* 4707; 5489 from Dibio: "nauta Araricus."

97. *CIL* 13.2009. See also *AE* 1975.613 and 1976.445.

98. *CIL* 13.1688; 1695; 1918; 1966 = *ILS* 7028.

99. *CIL* 13.1960; cf. 1979.

100. *AE* 1972.352.

101. *CIL* 13.1709 = *ILS* 7020; *ILS* 7021. The Arecarii are unidentified. For the importance of the confluence of rivers, see chapter 2 at n. 155. And note *CIL* 13.1541; 1702; 1710; 1712; 1719; 2940; 3144.

102. *CIL* 12.3316 = *ILS* 5656; cf. *CIL* 3317; 4107 (St. Gilles): "curat. Nautae Atr(iciae) et Ovidis et utriclarii Arelatenses"; *ILGN* 515–16. See Rivet (1988), 167, 174; Burnand (1971).

103. *CIL* 12.721, 731.

104. *CIL* 12.982; Rivet (1988), 203.

105. *CIL* 13.5096, and see below, nn. 141, 187.

106. *CIL* 13.3105, 3106 = *ILS* 7052; 3114.

107. *CIL* 13.4335 from Mediomatrici in Gallia Belgica.

108. *CIL* 13.3026a, *nautae Parisiaci* from Parisii.

109. *CIL* 13.3105 = *ILS* 7052; Drinkwater (1983), 203–4: this seems to me to go further than the evidence justifies.

110. *CIL* 12.2597; *ILGN* 361.

111. De Izarra (1993), 54–66.

112. See chapter 6, section 5.

113. Rivet (1988), 195–96, pl. 27; de Izarra (1993), 71.

114. Rivet (1988), 190–96; de Izarra (1993), 55–56; Gorgues, Long, and Rico (2004), 44–46.

115. Frank (1959), 476–79. For Arelate's importance as a port, see Rougé (1966), 95, 142; *fossa Mariana*, France (2001), 225–26.

116. Meiggs (1960), 285–86, on the mosaics in the Piazzale delle Corporazioni; Dunbabin (1999), 62–65. For the *portorium*, see below at n. 165.

117. *ILS* 6987.

118. Strabo 4.6.11 (208). Drinkwater (1975) argues that it was largely the determination of Augustus and his financial investment that made Lugdunum great, since it was not naturally a good site. For transverse communication from the Rhône corridor, see Burnand (1971).

119. In general, see Frank (1959), 479–86. For the port at Lugdunum, see Audin and Le Glay (1966).

120. *CIL* 13.1954, 1960, 1966.

121. Condate was a Celtic place-name meaning *confluence*, and about thirty examples are known.

122. *AE* 1982.702, with Le Glay (1980–81).

123. *CIL* 13.1709; see in general Drinkwater (1975); Audin (1979).

124. King (1990), 112. Middleton (1979), 84, argues that shippers and boatmen in Gaul were directly associated with military supply lines, but this remains problematical; as Strabo saw, the Rhône was more important than other Gallic rivers for trade, quite apart from military supply routes. The argument that of *collegia* only groups outside the military zone were accorded this status because they were involved in military supply is *ex silentio*; the reason why there are *collegia* on the Rhône and not on the Rhine is because the former was more important for trade for a variety of reasons (as briefly discussed above). The supposed link between *nautae* and state supply is very tenuous; for the long-distance supply of armies, see also Whittaker (1994), 104–13.

125. For these themes, see Drinkwater (1983), 126–28; Goudineau (1980), (2000), especially 474–79, 484–85; King (1990), 110–31; Rüger (2000), 504–6.

126. For a general survey of Cologne, see Doppelfeld (1975), especially 740–43, for trade.

127. For a summary of the Rhône-Rhine axis, see Kneissl (1981); Desbat and Martin Kilcher (1989); for transhipment at Chalon, Bonnamour (1975); France (2001), 217–18.

128. See de Izarra (1993), 61–65. Strabo registers Bordeaux, Châlons Korbilon, Orléans, and Paris as emporia.

129. De Boe (1978), 23. See map 16 in this volume.

130. For types of boat, see chapter 6, section 3, noting particularly the dugouts and barges found near the Roman auxiliary fort at Zwammerdam. See also A. J. Parker (1992), 325–26; Suttor (2000). A log boat was discovered in Britain on the river Ancholme at its confluence with the Humber (second century B.C.), probably used for river transport. Cf. J. D. Anderson (1992), 83; for other finds in Britain including a steering oar from Newstead-on-Tweed, 85–87.

131. De Boe (1978), fig. 35; map 17.

132. See Hassall (1978), 44. For river traffic on the Meuse and its tributaries, see Corbiau (2000), noting evidence for rivercraft, landing stages, and work on the riverbank.

133. See below at n. 167.

134. *CIL* 13.1911 = *ILS* 7033. See in general de Izarra (1993), 220–27.

135. *CIL* 13.2033. See Verboven (2007), especially 295–302.

136. Drinkwater (1983), 167. Vines came late to many areas of Gaul, in some cases not until the third century.

137. De Izarra (1993), 169. This is the extension of the Rhône-Saône axis. See Desbat and Martin-Kilcher (1989) for amphorae in Gaul and the identification of trade routes.

138. Diodorus 5.26.7. For the supply of Italian wine to Gaul and Italian wine production, see Tchernia (1983).

139. See Peacock (1978), 49, tab. 3, fig. 44. For the relative cost of transport, see chapter 6, section 4. Remesal Rodríguez (2002), 301, argues for the importance of the Atlantic trade route for trade between Baetica, Germany, and Britain, though on rather weak grounds (such as the presence of a lighthouse at Coruña, and the fear of breakages that might have occurred along the Rhône route). Whittaker (1994), 100, doubts that oil from Baetica came to the Rhine via the Atlantic.

140. King (1990), 90–91.

141. Arnold (1978). See also Broise (1976), 608–21, for the ports of Geneva and Lausanne. For the inscriptions, see Howald and Meyer (1940):

Lausanne, p. 243, no. 152: "Numinibus August(orum) nautae [lac]u Lemanno qui Leuso[nn]ae consistent, l(ocus) d(atus) d(ecreto) d(ecurioinum)"; and p. 243 no. 154: "Neptuno nautae Leuson(nenses) ex inpen[sis . . .]."

Geneva, p. 221 no. 92: "Q. Decio Alpino (quattuor)viro nautae lacus Lemanni"; and p. 227, no. 108: "Deo Silvano pro salu[t]e ratiarior(um) superior(um) amicor(um) posuit L. Sanct(ius) Marcus civis Hel(vetius) V(otum) S(olvit) L(ibens) M(erito) [de suo] d(onum) d(edit)"

Aventicum, p. 264, no. 217: "In honorum domus divinae [n]autae Aruranci Aramici scholam de suo instruxerunt [l(ocus)] d(atus) d(ecreto) d(ecurionum)." See also nn. 105, 187.

142. See A. J. Parker (1992), 447, for the discovery at Vichy on the Allier of the remains of a boat laden with pottery (central Gaulish *terra sigillata*).

143. King (1990), 125–31. For the development of *terra sigillata*, see Greene (2000b), 745–47. See also Bémont and Jacob (1986), 31–120 (La Graufesenque), 137–44 (Lezoux), On Lugdunum, see Picon (1975). See M.-T. Raepsaet-Charlier and Raepsaet-Charlier (1988) for the interaction of water and road transport in the movement of pottery in northern Gaul.

144. See Middleton (1980). He argues that the pottery was shipped by the southern route using a mule train over the Causse du Larzac and on to Narbonne. Settlements at Ceilhes and Salèlles acted as "interface markets between upland and plain communities." The expansion of this route and the export of pottery to the Rhineland and Britain were boosted by Roman interest in the exploitation of local precious metals. For the de-

velopment of ports in Britain, see Cleere (1978), 36–40, who examines ways of identifying them; some could certainly be river harbors. He includes cases where settlements are located on navigable rivers of major estuaries. Important centers were London, Gloucester, and Lincoln, but other harbors will have been small with localized markets in their immediate hinterland. They were probably used by smaller vessels bringing goods not available in the immediate area.

145. King (1990), 119–25.

146. Middleton (1980).

147. Drinkwater (1983), 187–88.

148. In particular quarries for particularly large blocks of stone are almost all adjacent to rivers. Transport could be by water or by road down the river valley; Bedon (1984), 137–44.

149. King (1990), 124. On Seyssel, see Dufournet (1971), (1976), (1984); Bedon (1984), 28–30. For flat-bottomed craft with small displacement and high-load capacity (the "prams"), see Bockius (2004) 109–14; also chapter 6, n. 76.

150. Bedon (1984), 140 (accepting the view of Dufournet).

151. Bedon (1984), 139.

152. Bedon (1984), 142 and n. 73. See also Pineau (1970), especially 54–55. The Charente was a great route of penetration toward the Limousin at Périgord. It has a tide as far as La Baine, eight kilometers east of Saintes. Navigating by boat extended as far as Tonnay-Charente where high tide achieved 5.50 meters. The river may have been bigger in the ancient world.

153. See Ferdière (1977), (1979); Bedon (1984), 142, n. 74. Note Rigault (1977), arguing that the presence of a quarry might lead to the construction of a port.

154. Rostovtzeff (1957), p. 224, pl. 39.5. For the importance of the Moselle as described by Ausonius, see chapter 4 at n. 34; Bedon (2010).

155. For the export of textiles in bales by riverboat, see Wild (1978), 80–81. Note Ellmers (1978), 13–14, on the transfer of goods and packaging in transport.

156. Goudineau (2000), 476–77.

157. Wightman (1970), 139–50.

158. King (1990), 101; Leveau (1996); Bellamy and Hitchner (1996).

159. Strabo 4.1.8 (183).

160. See de Laet (1949), 125–73; France (2001).

161. For a possible river port on the Durentia at Bourguet de l'Escale, see Rolland (1962), (1964).

162. *CIL* 13.2252, 2227.

163. *AE* 1919.21.

164. *ILS* 9035. For a summary of all collecting posts in this area, see de Laet (1949), 145–60.

165. Arelate, *CIL* 12.717 = *ILS* 1565; discussion in France (2001), 24–27, 317–19; Ostia, *CIL* 14.4708.

166. De Laet (1949), 161; France (2001), 225–29, 318–21.

167. Cagnat (1882), 67 with n. 2; Grenier (1934), 646–63; de Laet (1949), 164–66; France (2001), 60–65 (lead seals), 54–60, 391–96, 411–12 (Lugdunum).

168. *CIL* 13.5697–99.

169. Strabo 4.3.2 (192).

170. De Laet (1949), 168–70.

171. Strabo 7.1.3 (290). Pliny, *NH* 4.101, 106, does not comment on navigability.

172. Strabo 7.1.3 (290).

173. Caesar, *BG* 1.1.

174. *BG* 2.3–4.

175. *BG* 1.28; 33.

176. *BG* 6.35 (crossing river by boats and rafts); Velleius 2.107 (using a canoe to cross river); Pliny, *NH* 16.203, speaks of hollowed out trunks used to ferry up to 30 people across the Rhine.

177. For the Rhine's modern course, see chapter 1, section 4.

178. *BG* 4.10, 17.

179. Cicero, *In Pisonem* 81.

180. Strabo, 4.3.3 (193).

181. Seneca, *Quaestiones Naturales* 6.7.1; Tacitus (*Historiae* 4.26) notes that during the revolt of Civilis in A.D. 69 the river was barely navigable, but that was very unusual as a result of an unprecedented drought. The Rhine in ancient times was probably wider and shallower than the modern river, and it did change course at times; Mons Brisiacus (Alt-Breisach) lay on the left bank in Roman times but later on the right bank (*CIL* 13.2, p. 62).

182. Haslam (1991), 127; see also chapter 1 at n. 98.

183. *ILS* 4757: "deae [Vir]adecd[i civ]es Tungri [et] nautae [qu]i Fectione [c]onsistunt."

184. *CIL* 13.6324.

185. *CIL* 13.6450: "pro sal. imp. gen. naut. C. Iul. Urbicus D D VSLLM."

186. *CIL* 13.7067; Blussus describes himself as a *nauta*.

187. See above, nn. 105, 141. The identity of the Aramus is uncertain; it could be a river or lake.

188. See above, section 2; map 5.

189. Note Bedon (1984), 134; Dufournet (1971), especially 71–76, on Seyssel, which was a port and depot. Perhaps powerful companies of boatmen had buildings here; it was a center where the road from Lugdunum met that from Vienna. The river was not navigable beyond this point; Dufournet (1984).

190. Rüger (2000), 508–9.

191. Rüger (2000), 504.

192. Bogaers (1983), 13–22.

193. Bogaers (1983), 13–17.

194. *CIL* 13.8164a = *ILS* 7522; Bogaers (1983) 17–21.

195. See *RE* XVI.2177–82, a Gallic German mother goddess, symbol of the fertility of plants. The recorded *dea Nehalennia* may be based on a local river. We may compare the

statues of gods in ports to which sailors made an offering on departure and as a gesture of gratitude on return.

196. Discussion in Bogaers (1983), 21–24; *AE* 1977.512; Frere, Hassall, and Tomlin (1977), 430–31. This Viducius can be identified with the Placidus son of Viducius, a citizen of Rouen and trader with Britain, who dedicated an altar to Nehalennia in the East Scheldt estuary.

197. *CIL* 13.8725 from Noviomagus.

198. See Bogaers (1971), 33–43, especially 41–42; *CIL* 13/5, p. 158; also Schlippschuh (1974), 92–93. *CIL* 13.8793 from Domburg, set up by dealer in chalk to Deae Nehalenniae "for properly protecting the merchandise"; cf. also 7300, a *negotiator* from Britain at Castellum Mattiacorum.

199. A. J. Parker (1992), 452.

200. See Horn (1987), 171–72.

201. See Hartley (1969), 236–39. For the incidence of this ware round Argentorate, see Middleton (1979), 89–90.

202. See Brandt and Slofstra (1983), 194, for a distribution map, based on Mildenberger (1972), especially p. 117, map 5.

203. Dopplefeld (1975), 741; Price (1978).

204. See above at n. 150.

205. See Röder (1974), especially 534–44; Horn (1987), 523–27. On the exploitation of quarries in Gaul, see Bedon (1984), especially 131–44, for the removal and transport of stone.

206. Forrer (1911); Hatt (1970b), 44. See A. J. Parker (1992), 451–52, on a barge propelled by punting, 25–26, on a rivercraft sunk on the Rhine; and 325–26, on Pommeroeul.

207. Bockius (2004), 112–13. There were perhaps as many as 450 shiploads needed to build the curtain pillars of the bridge at Trier; he estimates that flat-bottomed barges or "prams" of the type discovered in various locations had a capacity of around forty tons. Bockius (113–14) also speculates that stone columns from the quarry at Felsberg were brought down a small local river to the Rhine and then to the mouth of the Moselle, from which they were towed upstream to Trier.

208. Amiet (1952).

209. See Bedon (1984), 140; chapter 5 at n. 108.

210. Hatt (1954) describes archaeological finds showing that the bank had been reinforced by a series of wooden posts placed in a line; a large pile had been set in the river to provide mooring for the flat-bottomed craft of the type used up to the sixteenth century on the Rhine. He believes that there was a quay sloping down toward the river to facilitate the loading of boats. For the sanctuary, see Hatt (1970a).

211. See Höckmann (1986), 370–77. Also Wells (1972), 138–46. For a general survey of Mogontiacum, see Decker and Selzer (1976).

212. Petrikovits (1952), 138–57.

213. Brandt (1983), 129.

214. Bogaers and Haalebos (1981).

215. In general, see de Laet (1949), 125–74; and the reassessment of some of the evidence by France (2001), 115–27, 337–45.

216. *AE* 1930.29. de Laet (1949), 131–37, argues the putative customs posts along the Rhine are not specifically mentioned as being in the Quadragesima Galliarum and therefore associates them with the *portus Lirensis*.

217. *RE* IV.1.871–72; Wells (1972), 137–38. For the approximate date of the Rhine bridge at Confluentes (c. A.D. 10–56), see Mensching (1981).

218. See above, n. 211.

219. For this view, see France (2001), especially 337–45.

220. Wells (1972), 116–23.

221. Pliny, *NH* 9.44–45.

222. Brandt and Slofstra (1983), 135–36.

223. Mogontiacum, *CIL* 13.6797: "cives Romani manticulari negotiatores"; Aquae Mattiacorum, *CIL* 13.7271: "negotiatores c(ivitatis) M(attiacorum)."

224. *CIL* 13.7655; see p. 484 for a discussion of various readings and restorations of the text.

225. Setting of Colchester, Frere (1987), 34; *BAtlas* 8G3 (London), H3 (Camulodunum).

226. Frere (1987), 63; Jones and Mattingly (1990), 166; *BAtlas* 8F1, E3.

227. See Jones and Mattingly (1990), 3, 199, map 6.19. For wharves on the Dee at Chester, see Mason (1987), 153–55; for British rivers, see also chapter 1 at n. 90.

228. Selkirk (1983). For pound locks, see chapter 6 at n. 140.

229. Selkirk (1983), 131.

230. Most effectively by J. D. Anderson (1992).

231. J. D. Anderson (1992), 11, 17.

CHAPTER 8

1. See also chapter 1 at n. 97. Stefan (1987) discusses the changing morphology of the coast at the mouths of the Danube.

2. See Mócsy (1974), 131.

3. Scylax, *Periplous* 24; Strabo 7.5.5–7 (315–16).

4. Pliny, *NH* 4.79.

5. Arrian, *Anabasis* 1.3.6. For the dugout canoes on the Danube and its tributaries, see Dio 49.37.6; Ammianus 17.13.27.

6. See chapter 6 at n. 141.

7. *AE* 1973.475.

8. Aelianus, *De Natura Animalium* 14.26.

9. *CIL* 3.7485: "n]autae un[ive]rsi Dan["; cf. also Schlippschuh (1974), 88: "amnici navicularii."

10. *CIL* 3.13804.

11. *CIL* 3.1209: "collegiorum fabrum centonariorum et nautarum conductori pascui

salinarum et commerciorum." Note also *SEG* 40.597 from Odessos, Christian period, epitaph of a shipper, possibly from the mouth of the Danube.

12. A. J. Parker (1992), 291.

13. Strabo 5.1.8 (214). Alföldy (1974), 72, argues that goods from Noricum were exported through Aquileia.

14. Alföldy (1974), 13.

15. Alföldy (1974), 245–46. See also Wilkes (1998), 643, on river transport along the Danube (mainly military).

16. Gabler and Keleman (1984).

17. Mócsy (1974), 176.

18. Kellner (1961), especially 168–70.

19. Gabler (1983).

20. *CIL* 3.4153; 4499; Mócsy (1974), 177–78. In the end, Pacatus was unsuccessful, and the pottery closed down.

21. Mócsy (1974), 119–21 and fig. 19.

22. Mócsy (1974), 124–26.

23. *CIL* 3.10430.

24. *CIL* 3.10771. South of Emona in the peninsula of Histria, the valley of the river Formio (Risano) was potentially another route to the interior. See Labud (1995), especially 105–8, for possible ports and small-scale cabotage navigation.

25. *CIL* 5.1047 = *ILS* 7526.

26. See Mócsy (1974), 130; Gerov (1988), 48–59, discusses the colony at Deultum for veterans of the VIII Augusta.

27. Tudor (1966); see 63–65 for the bridge. For the *portoria* collecting station at Sucidava, see de Laet (1949), 218.

28. Mócsy (1974), 214–16.

29. Histria—*SEG* 1.329; 24.1109; coins depicting river-gods, Klementa (1993), 189–93; *BMC* III, pp. 84–85, nos. 395–99; *LIMC* III.1.

30. Dio 71.11.3; 15.

31. *CIL* 3.3653.

32. See De Laet (1949), 174–245.

33. De Laet (1949), 178–92. For routes from northern Italy across the eastern Alps toward the Danube, note the importance of river valleys; Verona to Augsburg, partly by the valley of the Athesis (Adige) to the confluence with the Isarcus (Eisack) and then along this river; Aquileia to Poetovio passing Emona and reaching the Dravus at Poetovio. Here the Ad Publicanos customs post controlled the traffic in the valley of the Savus.

34. See *CIL* 3.3937, 13408; de Laet (1949), 222.

35. Notably, Boiodurum, Brigetio, Aquincum, Intercisa, Altinum, Statio Confluentes near Singidunum, Margum, Viminacium, Ratiaria, Almus, Ostrovo(?), Oescus, Asamum, Dimum. And on the *ripa Thraciae*: Novae, Durostorum, Capidava, Histria, see de Laet (1949), 194–209.

36. Boiodurum was at the confluence of the Danube and the Aenus (Inn) at the boundary between Noricum and Raetia; Brigetio at mouth of the Neutra; Statio Confluentes at the confluence of the Savus and Danube; Viminacium near the Mlava; Ratiaria at confluence of the river Ratiaria (Artscher) and the Danube; Almus at confluence of the Almus river and Danube; Oescus at confluence of the Oescus river and Danube; Asamum at confluence of Asamus and Danube.

37. De Laet (1949), 214.

38. Other important river sites are Ampelum, Sucidava, and Romula.

39. For internal stations, see de Laet (1949), 219–29, also 242–45, discussing rather speculatively the amount of the *portoria* for the Illyrian circumscription.

40. Swoboda (1958); Mócsy (1974), 120; *RE* suppl. XII (1970), 1575 (H. Sightz).

41. Trathnigg (1966).

42. Strabo 7.3.15 (305).

43. Mela 2.6. See in more detail chapter 2 at n. 222; *BAtlas* 23F2.

44. Dio Chrysostomos, *Orationes* 36.3.

45. *BAtlas* 88B2; 90D1.

46. Strabo 11.3.2 (500); Alazonius, *BAtlas* 88D3.

47. Tanais, Strabo 2.4.5 (107); Sangarius, Strabo 12.3.7 (543); *BAtlas* 52G3.

48. Strabo 7, frag. 20; *BAtlas* 50B3.

49. Strabo 7, frag. 47 (48); *BAtlas* 51G1.

50. See Mócsy (1974), 322: "The Axius was a convenient and also the only water route connecting Dardania with the Mediterranean." Strabo refers to Homer's description of it as "wide-flowing" and accepts that it received many rivers, but he thought that it was muddy and does not mention that it was navigable, though his text is fragmentary at this point (7.23 and 23a).

51. Pausanias 4.34.1; 8.41.3.

52. *NH* 4.14; 30; *BAtlas* 54D4; 58A2, B2; Arachthos (also known as Aratthus), Strabo 7.7.6–8 (326–27).

53. Strabo 5.2.5 (222). Also in Umbria Pliny (*NH* 3.51) refers to the navigable Umbro (Ombrone), which rises in the Apennines north of Saena (Siena) and flows south before inclining west to meet the coast north of Heba.

54. Bruni (1999), especially 11–16; (2000), 40–51. The remains of sixteen vessels have been found in the harbor at Pisa, including at least three boats with straight sides and raised ends probably used on the river. See Bruni (2000), 88–90, for the navigability of inland waters in the Pisan lowlands, and 26–40 for possible harbors and landing places from the Etruscan to the imperial era.

55. Pasquinucci and Menchelli (1999), 131; Pasquinucci and Del Rio (2004).

56. Pasquinucci and Menchelli (1999), 126–27, 134. The port continued to be the center of imports and exports into the third century A.D.

57. Ruegg et al. (1995), 24. For the Liris, see Coarelli (1979). For a geological survey of the area, see Martini (1994). For roads and bridges in the Liris valley, see Wightman (1982).

58. *Digest* 19.2.13.

59. Ruegg et al. (1995), 6–7; *CIL* 10.5371, *architectus navalis*, found northeast of the town on the river Liris.

60. Ruegg (1988); Ruegg et al. (1995), 58–60, 73–76, 123–31; Coarelli (1989), 172–73; Gualtieri (1997), 351–52.

61. Gualtieri (1997), 353. For local inscriptions, see Pagano and Villucci (1985).

62. Crimaco (1991).

63. Crimaco (1991), 37; Frederiksen (1984), 18. Note also Livy 26.7.9: Hannibal captures boats he comes across on the Volturnus; these seem to be boats there for trading purposes. Ruegg et al. (1995), 130, speculate that there were port installations serving Capua that are yet to be discovered.

64. Crimaco (1991), 13–15.

65. Crimaco (1991), 26. But there is much more evidence at Minturnae, and his contention is weak. It is not clear from his map (tav. XXX) that the villas really were consistently spread along the banks of the river.

66. See Petts (1989), 113–25.

67. *BAtlas* 39F5, G5, G4, H5.

68. *BAtlas* 39A5, B3, A2, D3, E2, F2, H3.

69. *BAtlas* 19F3. Elsewhere in Italy, Strabo (6.3.9 (284)) refers to a navigable river in Apulia between Sipous/Sipontium and Salapia, possibly the Cerbalus (Cervalo), rising in the Apennines and emptying into the sea at Scalo dei Saraceni. Pliny (*NH* 3.103) singles out the river Fertur (Fortore) as forming a harbor. It flows from the Apennines through Teanum Apulum on its way to the Gulf of Garganus. In Bruttium, Pliny (3.96), giving a list of navigable rivers, cites the Carcinus (Corace), which flows from the Ager Teuranus to the Scyallaceus Sinus near Castra Hannibalis. Teura is the only inland settlement in the area. Further north are the Crotalus (Alli), the Simerus (Simeri), the Arocas (Crocchio), which rises near Mt. Femminamorte, and the Thagines (Tacina), which rises on Mt. Gariglione and flows to the coast through Tacina. In these cases, he must be referring to small-scale navigation. This group of rivers running in parallel from the mountains to the coast will have provided routes of communication for small remote communities for supplies and transport by the coastal road or possibly by sea.

70. *Varia* 12.24. Cassiodorus (c. A.D. 490–585) was a monk and administrator who served the Ostrogothic kings.

71. Pliny, *NH*. 3.120; Uggeri (1987), 307–9.

72. Alfieri (1959).

73. See chapter 5, section 4.

74. Uggeri (1987), 313; also (1978). See, in general, for the character of the valley and navigation, Chilver (1941), 28–32; A. J. Toynbee (1965), 2:252–60, arguing that in the lower Po most of the cities were not located on the banks of the river because of flooding; Peyre (1979), especially 69–72; Boffo (1977); Calzolari (1989), (1992); Traina (1988), 82–83, 94–96, and (1990), for an evocative survey of the landscapes of Italy. Spurr (1986), 7–8, notes that in the middle and lower parts of the Po valley there were finer alluvial soils, and

also on the southern limits of the Latin plain. See Spurr, 19, for the climate of the valley, with a high annual range of temperatures and summer rainstorms.

75. Strabo 5.1.4 (212).

76. Strabo 4.6.5 (203); 5.1.11 (217).

77. Polybius 2.16.

78. *NH* 3.117–19; 123. Pliny advised his readers that they ought to visit the source of the great river, which had at least thirty tributaries and over a short distance enormously increased its volume.

79. Strabo 5.1.8 (214).

80. Pliny, *NH*, 3.119; Vitruvius, *De Architectura* 1.4.11.

81. See chapter 6, n. 128, for work undertaken by Augustus near Patavium.

82. For earlier engineering, see chapter 6, section 6.

83. For a general survey of roads in the area, see chapter 6, section 5.

84. Antonini Itinerarium 126.6.

85. *CIL* 5.8002 = *ILS* 208.

86. *CIL* 9.5959 = *ILS* 209.

87. *ILS* 9371.

88. *CIL* 5.7989 = *ILS* 487; cf. 490.

89. *NH* 16.178.

90. See Uggeri (1987), 314, n. 37.

91. Lucan, *Pharsalia* 4.134.

92. Livy 10.2.1–7; Uggeri (1987), 309–11.

93. Uggeri (1990), 187–95.

94. Uggeri (1990), fig. 3.

95. For a possible example, see Uggeri (1990), 193 (dated to time of Augustus).

96. Evidence for boatmen depends on a restoration of a funeral inscription by Boffo (1977). For a survey of epigraphic evidence of inland navigation in the Cisalpine region, see Bargnesi (1997). For the importance of Ticinum as a road junction and river port, see Bargnesi (2004), especially 77–79, who notes that close to the original Roman bridge is a possible storehouse connected with the harbor; many finds of high-quality pottery in the area were probably connected with river-borne transport.

97. *CIL* 5.4015–16. See also *AE* 1977.298: "collegium naut(arum) B(enacensium)"; 1993.786 from Lazise: *collegium* possibly of *nautae* associated with the lake.

98. *CIL* 5.4017 (Verona): "Item dedit coll(egio) naut(arum) Arilic(ensium) HSXII milia numm" to celebrate his memory.

99. Boffo (1977), 625.

100. *CIL* 5.4990: "in memoriam eorum et sui coll(egio) n(autarum) b(rixianorum) ad rosas et profusiones . . . dedit."

101. *CIL* 5.5995; 5911 (Comum): "-coll(egium) naut(arum) Comens(ium)."

102. *ILS* 7265.

103. *CIL* 5.2315, in honor of a man who gave 400 sesterces to the *collegium* of sailors of the *municipium* of Adreia to celebrate him every year.

104. *CIL* 11.135; 138. This depends on the interpretation of *n* as *n(auta)* in these inscriptions.

105. Sidonius, *Epistulae* 1.5.3–5; Boffo (1977), 626.

106. *AE* 1988.899 (with further references).

107. Cremona had a market; Tacitus, *Historiae* 3.30; Gabba (1975), 158, on the position of Cremona.

108. Uggeri (1990), 184–87.

109. Uggeri (1987), 316–21, discusses the many products of the Padana, but without specifically relating them to river transport. Note the comments of Sallares (2002), 81–85, on the problems in the Po valley and Tiber valley, where alluviation created breeding grounds for mosquitoes.

110. Vitruvius, *De Architectura* 2.9.16.

111. However, Zaninović (1977), 798, discussing maritime traffic in the eastern Adriatic, emphasizes that there were some good harbors; see p. 800 on trade that was well developed between Salona and Aquileia, Ravenna, and Ostia.

112. As argued by Brunt (1971), 179–84; see also A. J. Toynbee (1965), 2:255–60.

113. See above at n. 13.

114. Bosio (1991), 133. For roads in the area, see chapter 6 at n. 129.

115. See n. 85.

116. *AE* 1987.191–92: "navicularii maris Hadriatici"; see also *CIL* 14.409; *ILS* 6146; 7277; *AE* 1988.178.

117. Sidonius, *Epistulae* 1.5.

118. Le Gall (1953a), 9–13, basing his figures on reports up to the 1930s. It is assumed here that the river hydrology did not change much from Roman times to this era, though of course subsequently there have been hydroelectric schemes. See also Heiken, Funiciello, and de Rita (2005), 65–68, 81–84 (Tiber delta); Aldrete (2006), 59–60.

119. Measurements taken between 1920 and 1930; Le Gall (1953a), 11.

120. Holland and Holland (1950) describe their voyage down the Tiber on a raft from Orte to Rome, commenting on the strong current (about three miles per hour) and the high banks. The width of the river varied from 60 to over 200 yards. For the general qualities of Italian rivers, see Walker (1967), 86–87.

121. See Potter (1976), 1–7, for a description of the topography north of Rome and the role of the river valleys.

122. Potter (1976), 14–17. The relatively gentle slope of the Tiber meant that surges of floodwater were slow to develop. For Tiber floods, see below at n. 202.

123. See chapter 4, section 5.

124. Cicero, *De Re Publica* 2.10.

125. Dionysius Periegetes 351–56.

126. Strabo 5.2.5 (222), 3.5 (231–32), 3.7 (234).

127. Dionysius, *Antiquitates Romanae* 3.44.

128. *NH*, 3.53.–4.

129. Pliny, *Epistulae* 5.6.12. See chapter 6 at n. 148.

130. Juvenal 7.121; Martial, *Epigrammata* 4.64.21–24. See also Quilici (1985–86), 198.

131. For *codicarii*, see below; *CIL* 6.131, 185. See Meiggs (1960), 293, n. 8, refuting Le Gall's contention (1953a, 257) that river traffic above Rome was confined to *lyntrarii*.

132. Pliny, *NH* 3.53.

133. Le Gall (1953a), 124, makes an explicit connection. For *nundinae*, see Gabba (1975), 146–49; Frayn (1993), 3; de Ligt (1993), 51–54, 111–17; and see further below at n. 141. For attempts to improve navigation in the Tiber valley, see chapter 6, section 6.

134. Holland and Holland (1950), 91. They also comment on the difficulty of rowing upstream.

135. S. A. Smith (1877), 34–35.

136. See H. Patterson and Millett (1998); J. R. Patterson (2004). Coarelli and Patterson (2009) was available too late for consideration here.

137. Discussion in H. Patterson and Millett (1998), 6–13. There is an attempt to link the ongoing research in the Tiber valley to a theoretical model for the relationship between a city situated in a flat plain and the surrounding territory. See also Morley (1996), 59–82; J. R. Patterson (2004).

138. Alvisi (1986), 11–12.

139. Gaffney, Patterson, and Roberts (2001), 59–60.

140. Malone, Stoddart, and Allegrucci (1994), 186, and see also 3–4.

141. Festus 176L.

142. Degrassi (1963), 300–307; Gabba (1975), 147.

143. Argued by Gabba (1975).

144. See above at n. 107.

145. Campi Macri, Gabba (1975), 156; Consilinum, Cassiodorus, *Varia* 8.33; Gabba (1975), 159.

146. For assessments of the Tiber as a route of communications and commercial corridor in relation to the archaeological evidence, see Mocchegiani Carpano (1981), (1982), (1984); Quilici (1985–86); Balbi de Caro and Mocchegiani Carpano (1987).

147. *CIL* 6.1785; Purcell (1985), 12, explains the name on the hypothesis that they were dockside cranes for loading and unloading; location, north of *pons Aelius*, La Rocca (1984), 60–65; Flambard (1987), 200–204; further upstream, Palmer (1980), 55–57; Steinby (1993), 1:267–69. For effects of decline in Campanian wine production, see Panella and Tchernia (1994), 155. For port installations north of the city at the Milvian Bridge, see below at n. 164.

148. See Steinby (1995), 2:360. The *portus vinarius* was first attested in A.D. 68; see Purcell (1985), 12. Note also official wine cellars mostly along the riverbank (Purcell, 1985, n. 54).

149. *CIL* 11.3156 = *ILS* 7504. See Di Stefano Manzella (1981), 122.

150. Tchernia (1986), 253–56; Panella (1989), 156–61; Lapadula (1997), 147–54. In this section I am much indebted to J. R. Patterson (2004).

151. Bergamini (1993).

152. Strabo 5.3.7 (234). For the supply of wood from the Tiber valley, see Meiggs (1982), 237–38, 243–46.

153. Mocchegiani Carpano (1984), 60; Quilici (1985–86), 209–13; Strabo 5.3.11 (238).

154. Quilici (1985–86), 212.

155. Cicero, *Pro Milone* 64; *Pro Roscio Amerino* 20.

156. See chapter 6 at n. 3.

157. Pliny, *Epistulae* 5.6; estate on the Aio, Mocchegiani Carpano (1984), 60, n. 49.

158. Le Gall (1953a), 260–61, is confident that the plaque was attached to a ship, but it might have been lost from a wagon and thrown in the river. See also Quilici and Quilici Gigli (1986), 427–28.

159. *ILS* 8848 (procurator of Claudius and Nero). Le Gall (1953a), 262, interprets *CIL* 10.7587 = *ILS* 1402 of the time of Hadrian ("proc . . . ad ripam") as a procurator responsible for imperial estates on the Tiber riverbank and movement of goods from there.

160. Mocchegiani Carpano (1975–76); Castagnoli (1980); Quilici (1985–86), 205–9; Alvisi (1986), 13; Colini (1980), on the port at Forum Boarium. For the military port of Rome, see Platner and Ashby (1926), 358–60; Steinby (1996), s.v. *Navalia*, 3:339–40. Recently Cozza and Tucci (2006), 197, have suggested the restoration [Nava]lia on the marble plan of Rome instead of [Aemi]lia (usually taken as referring to the *porticus* of the Aemilian family) and argued that the main ship sheds in the republic were situated on the left bank of Tiber at the foot of the Aventine Hill, a site adjacent to the main port of Rome; subsequently, the *navalia* were converted to different purposes associated with the port facilities.

161. Landing from a small boat on the Tiber can be difficult because of the high banks. See Holland and Holland (1950). The confluences of tributaries provide an area of calmer water and sometimes pebble beaches.

162. See Quilici (1985–86), 205–7; Potter (1976), 36–39, 118. See Nardi (1980), especially 126–27, 168–69, 306–7, for a cautious appraisal of possible landing places near Orte and at Baucche Basse opposite Ocriculum. For the Paglia port serving the pottery manufacture at Scoppieto, see Bergamini (1993).

163. Pietrangeli (1943), 31–42; Quilici (1985–86), 209.

164. Quilici (1985–86), 200–202.

165. For the import of grain, see Rickman (1980); Garnsey (1988), 218–43; Mattingly and Aldrete (2000), 146–49.

166. Florus 1.1.4.

167. Meiggs (1960); 8–10, 115; Rougé (1966), 124–26; Claridge and Gallina Zevi (1996).

168. Meiggs (1960), 290–91.

169. See chapter 6, section 3.

170. Seneca, *De Brevitate Vitae* 13.4.

171. Philostratus, *Vit. Apoll. Tyan.* 7.16; Le Gall (1953a), 257–58; Meiggs (1960), 289–98.

172. Propertius 1.14.1–4 (*rates*). He notes that *lintres* moved more quickly. Note also Varro *ap. Non* 106M (= vol. I, p. 151) and 451M (= vol. II, p. 723) (Lindsay, 1903): "nautici

equisones per viam quam ducerent loro"; Procopius, *De Bello Gothico* 1.26; Dionysius Halicarnassus 3.44.3. Also, Cassiodorus, *Varia* 12.24.2, describing the advantages of a ship towed up the river safe from storms.

173. Mattingly and Aldrete (2000), 154–55, calculated that Rome required 1,692 ship-loads arriving at Ostia to carry a year's supply of oil, wine, and grains (on an estimate of 1 million for Rome's population); to accomplish the trips along the Tiber, at least 116 *codicarii* would be needed. However, Rickman (1980), 19, reckoned on at least 4,500 boat-loads, on the basis of his estimate of 40 million *modii* of grain required for the city, and an average ship capacity of 68 tons.

174. Meiggs (1960), especially 263–336, has the best account of the vibrant trading and commercial activity at Ostia. For the extent of trade coming up the Tiber, see also Mocchegiani Carpano (1984), 47–59.

175. *AE* 1955.184: "[?naviculari et negotiantes qui]bus coire et alveo Tiberis [navigare?] [con]cessu(m) est." See further below at n. 184 for the possible role of the *curatores*.

176. Mocchegiani Carpano (1984), 27–39. For transport on the Tiber in the early period, see Le Gall (1977). For doubts over the identification of the *porticus Aemilia*, see above, n. 160.

177. Rickman (1980), 20.

178. Rickman (1985), 110. Gradually a virtually continuous set of docks and wharves developed stretching to the emporium district of Rome, twenty-five kilometers inland. See Mocchegiani Carpano (1984).

179. For types of riverboats, see chapter 6, section 3; *CIL* 14.170: "codicarii navicu-larii et quinq. corp. navigantes"; *CIL* 14.409 = *ILS* 6146: "Cn Sentius Felix. . . . quinq. curatorum navium marinarum . . . navicular. maris Hadriatici . . . corpor. scapharior. et lenuncularior"; Meiggs (1960), 314, and *CIL* 14. 4144: "patron of the lenuncularii"; *AE* 1974.123bis: *navicularius lyntarius* from Ostia, probably a freedman who became *sevir Augustalis*; *AE* 1993.55, boatmen on the Tiber.

180. *CIL* 14.185: "codicari nav(icularii) infra pontem S(ublicium)."

181. *AE* 1994.201.

182. Suetonius, *Augustus* 37, thought that Augustus actually set up the institution of the curators; his arrangements may have been more informal. He had also dredged the riverbed (*Augustus* 30). For flood control efforts in Rome, see Aldrete (2006), 166–203. Malissard (2008) has a valuable survey of attempts to manage the Tiber in Rome.

183. Tacitus, *Annales* 1.76; 79; and see chapter 4 at n. 1.

184. Dio 57.14.8. For discussion of the introduction of this board, see Palma (1980), 236.

185. *CIL* 6.31545 = *ILS* 5926 (A.D. 41–44).

186. See, e.g., *CIL* 6.31546 = *ILS* 5927, C. Calpetanus Rantius Quirinalis Valerius Festus (consul in 71). Le Gall (1953a), 137–45, examines the known curators. For updates to *CIL* 6, see Alföldy (1996), ad loc. Doria and Cascione (2010) discuss the role of the *curatores* in managing river water and coping with floods.

187. Pliny, *Epistulae* 5.14; *CIL* 5.5262 = *ILS* 2927.

188. *CIL* 6.31549 = *ILS* 5930. On other activity of Ferox, see *AE* 1999.316 (A.D. 101): "Ti. Julius ferox curator terminavit ripam r(ecto) r(igore) ad prox(imum) cipp(um) p(edes) XXX s(emis)."

189. *CIL* 10.797 (Pompeii).

190. *CIL* 14.172 = *ILS* 1429; Pflaum (1960–61), no. 201. The earliest known example is L. Vibius Apronianus, between 96 and 161 (Pflaum, no. 160).

191. See *CIL* 6.1224 referring to "statio al[vei Tiberis et] cloacaru[m sacrae urbis]." For the *statio* at Ostia, see *CIL* 14.5384.

192. *CIL* 2.6085.

193. See Robinson (1992), 86–89. Cf. now Aldrete (2006), 192–202, who argues that constructions along the banks were primarily intended for port facilities and were ineffective for preventing serious flooding.

194. Le Gall (1953a), 176.

195. *CIL* 14.5320; cf. 14.254; Le Gall (1953a), 180–81. Meiggs (1960), 303–4, thinks that it is unlikely that the curator exercised a general control over all guilds of river boatmen; he may be principally concerned with constructions on the banks.

196. *CIL* 6.31556.

197. *CIL* 6.30841 a–b.

198. The earliest example is from 85/84 B.C. when the censors M. Valerius Messalla and P. Servilius Isauricus were at work; *CIL* 6.31540 = *ILS* 5922a.

199. *CIL* 6.31542k = *ILS* 5924a.

200. *CIL* 6.1240c = *ILS* 5931.

201. *CIL* 6.31553 = *ILS* 5932. For the work of Ferox, see *CIL* 6.31549f = *ILS* 5930. For the work of Trajan in regulating the banks of the Tiber, see Blake, Bishop, and Bishop (1973), 37.

202. Aldrete (2006), 10–90, surveys the evidence for floods in Rome; see also Chassignet (2005), 339. On the flood of 23 B.C., see Dio 53.33.5.

203. Aldrete (2006), 217–31.

204. Pliny, *NH* 5.124; Strabo 14.2.2 (651); *BAtlas* 56C2; 65A4.

205. Strabo 14.3.6 (666); *BAtlas* 56C2.

206. Strabo 14.3.7 (666); *BAtlas* 65D5.

207. Mela 1.78–79; *BAtlas* 65E3.

208. *NH* 5.96; Strabo 14.4.2 (667); Mela 1.78; *BAtlas* 65F3. The river Melas was also navigable.

209. *BAtlas* 66D4.

210. Pausanias 16.2.7 (751); 8.29.3; see chapter 6 at n. 137. For dredging on the Orontes, see *C.Th.* 10.23, assist navigation to Antioch; dredging work at Portus, *CIL* 14.4449. Strabo 14.5.4 (670) describes the navigability of the Calycadnus, which offered a route to the city of Seleukeia.

211. *AE* 1983.927; Berchem (1983), (1985), 53–61; *IGLS* 3.1131–34; cf. 1135–40. The Dipotamia seems to be the area north of Antioch at the confluence of the Orontes and the Arkeuthos (Berchem, 1983, 186). Since soldiers were used in the construction, the inten-

tion may have been partly to facilitate the transport of military supplies to the interior of Syria.

212. *AE* 1986.694 (A.D. 73/4) = *SEG* XXXV 1483; Feissel (1985).

213. Strabo 14.2.29 (663).

214. See Pliny, *NH* 5.113.

215. See Brückner (2003), 121–42, 133–35, for Miletus and Priene. For ancient sources and alluviation, see chapter 1 at n. 132.

216. Eisma (1964), (1978); Pausanias 8.24.11. Typical features of alluvial activity that can be noted in the Maeander are that the lower valley has alluvial fans spreading out from the hillsides; a flat alluvial plain is rarely flooded by the river at 5–10 meters above the present riverbed; a broad floodplain near the river mouth is flooded in winter; lagoons and beach ridges and dunes form along the coast; and the river changes course frequently on the way through the floodplain. For alluvial morphology, see R. J. Russell (1954); Vita-Finzi (1969). The sea level around western Turkey has risen steadily in historical times and does not seem to have influenced stream depositions.

217. Severyns (1927), 234–38; Robert (1937), 416–17 at n. 7; Thompson (2003), 62–63.

218. For ferries on the Maeander, see Strabo 12.8.19 (578); Robert (1966), 44–52 (Cilicia). See also *I. Milet* 1.3 (Delphinion) 150.99–105 (ferry lease); *Inschr. v. Metropolis I.B.* 18–20 (lease); *Inscr. v. Smyrna* 712 (a cartel); *OGIS* 572 (Myra). In what follows I am greatly indebted to advice from Peter Thonemann. See now Thonemann (2011).

219. Strabo 12.8.15 (578).

220. Strabo 12.8.17 (578). See chapter 9 for hot springs.

221. For the fish, see Scholiast to Aristophanes, *Eq.* 361; Athenaeus 7.311 a–e. In the opinion of Archestratus of Gela in the fourth century B.C., the gray mullet and sea bass were superb.

222. See chapter 3 at n. 151. Epikrates secured Milesian ownership of "the land newly turned to earth by the Maeander, and the sandbanks."

223. *I. Magnesia* 116.35.

224. See Traina (1992). It is possible that the extensive, flat Maeander delta facilitated the construction of salt pans.

225. *I. Priene* 111.112–23, 134–43; see also Holleaux (1938), 309–11.

226. We may compare the dispute at Ephesus over the tax-exempt status of Lake Selinusia and a neighboring lake, north of the mouth of the river Cayster (Strabo 14.1.26), both of which produced great revenues, which were coveted by the tax collectors. One Artemidorus went on an embassy to Rome and secured acceptance that the lakes were sacred to Artemis.

227. See chapter 3 at n. 151.

228. Himerios, *Oratio* 35.73–95 (edited by Colonna, 1951).

229. *SEG* 29.1139. See Roueché (2004), 65, for Vitianus.

230. *I. Milet* 343. Hesychius may be the historian Hesychius Illustris who lived in the first part of the sixth century A.D., or his father (*PLRE* II, p. 555, s.v. 14; *RE* VIII.1322–27, s.v. 11).

231. Head (1911), 608–9 (Antioch—the Morsynos was also represented); 659–61 (Tralles); 661 (Tripolis); 590 (Priene); 581–82 (Magnesia ad Maeandrum); 665–67 (Apamea); 671 (Dionysopolis); 677 (Hyrgaleis). For depiction of the river-god and the city of Antioch, see *BMC* III, p. 440, no. 1350.

232. Head (1906), xxxix–xl.

233. See chapter 4, n. 271.

234. Head (1906), p. 317, no. 228.

235. Head (1906), p. 296, nos. 111–12.

236. Head (1906), p. 234, no. 43.

237. For these themes, see Thonemann (2006), arguing that Mandros was a potamo-nym. I am much indebted to Peter Thonemann, who kindly allowed me to see this material before publication. Note particularly "Mandros drinker." An inscription of the third century A.D. from the vicinity of a village in the lower Maeander plain refers to the "village of the Mandragoreitai" (*SEG* 32.1149); it perhaps took its name from an individual called Mandragores. Toponyms deriving from Mandros are all located in valley between Miletus and Magnesia.

238. Strabo 16.1.9 (740); *BAtlas* 67C4.

239. *NH* 5.83; Sartona, *BAtlas* 64G3; Melitene, 64G4.

240. Strabo 16.1.9 (740), 15.35 (739).

241. Strabo 2.1.15 (73); *BAtlas* 98–99.

242. There is a useful survey in Adams (2001) and (2007), chap. 2 and 142–54; *BAtlas* 74–75, 77.

243. *P. Oxy.* 9.1197 (A.D. 211); 30.2568 (A.D. 264). See Adams (2007), 159–95, for state grain transport.

244. For river boatmen on the Nile, see *P. Giss.* 40; one of the collection of documents deals with expulsions from Alexandria and refers to the exemption of river boatmen and those bringing down reeds; note also *IGR* 1.1279.

245. *P. Oxy.* 1.112 (third or fourth century A.D.), a lady with the choice of traveling by boat; *BGU* 16.2604, passage on cargo ship; *O. Florida.* 17 (second century A.D.), a soldier sends his wife sixty drachmae so that she can travel to him by boat.

246. *P. Oxy.* 18.2182 (A.D. 166).

247. On travel on the Nile at high water, see Bonneau (1964), 96–101. Note also the interesting discussion by R. K. French (1994), 110–13.

248. Diodorus Siculus 1.33.1.

249. Adams (2007), 22–27.

250. *NH* 5.5; *BAtlas* 28A5. For flooding in the Sebou wadi and the importance of river valleys for human settlement in the area, see Akerraz, Brouquier-Reddé, and Lenoir (2010), 91–97.

251. *NH* 5.18; *BAtlas* 28D2–3.

CHAPTER 9

1. Lucan, *Pharsalia* 4.115–17.

2. Seneca, *Epistulae morales* 41.3.

3. There is a useful discussion of the control of water for the aquatic pleasures of the ruling people in Malissard (1994), 75–102. See p. 96 for water as spectacle. For an example of water as a plaything, see *CIL* 8.1828: "fontes perducti ad ornamentum."

4. Isaiah 66.12.

5. For a general survey of water used for relaxation, see Malissard (1994), 103–33.

6. Cicero, *De Legibus* 2.1.1–3.

7. Cicero, *Tusculanae Disputationes* 5.74.

8. *NH* 3.54–55.

9. Pliny, *Epistulae* 4.2.5.

10. Varro, *De Re Rustica* 3.5.9.

11. Statius, *Silvae* 1.3. See also chapter 4 at n. 30.

12. For the design and organization of Roman gardens in general, see Grimal (1969), 293–99, emphasizing the importance of springs and fountains; MacDougall (1987); Farrar (1998), especially 64–96.

13. Ricotti (1987), 181.

14. Purcell (1987) examines the relations between gardens, architecture, and landscape in Roman thinking, and how they accommodated buildings and the city itself in concepts of the natural landscape.

15. Clitumnus, Pliny, *Epistulae* 8.8; Martial, *Epigrammata* 3.20.20; Statius, *Silvae* 4.3.113 (Lucrine Lake); Pliny, *Epistulae* 6.24.2 (Lake Como).

16. Propertius 1.11.9–12 (adapted from the translation of A. E. Watts (Penguin, 1966)).

17. Pliny, *Epistulae* 9.33.

18. For discussion of methods of travel, with scant reference to rivers, see Casson (1971), (1974).

19. Strabo 17.1.16 (800) describes the canals leading from Alexandria to Canopus and then on the Schedia on the way to the Nile. For a survey of the Nile as a transport route in Egypt in relation to roads, see Adams (2007), 21–29.

20. Adams (2001), 157; and see chapter 8, section 5.

21. Strabo 17.1.17 (800).

22. *P. Oxy.* XVII.3052 (first century A.D.).

23. Horace, *Sermones* 1.5.

24. Strabo (5.3.6 (233)) observes that travelers preferred the night journey so that they could disembark early next morning and continue their journey. The canal was fed by local marshes and rivers.

25. Ausonius 35–42, 189–99, 341–48, and 240–58. See also chapter 4 at n. 34.

26. Suetonius, *Nero* 27.3.

27. Suetonius, *Vitellius* 10.2.

28. *Aeneid* 4.4. for Catullus's sailing exploits, see chapter 8 at n. 90.

29. *Sylloge*³ 1055 (Athens); *SEG* 33.1053 (Cyzicus, second century B.C.).

30. Stephanus of Byzantium (ed. Billerbeck, 2006), p. 126, no. 177; Strabo 7.7.6 (325); Dio 51.1. See in general Harris (1972), 126–32.

31. Pausanias 2.35.1.

32. Cicero, *Pro Caelio* 35; 38; 47–50; Martial, *Epigrammata* 4.57.6–10.

33. Aelian, *Varia Historia* 3.1. For the pleasures of Baiae, see below, section 10.

34. Suetonius, *Caligula* 54.2.

35. See below, section 3.

36. Vegetius, *Epitome of Military Science* 1.10.

37. Ibid.

38. Plutarch, *Cato the Elder* 20.

39. Cicero, *Pro Caelio* 36.

40. Suetonius, *Julius Caesar* 64. For the swimming strokes used by the Romans, see H. A. Harris (1972), 121–22.

41. Horace, *Carmina* 3.7.23–28; cf. 1.8.1–8.

42. Ovid, *Ars Amatoria* 3.385–86; cf. *Tristia* 3.12.19–22.

43. Suetonius, *Augustus* 64.

44. Pliny, *Epistulae* 8.8.

45. Tacitus, *Historiae* 2.93.

46. See chapter 5 at n. 34.

47. *Digest* 1.8.5; Buckland (1975), 185. See further chapter 3.

48. *Institutes* 2.1.2.

49. *Digest* 44.3.7 (Marcianus).

50. Pausanias 4.34.1–3. For the Rhine and the Danube, Pausanias seems to be referring to the giant European catfish. He does admit to sharks in the river Aoos in Thesprotis, but they came up from the sea. For the value of fish, both economic and cultural, in the ancient world, see Purcell (1995) and on personal angling, p. 137. For a catalog of the main types of fish caught in antiquity, see Gallant (1985), 49–70, referring to fish principally found in the open sea.

51. See chapter 4 at n. 160, for fishermen on the Tiber.

52. Plutarch, *Cato the Elder* 8.2.

53. Varro, *De Re Rustica* 3.3.9; Columella 8.16.3.

54. Varro, *De Re Rustica* 3.17.9.

55. Horace, *Sermones*, 2.2.120.

56. *CIL* 3, pp. 801–41; Frank (1959), 5:307–421.

57. *Mosella* 85–149. Symmachus (*Ep.* 1.14) noted that Ausonius never produced such fish when he dined with him.

58. *Mosella* 237–86; lines 283–86 translated by H. Isbell (Penguin, 1971). For a survey of the various ways of catching fish in the ancient world, see Gallant (1985), 12–25; Kron (2008), 207–10.

59. 2 Kings 5.10–14.

60. See above, n. 33.

61. Cicero, *De Oratore* 2.274.

62. Varro, *Lingua Latina* 5.71; Pliny, *Epistulae* 2.8; cf. 7.26.2.

63. Note, for example, *CIL* 3.1397, "Nymphae salutiferae"; 8167–68, "Nymphae salutares"; 10595, "Nymphae Medicae"; 10981; 10893, "Nymphae salutares"; 1397, "Nymphae salutiferae." By contrast Bruun (1992) has looked at some of the negative connotations of water in Roman thinking. These are limited but relate especially to curse tablets in wells and springs.

64. Jordanes, *De Origine Actibusque Getarum*, ed. T. Mommsen (Berlin, 1882), 20.109, p. 86.

65. Aelius, *Sacred Tales* 2.50; 3.43; Strabo 14.1.36 (645); Philostratus, *Heroicus* 299–300; Behr (1968), 23–47.

66. *Sacred Tales* 2.17; 18; 45; 51 (Asclepius); reference to doctor—e.g. 2.20. For Aristides' faith in Asclepius, see Festugière (1954), 85–104.

67. *Sacred Tales* 1.59; 2.18, 45, 50, 51, 59, 78; 5.42, 49–53.

68. *Sacred Tales* 2.18–21, probably the Kaleon.

69. *Sacred Tales* 2.51–53.

70. *Sacred Tales* 5.53–55.

71. *Sacred Tales* 5.42; 2.78.

72. *Sacred Tales* 5.11–13 in A.D. 166, and see further below.

73. Fagan (1999), 85–103, reviews the public baths and Roman medicine.

74. Vitruvius, *De Architectura* 8.3.1–28.

75. *De Architectura* 8.4.1.

76. *De Architectura* 8.3.26.

77. *De Architectura* 8.3.2.

78. Pliny (*NH* 31.28) refers to a spring at Tempe that eroded bronze and iron.

79. *De Architectura* 8.3.15; cf. 8.3.6 on Athens and Troezen.

80. *De Architectura* 8.3.5, 8, 17.

81. *NH* 31.41.

82. *NH* 31.8–12.

83. *NH* 31.11.

84. *NH* 31.11.

85. *NH* 31.52; 59.

86. *NH* 3.60, 151; 4.64; 5.71–72, 88.

87. Pliny provides other examples apart from those already cited: *NH* 18.114, eyesight, teeth, and wounds; 31.7, the eyes; 31.10, healing wounds; stomach, sinews, whole body; 31.15, variety of mental and physical changes; 35.179, healing disease in mules and also lighting lamps.

88. *NH* 31.13 ff.; Vitruvius, *De Architectura* 8.3.14, 16–17. Pliny has much colorful detail exploiting the remarkable character of springs. Some had very high temperature, for example, in the Alps, at Baiae, and on the river Liris; others bubbled up with cold water; others were intermittent, like the spring called "wait a bit" at Dodona, drying up and

flowing at certain times; and some increased and decreased with the flow and ebb of the tide (at Lake Como, a generous spring welled up and receded every hour). Some springs had a more dramatic effect such as the famous legend of the spring that on one day of the year tasted of wine (2.231). Similarly, Pomponius Mela, although he does not address the question of springs with healing properties, is interested in the miraculous and mythological such as the spring in Cyrene that managed to be cold during the day but heat up at night (1.39), or the sacred spring in Acarnania that had the capacity to put out a flaming torch but to rekindle one that had gone out (2.43). In Africa there were two fabulous springs, one of which could make people laugh themselves to death, while the draft from the other provided the antidote (3.102). For Pliny, springs also could cause death (2.131) or suck down anything thrown into them or enable those who drank to produce splendid oracles, though their life was shortened (2.232).

89. *NH* 31.21.

90. Pausanias 5.5.11.

91. Pausanias 6.22.7. Strabo noted the Alpheios and Anigros as a cure for leprosy (8.3.19 (347)); also the cold properties of the Kydnos helped swollen sinews in men and cattle (14.5.12 (673)).

92. Pausanias 4.35.10–12. The Romans called it Aquae Albulae. See Blake, Bishop, and Bishop (1973), 271. Baths were erected or extended by Hadrian at Aquae Albulae to take advantage of sulfurous springs.

93. Pausanias 2.2.3; cf. also 8.7.3, 41.4.

94. Pausanias 8.19.2–3.

95. Pausanias 4.31.4.

96. Pausanias 7.5.5.

97. Pausanias 7.23.2.

98. Pausanias 7.21.5.

99. Pausanias 1.34.3.

100. Pausanias 9.2.1 at Hysiae in Boeotia.

101. Pausanias 3.25.8 at Tinaron in Laconia.

102. Some springs had a curious effect on animals. If flocks drank from the river Torrent in Achaea in the spring, they usually had mainly male offspring. Herdsmen apparently varied their watering of the cattle accordingly (Pausanias 7.22.8); at Potniae there was a well that allegedly drove mares mad when they drank the water (9.8.1). Cf. Pliny (*NH* 25.94), who notes that the grass at Potniae drove both donkeys and horses mad. This may be a vague echo of some kind of attempt to prevent the grazing and watering of certain types of animal. Some springs or rivers were held to have an effect on the atmosphere. In time of drought, the priest of Lycaean Zeus dipped an olive branch in the Hagno spring and stirred it round. A vapor arose, and from this came a rain cloud (Pausanias 8.38.4). In the seventh century, Isidore of Seville was still able to list some of the most beneficial spas for health; *Etymologiarum sive Originum libri XX*, 13.13.5–6 (ed. Lindsay, 1911).

103. *Airs, Waters, Places* 9.4; 24.16.

104. *Airs, Waters, Places* 7.36 f. For general discussion of doctors' opinions on the cura-

tive properties of water, and medical practice and hot springs, see Jackson (1990), (1993), and (1999), 108–9, for illnesses that could be cured by water therapies. Note also Thevenot (1968), 211–17.

105. See Wasserstein (1982), G 36–37. For Galen's medical treatments, see now Mattern (2008).

106. Kühn (1821–33) 6.423–24; 11.393 (*De. Simp. Med.*). For Augustus's treatment, see below at n. 116.

107. Galen distinguished the various minerals in springs (Kühn (1821–33) 11.392K). For his view of the benefits of the baths, see Kühn (1821–33) 10.481, 708, 717, 723.

108. Celsus, *On Medicine* 1.1–4; 1.2.7; 1.3.5–6, 9–10; 1.7.1; 2.17.1, 3; 3.12; 3.15; 3.22; 3.27.1; 4.2; 4.12.7; 4.15; 4.31; 5.27; 5.28.19; 6.6; 7.26.5. For bathing and health, see also Heinz (1983), 157–75, 197–98.

109. *On Medicine* 3.27.1.

110. *On Medicine* 4.12.7; 2.17.1.

111. *On Medicine* 1.3.16; cf. the baths of Crassus Frugi in Baiae (below at n. 184).

112. Caelius Aurelianus, *On Chronic Diseases* 1.42. Caelius, from Sicca Veneria in Numidia, probably wrote in the fifth century and translated into Latin Soranus's work on acute and chronic diseases, which has not survived in the original Greek. For text and translation, see Drabkin (1950); Bendz (1990).

113. See Hanson and Green (1994). Note also Oribasius of Pergamum, the personal physician of the emperor Julian, who composed a medical encyclopedia, the tenth chapter of which dealt with the qualities and benefits of mineral waters.

114. See above, section 3.

115. Suetonius, *Augustus* 82.2.

116. Crinagoras (*Anthologia Graeca* 9.419).

117. *AE* 1982.805; 1989.870.

118. Horace, *Sermones* 2.3.288–95.

119. Lucian, *Alexander* 14–15.

120. For the Tiber as a healing river, see Le Gall (1988). Note the comments of Thiel (2000) on the interesting but little understood practice of offering weapons to river waters. For offerings to the Italic goddess Marica at the river seaport of Minturnae on the Liris, see Gualtieri (1997), 353.

121. Le Gall (1953b), 66–73; see chapter 4 at n. 159; also Le Gall (1988). Although it is possible that many of the votive finds in the river come from the Temple of Asclepius, Le Gall argues that the offerings were not all connected with Asclepius or made to Pater Tiberinus (a vague divinity with no healing qualities) but to the waters themselves. Many coins have been found in the river in quantities so large that they cannot have been dropped by accident. They presumably represent some kind of offering, possibly for safe passage across the river, but more likely for recovery from illness. However, Brown (1997), 190, has pointed out the difficulties of some of the evidence relating to artifacts in rivers; they could be the result of bank erosion and loss from boats and ferries as well as votive offerings. They might also have been moved downstream by the current.

122. Juvenal 6.522–26; see Le Gall, (1953b), 76–78.

123. Persius, *Satires* 2.15–16.

124. Above at n. 33.

125. Fauduet (1992) 202.

126. *CIL* 13.2861; see also 2862: "Deae Seq pro salute"; 2863–64; 2866; 11575.

127. For discussion of excavation and finds at the site, see Grenier (1960), 608–39; also King (1990), 142–43.

128. For example, *Genius Baetis* (*CIL* 2.2263). For dedications to rivers, see chapter 4.

129. Virgil, *Georgics* 2.147; Pliny, *Epistulae* 8.8.

130. See appendix 1.

131. In this I follow Houston (1992), 357.

132. T. J. Allen (2003), 406–7.

133. For a detailed survey of the topic, see especially Chevallier (1992), particularly 7–27; Grenier (1960); Jackson (1990); Yegül (1992).

134. Castagnoli (1977), 47–49, suggests that place names ending in *ernus* or *ernum* (e.g., Avernus, Liternum, Tifernum) might suggest the presence of springs.

135. See, e.g., Strabo 5.3.1 (228); Pliny, *NH* 31.9; Caelius Aurelianus, *On Chronic Diseases* 2.48; 5.77; Horace, *Epistulae* 1.15.8 (possibly referring to a shower); Seneca, *Epistulae* 51.5 criticizing the *fomenta Campaniae*, which he claims undid Hannibal. See also above, section 4.

136. Lugdunum, Strabo 4.2.1 (190); Autun, *Panegyrici Latini* 6.22.

137. Sidonius, *Epistulae* 5.14.

138. Pliny, *NH* 31.6–8, 12.

139. Pliny, *NH* 31.9; cf. Columella 10.1 on the fame of the springs at Stabiae. Nearby was *mons Lactarius*, famous for its milk, which also seemed to form an important part of the cure at Stabiae; see Symmachus 6.17; Galen, 10.363–66K.

140. *NH* 31.9. It assisted the treatment of gallstones and internal ulceration.

141. *On His Return* 1.251–55.

142. Caelius Aurelianus, *On Chronic Diseases* 2.48. Molto (1992) makes an interesting if speculative attempt to estimate the curative application of the thermal springs in Spain in antiquity.

143. Houston (1992), 359–60.

144. In Caelius Aurelianus, *On Chronic Diseases* 2.48.

145. Celsus, *On Medicine* 4.12.7. Cf. Pliny, *NH* 31.6 (for Aquae Cutiliae).

146. Rostovtzeff (1957), 1:212, pl. XXXV.2; Baratte (1992). The date is perhaps second century A.D.

147. Baratte (1992), 46.

148. Jackson (1990), 12 and pl. 5.

149. Croon (1967) notes that there is no evidence before circa 300 B.C. for hydrotherapy by hot mineral springs. But in the Hellenistic and Roman age the cult of Asclepius became increasingly connected with thermal springs, as these waters were more used for medicinal purposes and nature was adapted to suit popular requirements.

150. Strabo 5.2.3 (220).

151. Strabo 5.2.9 (227).

152. Aelius, *Sacred Tales* 5.11.

153. *CIL* 3.12336 = *Sylloge*³ 888. Note also 3.1335, *aquae calidae*.

154. Pliny, *Ep.* 9.33.

155. See appendix 1 and map 19. In addition, numerous sites not designated *aquae* or *fons* can be tentatively identified on the basis of literary or archaeological evidence.

156. *NH* 31.4.

157. See Jouffroy (1992), 92, 95.

158. Fauduet (1992), 200–201.

159. *BAtlas* 25D2; 24D3, D4.

160. See Schoppa (1974), 51–55.

161. Lazzaro (1981), 81–85.

162. Ortalli (1992).

163. Rémy and Buisson (1992).

164. Marini Calvani (1992), 306–7, nos. 12–16.

165. The goblets can possibly be dated between 7 B.C. and A.D. 47; see Heurgon (1952).

166. Discussion of the site by E. Künzl and S. Künzl (1992); for votive deposits, see *CIL* 11.3286–90.

167. Cuntz (1929).

168. Cuntz (1929), p. 65, 427, 4.

169. Cuntz (1929), p. 70, 457, 3.

170. See A. Levi and Levi (1967), 85–90.

171. Bosio (1983), 100; T. J. Allen (2003).

172. The basis for the inclusion of some spas and not others is not clear.

173. Talbert (2004c), especially 127–30; Talbert (2010), 118–20.

174. For the organization of operation of Roman baths, see Heinz (1983); Yegül (1992); Malissard (1994), 103–33; DeLaine and Johnston (1999); Hodge (2002) 261–72. Dunbabin (1989), 6–32, usefully analyzes the *ethos* of the baths and the importance of a sense of pleasure and beauty in bathing.

175. For the therapeutic value of normal water, see Fontaneille (1982); Fagan (1999), 85–103.

176. Pliny, *Epistulae* 6.4. For thermal springs in Campania, see Houston (1992).

177. Strabo 5.4.5 (244); Pliny, *NH* 31.5.

178. Cassius Dio 48.51.1–2. In the surrounding area of the Campi Flegrei there is a large area of small-scale volcanic activity with many hot springs and emissions of gas. The three most active craters have been Agnano, Solfatara, and Fondo di Baia; see Maiuri (1969); *I campi flegrei* (1977); Frederiksen (1984), 4; Amalfitano, Camodeca, and Medri (1990), 58–64, 70–73, 236.

179. Note that Naples (Neapolis) had thermal springs equal in quality if not in number to those at Baiae (Strabo 5.4.7 (246)). Houston (1992), 361, thinks that they perhaps

catered for the elderly and retired. See also D'Arms (1970); McKay (1988); Yegül (1992), 93–110; (1996).

180. Squatriti (1998), 52–63.

181. Horace, *Epistulae* 1.15.

182. Jackson (1990), 6–7; (1999), 115, fig. 4.

183. See Jackson (1999), and Yegül (1992), 93–110, for a good description. Yegül argues that the structures occupying the hillside development at Baiae were predominantly public in nature. Note that in thermal establishments a palaestra was usually missing; physical exercise was not usually recommended with hydrotherapeutic bathing. See also Blake, Bishop, and Bishop (1973), 268–70, who note that aqueducts and cisterns supplied the ordinary water pools and fountains, while pipes brought the mineral water or vapor to special chambers.

184. *CIL* 10.1063.

185. Claridge and Ward-Perkins (1976), 175, no. 228.

186. Plutarch, *Quaestiones Conviviales* 667C–D.

187. Plutarch, *De Fraterno Amore* 487F.

188. Plutarch, *Sulla* 26.3.

189. See Gregory (1979). Sabinus, *IG* IX.2.261.

190. Gregory (1979), 269, no. 13 = *IG* XII.9.1240.

191. *RE* I.1.940–41 (Hirschfeld). The site at Nymphaion (Selenicë) in Macedonia also attracted a lot of attention (Strabo 7.5.8 (316); Dio 41.45; Aelian, *Varia Historia* 13.16; Hammond, 1967, 231–34) because of the springs of warm water and asphalt, though it is not clear if it served as a curative center.

192. For example, the Romans built an artificial island to control springs that welled up from the bottom of the bay at Dikaiarchia (Puteoli), "so that they could have warm baths" (Pausanias 8.7.3); note also the channeling of the hot water through lead pipes (4.35.12).

193. Tacitus, *Annales* 12.66; Tigellinus, *Historiae* 1.72; for the spring's curative properties, Pliny, *NH* 31.8.

194. *CIL* 8.2583 = *ILS* 3893. It is unwise to take this inscription as evidence that people traveled to Sinuessa from long distances, as does T. J. Allen (2003), 411. It is more likely that Priscus erected the inscription in Africa in memory of a previous visit to the springs when he was in Italy; see also Houston (1992), 362; *CIL* 10, p. 464. Baths may have been established here by 217 B.C. An epigram refers to the hot springs at Sinuessa, ascribing the source of their heat to Aphrodite's son, Eros; *IG* XIV.889.9 ff.

195. Vespasian, Suetonius, *Vespasian* 24; Dio 66.17; Josephus, *BJ* 4.11. Titus, Suetonius, *Titus* 11; Dio 66.26; Pliny, *NH* 2.209.; 3.109; Seneca, *Quaestiones Naturales* 3.25.8; Strabo 5.3.1 (228).

196. See Reggiani (1979), 91–98. Aquae Cutiliae appears on the Peutinger Map, 5.4.

197. See in general Lazzaro (1981).

198. Lazzaro (1981), 72–78. However, the baths at Fons Aponi were in a state of decline by Cassiodorus's time.

199. There are two sites still in use today (at Abano and Montegrotto), which are closely related. In composition the water is salty bromine iodic, hyperthermal at a temperature of 36–38°C. The temperature, accentuated by the chemical compound of water, helps skin and muscular vascodilation, stretches muscles, and reduces artery pressure.

200. Lazzaro (1981), 93–106.

201. Lazzaro (1981), 156–63; many votive offerings are inscribed with A(quis) A(poni) though some think that AA stands for Apono Augusto (Lazzaro, 1981, 152). For a similar cross section of visitors at Aenaria (Ischia), see Houston (1992), 359 and 364.

202. See Heinz (1986); Yegül (1992), 112–16; Namatianus 1.249–56.

203. Livy 22.1.10; Strabo 5.2.3 (220); Cosentino (1992); Cosentino and Sabbatini Tumolesi (1989).

204. One visitor was a soldier; an inscription from Amelia (near Perugia) records that "P(ublius) Scribonius Proculus (centurion) of the VI cohort of Vigiles properly paid his vow to Jupiter and Hercules of the Spring of Caeretanae"; Cosentino and Sabbatini Tumolesi (1989), 21.

205. Houston (1992), 363. For a date from the second to early third century, see also Blake, Bishop, and Bishop (1973), 270. Springs of mineral water led to the establishment of an extensive bathing facility.

206. Houston (1992), 360–61. The original building probably dates from the first century A.D. Note also Aquae Statiellae (Acqui), where there was a large pool with three steps round the inside, which would have allowed visitors to sit in the thermal waters. See V. Mazzini, *Notizie dalle Scavi* 19 (1922): 200–202; G. Carducci, in *EAA* 1 (1958), 45–46, s.v. *Acqui*. In general Yegül (1992), 110–12, postulates three stages of development in thermal establishments: first, limited architectural development; second, an enclosed pool hall; and, third, a combination of a thermal area with a normal artificially heated area, for example, at Badenweiler (119).

207. See Jackson (1990), 7–8.

208. Sauer (1999).

209. Schoppa (1974), 45–51; see p. 35, fig. 9, for the swimming bath.

210. *AE* 1966.263.

211. Hugot (1963); Cüppers (1982), 5–7.

212. Wiedemeyer (1967); see also Yegül (1992), 111; Tacitus, *Historiae* 1.67.

213. Sauer (1999), 63–65. The local spring deities were Borvo and Damona. See also Grenier (1960), 445–49. It may have acted as a curative center for legionaries on the German campaigns.

214. Notably by Grenier (1960) and by various authors in Chevallier (1992). The methodology here is partly to identify modern thermal establishments and work back. This has yielded some interesting results, especially for France and Spain, though in some cases the evidence seems tenuous. In any case, it seems plausible that the Celtic god Apollo Granus is associated with healing springs (see *CIL* 13.5315, 6462 975, 8712; also 11.512; Jackson, 1990, 8). At Aix-les-Bains a cult statue of Hercules has been found; he

seems to have been the protecting divinity of the hot-water source there, perhaps assimilated to the Celtic god Borvo or Bormanus (*AE* 1963.150).

215. Boubon-L'Archambault, Grenier (1960), 442–43; Corrocher (1992), 177–82; Aquae Neri, Grenier (1960), 430–35; see also Desnoyers (1978), (1985); Yegül (1992), 120; Aquae Calidae, Grenier (1960), 435–42; Morlet (1957); Corrocher (1992), 182–85. For other important sites, see Grenier (1960): Aquae Sextiae (402–4); Aix-les-Bains (404–9); Aquae Onesiorum (411–13); Aquae Tarbellicae (414–17); Evaunum (417–23); Les Fontanes Salées (449–60); Badenweiler (460–68).

216. Cunliffe and Davenport (1985), 178–79. See also Yegül (1992), 118 with fig. 133. The date of the foundation of the establishment was A.D. 65–75, and there was a priest, *sacerdos deae Minervae* (*RIB* 155).

217. Cunliffe and Davenport (1985), 130–31; Cunliffe (1988). None of the votive offerings mentions a cure, but this need not imply that the spring did not possess curative properties.

218. See Dupré and Agorreta (1992); Diez de Velasco (1987), (1992) with a map of possible hot-water sources in Spain and an inventory of twenty-six sites. In many cases, there is insufficient evidence to decide if these sites functioned as spas.

219. Dupré and Pérex Agorreta (1992), 152.

220. Jouffroy (1992), 87–88.

221. Jouffroy (1992), 89–96, for a survey of thermal sites in Africa and Mauretania.

222. See Luquet (1964).

223. Note Bel Faïda (2002), 1717, for the thermal center at Aquae Thibilitanae; *CIL* 8.18810. See also Bel Faïda, 1723–27, for the persistence of the idea of the healing power of water.

224. Dvorjetski (1999), 117–22.

225. Dvorjetski (1999), 123–26; for a coin from Tiberias depicting Hygeia sitting on a rock from which flows water, see p. 128 and fig. 6. Josephus *BJ* 4.11; cf. 7.186–89 on the hot and cold springs at Machaerus, which, when mixed, produced a delightful bath.

226. Discussion and analysis of layout in Yegül (1992), 121–4; see also Hirschfeld and Solar (1981); Peleg (1991), 134–35. For Eudocia, see Dunbabin (1989), 15–16. See Elsner (2000), 190–92, for miraculous water sources in Palestine cited in the *Itinerarum Burdigalense*.

227. For Scaptopara, see above at n. 153; Salmacis, Vitruvius, *De Architectura* 2.8.12.

228. *AE* 1998.671.

229. We find a *beneficiarius consularis* at Aquae Balissae in Pannonia "pro se et suis" (*AE* 1978.657), and in Dacia at Ad Mediam a consular legate made a dedication to Hercules, the spirit of the place, and the hot springs (*CIL* 3.1566). Springs in Dacia, *CIL* 3, p. 225; 1395–96; 1397, Nymphae Salutiferae from Zazwaros. *CIL* 3, p. 227, for *aquae* in Pannonia; *CIL* 3, p. 521 XIII, for Aquae Iasae. On general expressions of gratitude for cures, for example, *Nymphae medicae* in Lower Pannonia set up by the governor, C. Julius Commodus Orfitianus, see *CIL* 3.10595. The important site at Aquae S. (Ilidza) near Sarajevo

perhaps had a hospital and a building from which the spa was administered (Wilkes, 1969, 275). For Haskovo and Augusta Traiana, see Yegül (1992), 111.

230. Velleius 2.25.4.

231. *CIL* 10.3828 = *ILS* 251. Presumably over the years the designated lands had been misappropriated by neighboring landholders.

232. *CIL* 10.3924 = *ILS* 6305.

233. Pliny, *Epistulae* 8.8.

234. *AE* 1977.769.

235. As conjectured by Houston (1992), 364.

236. See above at n. 146.

237. As argued by Talbert (2004c).

238. Robert (1948), 75–87.

CHAPTER 10

1. *Strategemata* 8.26.1. Polyaenus presents the Greek version, in which Semiramis was wife of Ninos, king of Nineveh and responsible for the building of Babylon. In fact, she was the wife of Shamshi-Adad V, an Assyrian king of the ninth century B.C.

2. Plutarch, *Alexander* 36.

3. *NH* 3.38: "Roma caput rerum"; 2.157–59.

4. *To Rome* 11. Rome received the produce of the tamed world: "ever supplying you with products from those regions. Here is brought from every land and sea all the crops of the seasons and the produce of each land, river, lake, as well as the arts of the Greeks and barbarians." (translation by Behr, 1981, 75).

5. *CIL* 2.4911 with *AE* 1960.158.

6. Pliny, *Epistulae* 10.61.5.

7. *Epistulae* 8.4.

8. *Works and Days* 737–41: "Never pass through, on foot, a lovely brook / of ever-flowing water, till you pray / and look into the beauty of the stream, / and in her clean, sweet water, wash your hands" (D. Wender, Penguin, 1973, p. 83).

9. Joshua 1.1–4.

10. Arrian, *Anabasis* 5.3.6.

11. Dio 60.19. Ocean was often regarded as a river.

12. Claudian, *De Bello Gothico* 80–82.

13. Livy 5.15; 16.9–10.

14. Livy 5.21.9.

15. Martial, *Epigrammata* 10.7. For a survey of the significance of representations of the Rhine by the Romans, see Vollkommer (1994); also chapter 7, section 3.

16. Tacitus, *Historiae* 5.17.

17. Tacitus, *Annales* 13.56.

18. *ILS* 8995.

19. Dio 55.1.3.

20. Statius, *Silvae* 4.3.95–100.

21. Kleiner (1991) emphasizes the importance in Roman ideology of the celebration of triumphs over nature.

22. *Tabula Siarensis*. See Crawford (1996), 1:528; González and Arce (1988); Lebek (1989). See further chapter 4 at n. 145.

23. Horace, *Carmina* 2.9.21–24; cf. Nisbet and Hubbard (1978), 158. We recall also Tacitus, *Annales* 1.79, where attempts to divert water from the Tiber are rejected partly so as not diminish the Tiber's majesty and standing.

24. *Aeneid* 8.722–28. Note that Propertius (4.3.35) speaks of the Araxes "that needs to be conquered."

25. Silius Italicus, *Punica* 3.446–65.

26. Ovid, *Fasti* 1.285–86.

27. Statius, *Silvae* 3.2.137–38.

28. Propertius 3.3.44–46. There is an element of literary commonplace in these sentiments going back to Homer and the Scamander in the plain of Troy, but in my view that does not detract from the significance of the use of rivers to express the defeat of peoples hostile to Rome.

29. Ammianus 16.12.57.

30. Pliny, *Panegyric* 82.4–5.

31. *Panegyric* 12.3–4.

32. *Panegyric* 16.5.

33. Cicero, *Pro Marcello* 28–29.

34. Lucan, *Pharsalia* 5.267–69.

35. *Pharsalia* 3.76–77.

36. Florus 2.13.88. The triumph for the conquest of Egypt included the Nile and the famous Pharos on moving platforms.

37. Caesar, *BG* 4.16.

38. Tacitus, *Annales* 2.41. For literary references to Roman triumphs, see de Saint-Denis (1981), 549; Coleman (1988), 120–27. For the triumph as a Roman institution, see Versnel (1970); Beard (2007).

39. For the traditional depiction of rivers, see chapter 4, section 3.

40. Ovid, *Tristia* 4.2.41–42.

41. Ovid, *Ex Ponto* 3.4.107.

42. Propertius 2.1.31–33.

43. See chapter 4 at n. 9.

44. Ennius, *Ann.* Frag. 63; Virgil, *Aeneid* 8.77; Fronto (C. R. Haines, Loeb, 2:111–12), quoting an unnamed orator. In general, see Murphy (2003), 313–21.

45. Propertius 3.4.4.

46. *Aeneid* 8.64; 77.

47. Sidonius 4.17.1.

48. *SEG* 11.922–23 = Ehrenberg and Jones (1976), no. 102 (A.D. 14/15).

49. See chapter 4, section 7.

50. *Sammelbuch* 8434.

51. Statius, *Silvae* 1.1, line 51, for the position of the horse's hoof; Martial, *Epigrammata* 8.44.6–8. Ahl (1984), 91–102, deals with the literary aspects of Statius's description of the statue; Bergeman (1990), 164–36 with taf. 92d, discusses the design of the statue. See also Platner and Ashby (1926), 201–2; L. Richardson (1992), 144–45. For depiction on coins, see Castagnoli (1953). Boyle and Dominik (2003), 219–20, provide a general impression. The statue was probably erected in 91.

52. Lepper and Frere (1988), pl. 6; Becatti (1957), no. 3; Birley (1966), 242, pl. 9.

53. This is the view of Hassel (1966), 18, n. 115, pls. 13; 16, 3–4; cf. Rotili, (1972), pl. 38.2. Toynbee (1934), 15–17, identified the kneeling female figure as Mesopotamia, with the rivers Tigris and Euphrates; she also wished to identify the Euphrates as one of the rivers in the spandrels and argued that the two figures representing (in her view) the Euphrates were female. This is rejected by Hassel; see also n. 55 below.

54. Toynbee (1934), 16, and n. 6; Brilliant (1967), 129–35 with pls. 42–43; Klementa (1993), 182–86.

55. See *LIMC* IV.1, 70–74, where J. C. Balty argues *contra* Toynbee that the Euphrates was not represented by a female figure.

56. See chapter 5, n. 154.

57. *LIMC* VII.1, 636. See Turcan (1984), and Abh. 1; the sarcophagus is decorated in the corners with river-gods, and the *genii* of the seasons; of the rivers, one holds a rose branch, the other an inverted urn.

58. See in general Ostrowski (1991), 47–59. For the importance of geographical symbols on coins in establishing local community identity, see Howgego, Heuchert, and Burnett (2005), 10–12. See also chapter 4, section 7, for a general survey of the depiction of rivers on coins.

59. *RIC* II, p. 283, no. 556, bronze (A.D. 103–11); *BMC* III, p. 168, no. 793–94, *sestertius* (A.D. 104–11).

60. *RIC* II, p. 251, no. 100 (A.D. 103–11). Cf. Imhoof-Blumer (1923), 529, Lucius Verus with river-gods and a kneeling enemy. Caracalla appears with the Rhine and two captives, *BMC* V, p. 259, no. 520, *virtus Augg* (A.D. 206–10). These were long-standing ideas; a medallion of Maximianus celebrating the "perpetual valor" of the emperor, shows the Rhine at his feet; Imhoof-Blumer (1923), 542.

61. *BMC* VI, pp. 82–83; 207, no. 949 (A.D. 233).

62. *BMC* II, p. 363, no. 298, *sesterius* (A.D. 85).

63. *RIC* II, p. 289, no. 642 (A.D. 114–17); *RIC*, III, p. 296, no. 1047 (A.D. 171–72).

64. Burnett, Amandry, and Ripollès (1992), p. 70, nos. 6 and 7; cf. no. 8; head of the river-god or river-goddess spitting water; legend: "with the permission of Caesar Augustus"; on the reverse an *aquila* between two standards; legend: "Em Aug"; p. 94, no. 160 (Carthago Nova, possibly time of Augustus), also shows a river-god spitting water. Cf. 8–9; see also p. 94, n. 160, from Carthago Nova, depicting the Hiberus.

65. Imhoof-Blumer (1923), no. 525; *BMC* III, p. 254, no. 99; p. 273, no. 274.

66. Imhoof-Blumer (1923), no. 526.

67. *BMC* III, p. 184, no. 873 (A.D. 104–11).

68. *BMC* III, p. 514, nos. 1769–78; *RIC* II, p. 375, nos. 308–14; Toynbee (1934), 30–31.

69. See chapter 4 at n. 251.

70. *BMC* III, p. 440, no. 1350. Note also the iconography linking the Orontes and Antioch, which the Romans seem to take over from Seleukos Nikator; the Tyche of Antioch is traditionally represented seated on a rock standing on the shoulder of the river in a dominant attitude. For examples, see *LIMC* I.I, 840; cf. the vignette from the Peutinger Map, Levi and Levi (1967), 154–56, sec. ix.5. Coins that depict rivers are important for proclaiming the identity and status of cities; this fits in well with the Roman use of coins to show major rivers working with Rome or subdued by Rome. Within that imperial structure, rivers then could work to sustain the cities that made up the framework of the empire.

71. See C. P. Jones (1991), 116–17.

72. Imhoof-Blumer (1923), nos. 238, 185, 220, 145; cf. 204 Hadrian (Elis); 146 Commodus (Nicopolis ad Istrum); 168 (Pantalia); 190 Marcus Aurelius (Augusta Traiana); 233 Marcus Aurelius (Prusias ad Hypios); 230 Commodus (Prusa); 167 Caracalla (Nicopolis ad Mestos); 186 Caracalla (Serdica). See chapter 4, especially at n. 270, for a general survey of the river symbols on coins of Greek cities.

73. Imhoof-Blumer (1923), nos. 210, 218.

74. Temporini (1982).

75. See Imhoof-Blumer (1923), 245; Ostrowski (1991), 57–58.

76. *RIC* VII.584, no. 100; A.D. 335; legend: "felicitas publica"; 589–90, nos. 145–48; *Epit. De Caes.* 41.20.

77. Cohen (1880–92) VII, p. 285, no. 483; Imhoof-Blumer (1923), no. 527; cf. no. 541, coin of Postumus with a personification of the Rhine and the legend "salus provinciarum," perhaps referring to the repulse of German tribes beyond the river.

78. *Panegyrici Latini* 12.17–18.

79. In what follows, I owe much to the suggestive analysis of Purcell (1996a), 205–9.

80. Isaiah 8.6–8.

81. *Concerning His Return* 35–40 (translation by H. Isbell, Penguin, 1971, 222).

82. Campbell (2000), 256–59. See Heurgon (1959), for the possible context of the prophecy in the first century B.C. For the hostile or damaging side of water, see Bruun (1991), 74.

83. Babylonian Talmud Sabbath 33b; translated by M. Hadas, *Philological Quarterly* 8 (1929), 373.

84. Revelation 16.4, 12, 17–20.

85. Pseudo-Sibylline Oracles 1.13–15. This is the third day of the creation. See J. L. Lightfoot (2007), 329–30, and on the nature of Sibylline prophecy, part I.

86. Pseudo-Sibylline Oracles 5.230.

87. Pseudo-Sibylline Oracles 14.129–32.

88. Pseudo-Sibylline Oracles 4.229–30; 7.166–73.

89. Arrian, *Periplous* 8.

90. Part of an inscription crudely scratched on a rock in the Wadi Rum in southern Jordan, south of Petra. See the "Aqaba-Ma'an Archaeological and Epigraphical Survey, 1988–90," *Syria* 70 (1993): 244.

91. Caesar, *BG* 4.16–17.

92. Ammianus 24.20.

BIBLIOGRAPHY

Abad Casal, L. 1975. *El Guadalquivir, Vía fluvial Romana*. Seville.

Ackerman, H. C., and Gisler, J.-R. (eds.). 1981–. *Lexicon Iconographicum Mythologiae Classicae*. 8 vols. Zurich.

Adamietz, J. M. F. 1966. *Quintiliani Institutionis Oratoriae Liber III*. Munich.

Adams, C. 2001. "There and Back Again." In Adams and Laurence, *Travel and Geography in the Roman World*, 138–66.

———. 2007. *Land Transport in Roman Egypt: A Study of Economics and Administration in a Roman Province*. Oxford.

Adams, C., and Laurence, R. (eds.). 2001. *Travel and Geography in the Roman World*. London and New York.

Ager, D. V. 1980. *The Geology of Europe*. Maidenhead.

Ahl, F. M. 1984. "The Rider and the Horse: Politics and Power in Roman Poetry from Horace to Statius." *ANRW* 2.32.1, 40–110.

Akerraz, A., Brouquier-Reddé, V., and Lenoir, E. 2010. "Rivages de Maurétanie Tingitane." In Hermon, *Riparia dans L'Empire romain*, 85–100.

Alberich, J. B., Ribera i Lacomba, A., and Serrano Marco, M. 2004. "A Fluvial Harbour of the Roman Period at Valentia (Hispania Tarraconensis)." In Pasquinucci and Weski, *Close Encounters*, 129–37.

Alcock, S. E. 1993. *Graecia Capta: The Landscapes of Roman Greece*. Cambridge.

Alcock, S. E., Cherry, J. F., and Elsner, J. (eds.). 2001. *Pausanias: Travel and Memory in Roman Greece*. Oxford.

Alcock, S. E., and Osborne, R. (eds.). 1994. *Placing the Gods: Sanctuaries and Sacred Space in Ancient Greece*. Oxford.

Aldrete, G. S. 2006. *Floods of the Tiber in Ancient Rome*. Baltimore.

Alfieri, N. 1959. "Spina e le nuove scoperte, problemi archeologici e urbanistici." *Atti Spina*, suppl. *Studi Etruschi* 25: 31–38.

Alföldi, A. 1952. "The Moral Frontier on Rhine and Danube." In *Limeskongress* I. Durham, 1–16.

Alföldy, G. 1974. *Noricum*. London.

———. 1975. *Die römischen Inschriften von Tarraco*. Berlin.

———. 1992. "Die inschrift des Aquäduktes von Segovia. Ein vorbericht." *ZPE* 94: 231–48.

——— (ed.). 1996. *Corpus Inscriptionum Latinarum*. Vol. VI, part VIII, fasc. II. Berlin and New York.

——— (ed.). 2000a. *Corpus Inscriptionum Latinarum*. Vol. VI, part VIII, fasc. III. Berlin and New York.

———. 2000b. "Das neue Edikt des Augustus aus El Bierzo in Hispanien." *ZPE* 131: 177–205.

Allen, J. R. L., and Fulford, M. G. 1986. "The Wentlooge Level: A Romano-British Saltmarsh Reclamation in Southwest Wales." *Britannia* 17: 91–117.

———. 1990. "Roman-British Wetland Reclamations at Longney, Gloucestershire, and Evidence for the Early Settlement of the Inner Severn Estuary." *Antiquaries Journal* 70.2: 288–326.

Allen, J. R. L., Fulford, M. G., and Rippin, S. J. 1994. "The Settlement and Drainage of the Wentlooge Level, Gwent: Excavation and Survey at Rumney Great Marsh 1992." *Britannia* 25: 175–211.

Allen, T. J. 2003. "Roman Healing Spas in Italy: The Peutinger Map Revisited." *Athenaeum* 91: 403–16.

Almagro Moltó, L. 1992. "Aguas minero-medicinales en los yacimientos termales de Hispania." In Chevallier, *Les eaux thermales*, 117–32.

Alvarez Martínez, J. M. 1983. *El Puente romano de Mérida. Monografías Emeritenses* 1. Badajoz.

Alvisi, G. 1986. "Il medio corso de Tevere e il suo rapporto con gli abitati della riva sinistra." *Acta Archaeologica Lovaniensia* 25: 11–17.

Amalfitano, P., Camodeca, G., and Medri, M. (eds.). 1990. *I campi flegrei: un itinerario archeologico*. Venice.

Amboise, R., et al. 1989. *Paysages de terrasses*. Aix-en-Provence.

Amiet, P. 1952. "Un port de rivière romain sur la bruche à la Montagne-vert." *Cahiers d'archéologie et d'histoire d'Alsace* 132: 89–98.

Anderson, J. D. 1992. *Roman Military Supply in North East England: An analysis of and an Alternative to the Piercebridge Formula*. BAR British Series 224. Oxford.

Anderson, J. G. C. 1938. *Cornelii Taciti de Origine et Situ Germanorum*. Oxford.

André, J. 1977. *Ovide, Pontiques*. Paris.

Ankum, H. 1980. "Afrikan *Dig.* 19.2.33: Haftung und Gefahr bei der publication eines verpachteten oder verkauften Grundstücks." *ZSS* 97: 157–80.

Antico Gallina, M. V. 1980–81. "*Sibrium*." Centro di studi Preistorici ed Archeologici, Varese. 15, 139–49.

———. 1986. "Repertorio dei ritrovamenti archeologici nella provincia di Alessandria." *Revue des études ligures* 52: 59–150.

Arafat, K. 1996. *Pausanias' Greece: Ancient Artists and Roman Rulers*. Cambridge.

Archi, A., Pecorella, P. E., and Salvini, M. 1971. *Gaziantep e la sua regione*. Rome.

Argoud, G., et al. (eds.). 1992. *L'Eau et les hommes en Méditerranée et en Mer noire dans l'Antiquité de l'Époque Mycénienne au règne de Justinien. Actes de Congrès international Athènes, 20–24 mai 1988*. Athens.

Arnaud, P. 1993. "L'itineraire d'Antonin: un témoin de la literature du Bas Empire." *Geographia Antica* 2: 33–49.

Arnold, B. 1978. "Gallo-Roman Boat Finds in Switzerland." In du Plat Taylor and Cleere, *Roman Shipping and Trade*, 31–35.

Arthur, P. 1991. *Romans in Northern Campania: Settlement and Land-Use around the Massico and the Garigliano Basin*. London.

Ashmole, B. 1972. *Architect and Sculptor in Classical Greece*. London.

Astin, A. E. 1961. "Water to the Capitol: A Note on Frontinus *De Aquis* 1.7.5." *Latomus* 20: 541–48.

———. 1983. "Observations on the *De Rebus Bellicis*." *Collections Latomus 180, Studies in Latin Literature and Roman History* III. Brussels, 388–439.

Audin, A. 1979. *Lyon: miroir de Rome dans les Gaules*. Paris.

Audin, A., and Le Glay, M. 1966. "Découvertes archéologiques récentes à Lugdunum, métropole des Gaules." *BAF* 67: 95–109.

Aupert, P. 1974. *La nymphée de Tipasa et les nymphées et "septizonia" nord-africaines*. Rome.

Aurigemma, S., and de Sanctis, A. 1955. *Gaeta, Formia, Minturno*. Rome.

Austin, N. J. E., and Rankov, N. B. 1995. *Exploratio: Military and Political Intelligence in the Roman World from the Second Punic War to the Battle of Adrianople*. London and New York.

Avitsur, Sh. 1960. "On the History of the Exploitation of Water Power in Eretz-Israel." *Israel Exploration Journal* 10: 37–45.

Avi-Yonah, M. 1984. *Historical Geography of Palestine*. 4th ed. Jerusalem.

Balbi de Caro, S., and Mocchegiani Carpano, C. 1987. *Tevere: archeologica e commercio*. Rome.

Baldacci, P., et al. 1972. "Importazioni cisalpine e produzione apula." *CEFR* 10: 7–28.

Baldassarre, I. (ed.). 1990–. *Pompei, pitture e mosaici*. 10 vols. Rome.

Baldwin, M., and Burton, A. 1984. *Canals: A New Look; Studies in Honour of Charles Hadfield*. Chichester.

Balil, A. 1977. "Fuentes y fontanas romanas de la Peninsula ibérica." In *Symposium de arqueologia romana*. Barcelona, 77–89.

Ballance, M. K. 1951. "The Roman Bridges of the Via Flaminia." *PBSR* 19: 78–117.

Baradez, J. 1949. *Fossatum Africae: recherches aériennes sur l'organisation des confines sahariens à l'époque romaine*. Paris.

Baratte, F. 1992. "La coupe en argent de Castro Urdiales." In Chevallier, *Les eaux thermales*, 43–54.

Bargnesi, R. 1997. "La testimonianza dell'epigrafia sulla navigazione interna nella Cisalpina romana." *Rivista Archeologica dell'Antica Provincia e Diocesi di Como* 179: 93–108.

———. 2004. "Inland Navigation in Ancient Northern Italy: The Port of Ticinum." In Pasquinucci and Weski, *Close Encounters*, 75–84.

Barker, G., and Lloyd, J. (eds.). 1991. *Roman Landscapes: Archaeological Survey in the Mediterranean Region*. British School at Rome Archaeological Monographs, 2. London.

Barker, G., et al. 1995. *A Mediterranean Valley: Landscape Archaeology and "Annales" History in the Biferno Valley*. Leicester.

Bass, G. F. 1966. *Archaeology under Water*. New York.

Batty, R. 2000. "Mela's Phoenician Geography." *JRS* 90: 70–94.

Bauer, A. 1955. *Hippolytus Werke* IV: *Die Chronik.* 2nd ed. Revised by R. W. O. Helm, *Die Griechischen christlichen Schriftsteller der ersten drei Jahrhunderte* 46. Berlin, set. IV.9, 43–69.

Bauer, H. 1985. "Ricerche sul muro perimetrale e sul portico del Foro di Augusto." In *Roma. Archeologia nel Centro,* 229–40.

Beagon, M. 1992. *Roman Nature: The Thought of Pliny the Elder.* Oxford.

Beard, M. 2007. *The Roman Triumph.* Cambridge, Mass., and London.

Beard, M., North, J., and Price, S. 1998. *Religions of Rome.* Vol. 1: *History*; vol. 2: *Sourcebook.* Cambridge.

Bearzot, C. 1992. *Storia e storiografia ellenistica in Pausanias il Perigeta.* Venice.

Becatti, G. 1957. *La colonna di Marco Aurelio.* Milan.

———. 1971. "Ninfe e divinità marine. Ricerche mitologiche iconografiche e stilistiche." *Studi Miscellanei,* 17–58.

Bedon, R. 1984. *Les carrières et les carriers de la Gaul romaine.* Paris.

———. 2010. "Les rives de la Moselle dans l'oeuvre d'Ausone: une illustration idéalisée de la gestion intégrée des bords de l'eau." In Hermon, *Riparia dans L'Empire romain,* 191–200.

Bedon, R., and Hermon, E. (eds.). 2005. *Concepts, pratiques et enjeux environnementaux dans l'Empire romain. Caesarodunum* 39. Limoges.

Begni Perina, G., Caretta, C., Incitti, M., and Catali, F. 1986. "Il porta sul Tevere in località." In *Tevere un'antica via per il mediterraneo.* Ministero per i Beni Culturali e Ambientali e Comune di Roma. Rome, 184–90.

Behr, C. A. 1968. *Aelius Aristides and the Sacred Tales.* Amsterdam.

———. 1981. *P. Aelius Aristides: The Complete Works.* Vol. II. *Orations XVII–LII.* Leiden.

Behrends, O., et al. 1998. *Frontin. L'Oeuvre gromatique.* Luxembourg.

———. 2000. *Hygin. L'Oeuvre gromatique.* Luxembourg.

Bel Faïda, A. 2002. "Eau et sacré en Afrique romaine." In Khanoussi, Ruggeri, and Vismara, *L'Africa Romana,* 1715–28.

Bell, M. 1994. "An Imperial Flour Mill on the Janiculum." In *Le ravitaillement en blé de Rome,* 73–87.

Bell, M., and Boardman, J. (eds.). 1992. *Past and Present Soil Erosion: Archaeological and Geographical Perspectives.* Oxford.

Bell, R. E. 1989. *Place Names in Classical Mythology.* Santa Barbara.

Bellamy, P. S., and Hitchner, R. B. 1996. "The Villas of the Vallée des Baux and the Barbegal Mill: Excavations at la Mérindole Villa and Cemetery." *JRA* 9: 154–76.

Beltrán Lloris, F. 2006. "An Irrigation Decree from Roman Spain: *The Lex Rivi Hiberiensis.*" *JRS* 96: 147–97.

Beltrán Lloris, F., Martín-Bueno, M., and Pina Polo, F. 2000. *Roma en la cuenca media del Ebro. La romanización en Aragón.* Zaragosa.

Beltrán Lloris, M. 1970. *Las ánforas romanas en España.* Zaragosa.

———. 1985. "La arqueológia romana del valle medio del Ebro." *XVII Congreso Nacional de Arqueológia 1983. Logroño.* Zaragoza, 274–84.

———. 1990. *Guía de la cerámica romana*. Zaragoza.

Beltrán Martínez, A. 1950. *Curso de Numismatica*. 2nd ed. Cartagena.

Bémont, C., and Jacob, J.-P. 1986. *La Terre sigillée gallo-romaine*. Paris.

Benario, H. W. 1978. "Vergil and the River Tiber." *Vergilius* 24: 4–14.

Bendz, G. (ed.). 1990. *Caelius Aurelianus: Akute Krankheiten Buch I–III; Chronische Krankheiten Buch I–V*. 2 vols. Berlin.

Berchem, D. van. 1952. *L'Armée de Dioclétien et la réforme constantinienne*. Paris.

———. 1983. "Une inscription flavienne du Musée d'Antioche." *Museum Helveticum* 40: 185–96.

———. 1985. "Le port de Séleucie de Piérie et l'infrastructure logistique des guerres parthiques." *BJ* 185: 47–87.

Bergamini, M. 1993. "Un insediamento produttivo sul Tevere in territorio tudertino." *Journal of Ancient Topography* 3: 179–94.

Bergeman, J. 1990. *Römische Reiterstatuen: Ehrendenkmäler im öffentlichen Bereich*. Mainz am Rhein.

Berger, H. 1880. *Die geographischen Fragmente des Eratosthenes*. Repr., Leipzig, 1964.

Berggren, J. L., and Jones, A. 2000. *Ptolemy's Geography: An Anotated Translation of the Theoretical Chapters*. Princeton and Oxford.

Bergier, J.-F. (ed.). 1989. *Montagnes, fleuves, forêts dans l'histoire: barriers ou lignes de convergence?* St. Katharinen.

Berti, F. 1985. *La nave romana di Valle Ponti (Comacchio)*. RSL 51.4, 553–70.

Beschaouch, A. 1974–75. "Trois inscriptions romaines récemment découvertes en Tunisie." *BCTH*, n.s., 10–11B: 193–94.

Billerbeck, M. (ed.). 2006. *Stephani Byzantii Ethnica*. Berlin and New York.

Bintliff, J. L. 1992. "Erosion in the Mediterranean Lands: A Reconsideration of Pattern, Process and Methodology." In Bell and Boardman, *Past and Present Soil Erosion*, 125–32.

Birebent, J. 1962. *Aquae Romanae*. Algeria.

Birks, P., Rodger, A., and Richardson, J. S. 1984. "Further Aspects of the Tabula Contrebiensis." *JRS* 74: 45–73.

Birley, A. R. 1966. *Marcus Aurelius*. London.

Bispham, E. 2006. "*Coloniam deducere*: How Roman Was Colonization during the Middle Republic?" In Bradley and Wilson, *Greek and Roman Colonization*, 73–160.

Biswas, A. K. 1970. *History of Hydrology*. Amsterdam and London.

———. 1982. "Ancient Harbours in the Mediterranean." *IJNA* 11: 79–104, 185–211.

Blackman, D. J. (ed.). 1973. *Marine Archaeology. Proceedings of the Twenty-third Symposium of the Colston Research Society Held in the University of Bristol, April 4th to 8th, 1971*. London.

———. 2008. "Sea Transport, Part 2: Harbours." In Oleson, *The Oxford Handbook of Engineering and Technology*, 638–70.

Blackman, D. R., and Hodge, A. T. 2000. *Frontinus' Legacy*. Ann Arbor.

Blagg, T. F. C., and Millett, M. (eds.). 1990. *The Early Roman Empire in the West*. Oxford.

Blake, M. E., Bishop, D. T., and Bishop, J. D. 1973. *Roman Construction in Italy from Nerva through the Antonines*. Philadelphia.

Blázquez Martínez, J. M. 1980. "La exportación del aceite hispano en el imperio romano: estado de la cuestión." In Blásquez Martínez and Remesal Rodríguez, *Producción*, 19–46.

Blázquez Martínez, J. M., and Remesal Rodríguez, J. (eds.). 1980–83. *Producción y comercio del aceite en la antigüedad* I and II. Madrid.

———— (eds.). 1999–2007. *Estudios sobre el monte Testaccio (Roma)*. 4 vols. Barcelona.

Bloemers, J. H. F. 1983. "Acculturation in the Rhine/Meuse Basin in the Roman Period." In Brandt and Slofstra, *Roman and Native in the Low Countries*, 159–210.

Blouin, K. 2010. "Fleuve mouvant, rives mouvantes: les terres 'transportées par le fleuve' dans l'Egypt hellénistique et romaine d'après la documentation papyrologique." In Hermon, *Riparia dans L'Empire romain*, 153–64.

Boatwright, M. T. 1989. "Hadrian and the Italian cities." *Chiron* 19, 235–71.

Bockius, R. 2002. *Die römerzeitlichen Schiffsfunde von Oberstimm (Bayern)*. Mainz.

————. 2004. "Ancient Riverborne Transport of Heavy Loads." In Pasquinucci and Weski, *Roman and Native in the Low Countries*, 105–15.

Bodel, J. 1997. "Monumental Villas and Villa Monuments." *JRA* 10: 8–35.

Boffo, L. 1977. "Per la storia della antica navigazione fluviale Padana. Un collegium nautarum o naviculariorum a Ticinum in età imperial." *RAL* 32: 623–32.

Bogaers, J. E. 1971. "Nehalennia en de epigrafische Gegevens." In *Deae Nehalenniae: gids bij de tentoonstelling Nehalennia de zeeuwse godin, Zeeland in de Romeinse tijd, Romeinse monumenten uit de Oosterschelde, Stadhuis Middelburg 17/6–29/8 1971*. Middelburg.

————. 1983. "Foreign affairs." In Hartley and Wacher, *Rome and her Northern Frontiers*, 13–27.

Bogaers, J. E., and Haalebos, J. K. 1981. "Woerden." *Bulletin Knob* 80: 106–11.

Bömer, F. P. 1969–2006. *Ovidius Naso Metamorphosen*. 8 vols. Heidelberg.

Boni, C., Bobno, P., and Capelli, G. 1987. *Hydrogeological Scheme of Central Italy: Map and Tables*. Centro di studio per la geologia dell'Italia central. Rome.

Bonnamour, L. 1975. "Le port gauloise et gallo-romaine de Chalon: état de la recherche." *Mémoires de la Sociéte d'Histoire et d'Archéologie de Chalon-sur-Saône* 45: 61–73.

————. 1981. *La Saône, une rivière, des hommes*. Le Puy.

———— (ed.). 2000. *Archéologie des fleuves et des rivières*. Paris.

Bonnard, L. 1908. *La Gaule thermale. Sources et stations thermals et minerals de la Gaule a l'époque gallo-romaine*. Paris.

————. 1913. *La navigation intérieur de la Gaule à l'époque gallo-romaine*. Paris.

Bonneau, D. 1964. *La crue du Nil, divinité Égyptienne à travers mille ans d'histoire*. Études et commentaires 52. Paris.

————. 1981. "La haute administration des eaux en Egypte." In R. Bagnall et al. (eds.),

Proceeedings of Sixteenth International Congres of Papyrology (New York 1980).
Chicago, 321–28.

———. 1984. "Les servitudes de l'eau dans la documentation papyrologique." In
Sodalitas. Scritti in onore di Antonio Guarino. Naples, 2273–85.

———. 1993. *Le regime administrative de l'eau du Nil dans l'Égypte grecque, romaine et
Byzantine*. Leiden.

———. 1994. "Usage et usages de l'eau dans l'Égypte ptolémaïque et romaine." In
Menu, *Les problèmes institutionnels*, 47–71.

Borthwick, E. K. 1963, "The Oxyrhynchus Musical Monody and Some Ancient Fertility
Superstitions." *AJP* 84, 225–43.

Bosio, L. 1983. *La Tabula Peutingeriana*. Rimini.

———. 1991. *Le strade Romane della Venetia e dell'Histria*. Padua.

Bouma, J. 1993. *Marcus Iunius Nypsus. Fluminis varatio, Limitis Repositio. Introduction,
Text, Translation and Commentary*. Frankfurt am Main.

Bowman, A. 1986. *Egypt after the Pharaohs, 332 B.C.–A.D. 642*. London.

Bowman, A., Champlin, E., and Lintott, A. (eds.). 1996. *Cambridge Ancient History*².
Vol. X: *The Augustan Empire, 31 B.C.–A.D. 69*. Cambridge.

Bowman, A., Garnsey, P., and Cameron, A. (eds.). 2005. *Cambridge Ancient History*²,
Vol. XII: *The Crisis of Empire, A.D. 193–337*. Cambridge.

Bowman, A., Garnsey, P., and Rathbone, D. (eds.). 2000. *Cambridge Ancient History*².
Vol. XI: *The High Empire, A.D. 70–192*. Cambridge.

Boyle, A. J., and Dominik, W. J. (eds.). 2003. *Flavian Rome: Culture, Image, Text*. Leiden
and Boston.

Bradley, G., and Wilson, J.-P. (eds.). 2006. *Greek and Roman Colonization: Origins,
Ideologies and Interactions*. Swansea.

Bradley, M. 2002. "'It all comes out in the wash': Looking Harder at the Roman
fullonica." *JRA* 15: 20–44.

Braemer, F. 1989. "La coordination de la voie d'eau et de la route terrestre dans
l'Antiquité romaine. Villes de transbordement." In *La ville et le fleuve*, 109–21.

Brandt, R. 1983. "A Brief Encounter along the Northern Frontier." In Brandt and
Slofstra, *Roman and Native in the Low Countries*, 129–45.

Brandt, R., and Slofstra, J. (eds.). 1983. *Roman and Native in the Low Countries: Spheres
of Interaction*. BAR International Series 184. Oxford.

Braudel, F. 2001. *The Mediterranean in the Ancient World*. Translated by Sîan Reynolds.
London. Originally published as *Les Memoires de la Méditerranée* (1998).

Braund. D. 1984. *Rome and the Friendly King: The Character of Client Kingship*. London,
Canberra, and New York.

———. 1996. "River Frontiers in the Environmental Psychology of the Roman World."
In D. L. Kennedy (ed.), *The Roman Army in the East*. Journal of Roman Archaeology
Supplementary Series 18. Ann Arbor, 43–47.

Breeze, D. J. 2011. *The Frontiers of Imperial Rome*. Barnsley.

Bremmer, J., and Horsfall, N. (eds.). 1987. *Roman Myth and Mythography*. London.

Brewster, H. 1997. *The River Gods of Greece*. London and New York.

Brice, W. C. (ed.). 1978. *The Environmental History of the Near and Middle East*. London.

Brilliant, R. 1963. *Gesture and Rank in Roman Art: The Use of Gestures to Denote Status in Roman Sculpture and Coinage*. New Haven.

———. 1967. *The Arch of Septimius Severus in the Roman Forum*. Rome.

Brink, C. O. 1963. *Horace on Poetry: Prolegomena to the Literary Epistles*. Cambridge.

Brittain, R. 1958. *Rivers and Man*. London, New York, and Toronto.

Brodersen, K. 1994. *Pomponius Mela: Kreuzfahrt durch die antike Welt*. Darmstadt.

Broise, P. 1976. "L'urbanisme vicinal aux confines de la Viennoise et de la Séquannaise." *ANRW* II.5.2, 602–29.

Brookes, A. C. 1974. "Minturnae: the Via Appia Bridge." *AJA* 78, 41–48.

Brown, A. G. 1997. *Alluvial Geoarchaeology: Floodplain Archaeology and Environmental Change*. Cambridge.

Brown, A. G., and Ellis, C. 1995. "People, Climate and Alluviation: Theory, Research Design and New Sedimentological and Stratigraphical Data from Etruria." *PBSR* 63: 45–73.

Brückner, H. 1986. "Man's Impact on the Evolution of the Physical Environment in the Mediterranean Region in Historical Times." *Geographical Journal* 13: 7–17.

———. 2003. "Delta Evolution and Culture. Aspects of Geoarchaeological Research in Miletos and Priene." In Wagner, Pernicka, and Verpmann, *Troia and the Troad*, 121–42.

Brugi, B. 1897. *Le dottrine giuridiche degli agrimensori Romani comparate a quelle del Digesto*. Verona-Padua.

———. 1930 "Fiumi compresi nei lotti dei coloni Romani." In *Studi in onore di Pietro Bonfante nel XL anno d'insegnamento*, vol. I. Milan, 361–66.

Bruni, S. (ed.). 1999. *Le navi antiche di S. Rossore: Pisa, Arsenali Medicei, 25 giugno–6 agosto 1999*. Pisa.

——— (ed.). 2000. *Le navi antiche di Pisa: ad un anno dall'inizio delle ricerche*. Florence.

Brunt, P. A. 1963. "Augustan Imperialism." Review of H. D. Meyer, *Die Aussenpolitik des Augustus und die Augusteische Dichtung* (1961). *JRS* 53: 170–76 = Brunt, *Roman Imperial Themes* (1990), 96–109.

———. 1971. *Italian Manpower*. Oxford.

———. 1990. *Roman Imperial Themes*. Oxford.

Bruun, C. 1991. *The Water Supply of Ancient Rome: A Study of Roman Imperial Administration*. Helsinki.

———. 1992. "Water as a Cruel Element in the Roman World." In Viljamaa, T., Timonen, A., and Krötzl, C. (eds.), *Crudelitas: The Politics of Cruelty in the Ancient and Medieval World. Proceedings of the International Conference Turku (Finland), May 1991*. Krems, 74–80.

Buckland, W. W. 1975. *A Textbook of Roman Law from Augustus to Justinian*. 3rd ed. Revised by P. Stein. Cambridge.

Buonocore, M. 1994. "Tra epigrafia e topografia. L'acquedotto di Amiternum." *Journal of Ancient Topography* 4: 185–94.

——— (ed.). 1996. *Vedere I classici. L'illustrazione libraria dei testi antichi dell'età romana al tardo medioevo*. Biblioteca Apostolica Vaticana. Rome.

Burford, A. 1960. "Heavy Transport in Classical Antiquity." *Economic History Review* 13: 1–18.

———. 1972. *Craftsmen in Greek and Roman Society*. London.

———. 1993. *Land and Labor in the Greek World*. Baltimore and London.

Burnand, Y. 1971. "Un aspect de la géographie des transports dans la Narbonnaise rhodanienne. Les nautes de l'Ardèche et de l'Ouvèze." *Revue archéologique de Narbonnaise* 4: 149–58.

———. 1977. "Le role des communications fluviales dans la genèse et le développement des villes antiques du sud-est de la Gaule." In Duval and Frézouls, *Thèmes de recherches*, 279–305.

Burnett, A., Amandry, M., and Ripollès, P. P. 1992. *Roman Provincial Coinage*. Vol. 1: *From the Death of Caesar to the Death of Vitellius (44 B.C.–A.D. 69)*. Part I: *Introduction and Catalogue*; part II: *Indexes and Plates*. London and Paris.

Burnham, B., and Johnson, H. (eds.). 1979. *Invasion and response: The Case of Roman Britain*. Oxford.

Burnham, B., and Wacher, J. S. 1990. *The "Small Towns" of Roman Britain*. London.

Burstein, S. M. 1989. *Agatharchides of Cnidus: On the Erythraean Sea*. London.

Burton, G. 2000. "The Resolution of Territorial Disputes in the Provinces of the Roman Empire." *Chiron* 30: 195–215.

Butler, H. C. 1901. "The Aqueduct of Minturnae." *AJA* 5: 187–92.

Butzer, K. 1972. *Environment and Archaeology*. London.

Buxton, R. 1994. *Imaginary Greece: The Contexts of Mythology*. Cambridge.

Cagnat, R. 1882. *Étude historique sur les impôts indirects chez les Romains jusu'aux invasions des barbares: d'aprés les documents littéraires et épigraphiques*. Paris.

Calvani, M. 1992. "Acque minerali, risorsa storica dell'Emilia occidentale." In Chevallier, *Les eaux thermales*, 297–309.

Calzolari, M. 1989. *Padania Romana. Ricerche archeologiche e paleoambientali nella pianura tra il Mincio e il Tartaro*. Mantua.

———. 1992. "Le idrovie della Padana in epoca romana: il Po e il Tartaro." *Quaderni del Gruppo Archeologico Ostigliense* 2: 85–110.

———. 1996. "Introduzione allo studio delle rete stradale dell'Italia romana: L'Itinerarium Antonini." *Atti dell' Accademia Nazionale dei Lincei: Memorie*, ser. 9, 7: 369–520.

Campbell, J. B. 1987. "Teach Yourself How to Be a General." *JRS* 77: 13–29.

———. 1993. "War and Diplomacy: Rome and Parthia, 31 B.C.–A.D. 235." In Rich and Shipley, *War and Society*, 213–40.

———. 1994. *The Roman Army, 31 B.C.–A.D. 337: A Sourcebook*. London and New York.

———. 1996. "Shaping the Rural Environment: Surveyors in Ancient Rome." *JRS* 86: 74–99.

———. 2000. *The Writings of the Roman Land Surveyors. Introduction, Text, Translation and Commentary*. London.

———. 2005a. "Surveyors, Topography, and Definitions of Landholding in Ancient Rome." In Conso, Gonzalez, and Guillaumin, *Les vocabularies techniques*, 173–82.

———. 2005b. "'Setting up true boundaries': Land Disputes in the Roman Empire." *MedAnt* 8.1: 307–43.

———. 2009. "River Definitions in Roman Technical Literature." In Gianfelice, *Atti del Convegno Internazionale, Sistemi centuriali e opere di assetto agrario tra età romana e primo medioevo*, 95–99.

Canal, A. 1992. "Aix-les Bains: de l'âge du fer à la période contemporaine." In Chevallier, *Les eaux thermales*, 172–77.

Capini, S. 1999. *Molise: repertorio delle iscrizioni latine*. Vol. 7: *Venafrum*. Campobasso.

Capogrossi Colognesi, L. 1966. *Ricerche sulla struttura delle servitù d'acqua in diritto romana*. Milan.

——— (ed.). 1982. *L'agricoltura romana*. Rome and Bari.

———. 2002. "*Pagi, vici* e *fundi* nell'Italia romana." *Athenaeum* 90.1: 5–48.

Carafa, P. 2004. "Il paesaggio Etrusco-Italico." In H. Patterson, *Bridging the Tiber*, 45–59.

Carter, J. C. 1994. "Sanctuaries in the Chora of Metaponto." In Alcock and Osborne, *Placing the Gods*, 161–98.

Casado, C. F. 1933. "Las presas romanas en España." In *Revista de Obras Publicas*, 449–54.

———. 1972. *Acueductos romanos en España*. Madrid.

Casson, L. 1965. "Harbour and River Boats of Ancient Rome." *JRS* 55: 31–39.

———. 1971. *Ships and Seamanship in the Ancient World*. Princeton.

———. 1974. *Travel in the Ancient World*. London.

———. 1984. *Ancient Trade and Society*. Detroit.

———. 1989. *The Periplus Maris Erythraei*. Princeton.

Castagnoli, F. 1953. "Note numismatiche." *Archeologia Classica* 5: 104–11.

———. 1977. "Topografia dei campi flegrei." In *I Campi Flegrei nell'archeologia e nella storia*. Rome, 41–79.

———. 1980. "Installazioni portuali a Roma." In D'Arms and Kopff, *The Seaborne Commerce of Ancient Rome*, 35–43.

Castella, D. (ed.). 1994. *Le Moulin hydraulique gallo-romain d'Avenches "en Chaplix": fouilles 1990–1991*. Lausanne.

Cavuoto, P. 1982. "Inscrizioni latine di Minturno." *Ottava Miscellanea Graeca e Romana* 33: 489–585.

Champlin, E. 1982. "The Suburbium of Rome." *AJAH* 7, 97–117.

Chassignet, M. 2005. "Les catastrophes naturelles et leur gestion dans l'*Ab Urbe Condita de Tite-Live*." In Bedon and Hermon, *Concepts*, 337–52.

Chaunu, P. 1959. *Séville et l'Atlantique (1504–1650)*. Paris.

Cherkauer, D. 1976. "The Stratigraphy and Chronology of the River Treia Alluvial Deposits." In Potter, *A Faliscan Town in South Etruria*, 106–20.

Chevallier, R. (ed.). 1974. *Littérature gréco-romaine et géographie historique: Mélanges offerts à Roger Dion*. Paris.

———. 1975. "Les eaux en Gaule. Rivages, sources, fleuves et vallées." *Caesarodunum* 10: 7–41.

———. 1976. *Roman Roads*. Translated by N. H. Field. London, 1989. Revised paperback edition. London.

———. 1980–81. "Recherches archéologiques Gallo-romaines sur le Haut-Rhône. Notes de topographie historique sur une zone-frontière." *Bulletin de la Société nationale des Antiquaires de France*, 152–63.

——— (ed.). 1992. *Les eaux thermales et les cultes des eaux en Gaule et dans les provinces voisines. Actes du colloque 28–30 septembre 1990, Aix-les-Bains*. Tours.

Chic García, G. 1984. "El trafico en el Guadalquivir y el transporte de las anforas." *AnUCA*, 33–44.

———. 1988. *Epigrafía anfórica de la Bética* II. Seville.

———. 1997. *Historia económica de la Bética en la época de Augusto*. Seville.

Chilver, G. 1941. *Cisalpine Gaul*. Oxford.

Christie, N. (ed.). 1995. *Settlement and Economy in Italy, 1500 B.C. to A.D. 1500*. Papers of the Fifth Conference of Italian Archaeology. Oxbow Monograph 41. Oxford.

Christol, M., and Fiches, J.-L. 1999. "Batellerie et commerce dans l'Antiquité." *Gallia* 56: 141–55.

"Chronique archéologique." 1993. *Syria* 70: 244.

Cifani, G., and Munzi, M. 2002. "Fonti letterarie e archeologiche per la storia del Kinyps (Libia)," In Khanoussi, Ruggeri and Vismara, *L'Africa Romana*, 1901–18.

Città di Montegrotto Terme. 1997. Soprintendenza Archeologica per il Veneto. Montegrotto Terme.

Claridge, A. 1998. *Rome: An Oxford Archaeological Guide*. Oxford.

Claridge, A., and Gallina Zevi, A. (eds.). 1996. *Roman Ostia Revisited: Archaeological and Historical Papers in Memory of Russell Meiggs*. London.

Claridge, A., and Ward-Perkins, J. B. 1976. *Pompeii, A.D. 79*. London.

Clarke, K. 1999. *Between Geography and History: Hellenistic Constructions of the Roman World*. Oxford.

Clavel-Lévêque, M., et al. 1993. *Siculus Flaccus. Les conditions des terres*. Naples.

———. 1996. *Hygin l'Arpenteur. L'Établissement des Limites*. Naples.

Cleere, H. 1978. "Roman Harbours in Britain South of Hadrian's Wall." In du Plat Taylor and Cleere, *Roman Shipping and Trade*, 36–40.

Coarelli, F. 1979. "Fregellae e la colonizzazione Latina nella valle del Liri." *AL* 2: 197–204.

———. 1982. *Guide archeologiche Laterza: Lazio.* Bari and Rome.

———. 1986. "L'urbs e il suburbia." In A. Giardina (ed.), *Società romana e impero tardoantico* II. Rome and Bari, 1–58.

———. 1988a. "I santuari, il fiume, gli emporia." In *Storia di Roma*, 127–51.

———. 1988b. "Colonizzazione romana e viabilità." *Dialoghi di Archeologia* 10: 35–48.

——— (ed.). 1989. *Minturnae.* Rome.

———. 2005. "P. Faianius Plebeius, Forum Novum and Tacitus." *PBSR* 73: 85–98.

Coarelli, F., and Patterson, H. (eds.). 2009. *Mercator Placidissimus: The Tiber Valley in Antiquity; New Research in the Upper and Middle Valley.* Rome.

Coen, A., and Quilici Gigli, S. (eds.). 1997. *Uomo acqua e paesaggio. Atti dell'Incontro di studio sul tema "Irreggimentazione delle acque e transformazione del paesaggio antico," S. Maria Capua Vetere—22–23 novembre 1996.* Atlante tematico di topografia antica, supplemento 2. Rome.

Cohen, H. 1880–92. *Description historique des monnaies frappées sous l'Empire romain communément appelées, médailles imperials.* 8 vols. 2nd ed. Paris.

Cole, S. G. 1994. "Demeter in the Ancient Greek City and Its Countryside." In Alcock and Osborne, *Placing the Gods*, 199–216.

Coleman, K. M. 1988. *Silvae IV Edited with an English Translation and Commentary.* Oxford.

Coles, B. J. 1994. "Trisantona Rivers: A Landscape Approach to the Interpretation of River Names." *OJA* 13: 295–311.

Colini, A. M. 1980. "Il porto fluviale del foro boario a Roma." In D'Arms and Kopff, *The Seaborne Commerce of Ancient Rome*, 43–53.

Collingwood, R. G., and Richmond, I. 1969. *The Archaeology of Roman Britain.* London and New York.

Colls, D., Etienne, R., Lequément, R., Liou, B., and Mayet, F. 1977. *L'Epave Port-Vendre II et le commerce de la Bétique en l'époque de Claude.* ArchaeoNautica 1. Paris.

Colonna, A. 1951. *Himerii Declamationes et Orationes cum Deperditarum Fragmentis.* Rome.

Colwell, F. S. 1989. *Rivermen: A Romantic Iconography of the River and the Source.* Kingston and London.

Congès, A. 2005. "Nature et authenticité des Casae Litterarum d'après l'analyse de leur vocabulaire." In Conso, Gonzales, and Guillaumin, *Les vocabularies techniques*, 71–124.

Conso, D., Gonzales, A., and Guillaumin, J.-Y. (eds.). 2005. *Les vocabularies techniques des arpenteurs romains.* Besançon.

Conta, G. 1987. "La stazione termale di Ad Aquas lungo la Via Salaria." In *Le strade nelle Marche. Il problema nel tempo, Atti del convegno, Fano, Fabriano, Pesaro, Ancona, 11–14 ottobre 1984*, 431–36. Ancona.

Cook, J. M. 1973. *The Troad: An Archaeological and Topographical Survey.* Oxford.

Corbiau, M.-H. 2000. "Les cours d'eau au sein des communications antiques. Les témoignages de l'archéologie en Belgique." In Bonnamour, *Archéologie des fleuves*, 94–98.

Corbier, M. 1984. "De Volsinii a Sestinum: Cura aquae et évergétisme municipal de l'eau en Italie." *Revue des Études latines* 62: 236–74.

Cordano, F. 1992. *La geografia degli antichi*. Rome and Bari.

Cornell, T. J. 1989. "The Conquest of Italy." In Walbank et al., *Cambridge Ancient History*, 351–419.

———. 1995. *The Beginnings of Rome: Italy and Rome from the Bronze Age to the Punic Wars (c. 1000–264 B.C.)*. London and New York.

Corrocher, J. 1992. "Sources et installations thermals en Bourbonnais." In Chevallier, *Les eaux thermales*, 177–98.

Cosentino, R. 1992. "Il complesso termale di Aquae Caeretanae." In E. Herring, R. Whitehouse, and J. Wilkins, *Papers*, 17–22.

Cosentino, R., and Sabbatini Tumolesi, P. 1989. "L'edificio termale delle Aquae Caeretanae." *Miscellanea Ceretana, I, Quaderni del Centro di Studio per l'Archeologia Etrusco-Italica*, 95–112.

Cosgrove, D., and Petts, G. 1990. *Water, Engineering and Landscape: Water Control and Landscape Transformation in the Modern Period*. London and New York.

Coulson, J., and Dodge, H. (eds.). 2000. *Ancient Rome: The Archaeology of the Eternal City*. Oxford University School of Archaeology Monograph 54. Oxford.

Courtney, E. 1980. *A Commentary on the Satires of Juvenal*. London.

Cozza, L., and Tucci, P. L. 2006. "Navalia." *Archeologia Classica*, n.s. 7, 57: 175–201.

Crawford, M. H. 1992. *The Roman Republic*. 2nd ed. London.

——— (ed.). 1996. *Roman Statutes*. 2 vols. London.

———. 2003. "Language and Geography in the *Sententia Minuciorum*." *Athenaeum* 91: 204–10.

———. 2005. "Transhumance in Italy: Its History and Historians." In W. V. Harris and E. Lo Cascio (eds.), *Noctes Campanae. Studi di storia antica ed archeologia dell'Italia preromana e romana in memoria di Martin W. Frederiksen*. Naples, 159–79.

Crawford, M. H., and Keppie, L. (1984). "Excavations at Fregellae, 1978–84." *PBSR* 52: 21–35.

Crimaco, L. 1991. *Volturnum*. Rome.

Criniti, N. 1991. *La Tabula alimentaria di Veleia*. Parma.

Croon, J. H. 1952. "The Palici. An autochthonous cult in ancient Sicily." *Mnemosyne* 5: 116–29.

———. 1953. "Heracles at Lindus." *Mnemosyne* 6: 283–99.

———. 1955. "The Mask of the Underworld Daemon—Some Remarks on the Perseus-Gorgon Story." *JHS* 75: 9–16.

———. 1956. "Artemis Thermaia and Apollo Thermios." *Mnemosyne* 4: 193–220.

———. 1961. "Hot Springs and Healing: A Preliminary Answer." *Mnemosyne* 14: 140–41.

———. 1967. "Hot Springs and Healing Gods." *Mnemosyne* 20: 225–46.

Crouch, D. P. 1975. "The Water Supply of Palmyra." *Studia Palmyrenskie* 7: 153–86.

———. 1984. "The Hellenistic Water System of Morgantina in Sicily." *AJA* 88: 353–65.

———. 1993. *Water Management in Ancient Greek Cities*. Oxford.

Cuinet, V. 1894. *La Turquie d'Asie*. Paris.

Cunliffe, B. 1970. *Roman Bath*. London.

——— (ed.). 1988. *The Temple of Sulis Minerva at Bath*. Vol. 2. Oxford.

Cunliffe, B., and Davenport, P. 1985. *The Temple of Sulis Minerva at Bath*. Vol. 1. Oxford.

Cuntz, O. 1929. *Itineraria Romana*. Vol. I: *Itinerarium Antonini Augusti et Burdigalense*. Lepizig. Repr., with revised bibliography by G. Wirth (Stuttgart, 1990).

Cüppers, H. 1982. "Beiträge zur Geschichte des römischen Kurund Badeortes Aachen." In H. Cüppers et al., *Aquae Granni*. Beiträge zur archäologie von Aachen. Rheinische Ausgrabungen 22. Cologne-Bonn, 1–75.

———. 1990. *Die Römer in Rheinland-Pflaz*. Stuttgart.

Curbera, J. B. 1998. "Onomastics and River-Gods in Sicily." *Philologus* 142: 52–60.

Curchin, L. 1991. *Roman Spain: Conquest and Assimilation*. London.

Dabrowa, E. (ed.). 1994. *The Roman and Byzantine Army in the East*. Krakow.

Dalby, A. 2000. *Empire of Pleasures: Luxury and Indulgence in the Roman World*. London and New York.

Darby, W. J., Ghalioungi, P., and Grivetti, L. 1977. *Food: The Gift of Osiris*. London.

D'Arms, J. H. 1970. *Romans on the Bay of Naples: A Social and Cultural History of the Villas and Their Owners from 150 B.C. to A.D. 400*. Cambridge, Mass.

D'Arms, J. H., and Kopff, E. C. (eds.). 1980. *The Seaborne Commerce of Ancient Rome: Studies in Archaeology and History*. MAAR, vol. 36. Rome.

Davis, J. 1977. *People of the Mediterranean: An Essay in Comparative Social Anthropology*. London, Henley, and Boston.

De Alarcão, J. 1988. *Roman Portugal*. 2 vols. Warminster.

De Blois, L., and Lo Cascio, E. (eds.). 2007. *The Impact of the Roman Army (200 B.C.– A.D. 476)*. Leiden and Boston.

De Boe, G. 1978. "Roman Boats from a Small River Harbour at Pommeroeul, Belgium." In du Plat Taylor and Cleere, *Roman Shipping and Trade*, 22–30.

De Caro, S., and Greco, A. 1981. *Guide archeologiche Laterza: Campania*. Bari and Rome.

Decker, K.-V., and Selzer, W. 1976. "Mogontiacum: Mainz von der Zeit des Augustus bis zum Ende der römischen Herrschaft." *ANRW* II.5.1, 457–559.

Degrassi, A. 1963. *Inscriptiones Italiae*. Vol. XIII.II: *Fasti Anni Numani et Iuliani*. Rome.

De Haan, N., and Jansen, G. C. M. 1996. *Cura Aquarum in Campania. Proceedings of the Ninth International Congress on the History of Water Management and Hydraulic Engineering in the Mediterranean Region, Pompeii, 1–8 October 1994*. Leiden.

De Izarra, F. 1993. *Hommes et fleuves en Gaule romaine*. Paris.

De Laet, S. J. 1949. *Portorium. Étude sur l'organisation douanière chez les romains surtout à l'époque du haute-empire*. Bruges.

DeLaine, J. 1995. "The Supply of Building Material to the City of Rome." In N. Christie

(ed.), *Settlement and Economy in Italy 1500 B.C.–A.D. 1500.* Papers of the Fifth
 Conference of Italian Archaeology. Oxford, 555–62.

———. 1999. "Bathing and Society." In J. DeLaine and D. E. Johnston, *Roman Baths,*
 7–16.

DeLaine, J., and Johnston, D. E. (eds.). 1999. *Roman Baths and Bathing. Proceedings
 of the First International Conference on Roman Baths held at Bath, England,
 30 March–4 April 1992.* Part 1: *Bathing and Society.* Part 2: *Design and Content.*
 Journal of Roman Archaeology Supplementary Series 37. Portsmouth, Rhode Island.

Delano Smith, C. 1978. *Daunia Vetus: vita e mutamenti sulle coste del Tavoliere.* Foggia.

———. 1979. *Western Mediterranean Europe: A Historical Geography of Italy, Spain and
 Southern France since the Neolithic.* London and New York.

De Ligt, L. 1993. *Fairs and Markets in the Roman Empire.* Amsterdam.

Deman, A. 1987. "Reflexions sur la navigation fluvial dans l'antiquité romaine." In
 Hackens and Marchetti, *Histoire économique de l'antiquité,* 79–106.

Demangeon, A., and Febvre, L. 1935. *Le Rhin. Problems d'histoire et d'economie.* Paris.

Demougeot, E. 1983. "Constantin et Dacie." In Frézouls, *Crise et redressement,* 91–112.

De Neeve, P. W. 1984. *Peasants in Peril: Location and Economy in Italy in the Second
 Century B.C.* Amsterdam.

———. 1990. "A Roman Landowner and His Estates." *Athenaeum* 78: 363–402.

*Déplacements des lignes de rivage en Méditerranée d'après les données de l'archéologie.
 Aix-en-Provence 5–7 septembre 1985.* 1987. Paris.

De Robertis, F. M. 1936. *L'espropriazione per pubblica utilità.* Bari.

———. 1945–46. "Emptio ab invito: sul problema della espropriazione nel diritto
 romano." *Annali della Facoltà di Lettere e Filosofia di Bari* 7–8: 153–224.

De Saint-Denis, E. 1981. "Le Rhône vu par les Grecs et les Latins de l'Antiquité."
 Latomus 40: 545–70.

Desbat, A., and Martin-Kilcher, S. 1989. *Les amphores sur l'axe Rhône-Rhin.* Rome.

Desnoyers, M. 1978. *Neris antique. Nouvelle recherche sur l'histoire de Neris.* Montlucon.

———. 1985. "Néris-les-Bains (Allier), ville therme gallo-romaine." In A. Pelletier
 (ed.), *La medicine en Gaule.* Paris, 39–62.

Devijver, H., and van Wonterghem, F. 1981. "Il *campus* nell'impianto urbanistico delle
 città romane: testimonianze epigrafiche e resti archeologici." *Acta Archaeologica
 Lovaniensia* 20: 33–68.

De Vries, B. 1998. *Umm El-Jimal: A Frontier Town and Its Landscape in Nothern Jordan.*
 Vol. 1. Portsmouth, Rhode Island.

De Weerd, M. D. 1978. "Ships of the Roman Period at Zwammerdam/Nigrum Paulum,
 Germania Inferior." In Du Plat Taylor and Cleere, *Roman Shipping and Trade,* 15–21.

Deyts, S. 1992. "Sources sacrées, stations thermales et ex-voto de guérison en Gaule
 romaine." In Chevallier, *Les eaux thermales,* 55–66.

Dias Andreu, K., and Keay, S. J. 1996. *The Dynamics of Change: The Case of the Iberian
 Peninsula.* London.

Diego, F. 1986. *Inscripciones romanas de la provincial de Léon.* Léon.

Diez de Velasco, F. 1987. *Balnearios y divinidades de las aguas termales en la Península Ibérica en época romana*. Madrid.

———. 1992. "Divinités des eaux thermals dans le Nord-Ouest de la Provincia Tarraconensis et dans le Nord de la Provincia Lusitania." In Chevallier, *Les eaux thermales*, 133–50.

Diggle, J. 1970. *Euripides: Phaethon, Edited with Prolegomena and Commentary*. Cambridge.

Dilke, O. A. W. 1971. *The Roman Land Surveyors*. Newton Abbot.

———. 1985. *Greek and Roman Maps*. London.

———. 1987a. "Maps in Service of the State: Roman Cartography to the End of the Augustan Era." In Harley and Woodward, *The History of Cartography*, 201–11.

———. 1987b. "Roman Large-Scale Mapping in the Early Empire." In Harley and Woodward, *The History of Cartography*, 213–33.

———. 1987c. "Itineraries and Geographical Maps in the Early and Late Roman Empires." In Harley and Woodward, *The History of Cartography*, 234–57.

Dillemann, L. 1962. *Haute Mésopotamie orientale et pays adjacentes. Contribution à la géographie historique de la region, du Ve s. avant l'ère chrétienne au VIe s. de cette ère*. Paris.

Diller, A. 1952. *The Tradition of the Minor Greek Geographers*. APA Monographs 14. Philadelphia.

Di Stefano Manzella, I. 1981. *Falerii Novi*. Supplementa Italica 1, 101–76.

Doblhofer, E. 1972–77. *Rutilius Namatianus, De reditu suo Iter Gallicum*. 2 vols. Heidelberg.

Dollinger, P. (ed.). 1970. *Histoire de l'Alsace*. Toulouse.

Domergue, C. 1998. "A View of Baetica's External Commerce in the 1st C. A.D. based on Its Trade in Metals." In Keay, *The Archaeology of Early Roman Baetica*, 201–15.

Donati, F. 2002. "Il fiume Cecina tra navigazione costiera e fluviale. La villa romana di San Vincenzino a Cecina e l'origine del toponimo Albini Villa." In Khanoussi, Ruggeri, and Vismara, *L'Africa Romana*, 11–19.

D'Onofrio, C. 1970. *Il Tevere e Roma*. Rome.

Doppelfeld, O. 1975. "Das römische Köln. I. Ubier-Oppidum und Colonia Agrippinensium." In *ANRW* II.4, 715–82.

Doppler, H. W. 1976. *Der römische Vicus Aquae Helveticae Baden*. Archäologische Führer der Schweiz 8. Basel.

Dorcey, P. F. 1992. *The Cult of Silvanus: A Study in Roman Folk Religion*. Leiden and New York.

Doria, C. M., and Cascione, C. 2010. "*Cura riparum*." In Hermon, *Riparia dans L'Empire romain*, 283–94.

Doumas, C. (ed.). 1978. *Thera and the Aegean World* I. *Papers Presented at the Second International Scientific Congress, Santorini, Greece, August 1978*. London.

Dowden, K. 1992. *The Uses of Greek Mythology*. London and New York.

Downey, G. 1961. *A History of Antioch*. Oxford.

Downs, R. M., and Stea, D. 1973. *Image and Environment: Cogitive Mapping and Spatial Behaviour*. London.

Downs, R. M., and Stea, D. 1977. *Maps in Minds: Reflections on Cogitive Mapping*. New York.

Drabkin, I. E. 1950. *Caelius Aurelianus: On Acute Diseases and On Chronic Diseases*. Chicago.

Drinkwater, J. F. 1975. "Lugdunum: Natural Capital of Gaul?" *Britannia* 6: 133–40.

———. 1983. *Roman Gaul: The Three Provinces, 58 B.C.–A.D. 260*. London.

Duby, G. (ed.). 1980. *Histoire de la France urbaine*. 1: *La Ville antique*. Paris.

Ducrey, P. 1969. "Trois nouvelles inscriptions crétoises." *BCH* 93: 846–52.

Ducrey, P., and van Effenterre, H. 1973. "Un reglement d'epoque romaine sur les bains d'Arcades." *Kretica Chronika* 25: 281–90.

Dueck, D. 2000. *Strabo of Amasia*. London and New York.

Dufournet, P. 1968. "Navigation sur le Rhône supérieur. Témoignages archéologiques sur deux elements du traffic. Les établissements portuaires. Condate, port et emporium. Liaisons voies d'eau—voies de terre dans le basin de Seyssel." *Actes du 91e congrès national des sociétés savants, section d'archéologie, Rennes, 1966*. Paris, 99–155.

———. 1971. "Le carrefour fluvio-routier de Seyssel dans l'antiquité." *Actes du colloque sur les cols des Alps dans l'antiquité et le Moyen Age, Bourg-en-Bresse, 13–15 mars 1969*. Orléans, 59–85.

———. 1976. "Pierre blanche et carrières antiques de Seyssel." *Actes 96e CNSS, Toulouse, 1971*, Paris, 245–72.

———. 1984. "Survivances antiques à Seyssel et val du Rhône (Haute-Savoie, Ain)." *Caesarodunum* 19: 133–41.

Dumézil, G. 1966. *La religion romaine archaïque*. Paris.

Dunbabin, K. M. D. 1978. *The Mosaics of Roman North Africa: Studies in Iconography and Patronage*. Oxford.

———. 1989. "*Baiarum grata voluptas*." *PBSR* 57: 6–46.

———. 1999. *Mosaics of the Greek and Roman World*. Cambridge.

Duncan-Jones, R. 1974. *The Economy of the Roman Empire: Quantitatve Studies*. Cambridge.

———. 1990. *Structure and Scale in the Roman Economy*. Cambridge.

Du Plat Taylor, J., and Cleere, H. (eds.). 1978. *Roman Shipping and Trade: Britain and the Rhine Provinces*. Council for British Archaeology Research Report, no. 24. London.

Dupré, N. 1973. "La place de la vallée de l'Erbe dans l'Espagne romaine. Recherches de géographie historique." *Mélanges de la Casa de Velázquez* 9: 133–75.

———. 1983. "La vallée de l'Erbe et les routes transpyrenéennes antiques." *Caesarodunum* 18: 393–411.

———. 1987. "Evolution de la ligne de ravage à l'embouchure de l'Ebre." In *Déplacements*, 25–34.

Dupré, N., and Pérex Agorreta, M. J. 1992. "Thermalisme et religion dans le Nord de l'Hispania (Des Pyrénées à l'Erbe)." In Chevallier, *Les eaux thermales*, 152–70.

Dussot, D. 1989. *Carte archéologique de la Gaule 23. La Creuse*. Paris.

Duval, P. M., and Frézouls, E. (eds.). 1977. *Thèmes de recherches sur les villes antiques d'occident, Strasbourg 1971*. Paris.

Duval, P. M., and Lavagne, H. 1981. "Chronique Gallo-romaine." *Revue des Études Anciennes* 83: 291–318.

Dvorjetski, E. 1999. "Social and Cultural Aspects of Medicinal Roman Baths in Israel according to Rabbinic Sources." In J. DeLaine and D. E. Johnston, *Baths*, 117–29.

Dyson, S. L. 1992. *Community and Society in Roman Italy*. Baltimore.

Eckoldt, M. 1980. *Schiffahrt auf kleinen Flüssen Mitteleuropas in römerzeit und Mittelalter*. Oldenburg, Hamburg, and Munich.

———. 1984. "Navigation on Small Rivers in Central Europe in Roman and Medieval times." *IJNA* 13.1: 3–10.

Edlund-Berry, I. E. M. 1987. *The Gods and the Place: Location and Function of Sanctuaries in the Countryside of Etruria and Magna Graecia (700–400 B.C.)*. Stockholm.

Edmondson, J. 1987. *Two Industries in Roman Lusitania: Mining and Garum Production*. BAR International Series 362. Oxford.

Edwards, C. 1996. *Writing Rome: Textual Approaches to the City*. Cambridge.

Ehrenberg, V., and Jones, A. H. M. 1976. *Documents Illustrating the Reigns of Augustus and Tiberius*. 2nd, enlarged ed. Oxford.

Eisma, D. 1964. "Stream Deposition in the Mediterranean Area in Historical Times." *Nature* 203: 1061.

———. 1978. "Stream Deposition and Erosion by the Eastern Shore of the Aegean." In Brice, *The Environmental History*, 67–81.

Ekwall, E. 1928. *English River-Names*. Oxford.

Ellmers, D. 1978. "Shipping on the Rhine during the Roman Period: The Pictorial Evidence." In du Plat Taylor and Cleere, *Roman Shipping and Trade*, 1–14.

Elsner, J. 1992. "Pausanias: A Greek Pilgrim in the Roman World." *Past and Present* 135: 3–29.

———. 2000. "The *Itinerarium Burdigalense*: Politics and Salvation in the Geography of Constantine's Empire." *JRS* 90: 181–95.

Enei, F. 1995. "Ricognizioni archeologiche nell' Ager Caeretanus, 1990–1992." In Christie, *Settlement and Economy*, 63–79.

Erdkamp, P. 1998. *Hunger and the Sword: Warfare and Food Supply in Roman Republican Wars (264–30 B.C.)*. Amsterdam.

——— (ed.). 2002. *The Roman Army and the Economy*. Amsterdam.

——— (ed.). 2007. *A Companion to the Roman Army*. Oxford.

Esch, A. 1990. "Die Via Cassia in der Landschaft." *AW* 21: 134–58.

Étienne, R. 1977. "Burdigala et Garumna." In Duval and Frézouls, *Thèmes de recherches*, 329–40.

———. 1989. "Lyon, emporion des Gaules; la ville et le fleuve chez Strabon, géographe du Ier siècle après Jésus Christ." In *La ville et fleuve*, 125–32.

Evans, H. B. 1982. "Agrippa's water plan." *AJA* 86, 401–11.

———. 1994. *Water Distribution in Ancient Rome*. Ann Arbor.

Fagan, G. G. 1999. *Bathing in Public in the Roman World*. Ann Arbor.

———. 2006. "Bathing for Health with Celsus and Pliny the Elder." *CQ* 56.1: 190–207.

Fahlbusch, H. 1987. "Side." *WAS* 2: 218–21.

Farrar, L. 1998. *Ancient Roman Gardens*. Stroud.

Fauduet, I. 1992. "Sanctuaires associés à l'eau en Gaule central." In Chevallier, *Les eaux thermales*, 199–206.

Favory, F. 2005. "Limites et territories d'après le corpus gromatique." In Bedon and Hermon, *Concepts*, 153–95.

Favory, F., and Fiches, J.-L. (eds.). 1994. *Les campagnes de la France méditerranéenne dans l'antiquité et le haut moyen âge: études microrégionales*. Paris.

Favro, D. 1996. *The Urban Image of Augustan Rome*. Cambridge.

Feissel, D. 1985. "Deux listes de quartiers d'Antioche astreints au creusement d'un canal (73–74 ap. J.-C.)." *Syria* 62: 77–103.

———. 2004. "Un rescrit de Justinien découvert à Didymus (1er avril 533)." *Chiron* 34: 285–365.

Fentress, E., et al. 1983. "Excavations at Fosso della Crescenza, 1962." *PBSR* 51: 58–101.

Ferdière, A. 1977. "Découverte d'un quai romain à Bourges 'Lazenay' (Cher)." *Caesarodunum* 12: 326–32.

———. 1979. "Un quai romain découvert à Bourges." *Archéologia* 132: 42–44.

Fernández de Avilés, A. 1961. "Prospección arqueológica en las Fontes Tamarici (Velilla-Palencia)." *Revista de Archivos, Bibliotecas y Museos* 69: 263–68.

Ferrari, G. 1957. *Early Roman Monastries*. Vatican City.

Festugière, A. J. 1954. *Personal Religion among the Greeks*. Berkeley and Los Angeles.

Filgueira, J., and D'Ors, A. 1955. *Inscripciones romanas de Galicia* III. Santiago.

Fink, R. O. 1971. *Roman Military Records on Papyrus*. Cleveland.

Finley, M. I. 1965. "Technical Innovation and Economic Progress in the Ancient World." *Economic History Review*, 2nd ser., 18: 29–45.

———. 1975. *The Use and Abuse of History*. Harmondsworth. Repr., 1987.

———. 1985. *Ancient History: Evidence and Models*. London.

Fischer, F. 1997. "Rheinquellen und Rheinanliegen bei Caesar und Strabon." *Germania* 75: 597–606.

Fischer, J. 1932. *Claudii Ptolemaei Geographiae Codex Urbinas Graecus 82*. Leiden, Leipzig, and Turin.

Fishwick, D. 1972. "The Temple of the Three Gauls." *JRS* 62: 46–52.

———. 1978. "The Development of Provincial Ruler Worship in the Western Roman Empire." *ANRW* 2.16.2, 1201–53.

Fitch, G. 1907. "The Missouri River: Its Habits and Eccentricities Described by a Personal Friend." *American Magazine* 53.6: 637–40.

Flambard, J.-M. 1987. "Deux toponymes du Champ de Mars: ad Ciconias, ad Nixas." In *L'Urbs: espace urbain et histoire*. Collection de l'École française de Rome 98. Rome, 191–210.

Fleming, N. C. 1969. "Archaeological Evidence for Eustatic Changes of Sea Level and Earth Movements in the Western Mediterranean in the Last 2,000 Years." *Geological Society of America. Special Paper* 109.

——. 1978. "Thera as the Tectonic Focus of the Southern Aegean: Archaeological Evidence from the Aegean Margin." In Doumas, *Thera and the Aegean World*, 81–84.

Fontana, S. 1995. "Un impianto per la produzione di calce presso Lucus Feroniae." In Christie, *Settlement and Economy*, 563–70.

Fontaneille, M. T. 1982. "Les bains dans la medicine gréco-romaine." *Revue Archéologique du Centre de la France* 21: 121–30.

Foraboschi, D. 1988. "Strabone e la geografia economica dell'Italia." In Maddoli, *Strabone e l'Italia antica*, 177–87.

Forbes, R. J. 1965. *Studies in Ancient Technology*. Vol. 2. Leiden.

Fornell Muñoz, A. 1997. "La navegabilidad en el curso alto del Guadalquivir en época romana." *Florentia Iliberritana* 8: 125–47.

Forrer, R. 1911. "Ein versunkener spätantike Mühlsteintransport in Wanzenau bei Strassburg." *Cahiers d'Archéologie et d'Histoire d'Alsace* 7–8: 131–43.

Fossey, J. M. 1979. "The Cities of the Copaïs in the Roman Period." *ANRW* 2.7.1, 549–91.

Fowden, G. 1990. "Religious Developments in Late Roman Lycia: Topographical Preliminaries." *Meletemata* 10: 343–70.

Foxhall, L. 1996. "Feeling the Earth Move: Cultivation Techniques on Steep Slopes in Classical Antiquity." In Shipley and Salmon, *Human Landscapes*, 44–67.

France, J. 2001. *Quadragesima Galliarum. L'Organisation douanière des Provinces Alpestres, Gauloises et Germaniques de l'Empire romain*. École française de Rome. Rome.

Frank, T. (ed.). 1959. *An Economic Survey of Ancient Rome*. 6 vols. Paterson, New Jersey.

Frayn, J. M. 1975. "Wild and Cultivated Plants: A Note on the Peasant Economy of Roman Italy." *JRS* 65: 32–39.

——. 1984. *Sheep-Rearing and the Wool-Trade in Italy during the Roman Period*. Liverpool.

——. 1993. *Markets and Fairs in Roman Italy*. Oxford.

Frazer, J. G. 1898. *Pausanias's Description of Greece*. 6 vols. London.

Frederiksen, M. 1984. *Campania*. Edited by N. Purcell. London.

French, D. H. 1994. "Legio III Gallica." In Dabrowa, *The Roman and Byzantine Army*, 29–46.

French, R. K. 1994. *Ancient Natural History: Histories of Nature*. London.

Frenz, H. G. 1989. "The Honorary Arch at Mainz-Kastel." *JRA* 2: 120–25.

Frere, S. 1987. *Britannia: A History of Roman Britain*. 3rd ed. London.

Frere, S., Hassall, M., and Tomlin, R. S. O. 1977. "Roman Britain in 1976." *Britannia* 8: 356–449.

Frézouls, E. (ed.). 1983. *Crise et redressement dans les provinces européennes de l'empire (milieu du IIIe–IVe siècle ap. J.C.)*. Strasbourg.

Frick, C. 1880. *Pomponii Melae de Chorographia Libri Tres*. Stuttgart. Repr., 1967.

Frier, B. 1969. "Points on the Topography of Minturnae." *Historia* 18: 510–12.

Fulford, M. G. 1978. "The Interpretation of Britain's Late Roman Trade: The Scope of Medieval Historical and Archaeological Analogy." In du Plat Taylor and Cleere, *Roman Shipping and Trade*, 59–69.

———. 1987. "Economic Interdependence among Urban Communities of the Roman Mediterranean." *WA* 19: 58–75.

Fulford, M. G., et al. 1994. "The Settlement and Drainage of the Wentlooge Level, Gwent: Excavation and Survey at Romney Great Wharf 1992." *Britannia* 25: 175–211.

Fustier, P. 1967. "Étude sur les liaisons routières entre Loire et Saône." *Archéocivilisation*, 43–51.

Gabba, E. 1975. "Mercati e fiere nell'Italia romana." *Studi Classici e Orientali* 24: 141–63.

Gabba, E., and Pasquinucci, M. 1979. *Struture agrarie e allevamento transumante nell'Italia romana (III–I sec. a. C.)*. Pisa.

Gabler, D. 1983. "Rapporti commerciali fra Italia e Pannonia in età Romana." *Archeologia Classica* 35: 88–117.

Gabler, D., and Keleman, M. H. 1984. "Olio betico in Pannonia. Anfore ispaniche nella valle danubiana." *AEA* 57: 121–42.

Gaffney, V., Patterson, H., and Roberts, P. 2001. "Forum Novum-Vescovio: Studying Urbanism in the Tiber Valley." *JRA* 14: 59–79.

———. 2004. "*Forum Novum* (Vescovio): A New Study of the Town and Bishopric." In H. Patterson, *Bridging the Tiber*, 237–51.

Gallant, T. W. 1985. *A Fisherman's Tale*. Ghent.

Garbrecht, G. 1987. "Irrigation throughout History—Problems and Solutions." In Wunderlich, W. O., and Prins, J. E. (eds), *Water Resources Developments in Perspective*. Rotterdam, 3–18.

García Iglesias, L. 1971. "La Beturia. Un problema geografico de la Hispania Antigua." *Archivo Español de Arquelogia* 44: 86–108.

García y Bellido, A. 1945. "La navigabilidad de los ríos de la Península ibérica en la Antigüedad." *Ivestigación y Progreso* 16: 115–22.

Garnsey, P. 1988. *Famine and Food Supply in the Graeco-Roman World: Responses to Risk and Crisis*. Cambridge.

Garnsey, P., Hopkins, K., and Whittaker, C. (eds.). 1983. *Trade in the Ancient Economy*. Berkeley.

Garnsey, P., and Saller, R. 1987. *The Roman Empire: Economy, Society, Culture*. London.

Garnsey, P., and Whittaker, C. (eds.). 1983. *Trade and Famine in Classical Antiquity*. Cambridge.

Garzyra, A. 1963. *Dionysii Ixeuticon*. Leipzig.

Gauthier, M. 1981. "Circumscription d'Aquitaine." *Gallia* 39: 494–95.

Gazzola, P. 1963. *Ponti romani.* 2 vols. Florence.

George, J. W. 1992. *Venantius Fortunatus: A Latin Poet in Merovingian Gaul.* Oxford.

———. 1995. *Venantius Fortunatus: Personal and Political Poems; Translated with Notes and Introduction.* Liverpool.

Gerlach, R., et al. 2008. "Das Rhein-Limes Projekt—Wo lag der Rhein zur Römerzeit." *Beiträge zum Welterbe Limes,* 3:9–17. Stuttgart.

Gerov, B. 1988. *Land Ownership in Roman Thracia and Moesia (1st-3rd century).* Amsterdam.

Geyer, B. (ed.). 1990. *Techniques et pratiques hydro-agricoles traditionnelles en domaine irrigué: approche pluridisciplinaire des modes de culture avant la motorisation en Syrie. Actes du Colloque de Damas, 1987.* Paris, 63–254.

Gianfelice, R. (ed.) 2009. *Atti del Convegno Internazionale, Sistemi centuriali e opere di assetto agrario tra età romana e primo medioevo. Aspetti metodologici ricostruttivi ed interpretativi, Borgoricco (Padova)-Lugo (Ravenna) 10-12 settembre 2009, Agri Centuriati,* in *An International Journal of Landscape Archaeology* 6 (2009).

Giannelli, G. 1963. *Culti e miti della Maga Grecia.* 2nd ed. Florence.

Giglioli, C. Q. 1911. "Note archeologiche sul 'Latium Novum'" I. Aquae Vescinae." *Ausonia* 6: 39–60.

Gimard, G. 1992. "Les sources salées thermales de la Tarentaise depuis les temps anciens." In Chevallier, *Les eaux thermales,* 207–14.

Ginouvès, R., et al. (eds.). 1994. *L'eau, la santé et la maladie dans the monde grec.* BCH suppl. 28. Paris.

Giovannini, A. 1985. "Le sel et la fortune de Rome." *Athenaeum* 63: 373–87.

Giovannoni, G. 1935. "L'aquedotto romano di Angita." *RPAA* 9: 63–80.

Giustolisi, V. 1976. *Parthenicum e le Aquae Segestanae.* Palermo.

Glaser, F. 1987. "Brunnen und Nymphäen." *WAS* 2: 103.

Gnecchi, F. 1912. *I Medaglioni Romani.* Vol. II. Bologna.

Goldworthy, A., and Haynes, I. (eds.). 1999. *The Roman Army as a Community.* Journal of Roman Archaeology Supplementary Series 34. Portsmouth, Rhode Island.

Gómez Fraile, J. M. 2002. "La representación geográfica de la Península Ibérica en la *Chorographia* de Pomponio Mela y en la *Naturalis Historia.* Una aproximación al espacio maritime del Mediterráneo occidental." In Khanoussi, Ruggeri, and Vismara, *L'Africa Romana,* 1515–28.

Gómez Moreno, M. 1967. *Catálogo monumental de España; provincia de Salamanca.* Madrid.

González, J. 1986. "The Lex Irnitana: A New Copy of the Flavian Municipal Law." *JRS* 76: 147–243.

González, J., and Arce, J. (eds.). 1988. *Estudios sobra la Tabula Siarensis.* Madrid.

González Román, C., and Padilla Arroba, A. (eds.). 2002. *Estudios sobre las ciudades de la Bética.* Granada.

Good, G. L., et al. 1991. *Waterfront Archaeology. Proceedings of the Third International Conference on Waterfront Archaeology held at Bristol 23-26 September 1988.* London.

Goodfellow, M. S. 1981. "North Italian Rivers and Lakes in the Georgics." *Vergilius* 27: 12–22.

Gorgues, A., Long, L., and Rico, C. 2004. "Two Major Trading Routes of the Roman Antiquity in Southern Gaul: The Narbonne-Toulouse Road and the Rhône Way towards Arles." In Pasquinucci and Weski, *Close Encounters*, 39–52.

Goudineau, C. 1980. "Les villes de la paix romaine." In Duby, *Histoire de la France urbaine*, 42–69.

———. 2000. "Gaul." In Bowman, Garnsey, and Rathbone, *Cambridge Ancient History*, 462–95.

Gowers E. 1995. "The Anatomy of Rome from Capitol to *Cloaca*." *JRS* 85: 23–32.

Grais, R. M. 1978. "Some Problems of River-God Iconography." *AJA* 82: 355–70.

Greene, K. 1986. *The Archaeology of the Roman Economy*. London.

———. 2000a. "Technological Innovation and Economic Progress in the Ancient World: M. I. Finley Re-considered." *Economic History Review* 53: 29–59.

———. 2000b. "Industry and Technology." In Bowman, Garnsey, and Rathbone, *Cambridge Ancient History*, 741–68.

Gregory, T. E. 1979. "Roman Inscriptions from Aidepsos." *GRBS* 20: 255–77.

Grenier, A. 1934. *Manuel d'archéologie Gallo-romaine*. Vol. II.2: *L'archéolgie du sol*. Paris.

———. 1960. *Manuel d'archéologie Gallo-romaine*. Vol. IV: *Les monuments des eaux. Villes d'eau et sanctuaires de l'eau*. Paris.

Grewe, K. 1988. "Die Wasserversorgung von zivilen Siedlungsplätzen und Kolonien: Lutetia Parisiorum/Paris." *WAS* 3: 78–79.

Grimal, P. 1969. *Les jardins romains*. Paris.

Gros, P. 1987. "Un programme augustéen. Le centre monumentale de la colonie d'Arles." *Jahrbuch des Deutschen Archäologischen Instituts* 102: 339–63.

Gruen, E. 1996. "The Expansion of the Empire under Augustus." In Bowman, Champlin, and Lintott, *Cambridge Ancient History*, 147–97.

Grünhagen, W. 1978. "Farbiger marmor aus Munigua." *Mitteilungen des Deutschen Archäologischen Instituts* (*Abt. Madrid*) 19: 290–306.

Gsell, S. 1911. *Atlas archéologique de l'Algérie*. Algiers and Paris.

Gualtieri, M. 1997. "A River-Seaport, the Via Appia Bridge and River Deposits at Minturnae." *JRA* 10: 347–54.

Gudea, N. (ed.). 1999. *Roman Frontier Studies. Proceedings of the XVII International Congress of Roman Frontier Studies*. Zalau.

Guillaumin, J.-Y. 1996. *Balbus. Présentation systématique de toutes les figures*. Naples.

Guillerme, A. 1983. *Les temps de l'eau: la cité, l'eau et les techniques: nord de la France: fin IIIe–début XIXe siècle*. Paris.

Haas, P. 1998. *Der locus amoenus in der antiken Literatur: zu Theorie und Geschichte eines literarischen Motivs*. Bamberg.

Habicht, C. 1985. *Pausianias' Guide to Ancient Greece*. Berkeley, Los Angeles, and London.

Hackens, A., and Marchetti, P. 1987. *Histoire économique de l'antiquité: bilans et contributions de savants belges presents dans une reunion interuniversitaire à Anvers/ Antwerpen, Universitaire Fakulteiten Sint-Ignatius*. Louvain-la-neuve.

Haensch, R., and Heinrichs, J. 2007. *Herrschen und Verwalten. Der Alltag der römischen Administration in der Hohen Kaiserzeit*. Cologne.

Haley, E. W. 2003. *Baetica Felix: People and Prosperity in Southern Spain from Caesar to Septimius Severus*. Austin.

Hallof, K. 1994. "Die Inschrift von Skaptopara: neue dokumente und neue Lesungen." *Chiron* 24: 405–41.

Halstead, P., and O'Shea, J. 1989. *Bad year Economics: Cultural Responses to Risk and Uncertainty*. Cambridge.

Hammond, N. G. L. 1967. *Epirus. The Geography, the Ancient Remains, the History and the Topography of Epirus and Adjacent Areas*. Oxford.

Hanson, A. E., and Green, M. H. 1994. "Soranus of Ephesus: '*Methodicorum Princeps*,'" *ANRW* 37.2, 968–1075.

Hanson, W. S. (ed.). 2009. *The Army and Frontiers of Rome*. Journal of Roman Archaeology Supplementary Series, 74. Portsmouth, Rhode Island.

Harley, J. B., and Woodward, D. (eds.). 1987. *The History of Cartography*. Vol. 1: *Cartography in Prehistoric, Ancient, and Medieval Europe and the Mediterranean*. Chicago and London.

Harris, H. A. 1972. *Sport in Greece and Rome*. London.

Harris, W. V. 1979. *War and Imperialism in Republican Rome, 327–70 B.C.* Oxford.

———. 1989. "Trade and the River Po: A Problem in the Economic History of the Roman Empire." In Bergier, *Montagnes, fleuves, forêts*, 123–34.

Hartley, B. R. 1969. "Samian ware or *terra sigillata*." In R. G. Collingwood and I. Richmond, *The Archaeology of Roman Britain*, 235–51.

Hartley, B. R., and Wacher, J. S. (eds.). 1983. *Rome and Her Northern Frontiers*. Gloucester.

Haselberger, L., Romano, D. G., and Dumser, E. A. (ed.). 2002. *Mapping Augustan Rome*, Journal of Roman Archaeology Supplementary Series 50. Portsmouth, Rhode Island.

Haslam, S. M. 1991. *The Historic River: Rivers and Culture Down the Ages*. Cambridge.

———. 1997. *The River Scene: Ecology and Cultural Heritage*. Cambridge.

Hassall, M. 1978. "Britain and the Rhine Provinces: Epigraphic Evidence for Roman Trade." In du Plat Taylor and Cleere, *Roman Shipping and Trade*, 41–48.

Hassel, F. J. 1966. *Der Trajansbogen in Benevent. Ein Bauwerk des römischen Senates*. Mainz.

Hatt, J.-J. 1954. "Les fouilles de Strasbourg en 1953 et 1954." *Gallia* 12: 323–43.

———. 1970a. "Découverts archéologiques à Strasbourg Rue du Puits." *CAAH* 14: 91–100.

———. 1970b. "L'Alsace romaine." In Dollinger, *Histoire de l'Alsace*, 27–55.

Hauck, G. 1988. *The Aqueduct of Nemausus*. Jefferson, N.C., and London.

Hayes, J. W., and Martini, I. P. (eds.). 1994. *Archaeological Survey in the Lower Liri Valley, Central Italy*. BAR International Series 595. Oxford.

Head, B. V. 1892. *Catalogue of Greek Coins of Ionia*. London.

———. 1897. *Catalogue of Greek Coins of Caria in British Museum*. London.

———. 1901. *Catalogue of Greek Coins of Lydia in British Museum*. London.

———. 1906. *Catalogue of Greek Coins of Phrygia in British Museum*. London.

———. 1911. *Historia Nummorum*. 2nd ed. London.

Healy, J. F. 1975. *Mining and Metallurgy in the Greek and Roman World*. London.

———. 1999. *Pliny the Elder on Science and Technology*. Oxford.

Heicheleim, F. M. 1940. "The Text of the Constitutio Antoniniana and the Three Other Decrees of the Emperor Caracalla Contained in *Papyrus Gissensis* 40." *JEA* 26: 10–22.

Heiken, G., Funiciello, R., and de Rita, D. 2005. *The Seven Hills of Rome: A Geological Tour of the Eternal City*. Princeton and Oxford.

Heinz, W. H. 1983. *Römische Thermen: Badenwesen und Badeluxus im römischen Reich*. Munich.

———. 1986. "Die 'Terme Taurine' von Civitavecchia—ein römisches Heilbad." *AW* 17.4: 22–43.

———. 1999. "Subtlety and Ingenuity in Architecture: The Roman Spa of Badenweiler." In DeLaine and Johnston, *Roman Baths*, 185–89.

Hermann, P. 1994. "Milet unter Augustus. C. Iulius Epikrates und die Anfänge des Kaiserkults." *Mitteilungen des Deutschen Archäologischen Instituts* (*Abt. Istanbul*) 44: 203–36.

Hermon, E. (ed.) 1999. *La question agraire à Rome: droit romain et société*. Perceptions historiques et historiographiques. Como.

———. 2001. *Habiter et partager les terres avant les Gracques*. Collection de l'école française de Rome 286. Rome.

———. 2008a. "Les savoirs traditionnels et la perception de l'eau comme patrimonie naturel et culturel dans le *Corpus Agrimensorum Romanorum*." In Hermon, *L'eau comme patrimonie*, 441–60.

——— (ed.). 2008b. *L'eau comme patrimonie de la Méditerranée à l'Amérique du Nord*. Quebec.

——— (ed.). 2009. *Société et Climats dans L'Empire romain. Pour une Perspective historique et systématique de la Gestion des Ressources en Eau dans L'Empire romain*. Naples.

——— (ed.). 2010. *Riparia dans L'Empire romain: pour la définition du concept. Actes des Journées d'Étude de Québec, 29–31 Octobre 2009*. BAR International Series 2066. Oxford.

Herring, E., Whitehouse, R., and Wilkins, J. 1992. *Papers of the Fourth Conference of Italian Archaeology. New developments in Italian Archaeology*, part 2. London.

Heurgon, J. 1952. "Le date des goblets de Vicarello." *Revue des Études Anciennes* 54: 39–50.

———. 1959. "The Date of Vergoia's Prophecy." *JRS* 49: 41–45.

Hilali, A. 2010. "*Castra et flumen* en Afrique romaine." In Hermon, *Riparia dans L'Empire romain*, 101–12.

Hinrichs, F. T. 1974. *Die Geschichte der gromatischen Institutionen*. Wiesbaden.

Hirschfeld, Y. 1997. *The Roman Baths at Hammat Gader: Final Report*. Jerusalem.

Hirschfeld, Y., and Solar, G. 1981. "The Roman Thermae at Hammat Gader: Preliminary Report of Three Seasons of Excavation." *IEJ* 31: 197–219.

Höckmann, O. 1986. "Römischer Schiffsverbände auf dem über und mittelrhein und die Verteigigung der Rheingrenze in der Spätantike." *Jahrbuch des römisch-germanischen Zentralmuseums Mainz* 33: 369–419.

———. 1993. "Late Roman Rhine Vessels from Mainz, Germany." *IJNA* 22: 125–35.

Hoddinott, R. F. 1975. *Bulgaria in Antiquity*. New York.

Hodge, A. T. (ed.). 1991. *Future Currents in Aqueduct Studies*. Leeds.

———. 2002. *Roman Aqueducts*. 2nd ed. London.

Hodges, R. 1995. "The Archaeology of the Vicarello Estate, Lake Bracciano." *PBSR* 63, 245–49.

Holland, L. A. 1961. *Janus and the Bridge*. Papers and Monographs of the American Academy in Rome, vol. XXI. Rome.

Holland, L. A., and Holland, L. B. 1950. "Down the Tiber on a Raft." *Archaeology* 3: 87–94.

Holleaux, M. 1938. *Études d'épigraphie et d'histoire grecques*. Vol. 1. Paris.

Hopkins, K. 1982. "The Transport of Staples in the Roman Empire." *Eighth International Economic History Congress, Budapest 1982*. Budapest, 81–87.

Horden, P., and Purcell, N. 2000. *The Corrupting Sea: A Study of Mediterranean History*. Oxford.

Horn, H. G. (ed.). 1987. *Die Römer in Nordrhein-Westfalen*. Stuttgart.

Hornblower, S., and Matthews, E. (eds.). 2000. *Greek Personal Names: Their Value as Evidence*. Oxford.

Horsfall, N. 2000. *Virgil, Aeneid 7. A Commentary*. Leiden.

Houston, G. 1988a. "Ports in Perspective: Some Comparative Materials on Roman Merchant Ships and Ports." *AJA* 92: 553–64.

———. 1988b. "The administration of Italian Seaports during the First Three Centuries of the Roman Empire." In D'Arms and Kopff, *The Seaborne Commerce of Ancient Rome*, 157–71.

———. 1992. "The *Other* Spas of Ancient Campania." In Wilhelm and Jones, *The Two Worlds of the Poet*, 356–70.

Howald, E., and Meyer, E. (eds.). 1940. *Die römische Schweiz. Texte und Inschriften mit Übersetzung*. Zurich.

Howgego, C., Heuchert, V., and Burnett, A. (eds.). 2005. *Coinage and Identity in the Roman Provinces*. Oxford.

Hoyos, D. 1979. "Pliny the Elder's Titled Baetican Towns: Obscurities, Errors and Origins." *Historia* 28: 439–71.

Hugot, L. 1963. "Die römischen Büchelthermen in Aachen." *BJ* 163: 188–97.

Hunt, E. D. 1982. *Holy Land Pilgrimage in the Later Roman Empire, A.D. 312–460.* Oxford.

Huntingford, G. W. B. 1980. *The Periplus of the Erythraean Sea.* London.

Hyde, K. van der. 1932. "*Flumen, fluvius, amnis.*" *Mnemosyne* 60: 135–46.

I campi flegrei nell'archeologia e nella storia: Atti del convegno dei Lincei, Roma 4–7 maggio 1976. 1977. Rome.

Imhoof-Blumer, F. 1923. "Fluss und Meergötter auf griechischen und römischen Münzen." *RSNum* 23: 173–421.

Ireland, R. 1984. *Anonymi Auctoris De Rebus Bellicis.* Leipzig.

Isaac, B. 1988. "The Meaning of the Terms *limes* and *limitanei.*" *JRS* 78: 125–47.

———. 1992. *The Limits of Empire: The Roman Army in the East.* Oxford.

Isler, H. P. 1970. *Acheloos.* Bern.

Jackson, R. 1990. "Waters and Spas in the Classical World." In Porter, *The Medical History of Waters and Spas*, 1–14.

———. 1993. "Roman Medicine: The Practitioners and Their Practices." In *ANRW* II.37.1, 79–111.

———. 1999. "Spas, Waters, and Hydrotherapy in the Roman World." In DeLaine and Johnston, *Roman Baths*, 107–16.

Jacob, C. 1991. *Géographie et ethnographie en Grèce ancienne.* Paris.

Jalabert, L., Mouterde, R., et al. 1929–. *Inscriptions grecques et latines de la Syrie.* Paris.

Jalmain, D. 1972. "Étude des voies romaines entre Seine et Loire." *Colloque international sur la Cartographie archéologique et historique, Paris 1970.* Tours, 111–14.

Janni, P. 1984. *La mappa e il Periplo.* Rome.

Jeskins, P. 1998. *The Environment and the Classical World.* London.

Jiménez, A. 1976. "Los acueductos de Mérida." *Symposium.* Madrid, 11–25.

Johannowsky, W. 1994. "Canali e fiumi per il trasporti del grano." In *Le ravitaillement en blé de Rome*, 159–65.

Johnson, A. C., Coleman-Norton, A. R., and Bourne, F. C. 1961. *Ancient Roman Statutes. A Translation with Introduction, Commentary, Glossary, and Index.* Austin.

Johnson, F. 1983. *Late Roman Fortifications.* London.

Johnson, J. 1933. *Excavations at Minturnae.* Vol. 2. Philadelphia.

———. 1935. *Excavations at Minturnae.* Vol. 1. Philadelphia.

———. 1940. *RE* Suppl. VII, *Minturnae*, 458–94.

Johnston, D. E. (ed.). 1977. *The Saxon Shore.* London.

Jones, A. H. M. 1964. *The Later Roman Empire, 284–602.* 2 vols. Oxford.

Jones, B., and Mattingly, D. J. 1990. *An Atlas of Roman Britain.* Oxford.

Jones, C. P. 1991. "Aelius Aristides on the water in Pergamon." *AA*, 111–17.

———. 2003. "Editing and understanding Pausanias" (review of Knoepfler and Piérart, 2001). *JRA* 16: 673–76.

———. 2006. "A Letter of Hadrian to Naryka (Eastern Locris)." *JRA* 19: 151–62.

Jones, G. D. B. 1962. "Capena and the Ager Capenas I." *PBSR* 30: 116–207.

———. 1963. "Capena and the Ager Capenas II." *PBSR* 31: 100–158.

———. 1980. "The Roman Mines at Rio Tinto." *JRS* 70: 146–65.

Jones, H. L. 1918–35. *Strabo. Geography, with an English Translation.* 8 vols. Cambridge, Mass., and London.

Jones, P. J. 2005. *Reading Rivers in Roman Literature and Culture.* Lanham, Boulder, New York, Toronto, and Oxford.

Jouffroy, H. 1986. *La construction publique en Italie et dans l'Afrique romaine.* Strasbourg, 1986.

———. 1992. "Les *Aquae* africaines." In Chevallier, *Les eaux thermales,* 87–99.

Judson, S., and Kahane, A. 1961. "Underground Drainageways in Southern Etruria." *PBSR* 29: 47–52.

Kahane, A., Threipland, M., and Ward-Perkins, J. B. 1968. "The Ager Veietanus, North and East of Veii." *PBSR* 36: 1–218.

Karanjac, J., and Günay, G. 1980. "Dumanli Spring, Turkey—the Largest Spring in the World?" *Journal of Hydrology* 45: 19–35.

Keay, S. J. 1988. *Roman Spain.* London.

———. 1998a. "Introduction. Early Roman Baetica." In Keay, *The Archaeology of Early Roman Baetica,* 11–22.

———. 1998b. "The Development of Towns in Early Roman Baetica." In Keay, *The Archaeology of Early Roman Baetica,* 55–86.

——— (ed.). 1998c. *The Archaeology of Early Roman Baetica.* Journal of Roman Archaeology Supplementary Series 29. Portsmouth, Rhode Island.

Keay, S. J., Millett, M., Paroli, L., and Strutt, K. 2005. *Portus: An Archaeological Survey of the Port of Imperial Rome.* Archaeological Monographs of the British School at Rome 15. London.

Keay, S. J., and Terrenato, N. (eds.). 2001. *Italy and the West: Comparative Issues in Romanization.* Oxford.

Keay, S. J., et al. 2004. "New Approaches to Roman Urbanism in the Tiber Valley." In H. Patterson, *Bridging the Tiber,* 223–36.

Kehoe, D. P. 1988. *The Economics of Agriculture on Roman Imperial Estates in North Africa.* Göttingen.

Kellner, H. J. 1961. "Zur Sigillata-Töpferei von Westerndorf." *Bayerische Vorgeschichtsblätter* 26: 165–203.

Kennedy, D. (ed.). 1996. *The Roman Army in the East.* Journal of Roman Archaeology Supplementary Series 18. Ann Arbor.

———. 1998. *The Twin Towns of Zeugma on the Euphrates: Rescue Work and Historical Studies.* Journal of Roman Archaeology Supplementary Series 27. Portsmouth, Rhode Island.

Keppie, L. 1983. *Colonisation and Veteran Settlement in Italy, 47–14 B.C.* London.

———. 1991. *Understanding Roman Inscriptions* London.

Khanoussi, M., Ruggeri, P., and Vismara, C. 2002. *L'Africa Romana. Lo spazio marittimo* del Mediterraneo occidentale: geografia storica ed economia. Atti del XIV convegno di studio Sassari, 7–10 dicembre 2000. Sassari.

King, A. 1990. *Roman Gaul and Germany*. London.

Kleiner, F. S. 1991. "The Trophy on the Bridge and the Roman Triumph over Nature." *AC* 60: 182–92.

Klementa, S. 1993. *Gelagerte Flussgötter des Späthellenismus und der römischen Kaiserzeit*. Cologne.

Kneissl, P. 1981. "Die Utriclarii: ihr Rolle im gallo-römischen Transportwesen und Weinhandel." *BJ* 181: 169–204.

Knoepfler, D. 2000. "Oropodorus. Anthroponomy, Geography, History." In Hornblower and Matthews, *Greek Personal Names*, 81–98.

Knoepfler, D., and Piérart, M. 2001. *Éditer, traduire, commenter Pausanias en l'an 2000. Actes du Colloque de Neuchâtel et de Fribourg 18–22 Sept. 1998*. Neuchâtel.

Kockel, V. 1985. "Beobachtungen zum Tempel des Mars Ultor und zum Forum des Augustus." *Mitteilungen des Deutschen Archäologischen Instituts (Röm. Abt.)* 92: 201–19.

Koller, H., and Doswald, C. 1996. *Aquae Helveticae-Baden*. Veröffentlichungen der Gesellschaft pro Vindonissa 13. Baden.

Kolowski-Ostrow, A., et al. 1997. "Water in the Roman Town." *JRA* 10: 181–91.

Konen, H. 2000. *Classis Germanica. Die römischen Rheinflotte im 1.–3. Jahrhundert n. Chr.* St. Katharinen.

———. 2002 "Die ökonomische Bedeutung der Provinzialflotten während der Zeit des Prinzipates." In Erdkamp, *The Roman Army and the Economy*, 309–42.

Kron, G. 2005. "Sustainable Roman Intensive Mixed Farming Methods: Water Conservation and Erosion Control." In Bedon and Hermon, *Concepts*, 285–308.

———. 2008. "Animal Husbandry, Hunting, Fishing and Fish Production." In Oleson, *The Oxford Handbook of Engineering and Technology*, 175–222.

Kühn, C. G. 1821–33. *Claudii Galeni Opera Omnia*. Leipzig. Repr., 1964–65.

Künzl, E., and Künzl, S. 1992. "Aquae Apollinares/Vicarello (Italien)." In Chevallier, *Les eaux thermales*, 273–96.

La Baume, P. 1975. *The Romans on the Rhine*. 3rd ed. Translated by B. Jones. Bonn.

Labisch, A. 1975. *Frumentum Commeatusque: Die Nahrungsmittelversorgung der Heere Caesars*. Beiträge zur Klassischen Philogie 69. Meisenheim an Glan.

Labrousse, M. 1977. "Une ville et un fleuve: Toulouse et la Garonne." In Duval and Frézouls, *Thèmes de recherches*, 325–28.

Labud, G. 1995. *Ricerche archeologico-ambientali dell'Istria settentrionale: la valle del fiume Risano*. Jonsered.

Lacroix, B. 1964. "Une installation artisanale aux Fontaines Salées (Yonne)." *Gallia* 22: 111–35.

Lacroix, L. 1953. "Fleuves et nymphes eponyms sur les monnaies antiques de la Sicile." *RBN* 99: 5–21.

Lafond, Y. 2001. "Lire Pausanias a l'époque des Antonins. Réflexions sur la place de la *Périégèse* dans l'histoire culturelle, religieuse et sociale de la Grèce romaine." In Knoepfler and Piérart, *Éditer*, 387–406.

Lambeck, K. 1996. "Sea-Level Change and Shore-Line Evolution: Aegean Greece since the Upper Paleolithic." *Antiquity* 269: 588–611.

La mobilité des paysages mediterranéens: Hommage à Pierre Birot. 1984. Toulouse.

Landels, J. 1978. *Engineering in the Ancient World*. New edition, 1997. London.

Lapadula, E. 1997. "Le anfore di Spello nelle Regiones VI e VII." *PBSR* 65: 127–56.

La Rocca, E. 1984. *La riva a mezzaluna*. Rome.

Laubenheimer, F. (ed.). 1992. *Les amphores en Gaulle. Production et Circulation*. Annales littéraires de l'Université de Besançon. Paris.

Lauffer, S. 1985. "Problèmes de Copaïs, solutions et énigmes." In *La Béotie antique*. Paris, 101–8.

———— (ed.). 1989. *Griechenland. Lexicon der historischen Stätten*. Munich.

Laurence, R. 1998. "Land Transport in Roman Italy: Costs, Practice and the Economy." In Parkins and Smith, *Trade*, 129–48.

————. 1999. *The Roads of Roman Italy: Mobility and Cultural Change*. London.

————. 2004. "The Economic Exploitation of Geological Resources in the Tiber Valley: Road Building." In H. Patterson, *Bridging the Tiber*, 285–95.

La ville et le fleuve. Colloque tenu dans le cadre du 112e Congrès national des Sociétés savants, Lyon, 21–25 avril 1987. 1989. Paris.

Lazzaro, L. 1981. *Fons Aponi. Abano e Montegrotto nell'antichità*. Padua.

Leach, E. W. 1988. *The Rhetoric of Space: Literacy and Artistic Representation of Landscape in Republican and Augustan Rome*. Princeton.

Lebek, W. D. 1989. "Die Mainzer Ehrungen für Germanicus, der älteren Drusus und Domitian." *ZPE* 78: 45–82.

Lebel, P. 1950. "Noms de rivières et migrations préhistoriques." *RAE* 1: 236–42.

Le Gall, J. 1953a. *Le Tibre, fleuve de Rome dans l'antiquité*. Paris.

————. 1953b. *Recherches sur le culte du Tibre*. Paris.

————. 1977. "Le Tibre et Rome pendant les siècles obscurs, esquisse d'une revision." In Duval and Frézouls, *Thèmes de recherches*, 273–78.

————. 1983. "La diffusion de l'huile espagnole dans la Gaule du Nord." In Blázquez Martínez and Remesal Rodríguez, *Producción y comercio del aceite en la antigüedad. Secondo congreso internacional*, 213–23.

————. 1988. "Le Tibre, fleuve guérisseur." *Dossier d'histoire et d'archéologie* 123, 16–21.

————. 1994. "Un mode de transport méconnu: les animaux de bât." In *Le ravitaillement en blé de Rome*, 69–72.

Leggio, T. 2004. "Il Tevere e le vie di terra nell'alto medioevo." In H. Patterson, *Bridging the Tiber*, 297–305.

Le Glay, M. 1977. "Le Rhône dans la gènese et le development de Vienne." In Duval and Frézouls, *Thèmes de recherches*, 307–17.

———. 1980–81. "Une nouvelle inscription Lyonnaise." *Bulletin de la Société nationale des Antiquaires de France*, 295–304.

Le Lannou, M. 1977. "Le role des communications fluviales dans la gènese et le développement des villes antiques." In Duval and Frézouls, *Thèmes de recherches*, 29–34.

Lengyel, A., and Raban, G. T. B. (eds.). 1980. *The Archaeology of Roman Pannonia*. Budapest.

Lenoir, M., Manacorda, D., and Panella, C. (eds.). 1989. *Amphores romaines et histoire économique: dix ans de recherche*. Collection de L'École Française de Rome 114. Rome, 590–93.

Lepore, E. 1977. "Fiumi e città nella colonizzazione greca in occidente, con speciale riguardo alla Maga Grecia." In Duval and Frézouls, *Thèmes de recherches*, 267–72.

Lepper, F., and Frere, S. 1988. *Trajan's Column*. Gloucester.

Le ravitaillement en blé de Rome et des centres urbains des débuts de la république jusqu'au haut empire. Actes du colloque international organisé par le Centre Jean Bérard et l'URA 994 du CNRS, Naples, 14–16 Février 1991. 1994. Naples and Rome.

Letta, C. 1972. *I Marsi e il Fucino nell'antichità*. Milan.

Leveau, P. 1988. "Saldae." *WAS* 3: 215–18.

———. 1993. "Mentalité économique et grands traveaux hydrauliques: le drainage du lac Fucin aux origins d'un modèle." *Annales ESC* 48.1: 3–16.

———. 1996. "The Barbegal Water Mill in Its Environment: Archaeology and the Economic and Social History of Antiquity." *JRA* 9: 137–53.

———. 2005a. "Frontières internes dans l'Empire romain et écologie d'un delta méditerranéen. Le cas du Rhône." In Bedon at Hermon, *Concepts*, 103–23.

———. 2005b. "Comprendre les environnements pour prévenir les catastrophes: la place de l'historien et de l'archéologue dans l'evaluation du risque." In Bedon and Hermon, *Concepts*, 377–98.

Leveau, P., and Provansal, M. 1991. "Construction Deltaïque et histoire des systems agricoles, le cas d'un petit delta: L'arc, étang de Berre." *RAN* 24: 111–31.

Leveau, P., et al. 1999. "Le Rhône romain: dynamiques fluviales, dynamiques territoriales." *Gallia* 56: 1–175.

Levi, A., and Levi, M. 1967. *Itineraria Picta. Contributo allo studio della Tabula Peutingeriana*. Rome.

Levi, P. 1971. *Pausanias, Guide to Greece*. Harmondsworth.

Levick, B. 1990. *Claudius*. London.

Lewis, A. 1983. "The Meaning of Institutes II.1.20." In Stein and Lewis, *Studies in Justinian's Institutes*, 87–95.

Lewis, M. J. T. 1997. *Millstone and Hammer: The Origins of Water Power*. Hull.

———. 2001. *Surveying Instruments of Greece and Rome*. Cambridge.

Lewis, P. R., and Jones, G. D. B. 1969. "The Dolaucothi Gold Mines, 1: The Surface Evidence." *Antiquaries Journal* 49: 244–72.

———. 1970. "Roman Gold Mining in North-West Spain." *JRS* 60: 169–85.

Lewit, T. 1991. *Agricultural Production in the Roman Economy*. Oxford.

Lightfoot, C. S. 1990. "Trajan's Parthian War and the Fourth-Century Perspective." *JRS* 80: 115–26.

Lightfoot, J. L. 2002. *Lucian on the Syrian Goddess. Edited with Introduction, Translation and Commentary*. Oxford.

———. 2007. *The Sibylline Oracles. With Introduction, Translation and Commentary on the First and Second Books*. Oxford.

Lindsay, W. M. (ed.). 1903. *Nonii Marcelli De Conpendiosa Doctrina Libri XX*. Leipzig.

———. 1911. *Isidori Hispalensis Episcopi Etymologiarum sive Originum libri XX*. Oxford.

Liverani, P. 1987. *Municipium Augustum Veiens: Veio in età imperiale attraverso gli scavi Giorgi (1811–1813)*. Rome.

Livingstone, D. 1995. "The Polity of Nature: Representation, Virtue, Strategy." *Ecumene* 2: 353–77.

Löhberg, B. 2006. *Das "Itinerarium provinciarum Antonini Augusti": Ein kaiserzeitliches Straßenverzeichnis des römischen Reiches—Überlieferung, Strecken, Kommentare, Karten*. 2 vols. Berlin.

López Monteagudo, G. 2002. "El impacto del comercio maritime en tres ciudades del interior de la Bética, a través de los mosaicos." In Khanoussi, Ruggeri, and Vismara, *L'Africa Romana*, 595–626.

Löringhoff, B., Mannsperger, D., and Prayon, F. (eds.). 1982. *Praestant Interna. Festschrift für Ulrich Hausmann*. Tübingen.

Lowenthal, D. and. Bowden M. (eds.). 1976. *Geographies of the Mind: Essays in Historical Geosophy in Honor of John Kirkland Wright*. Oxford.

Luquet, A. 1964. "Moulay-Yakoub: bains romains." *BAM* 5: 357.

L'Urbs: espace urbain et histoire (Ier siècle av. J.-C.–IIIe siècle ap. J.C.): actes du colloque international organisé par le Centre national de la recherche scientifique et l'École française de Rome (Rome, 8–12 mai 1985). 1987. Rome.

Lussault, A. 1997. *Carte archéologique de la Gaule 65. Hautes-Pyrénées*. Paris.

Luttwak, E. N. 1976. *The Grand Strategy of the Roman Empire from the First Century* A.D. *to the Third*. Baltimore and London.

MacDougall, E. B. (ed.). 1987. *Ancient Roman Villa Gardens*. Dumbarton Oaks Colloquium on the History of Landscape Architecture X. Washington, D.C.

Maddalena, P. 1970. *Gli incrementi fluviali nella visione giurisprudenziale classica*. Naples.

Maddoli, G. (ed.). 1988. *Strabone e l'Italia antica. Incontri Perugini di storia della storiografia antica e sul mondo antico. II Acquasparta Palazzo Cesi, 25–27 Maggio 1987*. Naples.

Maganzani, L. 2010. "*Riparia* et phénomènes fluviaux entre histoire, archéologie et droit." In Hermon, *Riparia dans L'Empire romain*, 247–62.

Magie, D. 1950. *Roman Rule in Asia Minor*. 2 vols. Princeton.

Maiuri, A. 1969. *The Phlegraean Fields*. Rome.

Malissard, A. 1994. *Les romains et l'eau: fontaines, salles de bains, thermes, égouts, aqueducs*. Paris.

———. 2008. "Un example de creation urbaine en milieu humide: Rome." In Hermon, *L'eau comme patrimonie*, 237–56.

Malone, C., Stoddart, S., and Allegrucci, F. (eds.). 1994. *Territory, Time and State: The Archaeological Development of the Gubbio Basin*. Cambridge.

Maltby, R. 2002. *Tibullus: Elegies. Text, Introduction and Commentary*. Cambridge.

Manconi, D. 1989. "Anfore romane in Umbria alla sinistra riva del Tevere." In Lenoir, Manacorda, and Panella, *Amphores romaines*, 590–93.

Manière, G. 1980. "La station Gallo-romaine des *Aquae Siccae à Saint-Cizy (Haute-Garonne)*." *Gallia* 38: 137–68.

Mann, J. C. 1974. "The Frontiers of the Principate." *ANRW* II.1, 508–33.

———. 1977. "*Duces* and *comites* in the Fourth Century." In Johnston, *The Saxon Shore*, 11–14.

———. 1979. "Power, Force and the Frontiers of the Empire." *JRS* 69: 175–83.

Mann, R. 1973. *Rivers in the City*. Newton Abbot.

Marazzi, F. 2004. "La valle del Tevere nella tarda antichità: inquadramento dei problemi archeologici." In H. Patterson, *Bridging the Tiber*, 103–9.

Marchese, R. T. 1986. *The Lower Maeander Flood Plain: A Regional Settlement Study*. 2 vols. BAR International Series 292. Oxford.

Mari, Z. 1991. "Nuovi cippi degli acquedotti aniensi. Considerazioni sull'uso dei cippi acquari." *PBSR* 59: 151–75.

Marini Calvani, M. 1992. "Acque minerali, risorsa storica dell'Emilia occidentale." In Chevallier, *Les eaux thermales*, 297–307.

Martin, A. 1960. "Circonscription d'Dijon." *Gallia* 18: 356–60.

———. 1962. "Circonscription d'Dijon." *Gallia* 20: 467–71.

———. 1980. "Les activités commerciales en Gaule libre, en Bretagne et en Germanie: le témoignage du *Bellum Gallicum*." *Études Classiques* 48.4: 333–40.

Martín-Bueno, M. 2008. "Cisterns, Aqueducts, Channels and Transfers: Past and Present in Water Management in the Iberian Peninsula." In Hermon, *L'eau comme patrimonie*, 257–72.

Martini, I. P. 1994. "The Genesis of an Environment: Elements of Geology, Geomorphology and Land Use." In Hayes and Martini, *Archaeological Survey in the Lower Liri Valley*, 5–10.

Martyn, J. R. C. (ed.). 1972. *Cicero and Virgil. Studies in Honour of Harold Hunt*. Amsterdam.

Mason, D. J. P. 1987. "Chester: The Canabae Legionis." *Britannia* 18: 143–68.

Mattern, S. 1999. *Rome and the Enemy: Imperial Strategy in the Principate*. Berkeley, Los Angeles, and London.

———. 2008. *Galen and the Rhetoric of Healing*. Baltimore and London.

Mattingly, D. J. 1988. "Oil for Export? A Comparison of Libyan, Spanish and Tunisian Olive Oil Production in the Roman Empire." *JRA* 1: 33–56.

————. 1994. *Tripolitania*. Ann Arbor.

Mattingly, D. J., and Aldrete, S. 2000. "The Feeding of Imperial Rome: The Mechanics of the Food Supply System." In Coulson and Dodge, *Ancient Rome*, 142–65.

Mayer, M., and Rodà, I. 1998. "The Use of Marble and Decorative Stone in Roman Baetica." In Keay, *The Archaeology of Early Roman Baetica*, 217–34.

McCormick, M. 2001. *Origins of the European Economy. Communications and Commerce, A.D. 300–900*. Cambridge.

McGrail, S. 2008. "Sea transport, Part 1: Ships and Navigation." In Oleson, *The Oxford Handbook of Engineering and Technology*, 606–37.

McIntosh, R. P. 1985. *The Background of Ecology: Concept and Theory*. Cambridge.

McKay, A. G. 1972. "Vergil's Glorification of Italy (*Georgics* II.136–74)." In Martyn, *Cicero and Virgil*, 149–68.

————. 1988. "Pleasure Domes at Baiae." *Studia Pompeiana et Classica* 2: 155–72.

McKechnie, P. 2002. *Thinking like a Lawyer: Essays on Legal History and General History for John Crook on His Eightieth Birthday*. Leiden.

McKeown, J. C. 1987–89. *Ovid: Amores. Text, Prolegomena and Commentary*. 3 vols. Liverpool.

Meiggs, R. 1960. *Roman Ostia*. Oxford. 2nd ed., 1973.

————. 1982. *Trees and Timber in the Ancient Mediterranean World*. Oxford.

Meijer, F., and van Nijf, O. 1992. *Trade, Transport and Society in the Ancient World: A Sourcebook*. London and New York.

Meneghini, R. 1985. "Attività e installazione portuali lungo il Tevere. La Riva dell'Emporium." In *Misurare la terra: centuriazione e coloni nel mondo romano. Città, agricultura, commercio: materiali da Roma e dal suburbia*. Modena, 162–71.

Mensching, E. 1981. "Die Koblenzer Rehinbrücke, P. Pomponius Secundus und der Brüchkenbrau am Rhien und Mosel." *BJ* 181: 325–54.

Menu, B. (ed.). 1994. *Les problèmes institutionnels de l'eau en Égypte ancienne et dans l'antiquité méditerranéenne*. Cairo.

Merino, J., Nolla, J. M., and Santos, M. 1994. *Aquae Calidae, presència romana a la Selva, Santa Coloma de Farners*. La Selva.

Meshel, Z., et al. 1996. *The Water Supply of Susita*. Tel Aviv and Lubeck.

Mesqui, J. 1986. *Le pont en France avant le temps des ingénieurs*. Paris.

Middleton, P. 1979. "Army Supply in Roman Gaul: An Hypothesis for Roman Britain." In Burnham and Johnson, *Invasion and response*, 81–97.

————. 1980. "La Graufesenque: A Question of Marketing." *Athenaeum* 58: 186–91.

————. 1983. "The Roman Army and Long-Distance Trade." In Garnsey and Whittaker, *Trade and Famine*, 75–83.

Mildenberger, G. 1972. "Terra nigra aus Nordhessen." *Fundberichte aus Hessen* 12: 104–26.

Millar, F. 1988. "Imperial Ideology in the Tabula Siarensis." In González and Arce, *Estudios*, 11–19.

————. 1993. *The Roman Near East, 31 B.C.–A.D. 337*. Cambridge Mass.

Millett, M. 1991. "Roman Towns and Their Territories: An Archaeological Perspective."
    In Rich and Wallace-Hadrill, *City and Country*, 169–89.

Milne, G. 1985. *The Port of Roman London*. London.

Mitchell, S. 1982. "The Life of Saint Theodotus of Ancyra." *AS* 32: 93–113.

———. 1993. *Anatolia: Land, Men and Gods in Asia Minor*. Vol. 1. Oxford.

Moatti, C. 1993. *Archives et partage de la terre dans le monde romain (IIe siècle avant–Ie
    après J.-C)*. Rome.

Mocchegiani Carpano, C. 1975–76. "Rapporto preliminare sulle indagini nel tratto
    urbano del Tevere." *RPAA* 48: 239–62.

———. 1981. "Indagini archeologiche nel Tevere." *AL* 4: 142–55.

———. 1982. "Tevere. Premesse per una archeologia fluvial." *BdA*, suppl. 4: 150–70.

———. 1984. "Il Tevere: archeologia e commercio." *Bollettino di Numismatica* 2.2:
    21–81.

Mócsy, A. 1974. *Pannonia and Upper Moesia*. London.

Moitrieux, G. 1992. "Hercule et le culte des sources en Lorraine." In Chevallier, *Les eaux
    thermales*, 67–76.

Molto, A. 1992. "Aguas minero-medicinales en los yacimientos termales de Hispania."
    In Chevallier, *Les eaux thermales*, 117–27.

Momigliano, A. 1938. *Thybris Pater*. Turin.

Momigliano, A., and Schiavone, A. 1988. (eds.). *Storia di Roma*, I: *Roma in Italia*. Turin.

Mommsen, Th. 1963. *Römisches Staatsrecht*. 3 vols. Repr., Basel and Stuttgart.

Moore, F. G. 1950. "Three Canal Projects, Roman and Byzantine." *AJA* 54: 97–111.

Mora, G. 1981. "Las termas romanas en Hispania." *AEA* 54: 37–90.

Moreau, J. 1972. *Dictionnaire de géographie historique de la Gaul et de la France*. Paris.

Morlet, A. 1957. *Vichy Gallo-Romain*. Macon.

Morley, N. 1996. *Metropolis and Hinterland: The City of Rome and the Italian Economy,
    200 B.C.–A.D. 200*. Cambridge.

Moynihan, R. 1985. "Geographical Mythology and Roman Imperial Ideology." In
    Winks, *The Age of Augustus*, 149–57.

Müller, C. 1854; 1861. *Geographi Graeci Minores*. 2 vols. Paris.

———. 1883–91. *Claudii Ptolemaei Geographia*. Vol. 1, parts 1–2. Paris.

———. 1901. *Claudii Ptolemaei Geographia: Tabulae XXXVI a Carolo Mullero
    Instructae*. Paris.

Murgatroyd, P. 1980. *Tibullus I. A Commentary on the First Book of the Elegies of Albius
    Tibullus*. Pietermaritzburg.

Murphy, T. 2003. "Pliny's *Naturalis Historia*: The Prodigal Text." In Boyle and Dominik,
    Flavian Rome, 301–22.

———. 2004. *Pliny the Elder's* Natural History: *The Empire in the Encyclopedia*. Oxford.

Muzzioli, M. P. 1985. "Capena e Lucus Feroniae." In *Misurare la terra: centuriazione
    e coloni nel mondo romano. Città, agricoltura, commercio: materiali da Roma e dal
    suburbia*. Modena, 53–58.

———. 1992. "La topografia della IX regione di Roma." *PBSR* 60, 179–211.

Nardi, G. 1980. *Le Antichità di Orte. Esame del territorio e dei materiali archeologici.* Rome.

Neboit, R, Dufaure, J.-J., Julian, M., Guigo, M., Holloway, N. D., and Holloway, R., 1984. "Facteurs naturels et humains dans la morphogenèse méditerranéenne." In *La mobilité*, 317–30.

Neuerburg, N. (1965). *L'architettura delle fontane e dei ninfei nell'Italia antica.* Naples.

Neumann, A. 1976–77. "Zu alten und neuen Funden aus Vindobona." *Jahreshefte des Österreichischen Archäologischen Instituts* 51: 141–55.

Neumann, J. 1985. "Climatic Change as a Topic in Classical Greek and Roman Literature." *Climate Change* 7: 441–54.

———. 1992. "Climatic Conditions in the Alps in the Years about the Year of Hannibal's Crossing (218 B.C.)." *Climate Change* 14: 139–50.

Newson, M. D. 1987. "Land and Water: The 'River Look' on the Face of Geography." Inaugural Lecture, University of Newcastle upon Tyne. Newcastle.

Nicolet, C. 1988. *L'Inventaire du monde.* Paris.

———. 1991. *Space, Geography and Politics in the Early Roman Empire.* Ann Arbor.

Nielsen, I. 1993. *Thermae et balnea. The Architecture and Cultural History of Roman Public Baths.* Aarhus.

Ninck, M. 1921. *Die Bedeutung des Wassers im Kult und Leben der Alten.* Repr., Leipzig, 1960. Philologus suppl. 14. Wiesbaden, 1960.

Nisbet, R. G. M., and Hubbard, M. 1970. *A Commentary on Horace: Odes Book I.* Oxford.

———. 1978. *A Commentary on Horace: Odes Book II.* Oxford.

Nisbet, R. G. M., and Rudd, N. 2004. *A Commentary on Horace: Odes Book III.* Oxford.

Nixon, C. E. V., and Rodgers, B. S. 1994. *In Praise of Later-Roman Emperors: The Panegyrici Latini.* Berkeley, Los Angeles, and Oxford.

Nowlan, N. 1970. *The Tiber.* London.

O'Connor, C. 1993. *Roman Bridges.* Cambridge.

Ogilvie, R. M. 1965. *A Commentary on Livy Books 1–5.* Oxford.

Oleson, J. P. 1984. *Greek and Roman Mechanical Water-Lifting Devices: The History of a Technology.* Phoenix Supplementary Volume 16. Toronto.

———. 2000. "Water-Lifting." In Wikander *Handbook of Ancient Water Technology*, 207–302.

——— (ed.). 2008. *The Oxford Handbook of Engineering and Technology in the Classical World.* Oxford.

Oliver, G. J., et al. 2000. *The Sea in Antiquity.* Oxford.

Oliver, J. H. 1989. *Greek Constitutions of Early Roman Emperors from Inscriptions and Papyri.* Philadelphia.

Orlin, L. L. (ed.). 1975. *Janus: Essays in Ancient and Modern Studies.* Ann Arbor.

Ortalli, J. 1992. "Aque e culti salutari dell'Appennino Romagnolo. Il Complesso termale di Bagno di Romagna." In Chevallier, *Les eaux thermales*, 317–47.

Ostrowski, J. A. 1991. *Personifications of Rivers in Greek and Roman Art*. Warsaw and Kraków.

Owens, E. J. 1992. "The Water Supply of Kremna, Pisidia." In Argoud et al., *L'Eau et les homes*, 371–81.

Pack, R. A (ed.) 1963. *Artemidori Daldiani Onirocriticon Libri V*. Leipzig.

Pagano, M. 1990. *Sinuessa, storia ed archeologia di una colonia romana*. Sessa Aurunca.

———. 1996. "Note su alcuni acquedotti romani in Campania." In de Haan and Jansen, *Cura Aquarum in Campania*, 101–7.

Pagano, M., and Villucci, A. M. 1985. "Nuove iscrizioni da Suessa e da Minturnae." *RPAA* 34: 49–63.

Painter, K. 1965. "Roman Flasks with Scenes of Baiae and Puteoli." *Journal of Glass Studies* 17: 54–67.

Palma, A. 1980. *Le curae pubbliche*. Naples.

Palmer, R. E. A. 1980. "Customs and Market Goods Imported in the City of Rome." In D'Arms and Kopff, *The Seaborne Commerce of Ancient Rome*, 217–33.

———. 1981. "The Topography and Social History of Rome's Trastevere." *Proceedings of the American Philosophical Society* 125: 68–97.

Panella, C. 1989. "Le anfore italiche del II secolo d.C." In Lenoir, Manacorda, and Panella, *Amphores romaines*, 139–78.

———. 1992. "Mercato di Roma e anfore galliche nella prima èta imperial." In Laubenheimer, *Les amphores de Gaule*, 185–206.

Panella, C., and Tchernia, A. 1994. "Produits agricoles transportés en amphores: l'huile et surtout le vin." In M. Lenoir (ed.), *L'Italie d'Auguste a Dioclétien. Collection de l'École française de Rome*. Rome, 145–65.

Parker, A. J. 1984. "Shipwrecks and Ancient Trade in the Mediterranean." *Archaeological Review from Cambridge* 3.2: 99–113.

———. 1992. *Ancient Shipwrecks of the Mediterranean and the Roman Provinces*. BAR International Series 580. Oxford.

———. 1996. "Sea Transport and Trade in the Ancient Mediterranean." In Rice, *The Sea and History*, 97–110.

Parker, R. 2000. "Theophoric Names and Greek Religion." In Hornblower and Matthews, *Greek Personal Names*, 53–79.

Parkins, H. M. (ed.). 1997. *Roman Urbanism: Beyond the Consumer City*. London.

Parkins, H. M., and Smith, C. 1998. *Trade, Traders and the Ancient City*. London and New York.

Parodi Álvarez, M. J. 2001. *Ríos y lagunas de Hispania como vías de communicación. La navegación interior en la Hispania romana*. Ecija.

Pascal, C. B. 1964. *The Cults of Cisalpine Gaul*. Collection Latomus 75. Brussells.

Pasqui, A. 1909. "Alveo del Tevere." *Notizie degli scavi di antichità*, 433–36.

Pasquinucci, M. 1988. "Strabone e l'Italia central." In Maddoli, *Strabone e l'Italia antica*, 47–59.

Pasquinucci, M., and Del Rio, A. 2004. "Commercial Flows, Ports and Hinterlands in North Coastal Etruria (Late Republican–Late Roman Period)." In Pasquinucci and Weski, *Close Encounters*, 53–66.

Pasquinucci, M., and Menchelli, S. 1999. "The Landscape and Economy of the Territories of *Pisae* and *Volaterrae* (Coastal North Etruria)." *JRA* 12: 122–41.

Pasquinucci, M., and Rossetti, G. 1988. "The Harbour Infrastructure and Portus Pisanus from Ancient Times until the Middle Ages." In Raban, *Archaeology of Coastal Change*, 137–56.

Pasquinucci, M., and Weski, T. (eds.). 2004. *Close Encounters: Sea- and Riverborne Trade, Ports and Hinterlands, Ship Construction and Navigation in Antiquity, the Middle ages and in Modern Time.* BAR International Series 1283. Oxford.

Paterson, J. J. 1998. "Trade and Traders in the Roman World: Scale, Structure, and Organisation." In Parkins and Smith, *Trade*, 149–67.

Patterson, H. (ed.) 2004. *Bridging the Tiber: Approaches to Regional Archaeology in the Middle Tiber Valley.* Archaeological Monographs of the British School at Rome 13. London.

Patterson, H., and Millett, M. 1998. "The Tiber Valley Project." *PBSR* 66: 1–20.

Patterson, H., et al. 2004. "The Re-evaluation of the South Etruria Survey: The First Results from Veii." In H. Patterson, *Bridging the Tiber*, 11–28.

Patterson, J. R. 2003. "The Emperor and the Cities of Italy." In Cornell and Lomas, *Euergetism and Municipal Patronage in Roman Italy*, 89–104.

———. 2004. "City, Territory and Metropolis: The Case of the Tiber Valley." In H. Patterson, *Bridging the Tiber*, 61–73.

———. 2006. "Colonization and Historiography: The Roman Republic." In Bradley and Wilson, *Greek and Roman Colonization*, 189–218.

Pauli, L. 1973. "Ein latenezeitliches Steinrelief aus Bormio am stilfser Joch." *Germania* 51: 85–120.

Pauni, D. 1992. "Eaux thermales et culte des eaux en Suisse à l'époche romaine." In Chevallier, *Les eaux thermales*, 385–404.

Pavese, M. P. 2004. *Fundus cum vadis et alluvionibus: gli incrementi fluviali fra documenti della prassi e riflessione giurisprudenziale romana.* Rome.

Pavolini, C. 1985. "I commerci di Roma e di Ostia nella prima età imperiale: merci d'accompagno e carichi di ritorno." In *Misurare la terra: centuriazione e coloni nel mondo romano. Città, agricoltura, commercio: materiali da Roma e dal suburbia.* Modena, 200–205.

Peacock, D. P. S. 1978. "The Rhine and the Problem of Gaulish Wine in Roman Britain." In du Plat Taylor and Cleere, *Roman Shipping and Trade*, 49–51.

———. 1982. *Pottery in the Roman World.* London.

Peacock, D. P. S., and Williams, D. F. 1986. *Amphorae and the Roman Economy.* London.

Peleg, Y. 1991. "Ancient Pipelines in Israel." In Hodge, *Future Currents*, 129–40.

Pensabene, P., Rizzo, M. A., Roghi, M., and Talamo, E. 1980. *Terracotte votive dal tevere.* Studi Miscellanei 25. Rome.

Peretti, A. 1979. *Il periplo di Scilace: studio sul primo portolano del Mediterraneo*. Pisa.

———. 1994. *Dall'Eridano di Esodio al retrone Vicentino: studio su un idronimo erratico*. Pisa.

Perrot, J. 1961. *Les dérivés Latins en -men et -mentum*. Paris.

Petrikovits, H. von. 1952. "Die ausgrabungen in der Colonia Traiana bei Xanten." *BJ* 152: 41–161.

———. 1968. "Aquae Iasae." *AArchSlov* 19, 89–93.

———. 1983. *Die römischen Provinzen am Rhin und an der ober und mittlerer Donau im 5 Jahrhundert n. Ch.* Abhandlungen der Heidelberger Akadamie der Wissenschaften. Heidelberg.

Petrović, P. 1977. "Fortresse romaine a l'embouchure de la rivière Porecka dans les Portes de Fer." In *Limeskongress XI*. Budapest, 259–75.

———. 1990. "Die römische Strasse in Djerdap: ein Rekonstruktionsversuch." *Limeskongress XIV*. Vienna, 883–95.

———. 1991. "Ein Donauhafen von Trajan bei dem Kastel Aquae (Moesia Superior)." *Limeskongress XV*. Exeter, 295–98.

Petry, F. 1992. "Sources sacrées et rochers sculptés dans le nord-est de la Gaule." In Chevallier, *Les eaux thermales*, 227–28.

Petts, G. E. (ed.). 1989. *Historical Change of Large Alluvial Rivers: Western Europe*. Chicester, New York, Brisbane, Toronto, amd Singapore.

Petts, G. E., and Foster, I. 1985. *Rivers and Landscape*. London.

Peyre, C. 1979. *La Cisalpine Gauloise du IIIe au 1er siècle avant J.-C.* Paris.

Pfeiffer, R. 1949–53. *Callimachus*. 2 vols. Oxford.

Pferdehirt, B. 1995. *Das Museum für Antike Schiffahrt* I. Mainz.

Pflaum, H. G. 1960–61. *Les carriers procuratoriennes équestres sous le haut-empire romain*. 3 vols. Paris.

Picon, M., et al. 1975. "A Lyons Branch of the Pottery-Making Firm of Ateius." *Archaeometry* 17: 45–59.

Pietrangeli, C. 1943. *Ocriculum (Otricoli)*. Rome.

Pineau, H. 1970. *La côte atlantique de la Bidassoa à Quiberon dans l'Antiquité*. Paris.

Pirazzoli, P. A. 1976. "Sea-Level Variations in the Northwest Mediterranean during Roman Times." *Science* 194: 519–21.

———. 1988. "Sea-Level Changes and Crustal Movements in the Hellenic Arc (Greece). The Contribution of Archaeological and Historical Data." In Raban, *Archaeology of Coastal Change*, 157–84.

Pirenne-Delforge, V. 2001. "Les rites sacrificiels dans la *Périégèse*." In Knoepfler and Piérart, *Éditer*, 109–34.

Platner, S. B., and Ashby, T. 1926. *A Topographical Dictionary of Ancient Rome*. Oxford.

Ponsich, M. 1974–1991. *Implantation rurale antique sur le bas-Guadalquivir*. Vol. I, Madrid; II, Paris; III, Paris; IV, Paris.

———. 1983a. "Nouvelles perspectives sur l'olivier du Bas-Guadalquivir dans l'Antiquité." In Blázquez Martínez and Remesal Rodríguez, *Producción y comercio del aceite en la antigüedad. Secondo congreso internacional*, 47–56.

———. 1983b. "Le facteur géographique dans les moyens de transport de l'huile de Bétique." In Blázquez Martínez and Remesal Rodríguez, *Producción y comercio del aceite en la antigüedad. Secondo congreso internacional*, 101–13.

———. 1988. *Aceite de oliva y salazones de pescado. Factores geo-económicos de Bética y Tingitana.* Madrid.

———. 1998. "The Rural Economy of Western Baetica." In Keay, *The Archaeology of Early Roman Baetica*, 171–82.

Ponsich, M., and Tarradell, M. 1965. *Garum et industries de salaison dans la Méditerranée occidentale.* Paris.

Porter, R. (ed.). 1990. *The Medical History of Waters and Spas.* Medical History, supplement 10. London.

Pöschl, V. 1964. *Bibliographie zur antiken Bildersprache.* Heidelberg.

Potenza, U. 1996. "Gli acquedotti romani di Serino." In de Haan and Jansen, *Cura Aquarum in Campania*, 93–100.

Potter, T. W. (ed.). 1976. *A Faliscan Town in South Etruria: Excavations at Narce, 1966–71.* London.

———. 1979. *The Changing Landscape of South Etruria.* London.

———. 1987. *Roman Italy.* London.

———. 1991. "Towns and Territories in Southern Etruria." In Rich and Wallace-Hadrill, *City and Country*, 191–209.

Price, J. 1978. "Trade in Glass." In du Plat Taylor and Cleere, *Roman Shipping and Trade*, 70–78.

Prieur, J. 1976. "Le Vicus thermal d'Aix-les-Bains." *Caesarodunum* 11: 156–66.

Prontera, F. 1983. *Geografia e geografi nel mondo antico: Guida storica e critica.* Rome.

Purcell, N. 1985. "Wine and Wealth in Ancient Italy." *JRS* 75: 1–19.

———. 1987. "Town in Country and Country in Town." In MacDougall, *Ancient Roman Villa Gardens*, 187–203.

———. 1990. "The Creation of the Provincial Landscape: The Roman Impact on Cisalpine Gaul." In Blagg and Millett, *The Early Roman Empire*, 6–29.

———. 1995. "Eating Fish, the Paradoxes of Seafood." In Wilkins, Harvey, and Dobson, *Food in Antiquity*, 132–49.

———. 1996a. "Rome and the Management of Water: Environment, Culture and Power." In Shipley and Salmon, *Ancient Landscapes*, 180–212.

———. 1996b. "The Ports of Rome: Evolution of a *façade maritime*." In Claridge and Gallina Zevi, *Roman Ostia Revisited*, 267–79.

Putnam, M. C. J. 1975. "Italian Virgil and the Idea of Rome." In Orlin, *Janus*, 171–99.

Quet, M-H. 1981. *La mosaïque cosmologique de Mérida. Propositions de lecture.* Paris.

Quilici, L. 1985–86. "Il Tevere e l'Aniene come vie d'acqua a monte di Roma in età imperial." In Quilici Gigli, *Il Tevere*, 198–217.

———. 2008. "Land Transport, Part 1: Roads and Bridges." In Oleson, *The Oxford Handbook of Engineering and Technology*, 551–79.

Quilici, L., and Quilici Gigli, S. 1978. *Antemnae*. Rome.

———. 1980. *Crustumerium*. Rome.

———. 1986. *Fidenae*. Rome.

Quilici Gigli, S. (ed.). 1985–86. *Il Tevere e le altre vie d'acqua del Lazio antico*. Archeologia Laziale VII. Settimo incontro di studio del comitato per l'archeologie Laziale. Rome.

———. 1997. *Uomo acqua e paesaggio*. Rome.

Raban, A. (ed.). 1985. *Harbour Archaeology*. BAR International Series 257. Oxford.

———. 1988. *Archaeology of Coastal Change. Proceedings of the First International Symposium "Cities on the Sea—Past and Present." Haifa, Israel, September 22–29, 1986*. BAR International Series 404. Oxford.

Rackham, O. 1996. "Ecology and Pseudo-ecology: The Example of Ancient Greece." In Shipley and Salmon, *Ancient Landscapes*, 16–43.

Raepsaet, G. 1987. "Aspects de l'organisation du commerce de la céramique sigillé dans le Nord de la Gaule au IIe et IIIe siècles de nôtre ère' I: 'les données matérielles.'" *Münstersche Beiträge zur Handelsgeschichte* 6.2: 1–29.

———. 2008. "Land Transport, Part 2: Riding, Harnasses and Vehicles." In Oleson, *The Oxford Handbook of Engineering and Technology*, 580–605.

Raepsaet-Charlier, M.-T., and Raepsaet-Charlier, G. 1975. "Gallia Belgica et Germania Inferior. Vingt-cinq années de recherches historiques et archéologiques." *ANRW* II.4, 3–299.

———. 1988. "Négociants et transporteurs. La géographie des activities commerciales." *MBAH* 7.2: 45–69.

Ramin, J. 1974. "L'espace économique en Gaule: les documents concernant les mines." In Chevallier, *Littérature gréco-romaine*, 417–37.

Rankov, B. 2005. "Do Rivers Make Good Frontiers?" In Visy, *Limes XIX*, 175–81.

Raus, L. 1974. *Minturno e la sua gente*. Minturno.

Reddé, M. 1986. *Mare Nostrum. Les infrastructures, le dispositif et l'histoire de la marine militaire sous l'empire romain*. Rome.

Reggiani, A. M. 1979. "La terme di Cotilia." *AL* 11: 91–98.

———. 1985. "La villa rustica nell'agro sabino." In *Misurare la terra. Centuriazione e coloni nel mondo romano. Città, agricoltura, commercio: materiali da Roma e dal suburbia*. Modena, 61–65.

Reifferscheid, A. 1860. *C. Suetoni Tranquilli Praeter Caesarum Libros Reliquiae*. Leipzig.

Remesal Rodríguez, J. 1998. "Baetical Olive Oil and the Roman Economy." In Keay, *The Archaeology of Early Roman Baetica*, 183–200.

———. 2002. "Baetica and Germania. Notes on the Concept of 'Provincial Interdependence' in the Roman Empire." In Erdkamp, *The Roman Army and the Economy*, 293–308.

Rémy, B., and Buisson, A. 1992. "Sources sacrées, cultes des eaux et eaux thermales dans la région Rhône-Alpes: essai d'inventaire." In Chevallier, *Les eaux thermales*, 229–50.

Renard, M. (ed.). 1962. *Hommages à Albert Grenier*. 3 vols. Collection Latomus 58. Brussels.

Renfrew, C., and Bahn, P. 1991. *Archaeology: Theories, Methods, and Practices*. London.

Rice, E. E. (ed.). 1996. *The Sea and History*. Stroud.

Rich, J. 1998. "Augustus's Parthian Honours, the Temple of Mars Ultor and the Arch in the Forum Romanum." *PBSR* 66: 71–128.

Rich, J., and Shipley, G. (eds.). 1993. *War and Society in the Roman World*. London and New York.

Rich, J., and Wallace-Hadrill, A. (eds.). 1991. *City and Country in the Ancient World*. London and New York.

Richardson, J. S. 1983. "The *Tabula Contrebiensis*: Roman Law in Spain in the Early First Century B.C." *JRS* 73: 33–41.

———. 1996. *The Romans in Spain*. Oxford.

Richardson, L., Jr. 1992. *A New Topographical Dictionary of Ancient Rome*. Baltimore and London.

Richmond, I. A. 1982. *Trajan's Army on Trajan's Column*. With a Preface and Bibliography by M. Hassall. British School at Rome. London.

Rickman, G. 1980. *The Corn Supply of Ancient Rome*. Oxford.

———. 1988a. "Towards a Study of Roman Ports." In Raban, *Archaeology of Coastal Change*, 105–14.

———. 1988b. "The Archaeology and History of Roman Ports." *IJNA* 17: 257–67.

———. 1996. "Portus in Perspective." In Claridge and Gallina Zevi, *Roman Ostia Revisited*, 281–91.

Ricotti, E. 1987. "Water in Roman Garden Triclinia." In MacDougal, *Ancient Roman Villa Gardens*, 137–84.

Riera, I. (ed.). 1994. *Utilitas necessaria: sistemi idraulici nell'Italia Romana*. Milan.

Riese, A. 1878. *Geographi Latini Minores*. Heilbronn.

Rigault, R. 1977. "L'ecluse de Creil—commune de Saint Maximin, Oise et son Port romain." *Caesarodunum* 12: 371–88.

Rivet, A. L. F. 1970. "The British Section of the Antonine Itinerary." *Britannia* 1: 34–82.

———. 1988. *Gallia Narbonensis: Southern Gaul in Roman Times*. London.

Rivet, A. L. F., and Smith, C. 1979. *The Place-Names of Roman Britain*. London.

Robert, L. 1937. *Études anatoliennes: recherche sur les inscriptions grecques de l'Asie mineure*. Paris.

———. 1948. *Hellenica. Recueil d'épigraphie de numismatique et d'antiquités grecques*, vol. IV: *Épigrammes du Bas-Empire*. Paris.

———. 1962. *Villes d'Asie mineure*. 2nd ed. Paris.

———. 1966. *Documents de l'Asie mineure méridionale: inscriptions, monnaies et géographie*. Geneva and Paris.

———. 1969. *Opera Minora Selecta*. Vol. I. Amsterdam.

———. 1974. "Les inscriptions de Thessalonique." *RPh* 48, 180–246.

———. 1979. "Un voyage d'Antiphilos de Byzance." *JSav*, 257–94.

———. 1980. *A travers l'Asie Mineure: poètes et prosateurs, monnaies grecques, voyageurs et géographie*. Paris, 239.

———. 1982. "Documents de l'Asie Mineure XXIII: Sardes et les roseaux du lac Koloe." *BCH* 107: 334–59.

Roberti, M. 1992. "Le terme romane di Monfalcone." In Chevallier, *Les eaux thermales*, 311–13.

Robinson, O. F. 1980. "The Water Supply of Rome." *Studia et Documenta Historia et Iuris* 46: 44–86.

———. 1992. *Ancient Rome: City Planning and Administration*. London and New York.

———. 1997. *The Sources of Roman Law: Problems and Methods for Ancient Historians*. London and New York.

Rocha-Pereira, M. H. 1973–81. *Pausaniae Graeciae Descriptio*. 3 vols. Leipzig.

Röder, J. 1974. "Römische Steinbruchtätigkeit am Drachenfels." *BJ* 174: 509–44.

Rodger, A. 1970. "Roman Rain-Water." *Revue d'Histoire du Droit* 38: 417–31.

———. 1972. *Owners and Neighbours in Roman Law*. Oxford.

Rodgers, R. H. 2004. *Frontinus: De Aquaeductu Urbis Romae. Edited with Introduction and Commentary*. Cambridge.

Rodríguez-Almeida, E. 1981. *Forma Urbis Marmorea: aggiornamento generale 1980*. 2 vols. Rome.

———. 1984. *Il Monte Testaccio. Ambiente, storia, materiali*. Rome.

Rodríguez Colmero, A. 2002. "Polivalencia del vocablo *gens* en la epigrafía hispánica. Nota a propósito de la *gens Gigurrorum* en la Tabula Paemeiobrigensium." In Khanoussi, Ruggeri and Vismara, *L'Africa Romana*, 1743–56.

Rolland, H. 1962. "Informations archéologiques." *Gallia* 20: 657–60.

———. 1964. "Informations archéologiques." *Gallia* 22: 530–31.

Roma. 1985. *Archeologia nel Centro*. Vol. 1: *L'area archeologica centrale*. Rome.

Roman, Y. 1989. "Un exemple de géographie voluntaire: les Romans, le Rhône et le Garonne." In *La ville et fleuve*, 135–45.

Rosenstein, N., and Morstein-Marx, R. 2006. *A Companion to the Roman Republic*. Oxford.

Rossi, M., and Gattiglia, A. 1992. "Les eaux thermales du Briançonnais: état de la question." In Chevallier, *Les eaux thermales*, 251–72.

Rostovtzeff, M. 1957. *The Social and Economic History of the Roman Empire*. 2 vols. 2nd ed., revised by P. M. Fraser. Oxford.

Roth, C. L. 1875. *C. Suetoni Tranquilli Quae Supersunt Omnia*. Leipzig.

Roth, J. 1999. *The Logistics of the Roman Army at War (264 B.C.–A.D. 235)*. Leiden, Boston, and Cologne.

Rotili, M. 1972. *L'arco di Traiano a Benevento*. Rome.

Roueché, C. 2004. *Aphrodisias in Late Antiquity: The Late Roman and Byzantine Inscriptions*. 2nd ed. London.

Rougé, J. 1966. *Recherches sur l'organisation du commerce maritime en Méditerranée sous l'Empire romain*. Paris.

———. 1975. *La marine dans l'Antiquité*. Paris Translated by S. Frazer as *Ships and Fleets of the Ancient Mediterranean*. Middletown, Conn., 1981.

Rowland, R. J., Jr. 1981. *I ritrovamenti romani in sardegna*. Studia Archaeologica 28. Rome.

Ruegg, S. D. 1988. "Minturnae: A Roman River Depot on the Garigliano, Italy." In Raban, *Archaeology of Coastal Change*, 209–28.

Ruegg, S. D., et al. 1995. *Underwater Investigations at Roman Minturnae: Liris-Garigliano River*. Part I: *Report*; part II: *Catalogue of Artifacts*. Goteborg.

Rüger, C. 2000. "Roman Germany." In Bowman, Garnsey, and Rathbone, *Cambridge Ancient History*, 496–513.

Russell, D. A., and Wilson, N. G. 1981. *Menander Rhetor*. Oxford.

Russell, R. J. 1942. "Geomorphology of the Rhône Delta." *AAAG* 32: 149–254.

———. 1954. "Alluvial Morphology of Anatolian Rivers." *AAAG* 44: 363–91.

Rutman, D. B. 1986. "History and Anthropology: Clio's Dalliances." *Historical Methods* 19: 120–23.

Saddington, D. B. 2007. "*Classes*. The Evolution of the Roman Imperial Fleets." In Erdkamp, *A Companion to the Roman Army*, 201–17.

Sáez Fernández, P. 1990. "Estudio sobre un inscripción catastral colindante con Lacimurga." *Habis* 21: 205–27.

Sallares, R. 1991. *The Ecology of the Ancient Greek World*. London.

———. 2002. *Malaria and Rome: A History of Malaria in Ancient Italy*. Oxford.

Salmon, E. T. 1969. *Roman Colonization under the Republic*. London.

Salway, P. 1981. *Roman Britain*. Oxford.

Salway, R. W. B. 2001. "Travel, Itineraria and Tabellaria." In Adams and Laurence, *Travel and Geography in the Roman World*, 36–47.

———. 2004. "Sea and River Travel in the Roman Itinerary Literature." In Talbert and Brodersen, *Space in the Roman World*, 43–96.

Samesereuther, E. 1938. *Römische Wasseerleitungen in den Rheinlanden*. Berlin.

Sánchez-Osty, Á. 1999. *Tabula Siarensis. Edición, Tradución y Commentario*. Pamplona.

San Nicolás Pedraz, M. P. 2002. "El transporte marítimo en los mosaicos romanos." In Khanoussi, Ruggeri, and Vismara, *L'Africa Romana*, 271–86.

Sargenti, M. 1965. "Il regime dell'alveo derelitto nelle fonti romane." *BIDR* 68, 195–273.

Šašel, J. 1973. "Trajan's Canal at the Iron Gate." *JRS* 63: 80–85.

Sauer, E. 1999. "The Augustan spa at Bourbonne-les-Bains." In Goldsworthy and Haynes, *The Roman Army as a Community*, 53–79.

Schama, S. 1995. *Landscape and Memory*. Bath.

Schelia, R. von. 1931. *Die Wassergrenze in Altertum*. Breslau.

Schiøler, T., and Wikander, Ö. 1983. "A Roman Water-Mill in the Baths of Caracalla." *Opuscula Romana* 14.4: 47–64. Stockholm.

Schlippschuh, O. 1974. *Die Händler im römischen Kaiserreich in Gallien, Germanien und der Donauprovinzen, Rätien, Noricum und Pannonien.* Amsterdam.

Schmiedt, G. (ed.). 1972. *Il livello antico del Mar Tirreno. Testimonianze dei resti archeologici.* Florence.

Schneider, H. 2007. *Geschichte der antiken Technik.* Munich.

Schnitter, N. 1978. "Römische Talsperren." *AW* 2: 25–32.

———. 1983. "Barrages romains." In Boucher, J.-P. (ed.), *Journées d'Études sur les Aqueducs romains/Tagung über römische Wasserversorgungsanlagen, Lyon (26–28 mai 1977).* Paris, 333–47.

Schönbeck, G. 1962. *Der locus amoenus von Homer bis Horaz.* Cologne.

Schoppa, H. 1974. *Aquae Mattiacae. Wiesbadens römische und alamannisch-merowingische Vergangenheit.* Wiesbaden.

Schulten, A. 1955–57. *Iberische Landeskunde: Geographie des antiken Spanien.* 2 vols. Strasbourg.

Scobie, A. 1986. "Slums, Sanitation and Mortality in the Roman World." *Klio* 68.2: 399–43.

Scott, M. 1991. *The River Gods.* Bray.

Sears, M. and Merriman, D. 1980. *Oceanography: The Past.* Woods Hole.

Seelye, J. D. 1977. *Prophetic Waters: the River in Early American Life and Literature.* Oxford and New York.

Segre, A. G. 1990. "Considerazioni sul Tevere e sull' Aniene nel quaternario." *AL* VII.2: 9–22.

Selkirk, R. 1983. *The Piercebridge Formula: A Dramatic New View of Roman History.* Cambridge.

Sellin, R. H. J. 1983. "The Large Roman Water Mill at Barbegal (France)." *History of Technology* 8: 91–109.

Semple, E. C. 1932. *The Geography of the Mediterranean Region: Its Relation to Ancient History.* London.

Settis, S. 1973. "Esedra e 'ninfeo' nella terminologia architettonica del mondo romano. Dall'età republican alla tardà antichità." *ANRW* 1.4, 661–745.

Severyns, A. 1927. "Deux 'Graffiti' de Délos." *BCH* 51: 234–43.

Shaw, B. D. 1976. "Climate, Environment and Prehistory in the Sahara." *World Archaeology* 8: 133–48 = Shaw, *Environment and Society in Roman North Africa* (1995), II.

———. 1981a. "Climate, Environment, and History: The Case of Roman North Africa." In Wigley et al., *Climate and History* = Shaw, *Environment and Society in Roman North Africa* (1995), III.

———. 1981b. "The Elder Pliny's African Geography." *Historia* 30: 424–71.

———. 1982. "Lambasa: An Ancient Irrigation Community." *AA* 18: 61–103 = Shaw, *Environment and Society in Roman North Africa* (1995), VI.

———. 1984. "Water and Society in the Ancient Maghrib: Technology, Property and

Development." *AA* 20: 121–73 = Shaw, *Environment and Society in Roman North Africa* (1995), V.

———. 1991. "The Noblest Monuments and the Smallest Things: Wells, Walls and Aqueducts in the Making of Roman Africa." In Hodge, 63–91 = Shaw, *Environment and Society in Roman North Africa* (1995), VII.

———. 1995. *Environment and Society in Roman North Africa.* Aldershot.

Shaw, J. W. 1966. "Greek and Roman Harbourworks." In Bass, *Archaeology under Water*, 87–112.

Sherk, R. W. 1974. "Roman Geographical Exploration and Military Maps." *ANRW* II.1, 534–62.

Sherwin-White, A. N. 1966. *The Letters of Pliny: A Historical and Social Commentary.* Oxford.

Shipley, G., and Salmon, J. (eds.). 1966. *Human Landscapes in Classical Antiquity.* London and New York.

Silberman, A. 1988. *Chorographie / Pomponius Mela; texte établi, traduit et annoté.* Paris.

———. 1995. *Arrien, Périple du Pont-Euxin.* Paris.

Sillières, P. 1990. *Les voies de communication de l'Hispanie meridionale.* Paris.

Silverman, S. F. 1986. "Anthropology and History: Understanding the Boundaries." *Historical Methods* 9: 123–26.

Simms, D. L. 1983. "Water-Driven Saws, Ausonius and the Authenticity of the Mosella." *Technology and Culture* 24: 635–43.

Slim, H. 1992. "Maitrise de l'eau en Tunisie a l'époque romaine." In Argoud et al., *L'Eau et les homes*, 513–31.

Smallwood, E. M. 1966. *Documents Illustrating the Principates of Nerva Trajan and Hadrian.* Cambridge.

Smith, N. A. F. 1970. "The Roman Dams of Subiaco." *Techology and Culture* 22: 58–68.

———. 1971. *A History of Dams.* London.

———. 1976. *Man and Water.* London.

———. 1977–78. "Roman Canals." *Transactions of the Newcomen Society for the History of Engineering* 49: 75–86.

———. 1983–84. "The Origins of Water Power: A Problem of Evidence and Expectations." *Transactions of the Newcomen Society* 55: 67–84.

———. 1991. "Problems of Design and Analysis." In Hodge, *Future Currents*, 113–28.

Smith, S. A. 1877. *The Tiber and Its Tributaries, Their Natural History and Their Classical Associations.* London.

Sommer, C. S. 2009. "Why There? The Positioning of Forts along the Riverine Frontiers of the Roman Empire." In W. S. Hanson, *Army and Frontiers of Rome*, 103–14.

Sordi, M. (ed.). 1988. *Geografia e storiografia nel mondo classico.* Milan.

Southern, P., and Dixon, K. 1996. *The Late Roman Army.* New Haven and London.

Spurr, M. S. 1986. *Arable Cultivation in Roman Italy, ca. 200 B.C.–ca. A.D. 200.* London.

Squatriti, P. 1998. *Water and Society in Early Medieval Italy, A.D. 400–1000.* Cambridge.

Stanco, E. A. 1986. "Il Tevere e il territorio falisco-capenate in età romana." In *Tevere un' antica via per il Mediterraneo. Ministerio per i Beni Culturali e Ambientale, Comune di Roma.* Rome, 181–82.

Starr, C. 1960. *The Roman Imperial Navy, 31 B.C.–A.D. 324.* 2nd ed. Cambridge.

Stefan, A.-S. 1987. "Évolution de la côte dans la zone des bouches du Danube durant l'antiquité." In *Déplacements*, 191–210.

Stein, P. G., and Lewis, A. D. E. 1983. *Studies in Justinian's Institutes in Memory of J. A. C. Thomas.* London.

Steinby, E. M. (ed.). 1993–99. *Lexicon Topographicum Urbis Romae.* Vols. I–V. Rome.

Stephens, G. R. 1985. "Civic Aqueducts in Britain." *Britannia* 16: 197–208.

Stevenson, E. L. 1932. *Claudius Ptolemy, The Geography.* New York. Repr., 1991.

Stiglitz, H., Kandler, M., and Werner, J. 1977. "Carnuntum." *ANRW* II.6, 583–730.

Stillwell, R., MacDonald, W. L., and McAllister, M. H. (eds.). 1976. *The Princeton Encyclopedia of Classical Sites.* Princeton.

Stoddard, S. 2006. "The Physical Geography and Environment of Republican Italy." In Rosenstein and Morstein-Marx, *A Companion to the Roman Republic*, 102–21.

Stückelberger, A. 2004. "Ptolemy and the Problem of Scientific Perception of Space." In Talbert and Brodersen, *Space in the Roman World*, 27–40.

Stückelberger, A., and Graßhoff, G. (eds.). 2006. *Klaudios Ptolemaios Handbuch der Geographie: griechisch-deutsch.* 2 vols. Basel.

Suttor, M. 2000. "Écrire l'histoire d'un fleuve: sources et méthodologie." In Bonnamour, *Archéologie des fleuves et des rivières*, 14–17.

Swoboda, E. 1958. *Carnuntum. Seine Gechichte und seine Denkmäler.* 3rd ed. Graz and Cologne.

Syme, R. 1969. "Pliny the Procurator." *HSCP* 73: 201–36. Reprinted in E. Badian (ed.), *Roman Papers*, vol. II (Oxford, 1979), 742–73.

———. 1995. *Anatolica: Studies in Strabo.* Edited by A. Birley. Oxford.

Talbert, R. (ed.). 2000. *Barrington Atlas of the Greek and Roman World.* Princeton.

———. 2002. Review of Adams and Laurence (2001). *AJPh* 123.3: 529–34.

———. 2004a. "Rome's Provinces as Framework for World-View." In L. de Ligt, E. A. Hemelrijk, and H. W. Singor, *Roman Rule and Civic Life: Local and Regional Perspectives. Proceedings of the Fourth Workshop of the International Network Impact of Empire (Roman Empire, c. 200 B.C.–A.D. 476), Leiden, June 25–28, 2003.* Amsterdam, 21–37.

———. 2004b. "Small-Town Sources of Geographical Information in the World of Imperial Rome." *Classical Bulletin* 80.1: 15–25.

———. 2004c. "Cartography and Taste in Peutinger's Roman Map." In Talbert and Brodersen, *Space in the Roman World*, 113–41.

———. 2005. "'*Ubique fines*': Boundaries within the Roman Empire." In Bedon and Hermon, *Concepts*, 93–101.

———. 2007. "Author, Audience and the Roman Empire in the Antonine Itinerary." In Haensch and Heinrichs, *Herrschen und Verwalten*, 256–70.

———. 2010. *Rome's World: The Peutinger Map Reconsidered.* Cambridge.

Talbert, R., and Brodersen K. (eds.). 2004. *Space in the Roman World: Its Perception and Presentation.* Münster.

Taubenschlag, R. 1955. *The Law of Greco-Roman Egypt in the Light of the Papyri, 332 B.C.–640 A.D.* Warsaw.

Taylor, L. R. 1960. *The Voting Districts of the Roman Republic: The Thirty-five Urban and Rural Tribes.* Rome.

Taylor, R. 1995. "*A citeriore ripa aquae*: Aqueduct River Crossings in the Ancient City of Rome." *PBSR* 63: 75–103.

———. 2000. *Public Needs and Private Pleasures: Water Distribution, the River Tiber and the Urban Development of Ancient Rome.* Rome.

Tchernia, A. 1980. "D. Caecilius Hospitalis et M. Iulius Hermesianus (*CIL* VI 1625b et 20742)." In Blázquez Martínez and Remesal Rodríguez, *Producción y comercio,* 155–60.

———. 1983. "Italian Wine in Gaul at the End of the Republic." In Garnsey et al., *Trade in the Ancient Economy,* 87–104.

———. 1986. *Le vin de l'Italie romaine: essai d'histoire économique d'après les amphores.* Bibliothèque des Écoles françaises d'Athènes et de Rome 261. Rome.

Tejara Gaspar, A. 1977. "Panorama arqueologico de la marisma del Guadalquivir." *Habis* 8: 207–15.

Temporini, H. 1982. "Die milesischen Münzen der jüngeren Faustina zur Vorlage eines Ineditum der Tübinger Sammlung." In Löringhoff et al., *Praestant Interna,* 349–63.

Terras, V. 1965. *Boris Godunov with Introduction, Notes and Vocabulary.* Letchworth.

Thévenard, J.-J. 1996. *Carte archéologique de la Gaule 52. La Haute-Marne.* Paris.

Thevenot, E. 1948. "La station antique des Bolards à Nuits Saint-Georges." *Gallia* 6.2: 289–347.

———. 1968. *Divinities et sanctuaires de la Gaule.* Paris.

———. 1971. "La voie d'Autin vers la Séquanie." *Latomus* 30: 1124–33.

Thiel, A. 2000. "Römische waffenfunde der frühen Kaiserzeit aus gewässern." In Bonnamour, *Archéologie des fleuves,* 70–74.

Thomas, K. 1963. "History and Anthropology." *PP* 24: 3–24.

Thomas, R. G., and Wilson, A. I. 1994. "Water Supply for Roman Farms in Latium and South Etruria." *PBSR* 62: 139–96.

Thompson, F. H. 2003. *The Archaeology of Greek and Roman Slavery.* London.

Thomson, D. F. S. 1978. *Catullus: A Critical Edition.* Chapel Hill.

Thonemann, P. 2006. "Neilomandros. A Contribution to the History of Greek Personal Names." *Chiron* 36: 11–43.

———. 2011. *The Maeander Valley: A Historical Geography from Antiquity to Byzantium.* Cambridge.

Thulin, C. 1913. *Corpus Agrimensorum Romanorum.* Leipzig. Repr., Stuttgart, 1971.

Tischler, J. 1977. *Kleinasiatische Hydronomie. Semantische und morphologische Analyse der griechischen Gewässernamen.* Wiesbaden.

Tölle-Kastenbein, R. 1990. *Antike Wasserkultur.* Munich.

Torbrügge, W. 1970–71. "Vor-und frühgeschichtliche Flußfunde. Zur ordnung und Bestimmung einer Denkmälergruppe." *BRGK* 51–52: 1–146.

Torelli, M. 1999. *Tota Italia: Essays in the Cultural Formation of Roman Italy.* Oxford.

Toutain, J. 1926. "Le culte des fleuves, sa forme primitive et ses principaux rites chez les peuples de l'antiquité classique." *L'ethnographie,* n.s., 13–14: 1–7.

Tovar, A. 1974–89. *Iberische Landeskunde,* 3 vols. Baden-Baden.

Toynbee, A. J. 1965. *Hannibal's Legacy: The Hannibalic War's Effects on Roman Life.* 2 vols. Oxford.

Toynbee, J. M. C. 1934. *The Hadrianic School: A Chapter in the History of Greek Art.* Cambridge.

Tozzi, P. 1988. "L'Italia settentrionale di Strabone." In Maddoli, *Strabone e l'Italia antica,* 25–43.

Traina, G. 1988. *Paludi e bonifiche del mondo antico.* Rome.

———. 1990. *Ambiente e paesaggi di Roma antica.* Rome.

———. 1992. "Sale e saline nel mediterraneo antico." *PP* 47: 363–78.

Tranoy, A. 1981. *La Galice romaine: recherches sur le nord-ouest de la péninsule Ibérique dans l'Antiquité.* Paris.

Trathnigg, G. 1966. "Beiträge zur Topographie des römischen Welt." *Jahreshefte des Österreichischen Archäologischen Instituts Beiblatt* 48: 108–66.

Troisgros, H. 1975. *Borvo et Damona. Divinités gallo-romaines des eaux thermales.* Bourbonne-les-Bains.

Tuan, Y. F. 1968. *The Hydrological Cycle and the Wisdom of God.* Toronto.

———. 1974. *Topophilia: A Study of Environmental Perception, Attitudes, and Values.* Englewood Cliffs, N.J.

———. 1976. "Geopiety: A Theme in Man's Attachment to Nature and to Place." In Lowenthal and Bowden, *Geographies of the Mind,* 11–39.

Tuccillo, F. 2010. "'Iter usque ad aquam': 'servitus' et 'ripa' dans l'expérience juridique romaine." In Hermon, *Riparia dans L'Empire romain,* 295–304.

Tudor, D. 1966. *Sucidava.* Bucharest.

Turcan, R. 1984. "Le sarcophage de l'Ile-Barbe (Lyon)." *Bulletin de Liaison de la Société des Amis de la Bibliothèque Salomon Reinach* 2: 19–23.

Uggeri, G. 1978. "Vie di terra e vie d'acqua tra Aquileia e Ravenna in età Romana." *Antichità Altoadriatiche* 13: 45–79.

———. 1987. "La navigazione interna della Cisalpina in età romana." *Antichità Altoadriatiche* 29.II: 305–54.

———. 1990. "Aspetti archeologici della navigazione interna nella Cisalpina." *Antichità Altoadriatiche* 36: 175–96.

Vallat, J.-P. 1981. "La cité des Ségusiaves à l'époque romaine (1er siècle av. J.C.-IVe ap. J.C.)." In S. Walker (ed.), *Récents recherches en archéologie gallo-romaine et paléochrétienne sur Lyon et sa region.* BAR International Series 108. Oxford, 168–277.

Van Buren, A. W., and Stevens, G. P. 1915–16. "The Aqua Traiana and the Mills on the Janiculum." *MAAR* 1: 59–62.

————. 1927. "The Aqua Traiana and the Mills on the Janiculum." *MAAR* 6: 137–46.

Ventriglia, U. 1971. *La geologia della città di Roma*. Rome.

Ventura, A., León, P., and Márquez, C. 1998. "Roman Cordoba in the Light of Recent Archaeological Research." In Keay, *The Archaeology of Early Roman Baetica*, 87–99.

Verboven, K. S. 2007. "Good for Business. The Roman Army and the Emergence of a 'Business Class' in the Northwestern Provinces of the Roman Empire (1st Century B.C.E.–3rd century C.E.)." In de Blois and Lo Cascio, *The Impact of the Roman Army*, 295–313.

Versnel, H. S. 1970. *Triumphus: An Enquiry into the Origin, Development and Meaning of the Roman Triumph*. Leiden.

Veyne, P. 1957. "La Table des Ligures Baebiani et l'institution alimentaire de Trajan." *MEFR* 69: 81–135.

Vigneron, P. 1968. *Le cheval dans l'antiquité gréco-romain*. Nancy.

Visy, Z. (ed.) 2005. *Limes XIX. Proceedings of the XIXth International Congress of Roman Frontier Studies. Pécs, Hungary, September 2003*. Pécs.

Vita-Finzi, C. 1961. "Roman Dams in Tripolitania." *Antiquity* 35: 14–20.

————. 1969. *The Mediterranean Valleys*. Cambridge.

Vodret, A., and Bauer, H. 1985. "Foro di Augusto e Porticus Absidata: il progetto di consolidamento e restauro." In *Roma. Archeologia nel Centro*, 224–28.

Vollkommen, R. 1994. "Vater Rhein und seine römischen Darstellungen." *BJ* 194: 1–42.

Vorbeck, E., and Beckel, L. 1973. *Carnuntum. Rom am der Donau*. Salzburg.

Voute, P. 1972. "Notes sur l'iconographie d'Océan." *MEFRA* 84.2: 639–74.

Wagner, G., Pernicka, E., and Verpmann, H.-P. (eds.). 2003. *Troia and the Troad: Scientific Approaches*. Berlin and New York.

Wagstaff, J. M. 1981. "Buried Assumptions: Some Problems in the Interpretation of the 'Younger Fill' Raised by Recent Data from Greece." *JAS* 8: 247–64.

Walbank, F. 1967. *A Commentary on Polybius*. Vol. II. Oxford.

Walbank, F., Astin, A. E., Frederiksen, M. W., Ogilvie, R. M., and Drumond, A. 1989. *Cambridge Ancient History*. Vol. VII.2: *The Rise of Rome to 220 B.C.* 2nd ed. Cambridge.

Walker, D. S. 1967. *A Geography of Italy*. 2nd ed. London.

Ward-Perkins, J. B. 1955. "The Aqueduct of Aspendos," *PBSR* 23: 115–23.

————. 1961. "Veii: The Historical Topography of the Ancient City." *PBSR* 29: 1–123.

————. 1962. "Etruscan Engineering: Road-Building, Water Supply and Drainage." In Renard, *Hommages à Albert Grenier*, 1636–43.

Wasserstein, A. 1982. *Galen's Commentary on the Hippocratic Treatise Airs, Waters, Places in the Hebrew Translation of Solomon ha-Me'ati*. Israeli Academy of Sciences and Humanities, vol. VI.3. Jerusalem.

Weber, E. 1976. *Tabula Peutingeriana: Codex Vindobonnensis 324. Kommentar/ Vollständige Faksimil-Ausgabe im Originalformat*. Graz.

Wells, C. 1972. *The German Policy of Augustus*. Oxford.

Wheeler, E. L. 1993. "Methodological Limits and the Mirage of Roman Strategy." *Journal of Military History* 57: 7–41, 215–40.

White, K. D. 1970. *Roman Farming*. London.

———. 1984. *Greek and Roman Technology*. Ithaca.

Whitehead, D. 1990. *How to Survive under Siege. Aeneas the Tactician, Translated with an Introduction and Commentary*. Oxford.

Whittaker, C. R. 1989. *Les frontières de l'empire romain*. Paris.

———. 1990. "The Consumer City Revisited: The *Vicus* and the City." *JRA* 3: 110–18.

———. 1994. *Frontiers of the Roman Empire: A Social and Economic Study*. A reworking of the French edition (1989). Baltimore and London.

———. 1996. "Where Are the Frontiers Now?" In Kennedy, *The Roman Army in the East*, 25–41.

———. 2000. "Frontiers." In Bowman, Garnsey, and Rathbone, *Cambridge Ancient History*, 293–319.

———. 2002. "Mental Maps: Seeing Like a Roman." In McKechnie, *Thinking like a Lawyer*, 81–112.

———. 2004. *Rome and Its Frontiers: The Dynamics of Empire*. London and New York.

Wiedemeyer, H. R. 1967. "Die entdeckung der römischen Heilthermen von Baden—Aquae Helveticae 1967." *Jahresbericht Gesellschaft Pro Vindonissa*, 83–93.

Wightman, E. 1970. *Roman Trier and the Treveri*. London.

———. 1982. "McMaster University Liri Valley Project." *Classical Views* 26: 214–19.

———. 1994. "Communications." In Hayes and Martini, *Archaeological Survey in the Lower Liri Valley*, 30–33.

Wightman, E., and Hayes, J. W. 1994. "Settlement Patterns and Society." In Hayes and Martini, *Archaeological Survey in the Lower Liri Valley*, 34–40.

Wigley, T. M. L., Ingram, M. J., and Farmer, G. (eds.). 1981. *Climate and History: Studies in Past Climates and Their Impact on Man*. Cambridge.

Wikander, Ö. 1979. "Water Mills in Ancient Rome." *Opuscula Romana* 12.2. Stockholm.

———. 1991. "Water Mills and Aqueducts." In Hodge, *Future Currents*, 141–48.

———. 2000a. "The Water-Mill." In Ö. Wikander, *Handbook of Ancient Water Technology*, 371–400.

——— (ed.). 2000b. *Handbook of Ancient Water Technology*. Technology and Change in History 2. Leiden.

Wild, J. P. 1978. "Cross-Channel Trade and the Textile Industry." In du Plat Taylor and Cleere, *Roman Shipping and Trade*, 79–81.

Wilhelm, R. M., and Jones, H. (eds.). 1992. *The Two Worlds of the Poet: New Perspectives on Virgil*. Detroit.

Wilkes, J. J. 1969. *Dalmatia*. London.

———. 1998. "Recent Work along the Lower and Middle Danube." *JRA* 11, 635–43.

———. 2005. "Provinces and Frontiers." In Bowman, Garnsey, and Cameron, *Cambridge Ancient History*, 212–68.

Wilkins, J., Harvey, D., and Dobson, M. (eds.). 1995. *Food in Antiquity*. Exeter.

Willems, W. J. H. 1983. "Romans and Batavians; Regional Developments at the Imperial Frontier." In Brandt and Slofstra, *Roman and Native in the Low Countries*, 105–28.

Williams, D. F., and Peacock, D. P. S. 1983. "The Importation of Olive-Oil into Iron Age and Roman Britain," In Blázquez Martínez and Remesal Rodríguez, *Producción y comercio del aceite en la antigüedad. Secondo congreso internacional*, 263–80.

Williams, F. 1978. *Callimachus Hymn to Apollo. A Commentary*. Oxford.

Williams, G. 1968. *Tradition and Originality in Roman Poetry*. Oxford.

———. 1969. *The Third Book of Horaces's Odes*. Oxford.

Wilson, A. I. 1995. "Water-Power in North Africa and the Development of the Horizontal Water-Wheel." *JRA* 8: 499–510.

———. 1999. "Deliveries *extra urbem*: Aqueducts and the Countryside." *JRA* 12, 314–31.

———. 2001. "Water-Mills at Amida: Ammianus Marcellinus 18.8.11." *CQ*, n.s., 51, no. 1: 231–36.

———. 2002. "Machines, Power and the Ancient Economy." *JRS* 92: 1–32.

———. 2003. "The Archaeology of the Roman *fullonica*." *JRA* 16: 442–46.

Wilson, R. J. A. 1990. *Sicily under the Roman Empire: The Archaeology of a Roman Province, 36 B.C.–A.D. 535*. Warminster.

———. 1996. "Tot aquarum tam multis necessariis molibus . . . ; Recent Studies on Aqueducts and Water Supply." *JRA* 9: 5–29.

Winkes, R. (ed.) 1985. *The Age of Augustus. Interdisciplinary Conference held at Brown University, April 30–May 2, 1982*. Louvain-la Neuve.

Wiseman, P. 1995. *Remus: A Roman Myth*. Cambridge.

———. 2004. *The Myths of Rome*. Exeter.

Wolodkiewicz, W. 2005. "Protection de l'environnement naturel et gestion de l'eau d'heir et d'aujourd'hui." In Bedon and Hermon, *Concepts*, 53–66.

Yegül, F. 1992. *Baths and Bathing in Classical Antiquity*. Cambridge, Mass., and London.

———. 1996. "The Thermo-Mineral Complex at Baiae." *Art Bulletin* 78.1: 137–61.

Zaninović, M. 1977. "The Economy of Roman Dalmatia." *ANRW* II.6, 767–809.

Zanker, P. 1988. *The Power of Images in the Age of Augustus*. Translated by A. Shapiro. Ann Arbor.

Zerbini, L. 2002. "Problemi sulla navigazione e la rota della nave romana di Comacchio." In Khanoussi, Ruggeri, and Vismara, *L'Africa Romana*, 821–28.

INDEX OF PERSONS

Attalus (perfume dealer at Lugdunum), 270

Atusius Priscus, Sex., sets up altar to Tiberinus, 142

Augustus: and aqua Alsietina, 236; and aqua Augusta, 239–40; and banks of Tiber, 319; conquests of celebrated, 373; and Diana Tifatina, 366; diverts river in Egypt, 240; forum of, 97; and Hispellum, 131, 366; and Maeander, 115; mausoleum of, 15; nominates curators, 91; repairs channels of aqueducts, 93, 237; rivers in his *Res Gestae*, 128, 188; stages boat races, 334; takes land from Capua, 92; teaches grandchildren swimming, 335; and Venafrum, 94

Aulus Gellius: on clearing river, 215; on major rivers of empire, xiii

Aurelius Faustinus, freedman official associated with Tiber, 318–19

Aurelius Verus, C. (merchant), 283

Baebius Modestus, Q., honors Aquae Hypsitanae, 366

Bagaudae, revolt of, 186

Betilienus Vaarus, L., brings water to Aletrium, 242–43

Blussus, funeral monument of, 267, 282

Bourdiga (deity), 444 (n. 149)

Caecilius Metellus Macedonicus, Q., diverts river into enemy camp, 162

Caecina Severus, A., and use of rivers, 162

Caelius Aurelianus (medical writer), 496 (n. 112)

Caesennius Paetus, L., forced to build bridge, 198

Calpetanus Rantius Quirinalis Valerius Festus, C. (curator), establishes boundary stones on Tiber, 458 (n. 186)

Calpurnius Piso, Cn., journey of through Italy, 219

Caninius, C., erects boundary stones in Ostia, 87

Caracalla (emperor), repairs aqueduct, 237

Carisius, P., founds Augusta Emerita, 171

Cassiodorus: describes Padus, 303; observations of on Fons Aponi, 362

Cassius Longinus, C., opinion of on river actions, 87, 101, 112

Cassius Severus, pays respects to Aquae Aponi, 362

Castor and Pollux (deities), shrine of, 15

Caunius Priscus, T., honors Aquae Sinuessanae, 362

Claudius (emperor), establishes military colony, 176

Claudius II (emperor), replies to petition, 90

Claudius Aelianus (Aelian): describes boats on Danube, 293; describes Peneios, 123

Claudius Caecus, Appius, constructs an aqueduct, 236

Claudius Marcellinus, makes vow to Rhine, 133

Claudius Ptolemaeus (Ptolemy): geographical work of, 46–47; rivers in work of, 58–59, 80–81

Commodus (emperor), builds forts along Danube, 183

Constantine (emperor): and battle of Milvian Bridge, 383; builds bridge on Danube, 196; builds fort on Rhine, 195–96; celebrates crossing Danube, 382; celebrates Hannibalianus as king of Pontus and Armenia, 382; and Danube, 186; and Euphrates, 382; sails down Rhône, 186

Cornelius Celsus, A., on benefits of water, 344

Cornelius Gallus, C. (prefect of Egypt), refers to Nile, 372

Cornelius Nepos, and Padus, 65

Cornelius Restitutus, L. (prefect of classis Pannonica), 183

Cornelius Sulla Felix, L.: dedicates springs, 366; visits Aidepsos, 361

Cornelius Tacitus: describes problems of Tiber, 118–19; discusses Rhine, 372

Coventina (deity), 139

Crassus Frugi, M., owns baths at Baiae, 360

Curius Dentatus, M.: and Old Anio, 20; and Veline Lake, 20

Decimus Magnus Ausonius, writes about Moselle, 125–26

Diana Tifatina (deity), 366

Dio Chrysostomos: addresses people of Tarsus, 126; on depiction of rivers, 151

Diocletian (emperor): celebrates building at Zanes, 196; creates river fleets, 185; reorganizes provinces, 65

Diogenianos, visits Aidepsos, 361

Dionysios of Halicarnassus, on Tiber, 310

Dionysios Perigetes, on Tiber, 46, 310

Domitian (emperor): builds bridge across Liris, 373; equestrian statue of, 377; Rhine depicted on coin of, 379

Domitius Corbulo, C.: builds canal, 183; guards Euphrates, 190

Draco (deity), 134, 140

Dusmia Numisilla, restores water supply, 243

Duvius Avitus, response of to Ampsivarii, 372

Elagabalus (emperor), and river god of Marcianopolis, 382

Ennius, describes Tiber, 375

Ennodius, on Fons Aponi, 362

Epictetus, and rivers, 121, 303

Etruscans, work of in Padana, 303

Eudocia, praises springs at Hammat Gader, 365–66

Eumenius, comments on value of maps, 80

Eunapius, comments of on hot springs, 365

Fabius, C., uses river against Gauls, 164

Faianius Plebeius, P., supplies water to Forum Novum, 243

Faustina the Younger (wife of Marcus Aurelius), on coins of Amaseia and Miletus, 382

Faustulus, and story of foundation of Rome, 13

Flavius Arrianus, L.: describes qualities of Phasis, 385; describes Roman bridge building, 167; writes about Black Sea, 385

Flavius Vegetius Renatus, on importance of teaching recruits to swim, 165

Frontonius Euporus, M. (patron of boatmen), 267

Fufius Alexander, erects altar to Fontanus, 134

Fulvius Charetes (debt collector), 314

Fulvius Nobilior, uses river in ambush, 164

Gaius (jurist), on problems of rivers and alluviation, 86, 108–9, 113

Galen, on benefits of water, 343

Granius Priscus, L., makes offering to nymphs, 133

Hadrian (emperor): letter of to Naryka, 150; and Nile, 380; organizes drainage work, 233–34; villa of at Tibur, and water features, 332

Hannibal: at siege of Casilinum, 163; supply base of, 178; uses Volturnus, 163

Hercules of Gades, 379–80

Lucius Verus (emperor), repairs river damage, 117

Lucretius Carus, T., on rivers, 120, 122, 123

Lutatius Catulus, Q., tactics of on riverbank, 164

Mahudus, makes dedication to nymphs, 139

Mamertinus, on rivers as defense, 196

Manilius Vopsicus, river villa of, 124, 332

Marcius Rex, Q., builds *aqua Marcia*, 236

Marcomanni, negotiate with Marcus Aurelius, 296

Marcus Aurelius (emperor): column of, 182; dealings of with Marcomanni and Iazyges, 190, 296; organizes supplies on Danube, 182–83; repairs river damage, 117

Marius, C., builds *fossa Mariana*, 178, 224, 278

Mars Ultor (deity), temple of and Tiber, 143

Martial. *See* Valerius Martialis, M.

Matrebo Namausikabo (deity), 443 (n. 149)

Matres Almahae (deities), 443 (n. 149)

Matres Ubelnae (deities), 443 (n. 149)

Matrona, sets up memorial for boatman, 268

Matronae Aufaniae (deities), 444 (n. 149)

Maxentius (emperor), drowned in Tiber, 383

Maximian (emperor), revolt of, 186

Maximinus (emperor), and Aquileia, 305

Messius Rusticus, L. (curator), restores boundary of Tiber, 320

Metrodorus, comments on name of Padus, 68

Mucius Scaevola, C., meadows of in Rome, 19

Mummius Niger Valerius Vegetus, provides water to private estate, 96

Munatius Plancus, L., river in tactical thinking of, 165

Murranius Verus (dealer in wine and pottery), 272

Mussolini, and Tiber, 4

Naaman, bathes in Jordan, 337

Narcissus, visits Aquae Sinuesssanae, 362

Nehalennia (deity), 283, 444 (n. 149)

Nero (emperor): builds dams, 227; plans to build canal, 220; water features in Golden House of, 332

Nero Claudius Drusus: sails down Rhine, 183; sets up trophies on Elbe, 373

Nikolaos of Damascus, intervenes to help Ilium, 1

Nonius Datus, engineers water tunnel, 240–41

Numa, tomb of, 17

Numitor, and stories of foundation of Rome, 13

Nymphs, 132–36 passim

Otacilius Cerialis (patron of boatmen of Rhône and Saône), 268

Ovidius Naso, P. (Ovid): has lover address river, 124; and river legends, 149–50; on rivers and victory, 373

Papinius Statius, P.: describes riverside villa, 124; on Domitian's statue, 377; on wars in the east, 373–74

Papirius Maso, Cn., dedicates shrine to Fons, 17

Pausanias: character of work of, 50–51; on healing waters, 342–43; on importance of rivers, 66–68; on rivers in geographical descriptions, 71–72; on river legends, 143–50 passim

Petillius Cerialis Caesius Rufus, Q., fights Civilis on Rhine, 184

Petronius Honoratus, M. (patron of traders in olive oil), 260

Petronius Melior, Q. (*adiutor* of curators), 318

Platorius Nepos, A. (curator of banks of Tiber), 320

Plautius, C., helps construct Appia Claudia aqueduct, 236

Plautius Silvanus Aelianus, Ti., transfers people across Danube, 189

Plinius Caecilius Secundus, C. (Pliny the Younger): on Trajan and Danube, 374; writes to Trajan about Lake Sophon, 216, 224; writes to Trajan about technical achievements, 370

Plinius Secundus, C. (Pliny the Elder): character of work of, 49–50; on healing waters, 341; on importance of rivers, 55–57, 60–62, 75–77; on name of Padus, 68; praises Tiber, 15

Plutarch, describes spring at Aidepsos, 360–61

Polyaenus, and use of rivers in war, 162

Polybius, comments of on Padus, 304

Pompeius Paulinus, builds embankment in Germany, 223

Pomponius Cornelianus, celebrates return of water at Vicetia, 134

Pomponius Mela: character of work of, 50; and importance of rivers, 56, 66, 77–78

Pontilius Duurus, L., sets up dedication to spring, 133

Poppaeus Sabinus, C. (governor of Moesia), visits Aidepsos, 361

Porcius Cato, M., advice of on location of farm, 200

Porcius Rufianus, T., honors Aquae Mattiacorum, 363

Poseidon (deity), 443 (n. 140), 447 (n. 228)

Postumius Africanus, arranges for construction of aqueduct, 98

Postumius Albinus, L., organizes centuriation in Campania, 170

Praeconius Ventidius Magnus, C., restores waterlogged land, 233

Propertius, Sex.: on Cynthia and boats, 332; on defeated Rhine, 374; on Nile, 375

Pseudo-Plutarch, work of on names of rivers, 120

Ptolemy. *See* Claudius Ptolemaeus

Quinctilius Varus, P., consequences of defeat of, 191

Quinctius Cincinnatus, L., meadow of in Rome, 19

Raecius Leo, provides supply of water, 135

Rhea Silvia, and stories of foundation of Rome, 13

Rufius Catullus, M. (curator of sailors of Rhône), 268

Rutilius Claudius Namatianus: comments on Aquae Tauri, 352; describes his return to Gaul, 384

Salassi, exploits Duria, 201

Salluienses, involved in land dispute, 95–96

Saturninus, Cn., and water supply for Nicopolis, 239

Scylax, and *periplous* of Mediterranean, 51

Segomo (deity), 443 (n. 149)

Seleukos Nikator, founds colonies, 218

Semiramis, declares control over rivers, 369

Sempronius Tuditanus, P., makes offering to Timavus, 138

Septimius Severus (emperor), arch of in Rome, 378

Sequana (deity), 346

Sertorius, gets his troops across river, 164

Servilius Rullus, P., agrarian bill of, 96–97

Servius, comments of on sacred springs, 128

Severus Alexander (emperor): and aqueduct, 237; commemorates war against Persians, 378

Siculus Flaccus, comments on landholding and rivers, 89, 103, 104

Sidonius Apollinaris: describes journey on Padus, 305; writes to Arbogastes, 376

Silius Italicus, and Rhône, 373

Silvanus (deity), 440 (n. 90)

Simeon ben Yohai (rabbi), comments of on Rome, 384

Sirona (deity), 444 (n. 149)

Soranus, on benefits of water, 344

Sosinestani, involved in land dispute, 95–96

Statilius Taurus, T., receives letter on water dispute, 89

Statius. See Papinius Statius, P.

Strabo: character of geography of, 47–49; describes view from Campus Martius in Rome, 15; importance of rivers in work of, 53–82 passim, 247–62 passim; on Euphrates, 326; on Maeander, 323; on Padus, 304; and river silting, 38–39; on Tiber, 310; on Xanthos, 320

Strato, views of on Black Sea, 74

Suetonius Tranquillus, C., work of on rivers, 120

Suiones, river boats of, 211

Sulpicius Similis (prefect of Egypt), names spring after Trajan, 134

Tacitus. See Cornelius Tacitus

Terentius Varro, M.: notes origin of words for rivers, 64; villa of, 332

Theodoric, undertakes drainage work, 235

Theodosius (emperor), 115

Tiberinus (deity), appears to Aeneas, 142–43

Tiberius (emperor), organizes water supply at Nicopolis, 239

Tigellinus, visits Aquae Sinuessanae, 362

Titus (emperor), visits Aquae Cutiliae, 362

Trajan (emperor): arch of, 377–78; and building of canal in Bithynia, 224–25; builds towpath at Danube, 293; canal of at Iron Gate Pass, 225; celebrates aqua Traiana, 380; depicts Euphrates and Tigris on coins, 379; harbor of, 220

Trebius Secundus, L., restores water supply, 243

Tullius Cicero, M.: on Caesar's victories, 374; on restorative qualities of water, 337; on Rhine, 281; on rivers, 124, 331; on Rullus's land bill, 96; on site of Rome, 310

Tullius Maximus (governor of Thrace), and inscription from Augusta Traiana, 366

Turranius Proculus Gellianus, Sp. (prefect of curators), 318

Ulpius Diadumenus, M., procurator of imperial estates on Tiber, 315

Ulpius Firmus, M., funeral monument of, 135

Ulpius Hieronymus, provides bathing establishment for Augusta Traiana, 366–67

Ulpius Nymphicus, mourns death of his son, 135

Ulpius Traianus, M.: canal of at Mt. Amanus, 321; constructs Dipotamia, 321

Valens (emperor), negotiates treaty with Goths, 197

Valeria Frontonilla, benefactions of to Augusta Traiana, 366–67

Valerius Catullus, C., yacht of, 334

Valerius Martialis, M. (Martial), describes Tiber, 142, 311

INDEX OF PLACES

Note: Modern river names, where known, are given in parentheses.

Antunnacum, 285

Apamea, 218

Aphrodisias, 199

Apollonia, 382

Appia Claudia, 236

Apulum, 293, 295

Aqua Acidula, 352

Aqua Alexandriana, 237

Aqua Alsietina, 236, 238

Aqua Anio Novus, 236

Aqua Anio Vetus, 236

Aqua Augusta, 239

Aqua Claudia, 237

Aqua Crabra, 90

Aquae. *See* Appendix 1 (*individual sites
    are not cited in index unless of special
    significance*)

Aquae Albulae, 343, 344

Aquae Apollinares Novae, 357

Aquae Aponi, 133

Aquae Balissae, 366

Aquae Bormonis, 356

Aquae Caeretanae, 133, 363

Aquae Calidae (Vichy), 356, 364

Aquae Cutiliae, 362

Aquae Flaviae, 356

Aquae Granni, 363

Aquae Helveticae, 363–64

Aquae Hypsitanae, 366

Aquae Mattiacae/Mattiacorum, 363

Aquae Neri, 364

Aquae Originae, 356

Aquae Quarquernae, 356

Aquae Regiae, 356

Aquae Sextiae, 355

Aquae Sinuessanae, 340, 362

Aquae Sulis, 135, 364–65

Aquae Tarbellicae/Terebellicae, 340, 356

Aquae Tauri, 352, 362–63

Aquae Thibilitanae, 356

Aquae Vescinae, 301

Aquae Vesevinae, 352

Aqua Julia, 237

Aqua Marcia, 236, 340

Aqua Tepula, 236

Aqua Traiana, 380

Aqua Virgo, 97, 237, 335

Aquileia, 60, 171, 294, 304, 305

Aquincum, 134, 138, 294, 295

Aquinum, 313

Aquitania, boundary of, 63

Ara Ubiorum. *See* Colonia Claudia Ara
    Agrippinensium

Arachthos (Arta), 300

Arar (Saône), 23, 58, 69, 70, 165, 186, 263,
    266–69 passim

Arara (Aar), 282

Arausio, 80

Araxes, 77

Arba, 134

Arco Felice, 352

Ar(e)lape (Erlauf), 27

Arelate, 224, 267, 269–70

Areva, 65

Argentorate, 176, 281, 285

Argos Amphilochikon, 66

Argyra, 146

Ariminum, 170, 219

Ariminus (Marecchia), 170, 219

Arna, 62

Arnus (Arno), 300

Arrabon, 59

Arretium, 81, 135

Arsanias, 198

Arsia, 55

Arun (Britain), 206

Arva, 252

Asamum, 482 (n. 36)

Asamus (Osum), 482 (n. 36)

Asana, 205

Asia Minor, geographical characteristics
    of, 27–28

Asisium, 62

Askouros, 54

Asopos (Asopos), 66, 68, 145, 151, 230

Aspendos, 321

Asterion, 145

Astigi, 260

Atax (Aude), 23, 203

Athesis (Adige), 193, 306

Atria, 303

Atrica (Ardèche?), 269

Attidium, 62

Aufidus, 170

Augusta Emerita, 63, 80, 104, 171, 213, 228,
 240, 262

Augusta Euphratensis, 65

Augusta Praetoria Salassorum, 171

Augusta Raurica, 282, 306

Augusta Taurinorum, 171, 285

Augusta Traiana, 366

Augusta Vindeliciorum, 308

Augustodunum, 80

Augustonemetum, 265

Auser (Serchio), 300

Automula, 205

Avennio, 263

Avens (Velino), 29

Aventicum, 282, 306

Aventine Hill, 18

Axati, 252

Axima/Forum Claudii Ceutronum, 117

Axiopolis, 293

Axios, 72

Axona (Aisne), 164, 179

Ayni, 457 (n. 154)

Baetica, 39, 247–61 passim

Baetis (Guadalquivir), 22, 58, 63, 65, 75,
 122, 138, 158, 205, 207, 213, 223, 247–61
 passim, 380

Bagrada (Oued Medjerda), 28, 64

Baiae, 332, 334, 344, 359–60

Balyra (Basiliko), 147

Bandusia, 123

Barbegal, 278

Barbesula (Guadiaro), 207

Bedriacum, 303

Beneventum, 170, 313

Bernesga, 176

Bingium, 286

Bithynia-Pontus, boundary of, 52, 63–64

Black Sea, characteristics of water of, 74

Bodincomagum, 68

Bodincus. See Padus

Bonna, 176, 286

Borysthenes (Dnieper), 56, 71, 78, 298

Bourbon-l'Archambault, 364

Bourbonne-les-Bains, 364

Branodunum, 289

Brenes, 252

Brigantio, 263

Brigetio, 176, 294, 297

Britain, geographical characteristics of, 24

Brixellum, 306

Brixia, 306

Brohl, 285

Bruttium, 75

Buridava, 192

Burrus (Rienz), 26

Cabellio, 263

Cabilonnum, 180

Caecina (Cecina), 301

Caelian Hill, 17

Caere, 133

Caesaraugusta, 62, 261

Caesarodunum, 265

Calagurris (Nassica) Iulia, 261

Cales, 168

Calor (Calore), 170

Calycadnus (Göksu), 321

Camerinum, 62

Campi Flegrei, 498 (n. 178)

Jerusalem, 69
Juliopolis, 382
Justinianopolis, 114–15

Kaikinos (Amendolea or Laverde), 145
Kaikos, 450 (n. 270)
Kalbis (Dalyan Çay), 320
Kal(l)ipous (Sado), 249
Kalliroe (Kryoneri?), 71
Kalos (İyi Dere), 54
Kanathos, 147
Kapros (Basli Çay), 325
Karoura, 323
Kastalian Spring, 132
Katarraktes (Anapodaris in Greece), 72
Kenchreai, 342
Kephisos: in Attica, 57, 72, 132, 145, 151; in
    Boeotia, 72, 234; in Phocis, 72
Kereus, 73
Kestros (Aksu), 320
Khaironeia, 234
Kladeos (Kladeos), 131
Kolophon, 71
Koroneia, 70, 234
Kotilion, Mount, 51
Krathis (Krathis), 70, 341
Kremisos, 151
Kruft, 285
Kynaitha, 342
Kyros (Kura), 299, 326

Lacus Artynia, 64
Lacus Benacus (Lake Como), 306, 332
Lacus Eburodunensis, 282
Lacus Flevum, 183
Lacus Juturnae, 15
Lacus Lemanus, 269, 279
Lacus Lychnidus, 292
Lacus Sabatinus, 19, 237
Lacus Velinus, 20, 220
Lacus Verbanus, 303
Ladon (Ladonas), 71–72

Lago Salso, 29
Lake Kopais, 233
Lake Regillus, 15
Lake Selinusia, 490 (n. 226)
Lake Sophon, 216, 224
Lamasba, 228
Lambaesis, 135
Lambrus (Lambro), 303
Lamia, 100
Laodicea (in Caria), 205, 325
Laud, 328
Lauriacum, 298
Lausanne, 476 (n. 141)
Lavinium, 14
Ledosus, 276
Legio, 134, 176
Lepinus, Mount, 20
Lepreon, 68
Leptis, 228
Lerna, 66
Lethe, 149
Leucogaei Fontes, 352
Libanus, Mount, 147
Liger (Loire), 23, 63, 64, 180, 265
Limyra, 66
Limyros (Limyros), 66
Lindum, 223
Liparis, 339
Liquentia (Livenza), 60
Liris (Garigliano), 20, 168, 301
Litas (Litani), 27
Liternum, 170
Lixus (Loukkos), 149
Londinium, 289
Loudias (Loudias), 299
Lousios (Lousios), 147
Lucus Feroniae, 59, 315, 333
Lugdunensis, 64
Lugdunum, 58, 171, 224, 240, 268, 270–76,
    351
Lupia (Lippe), 176, 183
Lutetia, 180

Nepet, 168
Neronia, 221
Nicer (Neckar), 282
Nicomedia, 216, 224, 242, 370
Nicopolis, 239
Niedermendig, 285
Nilus (Nile), 28–29, 38, 73, 136–37, 153, 157, 230, 326–28, 375, 376, 380
Norba, 171
Noreia, 294
Noricum, boundary of, 63–64
Noricum Ripensis, 65
Novae, 176, 182
Novaesium, 176, 184
Noviodunum, 180, 182
Noviomagus, 176, 184, 265
Nuceria, 136
Numicus, 15

Oberstimm, 293
Oceanos, 153
Ocriculum, 315
Oeroe, 68
Oescus, 176
Olana, 77
Olbia, 298
Olisipo, 178, 262
Ollius (Oglio), 303
Onoba, 249
Ophis (Pheidias), 53, 162
Opitergium, 60, 304
Orgas (Norgaz Çay), 325
Orgus (Orco), 303
Orontes (Nahr el-Asi), 27, 127, 157, 321
Oropos, 343
Ortygia, 145
Osrhoene, 194
Ossonoba, 249
Ostia, 135, 213, 316–17
Ostium Philistina, 221
Ostium Sagis, 221

Ostium Volane, 221
Ostra, 62
Oufens, 20
Ovidis (Ouvèze), 207
Ovilava, 298
Oxus (Amu Darya), 326

Padus (Po), 29, 65, 68, 72, 76, 127, 156, 221, 230, 302–9 passim
Pagus Arusnatium, 133
Pagus Ianiculensis, 21
Pallia (Paglia), 315
Palma del Río, 252
Palus Caprae, 19
Pamisos (Pamisos), 132, 299, 336, 342
Pannonia, Lower, 59, 182
Pannonia, Upper, 182
Parthenios (Syit Su [Turkey]), 57
Parthenios (Bartin Su), 407
Parthia, 161, 178, 185, 190, 198
Pasitigris (Karun; Lower Tigris), 326
Patavium, 304, 306, 307
Pathissus (Tisza), 25, 63
Patrai, 342
Peirene, 146
Pellene, 71
Peneios (Peneios), 67–68, 72, 76, 146, 300, 337
Pergamum, 338, 380
Perusia, 59
Petronell, 298
Petronia, 17
Phalaros, 234
Phasis (Rioni), 72, 299, 385
Phrygia, 65
Phrygios (Kum Çay), 65
Phrystimus, 204
Picenum, 65
Piercebridge, 289
Piroboridava, 192
Pisae, 12, 300

Urvinum Metaurense, 62
Uxellodunum, 163

Vacua (Vouga), 247, 248
Vada Sabatia, 221
Vada Volaterrana, 301
Valentia, 261
Valeriana, 295
Varanus/Varamos (Varmo), 60
Varus (Var), 55, 56
Veii, 20
Veleia, 111, 133
Venafrum, 94–95
Venta, 289
Venusia, 170
Vercellae, 303
Vesontio, 168, 180
Vetera, 176, 184, 191, 286
Vettona, 62
Vetulonia, 59
Via Aemilia Scauri, 221, 305
Via Amerina, 62
Via Annia, 60
Via Appia, 235
Via Aurelia, 384
Via Cassia, 59
Via Claudia Augusta, 60, 221, 305
Via Domitia, 218
Via Egnatia, 57
Via Flaminia, 60, 62, 312
Via Hadriana, 328
Via Julia Augusta, 23
Via Postumia, 60

Via Praenestina, 236
Via Quinctia, 59
Via Salaria, 312
Vicetia, 134, 304
Vicus Camenarum, 17
Vicus Laci Fundani, 18
Vicus Piscinae publicae, 18
Vicus Tiberini, 141
Vienna, 58, 69
Villaviçosa, 136
Viminacium, 176, 293
Vindobona, 176
Vindonissa, 271
Viriodunum, 266
Visurgis (Weser), 26
Viterbo, 96
Volaterrae, 59
Volsinii Veteres, 309, 315
Volturnum, 170
Volturnus (Volturno), 15, 124, 163, 168,
    170, 178, 302
Vorogio, 265
Vulci, 59

Wentlooge Level, 235
Woerden, 283

Xanthos (Kinik), 320

Zagatis (Pazar Dere), 54
Zanes, 196
Zeugma, 52, 176, 194
Zwammerdam, 212

Ludi Piscatores, 141

Lusoria (boat), 209

Magistri Fontis, 19

Maps. *See* Rivers

Medical writing, on rivers and springs, 343–44

Mensales, purpose of, 98

Metals, transported by river, 257–58, 276

Military camps and settlements, choice of sites of, 172–77

Military supply, by rivers, 177–80

Military tactics, and rivers, 161–67

Mines, location of and rivers, 257–58

Ministri Fontis, 19

Miraculous events, and rivers and springs, 338–43

Modus fluminis, purpose of, 86

Mosaic from Althiburus, 208

Mules. *See* Pack animals

Mutatio alvei, importance of for land-holders, 106–9

Nautae (river boatmen): definition of, 210; role of, 267–72, 282, 306

Navalia, 315, 487 (n. 160)

Navicularii, definition of, 210

Navigable rivers, and ancient writers, 203–8, 405–9

Navigation. *See* Rivers

Nundinae (markets), and rivers, 312–13

Older Fill, significance of, 9–10

Olive oil, production and transport of on rivers, 250–53

Oracles. *See* Sibylline Oracles

Pack animals, carrying capacity of, 216–17

Palynology, 12

Patronage, and water resources, 237–44

Periegesis, and rivers, 50–51

Periploi, nature and importance of, 51–52

Periplous Maris Magni, 52

Periplous of Red Sea, 52

Periplous Pontis Euxini (Black Sea), 51–52

Peutinger Map: and designation of aquae sites, 357–59; significance of, 52–53

Placida (boat), 209

Platypegion (boat), 210

Ploion zeugmatikon (boat), 210

Polykopon (boat), 210

Pontifices, 21

Ponto (boat), 210

Pontonium (boat), 306

Port installations, on Tiber, 315–17

Portoria, collection of and rivers, 278–79, 286–87, 296–98

Ports (on rivers), role and importance of, 271–72, 285–86, 301–2

Pottery, manufacture of, and rivers, 252–55, 275–76, 283

Praefectus Annonae, 317

Procurator Baetis, 260

Procurator ripae Tiberis, 317

Propulsion, of river boats, 211–15

Provincial boundaries, demarcation of by rivers, 62–64

Quarries, location of and rivers, 257, 259, 283–86, 314, 323

Rainfall, and rivers, 4–7

Rainwater, 103

Ratiaria (boat), 209

Religious observances. *See* Rivers

Revelation (book of), and destruction of Rome, 384–85

Ripenses, 195

Rivalis, 32

River boats, 209–10

River fleets. *See classis* entries

Rivers: and alluviation, 109–16; in art

and writing, 120–56, 373–77, 383–85; and colonies and military settlements, 167–77; in community identity, 64–70; and control of by Rome, 369–83; crossing of, 371, 440 (n. 72); definitions of, 34–35, 86–90; and demarcation of peoples and communities, 55–62; and demarcation of provincial boundaries, 62–64; and demarcation of territory, 98–100; as depicted on coins, 157–59, 377–83; and deposition of silt, 9, 11–12, 38–40, 129; and divine, 128–42; exploitation of by Rome for water supply, 235–44; and flooding, 100–109; in frontier zones, 186–94; in frontier zones in Late Empire, 194–97; in geographical descriptions, 70–78; and geography of Roman empire, 22–30; in health and relaxation, 330–47; importance of deltas of, 9, 11–12, 23, 304–5, 321–22; individual rivers (*see* Index of Places); in legends, 143–50; and mapping, 78–81; in measurement of distance and space, 53–55; and military fleets, 180–86; and military operations, 161–67; and movement of people and goods, 246–90, 291–329 passim; names of and early Rome, 19–21; problems of navigation on, 201–3; problems of writing about, 30–40; and psychology of control, 371–73; as public property, 86–87; and religious observances, 123, 130, 131–40; and riverine environment, 9–13; and river rivalry, 71–72, 337; sediment in, 8–9; speed of travel on, 217; as symbol of life, 120–21; as symbols of nations, 372–74; and warfare, 161–67

Rivus, 32, 87, 98

Roads, and river routes, 218–19

Road transport, speed and cost of compared to rivers, 215–17

Rowing, methods of, 211

Runoff, significance of, 5–8

Salt-pans: on Maeander, 323–24; in Tiber valley, 21

Scapha (boat), 209

Sea level, changes in, 11–12

Servitude (*servitus*), and rivers, 89

Ships, tonnage and capacity of, 217

Sibylline Oracles, and predictions of destruction, 385

Silt, in river valleys. *See* Rivers

Soldiers, trained in swimming, 165

Space, measurement of. *See* Rivers

Spas (*aquae*), 347–68

Springs: association of Nymphs with, 132–36; character and healing properties of, 337–47; importance of in Rome, 15–19

Stadiasmus (*Periplous Maris Magni*), 52

Stlatta (boat), 209

Subseciua, 104–5

Swimming, in rivers, 334–35, 337–38

Tabula Contrebiensis, and land dispute, 95–96

Temples, position of in relation to rivers, 131

Terra nigra pottery, production and movement of by river, 283

Terra sigillata pottery, production and movement of by river, 261, 275, 283, 295

Topophilia, 126

Towing, of river boats, 212–14

Towing-path on Danube, 225

Transpiration, 5

Transport of goods by water, 246–329 passim

Travel, for pleasure by river, 332–34

Tribes (in Rome), association of with water and rivers, 19–20

Tributaries, importance of, 42, 75, 76–77,